W9-DGI-372

www.routledgesw.com

Alice A. Lieberman, The University of Kansas, Series Editor

An authentic breakthrough in social work education . . .

New Directions in Social Work is an innovative, integrated series of texts, website, and interactive case studies for generalist courses in the Social Work curriculum at both undergraduate and graduate levels. Instructors will find everything they need to build a comprehensive course that allows students to meet course outcomes, with these unique features:

- All texts, interactive cases, and test materials are **linked to the 2008 CSWE Policy and Accreditation Standards (EPAS).**

- **One web portal with easy access** for instructors and students from any computer—no codes, no CDs, no restrictions. Go to www.routledgesw.com and discover.

- **The series is flexible and can be easily adapted for use in online distance-learning courses as well as hybrid and bricks-and-mortar courses.**

- Each text and the website can be used **individually** or as an **entire series** to meet the needs of any social work program.

TITLES IN THE SERIES

Social Work and Social Welfare: An Invitation, Third Edition by Marla Berg-Weger

Human Behavior in the Social Environment, Third Edition by Anissa Taun Rogers

Research for Effective Social Work Practice, Third Edition by Judy L. Krysik and Jerry Finn

Social Policy for Effective Practice: A Strengths Approach, Third Edition by Rosemary K. Chapin

The Practice of Generalist Social Work, Third Edition by Julie Birkenmaier, Marla Berg-Weger and Martha P. Dewees

Social Policy for Effective Practice
A Strengths Approach

by Rosemary Chapin

This text is designed for use in foundation generalist social policy courses, either at the baccalaureate or master's level, students will learn the process of defining need, analyzing social policy, and developing new policy. A clear philosophical base and a common theoretical framework underlie the discussion of each component of the policy process. Four themes are interwoven throughout the book: the importance of thinking critically about social policy, the benefits of using the strengths perspective in policy analysis and development, the critical role social policy plays in all areas of practice, and the absolute responsibility of every social worker to engage in policy practice.

Routledgesw.com now contains six cases; the Sanchez case has been revised to include much more policy content. Instructor materials include extra readings, PowerPoints, test questions, annotated links, syllabi, and EPAS guidelines.

Adapting the Third Edition to Your Course Needs

As with the second edition, instructors can choose chapters relevant to their course and custom publish them at www.routledge.customgateway.com

Social Policy for Effective Practice

A Strengths Approach

Third Edition

Rosemary Chapin
University of Kansas

Routledge
Taylor & Francis Group

NEW YORK AND LONDON

PROPERTY OF W
SOCIAL WORK LIBRARY
DISCARD

First published 2014
by Routledge
711 Third Avenue, New York, NY 10017

and by Routledge
2 Park Square, Milton Park, Abingdon, Oxon OX14 4RN

Routledge is an imprint of the Taylor & Francis Group, an informa business

© 2014 Taylor & Francis

The right of Rosemary Chapin to be identified as author of this work has been asserted by her in accordance with sections 77 and 78 of the Copyright, Designs and Patents Act 1988.

All rights reserved. No part of this book may be reprinted or reproduced or utilized in any form or by any electronic, mechanical, or other means, now known or hereafter invented, including photocopying and recording, or in any information storage or retrieval system, without permission in writing from the publishers.

Trademark notice: Product or corporate names may be trademarks or registered trademarks, and are used only for identification and explanation without intent to infringe.

Library of Congress Cataloging in Publication Data
Chapin, Rosemary Kennedy.
Social policy for effective practice : a strengths approach /
by Rosemary Chapin. — [Third edition].
   pages cm — (New directions in social work)
Includes bibliographical references and index.
1. Social service — United States.   2. United States — Social policy.
3. Public welfare — United States.   4. Human services — United States.
I. Title.
HV95.C416 2007
361.973—dc23

                                                    2013025994

ISBN: 978-0-415-51991-5 (hbk)
ISBN: 978-0-415-51992-2 (pbk)
ISBN: 978-0-203-79476-0 (ebk)

Typeset in Stone Serif
by Swales & Willis Ltd, Exeter, Devon, UK

BRIEF CONTENTS

Preface   xxv

Acknowledgments   xxxvii

About the Author   xxxix

CHAPTER 1   *Social Work and Social Policy: A Strengths Perspective   1*

CHAPTER 2   *The Historical Context: Basic Concepts and Early Influences   29*

CHAPTER 3   *The Historical Context: Development of Our Current Welfare System   66*

CHAPTER 4   *The Economic and Political Contexts   120*

CHAPTER 5   *Basic Tools for Researching Need and Analyzing Social Policy   167*

CHAPTER 6   *Social Policy Development: Research and Policy Practice   200*

CHAPTER 7   *Civil Rights   254*

CHAPTER 8   *Income- and Asset-Based Social Policies and Programs   307*

CHAPTER 9   *Policies and Programs for Children and Families   360*

CHAPTER 10   *Health and Mental Health Policies and Programs   406*

CHAPTER 11   *Policies and Programs for Older Adults   469*

CHAPTER 12   *The Future   517*

References   R–1

Credits   C–1

Glossary/Index   I–1

DETAILED CONTENTS

Preface xxv

Acknowledgments xxxvii

About the Author xxxix

CHAPTER 1   *Social Work and Social Policy: A Strengths Perspective   1*

Social Work and Social Policy   3

  The Relationship Between Social Policy and Social Work Practice   3

  Social Work Values Integral to the Strengths Approach to Policy Practice   5

    The Social Worker's Responsibility for Policy Practice   6
    Connecting Social Policy to Personal Experience   8

Social Work and the Strengths Perspective   8

  Policy Practice Infused With the Strengths Perspective   10

    Recasting Human Needs and Social Problems   10
    Expanding the Client's Role   12
    Claims-Making   13

  Principles of Strengths Perspective Policy Practice   14

  Frameworks for Policy Development   15

  QUICK GUIDE 1: COMPARISON OF THE PROBLEM-CENTRED AND STRENGTHS-BASED
  APPROACHES TO POLICY DEVELOPMENT   16

Identifying and Developing Your Policy Practice Abilities   17

  Integrating a Strengths Perspective: Benefits and Cautions   19

    Benefits of the Strengths Perspective   20
    Cautions Regarding the Strengths Perspective   21

  Connecting Social Work Values to Policy Practice   22

Conclusion   23

Meet the Policy Group   23

Main Points   25

Exercises   26

CHAPTER 2   *The Historical Context: Basic Concepts and Early Influences*   29

The Genesis of Social Welfare Policy   30

Religious Traditions   30

Judaism   30

Islam   30

Buddhism   31

Confucianism   31

Native American Religions   31

Christianity   32

Current Implications   32

Conflicting Views Regarding Social Welfare   33

A Framework for Understanding How Historical Approaches Influence Current Policy   34

QUICK GUIDE 2: HISTORICAL QUESTIONS   34

English Poor Laws   36

Background of the Poor Law   37

Population Growth and Migration   37

Poverty   38

The Poor Law of 1601   38

Analyzing the Poor Law   39

Influence of the Poor Laws on U.S. Social Policy   39

Social Welfare Policy in the United States   40

The Colonial Era: Adapting the English System, 1600–1775   41

Social Welfare in the English Colonies   41

Almshouses and Workhouses   42

Slavery and Indentured Servitude   42

The American Revolution: Civil Rights in the New Nation, 1775–1800   43

The Constitution and Civil Rights   43

Expanding Federal, State, and Private Assistance   44

From Independence to Civil War: Racism, Expansion, and Immigration, 1800–1865   45

Treatment of African Americans   45

Native Americans   46

Hispanics/Latinos in the Southwest   47

Discrimination against Immigrants   47

Growth of Cities and Public Institutions   48

Mental Health Reform   48

The Civil War and Its Aftermath: Reconstruction, Segregation, and Homesteads, 1865–1900 50

Reconstruction 50

From Reconstruction to Jim Crow 51

The Homestead Act 51

The Origins of Modern Social Work 52

The Child-Saving Movement 52

The Charity Organization Society and Social Darwinism 54

The Settlement House Movement 54

Building the Social Work Profession 56

African American Social Workers 56

The Progressive Era and the Expansion of Social Welfare Policy, 1900–1920 58

Maternalistic Approaches and Mothers' Pensions 59

Child Welfare 60

The Volstead Act, Prohibition and Racial/Ethnic Discrimination 61

The New Immigration 62

Conclusion 62

Main Points 63

Exercises 64

CHAPTER 3   *The Historical Context: Development of Our Current Welfare System 66*

Expanding the Welfare State in War and Depression: 1917–1945 67

The New Deal 68

The Townsend Movement 72

The Social Security Act 72

The Impact of World War II 74

The Evolution of the Modern Welfare State: 1945–1970 75

The Struggle for African American Civil Rights 77

The Challenge to School Segregation 77

The Challenge to Jim Crow 78

Civil Rights Laws 79

The Struggle for Hispanic American Civil Rights 80

Mental Health and Mental Retardation Initiatives 81

The War on Poverty 82

New Frontier Anti-Poverty Programs 82

The Great Society and the War on Poverty 83

Medicare and Medicaid 84

The War on Poverty: Successes and Failures 85

Continuity and Change: The 1970s 87

Family Assistance Experiments 87

Social Service Reforms 88

Social Welfare Initiatives 88

Watergate and After 89

Women and Civil Rights 89

Native Americans and Civil Rights 90

Termination and Relocation 90

Militancy and the Struggle for Sovereignty 91

Child Welfare 91

Affirmative Action 92

Affirmative Action and Employment 92

Affirmative Action and Education 94

Changes in Social Work 94

Retrenchment to New Foundations: 1981 to the Present 95

Implementing a Conservative Agenda 96

New Federalism, OBRA, and Devolution 97

OBRA and Block Grants 97

Pressures to Reduce Social Service Spending 98

Equal Opportunity Initiatives Stalled 98

From Reagan to Bush 99

"New Democrats" and Social Welfare Policy 99

Family Leave and People with Disabilities 100

Health Care: The Reform That Did Not Happen 101

The Contract with America and the PRWORA 101

Asset-Based Approaches to Poverty 102

Poverty and the American Family 103

The New Century 104

Privatization and Faith-Based Initiatives 105

Tax Cuts and Reduced Benefits 105

Challenging Affirmative Action and Abortion Rights 106

The Promise of a New Foundation 107

Health Care and Immigration   108

The Federal Debt   110

Supreme Court Rulings   111

The Voting Rights Act Decision   112

The Affirmative Action Decision   112

Same-Sex Marriage Decisions   112

Lessons and Challenges   112

Conclusion   115

Main Points   116

Exercises   117

CHAPTER 4   *The Economic and Political Contexts   120*

Effect on Social Policy   121

Regulatory Policy   122

The Impetus for Social Programs   123

Institutional and Residual Approaches to Social Welfare   125

Institutional Approaches   125

Residual Approaches   125

Influences on the Social Welfare System   126

Competing Explanations for the Development of the Welfare System   126

The Industrialization-Welfare Hypothesis   127

The Maintenance of Capitalism Hypothesis   127

Social Conscience Hypotheses   128

The Marshall and Titmuss Hypotheses   128

Economic and Social Conscience Hypotheses: A Critique   129

The Enabling State and the Capacity Building State   130

Economic and Political Schools of Thought   133

Keynesian Economics   133

Supply-Side Economics   134

Democratic Socialism   134

New Approaches to Deal with Slowing Economic Growth   135

The Political Continuum   135

Conservatives and Liberals   135

Other Political Influences   137

The Three Branches of Government   138

The Impact of Funding Strategies   139

  Federal and State Budgets   139

    Mandatory Versus Discretionary Spending   140

  Tax Strategies   141

    Federal Spending   142

    State Spending Policies   145

  The Role of the Private Sector   147

  Benefits and Drawbacks of Different Combinations of Funding Strategies   148

Social Welfare Expenditures in the United States   149

  The Nature of United States Social Welfare Spending   150

    Social Welfare and Tax Expenditures   151

  Adequacy of Current Expenditures for Social Programs   154

    U.S. Expenditure Compared to Those of Other Countries   156

  The Ramifications of Globalization   158

The Economy of the Agency   161

Conclusion   162

Main Points   163

Exercises   164

CHAPTER 5   *Basic Tools for Researching Need and Analyzing Social Policy   167*

Policy Analysis Fundamentals   168

  Social Conditions and Social Problems   168

  Alternative Views   169

  Defining Needs and Problems: The Social Constructionist Approach   170

    The Social Construction of Teenage Pregnancy   171

    The Social Construction of Family Violence   171

    Understanding Different Views of Reality   172

Using Strengths Perspective Principles to Consider Needs Determination   173

QUICK GUIDE 3: PRINCIPLES OF STRENGTHS PERSPECTIVE POLICY   173

  Frameworks for Policy Development   173

Analyzing Social Problems from an Expanded Viewpoint   175

  Defining and Documenting Problems or Needs   175

  Values, Ideologies, and Self-Interest   179

Causal Theories   180

Claims-Making   182

    The Various Bases of Claims-Making   182

    Assumptions Embedded in Claims-Making   183

Using Strengths Perspective Principles to Consider the Claims-Making Process   185

A Framework for Policy Analysis   185

Policy Goals and Objectives   186

    Locating Goals and Objectives   187

    Manifest and Latent Goals   187

    Incorporating Clients' Perspectives   188

Benefits or Services Provided   189

Eligibility Rules   190

Service Delivery Systems   191

Financing   192

Cost-Effectiveness and Outcomes   193

Conclusion   194

Catching Up with the Policy Group   194

Main Points   196

Exercises   197

CHAPTER 6   *Social Policy Development: Research and Policy Practice   200*

Steps in Policy Development   202

QUICK GUIDE 4: POLICY ANALYSIS AND DEVELOPMENT OVERVIEW   203

Determining Need and Making Claims   205

    Groups Involved in Needs Determination and Claims-Making   206

    The Legislative Agenda   207

    Initial Steps in Policy Development: A Summary   208

Crafting Policy Goals   209

    Achieving Consensus   209

    Utilizing the Strengths Perspective   210

Values: Examining the Feasibility of Policy Alternatives   211

Enacting and Implementing Policy   213

Social Policy Research: Evaluating Policy Outcomes   215

Social Work Policy Practice and the Ecological Perspective   217

Policy Research and Practice: Basic Skills and Tasks   220

Identifying and Defining the Target Population   221

Examining Your Perspective   223

Getting on the Agenda   223

Getting on the Agenda: A Real-Life Scenario   224
Strategies for Utilizing the Strengths Approach   225
Working with Other Individuals and Groups   226

Identifying Policy Options that Include Client Perspectives   227

Negotiating Policy Goals   227

Helping to Get Policy Enacted   228

Considering Whether a New Law is Needed   228
Using the Policy Analysis Framework   229
Analyzing Costs   230

Evaluating Policy Based on Client Outcomes   231

A Place to Start   233

Seeking Support   234

Taking Action   236

Integrating Other People into Action Plans   237
Focusing Your Efforts   238
Interacting with Your Opposition   238
Supporting Client Groups   239
Interacting with Policy Makers   239
Facing Limits on Political Activism   240

Conclusion   241

Main Points   242

The Policy Group Takes Action   243

QUICK GUIDE 5: SAMPLE ACTION PLAN   244

Exercises   250

CHAPTER 7   *Civil Rights*   254

Background and History   255

Civil Rights Policies in the United States   260

Disenfranchised Groups and Civil Rights   261

African Americans   261
Native Americans   264

Hispanics/Latinos   266

Asian Americans   267

Sexual Orientation and Gender Identity   268

People with Disabilities   272

Older Adults   274

Women and Civil Rights   276

Affirmative Action   279

Major Policies and Programs   281

The Civil Rights Act of 1964   281

The Voting Rights Act of 1965   283

The Education for All Handicapped Children Act of 1975   285

The Americans with Disabilities Act of 1990   286

The Reauthorization of the Violence Against Women Act 2005 and 2013   288

The Lilly Ledbetter Fair Pay Act 2009   288

The Matthew Shepard and James Byrd, Jr. Hate Crimes Prevention Act 2009   289

Evaluating Civil Rights Policies and Programs   290

Discrimination Based on Ethnicity and Gender   291

Current Threats to Civil Rights and Human Rights   293

Next Steps   295

Reconsidering "Neutral" Policies   297

The Role of Social Workers   298

QUICK GUIDE 6: AGENCY ANALYSIS   300

Conclusion   301

Catching Up with the Policy Group   301

Main Points   303

Exercises   305

CHAPTER 8   *Income- and Asset-Based Social Policies and Programs*   307

Definitions of Poverty   308

The Poverty Line/Poverty Threshold   309

Poverty Guidelines   311

Alternative Poverty Measures   311

Income-Support Policies and Programs   312

Universal Programs   313

Old Age, Survivors, and Disability Insurance: How Young People Benefit 313

Unemployment Insurance 316

Workers' Compensation 318

Veterans' Benefits 319

Selective Programs 320

Temporary Assistance for Needy Families 321

History and Development of TANF 323
TANF Goals 324
Family Formation Goals 325
TANF Work Requirements and Sanctions 325

Non-Cash Programs That Assist Low-Income Families 327

SNAP 327
The WIC Nutrition Program 328
Public Housing 329
The Tenant-Based Housing Assistance Program 330

Supplemental Security Income 330

General Assistance 332

The Earned Income Tax Credit 333

Evaluation of Income-Support Policies and Programs 334

TANF and Poverty 336

Devolution and Recessions 338

Reforming TANF from a Strengths Perspective 340

OASDI from the Strengths Perspective 343

Women and OASDI 344
People of Color and OASDI 345
Is OASDI Regressive or Progressive? 345
How Solvent is OASDI? 346

Asset-Based Policies 347

Proposals for Fundamental Reform 350

Basic Income Grant 351
Asset-Based Reform 351

Poverty in the Global Context 352

QUICK GUIDE 7: INCOME- AND ASSET-BASED PROGRAMS 353

Conclusion 354

Main Points   355

Exercises   357

CHAPTER 9   *Policies and Programs for Children and Families*   *360*

History and Background of Programs Protecting Children and Families   360

Children and Families Today   364

Impact of Growing Poverty Rates on Child Welfare   *365*

The Child Welfare System   *367*

The Juvenile Justice System   *369*

Major Policies and Programs Affecting Child Welfare and Juvenile Justice   370

The Child Abuse Prevention and Treatment Act   *372*

The Juvenile Justice and Delinquency Prevention Act   *373*

The Indian Child Welfare Act   *375*

Adoption Assistance and Child Welfare Act   *377*

Family Preservation and Support Services   *378*

The Multi-Ethnic Placement Act   *379*

The Adoption and Safe Families Act   *381*

Independent Living Transition Services   *383*

The Child Support Enforcement Program   *384*

Legislation for Children with Special Educational Needs   *385*

QUICK GUIDE 8: CHILD WELFARE AND JUVENILE JUSTICE APPLICATION TOOL   386

Evaluating Policies and Programs for Children and Families   387

Child Protection Policy from the Strengths Perspective   *390*

Family Rights and Child Safety   390

Family Reunification   392

Teen Pregnancy   393

Privatization   394

Strategies for Supporting Families More Effectively   396

Juvenile Justice from the Strengths Perspective   *397*

The Role of Social Workers in the Child Welfare System   *399*

Conclusion   400

Catching Up with the Policy Group   401

Main Points   402

Exercises   404

CHAPTER 10   *Health and Mental Health Policies and Programs   406*

Health Care in the United States   407

The High Cost of Health Care   410

History and Background of Health Care Programs   412

Growing Federal Involvement in Health Care   413
Medicare, Medicaid, and Civil Rights   413
Background on Approaches to Health Care Finance and Cost Control   414
Health Reform in the 1990s   416

2010 National Health Care Reform   417

The 2012 Supreme Court Decision   417
Issues Left Unaddressed   418

Major Health Care Policies and Programs   419

Medicaid   419

Mandatory and Optional Coverage   421
Variations among States   422
Medicaid and the PRWORA   423
Medicaid and Managed Care   424
Medicaid and Health Care Access   425

Medicare   426

Medicare Part A, Hospital Insurance (HI)   428
Medicare Part B   428
Medicare Part C, Medicaire Advantage   429
Medicare Part D   429
The Centers for Medicare and Medicaid Services (CMS)   431

The Children's Health Insurance Program   432

QUICK GUIDE 9: HEALTH AND MENTAL HEALTH PROGRAMS   435

The 2010 Patient Protection and Affordable Care Act   435

Affordable Care Act: Financing and Cost Control Issues   438

Major Mental Health Policies and Programs   440

History and Background of Mental Health Programs   442

Community Mental Health and Deinstitutionalization   442
The Substance Abuse and Mental Health Services Administration   445
Mental Health Parity and Increased Attention to Preparing Mental Health Professionals   445
Growing Concerns Related to Children and Mental Health   446

Mental Health Policies   *447*

The Mental Retardation and Community Mental Health Centers
Construction Act   447

The State Comprehensive Mental Health Services Plan Act   448

Evaluating Health and Mental Health Policies and Programs   448

Challenges to the Medicare System   *450*

Ageism in the Medicare Health Care Cost Debate   451

Substance Abuse, Pandemics, and the Health Care System   *453*

Social Work Education and Health Care Reform   455

Next Steps for Promoting More Effective Health and Mental Health Policies   *455*

Medicare Reform   *456*

Mental Health Care   *457*

Strategies to Promote Recovery, Diversity, and Health   458

Social Workers and Health Care Reform   *458*

A Health Model   461

Conclusion   462

Catching Up with the Policy Group   462

Main Points   463

Exercises   465

CHAPTER 11   *Policies and Programs for Older Adults*   *469*

History and Background   473

Policy and Program Responses   *474*

Private Retirement Programs   474

Public Retirement Programs   474

Policies to Provide Health Care and Support Social Engagement   475

Changes to Job-Specific Pension Programs   476

Pensions at Risk   476

SSI for Older Adults   477

The National Institute on Aging   477

Mental Health Services   478

Mandatory Retirement   478

Long-Term Care   479

Prescription Drug Policy   480

Shortage of Gerontologically Trained Professionals   480

The Influence of Demographics   *481*

Poverty and Aging in the Community   485

Voting Patterns of Older Adults   486

Major Policies and Programs   486

The Older Americans Act   *486*

The Employee Retirement Income Security Act   *488*

*NO CLASS: The Loss of the Long-Term Care Provisions of the
Affordable Care Act*   *490*

Elder Justice Act and the Patient Safety and Abuse Prevention Act   *490*

Evaluating Policies and Programs for Older Adults   491

Economic Security   *493*

Health Care   *497*

End-of-life Planning   500

Social Engagement   *501*

Next Steps   503

Developing a Strengths-Based Agenda   *505*

Creating Needed Infrastructure   *508*

Conclusion   509

Catching Up with the Policy Group   510

Main Points   512

Exercises   514

CHAPTER 12   *The Future*   *517*

Future Forecasts   518

Guidelines for Understanding Future Forecasts   *518*

Analyze the Purpose   518

QUICK GUIDE 10: UNDERSTANDING FUTURE FORECASTS   519

Assess Underlying Assumptions and the Credibility of
Source Information   520

Thinking about the Future Using A Values Based Lens: The Strengths Approach   *523*

Factors That Will Shape Future Social Policies   525

Population Growth   *525*

Increasing Diversity in the U.S.   *527*

Medical and Technological Changes   *528*

Globalization and Environmental Degradation   530

The State of the Future Index   533

Future Policy Directions   534

Diversity and the Work-Based Safety Net   535

Wages, Jobs, and Retirement   537

Supporting the Intergenerational Family   538

Health   539

Climate Justice   540

Information Technology and Privacy   541

The Influence of Pluralism on Future Social Policy   542

Privatization   542

Reconsidering Core Values   544

Using the Electoral Process   546

The Strengths Perspective in a New Era   547

Conclusion   549

Main Points   550

Exercises   552

References   R–1

Credits   C–1

Glossary/Index   I–1

PREFACE

MAJOR CHANGES TO THE THIRD EDITION

Welcome to the third edition of *Social Policy for Effective Practice: A Strengths Approach*. This edition has been redesigned to be more explicitly an empowerment tool for your students. It contains a host of new features that will allow your students to immediately begin applying what they learn about policy and programs to improve conditions for our clients. These changes incorporate the feedback that many faculty and students have graciously taken time to share with me. Thank you.

Reaction to the second edition was very positive. However, both faculty and students reported that the transition of content from classroom to policy practice is still a struggle for many students. This third edition has been redesigned to help bridge that transition. In Chapter 1, readers will meet four student social workers who become friends in their social policy class. Then, in subsequent chapters we follow them into their first social work position in child welfare, schools, health, mental health, and aging services. Students will observe the challenges they meet when beginning to apply policy practice skills and will be given practical strategies for combining policy practice with their clinical and other job responsibilities.

This edition is chock-full of resources, including social media links and web-based tools to help students engage in policy practice. Quick Guides provide easy-to-use summaries of key content. Like the previous editions, this text provides students with a value-based approach to understanding social policy. The strengths approach to policy analysis and development is grounded in social work values of self-determination, social justice, and respect for diversity. The premise of this text is that a greater focus on the strengths and resources of people and their environments, rather than on their problems and pathologies, should be integrated into the social policy development process. Thus, unlike most other social policy books, a values and ethics focus permeates the entire text.

In addition to comprehensive coverage of major social policies and programs across fields of practice, the latest information on policy initiatives and reforms emanating from the Obama administration is presented and carefully analyzed for its potential impact. This edition provides new information on many policy initiatives including the Affordable Care Act, the Elder Justice Act, and securing rights for same-sex couples. I also discuss recent civil rights advances. This new information is integrated into several chapters, and the effect of the changes on current policy and on social work practice is explained. Throughout the text, I call attention to how language frames policy debates, and urge students to engage in re-languaging to, for example, talk about insurance benefits rather than entitlements in discussing OASDI (Old Age, Survivors, and Disability Insurance). Additionally, international content has been thoroughly integrated into each chapter. Aging content is infused throughout this text and the entire *New Directions in Social Work* series.

As in the last edition, I make sure that students know where to find trustworthy web sources that are unlikely to disappear, and urge them to use these websites to get the most up-to-date information on policies and to expand their knowledge beyond the content in the text. This information is not simply listed at the end of the chapter, but integrated into the chapter discussion at the point where students would be curious enough to want to learn more and actually go to the website. Each time students follow one of the text prompts, they will become more familiar with the network of online advocacy organizations and resources they can use as a policy practitioner.

Beginning with Chapter 1, students are challenged to think for themselves and find areas of policy practice that ignite their passion. I have found that, once students begin to think about policy practice as a tool that can be used to bring about changes they care about, they become much more interested in mastering the content in this text. In addition to learning about the historical, political, and economic contexts of social policies, they will learn skills needed for both policy analysis and policy development. They will then use those skills to become knowledgeable about the major policies and programs that impact their clients.

As a veteran policy practitioner, I see policy practice tools everywhere. I want students to begin to do the same kind of environmental scanning, to recognize policy practice tools and be innovative in using them. For example, I make the connection between solution focused techniques students are learning to use with individual clients, and focusing on potential solutions generated by client groups early in the policy development process. Such illustrations will help students make these kinds of connections themselves.

The book's chapters are peppered with actual examples of social work students who banded together and engaged in policy practice to improve services for their clients. The website materials accompanying this text also provide a wealth of new ideas. The enriched syllabi function as extensive instructors' resources and include video links, interactive classroom activities, and many other resources that reflect the way that today's students learn, and facilitate instructors' efforts to make policy come alive and ignite students' interest in policy practice. Many of these resources were created by Melinda Lewis, who teaches social policy at the BSW and MSW level. She is a gifted policy practitioner immersed in the use of social media, web-based tools, and other interactive resources in her advocacy work with the immigrant community. Be sure to check out *10 "Old" Ideas for Using Technology in Macro Practice in New Ways*.

For all the books in the *New Directions in Social Work* series, each addressing a foundational course in the social work curriculum, the publisher has created a unique teaching strategy that revolves around the printed book, but offers much more than the traditional text experience. The series website www.routledgesw.com leads to custom websites coordinated with each text that offer a variety of features to support instructors as they integrate the many facets of an education in social work.

At www.routledgesw.com, you will find a wealth of resources to help you create a dynamic, experiential introduction to social work for your students. The website houses companion readings linked to key concepts in each chapter, along with questions to encourage further thought and discussion; six interactive fictional cases with accompanying exercises that bring to life the concepts covered in the book, readings, and classroom discussions; a bank of exam questions (both objective and open-ended) and PowerPoint presentations; and annotated links to a treasure trove of articles, videos, and websites. You may find most useful a set of sample syllabi showing how *Social Policy for Effective Practice*, third edition, can be used in a variety of course structures. A master matrix demonstrates how the text and website used together through the course satisfy the Council on Social Work Educational Policy and Accreditation Standards (EPAS).

The organization and content of this book and companion website are such that students at the bachelor and master's levels can apply knowledge gained from studying the material to both generalist and specialized practice. The third edition can be used throughout a two-semester sequence as well as a one-semester course, and the integrated supplements and resources on the web make the text especially amenable to online distance-learning and hybrid courses. The rich variety of resources and links provided as part of the *Social Policy for Effective Practice* text and website makes it possible to expand or contract the content to fit the variety of time-frames and levels in which social policy courses are taught.

Readings (and accompanying questions) have been added to offer more breadth and depth to selected topics, giving students and instructors options about which topics to explore more thoroughly, and providing opportunities to explore the diversity and complexity associated with the social issues most important to social workers. These readings can also help students with more self-directed learning in areas about which they are particularly interested and may want to explore further. For example, in the area of juvenile justice, one of the readings examines policy reforms needed to break the school to prison pipeline.

ORGANIZATION OF THE BOOK

Please take a look at the table of contents for this book. The chapter titles reflect social policy topics that are basic for effective social work practice. In Chapters 1–6, we will examine different frameworks and contexts for understanding social policy as well as tools for analyzing and influencing social policy. We will also consider the influence of history and economics on social policy. Students will be helped to try on policy practice roles by following the work of the policy group, consisting of four students introduced in Chapter 1, who are engaging in policy practice. Chapters 7–11 provide students with a chance to build their skills using basic tools to analyze policies affecting major client groups in a variety of fields of practice. Information on older adults is infused throughout this text and specifically covered in Chapter 11. Moreover, each chapter incorporates a strengths approach so that students can begin to consider clients' strengths and resources as well as their needs when evaluating relevant policies. By learning how members of the policy group used their policy practice skills in their first jobs, students also get a chance to see how they may use their policy practice skills in their first social work jobs. In Chapter 12, the book concludes by looking to the future in an international context, and considering ideas about how social workers can effectively respond to projected changes in the 21st century.

The chapter descriptions below briefly introduce each of the chapters included in this book, with emphasis on the updated content.

Chapter 1

Social Work and Social Policy: A Strengths Perspective provides an overview of social policy and programs and introduces the basic concepts that are the foundation for the rest of the book. My goal in the first chapter is to help students understand why policy practice is critical to effective social work practice. I discuss the value base of the strengths perspective and explain how a strengths approach and solutions focused strategies change not only the policy product but also the policy analysis and development process. Students are challenged right away to find an issue they are passionate about and to begin to build policy practice skills. Integral to this chapter is the concept of dual assessments, whereby social workers are expected to also assess the specific policy issues that impact their clients and consider whether intervention requiring use of policy practice skills is necessary. By the end of the first chapter, I hope students will be excited about policy practice and interested in acquiring the knowledge and skills necessary to help influence social policies and programs.

In Chapter 1, four student social workers are introduced. We follow them through their first social policy class together. Then, in subsequent chapters we learn about how they tackle policy practice issues in their first social work positions in child welfare, schools, health, mental health, and aging services. Thinking about challenges these students meet when beginning to apply policy practice skills provides an opportunity for readers to anticipate how they can successfully meet similar challenges. They also get the chance to learn practical strategies for combining policy practice with their clinical and other job responsibilities.

Chapter 2

The Historical Context: Basic Concepts and Early Influences presents history as a policy practice tool, and provides an analytic framework to support that approach. This chapter examines the historical context for the development of social welfare policies and programs, discusses the genesis of social welfare in early societies, and traces the development of U.S. social policies through the early years of the 20th century. New to Chapter 2 is an expanded discussion of the origins of social work, discriminatory health and mental policies during this period, formation of the Democratic Republican Party, the importance of policy research done by pioneer social workers, and the pivotal role of women in social policy development during the 1800s and 1900s.

In Chapters 2 and 3, many readers suggested adding more material to make historical events and people come alive for students. In response, I have added several exhibits that provide pictures as well as intriguing details related to important milestones in social work to both chapters.

Chapter 3

The Historical Context: Development of Our Current Welfare System then begins with World War I and continues through the administration of Barack Obama. These chapters are premised on the idea that history is not merely a prologue to the present. Rather, the ways in which historical social policy approaches are understood and reinterpreted directly and immediately affect the social policy decisions made. Chapter 3 contains an expanded discussion of the civil rights movement and of income-support strategies enacted since World War II. The changes that brought us retrenchment and devolution during the Reagan era are examined and the effects of the Great Recession during the Bush and Obama administrations are discussed. I also chronicle the major events that have shaped social work since the second edition with particular attention to the impact of the 2012 presidential election and the implementation of the Affordable Care Act (ACA) including information on the ACA Supreme Court decision. The "capacity building state" is discussed. Finally, expanded examination of major state initiatives has been added, specifically focusing on recent state immigration laws, state challenges of the ACA, state policies on same-sex marriage, and state abortion policies. In the context of devolution, social policy is increasingly contested in state legislatures and governors' mansions, and the new text gives students some of the resources they need to navigate these arenas in their own practice.

Chapter 4

The Economic and Political Contexts helps students understand how economic fluctuations and political change interact with shifting social values to shape and reshape social policy. New to this chapter is a much greater emphasis on the international political and economic context that increasingly influences our social policy. Each topic has been revised and now includes the most current statistics. Lastly, a discussion on the impact of the increased focus on the growing federal debt crisis has been added.

Chapter 5

Basic Tools for Researching Need and Analyzing Social Policy illustrates for students how to use a policy analysis framework to analyze social policy and gives them a chance to do hands-on analysis of legislation passed under the Obama administration that addresses homelessness. Strength principles for policy analysis are explained and their application is discussed. I have also added more specific information on how to analyze social policy in response to faculty requests for greater detail to flesh out the basic framework provided. The examples provided in the "A Framework for Policy Analysis" section have been updated and carried throughout the entire section. Also, new tools to help students analyze social policy have been included. Finally, we catch up again with the students in the policy group that were introduced in Chapter 1. They are grappling with the task of completing a policy analysis related to child hunger.

Chapter 6

Social Policy Development: Research and Policy Practice examines the process of policy development in detail, and then focuses explicitly on the ways in which social workers can intervene in that process. Explanations of ways social workers engaged in policy practice can use strengths principles and solution focused approaches to policy development have been expanded. New exhibits with examples of social work students doing advocacy work (e.g. immigration and promoting diversity) have been added. The case study and Sample Action Plan, which lays out how to develop and implement strategies to influence social policies, now focuses on the work of the students in the policy group to reduce childhood hunger. Finally, Quick Guides have been added to this and other chapters that summarize major points to consider when engaging in policy practice.

Chapter 7

Civil Rights provides a detailed look at the groups who have experienced discrimination and oppression in the U.S. In this edition, I include much more information on recent state immigration laws. I also discuss the repeal of the "Don't Ask Don't Tell" policy, as well as President Obama's denouncement of the Defense of Marriage Act (DOMA), and the passage of state laws recognizing same-sex marriage. Analysis of recent measures in state and federal legislatures to introduce policies limiting women's civil rights, such as state anti-abortion laws, anti-contraceptive bills, and legislation defunding Planned Parenthood, has been added to the "Women and Civil Rights" section. The "Reconsidering 'Neutral' Policies" section has been revised to include discussion of the impact of the voting law changes of 2012. Increased emphasis is put on understanding how to analyze a seemingly neutral policy for negative impact on traditionally oppressed groups. Beginning in Chapter 7 and continuing through the remainder of the text, I analyze major policies in separate boxes using a simple policy analysis framework introduced in earlier chapters. This is done so that students can easily grasp the basic policy elements of goals, service delivery, and financing, and then can more readily understand later amendments.

Chapter 8

Income- and Asset-Based Social Policies and Programs examines the major government policies and programs designed to reduce poverty. This chapter emphasizes means-tested and insurance-based policies and programs that provide cash to clients. However, because SNAP, employment policy, and housing subsidies also directly help ameliorate the effects of poverty, I examine these policies and programs as well. I also analyze official definitions of poverty, and contrast universal with selective programs. Updated statistics have been incorporated throughout Chapter 8 and I have added information about the importance of extending benefit time limits during times of financial crisis. A discussion of SNAP and its effect on poverty rates during periods of economic crisis as well as the disappearance of the middle class have been incorporated into the chapter. Finally, in response to faculty feedback, asset-based policy is discussed in much greater detail.

Chapter 9

Policies and Programs for Children and Families focuses on policies and programs dealing with child protection, family preservation, permanency planning, adoption, foster care, and juvenile justice. Programs for children with special needs as well as child-support enforcement policies are also examined. In addition, all statistics and policies have been updated throughout the chapter. Discussion of the impact on children of recent immigration laws and the growing poverty crisis has been incorporated, as well as information on adoption by same-sex couples. More advocacy examples have been added throughout the chapter. This edition also contains an expanded discussion of how child welfare and family policy can be improved and includes content on family capacity building, as well as on international child welfare and family policy. In this chapter, the newly minted social workers we first met in Chapter 1 grapple with the demands of their first job, including forays into policy practice.

Chapter 10

Health and Mental Health Policies and Programs has been revised to include discussion of continuing threats from state and federal legislators working to dismantle the ACA. Information on how Medicaid and Medicare will change due to the ACA has also been included. The impact of states not choosing to participate in Medicaid expansion is analyzed, and the resulting likelihood of increasing disparities in health outcomes from state to state is examined. Negative consequences for health care for not just people with low incomes, but also for the rest of the state's citizens, are considered. Discussion of the debate to make Medicare a voucher program has been added to the "Challenges to the Medicare System" section. Also, updated material on the mental health parity law has been incorporated in the "Substance Abuse, Pandemics, and the Health Care System" section. Information focusing on prevention and on encouraging the development of healthy lifestyles to reduce health care costs and improve quality of life has also been included in the chapter. Students are provided with resources to stay up to the minute on policy and program changes resulting from implementation of health care reform legislation, and ways they can shape implementation are explained. Finally, we continue to follow members of the policy group as they move into initial jobs and become involved in policy practice.

Chapter 11

Policies and Programs for Older Adults provides an overview of key policy issues that influence older adults including the many changes resulting from the 2010 health care reform legislation. Changes discussed include the Elder Justice Act, repeal of the CLASS Act voluntary long-term care provisions, and improvements to Medicare. Implications for social work are detailed. I also discuss the merger of the Administration on Aging with the Office on Disability and the Administration on Developmental Disabilities to form the newly created Administration for Community Living (ACL) and the potential impact of this merger. Additionally, the discussion of the Older Americans Act reauthorization in the "Creating Needed Infrastructure" section has been updated. I also examine policy strategies to promote economic security, adequate health care, and social engagement, as well as ways to support intergenerational cooperation. Expanded discussion of wellness initiatives and of changing work patterns and participation among older adults has been incorporated into the chapter. Last of all, as in Chapter 10, we continue to follow the careers of the social work students introduced in Chapter 1.

Chapter 12

The Future focuses on strategies for dealing with future policy dilemmas. The policy basics covered in earlier chapters provide the foundation for thinking about how we might begin to address future challenges. This chapter has been revised to help students more effectively synthesize what they have learned and chart their own strategies to apply policy practice content in a rapidly changing political, physical, social, and economic environment. Information on how students can be involved in shaping the future of social policy has been included to assist with this synthesis. The likely impact of global economic instability on social benefits and services is briefly examined. Discussion of the changing role of family and religion in our society is highlighted and the dual role of religion as therapeutic and also supporting social change is examined. Updated information on initiatives to improve child well-being as well as new developments related to global warming and potential impact on financial stability have also been incorporated into this chapter. The text closes with a challenge to students to help develop a vision of the future that will energize the journey, and to work to improve policies and, ultimately, future outcomes for our clients.

INTERACTIVE CASES

The website www.routledgesw.com/cases presents six unique, in-depth, interactive, fictional cases with dynamic characters and real-life situations that students can easily access from any computer, and that provide a "learning by doing" format unavailable with any other text. Your students will have an advantage unlike any other they will experience in their social work training. Each of the interactive cases uses text, graphics, and video to help students learn about engagement, assessment, intervention, and evaluation and termination at multiple levels of social work practice. The "My Notebook" feature allows students to take and save notes, type in written responses to tasks, and share their work with classmates and instructors by email. Through the interactive cases, you can integrate the readings and classroom discussions by acquainting the students with:

The Sanchez Family: Systems, Strengths, and Stressors The ten individuals in this extended Latino family have numerous strengths but are faced with a variety of challenges. Students will have the opportunity to experience the phases of the social work intervention, grapple with ethical dilemmas, and identify strategies for addressing issues of diversity. This case has been updated especially for this edition with more policy content and a video specifically about policy practice.

Riverton: A Community Conundrum Riverton is a small Midwest city in which the social worker lives and works. The social worker identifies an issue—homelessness—that presents her community with a challenge. Students and instructors can work together to develop strategies for engaging, assessing, and intervening with the citizens of the social worker's neighborhood.

Carla Washburn: Loss, Aging, and Social Support Students will get to know Carla Washburn, an older African American woman who finds herself living alone after the loss of her grandson and in considerable pain from a recent accident. In this case, less complex than the Sanchez Family, students will apply their growing knowledge of gerontology and exercise the skills of culturally competent practice.

RAINN: Rape, Abuse and Incest National Network This interactive case gives students a chance to assess a new type of delivery system for human services: the internet. Internet-based hotlines are emerging as a new form of service delivery for victims of sexual assault, as well as for other client groups.

Hudson City: An Urban Community Affected by Disaster Our clients are experiencing the brunt of natural disasters and this interactive case gives students a chance to learn about disaster relief and psychological first aid. Thinking through the policy issues related to dealing with disasters is becoming increasingly important for our students.

Brickville A real estate developer has big plans to redevelop Brickville, a major metropolitan area that has suffered from generations of disinvestment and decay. The redevelopment plans have stirred major controversy among community residents, neighborhood service providers, politicians, faith communities, and invested outsiders. This case is community with a family case embedded; students will be challenged to think about two levels of client systems and the ways in which they influence one another.

This book takes full advantage of the interactive element as a unique learning opportunity by including exercises that require students to go to the website and use the cases. To maximize the learning experience, you might want to start the course by asking your students to explore each case by activating each button. The more the students are familiar with the presentation of information and the locations of the individual case files, the case study tools, and the questions and tasks contained within each phase of the case, the better they will be able to integrate the text with the online practice component.

IN SUM

Social Policy for Effective Practice provides an integrated approach to the policy making process. A clear philosophical base and a common theoretical framework underlie the discussion of each component of the policy process. The focus is on understanding how social policy can contribute to effective social work practice on a day-to-day basis across the gamut of social work settings. My aim is to spark students' desire to understand and influence social policy. In order to help reach this outcome, I have interwoven four essential themes throughout this book: (1) the importance of thinking critically about social policy, (2) the benefits of using the strengths perspective, a value-based approach, in policy analysis and development, (3) the vital role social policy plays in all areas of practice, and (4) the absolute responsibility of every social worker to engage in policy practice.

This new edition integrates new web tools and resources, many of which have been developed since the second edition was published. This text charts a new course for policy practice in the 21st century.

ACKNOWLEDGMENTS

Many people have helped shape this book. Faculty steeped in the strengths perspective here at the University of Kansas (KU) as well as colleagues at other universities generously reviewed content. Dr. Katharine Briar-Lawson from the University of Albany and Melinda Lewis from KU were particularly helpful in reviewing chapters and identifying needed additions and revisions.

Melinda Lewis, a policy practice expert who works with the immigrant community, also developed the amazing Instructor's Resources that makes it easy to create a first-rate course using my text. Additionally, she created a policy practice video for the Sanchez case and infused the interactive cases with policy content.

Kathy DePaolis, a doctoral student at KU, did a great deal of work on exhibits and other resources that are part of each chapter. She also edited chapter content and particularly contributed her expertise to Chapter 9, Policies and Programs for Children and Families. We worked closely together on this revision.

Alicia Sellon, also a doctoral student at KU, put together the readings for this revision.

My husband, Barry Chapin spent many long hours creating graphs and charts and updating references. Without his steady help and encouragement, this text would have been less rich.

Steve Rutter, Dr. Alice Lieberman, Samantha Barbaro, Margaret Moore, and Tamsin Ballard are part of the inventive editorial team that helped make this integrative series a reality. The other authors of the book series, Anissa Rogers, Julie Birkenmaier, Marla Berg-Weger, Judy Krysik, and Jerry Finn, have helped craft this innovative way of introducing core content to social work students.

A thank you to the reviewers:

Cynthia Moniz	Plymouth University
Mary Yager	Lancaster Bible College
Aislinn Conrad-Hiebner	University of Kansas
Deborah Adams	University of Kansas

Martha Byam	University of New Hampshire
Aracelis Francis	University of the Virgin Islands
Martha Bial	Fordham University
Jo Bailey	University of Houston, Downtown
Lara Vanderhoof	Tabor College
Johanna Thomas	University of Arkansas, Little Rock
Belinda Bruster	Florida Gulf Coast University

Thank you all for your help and encouragement.

ABOUT THE AUTHOR

Dr. Rosemary Kennedy Chapin is an award-winning teacher and researcher, possessing extensive program development experience in the social policy arena. After receiving her PhD, she worked as a Research/Policy Analyst for the Minnesota Department of Human Services, where she was involved in crafting numerous long-term care reform initiatives. In 1989, she joined the faculty at the University of Kansas, where she established and now directs the Office of Aging and Long Term Care (OALTC), which was created to improve social service practice and policy for older adults, particularly low-income elders. Her social policy research and strengths-based training initiatives can be viewed at www.oaltc.ku.edu. Dr. Chapin has been recognized at both the state and the federal level for her social policy research and advocacy. She recently won the prestigious Steeples Award for her policy practice work on behalf of older adults. In addition to numerous articles and book chapters on social policy, she has also co-authored a text and various book chapters on the use of the strengths approach in social work practice with older adults. She teaches social policy and social work and aging courses at the University of Kansas. Dr. Chapin and her husband have three children and live in Lawrence, Kansas.

CHAPTER 1

Social Work and Social Policy: A Strengths Perspective

The outreach health and social service center where I'm placed is seeing more and more homeless teens with STIs and substance abuse problems. Some are runaways, but some are just considered too old to stay in the family homeless shelters in the city.

The school where I have my field placement has a growing proportion of Hispanic students, many struggle with English, and I am one of the few staff who speak Spanish. What's up with that?

I have an 85-year-old client, Rosalie Pachta, who can still live in the community but needs some help with bathing and dressing. Her children live in other states, and she can't afford formal home and community based services (HCBS). All of the publicly funded HCBS services have long waiting lists. She may end up in a nursing facility because she can't continue to live in the community without services.

Social Work Students

SOCIAL WORK STUDENTS INVOLVED IN FIELDWORK are facing new dilemmas. A lengthy recession is straining state budgets and contributing to growing federal debt. Tax cuts enacted during the Bush administration and stimulus spending during the Obama administration exacerbated the federal deficit. Social service agencies are seeing increasing numbers of people in dire need and at the same time, many agencies are facing deep funding cuts. Students find themselves laboring harder than ever to fill the gaps, with efforts that are often inadequate to meet clients' needs. Some students may become so overwhelmed that they decide social work is just "too hard" and they leave the field. Even worse, other students decide they cannot fight "the system," so they tell their clients, "There is nothing to be done." However, you can make a different choice. You can choose to understand and influence the social policies that will shape your practice and your clients' lives. Your social policy knowledge and skills become additional tools that you bring to your practice of social work, increasing your ability to help your clients.

Social policies are the laws, rules, and regulations that govern the benefits and services provided by governmental and private organizations to assist people in meeting their needs. Although the term "needs" can mean different things to different people, social workers define a need as the gap between an existing condition and some societal standard or required condition. For example, our society has developed standards of adequate nutrition for children. When children do not have access to a sufficient variety of foods to meet those standards, then their nutritional needs are not being met. The term social justice refers to the equitable distribution of societal resources to all people as well as equity and fairness in the social, economic, and political spheres.

For the people described in the opening vignettes, social policy shapes their lives in clear ways. For social workers, social policy shapes almost every practice setting. Indeed, as a student, your own future may be dramatically influenced by rising tuition fees, lack of access to health care and financial aid, regressive tax policies, and increasing debt burdens that are a direct result of social policy changes. It does not take long to identify repressive and ineffective social policies that have negative effects on your clients' lives as well as your own. Social policies can also be instruments for promoting social justice and greatly improving clients' lives.

My purpose in writing this book is to provide you with clear and concise frameworks as well as the knowledge, skills, and, most importantly, the desire to become involved in developing social policies that incorporate the strengths perspective. The strengths perspective is a philosophical approach to social work positing that the goals, strengths, and resources of people and their environment, rather than their problems and pathologies should be the central focus of the helping process (Saleebey, 1992). In this text, the terms "strengths perspective" and "strengths approach" are used to refer to this philosophical approach. For additional information about the strengths perspective, visit the website of the Strengths Institute at the University of Kansas, School of Social Welfare (www.socwel.ku.edu/strengths).

I believe that a greater focus on people's strengths and resources—a strengths approach—should be integrated into social policy development. To begin this learning process, this chapter introduces and critiques some of the basic concepts and frameworks that will be the building blocks of your understanding of policy making. In addition, it explains how the ways in which we define and understand social problems shape the social policies and programs that we develop to address those problems. Social problems are concerns about the quality of life of large groups of people that are either held as a broad consensus among a population and/or voiced by social and economic elites (Chambers and Wedel, 2009). Social workers spend much of their professional careers attempting to reduce social problems and/or helping clients to deal with the effects of social problems. Examples of social problems are drug abuse, juvenile delinquency, and homelessness. Subsequent chapters—particularly Chapters 5 and 6—present detailed information on how social workers can help analyze and develop social policies designed to address these problems. In future chapters, you will also learn about the historical, political, and economic contexts that shape social policy, and about the major social policies that affect our clients. There are also five interactive cases available at www.routledgesw.com that will allow you to practice applying your new policy focused skills to work with clients. The Sanchez case is particularly rich in policy related content.

SOCIAL WORK AND SOCIAL POLICY

Social policies shape the social welfare system of the U.S. The term social welfare refers to a nation's system of programs, benefits, and services that help people meet the social, economic, educational, and health needs that are fundamental to the maintenance of society. Social policies make it possible for clients to receive benefits and services they might desperately need. When I use the term client, I am referring to the recipient of the direct service or benefit provided by the social worker rather than to the taxpayer or policy maker. Taxpayers and policy makers are important constituents, but clients are the social worker's main concern. The terms "client group" and "service users" also refer to the population that is the primary focus of a social policy or program. Therefore, these terms are used interchangeably throughout this book. In this text, we focus primarily on social policies that shape benefits and services for our clients.

In 1973, the National Association of Social Workers (NASW) defined social work as "the professional activity of helping individuals, groups or communities to enhance or restore their capacity for social functioning and creating societal conditions favorable to this goal" (NASW, 1973, p. 4). A further delineation of the mission of social work was developed in 1996 and is part of the NASW Code of Ethics (2008).

The primary mission of the social work profession is to enhance human well-being and help meet the basic human needs of all people, with particular attention to the needs and empowerment of people who are vulnerable, oppressed, and living in poverty. An historic and defining feature of social work is the profession's focus on individual well-being in a social context and the well-being of society. Fundamental to social work is attention to the environmental forces that create, contribute to, and address problems in living (NASW, 2009b, p. 381). Combating injustice through policy reform is our ethical obligation. The quality of the services we deliver is influenced by the policies that govern their delivery. Therefore, social workers interested in increasing service effectiveness need to become involved in developing social policy. Silence and cynicism are political acts; those opposed to changes that are needed in the service system count on public apathy to maintain the status quo or to even cut back vital services.

The Relationship Between Social Policy and Social Work Practice

In order to help you understand the relationship between social policy and social work practice more clearly, we can examine policies, programs, and practice in the area of child abuse and neglect. Social policies determine who may remove children from their homes, where the children can be placed, whether they can receive specialized counseling services, who can provide those services, and how much providers will be paid. Social policies create the social programs that shape social work. Social workers serving children as well as other client groups cannot hope to help their clients unless they understand these crucial parameters that shape how they practice. Social policies ultimately dictate the services offered by social workers through social programs.

The child in foster care, the older adult in a nursing facility, and the incarcerated teenager have all powerfully experienced the results of social policy. Social workers, whether in private practice, in public child welfare, in health care, or in any other setting, also experience the consequences of social policy. You can become a much more effective social worker if you have a basic understanding of how policy influences practice in your agency and in your community. These insights can also help you move beyond understanding how policies work and coping with the aftermath of social policy to become proactive in helping to shape policies. For example, foster children are at increased risk of being homeless as adults. As a social worker with knowledge of the challenges foster children face, you can help educate legislators about the need for programs to help foster children successfully transition to adulthood.

Social policies can be developed by both the public and the private sector. Public social policies are those policies created by federal, state, and local governments. Most social policy in the U.S. is public policy. Nevertheless, private entities such as businesses and religious organizations may also develop social policies and programs, such as child care and elder care programs. Indeed, it is often through policies formulated by the private agencies in which social workers practice that clients experience the impact of social policy most directly.

Social policies can benefit clients in many ways. They can help clients achieve their life goals. For example, they can help single mothers secure well-paying jobs by mandating equal opportunity in employment. Social policies can also help clients by creating social programs. Social programs are a specified set of activities that are designed to solve social problems and/or meet basic human needs. For example, public social policies that create childhood nutrition programs make it possible for children to receive adequate food. Social workers are often involved in delivering the services that are part of these programs. They are also constantly helping their clients to navigate the resources that these programs provide and to hurdle the gaps in programs.

Exhibit 1.1 illustrates the relationships between the social welfare system, social policy, and social workers. Our social welfare system includes benefits and services for families who have incomes that are insufficient to adequately nourish children. The Child Nutrition Act is the social policy that created the Special Supplemental Nutrition Program for Women, Infants, and Children (WIC). Clients who qualify receive food benefits as well as nutrition and health education and referrals to health and other social services when needed. Social workers deliver some of these

Social Welfare System

Our social welfare system includes benefits and services for families who have incomes that are insufficient to adequately nourish children.

Social Policy

The Child Nutrition Act created the Special Supplemental Nutrition Program for Women, Infants, and Children (WIC).

Social Workers

WIC Program provides food benefits as well as nutrition and health education and referrals to health and other social services when needed. Social workers deliver some of these services.

EXHIBIT 1.1

Relationship of Social Welfare System, Social Policy, and Social Workers

services. Note that the arrows between the boxes in Exhibit 1.1 go in both directions. Social workers are influenced by social policy, but they can also influence the development of social policy.

Although social policies and programs are often created to assist people, they can also be a means of oppression. For example, in the past, the U.S. enacted public social policies that mandated separate schools for people of color and denied them the right to vote. As a professional social worker, you will see first-hand the results of both failed and effective social policies. You will be expected to do more than simply complain about unjust and ineffective policies; you will be expected to engage in policy practice. Policy practice "encompasses professional efforts to influence the development, enactment, implementation, modification, or assessment of social policies, primarily to ensure social justice and equal access to basic social goods" (Barker, 2003, p. 330). Engaging in policy practice will enable you to help craft policies that support effective work with clients. This book begins and ends with a challenge to use the tools provided in these chapters to engage in policy practice that benefits our clients. You will use many of the same skills—assessing, engaging, relating, communicating—that serve you in direct practice, and your social work value base will be your guide here as elsewhere in practice.

Social Work Values Integral to the Strengths Approach to Policy Practice

The Code of Ethics, developed by the NASW (2008) to help guide our practice, requires us to implement core social work values into our practice. Two fundamental values that can guide our efforts to shape more effective policy are self-determination and social justice. Self-determination refers to people's control of their own destiny. As we shall see, this concept is essential to the strengths perspective, which argues that clients possess resources that can help them achieve their goals. Social justice involves the fair distribution of societal resources to all people. It focuses on the means by which societies allocate their resources, which consist of material goods and social benefits, rights, and protections. These values reinforce the proposition that people who are disadvantaged by the current social order should have equal access to resources and opportunities to meet their common human needs.

Respect for diversity is central to social work practice. Therefore, social workers are expected to campaign for societal action on behalf of disadvantaged groups, regardless of gender, race, age, disability, or other characteristics that have been the basis for being denied access to resources. Visit the website of the NASW and then go to Code of Ethics to view this document in its entirety (www.naswdc.org). Unlike many other approaches to social policy analysis, social work values are basic to the strengths approach.

The Social Worker's Responsibility for Policy Practice   Like the NASW, the Council on Social Work Education (CSWE) has developed standards that reinforce the responsibility of social workers to become proficient in the policy arena and to engage in policy practice. Learn more about these two key social work organizations by visiting their websites (www.naswdc.org and www.cswe.org). For example, CSWE accreditation standards for social work programs in colleges and universities require that the curriculum contains content on policy practice. Nevertheless, many social workers remain hesitant to engage in the policy making process at either the agency or governmental level. Social workers who are on the front line, working daily with clients, can provide valuable perspectives on the consequences of social policies. However, they often do not recognize the resources they can bring to the policy making arena, and they have little idea of how they can influence social policy.

You can be a different type of social worker. Whether you are already involved in a field placement, are still preparing for field placement, or have several years of social work practice experience, this book can help you build the skills necessary to use what you will hear and see to understand current policies and advocate for more effective ones. You will learn to be a "listening post" for the stories that could help policy makers understand more clearly the impact of their decisions. You will be better able to navigate the social policy landscape, to secure what your clients need and to identify areas of needed social change. Further, if you work as a clinician, you may become involved in piloting new clinical approaches. When you are involved in this kind of innovative practice, you are laying the foundation for new programs and policies. It is out of these kinds of practice pilots that many successful policy innovations grow. This book will show you how to make your voice and your clients' voices heard in the policy arena and how to be innovative in guiding the policy process.

Often, interest in social work grows from a basic desire to "help people." However, interest in how policy practice can help clients must also be developed. You are preparing for a career that focuses on people in their environments. People and their environments are interdependent. Social policies shape our clients' environments and thus influence our ability to help them. Social work courses will help you sort out what it means to assist people and will provide conceptual tools to guide your efforts. No matter where you practice social work, you will be involved in policy practice. As you engage and assess your clients, you also need to begin assessing the policies and programs that either help or create barriers to the achievement of their goals. (The interactive cases that accompany this text will provide examples of how that is done.) These policies and programs may be federal laws and major programs such as the Child Nutrition Act that created WIC, as previously discussed. However, rules and regulations at your agency may also be hindering or helping clients. To be effective in helping your clients, at minimum you will need to do this "dual assessment" so you can identify the specific policy issues that impact your clients and consider whether intervention requiring use of your policy practice skills is necessary. Then, look for patterns in your caseload where several clients are negatively influenced by the same policy. These patterns should serve as red flags to alert you to the need for action. Make the connection between individuals' needs and policy issues that impact their ability to meet their need; then also work to change those policies. This is referred to as moving from "case-to-cause."

As a strengths-based policy practitioner, you can plan and implement these policy interventions in ways that place your clients' strengths and needs center stage and that actively involve them in all phases of the change process. Even social workers in very clinical roles are increasingly describing themselves as activist clinicians as they engage in advocacy to improve policies and programs for their clients. Advocacy involves helping to make the needs of a group clear to people in decision-making positions in ways that are most effective with the targeted decision makers (for example, helping clients who want to tell their stories, public education campaigns, press releases, letters, demonstrations, and petitions). As an advocate, you will need to be willing to take risks and also to have realistic expectations because you will certainly not always succeed. However, each time you try, you will build your skill level. Further, even if you fall short of the ultimate policy goal, the effort can reap many benefits such as increased client engagement, clearer understanding of issues, and greater awareness on the part of policy makers.

Advocacy requires an array of skills which we cover in detail later in this text. They include: understanding how to help clients become involved in the policy development process, providing research and technical information, understanding policy makers' biases, having insights into all perspectives on the issues, and presenting issues in ways that can be embraced by policy makers (Reisch, 2000). Advocacy in the context of policy practice is the kind of advocacy we focus on in this text. This type of advocacy involves work to change policies which can include introducing new legislation, helping to bring legal challenges in court, and/or work to change programs so that they are more effective for your clients.

At the end of this chapter, you will meet four social work students who initially get acquainted while working in groups in their social policy class. By following their ups and downs as they develop policy practice skills, you will get practical ideas about how you can become an effective policy practitioner.

Connecting Social Policy to Personal Experience   Regardless of whether you are currently in field placement, you will most easily master the content of this text if you use it immediately and try to connect it with your personal experience. To help make those connections, let us reflect on a situation in which you tried to help another person. When you were working with that person, did you give any thought to how social policies may have influenced your ability to help? Even if you never considered this question, social policies undoubtedly affected your efforts. For example, if you were working for a social service agency, then the agency's policies determined who could receive what kinds of services, who could offer those services, and how those services would be financed. Even if you were trying to offer assistance on a less formal level, such as when friends were getting a divorce or a grandparent was injured, it is likely that policies governing marriage and divorce, child custody, or long-term care significantly influenced your ability to help secure resources for the person in need. If you learn how to analyze social policies and advocate for needed change, then your efforts to help people can become more effective.

You can begin practicing the skills you learn in this course by applying them to your own life. Social policies shape your life and the lives of your friends and family. Take the time to examine which policies irritate you and which ones actually work well, and you will develop your capacity to successfully negotiate a path to your goals. At the same time, you will be building the necessary skills to support your clients in attaining their goals.

SOCIAL WORK AND THE STRENGTHS PERSPECTIVE

At the direct interpersonal level, methods of developing social policies, like methods of social work intervention, typically have been problem-focused and generally were designed to detect deficiency or pathology in the person experiencing the problem. The understanding of problems as originating in individual pathology has its roots in the medical model in which identifying the individual's problem or pathology is basic to treatment. For example, a medical practitioner diagnoses a patient as having a pathological condition such as influenza or diabetes and then prescribes treatment.

Traditionally, many policy makers have employed a similar approach to understanding needs or problems. Like medical practitioners, they have focused on defining and assessing "problems" that characterize individuals and institutions within their community. This approach is not necessarily inappropriate. In fact, a careful analysis of core social problems needs to be done in order to craft and implement effective social policy. The problem is that this approach has seldom been coupled with similar attention to identifying the strengths of the people and environments that the policy targets (Chapin, 1995). Further, social problem analysis that focuses on the pathology of the person experiencing the problem often leads to policy strategies that blame the victim. For example, a homeless mother may be deemed unfit and lose custody of her children, even though there is no available housing in the community that she can afford.

You have probably also been taught to always begin with a thorough analysis of the problem at hand. However, it is unlikely that you have been taught to couple that careful analysis of problems with a thorough analysis of strengths and resources. Think for a moment about problems in your community such as teenage pregnancy and homelessness. When people assess these problems, they frequently focus immediately and solely on possible deficits, or shortcomings, of the people involved. Thus, homeless people are homeless because of drug addiction or laziness, and teenagers become pregnant because they lack self-control. Our understanding of a social problem is sometimes so negative that we are led to believe the problem is impossible to resolve. For example, some cities and towns feel there is little they can do to significantly diminish the size of their homeless community. In such cases, our perception of the problem needs to be re-examined. We may be asking the wrong questions: perceiving people's needs in new ways could lead us to new answers.

In contrast to the medical model, the strengths perspective examines the strengths, goals, and resources of individuals and their communities as well as the barriers to meeting needs that exist in the broader environment in which social problems develop. For example, social workers who examine homelessness from the strengths perspective would begin by looking carefully at the variety of people who are homeless and exploring their strengths and goals as well as resources in the community. They would also consider broader elements such as current economic conditions, the availability of affordable housing, the possibility of mental health problems among the homeless population, and the availability of government programs to assist people who have inadequate financial resources due to such factors as low wages and serious or chronic illness. Identifying and acquiring the resources necessary for homeless people to meet their goals are central to the strengths perspective. Similarly, viewing teenage pregnancy through this lens requires us to focus from the beginning on not only the problem itself but on the teenagers, their strengths and goals, and the resources they need. The strengths perspective asserts that homeless people and teenagers possess or have access to personal and environmental resources (or strengths) that can help them deal with and perhaps overcome these problems. The strengths perspective can help practitioners to implement a social justice model rather than a medical model when engaging with clients. Chapters 5 and 6 present a more detailed account of how social workers can use the strengths perspective to redefine social problems and devise more effective policies to address these problems.

The strengths perspective, which underpins the strengths approach, can be used to reformulate problem-centered approaches to understanding need and creating social policies. Consider, for example, a population that has historically been marginalized in U.S. society: people with disabilities. Based on the deficits approach, this population was labeled as "handicapped," and their capacity to perform a constructive role in society was minimized. However, employing a strengths-based strategy, people with disabilities, and their advocates insisted that these individuals could be employed and could utilize community resources if access to jobs and facilities rather than their disabilities became the central focus of relevant social policies. Their activism led to passage of the Americans with Disabilities Act (ADA), a 1990 law that bans discrimination against people with physical or mental disabilities in such areas as employment and transportation. Clearly, this type of result could not have been achieved until policy makers were convinced to abandon the traditional deficits approach in favor of a more positive focus on strengths and resources. Crucially, the ADA is also an example of how taking a strengths approach to policy development changes not just the product but also the process; here, individuals with disabilities played key roles in shaping the policy alternatives and advocating for changes in laws and regulations, and their leadership crafted a very different policy outcome than would have otherwise been realized.

Policy Practice Infused With the Strengths Perspective

When we understand there are alternatives to the view that social problems are rooted in individual or environmental pathology, we can explore new possibilities. In this section, we will consider how policy development could reflect a strengths-based approach. We will begin with the initial stage in the policy making process, which is defining needs, strengths, and goals. We will then focus on reconceptualizing social problems, involving clients in the policy development process, and convincing decision makers to allocate resources to meet those clients' needs. As you become familiar with how a strengths perspective can be used to guide policy development, consider carefully how the policy development process changes when infused with the strengths perspective, and how the policy produced is likely to change. In fact, it is the change in process that is likely to produce a more effective policy.

Recasting Human Needs and Social Problems   It is possible to recast the social problems foundation of the policy development process and reconnect with the basic human needs tradition promoted by social workers such as Charlotte Towle (1945/1987). Towle's most famous publication is *Common Human Needs*, a manual written for the Bureau of Public Assistance of the U.S. Social Security Board, which was originally published in 1945. Developed for public assistance workers, the manual is based on the premise that all people have common human needs. Building on this premise, we can view social policy as a tool for helping people meet these common needs. Using this perspective enables us to define social problems not in terms of human and environmental deficits but in terms of barriers that disadvantaged groups confront in attempting to satisfy such basic needs as food, shelter, and positive community participation.

"Further, the strengths perspective argues that many of these barriers result from discrimination and exclusion in educational, political, and economic spheres based on demographic characteristics such as race, gender, and socioeconomic status (SES), rather than on individual attributes" (Rappaport, Davidson, Wilson, and Mitchell, 1975). In times of economic downturn, when a greater percentage of people have lost homes or jobs, voters are more likely to recognize that factors external to the individual are making it difficult to satisfy basic needs. During such times, they may be more willing to support increased spending on health and social programs. Because crises also can create powerful opportunities for change, these periods can present additional chances to help restructure programs and even enact major policy reforms. Despite expansions in social supports sometimes realized during times of economic crisis, these downturns are often particularly devastating for those already economically marginalized. For them, the temporary decline in fortunes just adds to the significant barriers they faced even in "boom" times, leading to entrenched disadvantage from which it is difficult to exit.

An essential task of effective policy making, then, is to identify individual and community resources that can be used to remove these barriers and to create opportunities for people who have been excluded from full community participation so that they can meet their goals. For example, when working with people with mental illness, it is important to understand not only their disability but also their strengths as well as any available environmental resources that may contribute to their recovery. What brings joy to their lives? What are their goals? What policies hamper their recovery? How might these policies be reformulated to build on their strengths? The strengths and goals of the client are legitimate starting places in developing social policy. Problems and deficits should not be given center stage. When problems or needs are presented without any consideration of individual and community strengths and resources, policy makers are left to make decisions based on biases and prejudices. We can help construct new insights about problems and possibilities once we understand that our views of social problems are socially constructed. The social construction of social problems is discussed in detail in Chapter 5.

What types of resources might be available to disadvantaged groups? Perhaps the most fundamental are neighborhood and community institutions such as schools, community centers, health facilities, and self-help organizations. Appropriate social policies can both enhance these resources and increase the access of disadvantaged groups to them. When practicing social work, your assessment of the policies and programs that can help your clients reach their goals will help you identify resources available to your clients. Your assessment of the barriers and gaps in policy and programs that create stumbling blocks for many clients will help you focus your policy practice work. This is an example of the connection between social work skills, such as assessment, that are honed in micro work with individuals and families, and the primary tasks of policy practice.

Expanding the Client's Role   Approaching policy development from a strengths-based rather than a problem-centered perspective leads to an expanded role for clients and a corresponding shift in the role of the social worker. According to the strengths approach, the role of the professional helper, including the social worker, is not that of policy expert who informs the public and develops policy goals on her or his own. Rather, the social worker's role is to ensure that policy makers take clients' perspectives into account, to act as a resource person, and to collaborate with clients throughout the policy development process.

At the same time, a strengths-based strategy calls for a more active role on the part of the groups that are the target of the proposed policy. The strengths perspective recognizes that the definition of a need or problem shapes the policy options that are considered. In turn, social policy essentially determines the allocation of scarce resources. Therefore, it is crucial that clients be included in the processes whereby needs are identified, problems are defined, and policies are developed.

A fundamental belief of the social work profession is that policy makers must understand the programs and policies they create from the viewpoint of service users. For example, policy makers need to understand that homelessness has many causes, and hearing about or talking to a homeless mother who works hard but cannot find affordable housing can help them see the issue in a new light. Social workers know that any initiative that does not start "where the client is," will be more likely to fail.

Temporary Aid to Needy Families (TANF), the federal program that provides financial assistance to low-income parents, is an example of how the failure to focus on clients' perspectives can produce inappropriate policy. TANF included among its goals reducing the caseloads of the income assistance program, but not reducing child poverty, which would have likely been the top priority had clients' perspectives driven the development of the policy. TANF also has strict work requirements, but it had inadequate provisions for expanding existing child care programs. This type of flaw highlights the need for policy makers to understand clients' perceptions and community strengths. Had more policy makers believed that most clients who are single mothers relied on public assistance not because they were unwilling to work but because they had to care for their young children, or lacked the job skills needed to qualify for well-paid jobs that make child care affordable, they might have incorporated less stringent work stipulations into the law. In addition, they might have provided greater funding for child care centers, schools, and other community institutions that could care for children while their mothers worked. Providing their children with proper child care is a goal for many parents, and existing high-quality care is a community strength. When policy makers consider client goals and community strengths, as well as needs, more effective policies can be crafted. Your classes in community organization and development, which emphasizes social work with groups and communities to improve conditions in society, will also help you build skills that are used in policy practice.

Giving voice to the realities of service users can help policy makers who see recipients as the "other" to perceive the common human needs that they and the recipients share (Banerjee, 2002). Policy makers as well as TANF recipients are parents and recognize that children need care. Of course, there will not be consensus about needs among all recipients and policy makers. Such consensus is unnecessary. A variety of opinions and views typically are expressed when a policy is being formulated. However, consensus around broad goals, such as providing adequate care for children, can often be developed.

Claims-Making   Recognizing needs, strengths, and goals from the client's perspective creates a base for policy making. However, for social policy to be enacted, concerned individuals must make a successful claim that resources should be allocated to meet a recognized need. This process is known as claims-making. Claims are often influenced by values and are intended to establish rights to resources. For example, social workers make social justice claims for people with disabilities based on their strong belief that these individuals have the same right as other citizens to access community services. Claims-making that asserts the right to equal opportunity for all people is consistent with the strengths perspective. Moreover, the strengths approach requires that clients themselves be involved in the claims-making process. We examine claims-making in greater detail in Chapter 6. For now, you need to be aware that simply recognizing a need will not result in the enactment of social policies to address that need. There is, unfortunately, ample evidence of this in the history of social policy in our country. This can also be clearly seen today when you examine what currently makes it to the policy "agenda." Rather, concerned parties have to make a successful claim that the need deserves attention at the policy level in order to gain support for policy formulation.

When social workers attempt to engage in claims-making and influence policy formulation, there will be groups that oppose their ideas as well as groups that agree with them. Potential economic gain and loss and political ideology will influence their views. Chapter 4 examines this economic and political context, as well as the conflictive nature of policy making, in greater detail. In addition, the policy practice sections in Chapter 6 explore strategies and tactics for dealing with conflict and negotiating consensus. Working to resolve conflict and consensus building are essential parts of policy practice and, in fact, can be a great way to develop your own strengths. Involving clients in this work helps them increase their power, that is, to become empowered. The strengths approach, like other empowerment-based helping strategies, seeks to help client groups build skills that can lead to achieving more power over their lives. Joining with others to influence the policies that impact their own lives is a clear opportunity for truly empowering practice and can awaken latent capacities held within these resilient individuals. The work of the lesbian, gay, bisexual, transgendered, and questioning (LGBTQ) community to secure equal treatment, particularly in regard to same-sex marriage, is a clear example of a group that is developing its capacity to speak out against discrimination and influence social policy. This text has been designed to be an empowerment tool and I wrote it to help you know how to proceed in your work to combat injustice.

Principles of Strengths Perspective Policy Practice

As we have observed, the strengths perspective, which underpins the strengths approach, is rooted in a number of basic concepts and principles. The most important policy focused strengths perspective principles are listed below. These principles are discussed in depth in Chapter 5. Many of these principles are not unique to the strengths perspective. Social workers have discussed and used many of these principles to guide effective social work practice in the policy arena in the past. These strengths policy principles build on the work of Rapp, Pettus, and Goscha as well as other social workers who are searching for ways to incorporate social work values into the policy development process (Rapp, Pettus, and Goscha, 2006). The strengths perspective is a stance that puts social work values into action. For more information on the strengths perspective, see the companion readings on the text's website (www.routledgesw.com/policy).

- The strengths and goals of your clients are legitimate starting places in developing social policy. Problems and deficits should not be given center stage.

- Given that the definitions of social problems that typically guide policy and program development are socially constructed, our clients' perspectives concerning their problems, needs, strengths, and goals should be part of the social construction of need for policy development.

- Structural barriers that disadvantage our clients in meeting their needs and create unequal opportunities should be emphasized when claims for the right to benefits and services are made.

- The strengths perspective is premised on social work values of self-determination and social justice. Claims for benefits and services that allow people to overcome these additional barriers are made based on the right to equal access to resources and opportunities to meet needs and reach goals for citizens, regardless of gender, race, age, disability, sexual orientation, gender identity, or other characteristics that have been the basis for denying access.

- Social policies and programs should build on individual and community strengths and resources and remove structural barriers that disadvantage the target group.

- The role of the social worker is not that of the expert who helps shape policy for hapless victims. Rather, it is that of the collaborator and resource person who helps gain attention for the perspectives of the target group and supports clients in advocating for policies to improve their lives.

- Social policy goals and design should focus on access, choice, and opportunity that can help empower the target group in meeting their needs and goals.

- The target group should be involved in all phases of policy development. The process as well as the product, or outcome, of policy development will differ when clients are involved in all phases of your work.

- Evaluating the efficacy of social policy should include evaluation of outcomes for clients.

Frameworks for Policy Development

Now that we have examined basic concepts and principles, we can explore how the strengths perspective can be integrated into a framework for policy development. Note that I emphasize what the strengths perspective can add rather than claiming that other policy development frameworks should be abandoned. Approaches to policy development on which this book is based incorporate frameworks developed by a variety of authors, including Gilbert and Terrell (2001) and Chambers (2000). To compare these as well as other frameworks, explore the reading on policy analysis frameworks that accompany the text. Your instructor can provide you with a synopsis of these frameworks, available on the book's website (www.routledgesw. com/policy) in a reading titled "Policy Analysis Frameworks."

Quick Guide 1 compares a problem-centered framework with one infused with the strengths perspective. This comparison can help you explore the ways in which social problems are defined and social policies are developed. This box summarizes many of the ideas previously discussed in this chapter and illustrates how those ideas inform the various stages of policy development. Although the strengths perspective shifts the focus away from individual problems, it does not require that we deny deficit or misery. However, it does demand that we shift our perspective, attitude, and language to focus on possibility and opportunity and the potential of the individual, who has strengths as well as needs.

QUICK GUIDE 1   **Comparison of the Problem-Centered and Strengths-Based Approaches to Policy Development**

PROBLEM-CENTERED APPROACH	STRENGTHS-BASED APPROACH
Define problem. • A situation is labeled a problem to be corrected.	Define needs, goals, and barriers in partnership with clients. • Identify basic needs and barriers to meeting needs. • Identify client goals.
Analyze problem, causes, and consequences.	Formulate policy alternatives in partnership with clients. • Identify ways that barriers to reaching goals are currently overcome by clients (strengths) and through programs (best practice). Focus on solutions.
Inform the public. Engage in claims-making.	Claims-making is based on right to self-determination and social justice.
Develop policy goals.	Identify opportunities and resources necessary for people to meet their goals in partnership with clients. Formulate policy goals informed by consumer collaboration.
Legitimize policy goals by building consensus.	Legitimize policy goals by negotiating consensus.
Develop and implement policy/program.	Develop and implement policy/program in partnership with clients. • Program design informed by consumer collaboration. • Implementation informed by consumer involvement.
Evaluate and assess policy/program effectiveness.	Evaluate outcomes in partnership with clients. • Evaluation and assessment emphasizes client outcomes and client feedback to improve policy.

Source: Adapted from Chapin, 1995. Copyright © 1995 by National Association of Social Workers, Inc. Used with permission of NASW. Based on the work of Chambers, 2000; Gilbert, Specht, and Terrell, 1998; and Tice and Perkins, 2002.

The point of Quick Guide 1 is not to propose that only one of the formulations of the policy development process is correct or presents truth. Indeed, the problem-focused approach may more clearly reflect how policies have been, and are currently being, made. Rather, the presentation of the strengths-infused framework highlights the values that underlie this approach, the outcomes you can expect when you use this approach, and the direction this approach provides for understanding and developing social policy. This approach helps people discover strategies for effectively meeting their needs when confronted by barriers.

Social workers have a responsibility to ensure that policy reflects clients' realities and more policy makers need to understand these realities. So, for example, policy makers need to understand that students who fail to graduate from high school are not always making a conscious decision to "drop out." Instead, they may face significant barriers to continued school progress; these barriers could include health care, mental health, poverty, family crisis, and learning disabilities. Hearing about or talking to these young people can help policy makers see the problem in a new light. When social workers help initiate such an interaction, they are helping to negotiate an expanded understanding of the truth. Further, client groups can be asked about what solutions they can envision. Indeed focusing more on these potential solutions can help engender hope and energize the process of formulating new policy or improving existing policy and programs.

Moreover, once the policy has been negotiated and formulated, the strengths perspective mandates that clients be involved in implementing and evaluating the policy and programs that are enacted. This statement suggests that benefits and services, financing, and the service delivery system should be evaluated primarily on how effectively they help clients achieve their goals rather than solely on cost, ease of administration, or potential for creating profit in the private sector. In summary, then, the policy making process that includes the strengths approach strongly emphasizes that clients must be involved throughout all phases. It also recasts claims-making and the role of the social worker and it stresses the importance of focusing on client outcomes in evaluating policy effectiveness.

IDENTIFYING AND DEVELOPING YOUR POLICY PRACTICE ABILITIES

A good place to start to apply the strengths perspective is with yourself. Take a good look at yourself and identify your strengths, resources, and areas of expertise. Your instructor can provide you with a copy of a strengths assessment. Exploring your own strengths could lay the groundwork for discovering your clients' strengths. Recognizing that your clients possess expertise and can share stories of strength and resilience will enable you to examine policy from an expanded perspective. A perspective that includes this recognition is critical to effective policy practice using the strengths approach.

Consider becoming involved with grassroots efforts to develop services. Students in my policy classes often take me up on this challenge. For example, one group of students met with elder advocates and decided to help develop a home sharing program for older adults and students. The older adults indicated they had large homes and needed someone to help with upkeep. They were willing to have someone live with them for reduced rent if that person would help out. The students knew many others who needed housing and would be willing to help older adults with upkeep. Class members were encouraged to see themselves as competent, to look for strengths in the person and the environment, and to become involved in developing policies and programs in the community. Their project culminated with the presentation of a model program that was then modified and implemented with the support of the local senior center. The students also helped the center develop policies governing home sharing. Their work provided the class with a hands-on example of policy and program development that included careful attention to the older adult population's perceptions of its needs and goals, recognition of strengths and resources within the community, and a search for "evidence-guided" models in other communities. These students had essentially developed a small program pilot, and it is from such pilot work that new programs and policies often develop. Opportunities to get involved in such efforts exist in every community. There are examples of how social work students have influenced social policy throughout the text that will provide you with concrete ideas for how you can become involved in policy practice.

Such involvement will also give you a chance to learn first-hand about the economic and political considerations and conflicts that influence policy. If you have some personal experience dealing with such conflicts, you will find the content in coming chapters much easier to apply, and you will build your confidence and skills in tackling this part of social work practice.

No doubt there are many people in your community who can help you build policy practice skills. Think about the people you know. Is there someone who you believe is particularly savvy about how to shape social policy? The person you identify might be the person in your agency or college who interprets the rules and regulations when there is a question. Typically, there is latitude in interpretation, and this person understands what discretion is possible and, we hope, uses it to the benefit of clients or students. This person is shaping social policy. Your agency or college may also have a staff member who is assigned to lobby the legislature or make presentations at public hearings. Or you might have a friend or social work colleague who is passionate about a certain aspect of social policy and has become an advocate.

If you cannot identify anyone you currently know who you feel is particularly savvy, get to know someone who is effectively engaged in policy practice. This task is not difficult. Begin by considering your interest area. For example, if your primary interest is working with older adults or children, there are advocacy groups in your area that are led by people who are working to influence policy every day. Call them up. Take them to lunch. If you have time, volunteer to help with one of their initiatives. Then, observe what they do. Ask questions. If you develop an ongoing relationship, see if they will talk with you about the ideas presented in this book, how these ideas might apply to their work, and how you might implement some of them. As a volunteer, you can contribute a fresh perspective, help translate theories you are learning into practice, conduct background research, and help build coalitions among students, practitioners, and advocates (Sherraden, Slosar, and Sherraden, 2002).

Volunteering even a little time to a policy advocacy effort is a great way to network. Effective networking and relationship building is central to effective policy practice. Advocacy builds on the relational skills that are the foundation of social work practice.

In Chapter 6, in the sections on policy development, we will examine networking and many other specific strategies and tactics that are useful in influencing policy. However, if you are not already involved with people who are role models of effective policy practice, then begin now to build your network. You will learn to apply the content of this book much more easily if you know the specifics of actual policy practice efforts.

As a student and, later, as a practitioner, you will likely lead a very busy life. Some students will have jobs in which lobbying and client advocacy are primary job functions. Many of you will provide counseling and case management. However, in all social work roles, a practitioner who is alert to policy implications will be able to carve out some time to help shape policy. There are numerous ways that you can do so. For example, you can begin reshaping the views of fellow voters simply by speaking up when your clients are stereotyped. You can begin to apply solution focused approaches in your discussions with people who use services and benefits. Ask what a policy or program would look like that more effectively met their needs. Think about the services and benefits you may get, such as student loans, care at the student health clinic, and other elements of your educational experience governed by university policies, in the same way. Hopefully, thinking about potential solutions will help you develop fresh insights that will spur involvement in policy practice. You can also call or email your state legislator when you feel that policies are not working for your clients. You can use social media and letters to the editor to shape public perceptions of issues that matter to you. If you brainstorm with other students, all sorts of ideas for influencing policy that do not require great amounts of time or expertise will emerge.

You are not expected to craft new laws and get them passed single-handedly. Rather, most policy changes happen incrementally, and anything you can do is important for your clients. Many social workers feel as powerless as their clients. Effective involvement by a wider group of social workers can change that dynamic. The NASW Code of Ethics does not require that we make policy practice our full-time job, but it also does not excuse those who are "busy" from this responsibility.

Integrating a Strengths Perspective: Benefits and Cautions

A major goal of social work education is to foster critical thinking skills. With this precept in mind, you should adopt a healthy skepticism concerning the advantages of integrating a strengths perspective into your policy practice. I encourage you to weigh the potential benefits and drawbacks of the strengths perspective. I hope there will be time for just such a discussion in your class. The following discussion of benefits and cautions can serve as a starting point for your critique.

Benefits of the Strengths Perspective   When thinking about the merits of integrating a strengths perspective into social policy courses, I see many positive results, including the following benefits.

First, as previously discussed, the strengths perspective offers an antidote to victim blaming. Clients are not seen as problems. Problem admiration is not the order of the day. As we have seen, the strengths perspective requires workers to assertively look for strengths and resources in their clients as well as the clients' families and environment. Often, students are reluctant to ask people about their strengths and goals. It is instructive to note that asking clients about their capacity to go to the toilet or bathe is easier for students initially than asking about hopes, goals, and dreams. Fortunately, however, even students who were trained in the pathology-centered approach typically develop skills in identifying strengths rather quickly. Using a solution focused approach where you invite people to engage with you in envisioning their own solutions and then in developing strategies to attain those goals often improves outcomes.

Second, the strengths perspective provides a voice to populations whose views previously were ignored. Listening to traditionally oppressed groups, including people of color, women, gays and lesbians, and people with disabilities, explain how they have managed to survive and even flourish, can help students put into practice such basic social work values as social justice and respect for the individual. The emphasis on exploring strengths in the context of unique life experiences is appropriate across ethnic, cultural, and income groups (Chapin, Nelson-Becker, and Macmillan, 2006). Further, the insights gained from this approach can inform claims-making based on rights to equal access.

Third, once students move beyond the model of a professional who hears about deficits and lays out a solution, they generally become energized to listen to ideas that emerge from client groups and begin to uncover resources in the community. Students become engaged and shrug off the sense of hopelessness that I have observed too many times in students who focus primarily on what often appear to be overwhelming problems in oppressed communities. Indeed, after recognizing that clients frequently can identify solutions to their own problems, students become enthusiastic about working collaboratively to make whatever headway is possible. Students who engage with policymakers may find that when policy makers have a sense of the strengths in the target population, it may make them more motivated to do something about the problem.

Students from historically oppressed groups particularly seem to warm to the strengths approach. For example, a Native American student who was also a tribal leader on her reservation developed a strategy for using gambling proceeds to build a health and social services infrastructure based on the strengths perspective. She began by educating tribal leadership on how to use a strengths perspective to determine where tribal resources should be targeted. She then conducted an assessment of strengths and needs on the reservation. Healthy children and older adults were identified as major strengths. She then advocated for a change in tribal policy. She pressed for the use of gambling proceeds to build an infrastructure on the reservation to help keep children and older adults healthy. This infrastructure included daycare facilities and assisted living. She also collaborated with parents and older adults who were potential consumers of these services as well as with other tribal policy makers to influence policy.

Social workers who are committed to supporting client autonomy should seriously consider adopting an approach based on collaborating with consumers of services in trying to influence policy making. In summary, then, some of the benefits of using a strengths perspective are:

- it moves us away from victim blaming

- it reflects basic social work values

- it provides fresh ideas

- it involves consumers of services in policy making.

Cautions Regarding the Strengths Perspective   Despite all of the benefits we have just discussed, there are some concerns we need to consider when applying the strengths perspective to social policy. First, when we downplay clients' needs, we can also lose the sense of urgency to address these needs. Conversely, if we focus exclusively on the hungry child, the homeless family, or the bereft older person, then policy makers and taxpayers may be more likely to agree to spend tax dollars to help these people than if client strengths are emphasized as well. Social workers and clients must find ways to present needs effectively so that sufficient resources are provided to build on strengths. Surely it is possible to portray strengths as well as needs in a manner that can garner resources while avoiding victim blaming. The process of strengths-based social policy development, which emphasizes clients' roles in informing, implementing, and evaluating policy, can also be distorted to provide an excuse for social work professionals, policy makers, and other stakeholders to ignore our collective responsibilities to work together to solve social problems.

A second concern is that once students understand the strengths perspective they may come to believe that it is the only appropriate approach, no matter what the policy issue. The strengths approach adds a useful perspective, but it is not the only conceptual tool that social workers need to be effective at policy practice. Instead, successful policy practice requires mastery of a variety of concepts and skills, including a comprehensive understanding of how social problems are constructed and how to analyze need. This book focuses on building those skills.

Third, empirical research on the effectiveness of social work practice based on the strengths perspective is growing but still limited (Oko, 2006; Fukui et al., 2012; Saleebey, 2013). Although there is extensive anecdotal evidence that the strengths perspective is a useful tool, insufficient formal research has been conducted to provide empirical evidence of the specific mechanisms by which practice grounded in the strengths perspective influences client outcomes, and there is even less established knowledge about the outcomes of strengths-based policy development. Research is needed to show how the strengths approach operates in comparison to other strategies.

For all of these reasons, it is critical that you carefully scrutinize the benefits and drawbacks of all the conceptual tools you will be exposed to throughout your social work education, including those that integrate a strengths perspective. Every conceptual tool serves to illuminate some aspects of a situation and blind us to others. Think about what you might miss using a strengths perspective, as well as what you might see that was formerly overlooked.

Connecting Social Work Values to Policy Practice

In this chapter, we have considered how the strengths perspective builds on social work values and how a strengths approach can be incorporated into policy practice. Now, I challenge you to consider how you can incorporate social work values such as client self-determination, commitment to social justice, and a nonjudgmental approach into your policy practice work with clients. Remember, although social policies can be a powerful instrument for achieving social justice, social policies do not always help to meet clients' needs. In some cases, they create need, reinforce oppression, and undermine strengths.

As long as clients are disadvantaged by policies and resulting programs that do not reflect social work values, social workers must strive to mitigate those effects, to modify offensive policies, and to craft effective policy at the agency and legislative levels. So, here is a chance to try your hand at putting social work values into practice. What kinds of policy practice initiatives could help Rosalie Pachta, the Hispanic school children, or the homeless teens whose cases we considered at the beginning of this chapter? Remember, Rosalie Pachta may lose her independence, students are facing language barriers in public schools, and the numbers of homeless teens are growing. Recall the discussion about doing a dual assessment of your clients. Think about how policies are creating barriers to teens having a home. What policy practice initiatives might help them? Similarly, what policy practice strategies could help Rosalie Pachta get the home-based long-term care services she needs to avoid institutionalization or the elementary school children to overcome language barriers? Look back at the list of principles in Quick Guide 1 for ideas about how social work values can be put into action with these clients. What actions could you take to improve the policies that contribute to teen homelessness, unnecessary institutionalization of elders and disabled persons, and language barriers for elementary school children? What strengths might these individuals and groups possess—within themselves and in their environments—that could be utilized in your policy change strategies?

CONCLUSION

Social workers today face a challenging policy arena. As a student and future social worker, your commitment to help shape policies and programs that can provide resources, support, and opportunities for clients is vital. Social policies can be powerful tools for increasing social justice, and you can influence social policies. Integration of the strengths perspective into your understanding of social policy can help clarify your crucial role in shaping social policy, provide concrete guidance on how you can proceed in helping to craft effective policy, and can reinforce your responsibility to view the people with whom you work as collaborators and sources of expertise. Each time you begin to assess a new client, you also need to begin assessing the policies and programs that either help or create barriers to the achievement of their goals. This kind of dual assessment is basic to effective social work. The following chapters are designed to equip you with new tools for conceptualizing social needs or problems, a more inclusive approach to policy formulation, and an expanded array of policy options. You will learn how to analyze policy and programs and how they are developed. You will discover how the historical, political, and economic contexts affect social policy. You will learn about specific policies and programs in areas including child welfare, mental health, and work with older adults, and how these policies and programs influence social work practice. We will explore your role in policy practice. The text closes with a focus on the future. I invite you to share in the excitement of learning to understand and help shape social policies and programs that can potentially help thousands, and in some cases millions, of clients.

MEET THE POLICY GROUP

The four students who will be introduced to you here are on the same journey you are starting. You will see where they are as they begin studying social policy and trace their development in later chapters as they take a variety of social work jobs in child welfare, mental health, health, and aging services. Hopefully, their stories will help you understand how much you will need policy practice skills and inspire you to engage in policy practice.

Tiffany was trying to think through what was supposed to happen in this first small group experience in her social policy class. She was expecting it might be a pretty quiet interaction; more than half the class said listening was their greatest strength when the professor asked them earlier to introduce themselves and name

EXHIBIT 1.2

*First Meeting
of the Policy
Group*

one of their strengths. She guessed she was probably the youngest person in the group. The group was charged with discussing what they were passionate about and action strategies they might use to bring about policy change. Homelessness was the issue that caught her attention on the "Finding Your Passion" handout that provided facts and figures about domestic abuse, child trafficking, homelessness, economic and ethnic disparities, immigration, elder abuse, and other pressing concerns. She had volunteered time at a free health clinic last summer and had talked with people of all ages who were homeless, but really did not know what issues or groups held the most interest for her. However, what she was really passionate about was getting her social work degree and starting a career. She had student loans and a part-time job. Her parents could not contribute much more to her education than they already had. She knew they would be expected to develop group action plans later in the semester. She had told the class her greatest strength was that she was a good writer. Maybe she would suggest writing an editorial or doing something with a blog. She considers herself a follower and really plans to just work individually with people in her career.

Alejandro was a little nervous about working in a small group to complete not only this exercise but the other ones, like the action plan, that the teacher had mentioned while going over the syllabus. He hoped it was nothing like the experience he had last year while working in a small group for another class. The group members had had such different views that it was really hard to reach any kind of consensus on group tasks. Plus, a couple of the group members had never completed their part of the assignments and rarely provided any input during group exercises.

Alejandro was really excited about his practicum placement at a junior high school in the city. His mom is a school social worker and that is what he plans on doing when he graduates because he really enjoys working with kids. Hopefully, there is someone else in his group who likes working with kids as well so they have something in common that they could build on to complete assignments. He really does not know how policy fits with his career aspirations but his mom always talks about advocacy being a critical part of social work, so he is interested in learning more about policy practice.

Kelli was not excited about this policy small group exercise. This was her third class of the day and she was really tired from staying up late reading last night. Plus, she really does not see how policy relates to what she wants to do after graduation. She plans on starting in child welfare working with children who are in the foster care system but eventually plans on becoming a child therapist. The idea of macro practice has always intimidated her a bit and she really does not know how one person, like her, can bring about major social change. She tends to avoid politics. She did say that her strength was her technological savvy when she introduced herself at the beginning of class, so maybe she could just contribute to the group by suggesting ways to use technology in completing their group project that is due later in the semester.

Alice hoped this policy group exercise would not run long because she had to leave right on time to get to her son's baseball game. As usual, she was the only black student and the oldest person in her small group. When she first visited her field placement agency, a mental health center, she was struck by how few people of color were on staff, and it did not look like many more were in the student pipeline. The statistics on growing economic inequality in the "Finding Your Passion" handout came as no surprise to her. She could see that happening with her own family. She knew that she wanted to help people with mental health problems, and life had already taught her that was going to involve more than just one-to-one work. At her placement, she was working with elders with chronic mental illness. Many of them also had other physical illnesses and some were homeless. She was interested in policy practice and had a bunch of ideas about what needed attention. However, she was wary of adding much more to her already over packed schedule.

The group discussion was interesting and lots of ideas including using social media and making videos were suggested. The conversation was a bit diffuse, but the group seemed to click. They had identified a common interest in homeless children.

MAIN POINTS

- Social workers need to engage in policy practice in order to be effective practitioners. Students can and should choose to develop their policy practice skills.

- Social work values, including self-determination and social justice, are the foundation for policy practice and are integral to the strengths approach.

- Social policies can be tools for achieving social justice.

- This text is designed to be an empowerment tool that can help you know how to proceed in your work to combat injustice.

- A dual assessment involves examining your clients' goals as well as the policies and programs that either help or create barriers to the achievement of their goals. You can find resources for doing a dual assessment in the Sanchez interactive case.

- Problem-focused models for defining problems and developing policy can limit the social worker's ability to craft effective policies that build on clients' strengths.

- The strengths perspective can be used to reconceptualize the policy making process. In fact, it is the change in process that is likely to produce a more effective policy.

- The role of a social worker using the strengths perspective shifts from that of expert to collaborator and resource person. Identification of potential solutions and goals from the clients' perspective is key.

- There are benefits to integrating a strengths perspective as well as cautions that critical thinkers should consider.

- Begin now to build your policy practice skills. Becoming involved in policy practice in your community will enable you to try out the ideas that are presented in this book and begin to translate theory into practice.

EXERCISES

1. Go to www.routledgesw.com/cases and get to know the Sanchez family.
   Spend some time exploring the elements available in the case files. Look at the information in the Engage, Assess, Intervene, and Evaluate sections. After exploring the Sanchez family case, respond to the following questions:
   a. Do you feel you have cultural competency in working with Hispanic families? If not, how can you build that competency in the context of your university and home community? How is cultural competency essential for building a strong working relationship with the Sanchez family? How is it important for engaging in effective policy practice alongside an affected population?
   b. Complete a dual assessment of Hector, whereby you identify his needs, strengths, and goals, as well as the specific policy issues that influence him.

Identify three social policies that influence social work practice with Hector and the Sanchez family. Try to identify one federal, one state, and one agency policy. What are the policies, and how do they influence practice? You may want to view the companion video, which illustrates a social worker grappling with policies that impact the Sanchez family's access to food assistance, in particular. What skills and insights would you bring to a similar challenge?

c. Do you think Hector and Celia Sanchez would consider the policies you have identified effective? What improvements can you suggest?

d. What persons or groups do you think made these policies? If you could talk to these people, what would you like to tell them about the results of their decision to implement the policies? How might you ensure that the voices of the people affected by these policies, such as members of the Sanchez family, are taken into consideration by policy makers in ways that do not harm the service recipients?

2. Go to www.routledgesw.com/cases and become familiar with Riverton. Explore the interactive case by experimenting with the options. Imagine you are a social worker in this community. Your work with the Riverton community will undoubtedly involve policy practice. You will need to understand current city policies related to the homeless shelter as well as the policies of the homeless shelter, and how different groups in the community want these policies to change.

a. Thinking about what you have learned thus far about policy practice using the strengths perspective, where would you start?

b. Who would you talk to and what would you ask them?

c. What patterns do you see in terms of policies that are helping or hindering homeless men and women from finding temporary shelter and, ultimately, permanent homes?

d. Considering the different approaches to policy practice discussed in the text, how do you think social workers using the strengths approach would differ from those using a problem-centered approach in their work to craft more effective policies and programs in this community?

e. How would strengths-based social workers approach the community and what would the relationship and focus look like? What social work values could guide their work? Be as specific as possible.

3. Go to www.routledgesw.com/cases and meet Carla Washburn. You can begin to develop policy practice skills by completing the exercises that introduce you to the Carla Washburn interactive case.

a. What do you think are Mrs. Washburn's major needs?

b. Identify at least three strengths she has that could help her in meeting these needs.

c. Identify resources in the community that can potentially help Mrs. Washburn meet her needs.

d. What policies and programs are helping her meet her needs?

   e. Can you identify any policies that are making it more difficult for her to meet her needs?
4. Go to www.routledgesw.com/cases and become familiar with Brickville, the community, and the people who live there. This case will provide you the opportunity to develop your policy practice skills.
   a. How would you conduct a dual assessment of family systems to identify the specific policy issues that impact your clients and to determine whether intervention requiring use of your policy practice skills is necessary?
   b. Can you identify policies that are helping or hindering the people of Brickville in acquiring the resources they need?
   c. How do you think a social worker using a strengths approach might begin to help people in Brickville to address policy issues that impact their community?
5. Go to www.routledgesw.com/cases and familiarize yourself with Hudson City, an urban community affected by disaster. Complete the exercises that introduce you to this interactive case. Consider where you would start in completing a dual assessment of people who have experienced this disaster.
6. Go to www.routledgesw.com/cases and complete the exercises that introduce you to the RAINN interactive case. RAINN is a private, nonprofit organization. How do you think engaging in policy practice to influence programs such as RAINN would be different from working to change policies in the public sector?
7. Go to the website of NASW at www.socialworkers.org/. Explore the website, giving particular attention to the segments listed under Advocacy. You can also follow NASW on Twitter at www.twitter.com/nasw. Membership in this organization is a real bargain for students, so if you would like to get more involved in your chosen profession, please consider joining.

CHAPTER 2

The Historical Context:
Basic Concepts and Early Influences

Charity is not a proper function of the federal government. Private churches and voluntary organizations do a much better job of ministering to the needs of the poor.

Our elected officials need to focus more on personal responsibility and stop giving handouts to people who don't take care of themselves and their families.

Every citizen in this country should be guaranteed a minimum income and health care as a right of citizenship.

Social Work Students

I HAVE HEARD ALL OF THESE ASSERTIONS IN POLICY debates. All the speakers were convinced they were speaking the truth. You have probably heard some of these comments yourself. By the time you finish reading this chapter and thinking about how you will use what you learn in your future practice, you should be able to enter into the debate concerning issues such as these. This ability to shape opinion—yours and that of others—is basic to policy practice. In order to understand current social policies and to discuss options for change, however, you need to become familiar with the historical developments that have shaped our current approaches. This chapter provides historical background on social policies, the social welfare system, and the profession of social work.

Although many people might take our current social welfare policies for granted, they are actually the product of decades or, in some cases, centuries, of change, debate, and struggle. Your study of this historical context as part of your social work education will be much more useful for practice if you explicitly link what you are learning about history to the policies that shape contemporary social work practice. History is not merely a prologue to the present. Rather, the ways in which historical social policy approaches are understood and reinterpreted directly and immediately affect the social policy decisions made today. For example, religious teachings introduced thousands of years ago have immediate influence on moral choices that policy makers now face. Additionally, understanding that the policies which, today, form the backdrop of our social welfare system were, themselves, often hotly contested during their development underscores that policies are not unchangeable. It is my hope that the historical overview in this text will spark your curiosity and lead you to delve more deeply into the sources referenced in this chapter as you complete your course assignments and embark on your future social work practice.

THE GENESIS OF SOCIAL WELFARE POLICY

Because social workers' clients are often living in poverty, this chapter initially explores cultural practices in pre-industrial societies that gave rise to current programs for people who have low incomes. The major religions of these early cultures required their adherents to care for people who were poor. Although some people worked unceasingly to relieve the immediate poverty surrounding them, powerful members of the ruling elite were careful to maintain the social and economic barriers that oppressed the poorest people. Thus, the social welfare structures that evolved to address poverty also served as a means of social control and supported the society's dominant economic structures. This dynamic continues today. This relationship between social welfare and the economy, which applies to current social policy as well, is examined in greater detail in Chapter 4.

Religious Traditions

We will begin our discussion of the early historical mandates that shaped social policy for the poorest people in ancient societies and that continue to shape social policy in communities today by examining selected religious traditions from around the world. You can build on these examples to begin exploring other religious traditions that are influential in your community.

Judaism   Basic Jewish teaching and law, known as the Torah, contains numerous mandates to provide for people living in poverty within the context of the agrarian society of the time. For example, Leviticus 19:9–10 instructs:

> And when ye reap the harvest of your land, thou shalt not wholly reap the corners of thy field, neither shalt thou gather the gleanings of thy harvest. And thou shalt not glean thy vineyard, neither shalt thou gather the fallen fruit of thy vineyard; thou shalt leave them for the poor and for the stranger: I am the Lord your God.

Overall, the Torah instructs that justice be extended even to the most vulnerable members of society (Anderson, 1986). Significantly, the Torah also instructs justice be extended to "strangers" who are not of the community.

Islam   Similarly, all branches of Islam accept the fundamental tenet that the faithful are required to provide charity to people in need. The Koran (Qur'an) teaches that the faithful are to give up part of their wealth for the benefit of poor people and people with disabilities. This annual alms giving is called *zakat*. According to the Koran, when you give away part of your possessions, whatever is left will be blessed. "Piety does not lie in turning your face East or West. Piety lies in . . . disbursing your wealth . . . among your kin and the orphans, the wayfarers and mendicants, freeing the slaves . . . and in paying *zakat*" (Koran, 2:177).

Buddhism   In India, in the 6th century BC, Siddhartha Gautama, the Buddha, instructed the faithful to seek a "middle way" between human desires and a completely meditative life. The teachings of the Buddha, known as the *dharma*, maintain that people are reborn into successive lives until they attain complete wisdom. Further, good deeds toward others may help lead to rebirth as a more prosperous and wiser individual. Each person is expected to feel compassion for, and to assist, those whose burdens in life are the hardest. The focus is on the individual doer of good, and the belief is that giving will enrich the giver. From the beginning of the establishment of Buddhist monasteries, Buddhist monks have helped needy individuals and families in the surrounding community by giving food and alms. This work is considered an example to others of how they should behave. One of the teachings in the *Dhammapada* (the *dharma*) is: "They are true disciples who have trained their hands, feet, and speech to serve others" (Hays, 1989, p. 195).

Confucianism   Although more of a moral philosophy than a religion, Confucianism, which developed around 500 BC and is based on the teachings of the philosopher Confucius, has been highly influential in China. Confucianism is an extensive guide to living that stresses the individual's duty to society and the natural compassion of the human heart. It requires its adherents to care for the needs of their extended families, even if doing so requires self-sacrifice. In addition, the development of natural compassion is expected to lead an individual to help wherever she or he perceives need. Confucianism stresses individual development and does not address the role of the lord, state, or government in helping people in need. However, the emphasis on moral and decent behavior for individuals includes a duty to be helpful to others.

Native American Religions   The diverse religious traditions of Native Americans also emphasize the importance of caring for one's neighbor. Indeed, the basic social structures of Native American groups often reflect a collective approach to the use of the tribe's resources. Sharing with your neighbors was necessary for the survival of the tribe. For example, Puritan Edward Winslow, who recorded many of his observations of Wampanoag behavior in 1675, wrote that "every sachem (tribal leader) taketh care for the widow and fatherless, also for such as are aged and any way maimed, if their friends be dead, or not able to provide for them" (Segal and Stineback, 1977, p. 83). Native Americans as well as other ancient cultures recognized that the ability to work together as a group conferred a competitive advantage in the struggle for survival. Care by group members, one for another, strengthened the willingness to work together as a group.

Christianity   Christian religious teachings instruct that people serve God by caring for one another. Jesus told a parable about people entering the Kingdom of God.

> Then the righteous will answer him, saying, "Lord, when did we see you hungry and feed you, or thirsty and give you drink?" And the King will answer them, "Truly, I say to you, as you did it to one of the least of these my brothers, you did it to me."
> (Matthew 25:37, 40)

The apostle Paul wrote, "Faith, hope, and love [charity] are all important, but love is the greatest" (I Corinthians 13:13). Elevation of the importance of charity and the portrayal of poor people as just as worthy as rich people—or perhaps worthier—in the eyes of God to enter the Kingdom of Heaven, are themes reflected in early Christian biblical teachings.

Current Implications

Several common elements of these early religious teachings and practices have implications for the current U.S. social welfare system. First, each culture developed a system or an institutionalized method to provide for the social welfare of less fortunate people; that is, the system was mandated in writing and implemented in practice. Second, charity was defined as a religious duty, and a righteous person shared at least a portion of her or his wealth with people in need. Third, charitable actions were directed primarily toward local people in need. Finally, accepting charity was relatively non-stigmatizing; the recipient was neither criticized nor considered inferior. Of course, in all societies, the ideal and the actual practice vary widely for many reasons, including the generosity of the alms giver, community attitudes toward the specific people in need, and the economic conditions of the day. However, examining the written documents and the historical records of practices at the time provides insight into the guiding principles of the period.

The themes that characterized earlier cultures continue to influence social welfare to this day. For example, advocates for policies that redistribute resources often contrast the great wealth and conspicuous consumption of some U.S. citizens with the poverty of many children and elders. Watch for messages in the media that are based on the assumption that their audience does or should believe that people in need are worthy of help and that charity is important for both the giver and the receiver. I encourage you to examine the early religious writings discussed above as well as other religious teachings for additional examples of attitudes and practices related to social welfare and to consider how they do or do not relate to current social welfare practice.

Conflicting Views Regarding Social Welfare

Other, conflicting themes also emerge when we examine the history of social welfare. For example, although ancient Greek and Roman societies developed social welfare systems, Greek and Roman philosophers warned against rewarding paupers for begging rather than working. Similarly, by the 13th century, Christians were clearly differentiating between the "worthy poor" and people who were considered to be poor because they were unwilling to work. They were also questioning the appropriateness of help for strangers. Parallel tensions between the mandate to help all poor people versus willingness to help only those of the same religious background are clearly reflected in the social policies and social programs that determine how some religious organizations distribute charity today. Indeed, the distinction between the "worthy" and "unworthy" poor has permeated even secular social assistance.

In the U.S. in the 1800s, the wedding of Social Darwinism and the Protestant work ethic created further support for stigmatizing the poor as somehow different, unworthy, and even less fit to survive. Social Darwinism is a social philosophy that applies Darwin's theory of evolution based on natural selection to human societies (Day, 2009). Social Darwinists such as sociologists Herbert Spencer and William Graham Sumner proposed that poverty was part of natural selection: in a competitive society, those who were most capable and worked hardest would succeed, and others would fail. Therefore, helping people in poverty would only perpetuate laziness and benefit people who were unfit to survive. People who amassed great wealth were seen as living testaments to the correctness of these beliefs. Everyone was responsible for their own fate.

Not all Americans, however, embraced this harsh philosophy. Rather, countervailing beliefs developed within the religious communities themselves. For example, proponents of the "Social Gospel" that called for social justice for people in poverty were present in Protestant and Catholic denominations beginning in the late 1800s and early 1900s. They preached that just wages and profit sharing were necessary to alleviate the ills of poverty, overwork, and underpayment, and they spoke out against laissez-faire capitalism, concentration of wealth, and unrestrained competition (Swatos, 1998; Trattner, 1999). Laissez-faire is a doctrine that proposes minimal or no government regulation of economic activities.

It is clear that human societies have attempted to deal with poverty and inequality since the earliest times. History indicates that people in many societies have called for social justice. Unfortunately, it also demonstrates that these calls were often disregarded and that societies throughout history have justified inequality and poverty. As you read about historic and current social welfare practices, consider what future students might identify as the guiding principles of our current programs for assisting people in poverty.

A FRAMEWORK FOR UNDERSTANDING HOW HISTORICAL APPROACHES INFLUENCE CURRENT POLICY

Consider the questions in Quick Guide 2 as we examine the history of social welfare. These questions are designed to help you understand the implications of historical events for current social policy and social work practice. They have been raised by a number of social policy academicians (Chambers and Bonk, 2012; Chapin, 1995; Spano, 2000). You can ask and answer these questions for yourself as you build your historical knowledge base. For example, as discussed above, the ways in which we address the problems of hunger and need today are clearly influenced by historical approaches. Some answers to the questions posed in Quick Guide 2 are presented below. They focus on using the framework and information above to consider faith-based policy initiatives at the federal level. These initiatives give public funds to religious organizations so they can provide social services. Proponents of faith-based initiatives hope that churches and religious institutions can assume more of the burden of providing public welfare. Some proponents assert that if such faith-based approaches are implemented more widely, then private funding of social welfare programs may begin to replace public monies, thereby reducing the government's welfare role. Be aware that the answers presented below are not intended to be exhaustive but, rather, are meant to start you on your way.

QUICK GUIDE 2	A Framework for Linking History and Current Social Policy

- How do historical policy approaches to this social problem/need shape current policy?
- What was the cultural milieu at the time these historical approaches were taken? Is the current political and economic context the same or different?
- What were the group interests, and who were the key players involved in developing these historical policies?
- Is there any reason to think that historical approaches would work better or worse today?
- Did this historical policy approach build on the strengths of the target population?
- Alternatively, was it predicated on a pathology or deficit view of the people to be helped?
- How have definitions of the social problem/need and policy approaches changed over time?

- **How do historical policy approaches to this social problem/need shape current policy?**
  Religious and faith-based approaches to poverty have influenced social policy historically and continue to do so today. Support for social justice and aid to people in poverty, differentiation between the worthy and unworthy poor, and ambivalence toward strangers and immigrants are all historical themes that are reflected in current social policy. Today, religious organizations continue

to minister to the needs of people in poverty, and policy proposals to fund more faith-based organizations to provide public social services have many supporters.

- **What was the cultural milieu at the time these historical approaches were taken? Is the current political and economic context the same or different?**

Early approaches to social welfare developed in largely agrarian societies with rather homogeneous populations. Also, religious institutions typically played a major role in providing social welfare. As societies became more diverse, the issue of how to treat people who were not perceived as similar to oneself became highly divisive. This is even truer today, given that the U.S. is made up of people from a great variety of ethnic and cultural backgrounds. People with different religious backgrounds or those who do not identify with any religion may be wary of faith-based social services because of past experiences of intolerance and attempts to proselytize them. The challenge we have yet to meet in our society is to recognize similarities while respecting differences.

- **What were the group interests, and who were the key players involved in developing these historical policies?**

In very early cultures, particularly in desert societies in which many of the major religions first developed, it was clear that even those members who had relatively more resources would not survive without the help of the group. People were tied together through "status relationships" such as family member, lord, or serf. Powerful people such as tribal leaders, lords, and family heads had greater status and thus could develop systems that favored and maintained their positions. These leaders often influenced the systems of charity developed by religious institutions. Maintenance of social control by powerful elites as well as mutual aid motivated social welfare in these societies.

- **Is there any reason to think that the historical approach would work better or worse today?**

Contemporary U.S. society is highly complex, diverse, industrialized, and technologically advanced rather than primarily agrarian. Although religious institutions still play an important role in providing social welfare, many people do not belong to organized religious groups. Additionally, many church-based welfare services already receive large amounts of funding from federal and state governments and do not have sufficient private funds to take on more roles. For example, religiously affiliated nursing facilities often receive more than half of their income from Medicaid, a program jointly funded by the federal and state governments. Further, certain segments of the population, for example, the lesbian, gay, bisexual, transgender, and questioning (LGBTQ) community, have reason to be wary of transfer of money and authority for social services to faith-based communities that might not fully support their needs.

- Did this historical policy approach build on the strengths of the target population?

- Alternatively, was it predicated primarily on a pathology or deficit view of the people to be helped?

- How have definitions of the social problem/need and policy approaches changed over time?

In societies in which many people were living at subsistence levels, it appears that poverty held little stigma, and people provided help through religious organizations with the knowledge that they themselves could become needy if poor crops or sickness depleted their resources. Such societies viewed community members as having strengths as well as vulnerabilities. However, as the gap between rich and poor members of society widened, the belief that people in poverty were somehow different or unwilling to work became more widely accepted. It is easier to see strengths in people you perceive as similar to yourself and to magnify the deficits of people you see as very different. Although religiously affiliated organizations may do an excellent job of caring for members of their own faith community, critics of this policy express concern that people of differing cultural and religious backgrounds will not receive a culturally competent service. Additionally, there are limitations in the scale and scope of faith-based organizations' capacities compared to the significant social problems facing many societies today.

You can apply this same framework to what you learn about social policy as you read through the rest of this chapter. By using the framework questions, you will be able to look at historical information in new ways and develop new ideas about policies that might be more effective for your clients.

This short exploration of how earlier cultures and religions influenced current thinking about social welfare illustrates the impact of a variety of cultures from around the world on social policy today. We now turn to specific historical governmental approaches to caring for people in poverty that are generally recognized as having direct impact on current U.S. social policy. Because many specific elements of policy can be traced to social policies developed initially in England during the Middle Ages, this examination will begin with the English Poor Laws.

ENGLISH POOR LAWS

Trends and major social welfare events that took place in England from the Middle Ages to the enactment of the Poor Law of 1601 have greatly influenced U.S. social policy. The feudal system of the Early Middle Ages was based on a hierarchy in which the lord owned the land and the serfs farmed the land and received protection from the lord. In return, the serfs owed their labor and portions of their agricultural product to the lord. This agrarian economy produced very little surplus, and famine was common. Nevertheless, poor people were not considered deviant. In fact, Canon Law—the law directing church activities—demanded that each parish provide for the poor. Anyone who had extra resources was exhorted to share with the poor. However, the "willfully idle" were not to be assisted (Quigley, 1996a).

In general, treatment of serfs and peasants was at the discretion of the lord, and it varied greatly based on available resources and the lord's temperament. Prior to the Middle Ages, begging and giving had long been supported by Church teachings; however, after the 13th century, the Church began to view begging more negatively (Quigley, 1996a). During the Middle Ages, guilds, foundations, and hospitals contributed to the welfare infrastructure. Guilds were associations of merchants and artisans that provided mutual aid and disaster insurance for their members. Private foundations and churches played a major role in this society.

Background of the Poor Law

By 1500, English society was experiencing a dramatic economic, political, and social transformation. The feudal system had declined, and feudal relationships that bound serfs and lords were giving way (Reid, 1995). At the same time, although the majority of the population continued to make its living in agriculture, many small industries, particularly textiles, were beginning to develop. In addition, a stratum of society made up of tradesmen and merchants was emerging in which position was based on profession rather than birth. Contracts that specified the number of hours to be worked or the product to be delivered, rather than status, such as that of a lord or serf, increasingly defined relationships. Unlike farming, which was located primarily in small villages, the emerging industries were concentrated in the growing numbers of towns situated throughout the country. In that sense, England was undergoing the initial stages of the industrialization movement that reached fruition in later centuries.

Population Growth and Migration   At the same time that the growth of towns and industries was remaking English society, the country was experiencing a major population increase. Beginning in 1348, a series of outbreaks of plague, known as the "Black Death," claimed the lives of between one-third and one-half of England's overall population. As these epidemics subsided, however, the population began to rebound. During the period 1500–1700, the number of inhabitants nearly doubled (Clark and Slack, 1976). Unfortunately, in many agricultural villages, the number of residents was increasing at the same time that land was becoming scarcer. One reason for this was that landowners were enclosing lands that formerly were accessible to the community, for raising sheep to supply wool for the expanding textile industry. In addition, many agricultural families continued to practice primogeniture, which meant the eldest son inherited the entire estate. As a result, many villagers had to acquire land or seek employment elsewhere (Cannon, 1997; Clark and Slack, 1976).

Perhaps the major result of rural overpopulation was a massive migration to the towns. People from farming villages moved to towns in large numbers hoping to find work or, if work was unavailable, some type of charitable relief. Unfortunately, despite the growth of industry during this period, the towns also lacked sufficient jobs and housing for this migratory population. One result was subsistence migration, in which poor migrants moved from town to town, looking for work or begging for charity. By 1600, the number of vagrants and beggars in England may have been as high as 20,000. More serious than begging were the growing complaints of criminal behavior by these groups. Many concerned people began to associate vagrancy with an "underworld culture" that threatened the social and economic order (Singman, 1995, p. 17; Cannon, 1997; Clark and Slack, 1976).

Poverty Compounding the problems of crime and vagrancy were the increasing poverty rates of the 16th century. As we have already seen, the towns could not provide jobs and housing for all new arrivals. In addition, many workers who found jobs became victims of seasonal unemployment. They also lost their jobs during periods of economic downturn, which unfortunately were common throughout this period. Moreover, a series of poor harvests during the years 1594–1597 led to shortages of grain and higher grain prices, which in turn generated popular discontent. In many towns, at least 20 percent of the residents were unable to meet their basic needs (Singman, 1995). As poverty and unemployment increased, the demand for relief increased accordingly (Clark and Slack, 1976; Rowse, 1950).

The English government implemented some policies during the 16th century to address poverty. The Poor Law of 1536 required wealthier families to contribute money to assist people in need. Significantly, these efforts distinguished between the "deserving" poor, who were worthy of assistance, and the "able-bodied" poor, who were not. The "deserving" poor consisted of individuals who were poor through "no fault of their own" and could not work for a living. Included in this group were orphans, elderly people (especially widows), and women with children who had been abandoned by their husbands. In contrast, individuals who were capable of supporting themselves if they could find work were considered able-bodied. This category included workers who lost their jobs due to seasonal employment and men who were returning from service in the army and navy. The Poor Law denied direct monetary assistance to people who were able-bodied but poor, although monies collected under the law could be used to create jobs for this group.

The Poor Law of 1601 As poverty increased over the course of the 16th century, however, towns were unable to meet the growing demands for assistance. In addition, the taxes assessed to the wealthier people for the care of poor people became a burden to many taxpayers. Thus, by 1600, "poverty was the major concern of all urban governors" (Clark and Slack, 1976, p. 121). Consequently, local officials looked to the central government in London for support. Finally, in 1597, Parliament agreed to consider the issue. In 1601, the government passed the Act for the Relief of the Poor, more commonly called the Poor Law of 1601. This law created a uniform system for addressing the issues of poverty and unemployment by empowering justices of the peace in every parish to appoint officials known as overseers of the poor, who supervised the relief programs. The law further authorized the justices to levy a tax to raise funds for relief.

Analyzing the Poor Law   Although the Poor Law attempted to address the entire spectrum of poverty, it retained the distinction between the "worthy" and "unworthy" poor. Regarding the "worthy poor," the law instructed the towns to raise "competent sums of money for and towards the necessary relief of the lame, impotent, old, blind, and such other among them, being poor and not able to work" (Axinn and Stern, 2001, p. 10). Tax monies also could be used to assist unemployed people who were capable of working, but only by "setting to work all such persons" (Axinn and Stern, 2001, p. 10). Included in this group were children whose parents were unable to support them. These children either could be required to work or could be assigned as apprentices to learn a craft.

Relief took different forms. Many people without resources, particularly in agricultural villages, continued to receive outdoor relief, that is, aid provided to them in their homes or other non-institutional settings. In contrast, other recipients were required to enter workhouses and almshouses. Workhouses were publicly funded establishments in which large numbers of laborers were brought together to perform some type of work and sometimes to receive job training. Although workhouse residents were better off than unemployed workers and beggars, conditions were sufficiently harsh so that people looking for work would consider private employment of any type before applying for public charity. By contrast, almshouses were supported by private funds, and they were reserved for the "worthy poor," particularly elders. In reality, however, the distinctions became blurred, and many elderly people and unmarried mothers eventually sought refuge in workhouses because that was the only shelter available to them. Workhouses existed well into the 20th century. The workhouse pictured in Exhibit 2.1 was constructed in 1837 and the woman standing in front of the building is the matron of the workhouse.

The systems of relief described above provided the foundation for poor relief in England for several centuries. A subsequent law, the Act of Settlement of 1662, attempted to resolve the vagrancy problem by restricting assistance to people who had been born in the parish or were long-term residents. This law embodied the principle of local responsibility, which mandated that each locality was responsible for helping only its own residents. People who were not long-term residents had to return to the parish in which they were born in order to receive aid (Cannon, 1997; Clark and Slack, 1976; Olsen, 1999; and Rowse, 1950).

Influence of the Poor Laws on U.S. Social Policy   Because the U.S. based many of its laws on the systems in place in England, it is not surprising that our policies dealing with poor people reflect many of the elements found in the Poor Laws. For example,

EXHIBIT 2.1

*Image of Union
Workhouse in
Northgate with
Mrs. Morrant,
the Matron of
the Workhouse*

consider the designation of elders, people with disabilities, widows, and orphans as the "worthy poor," and the designation of other groups as "unworthy." We can see similar philosophies at work today if we contrast benefits provided by two current social welfare programs: Old Age, Survivors, and Disability Insurance (OASDI), popularly known as Social Security, and TANF. Social Security is intended for "worthy" recipients such as retired workers and families of deceased and disabled workers. In contrast, TANF provides assistance to low-income families with children. These parents are often depicted as unworthy of help. Does it surprise you to learn that the average monthly benefit in 2011 for a retired worker covered by OASDI exceeded $1,100, whereas the maximum monthly TANF payment for a family of three—the average size of TANF families—with no income ranged by state from $170 to $923? In addition, the legislation that instituted TANF contains strict work requirements.

Think about how these principles continue to be played out as you progress through the rest of this chapter and Chapter 3, which traces the development of social policies and social welfare systems in the U.S. from colonial times until the present day. Additionally, you can consider how these principles and philosophies influenced the history of the profession of social work, which is also presented in this chapter.

SOCIAL WELFARE POLICY IN THE UNITED STATES

Having examined the history of social welfare policy in England, we now shift our focus to the history of social welfare policies in the U.S. The remainder of this chapter traces the development of U.S. social policies through the early years of the 20th century. Chapter 3 then begins with World War I and continues through the administration of Barack Obama. You will see that, as our population grew and became more diverse, our economy more industrialized, and our society more urban, some of the responsibility for helping people in need gradually shifted from private institutions and state and local governments to the federal government. At the same time, social work emerged as a profession that applied both personal experience and scholarship in the social sciences to the task of assisting poor people and other marginalized groups. In recent decades, a conservative political philosophy emerged that challenged many of the social welfare policies established throughout the course of the 20th century. However, in the face of a severe economic downturn, Barack Obama was elected president in 2008 and successfully expanded the publicly funded health safety net with the passage of the Patient Protection and Affordable Health Care Act in 2010. Restructuring of health care as well as other elements of the publicly funded social safety net is a central issue for President Obama's second term.

The Colonial Era: Adapting the English System, 1600–1775

Native Americans, living in North America when the colonists arrived, were the first people to provide European immigrants with charity—the donation of goods and services to people in need—in what would become the United States. However, the struggle for control of the land by white settlers was marked by bloodshed, broken treaties, and oppression of native peoples. Colonialism began along the eastern shore in the 1600s when both Dutch and English settlers and merchants started the process of supplanting established Native American communities. In the southwest, Spanish invaders were accompanied by Catholic missionaries, who numbered 3,000 by the 1600s (Day, 2000). Native Americans, who were suffering the brunt of the invaders' demands for tribute, were tended in missions. The missions became a major welfare system that provided hospitals and shelters for homeless people, elders, and people with disabilities. They also provided hospice care and alms for poor people.

Social Welfare in the English Colonies   The English colonies that developed along the eastern seaboard categorized poor people in much the same way that England did, distinguishing between the "worthy" and the "unworthy" poor. Poor people frequently were expected to move in with relatives. In fact, the colonies passed laws that required families to "take in" their impoverished and disabled relatives and to post bond for emigrating relatives to ensure their support. Local government, churches, and private philanthropy offered support only when families could not provide for their relatives.

Public relief at the time was based strictly on a residual approach, that is, relief was provided only if the marketplace or family was unable to provide for a person's needs. Residual approaches are often contrasted with the institutional approach, which asserts that government should ensure that basic food, housing, health, income, employment, and education needs are met as a right of citizenship in advanced economies. These approaches to welfare provisions are discussed in more depth in Chapter 4. A residual approach reflected the values and culture of colonial society. Further, the fledgling colonies had neither the money nor the infrastructure to sustain an institutional approach.

Towns in the colonies developed their own policies for helping poor people. Whatever assistance was provided had to be funded through local resources. Reflecting the philosophy that underlay the English Act of Settlement, some towns instituted eligibility rules that restricted poor relief to people who owned property or had been residents for a specified number of years.

Almshouses and Workhouses   In 1658, the first workhouse was opened in Plymouth Colony (Quigley, 1996b). As the numbers of people needing care increased, the quest to find less costly means of providing help and the need to share fixed costs among a larger number of people or communities fueled the growth of institutions for the poor (Quigley, 1996a). Workhouses were also called "houses of correction" because their philosophy required people to work and they housed people who violated colonial laws (Quigley, 1996b). Many times, these institutions were not segregated by gender, age, or infirmity. All residents were expected to work when they could. Mortality rates were high. Almshouses and workhouses were the fore-runners of hospitals, penitentiaries, and reform schools (Day, 2009). Some alms-houses began to segregate people with mental illness from other residents. These institutions were the forerunners of asylums for people with mental illness.

In the U.S., as in England, policies governing the treatment of poor people were designed to ensure that everyone who could potentially work would be motivated to do so, even for meager or no wages. These policies helped provide a continuous supply of human labor for farms and industry. However, they also indicated that governments were assuming more responsibility for people in need. At the same time, ongoing efforts were made to find ways to reduce the costs of providing for poor people, and citizens expressed continual dissatisfaction with whatever system was being used to provide such assistance (Quigley, 1996b). The emphasis on work remains a central tenet of many of our social welfare policies. Although support of economic independence can be characterized as building on strengths, many poli-cies that reinforced the necessity of work were not designed to support or promote economic independence. Public dissatisfaction with systems to provide for those in poverty continues today, too, although economic downturns sometimes increase support for public programs to reduce poverty.

Slavery and Indentured Servitude   Slavery is the most extreme example of the control of human labor to benefit and profit the ruling class. In the colonies, slaves were defined as property by law.

Additionally, colonial societies contained a large population of indentured servants; people who were required to work for someone to pay off a debt. In fact, almost half of white immigrants to early colonies were indentured when they arrived in America. The typical term of indenture was five to seven years, although it doubled for political dissenters (Faragher, 1990). Many people agreed to be indentured in order to pay for their passage to America. In addition, England sent paupers, dependent children, beggars, convicts, and political dissenters to the colonies as indentured servants (Hymowitz and Weissman, 1980). Overall, approximately 350,000 indentured people came to America prior to 1775, predominantly boys and young men between the ages of 15 and 25. Although indentured servants were supposed to receive remuneration such as land or money when they completed their indenture, such payment was often meager, if it was provided at all.

When opportunities to own land, vote, receive an adequate education, share in the profits that result from your labor, and earn a living wage are denied, then policies with work requirements become oppressive tools that keep poor people locked in poverty. Underlying most of these policies was the assumption that poverty was a result of individual failure or misfortune, not of economic or societal structures or change. Therefore, policy reforms based on these assumptions could be instituted without disturbing the economic or societal status quo (Quigley, 1996b).

The American Revolution: Civil Rights in the New Nation, 1775–1800

The American Revolution ushered in a new system of government in the colonies. The writings of European intellectuals such as John Locke and Adam Smith, as well as earlier Protestant reformers such as Martin Luther, John Calvin, and John Wesley, contributed to the development of the classic "liberal" construct that stressed individualism, the moral importance of work, personal responsibility, and distrust of collectivism and centralized government, which was reflected in much of the social policy developed during this period (Reid, 1995). As detailed in Chapter 4, the term liberal as used today has taken on a different meaning.

The Constitution and Civil Rights   The Constitution was intended to increase the power of our central government while continuing to protect state and individual rights. The democratic political system instituted by our new Constitution specified that elected representatives would make policy decisions. Elections were to be decided by voters and, until the 20th century, voters were almost exclusively white men. Rights for women were ignored, despite pleas from influential women of the time, such as Abigail Adams, to "remember the ladies." White men also controlled most of the country's resources, and the social policies that the new nation developed reinforced this control. To gain insight into women's struggle for civil rights during the colonial era, read the letter Abigail Adams sent to John Adams in 1776 imploring him to "remember the ladies," at the Massachusetts Historical Society website (www.masshist.org), and be sure to also read the rebuke John Adams sent in reply which can be found at "Letter from John Adams to Abigail Adams, 14 April, 1776."

Although the Constitution initially protected only the rights of white, land-owning males, it established the basis for civil rights in the nation. Many framers of the Constitution believed that the ability of voters to choose their leaders would not be enough to protect their basic rights. Thomas Jefferson organized the Democratic Republican Party, which became the current Democratic Party, to press for a "bill of rights," a written bill that outlined exactly which freedoms were guaranteed to citizens. The bill was appended to the Constitution in 1791. The Bill of Rights comprises the first ten amendments to the Constitution, and it addresses such issues as freedom of speech and of the press, the right to trial by jury, and protection against unreasonable searches and seizures. Subsequent amendments as well as numerous judicial rulings have expanded and ensured constitutional rights that underpin the civil rights standard that we have today.

Civil rights protection for citizens is a cornerstone of social welfare. Without this protection, public benefits and opportunities can be arbitrarily withheld from certain groups, who are then left without legal recourse. Moreover, individuals and groups who are denied basic civil rights face substantial barriers to opportunities and limited access to society's resources. We will explore the relationship between civil rights and social welfare in greater detail in Chapter 7.

Although the newly established federal government was unwilling to address the plight of most categories of people in need, they were willing to provide assistance to men who had fought for their country. In 1790, Congress provided financial support for disabled veterans and widows and orphans of veterans (Axinn and Stern, 2001). Though small, these pensions continued to be provided with little debate for veterans of American wars.

Expanding Federal, State, and Private Assistance   The Constitution laid the groundwork for a system that held states primarily responsible for the social welfare of their citizens. However, in 1798, the federal government did establish the U.S. Public Health Service (Barker, 1999). The Public Health Service was a federal system of health care and hospitals designed for merchant seamen. In the 19th century, the agency's responsibilities were expanded to include medical examination and quarantine of immigrants. Currently, this agency is charged with responsibility for public health and safety. However, as the 18th century drew to a close and the 19th century dawned, much of the assistance to individuals was still provided through voluntary, charitable giving.

In their analysis of U.S. social welfare from the strengths perspective, Tice and Perkins (2002) pointed out that this tradition of private philanthropy helped to support educational programs, libraries, and community organizations such as emergency services and firefighting. There was growing awareness in both the public and the private sector that lack of education and health care were linked to poverty and that communities needed to develop health and social service systems in order to thrive. The U.S., then, has a long tradition of creating private–public partnerships to address these community needs.

From Independence to Civil War: Racism, Expansion, and Immigration, 1800–1865

During the first half of the 19th century, the new nation expanded dramatically in size. Its population also grew as large numbers of immigrants arrived from Europe, especially Ireland, Germany, and the Scandinavian countries. Abundant natural resources in the U.S. provided many immigrants, including free African immigrants, with opportunities to escape poverty. However, for people in slavery and for Native Americans, this economic growth and development meant greater oppression. At the same time, the debate over slavery raised questions about the role of race in society, and the federal government systematically removed Native Americans from desirable lands in the east.

Treatment of African Americans   By the early 19th century, the South was relying on the labor of increasing numbers of slaves to build its economic infrastructure. Slaves were considered the property of slave owners and were therefore ignored by the formal social service system. In 1857, the Supreme Court confirmed the lack of basic rights for African Americans. In *Dred Scott* vs. *Sandford* (1857), it ruled that any person of African ancestry, whether slave or free, could not be granted citizenship in the U.S. and thus could not sue in the federal courts. Dred Scott was a slave who had sued for his freedom because he had moved from a slave state to a free state. The *Dred Scott* ruling undermined rights for African Americans because they were unable to use the courts to protect themselves.

The rudimentary types of health and mental health treatment that were available during this period were often denied to African Americans, particularly in the South. For example, before 1861, mental asylums in the South seldom admitted African Americans. The justification was that they presumably exhibited milder forms of mental disorders. Some went so far as to suggest that the structured life of a slave helped to guard against mental illness (Lowe, 2006). In this vacuum, African Americans developed informal methods of self-help, and strong self-help organizations developed and continue to flourish in black communities to the present day. Support for self-help organizations and continuing mistrust of the formal social service system in the black community today are legacies of slavery. Further discrimination and unequal treatment characterized many social service interactions with African Americans throughout much of the 20th century. Social workers and policy makers who are unaware of the ramifications of this history will not be as effective in attempting to develop and implement policies and programs in the black community.

During this period, many black and white abolitionists campaigned for an official end to slavery. Frederick Douglass, an escaped slave, was a very influential speaker and writer in the movement. Escaped slave Harriet Tubman joined the abolitionist movement and played a significant role in the Underground Railroad, which assisted slaves to escape from the South, often to Canada. You can learn more about these early abolitionists at the Library of Congress website (www.loc.gov). Search for "Resource Guide for the Study of Black History and Culture," and read "Influence of Prominent Abolitionists."

It was also during this period that the present day Republican Party, or Grand Old Party (GOP) began to develop. It first came to power in 1860 with the election of Abraham Lincoln. The party started as a coalition of anti-slavery activists and other groups pressing for free distribution of frontier lands, protective tariffs, and the building of a transcontinental railroad, under the broad theme of commitment to liberty. Business and libertarian interests were part of the initial coalition and contributed to the evolution of the Republican Party from its original roots to its current philosophical opposition to big government.

Native Americans   Native Americans were driven from their traditional homelands as growing numbers of white settlers made their way westward. During the period between the Revolutionary War and the Civil War, most Native American peoples living east of the Mississippi River were forced to move. Violations of treaties with Native Americans were commonplace. In 1824, the government created the Bureau of Indian Affairs. The U.S. thus assumed legal responsibilities for Native Americans and promised material assistance, but oppression and decimation continued. In 1830, Congress passed the Indian Removal Act, which ultimately forced many tribes to abandon their traditional lands and move to reservations located west of the Mississippi (Hine and Faragher, 2000). In the 1831 Supreme Court decision *Cherokee Nation* vs. *Georgia*, Chief Justice John Marshall denied a claim by the Cherokee Indians in Georgia that they constituted a sovereign foreign nation. Rather, Marshall characterized Native American nations as "domestic dependent nations." Although conceding that Native American peoples should exercise some control over their lands, Marshall ruled that all Native Americans were "completely under the sovereignty and dominion of the U.S." He compared their relationship to the government to "that of a ward to his guardian" (Commager, 1958, pp. 256–257).

In 1838 and 1839, as part of President Andrew Jackson's Indian removal policy, the Cherokee nation was forced to give up its lands and migrate to an area in present-day Oklahoma. This journey became known as the "Trail of Tears." The Cherokees faced hunger, disease, and exhaustion, and over 4,000 died on the forced march (Hine and Faragher, 2000). By 1850, the removal was basically complete, and white settlers had appropriated the lands that the Indians previously inhabited (Kutler, 2003). In 1851, Congress passed the Indian Appropriation Act, which declared the lands to which the Indians had relocated to be official reservations (Nabokov, 1993).

As white settlers began to move west of the Mississippi, the push to confiscate Native American lands continued. An 1871 Act of Congress officially terminated the practice of entering into treaties with Native American peoples. Future dealings were to take the form of "agreements" and special laws. The Dawes Act, passed in

1887, eliminated the traditional system of tribal ownership of land by allotting plots of land to Native American individuals and families. These allotments were restricted to 160 acres, thereby confining Native Americans to smaller and smaller regions and eroding their communal way of life. "Excess" land was sold to white settlers. These policies effectively controlled and limited all aspects of Native American life (Nabokov, 1993).

The physical and mental health of Native Americans today continues to be negatively affected by the erosion of their cultural sovereignty and the loss of their land, economic base, and social structures. Many Native Americans distrust the government that was responsible for years of mistreatment, and they are reluctant to access government-provided health and social services. High rates of unemployment, poor mental health, and substance abuse problems among Native Americans today are thus lasting legacies of 19th-century policies.

Hispanics/Latinos in the Southwest   To accommodate westward expansion, the U.S. focused on gaining new territory and securing borders, especially its border with Mexico. In 1845, the U.S. officially annexed Texas after it had achieved independence from Mexico. A resulting conflict regarding the Texas–Mexico border led to war between the U.S. and Mexico.

In 1848, after two years of fighting, the two countries signed the Treaty of Guadalupe Hidalgo. Under the treaty, Mexico ceded a vast territory to the U.S., including present-day Arizona, California, and New Mexico and parts of Colorado, Nevada, and Utah as well as relinquishing all claims to Texas. As a result, the Hispanic/Latino population of the U.S. increased dramatically. The treaty further specified that Mexican nationals living within the new border would be granted citizenship and protection of property and civil rights. However, conflicts between new, non-Hispanic settlers and Mexican landowners frequently resulted in the Mexicans losing their lands in legal disputes. The treatment of Mexican Americans and the presence of legal and undocumented Mexican workers in the U.S. would become a major source of controversy and a key issue in social welfare policy, particularly in the areas of health and education policy, as we shall see in the next chapter.

Discrimination against Immigrants   Six million people, mostly poor people from Europe, emigrated to the U.S. between 1820 and 1860 (Coll, 1972). A large number of these immigrants were unskilled and faced stereotyping and discrimination. Many immigrant families lived in crowded urban slums. When work was available, parents and children often toiled long hours under harsh working conditions. Immigrant families who managed to acquire the resources necessary to move west also faced a daunting struggle to establish new homesteads and find ways of making a living in an often hostile environment.

Prejudice toward these immigrants from groups that were themselves descendants of immigrants during an earlier period made the transitions even more difficult. For example, some earlier immigrants claimed newly arrived Irish immigrants were lazy and Irish men could not be counted on to support their families. These derogatory stereotypes are similar to the prejudices faced by African Americans and are reflected in the anti-immigrant attitudes leveled at newer groups today. Despite these obstacles, some immigrant families managed to succeed and make a better life for themselves, although many remained in poverty. However, the essential difference that made the trajectory to becoming an accepted part of the larger society possible for the Irish, but much more difficult for all people of color, is that Irish immigrants could change their names and lose their accents. However, people of color cannot blend into white culture because their skin color will continue to be a marker. As detailed in Chapter 7, a different path to the acquisition of a fair share of social resources is necessary for them (Basch, 1998).

Growth of Cities and Public Institutions   Cities on the east coast grew rapidly during this period as waves of poor immigrants sought places to live and work. However, these cities failed to develop adequate sanitation or safety standards. Living conditions in the cities were deteriorating. Thus, by the 1820s, the U.S. was searching for reform options to improve living conditions and provide assistance to those in need. Some economists at the time argued that providing public welfare aid to poor people in their homes further impoverished them, made them feel even less capable, and decreased the standard of living for everyone (Trattner, 1999). People who considered poverty to be the result of individual failings tended to view poor communities as teeming with people who exerted negative influences that would continue to trap people in poverty. Urban slums were considered breeding grounds for criminals and slackers who might prey on upstanding citizens. Some influential people came to believe that poor and dependent people needed to be exposed to the "right environment" so that they could become "useful" (Reid, 1995). Institutions for the care of people who were impoverished or dependent began to be viewed as the best solution to all manner of social ills including misbehaving children, impoverished elders, people with disabilities, and unwanted infants. During this period, states began to enact social policies to regulate local government provision of social services and institutions. However, the federal government continued to reject a more active role in social welfare.

Mental Health Reform   Although mental illness was a recognized problem in colonial America, it became a public concern only when it jeopardized public safety or the survival of the afflicted person. Treatment varied depending on the cause to which mental illness was attributed. If sin was thought to be the root, prayer or even exorcism might be in order. Great misfortune, physiological afflictions such as digestive dysfunction, or even the alignment of the stars were suggested as potential causes. Bleeding and various medications were used to relieve symptoms. However, by the late 18th century, growing interest in curing mental illness led to the establishment of hospitals for the mentally ill in large cities. Private hospitals, where the emphasis was on creating a curative environment, were available for the affluent. The needs of minority groups were largely ignored. When mental illness led to public involvement, prison, rather than hospital care, was a more likely outcome. Mentally ill men and women were housed together in squalid conditions in jails and prisons.

The continuing reluctance of the federal government to become involved in providing for the health and social welfare of its citizens can be seen in the federal response to efforts by Dorothea Dix to expand services for people with mental illness. Dorothea Dix, a leader in the mental health reform movement, was instrumental in the establishment of state mental health institutions, including New Jersey's first mental hospital in 1845. She found that many states were either unwilling or unable to fund adequate care of the mentally ill. She concluded the federal government needed to take responsibility and submitted a proposal to Congress for funding for care of the indigent mentally ill (Day, 2009). In response, Congress passed a bill in 1854 providing for institutions, not only for people with mental illnesses, but also for people who were blind and deaf. President Franklin Pierce vetoed the bill, thus reaffirming that the states, and not the federal government, were responsible for providing social welfare. Pierce also feared that charitable provisions for the care of people who were mentally ill would imply that the government eventually had to care for all needy persons (Trattner, 1999).

EXHIBIT 2.2

Dorothea Dix

The Civil War and Its Aftermath: Reconstruction, Segregation, and Homesteads, 1865–1900

The Civil War (1861–1865) was fought to preserve the Union and to delineate states' rights. The Emancipation Proclamation, an executive order issued in 1863 by President Lincoln to the armed forces, directed the U.S. government to treat as free those enslaved in the states that were part of the Confederacy, which meant that emancipation followed the progress of the Union Army across the American South. Following the northern victory, congressional action abolished human slave labor throughout the United States, and changes were made to policies regarding the treatment of African Americans. The period immediately following the Civil War, known as Reconstruction, witnessed some real, if temporary, progress in African American civil rights. Also during this period, the federal government passed legislation to assist primarily white families in purchasing lands in the west.

Reconstruction   Perhaps the most significant development during this period was the ratification of three amendments to the Constitution, sometimes referred to as the "Reconstruction Amendments." In 1865, the 13th Amendment, which prohibited slavery, was ratified. In 1868, the 14th Amendment was ratified. This amendment guaranteed citizenship for "all persons born or naturalized in the U.S." and guaranteed all citizens the rights to "due process of law" and "equal protection of the laws."

Significantly, in 1884, the Supreme Court ruled in *Elk* vs. *Wilkins* (1884) that Indians were not covered by the 14th Amendment because they were not citizens. Citing, among other cases, *Cherokee Nation* vs. *Georgia*, the court affirmed that the Indian tribes, although not technically "foreign states," nevertheless were "alien nations" whose members "owed immediate allegiance to their several tribes" and "were in a dependent condition" to the U.S. government. Because tribal members were not citizens by birth, they could achieve citizenship only by separating from their tribes and becoming naturalized, like other subjects of foreign governments. Only those Indians who completed the naturalization process were entitled to the protections of the 14th Amendment (*Elk* vs. *Wilkins*, 112 US 94, 1884).

The 15th Amendment, which followed two years later, guaranteed voting rights for all male citizens, including former slaves. Female abolitionists had hoped that women would also attain the right to vote. However, the 15th Amendment extended the suffrage to African American men but not to women.

Opposition to black suffrage quickly emerged. Vigilante groups such as the Ku Klux Klan, organized in Tennessee in 1866, resorted to violence and intimidation to prevent the newly enfranchised voters from exercising their rights. In response, the federal government issued a series of Force Acts during 1870–1871 that authorized the government to use military force if necessary to enforce the 15th Amendment. As a result of these enforcement efforts, the freed men voted in large numbers, and African Americans filled many elected positions in the South and even won a handful of seats in Congress. However, Reconstruction ended when Northern Republicans compromised with Southern Democrats to elect their presidential candidate for 1876, Rutherford B. Hayes, in exchange for an end to the Northern military presence in the South. As we shall see, after the Northern military presence was removed, policies were enacted in the South to counteract the advances achieved during this period.

It was also during Reconstruction that the first federal welfare agency, the Freedmen's Bureau, was established. The Freedmen's Bureau was created to provide a variety of services to African Americans as they transitioned from slavery to freedom, such as establishing schools, providing food, educating former slaves regarding land ownership, and acting as an employment agency. The Bureau lasted only seven years and did not accomplish all of its intended goals. Nevertheless, it assisted many displaced African Americans, helped to establish a new economic role for former slaves, and outlined a potential role for the federal government in providing social services to needy populations, when localities were unable or unwilling to do so.

From Reconstruction to Jim Crow After Reconstruction ended, conditions for African Americans in the South deteriorated. By imposing a system of poll taxes and literacy tests, intimidating would-be voters, and by simply blocking the voting booths, white southerners eventually denied African Americans their rights as citizens throughout the South. This process, whereby most of the racial reforms instituted during Reconstruction were overturned, continued throughout the last decades of the 19th century. A critical step in this development occurred in 1896, when the Supreme Court ruled in *Plessy* vs. *Ferguson* that separate accommodations for African Americans were constitutional as long as they were judged to be "equal." In the wake of this decision, states and municipalities passed numerous "Jim Crow" laws that legally separated white people from black people in public areas and institutions, including schools, restaurants, theaters, hospitals, and parks (Knappman, Christianson, and Paddock, 2002). In addition to social, residential, and educational segregation, African Americans experienced discrimination in employment that often forced them into the least skilled, lowest-paying jobs. In this way, the Jim Crow laws worked to keep African Americans in poverty and also allowed people in power to profit at their expense. The Jim Crow laws are a classic example of social policies that perpetuate rather than alleviate poverty and oppression.

The Homestead Act Although the federal government did not enable most of the former slaves to become landowners, it did help white settlers to acquire home-steads. In 1862, Congress passed the Homestead Act, which allowed families to assume ownership of land—generally in the West—after they had lived on it for five years (Hine and Faragher, 2000). This enabled thousands of Americans, including veterans and widows of veterans, to become landowners. Unfortunately for Native Americans, this policy continued the uprooting that had begun decades earlier. The land made available to settlers was originally communal Native American land. So at the same time that the government sought to aid white settlers, native lands were plundered, and the rights of Native Americans disregarded.

The Origins of Modern Social Work

The years following the Civil War witnessed massive increases in immigration and urbanization, which magnified the need for social services. However, the federal government continued to leave social reform to the states, cities, counties, and private charities, and the job done by these entities was uneven. Programs for people in dire need were overburdening city, county, and state budgets. One response to these developments was the beginning of the modern social work profession. Pioneering foremothers of social work struggled during this period to change the way the needs of poor people were met. Social work traces its roots to the child-saving movement, the Charity Organizations Societies (COS), and the settlement house movement, all of which were privately organized and financed (Trattner, 1999).

The Child-Saving Movement   The child-saving movement developed in response to the growing numbers of children who were overcrowding institutions and living on the streets of the cities. Because there was very little assistance of any kind to maintain impoverished families, the children suffered. Although the belief that the family should not face interference from the state was widespread, there was also some popular support for child welfare initiatives because children had long been included among the "worthy poor," who were deemed deserving of assistance. At the same time, many citizens were also concerned that failing to intervene with poor children would lead to higher rates of crime, juvenile delinquency, and other social problems (Day, 2009).

In 1853, Charles Loring Brace, a Protestant minister, founded the first Children's Aid Society in New York. Similar child-saving societies were established in other cities and towns during this period (Day, 2009). Brace organized the famous "orphan trains" that carried thousands of children west to be placed with families across the U.S. between 1853 and 1929. Brace argued vehemently that children should be redeemed in a home environment that could provide for their needs and demonstrate adequate family life. This approach directly conflicted with the prevailing ideal of saving children through correctional or reformatory methods that were popular at the time. However, the reality of the orphan trains was that they were not necessarily more benevolent than institutions. Some of the relocated children were treated well in their new homes, but others were abused and made to work unmercifully. Further, these children were not necessarily orphans; some were children of single parents or immigrant families who were simply too poor to support them. Taking these children from their communities, even when parents were unable to care for them, engendered anger and resentment, especially among Catholic immigrants, whose families were often targeted for this intervention. To learn more about the fascinating history of the orphan trains and to read firsthand accounts of the children's lives in the

EXHIBIT 2.3

The Children's Aid Society

Charles Loring Brace, a minister and social reformer, together with other individuals inter-ested in social reform founded the Children's Aid Society in 1853. The Children's Aid Society (CAS) focused on homeless, delinquent, and neglected children. Brace and the other founders believed in nurture over nature. They felt that if children were taken off the streets or away from their parents who could not provide for them, and raised in a loving family home and given appropriate work and educational opportunities, they would turn into productive members of society. The accompanying picture shows young-sters who traveled on the orphan train. While Brace and the CAS may be most well-known for starting the orphan train movement, CAS also used funds raised from wealthy donors to open houses that lodged homeless youth and established schools to teach disadvan-taged youth useful trades such as cobbling and sewing. Once the focus shifted to family-saving rather than child-saving policies during the Progressive Era, the goals of the CAS also began to change such that one of the central goals of CAS in the early 20th century was the preservation of high-risk families/homes.

Source: The Social Welfare History Project; retrieved from http://www.socialwelfarehistory.com/organizations/childrens-aid-society-of-new-york/

West, explore the National Orphan Train Complex website and read Orphan Train Rider Stories (www.orphantraindepot.org).

This child-saving movement was the precursor of home foster care. Other child-saving efforts were also initiated during this period. The first Society for the Prevention of Cruelty to Children was founded in New York in 1875, and soon other cities established such organizations to prevent maltreatment of children. These organizations were the precursors of our current child protection system.

The Charity Organization Society and Social Darwinism   The Charity Organization Society (COS) began to develop in the U.S. in the late 1870s. The COS tried to organize diverse philanthropic groups to reduce the possibility that people were receiving assistance from more than one group and to provide "friendly visitors" to people in need. The COS developed the idea of "scientific charity," which involved the use of systematic procedures to assess who was in need and to determine the most effective and efficient strategies to address those needs. Early COS workers were influenced by the writings of Thomas Malthus, a British economist, who predicted that populations would multiply faster than the production of goods to meet their needs. They were also influenced by the Social Darwinist philosophy espoused by Herbert Spencer and William Graham Sumner. This "science" of the day was used to support the belief that giving money and provisions to people in poverty could interfere with the process whereby the fittest people were naturally selected for survival and reproduction.

The early COS workers reflected these views in their belief that poor people caused their own problems through spending thoughtlessly, neglecting responsibility, refusing to exert themselves, and drinking excessively. Therefore, providing direct financial assistance to these people would reinforce these negative behaviors rather than encourage initiative and self-help (Day, 2009). For this reason, early COS workers identified moral reform as the most effective anti-poverty policy. When Josephine Shaw Lowell, who was associated with the first COS, founded in 1877 in New York, was asked by a contributor how much money would go directly to people in poverty, she proudly replied, "Not one cent!" (Trattner, 1999, p. 90). However, as workers began to actually learn about the conditions of poor people first-hand, their understanding began to expand. The COS engaged in social research that broadened views of how science could inform charity, helped sustain and organize charitable giving during this period, organized record keeping, and developed training programs. Their emphasis was on the individual, not social reform, and they were pioneers in social casework. By the 1890s, the COS workers were interested in establishing themselves as a profession.

The Settlement House Movement   Social work also traces its roots to the settlement house movement. Although the first settlement house in the U.S. was not founded until 1886, we discuss this movement here to complete the discussion of the three major roots of social work.

Both scientific charity and the Progressive Era, discussed in the following section, influenced the settlement house movement (Reid, 1995). Stanton Coit started the first settlement house in the U.S. in New York in 1886 after he had resided at Toynbee Hall in England. Inspired by work at Toynbee Hall, well-known social reformers Jane Addams and Helen Gates Starr founded the famous Hull House in Chicago in 1889. Initially often funded by wealthy donors, settlement houses were established in working-class neighborhoods in the areas where reformers wanted to implement changes. The workers resided in these homes on a permanent basis. To learn more about Jane Addams see her biography (http://nobelprize.org/nobel_prizes/peace/laureates/1931/addams-bio.html).

Settlements house reformers documented the deplorable conditions in immigrant neighborhoods and worked to influence both public opinion and elected officials. The settlement house movement was not only influenced by the Progressive Era, which began in the late 1800s, but also had a profound impact on this period in American history. Settlement house workers were in the vanguard of reform in the Progressive Movement (Davis, 1984). They fought for child labor laws, occupational health and safety, safe housing, fair wages, and decent sanitation. They also battled prostitution and the saloon. The settlement house workers promoted both social justice and social control and believed that both were worthy goals. The settlement houses were also the training ground for many young people who would go on to assume positions of leadership in government, industry, and the universities.

Settlement house workers also were researchers who investigated working conditions in the factories and sweat shops where new immigrants and their children labored, and provided information that was used in the fight for fair labor practices. For example, Florence Kelley, who moved to Hull House in 1891, was later appointed to the Illinois State Bureau of Labor Statistics and involved the women of Hull House in her investigation of labor conditions (Day, 2009).

Significantly, settlement house workers put into practice many of the tenets that we identify with the strengths perspective. Work in the settlement houses was premised on the belief that need in impoverished communities arose from economic, educational, and political exclusion rather than from individual deficiencies. Consequently, in contrast to COS workers, settlement house workers focused much of their attention on social reform rather than individual casework. These early reformers sought to identify and marshal individual and community resources to find alternative ways to meet needs. They saw the common human needs of women, children, and laborers, and they were instrumental in starting preschools, and the juvenile court system, as well as in job creation for people in their communities. They also helped train workers, and find them jobs. Hull House settlement workers focused on helping immigrant families. However, here, as in other strands of social reform, the needs of African Americans were again largely ignored, and racism was clearly evident (Tice and Perkins, 2002).

Building the Social Work Profession   By the end of the 19th century, the social work profession was starting to gain public recognition. Training courses were offered to friendly visitors and settlement house workers, first called "social workers" by educator Simon N. Patten in 1900 (Barker, 2003). Remember, the work of the COS, the settlement houses, and the orphan trains was all privately funded and governed. Then as now, private philanthropy played an important role in funding new ideas and programs that can greatly influence future public social policy. During the late 19th and early 20th centuries, Progressive Era reformers pushed for publicly financed social services, and social workers were needed to provide these services. The Progressive Era thus created an environment conducive to the growth of social work.

Despite early separation of the settlement house movement and charity organizations, both groups were beginning to cooperate and even merge by the turn of the century (Trattner, 1999). In 1909, Jane Addams was elected president of the National Conference of Charities and Correction, an organization that was instrumental in establishing casework as a distinct field within the social services. In 1917, Mary Richmond published *Social Diagnosis*, which became a primary text for social workers. Richmond applied the medical model to social work and prescribed investigation, diagnosis, prognosis, and treatment focused on the individual. Casework began to overshadow the social reform movement with roots in the settlement houses (Tice and Perkins, 2002). Also in 1917, the first organization for social workers was established; it is currently called the National Association of Social Workers (NASW).

By the 1920s, training programs established by the COS began to develop into schools of social work. Although these programs emphasized the individual, they recognized that human problems also arose from deficiencies in the social structure, communities, and families. However, in addressing these problems, they taught social workers to provide social services rather than to advocate social reform. Case rather than class advocacy was the primary focus, and skills in class advocacy that resulted in reforms in arenas from child welfare to public sanitation in the late 19th and early 20th centuries, were seldom stressed. As a result, social casework rather than policy practice or community organization gained prominence. The drive for professionalization and wider recognition of the profession was characterized by an emphasis on clinical skills focused on working with the individual, rather than on policy practice skills.

African American Social Workers   African American pioneer social workers of this period recognized that racism was the major barrier that prevented African Americans from meeting their basic needs. Significantly, they focused on both helping individuals within their communities and addressing larger societal issues. Racism was at the center of these larger issues, and African American social workers directed their practice towards community and organizational change.

EXHIBIT 2.4

Dr. E. Franklin Frazier

Edward Franklin Frazier was born in Baltimore in 1894. After completing high school in Baltimore, Dr. Frazier went on to attend Howard University on a scholarship. After obtaining his undergraduate degree, Dr. Frazier taught high schools in several different states. After several years of teaching, he accepted a fellowship at Clark University in Massachusetts from where he later graduated with his master's degree in sociology. Dr. Frazier became a research fellow at the New York School of Social Work in 1920 before leaving to travel to Denmark that same year on a research fellowship. Upon his return Dr. Frazier began the doctoral program at the University of Chicago and graduated with his PhD in sociology in 1931. Once he obtained his doctoral degree, he continued his teaching at Fisk College until he accepted the position of Director of the Department of Sociology at Howard University in 1934. During his career Dr. Frazier wrote nine books and many articles and essays focusing on the black experience in America. Although some of Dr. Frazier's writings were seen as controversial, with one even leading to his departure from his position at Morehouse College, he was seen as a significant scholar in the field of race relations. While at Howard University, Dr. Frazier was also a strong advocate for social work education. He was a pioneer in championing the need for standards and proper training for social workers and he directed the first basic social work curriculum that was offered through the sociology department. As a result of Dr. Frazier and other individuals' advocacy efforts, the School of Social Work at Howard was officially established in 1935.

Source: E. Franklin Frazier (2000). Howard University, Social Work Library. Retrieved Nov. 14, 2012 from http://www.howard.edu/library/social_work_library/Franklin_Frazier.htm

The African American community developed its self-help efforts in the face of its exclusion from most services available in the white community. For example, women's clubs were organized throughout the country and communicated with one another about their goals, including promoting the education of women and children, improving family conditions, and promoting the civil rights of African Americans. The National Association of Colored Women's Clubs (NACWC) was formed in 1896 and enhanced solidarity. Many of these early social workers taught at "colored" colleges and finishing schools, as part of the tradition of teaching the African American community to advocate for itself. By the first quarter of the 20th century, some courses of social work study specifically for and about African Americans had been implemented. These pioneer social workers played an important role in improving life for members of the African American community. Their work continues to be a model for service delivery, focusing on mutual aid, racial solidarity, and self-help efforts (Carlton-LaNey, 1999). Dr. Franklin Frazier exemplifies this influence on social work literature and teaching. See a bibliography and description of the published works by Dr. Frazier (http://www.howard.edu/library/social_work_library/Franklin_Frazier.htm).

The Progressive Era and the Expansion of Social Welfare Policy, 1900–1920

The Progressive Era began in the late 1800s and continued through the first decades of the 1900s. During this time, more than 19 million immigrants entered the U.S. (Day, 2009). The majority came from Southern and Eastern Europe and many settled in the cities. They lived in tenements and worked in deplorable conditions in factories. The period leading up to the Progressive Era was one of strife between industrialists and laborers. Progressive leaders believed that an activist, morally responsible government, rather than laissez-faire government, was needed to constrain the negative economic and environmental impacts of unrestrained industrial capitalism. They advocated reform that would return the country to the democratic ideals that had helped to shape the nation. Consequently, the government engaged in several cases of "trust busting," and Congress passed the Clayton Antitrust Act in 1914 to limit the size and power of large corporations. Progressive reformers were interested in using the power of government to counter the ill effects of industrialization, particularly in burgeoning cities, and to preserve natural resources (Hofstadter, 1963). As an extension of the belief that government should protect its citizens, they advocated on behalf of the farmer and small businessman. They also were interested in developing the concept of social insurance, whereby society recognized the normal risks of living, and people and the government pooled money to help out when misfortune, such as unemployment, injury, or sickness, struck. This signaled a shift away from blaming the individual for not being able to either avoid or manage these risks unaided.

During the Progressive Era, the federal government started to assume responsibility for child protection, consumer protection, and progressive taxation to finance reforms and social welfare policy. It encouraged reform of urban governments and pressed for laws regulating working conditions for women and children. During the administration of President Theodore Roosevelt, Congress passed the Meat Inspection Act (1906) and the Pure Food and Drug Act (1906) to protect consumers against unsafe products. Also during this period, African Americans and women organized to improve their political and economic status. Two organizations that emerged during the Progressive Era—the National Association for the Advancement of Colored People (NAACP) and the National Urban League—played a major role in the struggle for African American civil rights and economic opportunities throughout the 20th century. In addition, women's suffrage advocates finally achieved their goal in 1920 with the ratification of the 19th Amendment, which extended the franchise to women. Ideals of equality for different ethnic groups, for women, and for workers guided many of the social reform movements of the Progressive Era. Support garnered for these ideals helped to build the base for future civil rights initiatives, and the changing electorate aided the advancement of new political agendas.

Progressive reformers had also laid the foundation for increased federal involvement in social welfare by successfully pressing for the establishment of a federal income tax, which was authorized by the 16th Amendment and ratified in 1913. The income tax was a progressive tax; that is, people with higher incomes paid a greater percentage of their income than low-income people did. Later administrations would use income tax revenues to fund programs for people in need as well as enhanced national defense and other federal priorities.

Women were at the forefront of reform movements ranging from child labor to sanitation. Indeed, the policies that created the foundation for support and protection of women and children were successfully enacted because women were willing to become activists and demand these changes. Their efforts in settlement houses, in city politics, and at the state and national levels, created the groundwork for modern social welfare policy and provided role models for activist women social workers today.

Maternalistic Approaches and Mothers' Pensions   Women activists pressed for public programs to provide cash assistance for poor mothers and children at the state level. Progressive pressure for mothers' pensions led to the establishment of programs to support mothers and children in most states between 1911 and 1919 and set the stage for the assumption of funding of many social welfare programs by the federal government in the 1930s. Establishment of state programs meant that access to help for these families would no longer be based on rules developed by private philanthropic organizations and that assistance would no longer be doled out as charity by well-to-do individuals with an attitude of superiority (Reid, 1995).

Leaders of the mothers' pension movement asserted that bringing up children was a civic duty for mothers, who should be allowed to devote full-time efforts to child rearing (Tice and Perkins, 2002). Unfortunately, these programs were never adequately funded, and they reached only a small proportion of eligible women. Applicants had to pass a means test, that is, they had to demonstrate financial need. In addition, they had to pass a morals test. For the most part, only single mothers who were judged not to have violated the moral codes of the community received pensions. Therefore, most of the pensions were awarded to widows, whereas single mothers generally were unable to pass the morals test. Moreover, Hispanics/Latinos, Native Americans, African Americans, and immigrant groups faced discrimination when applying for these benefits. When benefits were not just summarily denied to them, the arbitrary nature of these morals tests opened the door for all kinds of capricious actions against "undesirable" applicants.

Overall, the proportion of women receiving pensions was minimal compared to the need in the minority and immigrant communities. Even for those mothers who did qualify, the pensions were so small that many recipients still had to work (Gordon, 1998). Then, as now, critics feared that a program that put money into the hands of poor women who were unattached to male breadwinners would encourage more men to abandon their families. Some critics even characterized the pensions as a downward slide toward state socialism (Tice and Perkins, 2002).

Historians such as Theda Skocpol (1993) have defined the mothers' pension movement as an effort to establish a maternalistic, as opposed to a paternalistic, approach to family support. That is, this initiative was developed around mothers, in contrast to the later Social Security program, which reflected the male breadwinner model. (We will examine the Social Security Act in the next chapter.) Supporters lauded this maternalistic approach to family support for recognizing the importance of helping women provide for their children in the absence of male breadwinners. However, the state mothers' pensions declined and eventually collapsed in the face of the Great Depression of the 1930s, when it became clear that only the federal government had a sufficient tax base to support impoverished families during widespread economic downturn (Tice and Perkins, 2002).

Child Welfare   Another area in which the nation made progress during this period was child welfare. From the mid-19th through the early 20th century, reformers pressed vigorously for improved care for orphans, child labor laws, and programs to enhance children's health. Pioneer settlement house workers such as Jane Addams, Florence Kelley, and Lillian Wald were leaders in this effort (Tice and Perkins, 2002). Their efforts bore fruit as Congress passed a bill in 1912 establishing the Children's Bureau within the Department of Labor. Significantly, the Bureau was not allocated any regulatory authority. However, it was empowered to investigate and publicize the working and living conditions of the nation's children. As such, the Bureau represented the first agency within the federal government that focused exclusively on child welfare (Trattner, 1999).

EXHIBIT 2.5

Child Labor

One issue to which the Bureau's investigations drew attention was child labor. During this period, many very young children toiled long hours under appalling conditions. Congress enacted the Keating-Owen Child Labor Act in 1916 to regulate child labor. Although the bill was declared unconstitutional by the Supreme Court two years later for overreach of federal authority and condemned in some quarters as a threat to families' authority over children, it served as a model for subsequent state regulations. By 1930, every state, as well as Washington, DC, had enacted child protection laws (Day, 2009; Link and Catton, 1967).

The Volstead Act/Prohibition and Racial/Ethnic Discrimination Although the drinking and manufacture of alcoholic beverages were well-established parts of American culture, drinking and certainly alcoholism, had long been considered a sin or at least a social problem by crusaders for abstinence. The Temperance Movement grew in strength during the 1880s and culminated in the ratification of the 18th Amendment in 1919, which prohibited the manufacture, sale, or transportation of intoxicating liquors. The Volstead Act, which provided for the enforcement of the 18th Amendment, was also passed in 1919. Successful reform initiatives, then as now, are propelled forward by a variety of supporters. The Temperance Movement was supported by many of the women's groups and early social workers who also pressed for other social reforms. In the South, the Ku Klux Klan supported

Prohibition because of fears of uncontrolled behavior by African Americans, Native Americans, and/or immigrants brought about by drinking. An interest in improving the country's morals and for some, an interest in asserting white dominance over members of minority groups, propelled passage of this legislation. Parallels have been drawn between the differential and discriminatory enforcement of Prohibition and harsher enforcement of drug laws in the minority community today (Provine, 2007). The 18th Amendment was subsequently repealed, the only amendment to the Constitution that has suffered that fate. Its repeal was also propelled by a variety of forces, but the defeat of Prohibition can be considered part of the antidiscrimination movement of the 20th century.

The New Immigration Although Progressive Era advocates experienced some success in establishing more humane social welfare policies, racism and discrimination against certain groups actually increased during this period. In addition to racism and discrimination aimed at African Americans, the late 19th and early 20th centuries witnessed increased discrimination and prejudice against immigrants. Immigration patterns began to change, as immigrants increasingly came from countries in southern and eastern Europe, including Italy, Russia, Poland, and Greece, rather than northern and western Europe. Whereas the majority of "old immigrants," such as Germans and Scandinavians, were Protestant, many of the "new immigrants" were Catholic, Greek Orthodox, or Jewish. As in earlier periods, fear of greater competition for jobs combined with a general mistrust of people who spoke foreign languages and came from different cultural backgrounds, to create barriers to integration into U.S. society. Though very limited, nascent social work initiatives such as the settlement house movement worked to ease this transition. Nevertheless, in the 1920s, the government passed legislation that severely curtailed immigration to the U.S.

Legislation repealing prohibition, establishing mothers' pensions and providing some protections for women and children in the labor force built a foundation for the protection of vulnerable groups in our society. This Progressive Era legislation formed a beginning base for the battle for antidiscrimination laws passed in the later part of the 20th century. Consider how the controversies over the pieces of legislation discussed in this chapter are similar to current controversies over immigration and civil rights.

CONCLUSION

In this chapter, we have explored social welfare approaches from ancient cultures to the beginning of the 20th century. These approaches and historical events continue to influence social policy and programs today. If you take a few moments to reflect on the questions listed in Quick Guide 2 when considering a given policy or program, you will see these connections. Understanding historical approaches will help you identify and critique the motivation, values, and ideologies that drive current policies and programs. It will also enable you to identify similar policies and programs that were implemented in the past and to evaluate their results. Look back at the three quotes at the beginning of this chapter. Take some time to consider what you have learned in this chapter that would help you speak up during discussions of the topics highlighted in those quotes. Additionally, this chapter has highlighted our legacy of policy and service disparities based on race. We must own this history and work to eliminate these disparities. It is vital that social workers speak up when subjects critical to their clients' well-being are debated. The examination of historical policy initiatives provides valuable insights that can help social workers, as well as policy makers, to develop more effective policies and programs.

MAIN POINTS

- History is not just a prologue to the events of today but, rather, has a direct influence on current social policies and programs.

- The questions in the framework provided in this chapter (see Quick Guide 2) will help you explore the relationships between current social policies and programs and historical approaches.

- Poor Laws passed in the 1600s in England—which established public responsibility for paupers, categorized "worthy" and "unworthy" poor, and established residency rules—influence many of our current social policies and programs.

- Oppression of people of color throughout our history continues to influence social policies and programs.

- The social work profession traces its roots to the child-saving movement; the Charity Organization Society, which stressed casework and individual causality of poverty; and the settlement house movement, which advocated for structural change, including changes in sanitation and child labor laws.

- Historically, as well as in the present day, private philanthropy has an important role in funding new ideas and programs that can greatly influence future public social policy.

- Legislation passed during the Progressive Era laid the foundation for many of the social welfare and civil rights reforms of the later part of the 20th century.

- Women were at the forefront of Progressive reform movements ranging from women's suffrage to mothers' pensions. Indeed, the policies that created the foundation for support and protection of women and children were successfully enacted because women were willing to become activists and demand these changes.

- Passage of the 18th Amendment (Prohibition) was supported by a variety of groups including some early social workers and the Ku Klux Klan. Scholars have suggested that repeal of the 18th Amendment can be considered part of the antidiscrimination movement of the 20th century.

EXERCISES

1. Go to www.routledgesw.com/cases and continue to get to know Carla Washburn and her community. You will find that she is very reluctant to accept help from social service agencies such as the Area Agencies on Aging that provide services authorized by the Older Americans Act (1965), a social policy designed to help older adults continue to live in the community and avoid institutionalization.
   a. How do you think Mrs. Washburn's experiences and history as a person of color in the U.S. may contribute to her reluctance to accept social services?
   b. Can you think of provisions reflecting awareness of this potential cultural barrier to services that might be included in a policy to help increase service access for African American older adults?

2. Go to www.routledgesw.com/cases. As you become familiar with the Sanchez family, you will find that their church is an important source of support for them. Look back in this chapter at the discussion of the role of religious institutions in the provision of social welfare.
   a. What historic factors do you think contribute to the Sanchez family being more willing to receive help through their church than through public social service agencies?
   b. What are the potential benefits and drawbacks for the Sanchez family when public policy allows for the provision of publicly funded social services through their church?

3. Go to www.routledgesw.com/cases. Citizens in Riverton are concerned about homelessness in their city. Review how homelessness and vagrancy were dealt with under the English Poor Laws.
   a. How are the causes of contemporary homelessness similar to or different from those that contributed to homelessness in England at the time the Poor Laws were enacted?
   b. What similarities and differences do you see between Riverton's present day attempts to deal with homelessness and policies created by the Poor Laws?

4. Take time to visit the Social Work History Station at the Boise State University website (www.socialworkhistorystation.org), where you can learn about the conditions in our country that led to the development of our earliest institutions. Try to imagine what it would have been like to have been a small child in

one of the poorhouses (almshouses) in the U.S. in earlier centuries. Then imagine yourself as an older person living there. The strengths perspective insists that policies should be developed that take into account the point of view of the recipients of service. Considering the economic realities of the day, from your vantage point as a child or an older person in the poorhouse, what types of policies or programs might have been more helpful to you?

5. You can view a timeline of social welfare history from 1750 BC through the 1800s by going to the NASW website (www.naswdc.org), navigating to the Centennial Index, and then to Milestones in the Development of Social Work and Social Welfare. Moving through the timeline will give you a sense of how reforms in one period of history often build on earlier reforms. Pick one of the milestones that you find particularly interesting, investigate the event in more detail, and write a short essay on how that event influences social work practice today.

6. What similarities and differences do you see in current approaches to providing for children in need of care (orphans, neglected and abused children) when compared to the approaches originally developed by Charles Loring Brace and the Children's Aid Society (see Exhibit 2.3 for more detail)? After identifying similarities and differences, determine probable reasons why some elements have remained the same while other historical positions have shifted. What are the implications for current and future policy development? Do you think these early approaches were strengths-based? Why or why not?

CHAPTER 3

The Historical Context: Development of Our Current Welfare System

Let us never forget that government is ourselves and not an alien power over us.

Franklin D. Roosevelt

In this present crisis, government is not the solution to our problem; government is the problem.

Ronald Reagan

The danger of too much government is matched by the perils of too little.

Barack Obama

THIS CHAPTER CHRONICLES MAJOR POLICY INITIATIVES FROM World War I through the first part of the 21st century. As the quotes above illustrate, widely varying views of government shaped social policy during this period. We will examine how these shifts influenced social welfare policy and, ultimately, our well-being. In many ways, the nation made great strides during this period in helping people meet their basic needs and also made some progress in helping people build their capacity for long and productive lives. Life expectancy increased dramatically, and poverty rates and child mortality rates decreased as improved public sanitation and health care, labor laws, and pensions provided greater protection for people in the U.S. At the same time, as this chapter will chronicle, basic needs still go unmet for millions of Americans; growing numbers of our children do not have adequate food, shelter, and educational opportunities; and work to secure civil rights is a continuing battle.

EXPANDING THE WELFARE STATE IN WAR AND DEPRESSION: 1917–1945

As we saw in Chapter 2, Progressive reformers left a rich legacy of public sanitation, public health, child labor, and state-level mothers' pension laws. Additionally, women, who were at the forefront of these initiatives, secured the right to vote in 1920. These reforms set the stage for a major expansion of the welfare state during the New Deal of the 1930s, a topic we will discuss later in this chapter. However, the entry of the U.S. into World War I in 1917 generally drew attention away from domestic reform efforts, though the nation did approve the 18th Amendment, which established Prohibition, and the 19th Amendment, which extended the vote to women, in 1919 and 1920, respectively. Both of these reform efforts are discussed in detail later in the chapter. At the same time, the psychological problems experienced by many veterans of the war increased national attention on, and the allocation of resources for, mental health treatment provided by social workers. Mary Richmond and many of her colleagues were actively involved in efforts by the American Red Cross to provide casework services to displaced veterans and their

EXHIBIT 3.1

Women's Suffrage in Kansas: 1916 Photo

families after World War I. However, Jane Addams, as well as other prominent social reformers of the day, opposed World War I.

Although women finally secured the right to vote in all elections shortly after the end of the war, the struggle was long. A major milestone took place in 1848, when Elizabeth Cady Stanton and Lucretia Mott organized the first women's rights conference at Seneca Falls, New York. In the ensuing years, a number of women's rights groups were formed, the most prominent being the National American Woman Suffrage Association (NAWSA). As early as 1878, these groups called for a constitutional amendment to guarantee full voting rights for women. Although several states—particularly in the west—extended the franchise to women, many other states either restricted voting by women to certain elections or outlawed it completely.

During World War I, the NAWSA, under the leadership of Carrie Chapman Catt, led the final push for a women's suffrage amendment. This movement gained the support of President Woodrow Wilson, in part because of women's contribution to the war effort. Consequently, the 19th Amendment, which mandated that "the right of citizens of the U.S. to vote shall not be denied or abridged by the U.S. or by any State on account of sex," was finally ratified in 1920. Having secured the right to vote, some women's groups struggled for a broader guarantee of rights and opportunities. In 1923, the Equal Rights Amendment (ERA) was introduced into Congress for the first time. The ERA states that equality of rights under the law will not be denied on the basis of gender and provides Congress the authority to enforce the provisions of the amendment. It was defeated, but it was subsequently reintroduced every year until 1972, when it finally passed the Congress. However, it has never been ratified by a sufficient number of states to become part of the Constitution. The struggle over the ERA illustrates the degree to which women's rights continue to be a battleground in U.S. politics, almost a century after women won full voting equality.

Beginning in 1916, Margaret Sanger, an activist who worked to secure women's reproductive rights, opened family planning and birth control clinics in this country. Sanger believed women's rights should extend to control over their own bodies. She was a pioneer in an arena that also continues to be controversial to this day, as seen, for example, in the debate over requirements that contraception access be included in health insurance plans regulated according to the Affordable Care Act, passed in 2010.

The New Deal

The decade following World War I was a time of prosperity for many Americans, and the needs of those who did not share in that prosperity were largely ignored. Voters elected three successive Republican presidents: Warren G. Harding, Calvin Coolidge, and Herbert Hoover. However, unlike Progressive Republicans such as Theodore Roosevelt, these presidents were unwilling to engage in large-scale social reform.

The reluctance of the federal government to provide aid to people in need lessened markedly in the face of the stock market crash of 1929 and the dire

EXHIBIT 3.2

*Margaret
Sanger*

Margaret Higgins Sanger was born in 1879 into a devout Catholic family where she witnessed her mother go through 18 pregnancies in 22 years before eventually dying from tuberculosis and cervical cancer. Due to the influences of her youth and after witnessing the suffering of many young women because of frequent pregnancies and self-induced abortions while working as a nurse in New York, Sanger started a newsletter promoting contraception. Margaret believed that all women should have the right to determine when they became pregnant and shouldn't be driven to dangerous and illegal methods to terminate unwanted pregnancies. Margaret became a fervent birth control activist who was the first to use the term birth control and in 1916 opened the first family planning and birth control clinic in the country. In 1921, Sanger established the first birth control clinic in the United States staffed with all female doctors and social workers, as well as a clinic in Harlem staffed by all African Americans. Sanger's lobbying efforts regarding reproductive rights culminated in the 1936 Supreme Court decision which legalized contraception. In the early 1950s the International Committee on Planned Parenthood, which Sanger helped establish, became the International Planned Parenthood Federation. During this period Sanger persuaded donors to provide funding for research into the development of the birth control pill. Although Margaret Sanger had many opponents during her time due to her controversial beliefs, she still remains to this day a pivotal figure in the fight for reproductive rights in the United States and is viewed by many as being a critical influence in both the birth control and woman's rights movements.

Source: Library of Congress (Bain News Service was publisher)

economic conditions of the Great Depression of the 1930s. The influence of the larger economic environment on millions of Americans who were now without jobs could not be denied. Just as in practice with individuals, a crisis can also be an opportunity for change, so U.S. social policy at the time of the Great Depression changed in significant ways. Franklin Roosevelt, a Democrat, was elected president in 1932 and held the office until his death in 1945. The Roosevelt administration implemented a series of economic policies that reflected the theories of British economist John Maynard Keynes. Keynes advocated increased government spending and manipulation of interest rates in order to dampen inflation and manage recessions. We will examine Keynesian economics in greater detail in Chapter 4.

During the Roosevelt administration, the federal government initiated work relief programs and other forms of aid to people in need. These policy and program innovations are referred to collectively as the New Deal. The Works Progress Administration (WPA), the Civilian Conservation Corps (CCC), and the Civil Works Administration (CWA) were among the most prominent New Deal programs. These programs employed millions of people in such diverse activities as building roads, bridges, and other public works; planting trees and preserving forests; performing plays; and painting murals. The Great Depression and the New Deal marked a fundamental change in the way many people thought about need and the responsibility of the government to address need. The conviction that the federal government must assume some responsibility for people who are in need through no fault of their own replaced the principle that social welfare was largely a local and state responsibility. States could no longer afford the pension programs that some of them had developed, and even robust state efforts were inadequate to meet the growing demand created by the Great Depression. Because the states had shown themselves to be incapable of meeting such widespread need, federal aid to the states was now considered vital.

Social workers were leaders in the development of several New Deal programs. For example, Harry Hopkins (director of the Federal Emergency Relief Administration (FERA)), Frances Perkins (Secretary of Labor), and Martha Eliot (Children's Bureau), as well as many other social workers, helped develop and administer the new social policies of the era (Tice and Perkins, 2002). As discussed in Chapter 1, Charlotte Towle wrote *Common Human Needs*, a manual originally developed for the Bureau of Public Assistance of the Social Security Board (1945/1987). Although it was not actually published until 1945, it was intended to instruct workers involved in administering the Social Security Act of 1935. Towle's monograph was based on the premise that people have common human needs, and it helped articulate a more compassionate view of people who could not provide for themselves. Social work was distinguishing itself as a profession that addressed not only individual needs but also the need for policy reform at the state and national levels. To learn more about the work of these and other famous social workers, go to the website of the NASW (www.naswdc.org), search for Centennial Index, and then go to Social Work Leaders.

EXHIBIT 3.3

Harry Hopkins

Harry Hopkins was born in Sioux City, Iowa in 1890 and was raised in Grinnell, Iowa. Hopkins attended Grinnell College, where the curriculum was strongly influenced by the values of the Social Gospel Reform movement, and graduated in 1912. After graduation, Hopkins began his career as a social worker by working with the poor in New York as a friendly visitor. Hopkins eventually moved into a management position and in 1923 he was elected president for the American Association of Social Workers (AASW). The Governor of New York, Franklin Roosevelt, became aware of Hopkins and his work and asked him to be in charge of the Temporary Emergency Relief Administration (TERA). This was the first state run relief program in the country. The partnership between Hopkins and Roosevelt continued once Roosevelt became president and Hopkins was a principal developer of a collection of policies and programs that were known as the New Deal. The goal of these New Deal programs was to stimulate the economy and get workers back into the work-place. This legislation acknowledged the responsibility of the federal government in the provision of social welfare and was a major social change from past belief that state and local government were primarily responsible for developing and implementing social policy to address need. Some of the New Deal programs ended or were terminated. However, many of the programs for people with disabilities, children, families, and older adults created by the Social Security Act, are still in existence today.

Source: Library of Congress

The Townsend Movement   In the years leading up to the Depression, people were living longer, yet there were fewer and fewer jobs, particularly for older adults. Researchers estimated that three out of four people over the age of 65 were unable to support themselves. Also, as a result of societal changes, many families did not or were not able to support their elder members in the way that was previously expected.

Townsend outlined his plan in numerous letters to the editor of his local newspaper. He was associated with the Liberal Party, and his plan was popular in his native state, where its proponents supported those candidates who endorsed it. Nationally, the Townsend Movement had a strong following among elders, and it is credited with influencing President Roosevelt and Congress to pass the Social Security Act in 1935. The movement helped make clear that some sort of support for elders had become politically and economically necessary.

The Social Security Act   Partially in response to the Townsend Movement, in 1935, Congress enacted a major piece of social policy legislation, the Social Security Act. This law encompassed major social insurance and public assistance programs that have become integral to our social service system. The original Act made provisions for old-age benefits; financial assistance for aged and blind persons, and dependent and crippled children; maternal and child welfare; public health measures; and unemployment compensation. It provided benefits to retired workers through a system of social insurance, which replaced the more stigmatizing practice of public assistance. Policy makers realized that retired workers were people much like themselves, who obviously needed and deserved income security in their old age. As we will see, benefits for poor women and children were not viewed in a similar positive way.

The Old Age, Survivors, and Disability Insurance (OASDI) program, established by the Social Security Act and subsequent amendments, is a social insurance program that is based on the proposition that "worthy" workers and their employers can pool money to provide for retirement, disability, and surviving family members after a worker's death. This insurance approach changed the traditional paradigm whereby children and the elderly were both dependent groups who were expected to rely on the family for economic support. By paying OASDI insurance premiums, unfortunately currently labeled "payroll taxes," workers could now insure that they had an income even after they became elderly and could no longer work. However, linking worthiness to paid work in industries where men were the primary employees reinforced the role of the male breadwinner and built on historic ideals of willingness to work as a precondition for assistance. Because many jobs, such as farm worker and housekeeper, were not initially included in the program, it also meant that people of color, unmarried women, and their children often were not covered and were segregated into separate, less generous, needs-based public assistance programs, not based on the insurance principle.

Perhaps the most important public assistance program established by the Social Security Act was Aid to Dependent Children (ADC), which provided cash assistance for needy children. The law defined a "dependent child" as "a child under the age of 16 who has been deprived of parental support or care by reason of the death, continued absence from the home, or physical or mental incapacity of a parent," and who is living with the other parent or another relative. Initially, payments were made only for the care of children, not for their parents or other caretakers. Later, caretaker grants for parents of dependent children were added, and the name of the program was changed to Aid to Families with Dependent Children (AFDC). Overall, public assistance programs have been much more controversial, more punitive, and less generously funded than benefits for "worthy" retirees. Not surprisingly, then, these programs have also been less successful in achieving society's aims for them; OASDI is quite effective in reducing poverty among older adult retirees, while poverty among children whose families receive public assistance has increased, especially in recent years.

The provisions for retired workers contained in the Social Security Act were originally called Old Age Insurance (OAI). As the name implies, benefits were restricted to the retired workers themselves. However, amendments adopted in 1939 extended coverage to two additional categories of people: (1) the spouse and children of a retired worker, and (2) the survivors of a deceased covered worker. It was at this point that the name was changed to Old Age and Survivors' Insurance (OASI) (DeWitt, 2003). In 1956, disability insurance benefits were added for workers aged 50–64 and for adult children of retired or deceased workers with permanent and total disabilities. The program then became known as Old Age, Survivors, and Disability Insurance (OASDI). In 1960, workers of all ages and their dependents were made eligible for disability insurance benefits (Social Security Administration, 2009). To learn more about the fascinating history of the Social Security Act and all of the areas of economic security covered by the Act, visit the Social Security Administration website and search for Social Security History (www.socialsecurity.gov).

In the discussion in Chapter 8 on income support policies, we will critique legislation such as the Social Security Act on many levels. For now, it is important to recognize that passage of the Social Security Act represented a milestone in the development of public support for people in need. Significantly, those parts of the Act that provide social insurance were premised on the belief that people have common human needs, rather than on the idea that destitution is an indicator of individual deficits. The Act, therefore, brought new resources into communities to aid citizens in meeting their needs. In this sense, these social insurance provisions reflect a strengths perspective. At the same time, however, the public assistance programs established by the Act were means-tested and failed to address the structural barriers that keep people in poverty, such as lack of access to employment, adequate education, and health care. In total, then, the Act reinforced the gender, class, and racial divisions in U.S. social policy.

EXHIBIT 3.4

Frances Perkins

Frances Perkins was born Fannie Coralie Perkins in 1880. She legally changed her name to Frances in 1905. Frances obtained her undergraduate degree from Mount Holyoke College in 1902, where as part of her studies she visited factories in the local area and become interested in working conditions and labor law. She went on to complete her master's degree in economics and sociology from Columbia University. After witnessing the Triangle Shirtwaist Factory fire in 1911, Frances sat on several committees that were established to determine what had caused the fire and how to prevent it from occurring again. During this time Perkins became even more determined to bring about labor rights reform. In the late 1920s Governor Franklin D. Roosevelt asked Perkins to be the Commissioner of Labor for the State of New York. During her time as commissioner, Perkins implemented policy that reduced the work week for women to 48 hours and fostered the development of minimum wage laws. Once Roosevelt became president in 1932, he asked Perkins to be his Secretary of Labor and with this appointment Perkins became the first female cabinet secretary. In the course of her career Perkins was instrumental in the development of the New Deal legislation, the abolishment of child labor, the implementation of maximum-hour laws, and giving workers the right to organize and collective bargain through the enactment of the National Labor Relations Act of 1935. In addition, due to her efforts to nationalize unemployment and old age insurance, the Social Security Act was passed and became law in 1935. Frances Perkins was a dedicated activist for workers' rights and was instrumental in bringing about a variety of social reforms many of which are the cornerstone for current labor standards and laws.

Source: Library of Congress

The Impact of World War II

Just as World War I had diverted the nation from the Progressive Movement, the attack on Pearl Harbor in December 1941 drew national attention away from the social reforms of the New Deal. At the same time, the nation's entry into World War II had a profound effect on the economy. The federal government increased spending dramatically, creating jobs for millions of Americans in the armed services and in war-related industries. Consequently, the U.S. finally emerged from the Depression. As millions of men joined the military, women entered the workforce and often moved into non-traditional areas, such as manufacturing jobs in shipyards and aircraft factories.

When the war was over, however, the jobs and the supports such as work-site child care, largely disappeared, and women were once again bombarded with messages extolling the virtues of traditional gender roles. You can learn more about how women were drawn into new kinds of jobs and the dilemmas they faced by visiting the web page Rosie the Riveter: Women Working During World War II (www.nps.gov/pwro/collection/website/rosie.htm) and clicking on History. This is a National Park Service website.

Racism in the U.S. was again displayed as Japanese Americans, but not German Americans, were detained and then transported without trial to internment camps during World War II. However, the horrors of the Holocaust led many Americans to begin to reexamine beliefs that supported prejudice and discrimination in the U.S. The Holocaust illustrated that eugenics, which encourages the reproduction of people thought to have desirable genetic traits, has horrific consequences when taken to its logical end. These lessons contributed to the civil rights movement of the 1950s and 1960s.

THE EVOLUTION OF THE MODERN WELFARE STATE: 1945–1970

With the end of World War II in 1945, the federal government developed programs to address the mental health needs of veterans and to provide support for returning veterans. In this section, we will trace the effects of these initiatives on the larger society. We will also explore the strides made in securing civil rights in the 1950s and 1960s, and we will consider the successes and failures of federal anti-poverty programs during this period.

During the administration of Harry Truman (1945–1952), more people in the U.S. began to enjoy relative affluence in a period of prosperity. Significantly, the federal government played a vital role in promoting this prosperity. For example, in 1944, Congress passed the Servicemen's Readjustment Act, commonly referred to as the GI Bill of Rights, that helped returning soldiers build assets. The GI Bill provided loans for veterans to purchase a home or establish a business, and it provided money for tuition, which enabled many working- and middle-class veterans to attend college. The rationale for the bill was that veterans should be returned to civilian status in a way that would restore the opportunities they lost by serving in the war.

If the GI Bill is considered in the larger political and economic context, the education and training that the veterans received upgraded the overall quality of the workforce. In addition, the GI Bill reflected a strengths perspective, in that it focused not on individual deficits but rather on finding ways to overcome structural barriers by enhancing economic and educational opportunities and helping veterans build their assets. It is a good example of a policy that reflects a capacity building approach. Remember, *the capacity building approach* refers to policies and programs that focus on strengthening the skills, competencies, and abilities of people and communities and

EXHIBIT 3.5

Images of Strong Women Like Rosie the Riveter Were Used to Recruit Women Into Factory Jobs During World War II

on helping them secure the resources needed for full economic and social inclusion. We will discuss proposals to provide a "GI Bill approach" to ameliorating poverty for single mothers with children and people with disabilities in later chapters.

In addition to focusing on the economic needs of returning veterans, the federal government addressed the mental health needs of World War II draftees by passing the Mental Health Act of 1946, which created the National Institute of Mental Health (NIMH) and ultimately helped move public treatment out of state institutions and into community-based programs (Reid, 1995). The GI Bill and the Mental Health Act were evidence of the federal government's more activist role in social welfare. Although these efforts enjoyed some degree of success, many people did not benefit from these gains or participate in the nation's increasing affluence. For example, African Americans continued to struggle against Jim Crow laws, and poverty remained widespread for many traditionally oppressed groups.

Significantly, the social work profession continued to upgrade standards for social work education during the postwar period. The National Council on Social

Work Education was established in 1946 to study differences and relationships between bachelor- and master's-level education in social work. This organization was later renamed the Council on Social Work Education (CSWE). CSWE is the accrediting body for BSW and MSW programs today. This period also witnessed the consolidation of several social work associations to form the National Association of Social Workers, which took place in 1956. NASW remains social workers' major national professional association today.

The Struggle for African American Civil Rights

During the postwar years, individuals and institutions could legally discriminate against people based on skin color. Consequently, racial segregation in housing, education, employment, medical treatment, public accommodation, and even burial sites continued. However, war experiences with the extremes of Nazi racism led some white Americans to question racist practices in their communities. White liberal groups began forming coalitions with black civil rights groups. African Americans who had served in the war brought home European ideas about racial justice and an expectation of greater respect and opportunity in exchange for their military service. In addition, throughout the 1940s and 1950s, the large-scale migration of African Americans to northern cities, where they could vote, increased their political power.

The Challenge to School Segregation In a milestone event, the National Association for the Advancement of Colored People challenged the separate but equal doctrine via the court case *Brown* vs. *Board of Education of Topeka*. In 1954, the Supreme Court ruled that in "public education the doctrine of 'separate but equal' has no place." It further asserted that "separate educational facilities are inherently unequal" and therefore violated the 14th Amendment's guarantee of equal protection of the law (Knappman, Christianson, and Paddock, 2002). The *Brown* decision is an excellent example of how the judiciary generates social policy. Indeed, social workers engaged in policy practice often overlook the power of the judicial branch of government and fail to think about how it can be used to change unjust policies. The Brown ruling, which overturned the 1896 *Plessy* vs. *Ferguson* ruling that separate but equal facilities are constitutional, helped bring an end to the Jim Crow laws. For this reason, it is considered one of the most important civil rights rulings of the 20th century. However, resistance movements and legal challenges arose across the country and limited the immediate power of this ruling. As a result, it took several years for many states to even begin implementing the requirements of this ruling which highlights the limitations of the judiciary in social policy making. Ongoing racial and class segregation in housing has resulted in most black school children still being educated in schools where a majority of the students are from minority groups over 50 years after that landmark ruling. To learn more about the historic *Brown* vs. *Board of Education* ruling and its aftermath, you can visit the

Brown vs. Board of Education National Historic Site maintained by the National Park Service in Topeka, Kansas either online (www.nps.gov/brvb/index.htm) or in person.

The Challenge to Jim Crow   Beginning in the 1950s, African American civil rights activists and their white allies initiated a campaign of direct action to challenge the nation's system of racial subordination. On December 1, 1955, an African American woman named Rosa Parks refused to surrender her seat on a Montgomery, Alabama bus to a white person, in violation of local segregation laws. Her arrest led to black residents of Montgomery boycotting the city's bus system. They demanded an end to segregated seating, better treatment for black riders, and the hiring of black drivers. The boycott continued for almost a year until the Supreme Court ruled that Montgomery's segregation law violated the 14th Amendment. Not only was the boycott a landmark victory for advocates of social justice, but it brought attention to a new civil rights leader, Dr. Martin Luther King, Jr., and a new organization, the Southern Christian Leadership Conference (SCLC), that were willing to directly challenge the oppressive racial system of the South (Patterson, 1996).

Civil rights protests intensified in the 1960s. On February 1, 1960, four black college students in Greensboro, North Carolina, sat down at a lunch counter that was designated "whites only." They were not served, but their sit-in continued until closing time. Similar sit-ins to protest segregation in schools, colleges, theaters, churches, swimming pools, and stores occurred across the South, bringing the issue of segregation to white consciousness and politicizing a generation of black youth.

Black leadership in the South mobilized to press for civil rights. In May 1963, King and the SCLC led a major protest in Birmingham, Alabama, to demand an end to segregation and employment discrimination in the city. The Birmingham police eventually arrested hundreds of demonstrators—including hundreds of young children—and used water hoses and police dogs against them as a stunned nation followed these developments on television. Later that year, King delivered his famous "I have a dream" speech to a multiracial audience of 200,000 people in Washington, DC. If you have never heard Dr. Martin Luther King, Jr.'s speech, use your web browser to locate a video of the speech and treat yourself to this historic event.

While the civil rights movement was certainly not led by social workers, neither were social workers completely absent from these critical struggles in U.S. history. Dr. Dorothy I. Height, one of the world's most important social workers, was the only female team member in the United Civil Rights Leadership, which included Dr. Martin Luther King, Jr., Whitney Young, A. Philip Randolph, James Farmer, Roy Wilkins, and John Lewis. She was a civil rights legend who was a lifelong advocate for rights for women and people of color. Dr. Height died in 2010.

During the Kennedy presidency from 1960 to 1963, the civil rights movement intensified. In the first years of his presidency, Kennedy moved cautiously. However, the civil rights demonstrations and crises of 1963 led him to become more active and introduce comprehensive new legislation before his assassination on November

EXHIBIT 3.6

Rosa Parks

22, 1963. To learn more about the civil rights movement during the Kennedy presidency, go to the website of the John F. Kennedy Library and Museum and navigate to Leaders in the Struggle for Civil Rights (http://www.jfklibrary.org/Education/Students/Leaders-in-the-Struggle-for-Civil-Rights.aspx). Civil rights advocates, both black and white, were working hard for reform and faced violent opposition. In 1964, Mississippi segregationists murdered three civil rights workers: social worker Michael Schwerner, James Chaney, and Andrew Goodman.

Civil Rights Laws   One concrete goal for which most civil rights activists campaigned was the enactment of a comprehensive national law to protect the civil rights of African Americans. This objective was achieved with the passage of the Civil Rights Act of 1964, which prohibited employment discrimination on the basis of race, sex, or ethnicity; banned federal funding for institutions that practiced discrimination; and mandated equal access to public accommodations. By banning discrimination on the basis of race as well as gender, this legislation addressed intersectionality, which focuses on the interrelation or intersection of forms of oppression such as race and gender. These markers of oppression do not act independently of one another, and solving for racism or gender inequity alone is not as effective as comprehensive legislation which attacks multiple roots of oppression. We will examine the specific features of the Civil Rights Act of 1964 in Chapter 7. That same year, the 24th Amendment to the Constitution, which prohibited the use of poll taxes or any other taxes to deny voting rights in federal elections, was ratified. The following year, Congress passed the Voting Rights Act of 1965, which suspended literacy tests and assigned federal registrars to enroll voters. The Voting Rights Act essentially provided for enforcement of the 15th Amendment (see Chapter 2). Civil rights advocates used these laws and amendments to launch a successful assault on the Jim Crow system. As we will discuss more in subsequent chapters, full and equal political participation of people of color continues to be elusive. This is especially true in some parts of the country, as new state voter identification laws construct barriers to suffrage, 50 years after the passage of this landmark civil rights legislation.

The Struggle for Hispanic American Civil Rights

As discussed in Chapter 2, the annexation of Texas and the Treaty of Guadalupe Hidalgo that concluded the Mexican War significantly increased the Hispanic or Latino population of the United States. Throughout the southwest, native-born Hispanics, as well as legal and undocumented Mexican immigrants, were exploited to meet the demand for cheap farm labor. They received low wages and were forced to work and live under dangerous and unsanitary conditions. During the 20th century up until today, policy toward immigrant workers has fluctuated greatly, depending on economic conditions. During prosperous times, when the demand for labor rose, the government encouraged Mexican workers to enter the country, although only temporarily. Beginning in 1942, the Bracero Program (it roughly translates to "strong arm," in Spanish) brought Mexican men to America to work in field agriculture, to meet demand for labor when American men were deployed to fight in World War II. Like women, who were pressed to return to the home after World War II ended when their labor was no longer needed, these Bracero workers faced discrimination and even deportation when the program ended. This same pattern was also seen earlier during the Depression, when thousands of Mexican Americans were deported (Nash et al., 2004). Jim Crow-type laws regulated the lives of Latinos in the U.S. as well, including laws that segregated schools and public accommodations, laws on property holding, and laws against intermarriage with Caucasians.

Responding to discrimination and exploitation, Hispanic migrant workers began to demand decent wages and working conditions. In 1962, Cesar Chavez and Delores Huerta co-founded the National Farm Workers Association, which pressed for fairer treatment of these workers. Three years later, that group evolved into the United Farm Workers (UFW) and initiated La Huelga, a major strike of agricultural workers in California (Patterson, 1996). The struggle to improve conditions for these workers continues today, as agricultural workers receive among the lowest wages and have the fewest labor protections of any industry in the country.

EXHIBIT 3.7

Dolores Huerta, September 24, 1965, Delano, CA, Grape Strike

Today, immigrants from Central and South America, Cuba, Puerto Rico, Mexico, and Spain are represented in the Hispanic population of the U.S., along with people whose ancestors were indigenous to the southwest at the time the U.S. annexed that territory. As have immigrants from around the world for generations, these immigrants and their descendants have achieved considerable gains and carved out positions of power within government and commerce. However, as we will discuss more in Chapter 7, health and economic indicators such as higher infant mortality and poverty rates for Hispanic/Latino than for white, non-Hispanic households suggest that Hispanic Americans as a group remain disadvantaged. As the percentage of the U.S. population who are Hispanic continues to grow, initiatives to increase opportunities for Hispanic/Latino families in poverty and address discrimination are becoming increasingly important. The influence of Hispanic voters' support for President Obama in the 2008 and 2012 elections has underscored the need for politicians to deal with these issues. Polls suggest that the policy issues that most concern Hispanic Americans are similar to those of other demographic groups: primarily education, health care, and economic growth/jobs. However, the long waits, high costs, and increasing injustice of the nation's immigration policies are a special concern for this population, making comprehensive immigration reform a core policy debate, as we will discuss later.

Mental Health and Mental Retardation Initiatives

Recall that in 1946 Congress passed the Mental Health Act, which focused increased attention on the treatment of people with mental illness. During the early 1960s, advocates for people with mental retardation and mental illness pressured the federal government to allocate greater resources for their treatment and to increase opportunities for community-based care. Significantly, they found a powerful ally in President John Kennedy, who had a sister with mental retardation. Their efforts culminated in the passage of the Mental Retardation Facilities and Community Mental Health Centers Construction Act of 1963. This Act provided money to construct and staff community mental health centers and mental retardation facilities nationwide. Although the mental health centers were never sufficiently funded to meet the need for community-based services, the Act helped usher in an era of deinstitutionalization in which people with mental illness were reintegrated into the larger community rather than confined and treated in mental hospitals (Trattner, 1999). Where mental illness had been something to be hidden, work was under way to establish the new expectation that people suffering from mental illness should receive community-based treatment and that better mental health should be considered an attainable goal for all Americans.

The War on Poverty

Closely associated with the civil rights movement were a variety of initiatives by the federal government to address the problem of poverty. The administrations of Presidents John Kennedy (1961–1963) and Lyndon Johnson (1963–1968) implemented a number of programs to create jobs, improve education, and provide financial assistance to people in need. Kennedy was influenced in particular by *The Other America*, published in 1962 by political scientist Michael Harrington. Harrington's book helped open the eyes of the American people to the reality of structural poverty that arose from unemployment and lack of opportunities rather than individual deficits. *The Other America* is often credited with ushering in another discovery of poverty, a problem that had been given less attention following the Depression. The book focused public attention on people in depressed areas and on specific populations who had not benefited from the relative affluence of the 1950s.

New Frontier Anti-Poverty Programs   Kennedy's domestic program, known as the New Frontier, included several measures to help move people out of poverty. For example, the Area Redevelopment Act of 1961 allocated federal monies to depressed areas such as Appalachia. The following year, Congress approved the Manpower Development Training Act (MDTA) to train or retrain workers who lacked the skills necessary to succeed in a changing economy. Further, the Equal Pay Act of 1963 attempted to address the issue of gender-based wage discrimination by promoting the concept that women should receive equal wages for performing the same work as men. Although these initiatives were limited in both their scope and their funding, they symbolized a growing belief that the federal government should take action against poverty even during relatively prosperous periods (Patterson, 1996).

Of special significance for social workers were the 1962 Public Welfare Amendments to the Social Security Act, referred to as the Social Service Amendments. These amendments allocated federal support to the states so that local welfare departments could provide recipients of public assistance with casework, job training and placement, and other social services. Growing attention to psychiatric social work fueled support for this approach. Social workers who proposed ideas to the president for addressing the dependency of public welfare recipients and family breakdown, indicated that these interventions would promote motivation and family unity, which in turn would reduce the welfare rolls significantly (Day, 2009). Instead, the welfare rolls increased by nearly 50 percent between 1962 and 1967.

There were a variety of reasons for this increase. One reason was that during the 1960s, large numbers of African American mothers began to claim AFDC benefits. Formerly reluctant to claim such benefits as a right of citizenship and strongly discouraged by racist interpretations of welfare rules, black women now pressed for benefits so their children would not have to go without health care and could stay in school rather than go to work to help support their families (Tice and Perkins, 2002). In addition, social workers and other activists engaged in outreach in order to help more people living in poverty. A burgeoning welfare rights movement organized welfare recipients to protest unfair treatment and to use direct action to draw attention to the challenges faced by low-income single parents, in particular. At the same time, eligibility rules were relaxed, sometimes through Supreme Court decisions, so that more people could receive help. However, the low levels of public assistance did not provide clients with sufficient support to take advantage of expanded educational and social services (Reisch, 2000). For example, people lacking sufficient funds for transportation and day care could not attend job training and parenting classes.

Because social workers had advocated for the Social Service Amendments, when these programs failed to reduce the welfare rolls, it contributed to increased skepticism about the effectiveness of social services. Poverty is essentially a lack of money and other resources; therefore, ameliorating poverty requires focus not only on the personal problems of poor people but also overcoming the structural barriers they confront and reforming the major social service systems. The idea that welfare rolls would be significantly reduced by offering social services to individuals to lift themselves out of poverty without addressing the social conditions that caused their poverty was contrary to what many social workers knew about the interactions of people and their environment. However, in order to secure funding for programs that can help in individual cases, advocates often promise unrealistic outcomes. This disconnect between working with the individual, and the fundamental need for more attention to increasing economic opportunity, particularly in terms of availability of jobs that pay a living wage, continues to plague social work and efforts to address poverty. Unfortunately, unrealized promises accumulate and contribute to public cynicism regarding the efforts of both the government and social workers to assist those with low incomes.

The Great Society and the War on Poverty   The assassination of President Kennedy in November 1963 ushered in the presidency of Lyndon Johnson, who was able to work with Congress to pass civil rights, health, and anti-poverty legislation. These policies and the programs they created were core initiatives of Johnson's Great Society, which included his War on Poverty. The proposals for reform developed by Whitney Young, Jr., an African American social worker who was a leader in the Urban League, are widely credited as being the inspiration for the War on Poverty.

Like the Progressive Era and the New Deal period, the 1960s witnessed major social policy developments. As you read the following discussion of the Great Society and the War on Poverty, consider how these periods were both similar and different and identify the forces that helped bring all these periods of increased reform to an end.

The centerpiece of Johnson's War on Poverty was the Economic Opportunity Act of 1964. This landmark law focused on community organizing, social action, increasing economic opportunities, and empowering, rather than "fixing," the poor. Among the programs and agencies established by the Economic Opportunity Act were:

- The Office of Economic Opportunity (OEO), which oversaw the administration's anti-poverty activities.

- Volunteers in Service to America (VISTA), a program in which volunteers directly assist people in need, including migrant workers and individuals with mental illness or other disabilities.

- The Job Corps to train young people who were unemployed and lacked adequate job skills.

- Community action programs (CAPs), which provide services and resources such as education, housing, health care, and job training to impoverished communities while encouraging "maximum feasible participation" by the residents of those communities.

- Head Start, a program administered by OEO that provides medical care, nutrition, school preparation, and parental education to aid poor preschoolers (Bernstein, 1996).

The Economic Opportunity Act reflected the belief that poverty could not be overcome by changing individual characteristics of poor people but, instead, would require major changes in the way opportunities for education and employment were provided. These changes, in turn, could take place only as people in poverty and from traditionally oppressed groups such as inner-city African Americans and Hispanics or Latinos began to hold office and exercise political power, beginning with their vote. When viewed from this perspective, then, the Economic Opportunity Act reflected a strengths-based approach to combating poverty.

Anti-poverty programs created in the War on Poverty initially did not incorporate social workers because the intent was to rely less heavily on professionals and instead acknowledge that the target groups themselves were the experts on how to escape poverty. However, these groups soon brought in social workers to help with community organizing, administering anti-poverty programs, and providing direct services (Popple, 1995).

Medicare and Medicaid   Another feature of the Great Society that was intended to combat poverty was federal legislation to assist older adults and those with low incomes in meeting their medical expenses. In 1965, three decades of lobbying for incorporating health care into the Social Security Act finally resulted in the passage of Title XVIII, which established Medicare, and Title XIX, which established Medicaid. Although these programs did not provide universal health care for all citizens, they did ensure basic medical care for certain categories of citizens and laid the foundation of government responsibility for health care.

Medicare is a national health insurance program for people aged 65 and older who are eligible for Social Security and for certain categories of younger people with disabilities. Medicare focuses primarily on acute care and provides little coverage for long-term care. Medicare Part A provides hospital insurance, and Medicare Part B is an optional program that allows people aged 65 and over to purchase coverage for Medicare-eligible physician services, outpatient hospital services, certain home health services, and durable medical equipment. Medicare Part D, which went into effect in 2006, provides subsidies to allow older adults to purchase prescription drug coverage at reduced rates. The Medicare program is federally funded through payroll taxes.

In contrast, Medicaid provides health care for certain categories of people with very low incomes as part of public assistance. It is a means-tested program that is financed jointly by federal and state dollars. Medicaid is typically thought of as the source of health care for poor families with children. Indeed, Medicaid has greatly increased access to health care for children. However, Medicaid also pays more than half of nursing home costs nationally; many older people are impoverished by the costs of nursing home care and thus become eligible for Medicaid. Many younger people with disabilities also qualify for Medicaid. Although states can use Medicaid to make home- and community-based services available for some older adults and young people with severe disabilities, there are often long waiting lists for these services. You can visit the Centers for Medicare and Medicaid Services (CMS) website (www.cms.gov), and learn more about the history of Medicare and Medicaid.

The War on Poverty: Successes and Failures   As we would expect from any major reform effort, the War on Poverty experienced both successes and failures. This observation is significant because many people have overlooked the actual benefits of policies and programs that were created in the 1960s. Instead, they remember the anti-poverty efforts associated with this period only as failures—they did not completely end poverty—rather than as programs that promised too much and were inadequately funded but nonetheless generated some positive outcomes. Certainly, the civil rights legislation of this period attempted to address the structural problems created by discrimination. Significantly, the national poverty rate dropped from 22 percent in 1960 to 11 percent in 1974. Although the improving state of the economy was the major cause of this decline, anti-poverty programs contributed as well.

Furthermore, several of the anti-poverty policies and programs implemented during this period survived and are still important today. In addition to Medicare and Medicaid, these initiatives include Head Start, the Food Stamp Act of 1964, and the Older Americans Act of 1965. Through the Food Stamp Act, low-income families receive subsidies for the purchase of some additional, nutritious food. The Food Stamp Program is now known as the Supplemental Nutrition Assistance Program (SNAP). The Older Americans Act contains a number of provisions designed to promote social interaction and enhance independent living for older adults. For example, funding for congregate meals and transportation helps community-dwelling older adults meet their nutritional needs more adequately and lessens their social isolation. This law incorporated such strengths-based policy tenets as empowering clients, involving them in developing and providing services, and increasing opportunities for them. Take a moment to think about the lessons we can learn from examining the various policies and programs implemented during the 1960s and consider the implications for social policy reform today.

The major anti-poverty programs generally received inadequate funding and many of the Great Society anti-poverty initiatives came to an end. Most of these programs failed to address the social, economic, and demographic forces that were causing the welfare rolls to rise. For example, increasing numbers of low-income families were migrating from the south to urban areas in the north, where they found insufficient job opportunities, inadequate housing, and ineffective transportation systems. Critics who were not mindful of these underlying deficiencies classified the War on Poverty as a failure when welfare rolls increased and poverty continued, rather than pushing for structural reforms.

In their book *Regulating the Poor*, Frances Piven and Richard Cloward, a social worker, examined historical periods of increase in economic assistance for low-income citizens through the 1960s. They contend that programs providing economic support to poor people expanded, not in relation to need but, rather, as a tool for controlling unrest, particularly in cities in the U.S. (Piven and Cloward, 1971). Their analysis points to the outpouring of economic assistance during the period of civil unrest of the 1960s. They assert that the government provided temporary economic aid to regulate unrest rather than to address the structural problems of unemployment and discrimination that limited opportunity. Although their assertions are certainly open to debate, their critical analysis helped increase awareness of the multiple goals of anti-poverty initiatives.

The cutback of funding for anti-poverty programs led Martin Luther King, Jr. to wonder whether social and economic justice would ever become a reality for African Americans and poor people. Other black leaders, such as Malcolm X and Stokely Carmichael, openly rejected the premise that nonviolence and integration would produce racial equality. They rallied their followers with calls for "black power" and "black separatism." However, a coalition of white and black civil rights advocates opposed their ideas because they felt that black Americans did not control sufficient resources to establish a separate economy. Also, many people strongly supported nonviolent and inclusive action, even when frustrated with the very slow pace in which change occurred. Further, they continued to believe that integration could succeed. Indeed, despite continued resistance, there were many gains for civil and economic justice in the 1960s. However, a white backlash that emerged in response to the separatist rhetoric and to urban riots such as the one in the Watts section of Los Angeles in 1965 fueled a political turn to the right that contributed to the election of a Republican president, Richard Nixon, in 1968.

CONTINUITY AND CHANGE: THE 1970S

Richard Nixon presided over the tumultuous first years of the 1970s. Nixon's administration was marked by controversy that culminated in the president's resignation. However, his administration almost doubled spending on anti-poverty programs over that of the Kennedy and Johnson administrations (Tice and Perkins, 2002). Our discussion of the 1970s highlights experiments with a different approach to providing cash assistance to low-income people, the negative income tax. We will also consider the continuing push for greater civil rights. Building on the civil rights reforms of the 1960s, several marginalized groups struggled to improve their situation in the 1970s. We will focus on the struggles of two such groups—women and Native Americans— to achieve social justice. We will also consider social policies that were implemented to promote their civil rights and to enhance the resources available to them.

Family Assistance Experiments

Perhaps the major social welfare initiative of the Nixon administration was the Family Assistance Plan (FAP), proposed by presidential adviser Daniel Patrick Moynihan. The FAP would have established a minimum income for all families by providing cash assistance to families whose incomes fell below a certain level. This policy is sometimes referred to as a "negative income tax." Reflecting a philosophy that dates at least to the English Poor Laws, the FAP also would have required all able-bodied recipients to work or to participate in a job training program. If enacted, this plan would have replaced AFDC.

However, the FAP quickly became the target of criticism from across the political spectrum. Liberals pointed out that the minimum income level was actually less than the established poverty level. Moreover, they objected to the work requirements, in part because the "able-bodied" poor included mothers with children over three years of age. Meanwhile, many conservatives argued that the FAP would significantly increase federal spending on welfare, especially if other assistance programs, such as food stamps, were not eliminated as part of the plan. Nixon himself, who was more concerned with foreign policy, eventually lost interest in the FAP, and it never passed the Congress (Moynihan, 1973; Trattner, 1999). However, internationally, many countries in Western Europe have long had some form of child or family allowance. Examining the debates around the FAP in the context of policy considerations today illustrates the importance of political and economic environments in shaping "acceptable" policy alternatives; today, some of the provisions that were objectionable within the FAP are, for example, accepted components of Temporary

Assistance to Needy Families (TANF). If you would like to learn more about the early development of this less stigmatizing method of helping people in poverty, you can visit the University of Wisconsin Institute for Research on Poverty website (www.irp. wisc.edu) and find further information about the negative income tax.

Although not implemented nationally, these negative income tax experiments heightened interest in providing income to low-income families through the tax system. Reflecting this interest, Congress passed legislation in 1975 that established the Earned Income Tax Credit (EITC), which provided a refundable tax credit to families whose incomes fell below the federal poverty line even when supported by full-time workers. Even though this tax credit was modest and did not significantly reduce poverty, it established the principle of using the tax system, administered through the Internal Revenue Service (IRS), to provide resources to low-income citizens without undue stigmatization and, today, the value of the EITC, at the federal level and in many states, is such that it does lift millions of Americans out of poverty each year. The EITC is explained in detail in Chapter 8. This approach, similar to the tax incentives, mortgage deductions, and other welfare programs for wealthy and middle-class families, reduces the stigma of assistance. Hopefully, knowing about the EITC, and how the tax system generally is used to provide assistance, helps more people realize that the tax system is a method for providing welfare and that most people are likely to be welfare recipients themselves. For example, many families who are not low income receive the benefit of the child care deduction and the child tax credit.

Social Service Reforms

Although the 1970s are not considered a period of major social service reform, several measures introduced during the administrations of Richard Nixon and his successor, Gerald Ford, contributed to the social welfare of people in need. One reform involved child welfare. Child welfare advocates lobbied intensely for a national standard for child protection and, in response, Congress passed the Child Abuse Prevention and Treatment Act of 1974. This law also enabled child advocates to document national trends in child abuse and to publicize the need for protective services for the first time.

Social Welfare Initiatives   Other initiatives sought to increase assistance to low-income groups. For example, in 1972, Congress enacted legislation creating the Supplementary Security Income (SSI) program. Prior to 1972, states had a patchwork of programs to provide assistance to elderly people, blind people, and people with disabilities who had limited or no income. SSI replaced this arrangement with a uniform national system for very low-income people in these categories.

Proposals to provide a demogrant—"a uniform payment to certain categories of persons, identified only by demographic (usually age) characteristics" (Burns, 1965, p. 88)—were considered for both older adults and children as a way to create a universal safety net, but the idea was never sufficiently popular to be nationally implemented. Universal demogrants are non-stigmatizing. However, selectivity can be built in through taxation of the benefit for higher-income families. Nevertheless, the overwhelming preference in the U.S. is to link benefits to workforce participation, whenever possible, and to provide only minimal means-tested benefits to people not attached to the workforce, even when they fall into the category of "worthy poor," such as elders and children.

The Social Service Amendments of 1974, specifically Title XX, did make grants available to states to provide social services to welfare recipients as well as to people above the poverty line. Although the amount of money available for these programs was capped, states were given a great deal of latitude in determining how the services were to be provided. Social Security and SSI benefits were also indexed through an automatic cost-of-living adjustment (COLA). This means that the benefit amount increases when the cost of living rises.

Watergate and After   Despite these reforms, the Watergate scandal, which led to Nixon's resignation in August 1974, further undermined the public's belief in the positive power of government, thus mitigating against the expansion of social programs that had marked the 1960s and early 1970s. The next two presidents, Gerald Ford and Jimmy Carter, were focused on controlling the budget deficit and taming inflation as well as dealing with foreign policy crises. Significantly, President Carter did propose a guaranteed annual income plan that would have created an income safety net for all Americans, but it was not enacted (Tice and Perkins, 2002). Carter also signed into law the Food Stamp Act of 1977, a bipartisan effort to expand the food stamp program and reduce the unacceptable levels of hunger still experienced across the U.S. To learn more about the history of the Food Stamp Program, go to the Center on Budget and Policy Priorities (CBPP) website (www.cbpp.org) and watch the video "Making America Stronger: The Food Stamp Program."

Women and Civil Rights

The women's movement increased its advocacy efforts during this period. In 1966, a group of activists founded the National Organization for Women (NOW) to press for equal rights for women. Its first president, Betty Friedan, was the author of the landmark book *The Feminine Mystique*. This book helped increase awareness of societal stereotypes that limited women's roles and impeded their efforts to secure equal rights. Women's rights activists pressed for equal opportunities across a broad spectrum, including employment, education, and athletics.

As we saw earlier in the chapter, amendments to the Constitution to guarantee equal rights for women were introduced repeatedly in Congress, beginning in 1923. Finally, in 1972, Congress passed the ERA, mandating that "equality of rights under the law shall not be denied or abridged by the U.S. or by any State on account of sex." Supported by groups such as NOW, the amendment was passed by 21 states. However, opponents such as the Moral Majority—a faith-based organization espousing a conservative vision of U.S. family and social policy—raised fears of women and men using the same bathrooms and pregnant women and mothers being drafted in wartime. Consequently, the ERA never gained the approval of the 38 states needed for ratification.

However, other policy reforms influencing women's lives were more successful. For example, Title IX of the Education Amendments of 1972 banned discrimination and exclusion in schools on the basis of sex in both academic and sports arenas, thus opening wider the doors of opportunity for women (Title IX Education Amendments of 1972). To learn more about Title IX, go to the website of the Department of Labor (www.dol.gov) and search for Title IX, Education Amendments of 1972.

The following year, the Supreme Court decision *Roe* vs. *Wade* legalized abortion. The pattern of activism by women, so evident in the 1800s and early 1900s, continued to shape health, welfare, and civil rights policy during this period. However, despite the activist environment of the time and the preponderance of women in the social work profession, the NASW did not elect a woman president until 1980 (Hooyman, 1994).

Native Americans and Civil Rights

The 1970s also witnessed increased activism by Native American groups. Many of these actions focused on the status of American Indians within the broader political system. Recall from Chapter 2 that the *Cherokee Nation* vs. *Georgia* ruling of 1831 placed the various Indian tribes under the jurisdiction of the government, denying them the status of sovereign nations. Decades later, the Dawes Act replaced the traditional tribal system of land ownership with an individual and family system. In the 20th century, Native American activists and their advocates in the government began to challenge these arrangements. In 1934, as part of the New Deal, Congress passed the Indian Reorganization Act, which officially abolished the Dawes allotment policy and returned certain expropriated lands to various tribes. Moreover, it authorized the tribes to establish governments or councils that would exercise some degree of sovereignty (DeLoria, 1993).

Termination and Relocation   The New Deal reforms demonstrated greater sensitivity toward Native American autonomy and culture. However, in the more conservative political atmosphere of the 1950s, the government's focus shifted to incorporating Indian peoples into mainstream culture. To accomplish this objective, it pursued the policies of termination and relocation. Formally implemented by two congressional actions of 1953, termination involved abolishing the special status of tribes as wards of the federal government and authorizing the states to assume some of the functions of the tribal governments. One objective of this policy was "to cut off public aid to Indians and to get them to fend for themselves" (Patterson, 1996, p. 376). However, because the government failed to provide transition supports, many Native Americans suffered heavy financial and property losses. For example, when Native Americans were billed for property taxes they were unable to pay, they lost their homes, which in turn left them unable to support schools, sanitation systems, and highways in their communities.

Groups like the National Congress of American Indians (NCAI) vigorously opposed termination, characterizing it as just another form of oppression. The NCAI argued that Native Americans should exercise a dual identity as members of a tribe and as citizens of the U.S. By the time President Nixon ended the policy of termination in 1969, several dozen tribes had been terminated (DeLoria, 1993; Patterson, 1996; Tice and Perkins, 2002).

A related policy, relocation, encouraged Native Americans—primarily young people—to move from their reservations to cities. The purpose of this policy was not only to provide greater economic opportunity but to promote assimilation into "white" culture. Again, Native Americans were pressed to abandon their cultural roots. In practice, relocation "frequently involved nothing more than a trade of rural for urban poverty" (DeLoria, 1993, p. 427). Consequently, many disillusioned young people returned to the reservations, where they also faced myriad social problems.

Militancy and the Struggle for Sovereignty   Like other marginalized groups, Native Americans adopted the direct action strategies of the African American civil rights movement during the late 1960s and 1970s. In 1968, activists organized the American Indian Movement (AIM), which played a major role in many subsequent protests. The following year, a group of Indians from several tribes occupied Alcatraz Island, California. In 1972, activists organized the "Trail of Broken Treaties" caravan to Washington, DC, where a group of militants took over the headquarters of the Bureau of Indian Affairs (BIA).

Perhaps the most dramatic confrontation occurred in 1973 when an alliance of AIM members and Oglala Lakota (Sioux) people occupied several buildings in Wounded Knee, South Dakota, where many Lakota had been massacred by U.S. troops in 1890. Their objective was to publicize both the severe social problems that existed on the local reservation and the many treaties that the government had failed to honor over the years. Federal agents quickly encircled Wounded Knee, and shots were exchanged. The ensuing stand-off lasted more than two months. The occupation finally ended when the government agreed to review its treaties with the Lakota (DeLoria, 1993; Nash et al., 2004; Patterson, 1996).

In addition to direct action, activists also used the courts to press historical land claims that were supported by treaties but had never been honored. They used similar tactics to assert traditional water rights and fishing rights. These actions led to frequent confrontations with whites who claimed that Native Americans were receiving special treatment from the government (DeLoria, 1993; Nash et al., 2004).

Child Welfare   Another target of Native American activism was government policy regarding child welfare. During this period, Native American children were being removed from their homes and placed with white families, until almost 30 percent of Indian children were no longer being raised in Native American homes (Tice and Perkins, 2002). Child welfare policies and practices that were not culturally sensitive contributed to the wide-scale adoption and out-of-home placement of these children with little regard for preserving their native heritage. Leah Katherine Hicks Manning, a social worker who was a member of the Shoshone-Paiute tribe and a staff development specialist at the BIA in the 1960s, believed that adoption and foster care policy for Native American children should emphasize keeping them on their reservation or near their families to promote healthy development (*Encyclopedia of Social Work*, 2008). These are key components of the Indian Child Welfare Act, passed by Congress in 1978 in response to a coordinated effort by a number of tribes, with Manning playing a prominent role. The goal of the Act was to strengthen and preserve Native American families and culture, and it re-established tribal authority over the adoption of Native American children. In sum, Native American militancy was directed toward two related objectives: (1) reasserting traditional sovereignty, identities, and cultures, and (2) alleviating social problems such as poverty, unemployment, and alcohol abuse that were common on the reservations. To learn more about the history of the Indian Child Welfare Act, go to the website of the National Indian Child Welfare Association (www.nicwa.org).

EXHIBIT 3.8

Leah Katherine Hicks Manning

Leah Katherine Hicks Manning was born on the Nixon Reservation, Nevada in 1917. As a member of the Shoshone-Paiute tribe, Manning played a key role in bringing the needs of Indian families and their children to the attention of Congress, resulting in the enactment of the Indian Child Welfare Act in 1978. Manning attended high school in Oklahoma and attended college at several universities across the country. Manning taught at an American Indian primary school and in the early 1960s worked at the Bureau of Indian Affairs educating social workers on Native American culture and traditions. Manning began her social work master's degree studies at the University of Chicago before taking time off to marry a chairman of the Shoshone-Paiute tribe who actively advocated for treaty rights. After raising her family, Manning went back to school and obtained her master's in social work from the University of Utah in 1968. Manning is also responsible for creating what is thought to be the first program that provided social services to Native Americans in Nevada. Manning was the director of this program and American Indian professionals provided services such as: substance abuse prevention, family counseling, public health services, and financial assistance. Manning was named Social Worker of the Year in 1974 by the Nevada chapter of NASW and was a lifetime member at the National Congress of American Indians. On February 12, 1979, Manning, her daughter Tina, and Tina's three children were killed in a fire in Manning and her husband's home while they were all sleeping.

Source: Indian child welfare act is her legacy. (1998). NASW NEWS. Retrieved Nov 13, 2012 from http://www.socialworkers.org/profession/centennial/manning.htm

American Indians continue to struggle to change conditions that lead to poverty and substance abuse. Approximately 28 percent of Native Americans and Alaskan Natives lived in poverty in 2010 (U.S. Department of Health, the Office of Minority Health, 2012). In addition, American Indians and Alaskan Natives continue to suffer disproportionately from substance abuse disorders compared with other racial groups in the U.S. (Department of Justice, 2011). American Indian leaders are working to identify and implement effective strategies to bring about structural as well as individual change to help alleviate these problems.

Affirmative Action

One major development that affected the economic status and opportunities of all of the groups we have just discussed was the transition from a policy of simple nondiscrimination to affirmative action. Affirmative action is a general term that refers to policies and programs designed to compensate for discrimination against marginalized groups such as women and people of color. In order to redress losses to people who have suffered discrimination and to their descendants, and to ameliorate current discriminatory practices, affirmative action policies establish criteria that give these groups preferential access to opportunities, most importantly in education and employment.

Affirmative Action and Employment Title VII of the Civil Rights Act of 1964 prohibits employment discrimination based on race, color, religion, or national origin, and it empowers the federal courts to "order such affirmative action as may be appropriate" to remedy past injustices. In 1964, affirmative action referred only to such actions as reinstating employees who had been terminated due to discrimination. In the ensuing years, however, the concept of affirmative action was broadened to include specific actions designed to attract and retain female and minority-group workers. For example, Executive Order 11246, issued September 24, 1965, required all government contractors to submit written "Compliance Reports" that specify the number and percentage of minority workers on their projects (Weiss, 1997).

In 1969, the so-called "Philadelphia Plan" went even further, mandating that government contractors submit numerical goals and timetables for hiring minority workers. It also empowered the government to cancel the contracts of employers who failed to comply with these regulations and to prohibit them from receiving future contracts. Numerical hiring targets became an essential feature of many subsequent affirmative action plans in both public and private employment. They also led to charges of fixed quotas and reverse discrimination by opponents of these policies (Weiss, 1997). Reverse discrimination is defined as discrimination against the dominant group due to affirmative action policies designed to redress discrimination against minority groups.

Affirmative Action and Education   During the 1970s, affirmative action was extended to education as well as employment. In 1972, the federal government began to require colleges to prove that they were recruiting qualified women and minorities in order to keep federal funding. These policies also generated charges of reverse discrimination, as critics charged that white students were being denied admission in favor of women and minority students who were less qualified.

This conflict eventually found its way to the Supreme Court in the 1978 case of *The Regents of the University of California* vs. *Bakke*. Allan Bakke, a white male applicant, had been denied admission to the medical school at the University of California at Davis even though he had a higher grade point average than some minority candidates who were admitted. The Court ruling in the *Bakke* case can be interpreted as a partial victory for both sides. The Court struck down the use of strict racial quotas and Bakke was admitted to the medical school. However, the ruling upheld the use of race as one determinant of admission to higher education. Affirmative action thus evolved into one of the most controversial issues in the country. Opposition to this policy became a fundamental feature of the emerging conservative movement that characterized the 1980s, as state ballot measures turned into a battleground over the roles of race and discrimination in modern U.S. society and social policy.

Changes in Social Work

During the 1970s, the NASW developed a model licensure bill, and social workers lobbied for legislation that would require practitioners to be licensed at the state level. Proponents argued that licensure would protect the public, improve the status of the profession, protect social workers against competition from people without licenses, and enable social workers to be paid directly by health benefits programs for providing services. Most health benefits programs such as Medicaid will pay directly only for services provided by licensed professionals. However, licensure requirements can reduce the ability of low-income people and people of color, who often have limited access to the required education, to practice social work and can deny some populations and some parts of the country adequate access to social work services. Consequently, these requirements have led to charges that social work is an elitist profession. Despite these charges, all 50 states plus the District of Columbia now regulate the certification of social work practice and the use of the professional title. To learn more about state-specific licensure laws, go to the website for the Association of Social Work Boards, and navigate to Licensing Requirements (www.aswb.org).

Overall, the social service sector continued to grow during this period as the for-profit and voluntary sectors expanded (Reid, 1995). However, some analysts have asserted that social work moved further away from involvement with social policy by the end of this period largely because of shrinking funding for public sector casework (Tice and Perkins, 2002). Although social workers became more focused on clientele who could pay for services, the profession's historic emphasis on collective responsibility for poor and oppressed populations was not extinguished. In fact, if you examine NASW policy statements and social work journals throughout that period and up until today, you will find evidence of that continuing commitment alongside a growing interest in private practice.

RETRENCHMENT TO NEW FOUNDATIONS: 1981 TO THE PRESENT

Ronald Reagan, who became president in 1981, ushered in an era of conservative politics. Reagan did not cut spending on all social programs. For example, Medicare expenditures actually increased, and Social Security retirement benefits gained rhetorical protections in American politics. Rather, he targeted social welfare programs that were directed primarily toward low-income Americans. The conservative portrayal of the welfare state as a failed social experiment served to rationalize initiatives by the Reagan administration to curtail federal funding for these programs (Reid, 1995). Indeed, during the last decades of the 20th century, and in the beginning of the 21st century, we witnessed a shift in the locus of responsibility for assuring individual and social well-being in the U.S. Remember that implementation of New Deal legislation signaled movement away from blaming people who become unemployed, or did not have adequate retirement savings, for their plight. The government and employers assumed greater responsibility for protecting Americans against a range of contingent events; public programs to insure people against common risks to their future such as illness and inability to work were developed and expanded during the following several decades.

Since the 1980s, we have seen these trends partially reversed as conservative policy makers contended that America needed to encourage individual responsibility with the aim of realizing an "ownership" society (Hacker, 2006). Policies to promote ownership are often premised on the philosophy that the welfare of individuals is best promoted by increasing their ability to control their own lives and wealth, rather than relying on government transfer payments. In practice, however, this approach has been characterized as "on your ownership." Politicians on the right who have helped champion policy reforms designed to cut back health and welfare programs believe these changes have reduced the scope of government and encouraged personal responsibility. As Hacker (2006) has asserted, reductions in the public health and welfare safety net and in corporate provision of health and pension plans have indeed shifted more responsibility onto the backs of the American family.

Risk shifting can also be seen in federal initiatives to transfer more responsibilities for social welfare to the states. Reagan adopted the policy of devolution, whereby responsibility for social welfare increasingly would be transferred from the federal government to the states. He also sought to increase reliance on the private sector to provide social welfare services. This approach involved privatization, a policy that transfers ownership or control from government to private enterprise. Typically, in the U.S., privatization has meant allocating public funds to private profit-making or nonprofit entities that then provide the benefits or services. As a corollary to privatization, the administration sought to cut back some social programs with the rationale of reinvesting tax dollars in the private sector in order to increase economic growth. These efforts, endorsed by President Reagan and his Republican successors, George H. W. Bush and George W. Bush, will be examined in the following sections.

Implementing a Conservative Agenda

In addition to curtailing spending on social programs for low-income Americans, Reagan successfully lobbied Congress to reduce taxes, especially on higher earners, and increase defense spending. These policies, in turn, increased the federal deficit. Under these circumstances, curtailing social welfare spending could be justified as necessary to hold the deficit in check. It is important to note that endorsing tax cuts garners taxpayer support in a way that a direct attack on programs for older people and children living in poverty does not. However, tax cuts frequently translate into decreased services for vulnerable populations, by reducing the revenues available to pay for such services.

Reagan's approach, dubbed "supply-side economics," was supposed to dampen inflation and revive the sluggish economy. This approach sharply contrasted with Keynesian economics, which had informed the New Deal initiatives and endorsed increasing government spending and manipulating interest rates in order to combat inflation and manage recessions. The combination of tax cuts and reduced social welfare spending under the Reagan administration was also supposed to encourage wealthy recipients of the tax cuts to donate more money to charity. Thus, there would be much less need for the federal government to be involved in social welfare. In fact, it was asserted that some of the traditional social programs provided by government could be privatized, with these functions assumed by nonprofit entities, using their charitable contributions as revenue.

Under both the Reagan and the George H. W. Bush administrations, federal policies placed less emphasis on structural change that would increase opportunities for traditionally oppressed groups. They ignored the following realities:

- The minimum wage was so low that people working full-time for that wage could not lift their families out of poverty.

- Many traditional manufacturing jobs were relocating to countries where wages and environmental standards were even lower than in the U.S.

Instead, social policies re-emphasized individual pathology as the reason that people could not provide for themselves. Even people with disabilities were not spared. Applications for federal disability claims were turned down in unprecedented numbers and new rules defining disability restricted access for many with substance addictions and mental illnesses. People who were already on the disability rolls were afraid even to consider working or undertaking any sort of rehabilitation effort for fear that they would lose their benefits.

Many leaders from major religious and private charities, although interested in private/public partnerships, were aware that they could never garner sufficient private resources to replace major public social programs that serve millions of people. In reality, a major shift from public to private funding can lead to cutbacks in services and benefits for poor people under the guise of less government "interference." On the other hand, the private organizations that develop to provide health and social services can potentially be mobilized and become a powerful lobbying force for continued funding, although this depends on the level of politicization of these private providers. This is clearly the case with the mostly private nursing home industry, which receives the majority of its funding from public sources. Their national and state organizations are very powerful players in the area of Medicaid policy reform.

New Federalism, OBRA, and Devolution

The Reagan administration also sought to restructure the relationship between the federal and state governments. The administration's policy, labeled "New Federalism," transferred ever more responsibility to the states for the social welfare of their citizens. Specifically, Reagan proposed that the states assume all costs for the Food Stamp Program, SSI, and AFDC. However, the federal government would take full responsibility for Medicaid. Reagan also encouraged religious institutions to take over programs for people in need.

OBRA and Block Grants   Although the Reagan administration was unable to convert this vision into reality, it did preside over the passage of the Omnibus Budget Reconciliation Act (OBRA) of 1981, which reduced funding for social programs. For example, funding for food stamps was reduced 19 percent, and AFDC was reduced 11 percent. In addition, eligibility requirements for AFDC were tightened.

OBRA also transformed the nature of federal assistance to the states. Specifically, it consolidated dozens of categorical grants—in which the federal government strictly regulated how the monies were spent for programs such as community development services, mental health, alcohol and drug abuse, social services, and maternal and child health services—into a much smaller number of block grants, which allocated much of the decision-making authority to the states (Kenney, 1981). Under the changed funding structure, states no longer had to provide matching funds for any of the block grant programs in order to receive federal funds. The block grants allowed state and local governments greater latitude in directing federal funds toward specific social problems. On the negative side, however, the OBRA reduced federal funding for each block by between 25 and 30 percent.

Theoretically, the reorganization was supposed to offset these cuts by reducing duplication and increasing flexibility. In reality, programs were cut back not only because federal funding was reduced but also because the states were no longer required to provide matching funds in order to receive the same amounts of federal monies as they had in the past. In many cases, funding declined by 50 percent. By 1984, the poverty rate had risen to 15 percent, higher than in any previous period since the 1960s (Tice and Perkins, 2002).

Funding for community mental health centers was collapsed into block grants that could be used for a variety of mental health services. This development diminished the ability of community mental health centers to provide services necessary to enable people with serious mental illness to successfully live in the community. States were attempting to deinstitutionalize more people who had lived in state mental hospitals. Community mental health centers were unable to fulfill the promise of community treatment for people who were deinstitutionalized as state mental hospitals downsized and closed. Other institutions, such as prisons and nursing facilities, began to house increasing numbers of people with serious mental illness.

Pressures to Reduce Social Service Spending   Pressures to reduce social welfare spending intensified in this period. Congress and the president made the biggest cuts ever to funding for children's social services. In 1988, Congress did pass the Family Support Act with the stated intent of providing education and job training programs for AFDC recipients. However, then as now, the lack of well-paid jobs, combined with inadequate funding for child care and few resources to support needed skills training, prevented many female recipients from adequately supporting their children. These realities limited the effectiveness of the Act.

Equal Opportunity Initiatives Stalled   During this period, efforts to secure equal employment opportunity made little headway. The Civil Rights Act of 1964 established the Equal Employment Opportunity Commission (EEOC) to combat employment discrimination. However, people of color continued to experience much higher unemployment rates than white workers and earn much lower average wages, and this made it clear that equal employment opportunity was not being achieved. Women also made only limited progress toward achieving equal opportunities during these years. By 1970, more than 50 percent of all women aged 35–54 held jobs outside the home (Tice and Perkins, 2002). Although a major shift from service to white-collar jobs occurred for women between 1940 and 1981, women continued to be over-represented in low-paying jobs such as beautician, food preparation staff, nurse's aide, housekeeper, and child care worker. In 1986, the National

Commission on Working Women indicated that 77 percent of all employed women worked in low-paying occupations and industries. Nonetheless, by 1989, when conservatives achieved a majority, the Supreme Court backed away from its support of affirmative action (Axinn and Stern, 2001).

From Reagan to Bush   George H. W. Bush took office in 1989, vowing to follow in Reagan's footsteps by holding the line on domestic spending, avoiding a tax increase, promoting a conservative social agenda, and maintaining a strong national defense. However, circumstances and continued activism on the part of some marginalized groups sometimes pressured him to change course. For example, in 1991, mounting racial tension exploded into race riots in Los Angeles, following the acquittal of four white police officers who were videotaped beating Rodney King, an African American, after a high-speed chase. In November of that year, after two years of debates, vetoes, and threatened vetoes, President Bush reversed himself and signed the Civil Rights Act of 1991. This Act strengthened existing civil rights laws and provided for damages in cases of intentional employment discrimination. Two years later, gay rights advocates organized one of the largest civil rights demonstrations in U.S. history. Almost one million people participated in the third National March on Washington to demand equal rights for gays and lesbians and an end to discrimination based on sexual orientation. We will examine the struggle to end

EXHIBIT 3.9

President George H. W. Bush signing ADA

discrimination based on sexual orientation, from the development of gay and lesbian activist organizations in the 1950s until today, in Chapter 7.

One group who achieved a major breakthrough during the Bush years was people with physical and mental disabilities. In 1990, Congress passed the Americans with Disabilities Act (ADA), which prohibited discrimination against people with disabilities in employment, public accommodations, and transportation. The ADA provides a clear example of how legislation that builds on strengths can be passed in a conservative era. The Act had dedicated support from the disability advocacy community. At the same time, its emphasis on work and opportunity spoke to traditional American values and therefore attracted the endorsement of many conservatives. We will discuss the ADA in more detail in Chapter 7.

Advocates for people in need had hoped that, with the collapse of the Soviet Union and the fall of communism throughout Eastern Europe, defense spending would be reduced and domestic issues would receive more attention and funds. However, with the few exceptions discussed above, Bush generally maintained the policy priorities of the Reagan era and, in the face of a sluggish economy, was not re-elected.

"New Democrats" and Social Welfare Policy

Bill Clinton assumed office in 1993. He identified with the ascendant moderate wing of the Democratic Party. Clinton had helped co-found the Democratic Leadership Council (DLC) in 1985, which sought to establish middle ground between more traditional liberal Democrats, who favored income redistribution, civil rights legislation, and cutbacks in defense spending, and "new Democrats," who focused on a narrower range of economic reforms such as job training, infrastructure improvement, free trade, national standards in education, and balanced budgets. "New Democrats" focused more on the needs of the middle class, in part because they feared that the Democratic Party was losing voters who believed that the interests of low-income groups and racial minorities were more important to the party than their needs (Tice and Perkins, 2002).

Some of the social welfare policy initiatives of the Clinton administration provided much-needed help for diverse constituencies. In addition, the administration tried unsuccessfully to create a universal health care system for the U.S. At the same time, however, the passage of legislation that replaced AFDC with Temporary Assistance for Needy Families (TANF) represented a giant step backward in the effort to provide economic security for our nation's children.

Family Leave and People with Disabilities   The Clinton administration sponsored basic reform efforts that assisted families and people with disabilities. Regarding families, in 1993, Congress passed the Family and Medical Leave Act (FMLA). This law required larger employers to guarantee a 12-week unpaid leave period for workers following births or adoptions or in the event that the employee, a dependent, or an immediate family member (spouse, child, parent) has a serious health condition. In 1999, Congress passed the Ticket to Work and Work Incentives Improvement Act. This legislation allowed millions of Americans with disabilities to remain eligible for Medicaid or Medicare if they became employed. Prior to the passage of this law, many people with disabilities were reluctant to seek work out of fear of losing their health care coverage. It also provided vouchers to pay for vocational rehabilitation. This law thus enabled more Americans with disabilities to work and thereby lessen their dependence on public benefits (Social Security Administration, 2007, 2009).

Health Care: The Reform That Did Not Happen   In contrast, the administration experienced far less success in its efforts to reform health care. Many people hoped that the unfinished agenda of extending health care coverage beyond the categories of people covered by Medicare and Medicaid would be completed by instituting universal health care. In 1994, the Clinton administration supported the Health Security Act, which proposed extending medical coverage to 95 percent of Americans by 2000 and establishing a commission to devise a strategy to reach the remaining 5 percent. Under the plan many employers would be required to assume some of the costs of coverage. However, the effort failed, and in November 1994 voters elected a Republican Congress, ushering in the Contract with America.

The Contract with America and the PRWORA   The Contract with America was a series of conservative proposals sponsored by Speaker of the House, Republican Newt Gingrich. It included reducing taxes on capital gains and imposing a "gag rule" that prohibited medical practitioners who receive Medicaid payments from discussing abortion as an option with their female patients (Drew, 1996). A major focus of the Contract was to further decrease the role of the federal government in providing for social welfare. This agenda was a legacy of the Reagan administration. Its supporters, including President Clinton, helped propel the passage of the Personal Responsibility and Work Opportunity Reconciliation Act of 1996 (PRWORA). This law replaced AFDC with TANF, thereby canceling the federal guarantee of support for poor children that had been established by the 1935 Social Security Act. However, the debate surrounding TANF was carefully orchestrated to focus attention on women's morality (childbearing outside of marriage) and work, rather than on the needs of poor children or the impossibilities of the labor market for mothers with young children and few skills. The TANF legislation limited recipients to five years of lifetime support, promoted marriage, and had stringent work requirements. The TANF program can vary widely from state to state. If a state runs out of money, it can terminate all TANF payments.

Further, the PRWORA limited food stamps and SSI benefits for legal immigrants. It also left provision of Medicaid, TANF, and Title XX benefits for legal immigrants up to the discretion of each state's Department of Health and Human Services (USDHHS) or equivalent. Echoes of colonial poor laws could be seen in the return to an emphasis on local responsibility and limiting aid to "strangers."

Soon after PRWORA was passed, benefits were reinstated for legal immigrants residing in the U.S. prior to the passage of the Act in 1996. However, benefits were still denied to new immigrants entering the U.S., for their first five years of Lawful Permanent Residency. These actions underscored the belief that it was inhumane and unjust to terminate benefits already in place for legal immigrants, but it also indicated reduced national responsibility for "strangers" entering the country. People feared that large-scale immigration would drive up the costs of public education and public aid. These economic concerns replaced earlier fears of immigrants' religious and political ideas. We will examine both TANF and Social Security as currently configured in greater detail in Chapter 8, where we focus on income-based social policy.

Because of increased economic prosperity during the second Clinton administration, more low-income people were able to find jobs, which improved the financial standing of families with children, even in light of adverse policies. However, the safety net for low-income families had been greatly weakened. Many of these families were headed by single women. In 2010, 40.8 percent of all births were to single mothers, more than double the rate of 18 percent in 1980 (Martin et al., 2012). Although most single mothers support their children without ever receiving TANF benefits, most families receiving TANF are headed by single women. The lack of adequate child care and the inability of many of these women to move beyond minimum wage jobs, leave children in these families at great risk of negative outcomes such as poor health and not completing their high school education.

Some help in the area of children's health care was provided in 1997, when federal legislation to establish the State Children's Health Insurance Program (SCHIP) was passed. SCHIP authorizes states to offer health insurance to children, up to the age of 19, who are not already insured. This program, covered in detail in Chapter 10, has made health insurance for children much more widely available.

Asset-Based Approaches to Poverty   During the Clinton years, federal and state policy makers explored ways to help low-income families acquire assets. Much of the impetus for this approach came from social workers. One popular strategy was to institute public and private matched savings plans. These initiatives allow low-income people to save money to pursue their education, purchase homes, or start small businesses, and their savings are matched through either public or foundation funds. Asset-based policy will be discussed in more detail in Chapter 8.

These policies reflect the strengths perspective in that they build on the goals of the person in need and help her or him acquire resources in a non-stigmatizing manner. In fact, these policies have helped families build assets they could then use to keep themselves and their children out of poverty throughout their lifetime. These policies mirror structures in U.S. policy making that support the asset accumulation of higher-income families, such as the mortgage interest tax deduction and tax-preferred treatment of Individual Retirement Accounts. Recall that other asset-based programs, such as the Homestead Act and the GI Bill of Rights, similarly benefited previous generations of Americans. It is to be hoped that asset-building programs will assist increasing numbers of low-income families to secure a higher standard of living. Again, asset-building strategies are compatible with these other initiatives and may signal more emphasis on a capacity building state in contrast to a welfare state. However, when we examine the rates of poverty experienced by the American family in the last half of the 20th century and the first decades of the 21st century, it is clear that income inequality is increasing in our society and that existing policies, whether income- or asset-based, are not adequately addressing the problems of children who are growing up in poverty.

Poverty and the American Family

When the Social Security Administration first began to track poverty rates in 1959, it calculated that 22 percent of the population was poor. During the end of the 1960s, when the War on Poverty was initiated, and the 1970s, when spending on social services increased, the poverty rate was reduced approximately by half, to about 11–12 percent. It subsequently rose to 15 percent during the Reagan administration and then stabilized at around 13–14 percent. Following another peak of 15 percent in 1993, the poverty rate returned to 1970 rates of 11–12 percent from 1999 to 2001. However, by 2013, the poverty rate had risen above 15 percent (U.S. Census Bureau, 2013c). Although the majority of people in poverty are non-Hispanic whites, people of color have disproportionately borne the burden of poverty throughout modern U.S. history. Further, in many households with incomes below the poverty threshold today, someone is working full-time, but at a wage insufficient to lift the family out of poverty.

Income inequality has effects on society in addition to the impact of poverty. Income inequality often results in greater geographic separation of rich from poor, which in turn can contribute to inequality in schools, public services, and housing. Income inequality can erode the cohesiveness of society, as very low-income workers see that they have few prospects of sharing in the American Dream, and the very wealthy have fewer opportunities to see first-hand the plight of the poor. Income inequality decreased from 1947 to 1968; however, since that point, it has been increasing. Household inequality grew slowly in the 1970s and then rapidly in the 1980s. This trend has continued through the first decade of this century. The George W. Bush administration helped to increase income inequality by shifting tax burdens and making the rich richer: the top federal income tax bracket declined to 35 percent from nearly 40 percent, the estate tax on inherited wealth was reduced, and capital gains taxes paid on the sale of stocks, real estate, and bonds were lowered.

During this period, the economy was transitioning from an industrial base to a service and informational base. As a result, it produced many well-paying jobs in such fields as computing and finance. At the same time, however, it generated many low-paying jobs in service areas such as fast-food restaurants and department stores.

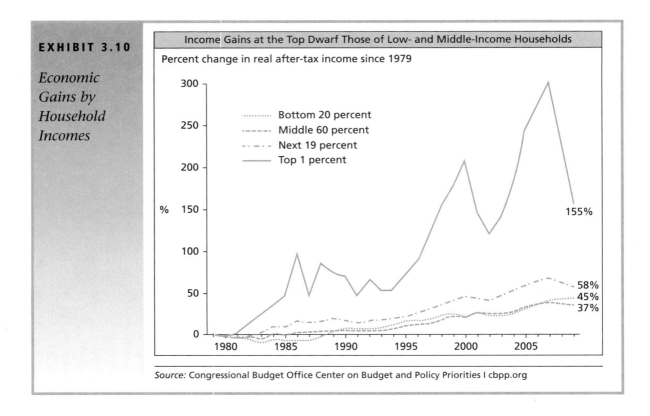

EXHIBIT 3.10

Economic Gains by Household Incomes

Income Gains at the Top Dwarf Those of Low- and Middle-Income Households

Percent change in real after-tax income since 1979

Bottom 20 percent
Middle 60 percent
Next 19 percent
Top 1 percent

155%

58%
45%
37%

Source: Congressional Budget Office Center on Budget and Policy Priorities I cbpp.org

In addition, changes in the configuration of the American family also affected the income distribution of households. For example, the divorce rate in the U.S. reached its peak of 5.3 divorces per every 1,000 people in 1981; it has since declined (Centers for Disease Control and Prevention, 2009). However, marriage rates also declined dramatically during this period. Correspondingly, the percentage of births to single white, African American, and Hispanic or Latino mothers rose during this period. Single-parent households typically have lower incomes compared to two-parent households and, thus, a higher prevalence of poverty (DeNavas-Walt, Proctor, and Mills, 2004).

The New Century

George W. Bush was the first president of the 21st century. The terrorist attacks on September 11, 2001, on military and economic centers in the U.S. turned our attention to long-standing conditions in the Middle East. This Bush administration was wracked by economic and political turmoil as the economy slumped and the U.S. went to war in Afghanistan and Iraq. Changing policies toward torture and concern about eroding civil rights, particularly for Muslims, marked this period. Conservative proposals to turn over many social welfare services to religious organizations and to limit abortion rights occupied the social policy agenda. With Republicans in control of the White House and both houses of Congress, and the public occupied with military and security concerns, resources and services for people in poverty, children, and elders were scaled back in many areas.

Privatization and Faith-Based Initiatives   Like the Reagan and first Bush presidencies, the administration of George W. Bush sought to increase the private sector's responsibility for social programs, thereby decreasing government responsibility and reducing public expectation that the government is responsible for the welfare of its people. Increased reliance on, and funding for, faith-based initiatives was a key component of the administration's privatization program. The assumption that the state, rather than religious institutions, could best provide social assistance was again under attack at a time when many Americans were not even affiliated with a religious denomination. Policy initiatives to strengthen faith-based social services received both support and criticism from religious institutions that were interested in expanding their ministry but were wary of assuming financial and organizational responsibilities they could not meet. State experiments with turning over adoption and foster care services to religiously based organizations had already driven some of these organizations into bankruptcy (Kansas Action for Children, 2001). As we saw in our examination of the Great Depression, relying on churches and nonprofit institutions for social services and benefits, particularly during economic downturns, is not economically viable or morally defensible social policy.

Medicare Part D, which began in 2006 under the Bush administration, used a private-sector strategy to provide prescription drug benefits for people receiving Medicare. Profit-making pharmaceutical and insurance companies lobbied hard for this legislation. In contrast to traditional Medicare insurance programs, in which the government generally chooses benefits and sets prices, for Medicare Part D, elders and people with disabilities must choose their plans from a large variety of often confusing private options. There is no question that this benefit helped many people afford costly but medically necessary prescription drugs. The challenge is to craft policies to make the program more cost-effective and sustainable that can gain enough bipartisan support to be enacted.

Tax Cuts and Reduced Benefits   By combining tax cuts with greatly increased defense spending, the Bush administration limited the amount of money available for maintaining social services without directly attacking popular programs that provided opportunities for poor children and elders. Hundreds of thousands of people across the nation who qualified for assistance were put on waiting lists or were turned away when they applied for help with child care, meals, utility bills, and housing (Claxton and Hansen, 2004). Further, because federal and state tax codes are often linked, diminished tax revenues also generate cutbacks at the state level. In general, as federal and state support for education and social services declines, the private sector and local governments must increase support, or opportunities will disappear. Traditionally poor and oppressed communities have the least capacity to fill this funding gap, so poor schools and people become poorer yet. In turn, structural barriers that keep people in poverty are reinforced, and the distance between the haves and the have-nots increases.

Challenging Affirmative Action and Abortion Rights   The Bush administration also supported legislative and judicial actions against two major social welfare policies of the 1970s: affirmative action and abortion rights. Regarding the former, in 2003, the Supreme Court overturned an affirmative action program at the University of Michigan, but it upheld a more flexible program at the university's law school. In both cases, Bush had called for abolishing the programs (Greenhouse, 2003).

Bush also signed into law two controversial congressional initiatives relating to abortion rights. The first bill, passed in 2003, banned so-called partial birth abortions. The second, passed the following year, in effect defined a violent federal crime against a pregnant woman as two crimes—one against the woman and one against the fetus. Critics charged that by affirming that a fetus has separate rights, Congress was contradicting the underlying philosophy of *Roe* vs. *Wade*. In addition, in 2001, Bush prohibited federal funding of any overseas programs that provide abortions or even counsel women regarding abortions, known as the "global gag rule" (Goldstein, 2004).

Both the policies governing aid to poor families, such as TANF, and the policies designed to make small changes in the economic and societal status quo, such as minority preferences at colleges and universities, were reconfigured under the conservative president, and their capacity to address social and economic inequities were reduced. Because Bush was re-elected for a second term, the U.S. Supreme Court, which has often been the champion of the oppressed, became more conservative as Chief Justice John Roberts replaced Chief Justice William Rehnquist and Justice Samuel Alito replaced Justice Sandra Day O'Connor. These conservative justices ruled, for example, against Lilly Ledbetter in her sex discrimination case and went on to rule against Jack Gross in his age discrimination case. In *Ledbetter* vs. *Goodyear Tire & Rubber Co.* Lilly Ledbetter sued Goodyear Tire after 20 years of service when she realized that, although she had the most experience, she was the lowest-paid supervisor. Although a jury had previously found that her employer had unlawfully discriminated against her based on sex, the Supreme Court rejected this ruling in a 5–4 decision on the basis that the lawsuit was not brought within 180 days of the discrimination—even though Ledbetter had no idea at the time that she was being discriminated against. To remedy this injustice, Congress passed The Lilly Ledbetter Fair Pay Act which allows individuals to bring about a lawsuit within 180 days of *any* issuance of a discriminatory paycheck. President Obama signed this legislation during his first year in office. In the case of Jack Gross, the Supreme Court's ruling made it much more difficult for a worker to win an age discrimination case.

EXHIBIT 3.11

President Obama and His Staff on the Day He Signed the Lilly Ledbetter Act

In 2008, the last full year of the Bush presidency, the increased poverty rate was accompanied by a decline in real median household income, from $52,163 to $50,303 (U.S. Census Bureau, 2009b). In the face of worldwide economic crisis brought on by the collapse of U.S. financial markets, surging home foreclosure rates and declining property values, and high unemployment, the free-market ideology and lack of regulation that had characterized the Bush presidency was being widely questioned, even by the former long-time chairman of the Federal Reserve Board, Alan Greenspan, who had helped shape economic policy for decades. Beset by growing economic turmoil and two ongoing wars, voters in 2008 elected Barack Obama, a Democrat, and the first African American president of the United States.

The Promise of a New Foundation

Barack Obama was elected President in 2008. He won 52 percent of the popular vote and took office with Democratic majorities in both houses of Congress. Although his campaign centered on the need for change in the regulation of financial markets, health care reform, and action to address climate change, it was the economic crises that became the main focus of the election. He promised a "new foundation" that would provide for economic growth and greater security for the citizenry. Health care reform and energy reform were two pillars of the new foundation. Repudiating the old conservative belief that public programs somehow harmed the social order, Obama asserted that basic public social programs such as universal health care were the building blocks of a sound economy. This is in keeping with the development of a capacity building state. Unlike President Reagan, Obama saw government as part of the solution: adequate, publicly funded income security and health care programs not only make it possible for citizens to weather an economic downturn, they also help to keep money flowing in the economy when unemployment is high.

Competent government employees are crucial if public programs are to be adequately administered and regulations such as those that might have prevented the disastrous 2010 British Petroleum (BP) oil spill in the Gulf of Mexico are to be effectively enforced. When the tone at the top is one of disregard for the potential of government to help solve our country's problems, government effectiveness is diminished.

As many middle-class families in the U.S. experienced job loss and loss of health insurance, more citizens realized that our public supports are inadequate. The tumult resulting from the collapse of the economy and wider realization of the inadequacies of our current system can create a catalyst for the reforms that will lead to greater social justice. However, just as during the period of social reform in the 1930s, when the U.S. was in the midst of the Great Depression, reform initiatives spark fierce debate. Many people oppose strengthening the public health and welfare safety net. Concern about rising national debt and its effects on overall economic stability is also a central issue.

At the other end of the spectrum from those who see government as part of the solution to society's problems are those who feel that government *is* the problem. This belief has traditionally been associated with the conservative movement and the Republican Party. However, historically, leading conservatives from Theodore Roosevelt to Barry Goldwater, William F. Buckley, and Robert Dole have believed in a virtuous government and supported the development of effective public programs. Nonetheless, at this point in history, it appears that the chasm between the Democratic and Republican parties has widened. With the ascendancy of the Tea Party movement and its role in influencing Republican primary election outcomes for very conservative candidates, fewer Republicans are willing to be counted as moderates, or even as conservatives in this historical sense. The Democratic majority in Congress set the stage for historical reform of the health and social service sector. However, President Obama also became president in the midst of one of the most serious economic downturns in recent history. Before leaving office, the Bush administration convinced Congress to provide $700 billion in additional funding to shore up failing financial markets. Additional federal legislation that provided $787 billion to stimulate economic recovery was hurriedly passed shortly after President Obama took office. However, economic recovery was slow. The federal government's budget deficit, which is calculated on a yearly basis, as well as the national debt, grew precipitously. Given the increasingly interconnected nature of the world's economies, a deepening financial crisis in Europe exacerbated problems in the United States.

Health Care and Immigration   Obama's strategy was to promote economic recovery by investing in infrastructure and job creation, particularly "green" jobs that would help produce cleaner energy. President Obama also moved aggressively to implement health care reform. The U.S. spends much more on health care per person than any other country and has poorer outcomes in many areas, such as infant mortality. Because many business and health care leaders, as well as hospitals and individual citizens, were very dissatisfied with the current system, it appeared that the time might be right to overhaul the health care system. Unlike the policy debate in 1992, however, Obama did not advocate direct government provision of health care. Rather, he pressed for a pluralistic system that included government and the private sector, where government would ensure all citizens had health care insurance and act as a check and balance, particularly in controlling ever-increasing health care costs. Such a pluralistic system is one that has historically been preferred in the U.S. President Obama's detractors incorrectly accused him of promoting socialized medicine, which involves government financing and direct provision of health care services. Indeed, health care reform advocates, including many social workers, pressed for a single-payer universal health care system like that provided in most other industrialized nations. Universal health care means all eligible residents of the country are guaranteed access to health care, and in a single-payer system, the government collects health care funding derived from a mixture of sources, including insurance premiums and government taxes, and then pays for health care services. People are still free to choose their own health care provider. Medicare is an example of a single-payer health care insurance system, but it is only available to elders and some people with disabilities.

Although single-payer health care systems are favored internationally because they can help control spiraling health care costs, it was clear there was insufficient congressional support to implement such a system in the U.S. Indeed, even a public insurance option that would have provided more choice for people buying insurance, created more competition for insurance companies, and helped to contain health care costs, could not garner widespread support. However, in 2010, the final comprehensive health reform law, the Patient Protection and Affordable Care Act of 2010 (Public Law 111–148) as modified by the Health Care and Education Affordability Reconciliation Act (H.R. 4872) was signed into law (Gorin, 2010). This was a major victory for the Obama administration and a major step toward ensuring health care for all Americans. This health care reform legislation builds on the insurance principle. Most Americans who receive health insurance through their employer will continue to do so. Public programs such as Medicaid and the Children's Health Insurance Program will be expanded. When the legislation is fully implemented, most Americans will benefit from its provisions. This legislation is discussed in detail in Chapter 10 and implications for social workers are detailed. Obama's reform efforts in the health insurance as well as in other areas are designed to stimulate economic growth. They are premised on the understanding that corporations are supported in wealth creation by social investment by the state, that is by development of a capacity building state. As unemployment remained high, job creation became a centerpiece in President Obama's reform agenda.

Buoyed by strong support and unprecedented voter turnout among the growing Latino and Asian-American electorates in 2008, then-candidate Obama promised to address the nation's broken immigration system during his first term. However, the struggling economy, battles over health care reform, continued anti-immigrant sentiment, and congressional reluctance to take up the complex and controversial legislation stymied the Obama administration's plans for a complex immigration overhaul. Instead, the first Obama administration saw a continuation, and even acceleration, of the immigration enforcement priorities of the Bush administration, with the resulting effects of uncertainty and oppression in immigrant communities. As the 2012 election loomed, immigrants and their advocates expressed frustration that President Obama had deported more individuals than any other chief executive, while failing to deliver the immigration reforms the nation so badly needed. At least partly in response, the Department of Homeland Security, in June 2012, used its existing authority to grant deferred action for some immigrants who arrived in the U.S. as children, thus protecting them from deportation and making them eligible for legal work. Building on this limited victory, advocates continued to press for legislation to prevent abusive labor practices and improve the nation's homeland security by comprehensively reforming immigration policy, including family reunification and a path to citizenship for long-term immigrant workers.

The economy failed to improve dramatically during President Obama's first term, and many more conservative Republicans swept into Congress in 2010. Repeal of the Affordable Care Act was a cornerstone of the Republican agenda, although most of the individual components of health reform legislation were quite popular with constituencies. In 2012, the Supreme Court upheld key provisions of the Affordable Care Act including the mandate for everyone to have insurance. Somewhat surprisingly, though, the Court struck down penalties for states if they do not implement the Medicaid expansion, to provide health care for all nonelderly people with an income below 133 percent of the poverty line (Kaiser Family Foundation, 2012a). This left governors who are ideologically opposed to President Obama's approach to health care reform with a choice between improving the health status of their populations, at no cost to the state, and rejecting significant federal dollars in order to stand on principle against the Affordable Care Act.

The Federal Debt   The 2012 presidential election, the first following the U.S. Supreme Court decision in *Citizens United* vs. *Federal Election Commission*—in which the Court ruled that corporations are people who, then, have a constitutional right to freedom of expression, which essentially negated limits on campaign spending—broke all previous records for campaign expenditures. The state of the economic recovery, including tax policy and deficit reduction, was the driving issue in the 2012 campaign and the early part of President Obama's second term, but critical incidents and pent-up frustration over congressional failures prompted the inclusion of other priorities on the agenda, too. Several horrific mass shootings sparked a push for gun control legislation, changing demographics helped to drive an emphasis on the need for immigration reform, and the continued influence of ultra-conservatives within the Republican Party ensured that social issues such as gay marriage and access to birth control would receive policy makers' attention, as well. President Obama was elected to a second term in 2012, despite ongoing concerns about the state and pace of the economic recovery. His grassroots campaign strategy to organize and appeal to a wide coalition of voters, including Latinos, African Americans, young people, and women, was successful and, in fact, Republican strategists widely acknowledged, following the defeat, that their party needed to address the concerns of these groups more effectively.

Large tax cuts in 2001 and 2003, the collapse of the financial markets in 2008 and the cost of two wars have increased the country's debt dramatically. President Obama faces the daunting challenge of reducing debt and also sustaining the educational, economic, health, and welfare infrastructure necessary to compete globally. Increasing recognition of the need to address climate change, particularly following major natural disasters that most scientists attribute, at least in part, to climate changes, will add to the complexity of developing effective social policy in the coming years. Terrorism, gun violence, and the tradeoffs between privacy and security are all issues demanding attention. Additionally, the deep and broad connections among the world's economies raise the stakes whenever a region experiences an economic crisis; at the same time there is potential for global advances in democracy and shared governance.

In the face of congressional gridlock, the Obama administration has moved on some fronts by use of executive orders. For example Defense Secretary Leon Panetta signed an executive order lifting a ban on women serving in combat. This is an example of how the executive branch can change social policy and it is expected President Obama will increasingly rely on the executive branch to move forward his policy agenda. Immigration reform and implementation of the Affordable Care Act continue to be major agenda items during his second term. The upward trajectory of health care costs has begun to bend down and this may, in part, be due to changes brought about by the Affordable Care Act.

Supreme Court Rulings

In 2013, the Supreme Court issued major decisions on voting rights, affirmative action, and same-sex marriage. Concerning voting rights, the Court responded to civil rights challenges to restrictive new voter registration laws with a ruling that Arizona's requirement that prospective voters submit proof of citizenship when registering violates federal law. Importantly, however, the 7–2 decision relied on the federal Motor Voter Act, not the Voting Rights Act, ruling that Arizona could not reject the federal voter registration form in favor of their own document requirements, but not ruling that requiring proof of citizenship is necessarily an undue infringement on voting rights. The ruling ensures that questions about voting and civil rights will continue in the 21st century. However, a second 2013 Supreme Court case has more direct and, likely, more far-reaching consequences for people concerned with protecting voting rights.

The Voting Rights Act Decision   Key issues in *Shelby County Alabama* vs. *Holder* was whether racial minorities continue to face barriers to voting in states with a history of discrimination and, further, should these states face particular scrutiny regarding their electoral rules. In a 5–4 decision the Court decided that nine states, mostly in the South, should no longer be required to receive advance federal approval to change their election laws. Now state voting restrictions will be subject only to after the fact litigation. This means the burden of proof will be on those alleging discrimination, instead of expecting states to demonstrate that their proposed changes will not deprive voters of their rights. By striking down a major segment of the Voting Rights Act of 1965, the Supreme Court stripped federal regulators and civil rights advocates of an important civil rights enforcement tool and raised concerns that many of the hard fought electoral victories of people of color, could be eroded over time. The ramifications of this change will be discussed in more detail in Chapter 7, Civil Rights.

The Affirmative Action Decision   In the 2013 affirmative action admissions case, *Fisher* vs. *University of Texas*, the Supreme Court did not challenge earlier rulings that struck down strict racial quotas but continued to allow the narrowly tailored use of race as a criterion in university admissions. However, the Court did reassert that consideration of race in admissions policy must be "narrowly tailored" and sent the case back to lower court for further consideration.

Same-Sex Marriage Decisions   In 2013, the Supreme Court struck down Section 3 of the Defense of Marriage Act (DOMA) which limited the definition of marriage to marriages between a man and a woman for the purposes of federal benefits. The Court ruled this was a violation of the U.S. Constitution's guarantee of equal protection under the law. The ruling was a great victory for advocates of marriage equality. Now, legally married couples will be able to claim the many federal benefits, rights, and burdens conferred under current U.S. law. However, regulations will need to be developed that specify how federal rights and benefits will be extended to same-sex couples. Because the states, not the federal government, currently dictate who is married, these regulations will be complex to craft. The full impact of this ruling will not be clear until these regulations are completed. A second Supreme Court case focused on California's Proposition 8 same-sex marriage ban. The Court ruled on procedural issues and let stand the lower court ruling that Proposition 8 was unconstitutional. However, the lack of a mandate to states to allow same-sex marriage means that the fight over same-sex marriage will continue in regional elections, in state legislatures, and in the courts.

LESSONS AND CHALLENGES

The U.S. has seen periods of tremendous ethnic diversity in its history, especially at the height of immigration at the end of the 19th and beginning of the 20th century.

Today, however, immigrants are arriving from all over the world, changing the ethnic compositions of the U.S., particularly in light of lower birthrates among Caucasian Americans. These demographics have implications for U.S. politics, as discussed above in relation to the 2008 and 2012 elections, but also for the economy, given the dependence of many industries—particularly agriculture, construction, food service/hospitality, and retail sales—on foreign-born people. As the U.S. contemplates how to best update our immigration policies to address the needs of new Americans and our social and economic imperatives, we must craft policy solutions that reconcile these sometimes competing aims. One of the great domestic policy challenges of the coming years will be to meet the nation's future needs in immigration policy while honoring our history.

In the second decade of the 21st century, we are facing greater demands for natural resources, uncertain economic conditions, and increasing need for health care as the average age in the U.S. rises. These challenges will require innovative strategies to build sustainable health and income support programs. Throughout U.S. history, social welfare policy has developed in the context of the culture of capitalism (Wilensky and Lebeaux, 1965). We have a system in which the governmental, corporate, and voluntary sectors coexist, creating a mixed welfare economy, financed primarily with public or government funds. This has resulted in an uneven patchwork of policies and programs that blend humanitarianism with an emphasis on self-reliance and competitiveness. These social policies and programs often benefit people in power and increase social control. However, it is also apparent that government can be used as an instrument of social justice. The Social Security Act and Medicare have clearly reduced poverty and increased life expectancy. Discriminatory practices decreased after the passage of civil rights protection. The success of these policies, and current uncertainty and turmoil in the private sector, have increased acceptance of the government's role in providing for the health and welfare of the people. However, we have yet to learn whether the demographic changes in our society, as each generation becomes more diverse, will translate into ongoing support for public programs and the higher taxes that will accompany them.

As Gilbert (2002) has asserted, increased emphasis on work and on viewing social benefits not so much as rights, but more as benefits linked to obligations, points to movement from a welfare state to an enabling state. An enabling state provides citizens with benefits, including health care and education, to enable them to be productive workers, and they are expected to work even when there are insufficient jobs or other structural barriers to employment. The challenge is to develop social welfare policies that assume the worthiness of all citizens and support all citizens in meeting their basic needs and developing their capacity to be engaged citizens.

As the needs of poor children continue to go unmet and the number of older adults grows with the aging of the "baby boomers" (people born between 1946 and 1964), we must take steps to ensure that young and old people are not pitted against each other in the struggle for necessary resources. Social insurance programs for older adults need to be reformed now, to ensure their solvency for future generations of elder beneficiaries, and to protect the health of the overall economy, so that the U.S. can continue to meet its obligations to other cohorts as well. As will be discussed in greater detail in subsequent chapters, the Medicare Trust Fund is currently projected to run out of money in 2017. In contrast, Social Security is solvent for a much longer time, and can be kept solvent for generations to come if some fairly modest changes in benefits, tax rates, and eligibility are made soon.

Unfortunately, if these modest changes are not made, large structural changes could undermine these very successful programs. For example, they could be dismantled entirely and replaced with means-tested programs, or with private-sector alternatives that rely on vouchers and would likely be inadequate to provide economic and health security for lower-income retirees. Indeed, many influential political groups initially fought the development of these programs, believing that family and religious institutions rather than government-administered social insurance programs should provide for the income and health care of elders.

People who still seek to reduce these programs have found allies by attempting to link poverty among children to spending on programs for elders, thus promoting intergenerational conflict. However, young versus old is a false dichotomy. If we are lucky, all of us will become old someday. Children are not poor because older adults receive Social Security; children are poor because many parents earn inadequate incomes and lack critical supports to provide economic security for their families, especially when mothers are parenting alone. Low wages result in poverty and contribute to inadequate income in old age because they severely limit workers' ability to save money and to contribute to a pension fund.

We are entering a unique time in history when four or five generations of many families will be alive at the same time. Therefore, our social policies need to ensure that the generations continue to live in harmony. The moral obligation of one generation to another can be combined with enlightened self-interest in crafting viable policies.

Environmental concerns also will influence the development of social policy in the new millennium. For example, social policies in the area of housing subsidies which contribute to urban sprawl lead to increased fuel consumption for transportation and the destruction of natural habitats. Therefore, social policies that help people live where they have easy access to jobs or public transportation will become even more critical. More people are recognizing that climate change has real immediate impact on our communities and economy, and are pressing for more effective policies to mitigate overwhelming costs at the local level necessary to deal with the effects of climate change. In general, a deteriorating environment will contribute to increased health problems, and careless use of our natural resources will lead to worldwide shortages. Both new and existing social policies will need to be examined from a transgenerational perspective. That is, policies will need to be analyzed not only for how they affect the environment and provide for needed benefits and services today, but also for what they mean for the environment and quality of life our children and grandchildren will experience. The growing federal deficit is of particular concern. We need social policies that are environmentally sound and also support the strengths of a diverse population. Such a capacity building approach will emphasize investing in people and infrastructure. Developing such policies and programs will take the same kind of imagination and resolve on the part of your generation of social workers that past social work leaders such as Jane Addams, Charlotte Towle, Dr. Dorothy Height, Whitney Young, Jr., and Harry Hopkins brought to bear when confronted with social and economic injustice.

CONCLUSION

You can use what you have learned about analyzing history when you encounter new social policy. Now it is time to return to the framework for linking historical and current policy that was introduced in Chapter 2. This framework can guide your investigation of new policy. The framework components are:

- How do historical policy approaches to this social problem/need shape current policy?

- What was the cultural milieu at the time these historical approaches were taken? Is the current political and economic context the same or different?

- What were the group interests, and who were the key players involved in developing these historical policies?

- Is there any reason to think that these historical approaches would work better or worse today?

- Did this historical policy approach build on the strengths of the target population?

- Alternatively, was it predicated on a pathology or deficit view of the people to be helped?

- How have definitions of the social problem/need and policy approaches changed over time?

As you confront new social policies in the field, take time to consider their historical precedents. History directly shapes social policy today. Armed with historical insight and knowledge of policy precedents that built on the strengths of target groups, you will be more capable of understanding the policy and advocating for the changes that are needed.

MAIN POINTS

- The 20th century ushered in important social policy initiatives, including child labor laws, women's right to vote, antidiscrimination laws, Social Security, Medicaid and Medicare legislation, and public health and sanitation laws. However, many basic needs, such as health care, were still unmet for a large number of Americans at the beginning of the 21st century.

- The Old Age, Survivors, and Disability Insurance (OASDI) program changed the traditional paradigm whereby children and the elderly were both dependent groups who were expected to rely on the family for economic support. By paying OASDI insurance premiums, unfortunately currently labeled "payroll taxes," workers could now insure that they had an income even after they became elderly and could no longer work.

- The first decade of the 21st century has been marked by terrorism, war, and worldwide economic turmoil. Although the widespread poverty experienced during the Great Depression of the 1930s helped create new consensus that supported the establishment of many major health and social service policies and programs, it is as yet unclear whether current conditions will spur development of a new consensus that will result in greatly expanded access to health care in all states, greater civil rights for marginalized populations, and more attention to creating environmentally sound health and welfare programs.

- New and existing policies need to be considered from a transgenerational perspective. That is, policies will need to be analyzed not only for how they affect the environment and provide for needed benefits and services today, but also for what they mean for the environment and quality of life our children and grandchildren will experience.

- Oppressed groups have struggled to eliminate discrimination on the basis of race, gender, disability, and sexual orientation. Although they were successful in gaining passage of important policy initiatives such as the Civil Rights Act, Title IX of the Education Act, and the Indian Child Welfare Act, discrimination persists.

- The War on Poverty experienced both successes—including significant investments in anti-poverty and human development programs that persist today—and failures.

- New Federalism is an initiative to return power to the states.

- The U.S. has a long history of public–private partnership in providing for people in need. The push for privatization of social welfare during the last decades of the 20th century reflected a growing reluctance on the part of the federal government to take responsibility for the welfare of its citizens. However, the election of Barack Obama in 2008 and his re-election in 2012 may signal growing support for expansion of federal health and welfare initiatives, and more emphasis on a capacity building approach.

- Certain policies, such as the GI Bill of Rights and the Americans with Disabilities Act, reflect the premise that people have strengths and will take advantage of opportunities if structural barriers are removed.

- Other policies, such as the Personal Responsibility and Work Opportunity Reconciliation Act of 1996, begin with the premise that people must be made to work and that social policy should therefore focus on strict work requirements and time limits rather than on removing structural barriers such as lack of access to needed education and training.

- In 2010, comprehensive health reform was signed into law. This was a major victory for the Obama administration and a major step toward ensuring health care for all Americans.

- The re-election of President Obama in 2012 means that implementation of the Affordable Care Act will continue. Immigration reform is also a priority.

EXERCISES

1. Go to the Sanchez case at www.routledgesw.com/cases. Could members of the Sanchez family qualify for TANF or Medicaid in your state? If so, which members?
   a. Where do you think Roberto could turn for medical care if he became seriously ill?
   b. What are the historical precedents for denial of benefits based on residency or citizenship? What do current rules around public assistance for non-citizens say about the ongoing influence of ideas about "worthy v. unworthy" poor?
   c. Will the Patient Protection and Affordable Health Care Act provide benefits for Roberto? Would he currently be eligible to purchase health insurance through the health insurance exchanges?
2. Go to the Carla Washburn case at www.routledgesw.com/cases. Mrs. Washburn receives Medicare and Social Security retirement benefits.
   a. How do you think she would be able to support herself and get medical care if these programs had not been enacted?
   b. Why do you think she is accepting of these programs but not of other public social benefits and services offered to her?

    c. What policy reforms do you think would make it more likely that people in need will actually access benefits and services?

3. Go to the Riverton case at www.routledgesw.com/cases. Homelessness in Riverton increases dramatically in periods of economic downturn.

    a. How would you expect attitudes toward homeless people in Riverton might change during economic downturns?

    b. Do you believe the people of Riverton might be more willing to fund homeless shelters during economic downturns? Why, or why not?

    c. Contact a homeless shelter in your community and find out how they are funded. What federal and state policies provide their funding? Is the funding increasing or decreasing? Can they suggest one or two policy changes that would improve conditions for people who are homeless in your community?

4. Consider what you know about the history of Brickville, as detailed in the Brickville interactive case. How do you think knowing about the history of Brickville could help you work more effectively with this community today?

5. Interview someone who remembers the Great Depression of the 1930s, World War II, and/or the civil rights movement. Ask her or his opinion on why these events happened and what it was like to experience them. Ask if this person thinks the social policies and programs that arose as a result of these events, such as the New Deal policies, the GI Bill, and school desegregation, were effective or not. Based on your study of history, do you agree or disagree with this person's opinion? Why or why not?

6. One of the lessons of history is the power of language. Examine current newspaper or magazine articles and note how the term "welfare" is used. How does the language surrounding the term lead readers to attach positive or negative connotations to it? Watch for other examples of how language is used to produce negative or positive portrayals of people, policies, and programs with which social workers are involved. What influence do you think this use of language has on efforts to develop strengths-based social welfare policies and programs?

7. Continue your exploration of the timeline of social welfare history and review historical milestones beginning in the 1900s by going to the NASW website (www.naswdc.org), searching for the Centennial Index, and then to "Milestones in the Development of Social Work and Social Welfare." Pick a social policy milestone from the 1900s that relates to a field of special interest to you (for example, child protection, mental health, substance abuse, services for older adults) and learn more about the policy. What were the factors that led to its passage? Does that policy milestone influence current policy in your field of special interest? If so, in what way?

8. You have just learned about how states were trying to address unemployment, poverty, and childhood hunger before the Great Depression, and about the new

policies implemented as part of the New Deal to address these problems. You have also personally experienced the major economic downturn of the last few years. Based on this experience, what would you say to people advocating turning the Food Stamp Program (now SNAP) over to states? Would you be for or against this change? Why?

CHAPTER 4

The Economic and Political Contexts

The size of the federal budget is not an appropriate barometer of social conscience or charitable concern.

President Ronald Reagan

Don't tell me what you value, show me your budget, and I'll tell you what you value.

Vice-President Joe Biden

The swirl of history, politics, and economics makes my head hurt. Can't you make this simpler? I just want to help people.

Social Work Student

OUR EXAMINATION OF THE HISTORICAL CONTEXT in the last two chapters made clear that economic fluctuations and political change interact with shifting social values to shape and reshape U.S. social policy. In order to understand how social policies and social programs are created and why they succeed or fail, you will need to become familiar with the economic and political contexts of social policy. As the social work student quoted at the beginning of the chapter pointed out, it can be complicated. However, developing the critical thinking skills to analyze how all these elements are woven together to create social policies is vital for you to become an effective social worker. The process whereby social policy is developed and implemented is not a technically oriented, politically neutral undertaking. Rather, it is strongly influenced by political and economic interests and ideologies. The economic context of social policy focuses on the production, distribution, and use of income, wealth, and resources. In contrast, the political context focuses on the pursuit and exercise of power in government or public affairs. Although these two terms have distinct meanings, they are typically enmeshed in the policy making process. Competition and conflict, inherent in economic and political processes, influence how, when, and what types of social policies and programs are developed and implemented. These factors, therefore, also influence the end result: whether social policy promotes social justice or, conversely, increases economic insecurity and inequitable treatment for historically vulnerable groups.

EFFECT ON SOCIAL POLICY

The economic and political contexts of social policy in the U.S. reflect the workings of a capitalist system. The U.S. has a marketplace economy, which means that citizens exchange goods and services, typically by working for a salary. Citizens may also possess assets such as stocks, property, and other investments that are sources of income. These income sources generate the money that is necessary for citizens to purchase goods and services. In a marketplace economy, this is how citizens are expected to meet their needs and wants. However, we know that many people in our society cannot work because of disability, discrimination, or sickness, or because of obstacles created by gaps in our social policy infrastructure, such as inadequate child care supports or poor quality education. Significantly, the market system contains no mechanisms to provide for their basic needs. Even for those who can work, jobs may be unavailable, or the compensation may be inadequate to meet the basic costs of food, shelter, and health care. Furthermore, the marketplace system intensifies inequality, which, even beyond absolute deprivation for some members of a society, has detrimental effects on disadvantaged individuals' relative well-being and on the overall social fabric. This asset and income inequality contributes to the development of an economic and political aristocracy which crafts and advocates for policies that sustain private wealth and maintain structural barriers to equal opportunity. Further, focusing primarily on the marketplace economy as a driver of public policy draws attention away from the non-monetized work that families (however defined) do involving caregiving, education, health care, etc. This work matters but is marginalized in public policy. For example, there is no family policy, per se.

The question then arises, "How should our society respond to people in need?" Not surprisingly, there is no overriding consensus on this question. As we saw in the previous chapters, individual responsibility and the work ethic are basic values that have influenced the development of social policy in the U.S. At the same time, however, social responsibility is also a traditional U.S. value. Reflecting this value, the U.S. has developed a social welfare system to help balance the mandates of the marketplace with the realities that

- some people are unable to work;

- economic cycles inevitably lead to unemployment and to shifts in the types and location of jobs that are available; and,

- family status, disability, inadequate education, and persistent discrimination create needs in the lives of some Americans that the market system cannot accommodate.

Political support for government policies and programs to assist people who are unable to meet their needs through the marketplace has waxed and waned over time. In general, when the economy is doing well, people may place increased emphasis on individual responsibility, as more individuals experience success in providing for their own needs. Conversely, when the economy is failing, people may be more likely to turn to the government for relief. However, with the shift in responsibility from federal to state and local governments since 1980, social programs have become more tightly bound by budget constraints and inequality among jurisdictions has intensified. These are topics we will examine later in the chapter. Further, governments are often called on to regulate private commerce as well as public entities in order to protect citizens from harm and provide for their well-being. Regulatory policy, as explained below, often gains support after a man-made disaster such as a coal mine collapse or a nuclear facility meltdown and is heavily influenced by the economic and political context of the period.

Regulatory Policy

Programs such as TANF and SSI, which are both parts of the Social Security Act, provide direct economic relief for people in need. Food Stamps, public housing, and publicly financed health care provide goods and services for people in need. Beyond this kind of provision of income and services, there are social regulations that can mandate benefits or protections or erect barriers for vulnerable groups. Legislation requiring certain employers to pay overtime wages and mandating workplace safety requirements are examples of regulatory policy, as are limitations on how much pollution companies can create and obligations that vehicles meet certain safety standards.

Regulatory policy can erect institutional barriers that discriminate against whole groups of people. Such policies can help to maintain a labor force that is willing to work for very low wages. An historical example is the "separate but equal" policy that allowed school districts to provide inadequate education for African American children. Although this policy was outlawed by the *Brown* vs. *Board of Education* decision, existing state school funding formulas that do not provide sufficient resources to adequately educate children of color in impoverished neighborhoods continue to cause these children to face lifelong barriers in securing jobs that pay adequate wages. Regulatory policy can also help to remove institutional barriers and to address health and social problems without raising taxes or greatly increasing public expenditure. For example, children living in poverty can benefit from child-support enforcement legislation that requires withholding support payment from wages in cases where court child-support orders were violated. Similarly, regulatory laws require that businesses be accessible to people with disabilities, making it possible for them to get the goods and services they need. This also expands the business's customer base. However, such programs are not without cost. Often, the private sector incurs the cost of complying with regulations.

Thinking beyond specific social welfare policies, the need for more effective public regulatory policies and oversight of banks, financial markets, and oil companies has become painfully clear in the U.S. recently. Indeed, more Americans may be moving away from the belief that corporations can be trusted to be self-regulating and that government should not interfere with their activities. The economic devastation wrought by the collapse of financial markets and environmental disasters related to nuclear, oil, and natural gas production have had a negative effect on the welfare of a great many Americans. Increases in disasters, both natural and man-made, may create new pressure for policy reform and innovation.

The Impetus for Social Programs

As shown in Chapter 1, two requirements generally must be met before a public social program develops in the U.S. First, there must be a clear indication of a social problem, or what some economists have termed a "market failure." A market failure is a "circumstance in which the pursuit of private interest does not lead to an efficient use of society's resources or a fair distribution of society's goods" (Weimer and Vining, 1999, p. 41).That is, the free market, the family, and other private entities are not providing for basic needs, such as education, health care, or retirement income, for a sizable segment of the population. Furthermore, people in power and their constituencies must recognize the problem and support political intervention to solve it. They must also be convinced that government action, as opposed to private intervention, will not do more harm than good (Waldfogel, 2000). The development of the federal Old Age, Survivors, and Disability Insurance program (OASDI), which is part of the Social Security Act, is an example of government creating a way for workers and employers to pay into an insurance program to provide income after retirement. This government program began in the wake of the financial collapse resulting in the Great Depression and is an example of a tremendously popular program that responds to a market failure—in this case, the inability of many older Americans to adequately sustain themselves in retirement without government support.

When determining whether government action is necessary, some economists posit that focusing on market failures does not sufficiently examine all costs involved when the government takes action. These economists suggest that transaction costs should also be included in determining when the government should intervene in a situation once a market failure has been defined (Zerbe and McCurdy, 2000). Transaction costs refer to all costs incurred during government interventions, including financial, economic, personal, and environmental costs. For example, when a city develops publicly funded low-income housing, there may be a financial impact on people who own low-cost rentals because they may no longer be able to rent their properties as quickly. People who are concerned about a social problem should weigh the transaction costs against the expected benefits of intervention to determine whether intervention is appropriate or desirable, and, if so, what type of intervention is preferable.

Going further, groups and individuals who examine options for intervention generally consider both economic efficiency and equity. The principle of economic efficiency focuses on three interrelated issues:

1.   the probable effect of the intervention on the overall economy, including the impact of increasing federal debt;

2.   the relative merits of spending on one social program rather than another; and,

3.   the ways in which the incentives and/or disincentives created by the program will likely influence individual behavior.

To understand how principles of economic efficiency can be applied to social policy, consider the debate over care for people with mental illness in institutions versus communities. Throughout much of our history, people with mental illness were generally treated in institutions such as poor houses and mental hospitals. Eventually, however, the high costs associated with state institutions and interests in pursuing greater efficiency, coupled with a concern for the well-being of these individuals, helped fuel growing interest in community-based care. Further, programs to integrate people with serious mental illness into the community were expected to help create access to employment and other support that makes it possible for these individuals to change their lives for the better. In addition, it was hoped that community residents would change their attitudes and behavior as they became more personally involved with individuals with mental illness. These factors all helped generate growing support for the policy of deinstitutionalization, whereby patients of state mental hospitals were moved into the community. Although the economy of the town where the mental hospital was located was often negatively affected as facilities downsized or closed and jobs were lost, the overall economic impact was mitigated because new jobs were created in the home communities of people with mental illness and because state economies benefited from reduced costs associated with institutionalization. If community-based care could be provided more economically and could achieve more positive outcomes for clients, then it would constitute a better use of society's resources and would be economically efficient.

The principle of equity revolves around an underlying question: will the policy treat all people with a particular need equally, a concept referred to as horizontal equity, or will it redistribute resources to people in need who possess fewer resources and/or greater need and thus exhibit vertical equity (Waldfogel, 2000)? Referring back to the provision of services for people with mental illness, horizontal equity would extend equal access to services to all people with mental illness irrespective of ethnicity, location, severity of diagnosis, socio-economic status (SES), or age. In contrast, social policy based on vertical equity might provide services to people with low incomes at no charge while requiring people with higher incomes to pay a fee.

Of course, many public policies actually create greater inequity, particularly in the economic sphere, when economic resources are taken from those who have less and redistributed to those who have more. An example of this is when average taxpayers are asked to shoulder the bill for bailout of the financial markets and wealthy business executives who head them, or when homeowners receive sizable tax deductions for the mortgage interest they pay, while renters receive no comparable subsidy. Wealth is thus redistributed from the middle class to those already enjoying positions of wealth and power, or from low-income households to more economically secure ones. On the other hand, public policy can promote political equity and opportunity by, for example, safeguarding the right to vote for all citizens.

Institutional and Residual Approaches to Social Welfare

Determining the best approach to addressing a social problem requires us to negotiate between efficiency and equity. In the U.S., two approaches to social welfare—institutional and residual—are continuously debated when social policy is formulated. Proponents of both approaches make claims about the efficiency and equity of their programs. Therefore, policy makers and social workers must evaluate these claims and determine which programs should be funded and implemented.

Institutional Approaches The institutional approach to social welfare policy asserts that the government should ensure that the basic needs of all citizens— particularly for food, housing, health, income, employment, and education—are adequately met. Advocates of the institutional approach focus on creating universal programs, funded through taxation, that address these common human needs. As their name suggests, universal programs provide services and benefits to all citizens in a broad category. For example, our public school system is a universal program because it makes education broadly available to all the country's children. Universal programs are generally considered more efficient than selective programs in determining eligibility. For example, when everyone in a broad category, such as children between the ages of 5 and 18, is automatically eligible, the eligibility determination process is greatly simplified, and administrative costs are significantly reduced. Consequently, more of the funding for the programs goes directly to beneficiaries. Because universal programs typically attempt to treat all aid recipients equally, they are identified with the concept of horizontal equity.

Residual Approaches In contrast to the institutional approach, the residual approach posits that the government should intervene only when the family, religious institutions, the marketplace, and other private entities are unable adequately to meet the needs of certain populations. Therefore, public assistance should be offered only in cases of dire need when all other support systems have failed. Moreover, tax dollars collected from a broad spectrum of citizens should be used to provide assistance that is narrowly targeted to those individuals or groups who possess the fewest resources. Thus, the residual approach reflects the principle of vertical equity because it redistributes resources to people with the greatest need. Residual policies tend to create selective programs, defined as programs that provide benefits and services only to those segments of a population that meet specific eligibility requirements. Furthermore, residual programs are often inadequately funded, such that some individuals who might theoretically meet the requirements are still unable to receive needed assistance. For example, whereas public education is a universal program because it is available to all children, Head Start is a residual program because it is designed specifically for low-income students and often has waiting lists. Another example is special education, designed specifically for those with recognized disabilities. This is a selective program offered within a universal program.

The residual approach often employs means tests, which base eligibility on income, to target benefits to people in need. This process cuts down on overall spending because the program does not support people who are able to assist themselves; however, administrative costs are often greater within residual programs, because of the expenses associated with verifying that individuals meet eligibility guidelines. With their differing eligibility requirements, the main intent of the programs is not to treat all people equally.

INFLUENCES ON THE SOCIAL WELFARE SYSTEM

When the U.S. was founded, independent farmers made up 80 percent of the labor force (Bell, 1987). The other 20 percent were primarily independent handicraftsmen and tradesmen. Today, the vast majority of the labor force is composed of wage and salary workers. Many of these workers are employed in service occupations, information technology, manufacturing, and white-collar, corporate work. In addition, the majority of working-age women participate in the labor force. Clearly, significant economic change has transformed our country.

Competing Explanations for the Development of the Welfare System

Over the centuries, our economy has evolved from an agricultural and small business base to a post-industrial base that encompasses service and information technology occupations. Many theorists argue that, in addition to transforming our way of life, the evolution of our economy gave rise to the modern social welfare state. We examine several of their theories and hypotheses below. This examination is informed by the work of James Midgley (2009), an international social policy scholar.

The Industrialization-Welfare Hypothesis   One explanation of the origins and functions of the welfare system, termed the *industrialization-welfare hypothesis*, emphasizes industrialization as a significant factor in the development of the welfare state. This hypothesis proposes that the traditional welfare functions performed by the family, church, and community in a pre-industrial society—for example, caring for elderly parents—are assumed by the government in industrial and post-industrial societies, not out of humanitarian motives, but because industrialization undermines these institutions. When families are uprooted as family members relocate in search of employment and opportunities, then poverty, deprivation, and social need increase. In response, the government establishes a variety of social programs designed to substitute for the traditional, informal welfare system.

The Maintenance of Capitalism Hypothesis   A second explanation of the development of the welfare state, termed the *maintenance of capitalism hypothesis*, also emphasizes the role of capitalist industrialization in the creation of the welfare state. However, this theory highlights the role of the welfare state in encouraging capitalism (Piven and Cloward, 1971). More specifically, it postulates that a "power elite," made up of people from the government and the private sector, exerts great control on all policy making for the purpose of maintaining their positions and wealth.

One variation of this hypothesis argues that social welfare policy is used to control women's lives (Abramovitz, 1996). For example, the type of caring work that women have traditionally done for their children and families at home is not defined as "work" for the purpose of securing benefits such as retirement income through Social Security. Consequently, women must either marry a person eligible for Social Security or enter the paid workforce, in addition to their informal caregiving responsibilities, to secure retirement benefits. Further, when social programs are not in place to make it financially possible for young single mothers to stay at home and care for their children, they must often take minimum wage jobs, thus ensuring a ready supply of low-paid workers. Recall from Chapters 2 and 3 that social policies are instituted both to assist people in need and to promote social control.

A related explanation of the relationship between social welfare and industrial capitalism posits that the government introduces welfare programs to promote both accumulation of capital by businesses and popular acceptance of the capitalist system (O'Connor, 1973). Accumulation of capital, and acceptance or legitimization of capitalism, are both necessary functions of the welfare state. The government's role is to introduce social programs that create an efficient yet inexpensive labor force. Public education is one example of a popularly accepted social program that leads to improvements in the capabilities of the workforce. Publicly financed health care also helps create a more productive workforce. When government assumes the cost of these programs, the result is lowered business costs and increased business profits. At the same time, programs such as Social Security, services for people with disabilities, and welfare payments can enhance social contentment and stability, thus creating an environment that is conducive to business growth. In this sense, the accumulation and legitimization functions of welfare capitalism benefit both the recipients and the capitalist system. On the negative side, however, the state's ability to provide the services that maintain the system eventually becomes exhausted, thereby precipitating a crisis. This will be particularly true if private enterprises in the country are unwilling to incur higher taxes to fund public social welfare programs and have the political might to undercut existing programs. Additionally, there are some who suggest that the availability of social welfare services may forestall greater agitation for social change among those oppressed within the capitalist system, thereby sustaining the same system responsible for perpetuating the inequities.

Social Conscience Hypotheses   Other popular explanations include the *social conscience* or *humanitarian impulse hypotheses*. According to these hypotheses, human beings have innate, altruistic concerns for other people. This natural drive in people has led to the creation of the modern welfare state. These explanations trace the roots of the modern welfare state to the charitable activities of ancient religious groups and early philanthropists. However, proponents of social conscience theory also argue that, due to industrialization, people are no longer as willing to assist others. People's desire to help others has been continually weakened by urbanization, the emphasis on individualism, disruption of traditional social ties, and increased competitiveness. Moreover, these factors have created additional social problems that cannot be resolved simply by humanitarian aid. Therefore, it is now much harder to garner support for the expansion of the welfare state, even though modern societies are experiencing serious social problems that require immediate attention.

The Marshall and Titmuss Hypotheses   British theorists T. H. Marshall and Richard Titmuss cast additional light on conceptions of social welfare when they developed arguments focused on legitimizing the social welfare function. Marshall (1950) argued that ensuring rights to an adequate education, housing, and income was part of the evolution of citizenship rights. As citizenship was granted, civil, political, and social rights were extended beyond the aristocracy. People in a democracy are not as capable of fulfilling their responsibilities of citizenship without legal protection of all of these basic rights. Furthermore, social rights should be accorded on the basis of citizenship and not be dependent on status as a worker or relationship to the workforce. He described the development of the welfare state as the subordination of the market to social justice.

Richard Titmuss (1974), of the London School of Economics, had a profound influence on the development of social policy, particularly the institutional approach. Titmuss argued that government actions to provide for the social welfare of its citizens have desirable moral consequences such as institutionalizing altruism, increasing solidarity, and promoting reciprocity and social responsibility. Titmuss further maintained that, unlike economic goods, such as scarce services or items such as cars and televisions that have a price when sold, social goods such as public education and streets should not be bought and sold in an open market. Titmuss played a major role in promoting social welfare as a social right and in encouraging the study of social policy.

Economic and Social Conscience Hypotheses: A Critique Current international evidence does not provide a great deal of support for any of these hypotheses in explaining the dynamics of social welfare. Instead, different hypotheses might cast light on the development of specific welfare policies and programs. For example, concern for quelling social unrest as embodied by the Townsend movement certainly influenced the passage of the Social Security Act of 1935. In addition, religious leaders have often spoken out in support of programs for the poor. Similarly, the impulse to control women's lives is unquestionably reflected in the debate surrounding work requirements and marriage incentives for recipients of TANF, as well as in the controversy about providing birth control/contraceptives under the Affordable Care Act. Further, the influence of labor unions must be recognized in the development of many public social benefits. Indeed, many people believe that benefits such as unemployment insurance and health and safety standards in the workplace would not have developed without pressure from the labor movement. All of these motivations, as well as others, are undoubtedly afoot in our society. If we can recognize these diverse motivations and not insist on characterizing people involved in the debate simplistically, this understanding can help us craft and enact strengths-based legislation.

There is increasing focus on how social policy and programs actually can be an engine for economic growth. For example, health and education programs are clearly vital to keep the economy growing. Social welfare policies that focus on creating opportunities for more people to help stimulate the economy are garnering increased support. This emphasis grows out of a social development approach which I will detail later in the chapter. These ideas are also basic to a capacity building approach which I have discussed in earlier chapters.

We cannot expect that all of the players involved in passing any legislation will be motivated by the same forces. For example, people favoring a residual approach to income-support programs, who generally champion free-market strategies and want to downsize the public sector, and people favoring an institutional approach to social welfare may find common ground and support public investment to prepare a well-educated workforce, which contributes to a healthy marketplace economy. We must understand the motivations of key actors in order to craft support for policies and programs that benefit our clients.

Examining the development of welfare states in different countries can help us to better understand our own. Esping-Andersen (2002) argues that welfare systems vary substantially depending on the role the market, the family, and the state—the three pillars of welfare—each play in providing for basic needs and managing risks such as unemployment, disability, and old age. Sweden and other Scandinavian countries have traditionally been pointed to as examples of countries in which citizens rely on the state to provide for basic needs as a right of citizenship. Other countries may rely more or less heavily on a combination of market and family resources; some use an insurance model, whereby citizens' contributions are pooled by both private and government agencies to ensure against risks. In the U.S., the concept of "welfare" initially meant well-being. The U.S. Constitution refers to the promotion of the general welfare, which was understood to mean the advancement of the well-being of the entire population (Katz, 2008). In the U.S., welfare has gradually been redefined until many people now equate welfare with means-tested public assistance programs such as TANF. In reality, the United States welfare system combines private and public components. Public components include public assistance, social insurance, public social services, and taxation. Private components include employee benefits, charities, foundations, and private social services (Katz, 2008). Our system is multi-faceted and fragmented. As a result, total spending as well as effectiveness can be difficult to measure. Countries adopt welfare models that grow from particular historical class relationships and are often heavily influenced by labor unions, and thus different countries ascribe different levels of importance to the moral obligation of the government versus that of families and individuals to prepare, save, and provide for an adequate standard of living. Countries also vary in the extent to which they integrate their public welfare system into their economic system, such that public benefits provide adequate protection in times of market failure and promote work and education to fill the need for employees when markets expand. No hypothesis developed to explain why countries have different types of welfare states is completely supported. Variations in the welfare programs created by different countries reflect the insight that it basically comes down to which type of society the people in power wish to create and live in, and how they decide to implement and sustain that vision.

The Enabling State and the Capacity Building State

Emphasis on social rights and citizen entitlements that influenced the development of welfare states, particularly in Europe, is now being replaced by increased emphasis on the responsibility of citizens to meet their own needs and contribute to society through working. Many industrialized nations, even those long viewed to have high standards for provision of social welfare programs, have made eligibility requirements stricter and fast-tracked the pace for exiting these programs. Some countries have also revised the criteria for continuing eligibility and are segmenting incoming recipients by certain characteristics to differentiate clients by their estimated needs and future ability to work.

Eligibility requirements for programs are increasingly moving from universal to selective criteria and becoming more restrictive in order to limit the number of individuals eligible for benefits. Many industrial nations have also tightened their definition of "citizen," in an effort to restrict immigrants' access to services, evidence of a further retrenchment of the social safety net.

Popular support has now decreased for the idea that eligibility for welfare benefits should not be linked to status as a worker but should, rather, be a fundamental right based on citizenship, thus liberating citizens from relying on wage labor to survive. We have instead seen the rise of the *enabling state*, whereby public benefits are provided to citizens in order to help them be more productive workers (Gilbert, 2002). People are expected to work to meet their own needs and those of their families. Governments provide benefits and services to children, including education and health care, to help them become productive adults. Older adults receive public benefits based on their prior relationship to the workforce. People who are able to work but are unemployed receive time-limited benefits designed to help them get back to work. Only those unable to work receive benefits not linked to work requirements, and even then they are regularly re-evaluated for potential to work and may receive rehabilitation services so they can go to work. Some countries are implementing policies that require beneficiaries of public support to develop individualized action plans in partnership with case workers to facilitate getting back into the workforce.

This approach has been criticized for "recommodifying labor." That is, labor becomes a commodity to be bought and sold in response to market forces. The value of a person lies in his or her capacity to fulfill the social contract as a worker rather than in her or his rights as a citizen. Thus people who are unable to work or for whom no jobs are available may be devalued.

Scandinavian countries that are credited with developing some of the most advanced welfare states, have long emphasized the connection between public benefits that enable citizens to be healthy and well educated and the obligation that citizens contribute to society. During a recent visit to Sweden and Finland, government policy makers confirmed to me that their emphasis is on "work, work, and more work." However, education and training are also encouraged and more heavily subsidized at the post-secondary level than is the case in the U.S. Thus public health, education, and welfare programs serve the needs of capitalism as well as of individual citizens and, in fact, spread the cost of capitalism across the citizenry.

When governments link benefits to obligations, we see more incentives for working and penalties for not working. As the global economy advances and integrates, education and training opportunities should also be made widely available and accessible. This is particularly important in areas facing deindustrialization as manufacturing jobs requiring fewer skills move to countries where wages are lower. Exhibit 4.1 illustrates the impact of deindustrialization in Detroit.

EXHIBIT 4.1

Detroit and Deindustrialization

The city of Detroit provides a clear example of the impact of deindustrialization. Once known as the epicenter for automobile manufacturing, Detroit was the fourth largest city in America between 1920 and 1950. During this time, working-class individuals in Detroit had the highest per capita income and percentage of home ownership in the country. Due to globalization, U.S. automakers began to face competition from other countries such as Germany and Japan. In response, these corporations began to move manufacturing jobs overseas to countries with cheaper labor costs. Dozens of factories were shut down, resulting in layoffs and substantial unemployment. As the jobs disappeared, the population of Detroit began to decline as well. Since 1950, Detroit's population has decreased by 60 percent and in 2012 was the lowest it has been since the 1910 census. Although some parts of Detroit are experiencing revitalization, abandoned factories, vacant buildings, and closed schools still continue to dot the city landscape.

Packard Automobile Factory 2009

Countries that do not invest in the health and education of their children as well as their workers risk developing even greater class divisions and losing the capacity to compete economically. Likewise, initiatives to encourage people to fulfill their civic duties and become politically involved can help reduce social stratification and promote social engagement. For example, in the U.S., community organizers are building grassroots political organizations as intermediate arenas for interactions between citizens and the state, using social media such as Facebook and Twitter that can break down barriers between people and politics. Barack Obama, who was a community organizer, understood the potential of this approach and used it extensively in his campaign for the presidency. Opportunities for social connection at the community level can increase social cohesion, and can also help support mental health and reduce social isolation. See the web link http://www.communityorganizer20.com/. These kinds of initiatives are in keeping with the development of a capacity building state which focuses on strengthening the skills, competencies and abilities of people and communities and on helping them secure the resources needed for full economic and social inclusion.

The capacity building state prioritizes investment in human capital and in building social connections wherever possible, rather than direct provision of economic maintenance. However, direct income support is necessary to support people who face significant structural barriers that still trap them in poverty. The voluntary and business sectors, as well as government, need to be mobilized to make greater social investments to improve educational outcomes and increase employment opportunities for groups that have been oppressed.

Economic and Political Schools of Thought

In addition to the groups and ideologies we have just discussed, major political and economic schools of thought have shaped social welfare policy in the U.S. The U.S. has a long history of pluralism. A pluralistic process of creating policy means that no one particular group holds all the power. Instead, many interest groups and citizens are actively involved in creating and implementing policies that they believe will benefit themselves and others. With any social policy, certain groups stand to gain or lose economically. A range of interest groups and political parties have developed both public and private approaches and strategies at the federal, state, and local levels that contribute to our social welfare system. A variety of economic philosophies have been developed to provide insight into the workings of economic systems. We begin our exploration of this topic by discussing three fundamental economic philosophies: Keynesian economics, supply-side economics, and democratic socialism. We will then shift our focus to the political arena and examine how different political philosophies and the three branches of government affect social welfare policy.

Keynesian Economics   The economic school of thought known as Keynesian economics, also referred to as *demand-side* or *consumer-side economics* is based on the writings of John Maynard Keynes, an English economist who published the book *The General Theory of Employment, Interest, and Money* in 1936. Keynes rejected the traditional laissez-faire philosophy that free-market competition would automatically facilitate full employment, making government intervention both unnecessary and undesirable. Instead, he posited that modern economies are not self-correcting; therefore, government stabilization efforts are necessary to keep a capitalist economy running smoothly. Specifically, Keynes argued that the government should stabilize the economy through the use of fiscal policy, that is, by increasing or decreasing spending and taxes in response to economic conditions. When individuals or private businesses do not consume or invest enough, then the

government must intervene. Demand-side economics also emphasizes the importance of public investment in human capital—that is, programs such as education,
health care, and job training that make people more productive—in order to increase
national wealth.

Keynes's theory was used to some extent to guide U.S. social policy during the
Great Depression and influenced the approach of the Obama administration to the
economic crises faced during both his first and second administrations. His ideas
clearly were reflected in the various New Deal programs that sought to increase
demand for goods and services—and, therefore, create jobs—by providing income
and work opportunities to people in need. Overall, Keynesian principles are integral
to liberalism and its efforts to develop a comprehensive public welfare state.
Liberalism is a political philosophy that endorses individual freedom and advocates
government intervention to ensure an adequate minimum living condition for all
people. The type of government activism on behalf of people in poverty that Keynes
proposed is most typically supported by the liberal wing of the Democratic Party.

Supply-Side Economics   In contrast, supply-side economics guides the conservative
political view of social welfare, represented in our political system today by some
within the Republican Party. In contrast to liberals, classic or traditional conservatives
oppose widespread change in the political sector and advocate a laissez-faire economy
and a minimal welfare state. Supply-side economics was greatly influenced by the
work of conservative economist Milton Friedman and his theories of monetary policy
or monetarism. Friedman argued that Keynesian strategies of using fiscal policy to
smooth out business cycles actually harm the economy and fuel instability. According
to Friedman, government policy should be restricted to promoting steady growth in
the nation's money supply, that is, the total amount of money that is circulating in
the economy, which is accomplished primarily through the levers of interest rates.

Influenced by Friedman, supply-side economics gained momentum in the
1980s. However, supply-side economists have increasingly rejected Friedman's idea
of gradually increasing the money supply and instead have focused on tax cuts as
engines of economic growth. They argue that tax cuts, particularly for wealthy
people, will lead to large increases in investment, spending, and savings, which in
turn will expand the economy and create jobs. Allowing people to retain a larger
portion of their income after taxes will encourage them to work more hours and
thereby increase the supply of goods and services available to consumers, hence the
term "supply-side" (Roberts, 1988). Ultimately, some of these benefits should
"trickle down" and improve economic conditions for low-income groups. Supply-
side economics provided the rationale for the large-scale tax cuts enacted during the
administrations of Ronald Reagan and George W. Bush, as well as experiments with
tax cuts in some states.

Democratic Socialism   A third philosophy, democratic socialism, adopts a
dramatically different stance. Advocates of democratic socialism argue that, because

capitalism is predicated on the pursuit of individual self-interest and profit, it inevitably increases social inequality and, therefore, cannot be relied upon to advance the public good. Democratic socialists further posit that the expansion of government in the social welfare arena comes about not through the actions of altruistic government officials but, rather, through the struggle of the working class and its allies. As their name suggests, democratic socialists believe in the democratic process, and they work to bring about change in the economic system. Because they define social problems as stemming from an unjust society, they view the expansion of social welfare as a step toward social justice. However, many democratic socialists maintain that welfare programs function as a flawed substitute for the fundamental social changes that are needed to achieve social justice.

New Approaches to Deal with Slowing Economic Growth

Current economic approaches are being re-evaluated in the face of depleted natural resources, climate changes, and slowing economic growth. Economic strategies that take into account finite natural resources and the cost of continued environmental degradation, and factor in declining rates of economic growth are needed. Economic approaches predicated on continued, uninterrupted economic growth may be less viable given these new realities, especially given the increasingly integrated nature of the global economy, which means that individual nation-states cannot expect to thrive in isolation. Policies to support economic growth which, in the long run, cannot promote the welfare and improve the quality of life of the citizenry, must be reconsidered.

The Political Continuum

Conservatives and Liberals   As we move from the economic to the political landscape, we now turn our attention to political philosophies. These philosophies fall along a continuum from conservative to liberal and, as you will see, different political perspectives also encompass different beliefs about how to organize an economy, since controlling economic resources is a critical tool for advancing political power. Although philosophical stances and labels have shifted over time, there are significant differences in the political agenda of people grouped under the label of *conservative* or *liberal*. Current differences are the primary focus of this discussion. Classical conservatives advocate a laissez-faire approach to economics. They traditionally focus on the economy, defense spending, and foreign affairs. However, in the 1970s, a new conservative movement took root. New conservatives seek to restrict the government's role in promoting social welfare, and they advocate the transfer of welfare responsibility from the government to the private sector. New conservatives insist that social welfare programs be compatible with traditional social values such as self-reliance and personal responsibility, as well as with a market economy. Consequently, they do not necessarily perceive high unemployment and low wages as problematic. These conservatives are sometimes labeled "neoconservatives," although that term has been used to describe a great variety of ideological stances. Cultural conservatives are also a part of this political landscape. They oppose recent social changes in areas such as abortion rights and same-sex marriage, and often support government action to promote their agenda. They assert traditional beliefs about the role of women in society and oppose government spending in ways they deem incompatible with their traditional beliefs, including teaching evolution and providing access to contraception.

By the late 1970s, cultural conservatives were beginning to assert power. Although classical conservatives, new conservatives, and cultural conservatives advocate a laissez-faire approach to economics and a minimal welfare state, classical conservatives are strict constitutionalists who believe strongly in the separation of church and state and in the rights of individuals to live their lives free of government intervention as long as they are not threatening the safety of others. Though fiscally conservative, both classic conservatives and new conservatives are often more socially liberal than cultural conservatives. To learn more about the proposals for public policy reforms supported by conservatives, go to the websites of the Hoover Institute (www.hoover.org), and the Heritage Foundation (www.heritage. org), two conservative think tanks. On the other hand, cultural conservatives support a domestic agenda in which the federal government provides increased support for faith-based social service initiatives, and moves aggressively to stem activities they consider immoral. Their capacity to rally voters around issues such as abortion and homosexuality has made them a potent, if sometimes divisive force, in the Republican Party.

In contrast to conservatives who believe the social order is often harmed by social programs, traditional liberals believe that the government can, in fact, provide the building blocks for a productive economy. However, although the term neoliberal has been used in a variety of sometimes contradictory ways, neoliberals are often associated with a more cautious approach toward social reforms and Keynesian-inspired government interference with interest rates, spending, and borrowing, They are concerned about obstructing the efficiency of the free market, and believe that welfare policy and economic policy should be more closely blended. They tend to support free-trade agreements in the belief that open markets can be a tool to promote economic development and greater prosperity. Thus, job training, education, and research should be prioritized and income-support programs such as TANF should be time-limited and work requirements should be strengthened.

Liberals have traditionally supported the goals of full employment, universal health care, and a guaranteed annual income. However, with the defeat of Jimmy Carter and the ascendance of Ronald Reagan, a new liberal consensus began to form. The new liberal consensus supports an active government role in achieving economic growth and social justice. Nevertheless, new liberals differ from traditional liberals in their belief that institutions other than the government need to play a bigger role. They advocate investment by corporations in human capital and social welfare, and they do not believe that the accumulation of corporate profits necessarily conflicts with the advancement of the social good. To learn more about the work of more liberal think tanks, go to the websites of the Brookings Institution (www.brookings. edu) and the Center on Budget and Policy Priorities (www.cbpp.org).

Other Political Influences   Communitarians, libertarians, and the Green Party are also part of our political landscape. Communitarians represent a mix of liberal and conservative traditions. They emphasize the need to rebuild communities, and they encourage two-parent families. Communitarians advocate for individual rights and equality; however, they also believe that communities and institutions need to build character and promote virtues of citizenship. This role can be more important than individual rights at any given time. They favor greater involvement of local government and communities in promoting social welfare. Another political group, libertarians, believes that government grows at the expense of individual freedom. Therefore, they are critical of taxation, and they reject the argument that government should be involved in social or economic activities. Instead, they seek to restrict or eliminate the public welfare system, and restore the roles of family, church, and other non-governmental entities in assisting people in need. The Tea Party, a grassroots political movement that helped to elect more conservative Republican candidates in 2012, has its roots in both the libertarian and the cultural conservative camps.

Although they are widely portrayed as being primarily interested in ecological awareness, the Green Party represents a much broader range of values and political views. Regarding social welfare policy, the Green Party advocates universal health care and financial support for children, families, people with disabilities, and care givers not in the workforce. They call for both personal and global responsibility, and they support local communities in developing environmentally sustainable approaches to alleviating poverty and hunger, rather than pressing for ever-more economic growth. To learn more about the Green Party and the Libertarian Party, visit their homepages (www.gp.org and www.lp.org) and compare and contrast their platforms and priorities.

We have briefly discussed some major schools of economics and political ideologies. Given this political and economic context, how can we use this information to understand the development of a particular policy or program at a given time? To answer this question, think back to the historical context of the New Deal social policies of the 1930s. Economic instability and deflation experienced during the Great Depression fueled some political initiatives informed by Keynesian economic thought. On the other hand, the sluggish economic growth and high inflation of the 1970s ushered in the conservative supply-side economics and political policies of the 1980s. The influence of popular values and the interplay of the economic and political context of these two periods brought about two very different approaches. In 2008, in the midst of a severe economic crisis, the country elected Barack Obama, who promised to reform the financial markets, the health care system, the immigration system, and U.S. environmental policy.

Because Obama garnered a sizeable proportion of the vote, and Democrats became the majority in Congress, he was seen as having the political capital or popularity with the citizenry, to press for major reforms in health and social policy. Similarly, in the wake of the September 11, 2001 attacks by al-Qaeda, President Bush was elected to a second term in 2004 and believed he had the political capital to implement additional national security reforms and pour increased funding into the wars in Iraq and Afghanistan. Political capital can have a dramatic effect on whether proposed policy reforms will actually be implemented. The political capital President Obama garnered from his successful re-election campaign in 2012 makes it more likely he will be able to successfully continue to implement health care and immigration reform.

At different periods in our history, various political parties have pressed for equality of opportunity, income redistribution, increased defense spending, and civil rights. The political process is conflictual. The two major political parties, Democrats and Republicans, spend a great deal of money and time vying for media attention and, ultimately, citizens' votes. Each party wants to control the legislative, executive, and judicial branches of government at both the federal and the state levels, in order to push policies that reflect their ideological approaches to governance. We turn now to the influence of these three branches of government on our social welfare system.

The Three Branches of Government

There are three branches of government at both the federal and the state level: the legislative, executive, and judicial branches. In theory, each branch performs separate and distinct functions. Simply put, the legislative branch makes laws; the executive branch concurs in law making, enforces the laws, and develops budgets; and the judicial branch interprets the laws. For a review of the structure of the three branches of government and the relationship between them, go to www.usa.gov and navigate to U.S. Federal Government. However, the reality is that all three branches create social policy and influence our social welfare system in complex and interrelated ways. Social workers who are aware that all three branches of government make social policy can craft strategies that are more effective at influencing social policy in each of these arenas. Chapter 6 provides guidelines for this process.

At the federal level, the executive branch includes the president, the vice-president, the cabinet, the president's advisers, and all of the offices and agencies that serve the president and execute federal policy. At the state level, the governor, the cabinet, and all of the offices and agencies charged with executing state policy belong to the executive branch. When they develop budgets, champion legislation, and create the rules and regulations necessary to implement laws, they are making social policy. Focusing on changing regulations via these agencies may yield quicker results, and indeed some policy analysts believe many issues can be dealt with much more easily at this level, alleviating the need for legislative action. Recall that in

Chapter 3 we discussed President Obama's use of the executive branch to change regulations such as the ban on women in combat.

Congress, the major component of the legislative branch, is bicameral; that is, it consists of two chambers, the House of Representatives and the Senate. Both chambers are charged with passing legislation. They are independent of each other, but they must agree on proposed legislation for it to become law. For a fun refresher on how a bill becomes a law, use your web browser to find the Schoolhouse Rock video *How a Bill Becomes a Law*. Most states also have a bicameral legislature. The judicial branch comprises the court system. Both federal and state judiciaries include a supreme court, a court of appeals, and district courts. When the judicial branch interprets legislation, rules on legal intent, or determines whether legislation violates the Constitution, it is actually exerting great influence over social policy. For example, in 2010, the Supreme Court conservative majority overturned well-established precedents with substantial bipartisan backing that supported campaign finance limits. They invoked protection of free speech for entities including corporations and labor unions to justify the ruling, which has clearly increased the capacity of corporations to influence candidates and thereby to shape policy debates, and ultimately to determine what policies are enacted. Similarly, you will see in future chapters how social work policy advocates have turned to the courts to seek redress of grievances when legislative and executive channels do not yield desired changes, and how the resulting legal decisions can reshape social policy for generations.

THE IMPACT OF FUNDING STRATEGIES

When considering the political context, it is important to remember that policy making is about rationing resources. Public policies influence public revenues by increasing or decreasing taxes and policies promote the growth or contraction of the economy. Social policies also determine who gets how much of the pie. You only have to observe one year's state legislative session to learn that dollars are finite. Although social workers should support efforts to expand the pie and draw upon untapped strengths, they must never lose sight of this reality. The amount of funding allocated to implementing social policies and programs determines the extent to which clients' needs can be met, today and in the future. If you examine the federal and state budgets and monitor the budgetary process, you can determine how different funding strategies shape outcomes for your clients.

Federal and State Budgets

Analysis of the federal budget provides insight into the priorities established and the values played out through the political process. Each year, the White House prepares a budget for the new federal fiscal year, from October 1 through September 30, through the Office of Management and Budget (OMB). It then submits the budget to Congress for authorization and appropriation. In fiscal year (FY) 2012, the federal government spent $3.79 trillion, or approximately 24.7 percent of the nation's gross domestic product (Congressional Budget Office, 2013a). Gross domestic product (GDP) is the total monetary value of all goods and services produced in a country annually. To learn more about the current budget, go to the website of the Congressional Budget Office (www.cbo.gov) and navigate to "The Budget and Economic Outlook." It is particularly important for social workers interested in shaping federal and state programs to track appropriations, because this is where the decisions are made concerning how much money will actually be spent on different programs.

Mandatory Versus Discretionary Spending   Although the size of the federal budget grows yearly, policy makers realistically can exercise control over only a part of it. The majority of the budget is earmarked for mandatory spending, which is government spending directed toward individuals and institutions that are legally entitled to it (entitlement programs), as well as interest payment on the national debt. Mandatory spending, then, is essentially outside of the control of appropriators during a given budget year and can only be influenced by enacting policies that change budget obligations more broadly. An entitlement program is one for which all citizens who meet the eligibility requirements legally qualify. Perhaps the most prominent examples are Social Security and Medicare. In theory, Congress possesses the power to limit or even reduce mandatory spending by modifying entitlement programs. For example, recall that AFDC was an entitlement program; however, the legislation that replaced AFDC with TANF abolished this entitlement. Generally speaking, however, Congress is not quick to tamper with the major entitlement programs because they benefit a majority of Americans and, therefore, are very popular with voters.

Consequently, congressional decision making focuses on that portion of the federal budget (approximately one-third) that is termed discretionary spending (CBO, 2013b). Discretionary spending at the federal level refers to all the spending authorized by the 13 appropriation bills that are passed each year by Congress and signed by the president. It includes funding for national defense, transportation, housing supports, educational and social programs such as Head Start, and agriculture, as well as spending on the basic operations of government. Each year, Congress and the White House struggle to establish priorities concerning which programs to fund and how much money to allocate to them. One difference between discretionary and mandatory spending is that the government imposes a ceiling on discretionary spending. If that money is completely used, then the government has no obligation to allocate an additional amount.

All discretionary spending and some mandatory spending, such as payment of interest on the national debt, are funded through general tax revenues. Other sources of funding are payroll taxes and tax expenditures, discussed in detail below, which also fundamentally influence the development of adequate public health and welfare services.

Tax Strategies

When you started filing income tax returns, you began to grapple with the complexity of the tax system in our country. Tax policy can be a powerful instrument for promoting social justice and ensuring that people's basic needs are adequately met, so it is important to understand some fundamentals of the tax system. You will see that tax policy can also be a tool for redistributing money from lower and middle socio-economic groups to the wealthy, or for eviscerating the revenue foundation on which strong social policy can be built.

We pay taxes to fund services and benefits received at the local, state, and federal levels. Taxes are either regressive or progressive. Regressive taxes require people with lower incomes to pay higher rates or proportions of their income. For example, sales taxes on food and clothing are regressive because low-income people spend a higher percentage of their income on these necessities. Sales taxes are typically used to fund services at the local level, although some states rely heavily on sales taxes, particularly as states have reduced income taxes in an attempt to appease higher earners. In contrast, progressive taxes require people with higher incomes to pay higher rates or proportions of their income. Federal or state income taxes that require people with higher incomes to pay a greater percentage in taxes are examples of progressive taxes, although tax deductions and other mechanisms can reduce the progressivity of income tax structures. Sales taxes, property taxes, income taxes are typically sources of general tax revenue. That is, general tax revenue is not dedicated automatically for functions such as road maintenance or paying for specific services or benefits, but it can be used for general purposes.

A type of tax that you began to pay when you started your first job is commonly called a "payroll tax," which your employer deducts from your pay and sends to the government before it issues your check. Some payroll taxes are not intended to be a source of revenue for the government and so are often not considered a true tax. Look at your payroll stub and note the amounts deducted for the Federal Insurance Contribution Act (FICA) and for Medicare. These deductions are premiums/contributions you are making to a public insurance program from which you are entitled to draw benefits if you become disabled or when you meet the age and work effort requirements for receiving a Social Security pension and Medicare. Only half of this payroll tax is paid by the employee. The other half is paid by the employer. Re-languaging the discussion of these payments made for OASDI and Medicare to refer to them as insurance premium payments rather than payroll taxes, highlights that these are public insurance programs. Nonetheless, many people pay more in insurance premiums/payroll taxes than they do in income taxes and, because these insurance premiums/payroll taxes are not assessed on some of the income of very high earners or on non-wage income, they are regressive.

An additional area of tax policy that exerts a powerful influence on social welfare is that which governs tax expenditures. Economists apply the term tax expenditures to tax deductions that the government extends to particular groups in order to assist them in obtaining services such as housing, health care, and education. Tax expenditures are the way most Americans receive support from the government. Most people do not enjoy paying taxes. In contrast, tax credits, tax deductions, and tax exemptions typically do not draw the attention and ire of citizens the way proposals to raise taxes do, even though they reduce the tax base and will ultimately result in reduced public services or higher taxes for those not fortunate enough to be the recipient of tax breaks. Therefore, tax breaks can be used by federal, state, and local policy makers to advance various social agendas.

For example, in our country there has been a consensus that widespread home ownership increases community and family stability. Our tax laws, therefore, favor home ownership by providing for a home mortgage interest deduction. Such deductions change the amount of taxes owed by those who fall into the preferred category. Similarly, corporations that provide pension and health coverage to their employers receive favorable tax treatment. The wealthy typically benefit more from tax exemptions and deductions because when you have more income and thus owe more taxes, deductions will save you more. Further, many tax expenditures benefit large corporations. However, tax expenditures can also be used to promote social justice. For example, the Earned Income Tax Credit, which is refundable, helps redistribute financial resources to low-income working families. Importantly, because it is administered through the tax code, the Earned Income Tax Credit (EITC) is able to lift households out of poverty without the stigma and sometimes high administrative costs that are part of some means-tested programs.

Taxes are also used to discourage certain behavior. For example, additional taxes are charged on tobacco and alcohol. Higher taxes on tobacco levied by states have been shown to be effective in reducing teen smoking. Of course, when the targeted behavior is actually dramatically discouraged, state revenues are reduced, making these taxes an effective policy lever but a poor long-term revenue source.

Federal Spending   The federal budget exerts a powerful influence on social welfare policy. It represents the priorities of our lawmakers. The federal government can raise funds across the country and provide funding for social and health programs in every state, even when problems such as a prolonged drought or the bankruptcy of major industries compromise the economic base of particular states. The federal government also has the capability to withhold valuable federal dollars from states. For example, the federal government can pass laws requiring states to implement certain policies as a condition for receiving federal funds. If a state fails to implement these social policies/laws, the federal government can withhold funds from that one particular state.

Look at Exhibit 4.2 to see how federal dollars were spent in FY 2012. Overall, most of the budget goes for defense, major health programs, and Social Security. The safety net programs included in the "Other Mandatory Spending" category include unemployment insurance, food stamps, the earned income tax credit program, TANF, school meals, SSI, programs providing aid to abused and neglected

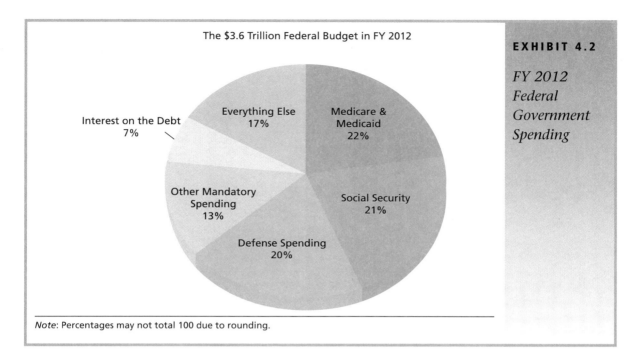

The $3.6 Trillion Federal Budget in FY 2012

EXHIBIT 4.2

FY 2012 Federal Government Spending

Note: Percentages may not total 100 due to rounding.

children, and various other programs that provide aid to people facing hardship. The 17 percent of spending grouped under "Everything Else" includes veterans' health care, medical and scientific research, disaster relief, transportation, and education as well as all other spending.

Conflicts over the allocation of our tax dollars revolve around three basic issues:

1. Who should pay?

2. Who should benefit?

3. Which programs should grow and which ones should shrink? (Schick, 2000)

Government spending is a redistributive process, meaning that some people gain and others lose. As an obvious example, when expenditures for defense escalate, fewer dollars are available for social programs unless lawmakers are willing to let the federal deficit increase dramatically, which was in fact the case during 2009 and 2010. Political differences over these three issues must be resolved—at least temporarily—before the budget can be approved.

A careful examination of the types and percentages of expenditures from year to year discloses clear shifts in spending. Exhibit 4.3 shows the shift in government spending as a proportion of GDP. Both mandatory and discretionary spending decreased since 2010 after a sharp increase in 2008. Because health care costs are expected to rise and millions of baby boomers will become eligible for Medicaid and

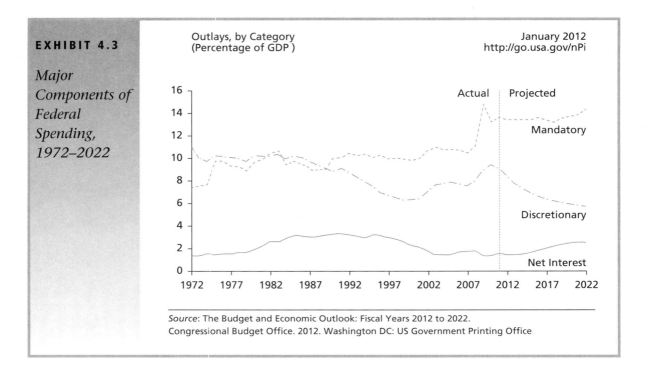

EXHIBIT 4.3

Major Components of Federal Spending, 1972–2022

Outlays, by Category
(Percentage of GDP)

January 2012
http://go.usa.gov/nPi

Source: The Budget and Economic Outlook: Fiscal Years 2012 to 2022.
Congressional Budget Office. 2012. Washington DC: US Government Printing Office

Medicare programs in the near future, there will likely be a continued increase in mandatory spending in the coming decades. Overall, federal government spending since 1970 decreased slightly as a percentage of GDP prior to this period of war and economic downturn in the first decade of the 21st century. However, in the wake of the recent severe economic downturn, federal spending has increased dramatically to provide the stimulus for recovery. Automatic increases in programs that always grow to meet rising need during economic downturns, such as food stamps and unemployment insurance, combined with spending on the stimulus package, shoring up financial institutions and banks, and other recovery-related spending together drove federal spending to almost 25 percent of GDP in FY 2012.

Beyond direct service spending, the government promotes social welfare through many other policies such as tax incentives that encourage savings for retirement, educational policies and expenditures, and antidiscrimination laws. At the same time, however, when the government offers a tax incentive, then tax dollars that normally would have been collected are not. As a result, a smaller amount of general tax revenue is available for other programs. Uncollected tax dollars leave fewer dollars available to pay for benefits and services without increasing the federal deficit.

President Obama has different spending priorities than did his predecessor, George W. Bush. However, the tax cuts passed during the Bush administration, the ongoing expense of two wars, and the large increase in the yearly federal deficit and in the long-term national debt (resulting from infusion of federal funds to rescue collapsing financial markets and failing corporations and to provide stimulus funds to the states) limit the funding available for Obama's priorities. To examine Obama's budget priorities, go to the OMB (www.whitehouse.gov/omb) and navigate to "The President's Budget." You may be particularly interested in his plans to increase funding opportunities for college students.

The federal government runs a surplus when the amount of all tax revenue exceeds the cost of mandatory and discretionary spending in a given year. Conversely, it runs a deficit when spending exceeds tax revenues. In FY 2009, the federal deficit totaled $1.4 trillion; for FY 2013, it was projected to be $901 billion (Office of Management and Budget, 2013). The federal deficit is calculated on a yearly basis. In contrast, the national debt is the total amount of federal debt which includes the sum of all previously incurred annual federal deficits. In FY 2013, the national debt exceeded $16 trillion (U.S. Department of the Treasury, 2013). To find out the current size of the national debt, visit the website of the U.S. Department of the Treasury (www.treasurydirect.gov), and search for "Debt to the Penny."

Although federal spending on the wars in Iraq and Afghanistan, as well as money spent to avert collapse of the financial markets and stimulate economic recovery have been immediate drivers of the increase in the national debt, Social Security and Medicare are often pointed to as sources of long-term increases in public debt. There is a great deal of confusion surrounding the funding of Social Security and Medicare, two entitlement programs that fall under the category of mandatory spending. Although these programs are included in the overall budget, they are designed in part on an insurance model and are funded through payroll taxes that flow into the Social Security Trust Fund and the Medicare Hospital Insurance Trust Fund. Although many critics complain about the percentage of the federal budget that is devoted to these programs, the current level of payment of payroll taxes/insurance premiums is sufficient to fund Social Security until 2033 (Social Security Administration, 2012). This is slightly sooner than previously estimated, due in part to the suspension of payroll taxes for two years, as part of the economic recovery measure, as well as higher rates of unemployment and stagnant wages, both of which depress collection of payroll taxes as well. However, even after that date, current policies are sufficient to fund three-quarters of the Trust Fund's obligations without further reform, suggesting that rather modest changes enacted soon could ensure long-term sustainability. Further, Social Security is not and never has been a driver of the federal debt or deficit. It was structured such that it is fully self-sustaining. The Medicare Hospital Trust Fund, in contrast, is in trouble because of spiraling health care costs in the U.S., which far exceed health care costs in any other country. We will examine the funding of Social Security in detail in Chapter 8 and discuss Medicare in Chapter 10.

State Spending Policies   State budgets also have important ramifications for social welfare policy. As discussed in Chapter 3, beginning with the Reagan administration, the federal government increasingly shifted responsibilities for social welfare programs to the states. Federal and state budgets are linked in that the states receive financial support and incentives for certain programs such as Medicaid for which they are required to provide matching funds. States that fail to provide these funds lose the federal monies. The amount of the match differs by state and is determined by a formula that takes into consideration the state's poverty rate. Also, state budgets are impacted by changes in the federal tax code, since most states link their tax policies to federal law. Since most states are required to balance their budgets, states have far less ability to respond to economic crises than does the federal government. This can have important implications for the devolution of responsibility for much social service programming.

As we saw in Chapter 3, for some programs, such as TANF, federal support takes the form of block grants, which allow the state more discretion over how federal monies will be spent. However, block grants typically are capped, so that if the need for services increases, the federal government will not automatically provide additional funding. Unfortunately, need often increases because the state or local economy declines. When this occurs, corporate profits fall, and workers are laid off. Consequently, the state tax base shrinks, and tax revenues decline. Because federal funds are capped, the federal government is under no legal obligation to compensate for the loss of state revenue. Moreover, most state governments, noted earlier, are required by law to balance their budgets, unlike the federal government. Consequently, states must adopt some combination of the following policies: increase taxes, reduce spending, and find new sources of revenue. Unfortunately, spending cuts often target social welfare programs, regardless of their effectiveness. Consequently devolution of responsibility for social programming may occur during economic downturns when discretionary programs are subject to cutbacks and elimination at the very time when people need them most. The federal government provided additional funds to lessen these cuts at the state level during the recent economic downturn. However, many states are still in dire financial straits and have had to make drastic cuts to their education and welfare programs. Because spending on children's development is mainly done at the state level via spending on education, this means children often bear the brunt of these cuts and educational inequities between states grow even larger. Powerful business interests in some states have successfully pressed to cut taxes even further based on the supply-side claim that lower taxes will spur economic growth. This means education and welfare programs, which make up a major portion of state spending, are subject to even deeper cuts. In a painful economic cycle, state budget cuts can actually deepen an economic recession in a state, as laid-off state workers and individuals whose benefits have been cut are less able to participate fully in state economic activity.

In general, a state's economic resources and political climate determine which programs will be cut and how drastically. As we would expect, the political power of interest groups at the state level strongly influences these decisions. Take a moment to think about what happens in your state in terms of the representation and influence of low-income people, particularly women and people of color. Because these groups are generally underrepresented in state legislatures, their interests often are not protected during economic hard times. Thus, the education and social programs designed to assist them are especially vulnerable to the pressures to reduce spending. To compound these difficulties, state governments are particularly vulnerable to business threats to downsize or relocate if the state raises taxes, even if the tax revenues would be used to finance necessary social programs.

For all of these reasons, the ability of individual states to help their citizens meet their basic needs is more limited than the federal government's ability to do so. Not surprisingly, then, in our history, the federal government has assumed the responsibility to protect the interests of those in the U.S.—particularly women and other minorities—at times when the states are struggling (Gordon, 1998). Overall, the federal government is more stable and can provide more substantial benefits to a larger number of people in need. Because the federal government can run a deficit, it is able to keep borrowing and spending, although tax revenues are insufficient to cover the increased spending. This enables the federal government to shore up states that can no longer fund basic programs because they are required to have a balanced budget. However, the increasing federal deficit and national debt can create economic instability, particularly if the countries from which the federal government borrows lose faith in the robustness of the U.S. economy. Further, national debt places a burden on our children and grandchildren. However, the major drivers of increased federal debt in the last decade are the combination of tax cuts, two wars that were not paid for, and the financial collapse, rather than increased social spending. Moreover, if the federal government invests heavily in education, transportation, health, and energy infrastructure that strengthens the economy, such spending can lead to long-term economic stability.

The Role of the Private Sector

Of course, not all social welfare programs are funded or administered by the government. Rather, many programs operate through the private or non-governmental sector. In fact, as discussed in Chapter 3, privatization has emerged as a major political trend since the 1980s. The private sector is composed of many profit-making organizations such as hospitals, nursing homes, substance abuse centers, and counseling centers. It also includes the not-for-profit sector which also owns hospitals, nursing homes, etc. and includes religious institutions, foundations, and other charitable organizations. Private sector initiatives can be very flexible, and they employ a variety of funding strategies. They often have a mix of clients, some of whom pay privately for their services and some who receive federal or state funding. For example, in a profit-making nursing home, it is not uncommon for more than half the residents to have their bills paid by taxpayers through Medicaid. Such profit-making facilities are able to serve private-paying clients more affordably and still make a profit because infrastructure and fixed costs are financed largely by public funding for clients who qualify for government programs in both profit-making and not-for-profit facilities.

Because the private sector does not simply draw on public funds to provide social services, the assets of these organizations typically increase in value when the economy is growing, so that private funding for social services can be enhanced. Even so, a relatively small proportion of funding for many not-for-profit agencies comes from charitable contributions. In addition, people are more able to pay privately for services when the economy is growing and more people can afford to make large contributions to charities and foundations. During economic downturns, the amount of services such organizations can provide is often constricted. Further, regardless of economic conditions, a substantial portion of funding for most private organizations comes from government sources. As with state governments, then, as need increases, the available resources decline. The private sector clearly does not have the capability to fund a welfare system that can effectively meet citizens' basic needs. If you want to find out more about the work of private charities in your area and how they are financed, go to www.charitynavigator.org.

Benefits and Drawbacks of Different Combinations of Funding Strategies

The U.S. has a long history of a pluralistic system, in which both public and private funding contribute to the provision of social welfare services, and creative use of both sources is often necessary to meet our clients' needs. Private funding and provision of services can be particularly important for innovative or controversial services from which public funding might be withheld, such as abortion counseling and shelters for gay and lesbian victims of domestic abuse. At the same time, however, private supporters can exclude people they consider "unworthy," and they can attach conditions many people might find objectionable. In pursuing these policies, they are not subject to the same public scrutiny or oversight as public programs. For these reasons, public funding and provision of services may be preferable when the service is either particularly important or not profitable, or when the population it serves is especially vulnerable. Protection against child and elder abuse is an example of such services. In such cases, public scrutiny and accountability become very important.

Public and private funds can also be combined to fund benefits and services. Your college or university might provide a good example of such a combination. For example, if you are attending a public university, it is likely that private contributors financed many of the buildings, private donors funded many scholarships, and even some of your professors might be partially paid through private endowments. If you are attending a private college, it is likely that public funds are being used to provide student loans to low-income students and that your professors are conducting research funded by the federal or state government. In considering the benefits and drawbacks of different funding combinations for social programs, many analysts emphasize that taxation can generate very large amounts of public funds, thereby ensuring more year-to-year stability. Indeed, it is the public sector that can realistically provide sufficient funds to mount major social welfare programs nationwide, although the private sector might provide the actual services. Private funding is generally much more limited. Also, it can be either restricted or very flexible, depending on the wishes of the people who control the funds. Private and public funding both have their advantages and disadvantages, and social workers need to consider both when attempting to develop funding strategies for needed services.

SOCIAL WELFARE EXPENDITURES IN THE UNITED STATES

When direct public welfare expenditures at the federal level in the United States are compared to other industrialized countries, the U.S. is often considered to have an underdeveloped welfare state. Direct public welfare expenditures as a percentage of GDP, particularly at the federal level, have been lower than that of other industrialized countries. Further, spending is often fragmented. For example, cities and counties may invest additional money in local health and social services separately from federal and state initiatives. Additionally, the U.S. is exceptional in that the corporate and the voluntary sectors have long been an integral part of our social welfare system. In the U.S., many people receive health and life insurance benefits through their place of employment and corporations receive hefty tax breaks for providing them. Many times, these expenditures go uncounted in international comparisons (Hacker, 2002). In fact, it has been argued that if tax expenditures and private social benefits are considered, the U.S. devotes a relatively high percentage of GDP to social welfare, and has a high per capita expenditure level on social welfare. Of course, private benefits can often be withdrawn, as we have seen with the drop in corporate-sponsored private pension plans and health benefits. Further, many benefits are lost when employment is lost. Thus, it is typically easier to shift risk back onto the individual when the benefits are provided by the private sector rather than the public sector. For example, when privatization of a portion of the Social Security pension program was proposed by the Bush administration, whereby a person's retirement benefits would vary based on success of individual investment strategies, a furor was raised by constituents. Consequently, the Social Security pension program continued as an exclusively guaranteed benefit program. Risk was not shifted to the individual as it has been by so many companies which changed from a guaranteed benefit to "defined contribution" plans, where benefits vary based on the level of employees' own contributions and how workers decide to invest employee and employer contributions to private retirement programs.

To evaluate social policy in the U.S., we must carefully consider the definition of social welfare expenditures. Typically, the term social welfare expenditures refers to all spending necessary to sustain the core federal and state social welfare programs. The core federal programs include TANF, Social Security, Medicaid, Medicare, SSI, food stamps (SNAP), Head Start, various housing programs, job training programs, educational grants, veterans' benefits, and unemployment benefits. State and local programs include education, programs for people with mental illness, health and social services for children and older adults, corrections programs, and workers' compensation. Although these programs are administered on a state or local level, they are often subsidized by the federal government.

Contrary to popular opinion, most social welfare spending in the U.S. is not for cash payments or other forms of assistance for poor people. Rather, the largest and most rapidly growing component of social welfare spending is social insurance. Significantly, most of the recipients of social insurance benefits are not poor, although many of them would fall into poverty were it not for these programs.

The Nature of United States Social Welfare Spending

Recall from Chapter 3 that, beginning in the 1980s, there was growing pressure for changes in the social welfare system, including curtailing welfare benefits, reconfiguring universal programs based on the insurance principle, and instituting strict means-tested programs that the majority of citizens do not expect to ever use. Support for cutbacks was fueled by a sluggish economy, increased mistrust of government, and growing pressure from globalization, a phenomenon we discuss later in the chapter. The conservative political philosophy that emerged during this period favored privatization of a variety of social welfare activities and the devolution of many fundamental services to the state and local levels.

The success of the various initiatives that evolved from this philosophy has been mixed at best. On the negative side, increased fragmentation in a welfare system already notorious for its lack of cohesion has been widely documented. As one example, piecemeal, uncoordinated public and private initiatives to feed and house adults and children who are no longer eligible for public financial assistance are being cobbled together at the local level to provide needed assistance. Though some programs were cut drastically, for the most part, overall funding for social welfare programs has been increasing on an annual basis.

Total federal spending increased during George W. Bush's administration. This increase included both mandatory spending on programs such as Social Security and Medicare and discretionary spending for defense, homeland security, and social welfare programs. Social welfare spending increased as a percentage of GDP, yet the Bush administration pressed for slower growth in social welfare programs. In fact, in the area of non-security related discretionary spending, which is primarily social welfare, by 2005, the increase declined to one percent, which was below the rate of inflation (Office of Management and Budget, 2005). Bush's strategy did not allow for adequate growth of programs that meet the needs of poor children and elders, particularly as the economy began to wane. In the later years of his administration, he pressed for cuts or elimination of many more social programs, including agencies that provide employment, education, and housing services to people with low incomes (House Budget Committee, 2005; Pear, 2005; Stevenson, 2005).

President Obama's election and high rates of job loss in 2008 and 2009 reversed spending trends on social welfare. The numbers of people applying for unemployment insurance increased dramatically and the time period for receiving unemployment benefits was extended. The Recovery Act also channeled more funds into social welfare programs. However, much of this spending was temporary and designed to end as the economic crisis lessened. Public health care expenditures will rise under the Affordable Care Act, but overall health care spending may slow down as policy shifts to incentives for more cost-effective preventative and coordinated care.

It is evident that the government has long been used to promote social welfare and will continue to be used that way. What is less evident is whether public resources will be spent primarily to enhance the social welfare of the middle and upper classes or will go to support basic, universal benefits for all citizens. For example, some critics contend that many middle- and upper-income citizens receive substantially more government support through the tax system than low-income citizens receive via social welfare programs targeted at specific needs such as poverty and unemployment.

Social Welfare and Tax Expenditures   When social welfare is defined broadly, it is clear that most social welfare expenditures are not targeted toward low-income people. However, the popular definition of social welfare often is limited to assistance for people categorized as needy or deficient and does not include the policies that benefit people with higher incomes. For example, social welfare expenditures inevitably include funding for public housing for low-income families, but they often overlook tax deductions for home mortgages. This practice is common despite the fact that both policies help families obtain housing they otherwise could not afford. Further, tax deductions for medical care, special tax breaks for large corporations, tax incentives for retirement savings, and tax deductions for college tuition all could be considered public social welfare expenditures. In fact, defining them as such helps draw attention to what has been termed "the upside-down welfare state."

Remember, tax expenditures are tax deductions that the government extends to particular groups for a great variety of reasons. They are extended to individuals as well as corporations and benefit people across income groups. Although tax expenditures typically are analyzed separately from social welfare expenditures, they represent lost revenue that the government is not able to use for other purposes, such as paying down the debt, providing more military funding, or increasing social welfare expenditures. The government determines that this money will remain with the person filing her or his taxes instead of being collected for other purposes. These tax breaks operate very much the same way as direct expenditures. Recall that mandatory spending (entitlements) does not go through a direct appropriations process each year, and neither do most tax expenditures. Rather they continue and may even expand without any vote taking place in Congress. In fact, tax expenditures are sometimes referred to as tax entitlements. Tax entitlements/tax expenditures also provide a direct benefit to the individual taxpayer but are much less visible than TANF or Social Security. In 2012, nearly $1.3 trillion in tax benefits went to individuals through this kind of tax benefit, including the tax exclusion for employer-provided health insurance and the mortgage interest deduction. Tax expenditures currently account for 5.3 percent of the GDP and are equal to approximately one-third of the projected revenue for 2012. The importance of tax expenditures is well recognized and, in fact, the president is required to submit a tax expenditure budget to Congress, which documents these types of uses of the tax system. Exhibit 4.4 illustrates the impact of tax expenditures at the federal level. As you can see, the tax expenditures category dwarfs spending on other social programs often labeled as "too expensive." Indeed, despite the popularity of these measures with powerful interests, the multitude of tax exemptions and deductions that are included under tax expenditures are increasingly being targeted for cutback in order to reduce federal and state deficits.

EXHIBIT 4.4

Cost of Tax Expenditures

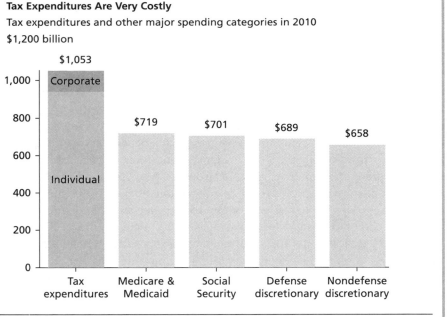

Tax Expenditures Are Very Costly

Tax expenditures and other major spending categories in 2010

$1,200 billion

Note: Tax expenditure figures exclude Recovery Act provisions that were allowed to expire, but include those that have been extended.

Source: Office of Management and Budget Center on Budget and Policy Priorities | cbpp.org

Exhibit 4.4 compares tax expenditures to other major spending categories such as: Medicare & Medicaid; Social Security; Defense; and Nondefense discretionary. Tax expenditures include items such as medical expense deductions, charitable contributions, employer-provided pension programs, employer-provided health care, the child tax credit, EITC, and mortgage interest deductions.

Note that tax expenditures are significantly higher than any of the other spending categories, including those social welfare expenditures which assist people or families with low or middle incomes. Now, consider Exhibit 4.5, which illustrates the percent distribution of tax entitlements, by income group. A clear, class-based pattern emerges from this analysis. Tax expenditures largely benefit the 20 percent of individuals or families with the highest incomes.

The major exception is the EITC, which generally benefits low-income taxpayers; importantly, the EITC has uniquely been threatened because of concerns about "fraud," despite its comparatively small size, three percent of tax expenditures. Further, many people assume that entitlement benefits go primarily to older Americans because large programs such as Social Security retirement insurance and Medicare primarily target this age group. However, when both these tax entitlements and spending entitlements are combined, a majority actually go to the under-65 (Gist, 2007).

Overall, then, when we analyze tax expenditures, we discover that expenditures going to middle- and upper-income families in non-stigmatizing ways often exceed

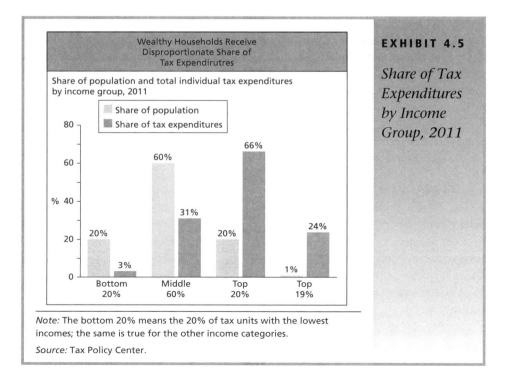

EXHIBIT 4.5

Share of Tax Expenditures by Income Group, 2011

Note: The bottom 20% means the 20% of tax units with the lowest incomes; the same is true for the other income categories.

Source: Tax Policy Center.

the amounts going to low-income families. This policy is sometimes justified by the argument that expenditures targeted to upper-income citizens will improve the economy. However, as discussed earlier, this reflects an ideological debate more than an economic fact. Expenditures for low-income people also provide an economic stimulus because they must spend most of the money immediately on necessities.

Adequacy of Current Expenditures for Social Programs

Earlier in this chapter, the principles of economic efficiency and equity were discussed in terms of evaluating interventions. Another important principle for social workers to consider is the adequacy of social welfare programs, including those provided by the tax system. Adequacy refers to the ability of social welfare programs to address and sufficiently meet the needs of the general public. Determining whether public expenditures on social welfare are adequate is a complex task. One way to assess social welfare programs in the U.S. is to look at equity, and adequacy in the context of income distribution.

Income distribution in the U.S. is highly unequal. In 2011, median household income in the U.S. was $50,054. However, the median income of households in the highest five percent of the population was $186,000 and most had two wage earners. At the same time, the median income of households in the lowest quintile was $20,262 (DeNavas-Walt, Proctor, and Smith, 2012). Income includes earned income, social welfare benefits, and capital gains, but it does not include tax deductions. The U.S. Census Bureau reports that the percentage of the nation's overall income received by households in the lowest and middle quintiles decreased in 2011, while the percentage going to the highest quintile increased (DeNavas-Walt et al., 2012). Equitable income distribution can be achieved by redistributing income through social welfare programs and tax strategies. Income inequality can be reduced by redistributing income from those with high incomes to those in poverty. Determining the need for redistribution of income can be understood by evaluating the adequacy of income for those with low to moderate incomes. The actual income level of the lowest quintile (after inflation adjustments) has increased since 1970, although its share of national income has decreased. Exhibit 4.6 illustrates the income disparity between the lowest 20 percent of households and the highest 5 percent as well as for the middle 20 percent of households in 2009. Growth in income provides households with more money to meet basic needs such as housing and food. However, this increase does not guarantee adequacy, because low-income households might not have been able to meet their needs prior to the increase. In addition, the cost of living escalated during this time period.

As Exhibit 4.7 indicates, the gap between the income classes has increased dramatically. Further, the people in the group with the highest incomes have experienced substantially greater growth in income than have the other groups.

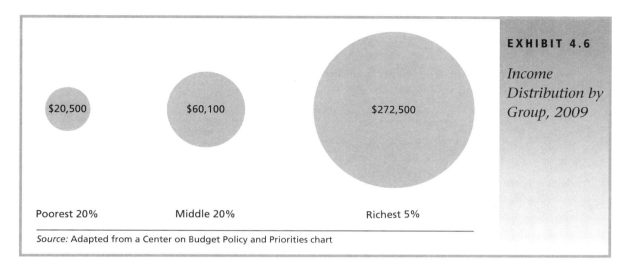

EXHIBIT 4.6

Income Distribution by Group, 2009

$20,500

$60,100

$272,500

Poorest 20%   Middle 20%   Richest 5%

Source: Adapted from a Center on Budget Policy and Priorities chart

In order to determine adequacy of income and social welfare programs in the U.S., it is important to look at how much it actually costs a household to live. However, this is a complicated process, because the cost of living in New York, for example, might be very different than it is in Missouri. Different families have different spending needs, depending, for example, on whether some members have disabilities. Also, different people might define basic needs and their costs in

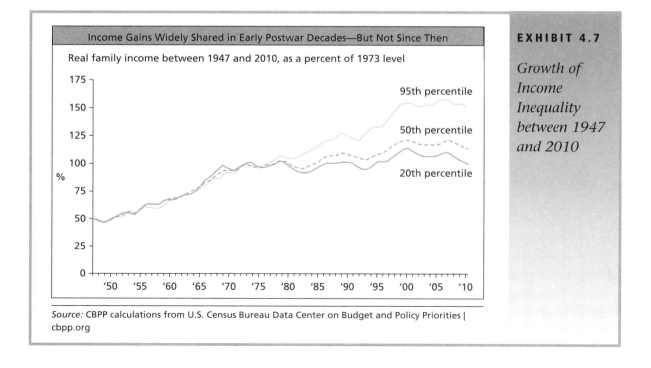

EXHIBIT 4.7

Growth of Income Inequality between 1947 and 2010

Income Gains Widely Shared in Early Postwar Decades—But Not Since Then

Real family income between 1947 and 2010, as a percent of 1973 level

95th percentile

50th percentile

20th percentile

Source: CBPP calculations from U.S. Census Bureau Data Center on Budget and Policy Priorities | cbpp.org

different ways. Understanding adequacy and equity in terms of income distribution and social welfare programs is important for evaluating policies. Another way to evaluate the adequacy of expenditures on social welfare programs in the U.S. is to examine social welfare expenditures and outcomes in other countries, a topic to which we now turn.

U.S. Expenditure Compared to Those of Other Countries   Although some critics contend that the problem with the U.S. economy is the high level of spending on social welfare, the reality is that, by international standards, social welfare spending in comparison to the size of the U.S. economy is not high. In fact, the U.S. has historically never provided the full array of social welfare protections that most Western governments do.

The Organization for Economic Co-operation and Development (OECD), an international organization devoted to promoting economic growth and world trade, has collected data on the social spending of various countries for 2013. The social expenditures fall into three broad categories:

1.   Pension payments such as old-age cash benefits, including survivors' benefits.

2.   Income-based support for working-age people who are experiencing need due to illness, disability, or loss of earnings.

3.   Health and other expenditures for children, older adults, and people with disabilities, as well as active programs that focus on training people to return to work.

Not included in these data are similar benefits provided by private sources or educational expenditures. The OECD also was unable to include an accurate representation of expenditures by all the many levels of government such as towns and counties (OECD, 2013). Note that because the U.S. relies more heavily on city-, county-, and state-level spending, as well as the participation of private entities, to provide social welfare services, these comparisons underestimate spending in the U.S. In addition, the OECD collected information about tax rates of different countries.

Exhibit 4.8 compares the U.S. to other countries in terms of social welfare expenditures and tax revenues. The chart compares tax revenues, expenditures, and GDP based on per capita spending. To ensure accuracy in these comparisons, per capita spending is adjusted for the purchasing power parity (PPP) of the various countries. Controlling for PPP when looking at per capita spending makes it possible to more realistically compare spending, GDP, or other economic measures between countries with very different populations and currencies. The chart clearly illustrates that the U.S. does spend a comparatively large share of taxes collected on social expenditures. The chart also shows that federal taxes in the U.S. are lower per person than in many

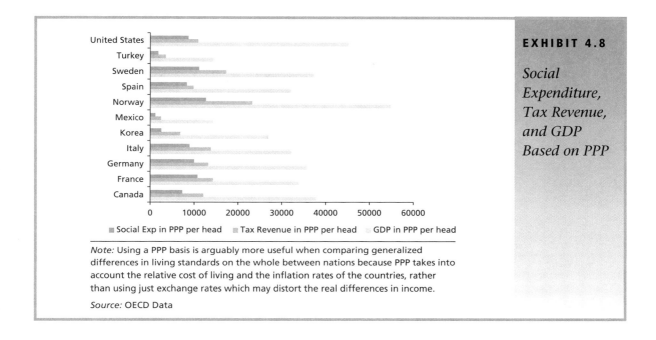

EXHIBIT 4.8

Social Expenditure, Tax Revenue, and GDP Based on PPP

Note: Using a PPP basis is arguably more useful when comparing generalized differences in living standards on the whole between nations because PPP takes into account the relative cost of living and the inflation rates of the countries, rather than using just exchange rates which may distort the real differences in income.

Source: OECD Data

other industrialized nations; thus the United States does not tax its citizens as heavily when compared to the countries that provide more extensive social welfare benefits. However, there is some evidence that other nations may be moving in the direction of constrained revenue policies, as in the U.S. In recent decades, most Western governments, like the U.S., have either reduced spending on specific social programs or arrested their growth in response to high rates of unemployment and inflation, changing demographics, sluggish economic growth, and increasing pressure to reduce what were considered to be excessive levels of taxation.

Due to its hesitance to fund more social welfare provisions, Wilensky and Lebeaux (1965) defined the U.S. as a "reluctant welfare state." However, welfare pluralists in this country reject the notion that the U.S. is a laggard in the social welfare arena. They do not believe that social needs should be met primarily by the government. Instead, they argue that people can and do enhance their well-being through their own efforts, with the help of neighbors or families, by purchasing services on the market, or by obtaining help from voluntary organizations.

The question thus arises, how do we assess whether the approaches used in the U.S. are as effective as the publicly financed programs in other countries at addressing citizens' needs? One strategy to use in answering this question is to examine basic indicators of the health and welfare of the citizenry, including infant mortality, childhood poverty, mental and physical health, and elder welfare. One such indicator, the infant mortality rate, is relatively high in the U.S.: it is 40th in the world in the latest international rankings, behind most European countries, as well as many other countries including Canada, Australia, New Zealand, Singapore, Japan, and Cuba (Kaiser Family Foundation, 2012h). Furthermore, our ranking is becoming worse rather than improving. This ranking undoubtedly reflects the lack of universal health care in the U.S., as well as the economic inequities that make some populations in the United States particularly vulnerable to these poor health outcomes. Related to this, the U.S. has a high rate of childhood poverty compared to other developed countries and childhood poverty is increasing. Of course, there is probably a variety of reasons why countries differ on these indicators. Nevertheless, the adequacy of the social welfare system certainly is one of them.

The willingness of the citizenry to pay taxes to support health and welfare programs influences these outcomes. Investing in the workforce by providing effective public education, health care, and other economic and social supports can increase competitiveness and improve health and economic outcomes. In fact, many of the developed countries with more comprehensive health and welfare programs and higher taxes are also very competitive in the global market. However, in the U.S., opposition to higher taxes and taxpayer revolts are often justified based on the belief that higher taxes will cause loss of global competitiveness. Actually, as illustrated above, U.S. taxpayers pay less tax than most of our global competitors. Nonetheless, more citizens will need to accept public as well as individual responsibility for producing more positive outcomes for children as well as other groups before they will consent to the higher taxes needed for universal public programs. Focus on policy outcomes is an integral part of the strengths perspective, and we will spend time examining outcomes for clients in the coming chapters. By focusing on outcomes, you can also begin to help voters understand the cost of failure by highlighting the cost of, for example, housing and feeding a former foster child who ends up in prison. This can be contrasted with the cost of providing effective transition programs to children aging out of foster care to aid them in becoming adequately housed and employed.

The Ramifications of Globalization

A final economic and political factor we will consider that affects social welfare policy in the U.S. is globalization. Globalization refers to the international economic, political, and social integration of the world's nations and, especially, its markets. This process of integration is transforming the economic and political context in the U.S. Globalization influences trade and labor markets. The increased ease of shipping, traveling and communication means that goods, services, information, and currency can be moved around the world more quickly. This movement allows companies to look for workers in other countries to perform jobs for wages lower than those paid in the U.S. In turn, this process exerts pressure on wages in the U.S. to remain low. Globalization also links the relative "health" of the U.S. economy with that of other nations, introducing a level of global vulnerability previously unseen. For example, as the U.S. struggled to emerge from recession, serious financial crises in Greece and elsewhere around the world threatened our precarious recovery and demonstrated the degree of interconnection between global markets.

The economic status of our citizenry is greatly influenced by decisions made by corporate policy makers. Many of these corporations operate globally, which means they are largely outside the control of any single government. Multilateral trade agreements, such as the North American Free Trade Agreement (NAFTA) explicitly give corporations the right to appeal government decisions that could usurp their profits, eroding the power of the nation-state. Moreover, when governments are unable to agree on regulations, such as international wage or pollution standards or the protection of basic human rights, the power of these corporations is further enhanced. In fact, concentration of wealth and power in the hands of giant multi-national corporations enables them to exert great influence over the operations of governments worldwide. Indeed, large transnational corporations have been successful in rewriting many of the rules of the global economy, asserting, for example, the right to challenge national policies that would threaten their global profit-making ability, even when governments are trying to act to protect the environmental or labor interests of their citizenry.

Globalization is exerting a significant impact on the health and well-being of our people. A global economy influences the growth and development of public social programs. All Western nations, including ours, are experiencing an increasing need to become competitive or stay competitive in the new global economy. One strategy to become more competitive is to reduce government spending so that tax burdens can be reduced. At the same time, companies want access to highly educated workforces, especially as technology evolves rapidly. It is difficult, of course, for countries to simultaneously hold down taxes and invest more in human capital, but these are the quandaries presented in the current context. However, countries can also learn about social innovations and the benefits of social policy reforms from other countries.

At the same time, however, as more and more workers become dislocated due to global economic change, the need for social services is increasing. As governments reduce spending on social programs in an attempt to make their economies more globally competitive, people in need suffer. In the current environment, the prospects for direct financial assistance for these people are becoming more remote. However, strategies that focus on the role of government in promoting social investment, so that people can more effectively participate in the productive economy and provide for their own social needs, may yet garner sufficient support to be enacted in the global economy as well as in the U.S. (Midgley, 2012b).

The social development approach is such a strategy. Initiated by social workers, the social development approach seeks to harmonize economic development with social welfare policy by redistributing wealth and resources in ways that also promote economic growth (Midgley and Sherraden, 2009). Social development also seeks new ways of removing barriers to economic participation so that resources are returned to the economy and human capital is developed to its fullest potential. This approach involves government intervention, but primarily in the form of social investment with positive rates of return. Among other things, government funds can be used to:

- train jobless people and persons with disabilities for real jobs within their communities;
- enhance community-held assets such as social infrastructure by encouraging local people to work with public agencies to build clinics and parks;
- support micro-level enterprise development;
- encourage recipients to maintain savings accounts, which are matched by the government and can be used to buy a home, pay for college, or start a business.

Significantly, the outcomes of social programs based on this approach can be carefully evaluated, which can then increase their effectiveness. The social development approach can also be a powerful tool to promote social inclusion (Sherraden and Ansong, 2013). To learn more about how the social development approach has been used in this country and around the world, go to the website for the Center for Social Development (csd.wustl.edu).The social development approach is a tool for capacity building.

Perhaps because the social development approach was shaped by social workers, it is not surprising that this strategy reflects the strengths principles of starting from common human needs, providing opportunities and garnering resources so that people can build on their strengths, identifying and removing barriers to self-sufficiency, and focusing on outcomes. If social investment in human capital enables people currently in poverty to train for real jobs, save money, own even a small share of community assets, save for college, and become productive and creative in their own businesses, then these people will become part of the functioning economy. So far, this approach has been adopted by several developing countries and is widely supported by the United Nations. In addition, support is increasing for governments to emphasize developing local approaches to providing adequate food and housing within a sustainable environment rather than fueling economic growth as a way of providing for low-income people. Further, we know that climate change, depletion of natural resources, and environmental disasters are influencing our health and welfare across national boundaries. Analyzing the relationship between the environment and social welfare policy will become increasingly important in crafting workable policy for the future and will be discussed further in Chapter 12.

THE ECONOMY OF THE AGENCY

It is important to apply the theories and concepts you learn in class to daily social work practice. In this chapter, we have discussed the economic and political context of social welfare policy. In terms of your actual practice, you should be aware that social work agencies also have an economic context. These parameters, of course, are in turn shaped by the economic pressures exerted by local, state, and federal governments. In order for an agency to provide benefits or services, it must have sufficient financial resources to pay staff salaries and benefits and to meet such basic costs as office space and supplies. These costs are beyond the actual tangible benefit that goes to the clients such as the TANF payments, housing subsidy, or foster care payment.

Every social service agency employs administrators who are responsible for ensuring that there are sufficient financial resources to meet these needs. In most agencies, these administrators also have the authority to make decisions that influence service or benefit delivery. For example, administrators of agencies funded primarily by private donations and private payments from clients realize that clients who cannot afford to pay can be served only if they attract sufficient donations and clients who pay privately. Similarly, in public and private agencies that are reimbursed on the basis of client diagnoses, administrators know they must carefully plan staffing and services so that they can meet their financial obligations based on these diagnoses. If they want to raise the rate of reimbursement, they will need to serve people with more severe diagnoses. This particular reality has led to the phenomenon of "charting for dollars," in which the diagnosis is made with an eye to which particular diagnosis will bring in sufficient funds to serve the client adequately. For example, a young person who may need family counseling could also be diagnosed as having a mental illness such as depression because of the greater reimbursement available to serve someone so diagnosed.

So, you might be asking yourself, what does all of this have to do with social policy? When you are having a difficult time grasping the logic of a national, state, or agency policy, one useful piece of advice is to "follow the money." Many agency programs and policies are heavily influenced by the financial ramifications of the policy that regulates how they are funded. Like many of the ideas presented in an initial social policy class, entire books could be written on this subject. However, you can begin to educate yourself in the area where you will practice social work. Ask how the agencies with which you are involved are funded. Are they publicly or privately funded, or do they receive both public and private funds? Is the agency public, private profit-making, not-for-profit, or volunteer? Think about how funding may be driving policy decisions. What incentives or disincentives are created for clients and workers by the way the agency is funded? Ask to see the agency budget. Ask questions about funding and financing. This can be done in the spirit of student inquiry. In fact, as a student, you are in the perfect position because you are expected to ask questions, and no question should be considered dumb. Of course, you will need to use the well-developed interpersonal skills you hopefully already have or are learning in your social work classes to make these inquiries in a respectful and nonthreatening way. You should also encourage approaches that involve clients, to the greatest extent possible, in making critical decisions about resource allocation. Social work agencies should be laboratories for the kind of social policy development we want to see in larger systems, and this begins with identifying ways to include those most affected by budget decisions in helping to inform them. If you begin to consider the economic context and to ask these questions, you will understand much more readily and be able to anticipate policy changes in your agency. Furthermore, your understanding of the state and federal budget and how changes in either can influence your agency will provide you with the knowledge base necessary to advocate for your client at the state and federal levels.

CONCLUSION

Policy makers as well as other citizens are faced with the task of restructuring the U.S. welfare state so it can respond more effectively to the changing political, economic, and social forces facing the country. Clearly, the severe recession that started in 2007 has made many people more aware of the big holes in our safety net, but social workers cannot expect that necessary investments in social programs will be automatically forthcoming as the economy improves. We need programs that increase economic productivity and human capital rather than restrict it. The values of reciprocity, responsibility, productivity, social integration, family and community cohesion, and social choice can be reflected in public social policy that also increases social justice. Advocates of social justice need to make clear to the public how social programs contribute to the overall well-being of society. Social responsibility is not the obligation solely of the poor.

It is too simplistic to believe that one type of program or the same incentives will work for all people. There is no reason to believe that all poor people, disabled people, or elders will respond to incentives or opportunities in the same way. It is to be expected that people in poverty differ, as do people who are not poor. It is naive to think that any one public welfare policy would make it possible for most people in poverty to become self-sufficient. Further, more acknowledgment of the interdependency that in fact is part of all of our lives, combined with greater recognition of interdependence as a worthy goal for social policy, are important to building a society where more people's basic needs are adequately met.

Policies are also needed that encourage social inclusion, These policies are designed to support participation of all people in society, regardless of background or other differences, which may include: race, language, culture, gender, disability, social status, age, and other factors. Well-funded public schools and public transportation policies are examples of policies promoting social inclusion. Such policies are vital to economic growth and stability and to reducing inequality. They also contribute to capacity building.

People have different strengths, needs, and resources. In charting new welfare policy, it is important to couple opportunities and incentives for self-sufficiency with a realistic assessment of the labor market's capacity to provide a sufficient number of jobs that allow families to live above the poverty level. Initiatives should also be evaluated in terms of their effect on environmental resources so that they continue to be sources of strength rather than problems. Valid outcome benchmarks are needed to measure the success of strategies that are touted as alternatives to traditional publicly sponsored social welfare approaches, and influential organizations need to regularly monitor those outcomes and widely publicize the results. Kids Count, a nationwide initiative to track the well-being of children in this country, sponsored by the Annie E. Casey Foundation, is an example of such an effort (Annie E. Casey Foundation, 2013).

As you have learned in this chapter, the political and economic context exerts great influence over what social policies are supported. Strategies that combine concerns about economic productivity and social welfare may appeal to a wider political spectrum. Social workers can help craft such policies by doing research and advocacy work that highlights the strengths and capacities of their clients. In a pluralistic society such as ours, where many groups vie to influence public social policy, crafting strategies around which consensus can be built is key.

MAIN POINTS

- Social workers cannot adequately understand the social policies that determine how they will practice and what benefits and services their clients will receive, unless they examine the economic and political contexts in which policies are developed.

- The economic context focuses on the production, distribution, and use of income, wealth, and resources. The political context focuses on power seeking in government or public affairs. Both exert powerful influences on social welfare policy.

- The U.S. is a capitalist system with a marketplace economy.

- Explanations of how the economic and political contexts have influenced the development of social welfare policy include hypotheses that focus on the use of welfare policy to even out economic cycles, control workers, and maintain capitalism. "Humanitarian impulses and social conscience," as well as activism by the working class also influenced social welfare policy.

- In the U.S., the private sector (both profit-making and nonprofit), as well as the public sector are actively involved in providing social welfare benefits and services.

- The legislative, executive, and judicial branches of government all create social policy and, as such, all are important arenas for social policy development and evaluation.

- The size of the federal budget, the size of the federal debt, compulsory spending required for entitlement programs, and interest on the federal debt all limit discretionary spending whereby the priorities of the current president and Congress can be reflected.

- U.S. social welfare policy and tax policy are contributing to the widening gap between rich and poor and to increasing poverty rates, particularly for children, in the 21st century.

- The severe recession beginning in 2007 has increased the recognition of gaps in our social safety net.

- The economic devastation resulting from collapse of the financial markets and environmental disasters such as major oil spills may increase support for more effective regulation of the corporate sector.

- Increased investment in strategies such as providing low-cost training for jobs that pay a living wage, is an example of a capacity building approach.

- A capacity building state focuses on strengthening the skills, competencies and abilities of people and communities and on helping them secure the resources needed for full economic and social inclusion.

- Globalization influences social policy and must be taken into account in developing a new consensus to support a more effective, pluralistic welfare system. Strength principles can be useful in evaluating new options.

EXERCISES

1. Go to the Sanchez case at www.routledgesw.com/cases.
   a. Identify a federal and a state social policy that influences the services or benefits for which members of the Sanchez family may be eligible. How would these benefits be affected by a growing federal deficit or state budget shortfalls?
   b. Choose a liberal publication such as *The American Prospect* or *The New Republic*, and a conservative publication, such as the *National Review* or *The American Spectator*. Pick one of the policies you identified when answer-

ing the question above, and compare how the policy is depicted in a conservative and in a liberal publication. How do you account for the differences?

2. Review background information about the Sanchez family. How do you think globalization influences their success in meeting their basic needs?

3. How does an approach to social welfare that bases eligibility on citizenship impact Sanchez family members who are non-citizens but who nonetheless contribute to the economy?

4. Go to the RAINN case at www.routledgesw.com/cases. Review the funding section of this interactive case and answer the questions.

   a. How do you think sources of funding impact the capacity of this private nonprofit organization to provide sexual assault services?

   b. What might be the opportunities and concerns related to providing these services through a private organization rather than a public one?

   c. How might you experience this organization differently, for example, as a LGBT individual or a person of color?

5. What federal and state policies would have direct impacts on RAINN and its services? What public agencies would be responsible for developing and enforcing regulations governing RAINN's services? How would the political context, particularly attitudes around the rights of women, potentially shape support for RAINN and its objectives?

6. Go to the Carla Washburn case at www.routledgesw.com/cases. Carla Washburn receives income and health benefits that are considered entitlements. What specific entitlement program benefits does she receive?

   a. How do these benefits contribute to the federal deficit? How do they contribute to the national debt?

   b. Although it might help to promote long-term solvency, how would changes in entitlements, such as raising the retirement age or requiring higher co pays for Medicare, doctors' visits and prescription drugs, likely impact Carla Washburn's daily life?

7. Go to the Riverton case at www.routledgesw.com/cases. Do you think the underlying philosophy of the enabling state is one that will promote social justice for people who are homeless such as those living in Riverton? Why, or why not?

   a. How is understanding the diverse circumstances of people experiencing homelessness important to crafting effective policy approaches to addressing this problem?

   b. How would reframing public expenditures in the area of housing to include tax expenditures, such as the mortgage interest deduction, potentially influence community attitudes about support for those who are homeless?

   c. Using the logic of the social development approach, what kinds of programs might you suggest for helping people who are homeless become capable of long-term financial independence?

8. Go to the homepage of the Democratic, Republican, Libertarian and Green parties. How do their platforms differ? What policies are they for and against? What factors can you identify (for example, average income level of supporters) that should be considered in order to understand the differences between these parties?

9. Write down three welfare benefits that you or your family has received. Discuss whether there was any stigma attached to the benefits and the reason for the presence of stigma or lack thereof for you or your family.

10. Listed below are a variety of federal initiatives. Do you believe that the expenditures made for any of these initiatives represent investments that will improve our economic well-being? Why, or why not? If not, how do you think the money could be better spent?
    a. The wars in Iraq and Afghanistan.
    b. The Emergency Economic Stabilization Act of 2008 (that is, the bailout of financial institutions).
    c. The American Recovery and Reinvestment Act of 2009.

11. Find out how your community has used tax exemptions to attract or keep business in your town in the last five years. How large were the tax exemptions? Did the community attract businesses that created jobs providing a livable wage (that is, not most minimum wage jobs), and did they stay? What were the benefits and who benefited?

12. Go to the websites of conservative think tanks such as the Heritage Foundation and the Hoover Institution and compare their articles on topics such as health reform, to those found on the websites of more liberal think tanks such as the Brookings Institution and the Center on Budget and Policy Priorities. Remember, these policy institute articles do not typically go through a peer-review process, so you should evaluate their conclusions carefully and verify them in peer-reviewed sources whenever possible.

CHAPTER 5

Basic Tools for Researching Need and Analyzing Social Policy

The significant problems we have cannot be solved at the same level of thinking with which we created them.

Albert Einstein

Research is formalized curiosity. It is poking and prying with a purpose.

Zora Neale Hurston

Social policy should be grounded in a clear understanding of the needs, strengths and goals of our clients.

Rosemary K. Chapin

NOW THAT WE HAVE CONSIDERED THE HISTORICAL, political, and economic contexts that shape social policy, it is time to delve into policy analysis in more depth. As new content on the policy analysis process is introduced, you can build your policy practice skills by applying what you have learned about the context of social policy. The purpose of this chapter is to explain the steps involved in doing research to analyze existing social policies and programs so that you can understand them and evaluate their effectiveness. The chapter initially explores needs determination, because needs determination is the foundation on which effective social policy is built. We will examine traditional problem analysis methods, and we will also explore how examining strengths, goals, and needs can build a foundation for more effective policy and programs. We will then link needs determination to other steps in the policy analysis process. This chapter also demonstrates how policies can be analyzed based on the strengths perspective.

We discussed some of the steps in policy analysis in Chapter 1. This chapter examines these steps in greater detail and presents a framework for analyzing social policy. Chapter 6 then builds on your understanding of policy analysis to consider the policy development process and policy practice in more depth.

POLICY ANALYSIS FUNDAMENTALS

As we have seen in previous chapters, social policies are designed both to meet the needs of the citizenry and to support the social order. Thus, they often have the dual purposes of alleviating social problems and maintaining social control.

Although social policy may address individual needs, it also typically benefits the host society. In fact, efforts to meet societal goals may cause the social welfare policy to be less effective in meeting your clients' goals. For example, a city may be willing to fund a homeless shelter not only to provide a haven for the homeless population but also to clear homeless people from around businesses. Therefore, it often establishes the shelter away from the business hub, where job possibilities are greatest. It is important to realize that social welfare policies are not a one-way street whereby taxpayers' hard-earned dollars flow to people in need with no hope of offering benefit to the society at large. In fact, just the opposite is typically the case.

You can identify the societal needs that are being met by examining how need is being defined. Consider the case described above. If we define the problem as homeless people discouraging shoppers and needing shelter, then establishing a policy to fund a homeless shelter away from the business hub is an obvious solution. In contrast, if we view the homeless population as people with strengths who face barriers to resources, we may decide to prioritize helping them find a permanent home quickly in order to create a base from which they can recover from the economic crises that have resulted in them being homeless.

Social Conditions and Social Problems

Indeed, the way that policy makers and the public view a situation determines whether any social policy is developed at all. For example, for years in our society, discrimination in employment was considered a social condition, simply "the way things are." When a woman or a person of color could not get a job that paid a living wage that was just a personal problem. Whereas a personal problem negatively affects an individual in a unique way, a social problem negatively and systematically influences a large group of people. Therefore, a social problem generally requires a structural or systemic solution rather than a primarily personal solution. A systemic solution affects the prevailing structure of society. Policies that prohibit discrimination in employment are examples of solutions that aim to bring about societal change in addition to improving conditions for individuals experiencing discrimination.

Before such social policies develop, it is usually necessary to convince at least a sizable segment of the public that a problem or need exists that warrants intervention. The actual size and seriousness of a problem does not determine whether public concern rises to the point of action. Rather, the critical element is the power, influence, and capacity of the group to tell a story that helps people "see" the problem (Mildred, 2003) and envision collective action. Very often, the people affected by the problem have played an active role in achieving this public recognition. For example, as we saw in Chapter 3, focusing public attention and outrage on the problem of discrimination was—and continues to be—a long and arduous struggle. The efforts of people of color and women, who were the targets of discrimination, were central to the struggle to change public perceptions.

Advocates have used a variety of strategies for increasing public recognition of a social problem, including:

- conducting research and collecting supporting data;

- building alliances with other groups, including those with greater access to power;

- identifying the barriers that the problem creates; and, most importantly,

- attracting public attention.

Advocates have also increased public recognition through litigation, direct action in the form of education (teach-ins, media events), physical confrontation and mass mobilization (rallies, marches, picketing, sit-ins), and economic tactics such as sanctions and boycotts. Once they gained recognition of the condition as a problem, they could garner public support for programs and services to alleviate the problem by publicizing the harmful effects of the problem for both the individual and society as a whole.

Many of the social policies that govern agencies where social workers are employed are designed to ration resources targeted to alleviate a condition that has been labeled a social problem. Social policies structure the services and ration the amount of funding and resources that go to agencies that address these problems. Social policies are necessary because human needs and wants are unlimited, whereas most resources are not. Existing social policies designed to address society's most pressing needs were created because these needs or problems were defined in such a way that resources to help alleviate the need were mobilized.

Alternative Views

When analyzing existing policy, it is vital to examine how policy makers and the public understood the social problem or need at the time the policy was made. At the same time, you should consider whether there are alternative ways of understanding those needs that might lead to more effective policy making, particularly where social problems are still largely neglected.

When you are thinking about alternative understandings of need, carefully consider the questions to be asked rather than quickly moving to gather facts or seek answers. For example, many of the policies we will study have been designed to address the problem of poverty. In considering poverty, the question that first must be addressed is, "Why are people poor?"

There are a variety of explanations for the causes of poverty. Some authors on the subject have argued that people are poor because they lack a work ethic or have impaired intellectual capacity. These authors ignore the structural causes of poverty, such as inadequate educational systems in poor neighborhoods, lack of jobs, and discrimination. These beliefs about the causes of poverty, in turn, lead to policy approaches that emphasize individual remediation and even sanctions for individual behavior, rather than social changes. It is true that some people have intellectual limitations, drug and alcohol addiction, and other personal challenges that keep them impoverished. Social workers know these challenges must be addressed and that policies designed to provide individual services are crucial. However, they also know that many of the structural causes of unemployment and poverty are not effectively addressed and, therefore, contribute to the development of, and lack of adequate treatment for, personal problems. For example, the lack of jobs that pay a living wage and provide health benefits in a community will increase the number of families who do not receive preventive health care and do not have access to treatment for mental health and substance abuse problems. Part of the preparation for being a social service professional is exposure to a wide variety of ways of understanding conditions in our society. Social workers must understand how others view the social problems that are the focus of their work and must be able to help key policy makers see the social problems from a perspective compatible with the real experiences of affected populations. Later in this chapter, we will explore how to apply the strengths perspective in reframing the questions used to examine poverty and find alternatives to existing policies.

Defining Needs and Problems: The Social Constructionist Approach

In this chapter, you will learn how to integrate the strengths perspective into the process whereby we define needs and social problems. To do this effectively, you will need some background information on the conceptual underpinnings of this perspective. The strengths perspective reflects a social constructionist approach to reality, which posits that our explanations of all human interactions—including social problems—are based on socially and personally constructed views of reality (Geertz, 1973; Gergen, 1999). The term "socially and personally constructed" suggests that personal beliefs and group consensus shape what a group of people consider to be real at a given time.

To comprehend the social construction of reality more easily, consider historical periods when the majority of people in some areas were convinced that witchcraft and personal sin caused both natural disasters and personal suffering. Over time, careful and more objective observations dispelled many of these beliefs. Even when we attempt to be objective, however, our observations are shaped by our preconceptions. Leaders in the natural sciences and in the social sciences acknowledge that the observer shapes all observations and the meanings she or he attaches to those observations. Thus, all observations regarding human situations that are classified as social problems are fundamentally shaped by the observer. Meaning is socially constructed.

For the purpose of integrating the strengths perspective into social policy, it is entirely unnecessary to enter into a lengthy debate about the existence of objective reality. However, it is important to understand how reality has been constructed and reconstructed in relation to core social policy issues basic to social work. Many factors, including values, ideology, and past experience, influence our interpretations of reality. The following discussion illustrates how different people interpret the same reality from very different perspectives based on these factors.

The Social Construction of Teenage Pregnancy The policy debate concerning teenage pregnancy provides an example of how reality is constructed based on the values and beliefs of the observer. Recall from Chapter 1 that different people identify different causes for this problem. For example, some people define teenage pregnancy in terms of moral failure; based on this construction of the problem, they are more likely to argue that abstinence is the only viable solution. In contrast, other people perceive the problem as a failure by our schools to provide adequate sex education; their proposed solution would be to provide teenagers with information about, and access to, contraceptives. Still others point to the structural disadvantages faced by teenagers of color and those coming from families in poverty and advocate for greater economic justice and improved pathways to educational opportunity as the best prevention against unplanned pregnancy. Advocates for the right to abortion might define a pregnancy in terms of lack of access to abortion facilities. For the teenage mother herself, the pregnancy may represent a rite of passage to womanhood or may reflect females' comparative powerlessness over sexual decision making in some contexts.

Clearly, our society has not achieved a consensus on the causes of teenage pregnancy. Consequently, we have developed often conflicting social policies related to sex education, contraception, adoption, child support, and public welfare based on differing views of why teenagers become pregnant and how to best solve the problem. Ultimately, the inability to understand that there is more than one correct way to view this issue limits our capacity to work effectively on behalf of the mother, her child, and our communities.

The Social Construction of Family Violence Although there are always differing beliefs within a society, at any given time there can also be widespread agreement, or consensus, about social issues. That consensus, in turn, shapes the society's responses to those issues. Significantly, however, this consensus also can change over time. As an example of shifting consensus, let us consider an issue of vital concern to social work: domestic violence. Until relatively recent times, violence against family members was widely perceived as the father's prerogative. Indeed, it was the father's duty to keep order in the home, and violence was an acceptable tool with which to accomplish that duty. Over time, however, that consensus changed. Today, a husband who beats his wife is guilty of committing a criminal act.

In many states, however, parents are still allowed to administer the same discipline to a wayward child. In fact, there are undoubtedly a sizable number of people in many U.S. communities whose view of reality supports physical punishment as an essential ingredient of successful child rearing. "Spare the rod and spoil the child" is a maxim many people still live by. Even beyond the home, some schools and religious institutions assert their right to use physical punishment for children, while similar claims are not made seriously regarding adult women. Thus, the consensus regarding the physical punishment of children in the United States has not changed as dramatically as the consensus regarding the physical punishment of a spouse.

Understanding Different Views of Reality   If you understand that views of reality differ over time as well as among people at any given time, you can begin to see definitions of needs and problems in a new light. People have different perspectives depending on their place in society and, therefore, interpret the same problem in fundamentally different and often conflicting ways. Defining a problem in a certain way may prevent a person from considering many possible policy alternatives. Armed with these insights, you can ask what motivates particular groups to define needs or problems in a certain way. You can also consider how that definition may shape social policy and lead to positive or negative outcomes for your clients.

Furthermore, certain conceptions of social problems are privileged. Our society gives experts the power to define reality for people. Groups empowered to define social problems in the policy arena because of their positions include political officeholders, religious leaders, lobbyists, media personalities, foundations, think tanks, and university researchers. Because their opinions are widely circulated, these opinions frequently become accepted by a large segment of the public, including members of the target population themselves. Conversely, the people in need generally are not privileged, and their opinions are often not taken into account when the problem is defined in the policy arena.

Understanding how social problems have been constructed will also help us identify the prevailing causal theories underpinning those definitions of the problems. Policies are supposed to result in intervention either to eliminate the causes or to lessen the consequences of a social problem. However, many times, little or no research has been conducted to support the supposed causal relationship, an issue we will discuss in more detail later in the chapter. Where there are significant gaps in our understanding about the causes of a problem, the intervention designed in response will almost inevitably be flawed.

USING STRENGTHS PERSPECTIVE PRINCIPLES TO CONSIDER NEEDS DETERMINATION

In Chapter 1, we discussed strengths perspective principles that you can use as tools to gain a broader perspective on need and to guide your social policy analysis. These principles are presented for review in Quick Guide 3. The primary focus of this chapter is on analysis of existing policy so that you can evaluate its merits. We will also discuss how strengths principles can be applied to help you consider alternative, and perhaps more effective, policy approaches. In this section of the chapter, we will consider how to apply the first two principles. Ways to use the other principles are discussed in subsequent sections.

QUICK GUIDE 3   **Principles of Strengths Perspective Policy**

1. The strengths and goals of your clients are legitimate starting places in developing social policy. Problems and deficits should not be given center stage.
2. Given that the definitions of social problems that typically guide policy and program development are socially constructed, our clients' perspectives concerning their problems, needs, strengths, and goals should be part of the social construction of need for policy development.
3. Structural barriers that disadvantage our clients in meeting their needs and create unequal opportunities should be emphasized when claims for the right to benefits and services are made.
4. The strengths perspective is premised on social work values of self-determination and social justice. Claims for benefits and services that allow people to overcome these additional barriers are made based on the right to equal access to resources and opportunities to meet needs and reach goals for citizens regardless of gender, race, age, disability, sexual orientation, gender identity, or other characteristics that have been the basis for denying access.
5. Social policies and programs should build on individual and community strengths and resources and remove structural barriers that disadvantage the target group.
6. The role of the social worker is not that of the expert who helps shape policy for hapless victims. Rather, it is that of the collaborator and resource person who helps gain attention for the perspectives of the target group.
7. Social policy goals and design should focus on access, choice, and opportunity that can help empower the target group in meeting its needs and goals. The target group should be involved in all phases of policy development.
8. Evaluation of the efficacy of social policy should include evaluation of outcomes for clients.

Note: These strengths policy principles build on the work of Rapp, Petus, and Goscha, as well as other social workers who are searching for ways to incorporate social work values into the policy development process (Rapp et al., 2006).

Frameworks for Policy Development

Strengths Perspective Principles 1 and 2 assert that (a) social policies should be developed based primarily on analysis of client strengths and goals rather than problems and deficits, and (b) the definition of need should incorporate clients' perspectives. You can apply these principles directly when you analyze the way in which a given policy defined need. Moreover, after you explore the definition of need, these principles can help you consider alternative definitions.

Policies that created high-rise public housing projects are excellent examples of how policy makers addressed a social problem—inadequate housing for low-income people—without considering the way members of the target population understood their needs and goals. If anyone had bothered to ask the low-income families who were inadequately housed, very few would have responded that they want to live on the ninth floor of a high-rise building surrounded by concrete and thousands of other low-income people. However, because policy makers, who likely did not want poor people in their neighborhoods, focused only on the problem as they saw it—creating affordable housing in an available location—they crafted ineffective, even inhumane, solutions. Although many of the policies we will analyze do not reflect a strengths approach, we can still use a strengths lens to evaluate the policy and determine its merits.

Social workers who utilize a strengths perspective perceive the client group or target population that is the subject of social policy as an interdependent component of the general population (Rapp et al., 2006). That is, they focus on how members of the larger society influence and, in turn, are influenced by the target group. Rather than placing our initial focus on the social problem, we should consider the needs, strengths, and goals of the target population as well as potential community resources.

As you analyze existing policy, you will uncover a variety of interpretations of social needs. However, if you take the time to also think about these strengths principles as part of that analysis, you can begin to recognize instances in which the experiences of the people in need have been distorted due to the historical emphasis on their alleged deficits or pathology. For example, when you analyze existing policies to reduce poverty, you can use these principles to reframe the questions about the causes of poverty. You could ask, "What resources or opportunities are necessary for people in our society to prepare for and succeed in jobs that will support a family above the poverty level? How many people do not have these opportunities? Why does this happen?" Further, a strengths-based, solutions focused approach is goal oriented. Client groups can be asked about their vision of appropriate goals early in the process. Some goals in relation to reducing poverty have already been articulated by client groups. They include improving schools in low-income areas and focusing on helping young people not going to college to get the technical training they need to get a job that pays a living wage. Such answers allow us to imagine a better alternative future state to work towards.

The answers to these questions and the policy options that they suggest are very different from those that arise from a deficits approach. They require people to consider why people are comparatively powerless and to examine which pathways to power are (and are not) available to various groups. Typically, people who are unable to meet their needs do not have access to the same resources and environment as other people. Just as a pathology and deficits-based approach provides policy makers with an understanding of need that does not lend itself to building on strengths, so a strengths approach provides a focus that does not dwell on individual deficits.

Social workers and students of social policy can find numerous examples of how an intense focus on deficits has not produced effective solutions for many clients. Indeed, this is one of the first lessons students encounter, often, in practice, as they come face-to-face with policies that are failing those they seek to help. Therefore, it is time to experiment with a different approach. However, lest we fall into the same mistakes that characterize the deficit-focused approach, it is important to remember that seeking a single cause or truth to explain complex problems such as poverty is too simplistic an approach.

ANALYZING SOCIAL PROBLEMS FROM AN EXPANDED VIEWPOINT

Previous content on defining need and using strengths principles has prepared you to analyze social problems from an expanded viewpoint. Examining the definitions of problems that laid the foundation for policy will help you uncover the assumptions that were made about the people the policy is designed to serve. This section examines social problem analysis and discusses how the strengths principles outlined above can be integrated into that analysis. The problem analysis approach discussed here builds on the work of a number of policy analysts (Chambers, 2000; Gilbert, Specht, and Terrell, 1998; McInnis-Dittrich, 1994).

In order to understand the definition of social problems or needs that shaped a social policy, you need to:

- examine how the problem or need was defined and documented;
- consider how values and self-interest shaped the definition and documentation;
- determine which causal theories have been developed based on the definition of social problems and what consequences are ascribed to the problem so defined.

Defining and Documenting Problems or Needs

To illustrate how a social problem such as homelessness is defined and documented within a policy, we will use the example of the Stewart B. McKinney Homeless

Assistance Act (Public Law 100–77). This Act, sometimes referred to as the McKinney-Vento Homeless Assistance Act, was originally passed in 1987. On May 20, 2009, President Obama signed into law the Homeless Emergency Assistance and Rapid Transition to Housing (HEARTH) Act, to expand upon and improve the McKinney-Vento Homeless Assistance programs sponsored by the Department of Housing and Urban Development (HUD). The HEARTH Act of 2009 is part of the Helping Families Save Their Home Act (Public Law 111–22). I will use elements of this Act to illustrate the policy analysis process throughout the chapter, and being familiar with the Act will help you understand the policy analysis framework. You can review the text of this legislation and become more proficient at using Thomas, a widely used link to legislation, by navigating to the Thomas website (thomas.loc. gov), clicking on Public Laws, and then going to the 111th Congress. Look up the Helping Families Save Their Home Act under Public Law 111–22. Scroll down to Division B, Homelessness Reform.

The McKinney-Vento Homeless Assistance Act, passed in 1987, was the first major piece of federal legislation designed to respond to homelessness. In the decades leading up to passage of this legislation, some towns and cities were experiencing difficulties coping with the growing homeless population, had documented the need, and were exerting pressure to have homelessness defined as a national problem. The original Act contained findings that homelessness is a national crisis and that states and localities need federal assistance to deal effectively with this crisis. Because homelessness previously had been considered largely a local problem, the redefinition of it as a national problem was critical to garnering federal resources for local initiatives. In the 2009 amendment, the findings section states:

The Congress finds that—

1. A lack of affordable housing and limited scale of housing assistance programs are the primary causes of homelessness; and
2. Homelessness affects all types of communities in the U.S., including rural, urban, and suburban areas (Public Law 111–22, Division B, Section 1002).

Note how the findings in the 2009 amendments focus on prevention by asserting that the primary causes of homelessness are lack of affordable housing and inadequate housing assistance programs. These causes can be addressed by structural changes whereby policies and programs are created to increase affordable housing and provide housing assistance to those experiencing or at risk of homelessness. Because many Americans were affected by the foreclosure crisis of 2009, homelessness was clearly being cast as part of the wider problem of people losing their homes. Indeed, making the HEARTH Act of 2009 part of the Helping Families Save Their Home Act is a way of making the connection between the housing insecurity faced by many families and the need to help people who are homeless. The emphasis in the HEARTH Act is on economic crises that lead to homelessness rather than on problems such as alcoholism, mental illness, and drug abuse as causes of homelessness. The main thrust of the HEARTH Act is to highlight and incentivize proven strategies for preventing and ending homelessness, such as rapidly getting people rehoused as soon as possible after they lose their home. These kinds of strategies recognize that an economic crisis (job loss, medical emergency, etc.) is the primary immediate cause of homelessness. Whereas many people who are homeless do have a history of alcohol or drug use, many do not. These problems are rarely the causes of homelessness, though they can be contributing factors. Focusing on strategies such as rapid rehousing allows us to move quickly to work towards solutions.

When examining legislation, it is important to take a look at the definitions segment. The definitions will give you insight into how need is being defined. In the original 1987 legislation, a homeless person was defined as:

> An individual who lacks a fixed, regular, and adequate nighttime residence; and an individual who has a primary nighttime residence that is a private or public place not designed for, or ordinarily used as, sleeping accommodation for human beings; an institution that provides a temporary residence for individuals intended to be institutionalized; or a supervised publicly or privately operated shelter designed to provide temporary living accommodations (including welfare hotels, congregate shelters, and transitional housing for the mentally ill).
>
> (McKinney-Vento Homeless Assistance Act, 1987)

This definition was criticized by those working with people at risk of homelessness as too limited to help those who need assistance to *prevent* their fall into homelessness. The definition of homelessness in the HEARTH Act of 2009 expands the definition to include people at imminent risk of losing housing so that some preventive work can be done with these groups.

To identify the official definition of the homelessness in the HEARTH Act of 2009, look first at the legislation itself. Sometimes, legislation contains a section called "general provisions," "legislative intent," or "findings" that provides this information. In the HEARTH Act, there is a section called "definitions of homelessness." The HEARTH Act "expands the statutory definition of homelessness" to include the following situations:

- People who lived in a shelter or a place not meant for human habitation prior to temporarily residing in an institutional care setting would be considered homeless upon their exit.

- People who will imminently lose their housing and lack the resources and support networks needed to find other housing, including those who are being evicted within 14 days, people living in a hotel or motel and who lack the resources to stay for more than 14 days, people who are doubled-up and must leave within 14 days.

- Unaccompanied youths and homeless families who have not lived independently for a long time, have experienced persistent instability, and will continue to experience instability because of disability, health problem, domestic violence, addiction, abuse, or multiple barriers to employment.

- People who are fleeing or attempting to flee domestic violence (National Alliance to End Homelessness, 2009).

For a summary of the changes made to the original legislation go to the website of the National Alliance to End Homelessness (www.endhomelessness.org) and navigate to the Summary of HEARTH Act. The new definition of homelessness puts increased emphasis on homeless families. Further, as you can see, the definition of need and the target population can be quite general and open to interpretation at the level at which the legislation is actually implemented.

Of course, as with the other social problems we have discussed, there are alternative definitions of homelessness. Even within the federal government, definitions vary, as the Department of Education uses different criteria to assess eligibility for homeless services for students, for example, than does the Department of Housing and Urban Development. The professional literature as well as sources such as homeless shelters and advocacy organizations might define homelessness in different ways. For example, many organizations, such as the National Alliance to End Homelessness, provide fact sheets with alternative definitions, and other resources that are helpful in understanding homelessness.

Once we have defined homelessness, we can count cases in order to document need. However, because different researchers will define the problem in diverse ways, research studies sometimes provide wildly divergent estimates of the size of the homeless population. For example, should a person who has been sleeping on her relative's couch for the last month and will continue to do so because her home was destroyed by fire, be classified as "homeless"? In such a case, would it matter if the person was an unaccompanied youth, instead of a working-age adult? Obviously, studies that include such cases will generate different numbers compared to studies that exclude such cases. Clearly, then, agreeing on a definition and then counting or documenting the number of homeless people in a given area is not an easy task. However, understanding how the problem or need was defined and documented is a key step in policy analysis.

This analysis of the diverse definitions of homelessness highlights the central point that all social policies—whether their overriding objective is social assistance, social control, or both—are based on socially constructed beliefs concerning people and social conditions (Loeske, 1995). Significantly, need often is not systematically documented until a condition is socially constructed as a problem. In the case of homelessness, for example, until the homeless population began to infringe on the business community, city officials seldom documented the numbers of homeless people. At that point, however, officials became more interested in gathering information to help in controlling homeless people, thus initiating the process whereby homelessness was defined as a national problem worthy of federal intervention.

Further, a social condition sometimes goes largely unnoticed by the larger society until it is identified as a problem. For example, emergency room staff can log the number of women injured by their spouses and the police can record the number of domestic violence calls to which they respond, but these numbers will not even be collected and analyzed until the social condition of intimate partner violence is labeled and identified as an indication of deviant behavior.

Defining the problem helps in identifying the number of people who have need and can help convince policy makers that they should take action. Focusing on negative outcomes for groups of people, such as higher rates of homelessness for veterans and former foster children or higher rates of poverty and lower life expectancy for people of color, calls attention to social justice issues without depicting the target population as pathological. Information on differential outcomes can often be accessed from statistical reports compiled by the U.S. Census Bureau, U.S. Justice Department, Centers for Disease Prevention and Control, and other government agencies; from professional literature; and from many organizational websites, particularly those dedicated to serving marginalized communities. When analyzing social policies, it is important to have an understanding of the problem that includes the dominant view as well as divergent views.

You also need to question whether the problem or need has been identified in ways that will make it possible to evaluate how outcomes for the target group have changed after policies were implemented. In the HEARTH Act, the defined problem is homelessness. Using a strengths perspective, we can evaluate the effectiveness of this policy in terms of clients' accomplishments in reaching goals. For example, how many formerly homeless people have now acquired adequate permanent housing? However, a second problem for communities attempting to effectively address homelessness is lack of coordination of service providers. Outcomes in terms of improved coordination will be harder to document. If you would like to learn more about national strategies to end homelessness, you can read the 2010 federal strategic plan, *Opening Doors* and the 2012 amendments at: www.usich.gov/opening_doors.

Values, Ideologies, and Self-Interest

Examining the values that define a condition as a social problem provides insight into the "should statement" that underlies the perception of that problem. Individualism, self-reliance, and equality are basic values in our culture. Our belief in self-reliance is reflected in the statement that people *should* work and meet their own needs. *Should* statements are implicit in most descriptions of social problems and in the resulting policies. Parents *should* care for their children. Children *should* have adequate food, clothing, and shelter. Teenagers *should* abstain from sex.

Women *should* have equal rights. Look for the *should* statements in the information you read depicting social problems and social policies. For example, the purpose statement of the original Homeless Assistance Act places special emphasis on homeless programs that serve families with children, elderly people, and veterans. These groups historically have been considered the "worthy" poor who should receive help.

Sometimes an entire body of belief or ideology develops in support of specific values. An ideology may guide a social movement. For example, members of the women's movement work hard to gain widespread acceptance of the *should* statement that women should have equal rights. They have generated large quantities of research and theory designed to support equal rights for women. Social movements can do a great deal to shape the definition of a problem and to document the problem in ways that reflect their values and ideologies. Self-interest is a strong motivator for people to take part in social movements. Altruism also motivates activism. By examining who wins or loses when a problem is defined in a specific way and the size of the gain or loss, you can often gain insight into which group was able to dominate the problem-definition process.

To draw on an example from the disabilities field, people with disabilities who are living in the community need social services as well as medical services. However, their medical needs garner the vast majority of attention and funding. Physicians' groups, whose members provide that medical care, are very influential in determining which needs receive attention. Social services providers are not as influential. This power imbalance helps explain why medical needs, not social service needs, receive greater attention and funding. Of course, if people with disabilities were driving the agenda regarding the prioritization of their needs, there might be a different emphasis entirely.

Professional groups, corporations, and myriad advocacy groups all lobby to promote a definition of the need or problem that is in their self-interest. In the case of the original Homeless Assistance Act, it was in the interest of states and localities that homelessness be defined as a federal issue, and they lobbied for that outcome. Similarly, social workers themselves often define needs for the target population that can be met by their services. For example, social workers have helped point out the special needs of homeless people who have mental illness and have pressed for policies that provide for outreach and case management services for homeless people who are mentally ill.

Causal Theories

It is necessary to understand the causes and consequences that policy makers attribute to a social problem because the policy is supposed to eliminate the causes or lessen the consequences of that problem. The findings section of the HEARTH Act asserts that a lack of affordable housing and the limited scale of housing assistance programs are the primary causes of homelessness. Given that definition, the

HEARTH Act focuses on getting more programs that have been proven effective, such as rapid rehousing, more widely implemented. Further, housing assistance programs are targeting immediate causes of homelessness such as inability to pay utilities, and helping families contend with these problems and thus avoid recurring episodes of homelessness. This stems both from successful advocacy on the part of advocates for people experiencing homelessness, as well as a growing recognition that preventing homelessness is by far the most cost-effective and successful approach to dealing with housing insecurity.

Further examination of our earlier example of teenage pregnancy provides another view of the complex nature of causes and consequences associated with a social problem. Lack of self-control on the part of adolescents, absence of parental supervision, the media and societal attitudes about sex, birth control, and the women's movement have all been identified as causes of teenage sexuality and teenage pregnancy. The consequences include unwanted pregnancies and abortions. Children who were unwanted and are not well cared for are more likely to become teenage parents themselves. Thus, causes and consequences are linked in a circular fashion by which the consequence becomes a cause.

However, consider that, historically, many women have been wives and mothers in their teens. Indeed, in many cultures, this was the expectation, not something to be abhorred. If you are mindful of this history, you can reconsider whether the problem is primarily teen sexuality and how and why societal and familial support of teen sexuality has changed. You can see that the business of determining cause and consequences is difficult, often circular, and can lead to redefinition of the social problem. Further, social policies based on some formulations of cause may create or exacerbate social problems rather than alleviate them. Policies that force schools to begin to exclude information on birth control from sex education efforts may lead to increases in teenage pregnancy.

Although a variety of causes and related interventions for a social problem may have been identified, adequate research to support the supposed causal chain and interventions frequently has not been conducted. Acknowledging this deficiency, researchers are now working hard to develop connections between problem, intervention, and outcome. As called for earlier in the chapter in regards to general policy practice, groups who are the subject of research are also increasingly engaging actively in the research process. For example, researchers are asking people who have successfully overcome a problem such as substance abuse how they did so and how other people can best be supported in these efforts. Other researchers are asking people who are still addicted to help identify the barriers to recovery. Involving the target population in the research is consistent with the strengths principle that people are experts on their own needs and goals, and this approach helps focus attention on successful strategies, even at the point of needs determination.

Some policies you will analyze reflect strengths-based thinking more clearly than others but may have elements that are not strengths-based and may have unintended negative consequences. However, when the goals of the target group are ignored and the primary emphasis is on meeting societal goals that continue to keep target members powerless, a policy is clearly not strengths-based. Remember, social policies can change. The voices of people in need can lead to revision of policies. You will learn how you can help encourage this process in Chapter 6.

Claims-Making

We now move our focus from analysis of problems and needs to the claims-making process. Claims-making connects the social problem or needs assessment and the resulting social policy. Even if policy makers agree that a need exists, they may not necessarily agree that the need deserves to be met, and they certainly may not agree about how to address the need. Instead, a compelling claim for resources, which takes into account the current social, political, and economic contexts, must be made. When you make a claim, you are asserting what needs to be done. Recall from Chapter 1 that claims-making is the process that promotes recognition of a social condition as deserving of action by policy makers. Values undergird claims. For example, the claim that stricter work requirements are needed for mothers receiving cash assistance is often linked to the value of personal responsibility. Claims often contain an underlying appeal to morality. Calls for compassion, social responsibility, and fairness speak to our sense of morality. Examples of claims-making are holding a demonstration to demand equal rights for Latinos or lobbying a member of Congress to provide prescription drug coverage for older adults. Engaging the client group in envisioning potential solutions as part of the claims-making process makes it possible to infuse the process with a beginning discussion of an effective way forward.

The Various Bases of Claims-Making   Claims can be made on a variety of bases. In some cases, claims are based on rights. For example, women could make a claim of domestic violence only after they won the right to be considered more than the property of their husbands. The claim of domestic violence is based on the assumption that spouses do not have the right to batter each other.

Power is the basis for claims-making in many situations. If individuals or groups are powerful enough, they can make a successful claim for policy changes. For example, policies that give large tax breaks to corporations are often passed because corporate executives have sufficient power and money to influence Congress members to support their claims for preferential treatment. People and groups with power can also help press for claims based on rights or other criteria. This is why advocates pressing a claim for new policies or programs typically attempt to mobilize a wide and powerful base of support. For example, advocates working for health care reform attempted to get the powerful pharmaceutical industry to back their reform efforts.

Other bases for claims include comparative disadvantage and, more broadly, an appeal for social justice. The claim may be made that public schools should provide free breakfasts for children from low-income families because these children are at a disadvantage when trying to learn on empty stomachs. Further, consider how claims are made on behalf of elders and children in general. Advocates for both groups claim that we should help elders and children because they are a part of our community and we are responsible for their well-being. This claim reflects our belief in social justice. In addition, we can make a further claim for children based on utility. Specifically, if we do not invest in our children, they will not be competent to take on important roles in our society, and we will all suffer. For elders, we can make a claim based on reciprocity. This population worked hard, fought our wars, and raised children. Now, they deserve to rest and receive our care. It is not only the need that propels action. It is the claim that the policy making entity has a responsibility to meet the need based on values held in common or, more typically, based on claims of utility in combination with appeals based on values.

When making claims that policies and programs need to change, it can be helpful to look carefully at the historical basis of claims for the original policies or programs. For example, recall that programs such as AFDC were underpinned by general agreement that society has a moral obligation to care for impoverished women and children. Stricter work requirements were pressed for in the 1990s and proponents of these stricter requirements claimed that welfare mothers needed to take more personal responsibility and work outside of the home. Note the language change. These proponents often used the term, "welfare mothers" rather than "women and children" to refer to people receiving assistance when making claims for stricter work requirements. Thus, the morality claims were shifted away from protecting vulnerable women and children. Further the term "welfare mother" was associated with the immorality of sloth and irresponsibility. This interplay of values, morality, and language needs to be carefully considered when social workers craft claims for policy reform or work to refute the claims of others who seek to undermine these claims.

Returning to the original McKinney-Vento Homeless Assistance Act of 1987, it is clear from the findings section that successful claims for federal involvement on behalf of homeless children and elders as well as other groups were made in order to get the law passed. By 2009, when the HEARTH Act passed, the need for federal involvement had already been established. The claim emphasized in the HEARTH Act was that much more evidence-based housing assistance should be provided to an expanded class of eligible recipients, in order to effectively combat homelessness. For legislation in general, information concerning the bases for claims-making often can be found in the initial sections of the law. Articles in journals and even popular media around the time legislation was being developed, as well as current publications that discuss the legislation, are also good sources for this information.

Assumptions Embedded in Claims-Making Claims-making is complex and nuanced. When you are considering claims-making, it is important for you to be aware of the assumptions embedded in the claim. For example, a claim for spending on older adults based on their deserving rest and care for past contributions will likely promote policies that increase funding for nursing homes rather than encourage employment opportunities. Keep in mind, however, that the population of adults ages 65 to 74 will bulge in the coming years. These individuals are often healthy enough to work and may need to work to pay their bills. Therefore, they will have a greater need for policies that support older workers and lessen age discrimination than for more retirement facilities. Consequently, advocates will have to craft a new claim that identifies the structural barriers confronting older workers and emphasizes the importance of removing those barriers. These claims will have to rest on somewhat different value bases, emphasizing equality of opportunity and the significant contributions elders can and do still make. This is another example of the importance of including the target populations influenced by the social policies, in their full spectrum of diversity, in crafting and advancing claims including preferred solutions.

We observed earlier that claims-making is often based on rights. Significantly, successful claims-making can also result in the establishment of rights. For example, eligible older adults now have the right to health care through Medicare and can take legal action if Medicare refuses to pay for covered care. Examining how such successful claims were structured, limited, and promoted helps us to understand current policy and to enact future policies.

When a claim is made that a need deserves to be met, it must compete for resources with other claims that may be more compelling. For example, after the terrorist attacks of September 11, 2001, claims for increased spending on defense were much more successful than claims for greater social spending. In earlier chapters, we examined key factors that influence whether claims-making succeeds and social policy is enacted. For example, the economy influences the definition of social problems and also the amount of resources available to address these problems. Similarly, history provides precedents and sets the stage for policies to emerge. Of course, politics influences who has power and who does not. Values and ideologies fuel social movements that press claims for certain policies. The interplay among these factors shapes both the claims-making process and the social policy that is developed.

As an example, recall our discussion of the Social Security Act of 1935 in Chapter 3, which explained how economic conditions during the Great Depression increased public acceptance of an expanded federal role in promoting social welfare. In addition, policy makers felt pressure to reduce the chance of the political upheaval that might be fueled by emerging social movements such as the Townsend Movement. Members of the Townsend Movement pressed the claim that people who had worked all their lives should not become paupers in their old age. In addition, people were living longer, which meant that they needed greater financial support in their post-retirement years. Finally, there were historical precedents for such intervention in the form of government-funded pensions for war veterans as well as international precedents because some European countries had already established public pension systems. The interplay among all these factors propelled passage of the landmark Social Security Act.

As you analyze the development of the major social policies that shape your practice, consider how the interplay of these key factors shaped the original policies and continues to shape efforts at reform. Articles in social work journals related to your area of practice often provide this background.

Using Strengths Perspective Principles to Consider the Claims-Making Process

After you explore the claims-making process for a particular policy, use Strengths Perspective Principles 3 and 4 (see Quick Guide 3) to help you evaluate the extent to which claims are strengths-focused. The principles essentially state that claims should (a) emphasize the structural barriers that prevent clients from meeting their needs; and (b) reflect the basic social work values of self-determination and social justice. If you determine that a claim does not meet these criteria, then you should consider alternative claims-making approaches that incorporate a strengths perspective.

A FRAMEWORK FOR POLICY ANALYSIS

In the previous section, we explored how the processes of need analysis and claims-making shape existing policy. You will need to keep the link between these processes in mind as we continue our exploration of the steps in policy analysis. These steps can be thought of as a framework made up of specific elements to help structure our analysis. Examining policies and programs using a policy and program analysis framework will help you determine why a policy is effective or ineffective.

Scholars have developed a variety of frameworks for the purpose of policy analysis (Chambers, 2009; Dobelstein, 2003; Gilbert and Terrell, 2009; Popple and Leighninger, 2004; McPhail, 2003). (Your instructor can provide you with a synopsis of these frameworks, available on the book's website (www.routledgesw.com/policy), in a reading titled "Policy Analysis Frameworks.") These frameworks as well as others vary extensively in terms of their length, focus, and intent. Some focus primarily on the historical context of the policy, on understanding the problem, on key policy elements, or on examining social policy through a gendered lens, while others focus on key policy elements, separately and in terms of how they interact with each other. When you are analyzing a policy or program, it is easy to become overwhelmed by the vast quantity of information that you can access. The framework presented below is a thorough and relatively simple way to begin analyzing policy. It draws on common elements shared by many of the frameworks. This framework will be used consistently in Chapter 7 through Chapter 11 to help you quickly grasp the major components of social policies. If you would like to see how the framework can be used, take a look now at the policy synopsis boxes in these chapters. This framework focuses on the essentials of policies and programs. Elements include:

- policy goals;
- benefits and services;
- eligibility rules;
- service delivery systems;
- financing.

Most frameworks focus, at least in part, on certain elements needed to implement and evaluate a policy such as those presented by Chambers (2009) and others discussed in more detail in this section. Frameworks vary greatly in their emphasis on strengths, but as a social worker with a general understanding of the strengths perspective, you can use these frameworks and the strengths perspective to analyze both social policies and programs.

The following section will familiarize you with the policy elements listed above. The discussion of factors to consider when analyzing each element also builds on selected portions of Chambers' analytical framework (Chambers, 2009).

After you become proficient in using the basic framework presented here, you may want to consider a variety of frameworks in more detail and begin to determine for yourself which elements and aspects of policy are most important when you are analyzing policies. For now, the framework presented here is easy to remember and will serve you well as a starting point.

Also, as you utilize this framework, you can use Strengths Perspective Principles 5, 7, and 8, from Quick Guide 3, to evaluate the extent to which policy and program goals, benefits and services, eligibility rules, service delivery systems, and financing reflect attention to client and community strengths. In regard to policy analysis, these principles affirm that social policies should (a) help remove structural barriers that limit your clients' full participation in the life of the community; (b) emphasize access, choice, and opportunities for clients that can lead to empowerment; and (c) be evaluated in terms of client outcomes. Note that Principle 5 builds on Principle 3, which focuses on claims-making based on structural disadvantages your clients face, in that Principle 5 asserts that social policies should help remove these structural barriers.

Policy Goals and Objectives

When analyzing a policy, it is essential to examine its goal and how the policy might alleviate the identified need or problem or achieve a desired condition. A policy goal is a statement of the desired human condition or social environment that is expected to result from implementation of the policy. A goal helps you understand what a policy is supposed to accomplish. For example, a goal of the legislation that established the Special Supplemental Nutrition Program for Women, Infants, and Children (WIC) is to safeguard the health of low-income women, infants, and children up to age five who are at risk of poor nutrition (Food and Nutrition Service, 2009).

Goals may be stated in general or abstract terms. In contrast, objectives spell out in more detail what is to be accomplished. Social policies often establish social programs. Objectives provide more specific detail about services and outcomes on which programs are evaluated so that program administrators can determine how to proceed. They are specific statements that operationalize desired outcomes. Several different objectives may be developed for the same goal. For example, one objective for the WIC policy discussed above is to increase the birth weight of infants in low-income families. Another objective is to increase breastfeeding among the mothers enrolled in the program. In the latter case, if the objective specifies a desired percentage of increase, then it provides a specific statement of expected outcome by which to evaluate the program's effectiveness.

Locating Goals and Objectives   As with claims and the definition of needs, the goals and objectives for a particular policy are often found in the preamble or general provisions of the enabling legislation which is usually accessible online. When researching goals and objectives, you can also look into the legislative history that contains the background material legislative committees use in framing the legislation. Law school libraries and the public document centers of university libraries have copies of legislative background information and well-versed librarians who will guide you to specific sources. In the case of state legislation, state legislative libraries are good sources of background information. In addition, many states have legislative library hotlines staffed by knowledgeable librarians who can often help you find this material online. Descriptions of programs, available from agencies that administer the programs created by the policy, also provide information on policy goals, and legislation is now easily accessed online, as are increasing quantities of legislative history materials, as governments move towards "paperless" operations. To locate the goals of the HEARTH Act [Public Law 111–22], you can find the Act on the Thomas website (thomas.loc.gov) and go to the Findings section. This section establishes a federal goal of ensuring that individuals and families who become homeless return to permanent housing within 30 days.

Manifest and Latent Goals   Goals can be both manifest and latent. Manifest goals typically are publicly stated, whereas latent goals are not. Latent goals may be intended by some of the policy makers, but they are often goals on which it would be difficult to achieve consensus or that would not be considered socially acceptable. Consequently, it is easier not to state them explicitly. For example, a manifest goal of the homeless assistance legislation we have been discussing is to provide funding for services for homeless people; a latent goal may be social control of homeless people so that they do not interfere with shoppers. As this example illustrates, it is possible for the manifest goal of a policy or program to be consistent with social work values and the strengths perspective, even if the latent goals are not, which is another reason it is important to critically analyze the intents and the effects of social policies in your area of practice.

When you examine the goals and objectives of a policy or program, you need to determine whether the goal is clearly stated, measurable, and concerned with ends rather than means. The goal of increased coordination in the original McKinney-Vento Homeless Assistance Act was concerned with the means of meeting the needs of the homeless population rather than the end of reducing homelessness. Although increased coordination may lead to a reduction of homelessness, when the stated goal is concerned with the means of reaching a goal, people can lose sight of the end goal and, instead, evaluate outcomes in terms of how many coordinating meetings were held rather than how many citizens are no longer homeless. Measuring and documenting increased coordination may also be difficult. However, the "purpose" section of the original legislation also contained the stated goal of meeting the needs of the homeless.

In addition, you should consider whether the goals can be accomplished by the activities prescribed by the policy. For example, one possible manifest goal of a program that promotes adequate nutrition for pregnant mothers is to improve the health status of their babies. Activities designed to achieve that goal, which could be specified in the policy, include identifying and distributing food and information that would help safeguard the health of both the mothers and their children. We could measure success in accomplishing this goal by comparing the percentages of low-birth-weight babies born before and after the policy was implemented in a specified area.

In contrast, if the specified goals and activities had been simply to distribute surplus food to pregnant women and children, program administrators could just distribute any surplus food rather than food and information that would improve the health of the target population. Under these circumstances, evaluation of the program would focus on how much food was distributed rather than the health of the mothers and their children. From a strengths perspective, it is important for us to examine what outcomes will result for clients if the goal is attained. In evaluating policies and programs, it is important to use data from reliable sources that are as objective as possible. Your instructor can provide resources to help you determine the reliability of data sources, particularly as it applies to information available on the web. Always, when you are relying on a given source of information, you should assess the ideological perspective(s) represented, so that you have a better sense of any biases that are reflected in the source's presentation of information.

Incorporating Clients' Perspectives   Typically, the goal of the policy as well as the type of intervention the policy prescribes are determined by policy makers who may not possess expertise in the underlying issue. In such cases, the policy makers turn to "experts" who often do not provide the perspective of the service users. As we discussed earlier in the chapter, these experts frequently are members of privileged or higher-status groups who may have little knowledge of the clients' reality. Failure to incorporate the clients' perspective often leads to the adoption of inappropriate and ineffective goals (Rapp et al., 2006).

For example, people with developmental disabilities who want a decent job may instead have received a lifetime of "vocational training" at a developmental achievement center because the prescribed policy goal was to provide them with such training. Not coincidentally, this goal reflected the input of the experts who ran the centers. In contrast, a policy developed using the strengths perspective would reflect the clients' goals of securing and maintaining a paying job. Although vocational training can certainly help people build on their strengths, when it becomes an end in itself rather than a means to attaining a paying job, many clients would not endorse vocational training as an appropriate end goal.

Benefits or Services Provided

Another component of social policies and programs that should be examined are the benefits or services provided by the policy or program. Benefits and services can include food stamps, counseling services, job coaching, a Social Security check, and the opportunity to vote. In certain cases, the benefits may be stigmatizing. For example, school systems sometimes provide vouchers that can be presented at specific local department stores to purchase back-to-school clothing. If the clothing voucher clearly marks the shopper as indigent, the child may feel ashamed and become stigmatized.

Analyzing benefits and services from a strengths perspective leads to a number of questions: Is the benefit or service designed to remove societal barriers that prevent people from meeting their needs? Alternatively, does the benefit or service focus primarily on correcting the behavior of the target population? How much consumer choice is allowed? Cash provides the most choice; however, if a service is unavailable, cash does not help. For example, if children with disabilities need therapeutic preschools and none are available, then the service must be developed to address the need.

The strengths perspective also raises the question of whether the benefits or services take into account the strengths and resources of the community. For example, policies may prescribe that nutrition programs for seniors serve a uniform menu across the city. Alternatively, they may permit local groups to develop different menus that comply with nutrition guidelines. Cooks who make the ethnic dishes long favored by elders in the community could be hired and consulted in developing a healthful menu built on their talents. A policy could also set nutrition guidelines and permit different communities to figure out how best to meet them without requiring uniform menus. In the case of the original McKinney-Vento

Homeless Assistance Act, funds were provided to a wide variety of programs that assist homeless people. Such an approach makes it possible to build on existing community resources and tailor programs to the community. On the negative side, however, the quality of the programs funded by the Act will also vary widely, and such customization may be more expensive, resulting in greater service gaps.

Finally, it is crucial to evaluate whether the benefit or service will alleviate the identified need and result in positive outcomes for your clients. For example, when the goal is to reduce substance abuse among teenagers and the service provided is a rack of pamphlets in each high school warning against drug use, the policy will probably be ineffective.

Eligibility Rules

Eligibility rules stipulate who receives the benefit or service. Some rules require that people may receive benefits only if they have made prior contributions. For example, Social Security retirement benefits are available only to workers who have been employed in a covered job and have paid into the system for the required amount of time; spouses and children of qualified workers are also eligible for certain benefits. Other benefits are available based on attachment to the workforce and do not require employee contribution. For example, workers' compensation is funded by employers, but workers in some industries or in the informal economy will not have these same protections. As a social worker, you should always consider social justice and equity issues when you examine eligibility rules. For example, historically, women have been disadvantaged when eligibility for public benefits was based on attachment to the workforce because they were less likely than men to have held paid jobs. Similarly, people of color were less likely to have worked in jobs that provide Social Security benefits.

The eligibility rules for many of the services and benefits received by your clients require a means test. For example, many policies provide for financial aid only to people who have income and assets below a certain level. In addition, some policies require functional need as well as financial need. For instance, older adults can receive Medicaid funding for nursing facility care only if they have exhausted their financial resources and are also severely functionally impaired. Means tests can be stigmatizing and can discourage people in need from applying for services. Asset tests, in particular, can force individuals in need to deplete even a small financial cushion, resulting, in the long run, in greater economic insecurity and dependence on public assistance. Processing eligibility determinations according to these means tests can be expensive, too; programs available only to select populations usually have higher administrative costs than those that are more universally available. At the same time, however, benefits provided with less stringent eligibility rules may lead to overwhelming cost. In the case of the HEARTH Act, programs that serve the homeless population and meet other specified requirements are eligible for funding, and the definition of homelessness is specified in the law.

Eligibility rules may also be based on judicial decisions. For example, a judge can rule that a family should receive services designed to prevent further child abuse. Similarly, a teenager may be assigned to probation during which he will receive the services of a probation officer. In addition, many health and mental health benefits require that licensed professionals certify the need for services. Although there typically are rules or guidelines, professionals, such as physicians, nurses, and social workers, have some discretion in deciding who will receive services.

When considering eligibility rules from a strengths perspective, you should examine the structure of these rules to determine if they create incentives for people to develop their capacity to meet their own needs. At the same time, you should ask whether such positive steps could result in loss of benefits. For example, do low-income parents automatically become ineligible for a day care subsidy if they manage to land higher-paying jobs?

Service Delivery Systems

The system for delivering services or benefits also influences policy effectiveness. Therefore, any comprehensive policy analysis includes an examination of the delivery system. Remember that services can be delivered by public or private agencies. In addition, publicly funded services can be provided by private institutions supervised by public agencies. For example, the publicly funded Medicaid program pays for long-term health care services that are often provided by private church-affiliated nursing facilities. Similarly, Medicaid-funded acute health care is often provided by private hospitals that are regulated by public agencies.

Services can be delivered in a variety of ways, for example, by social workers in a hospital, nursing facility, or family service center or by case managers working in a senior center. Clients can be trained to provide support to their peers, as is the case in many community mental health systems. In San Francisco, the public library hired a social worker to work with the many homeless people who seek refuge in the library during the day. Taking advantage of modern technology, social workers are now experimenting with delivering services such as case management, support groups, counseling, and family therapy online or via smart phones. In addition, certain benefits, such as Social Security payments, are routinely delivered through direct bank deposit.

As is true of the other topics we have examined, the delivery system can be analyzed from a strengths perspective. To do this, you need to consider whether the service delivery system is designed to build on assets that already exist in the community, such as schools, churches, medical services, and community centers. Alternatively, does the delivery system create separate structures for serving the target population? For example, separate schools and recreation facilities can be set up for people with disabilities, or, instead, existing schools and recreation facilities can be modified so that people with disabilities can use them. History has illustrated again and again that separate structures are inherently unequal.

Further, consider whether a service delivery system offers clients choice. For example, SNAP benefits allow people to shop in a variety of grocery stores. Alternatively, clients could be required to receive the service in only one place. Historically, people had to go to a surplus-food distribution site to receive publicly subsidized food benefits, and there were few options regarding the types of food provided, either.

Service delivery systems should be staffed by workers who reflect the ethnic diversity found within the target population, and services should be accessible to people of all ethnic backgrounds. For example, locating a program in an all-white neighborhood that does not have public transportation will limit access to that service by low-income people of color who do not have private transportation. Of course, policies can be designed to require service delivery systems that are not accessible to certain groups to change the way they provide services, perhaps by offering extended hours, providing in-home visits, or hiring multilingual staff. However, most policies focus change efforts on the individual clients rather than on problems in the service delivery system.

The most important question to ask when evaluating the effectiveness of a service delivery system is: "Can this system deliver services or benefits in a cost-effective manner that achieves the desired outcomes for clients?" It is crucial that we always return to the question of outcomes for clients. However, attention to outcomes must be coupled with attention to cost-effectiveness. Cost-effectiveness is critical to policy makers who will determine whether to continue the policy or program, and it is important in evaluating overall effectiveness. Particularly when budget crises are looming, if social workers have not considered cost-effectiveness of service delivery and do not have documentation of both cost-effectiveness and positive outcomes for clients, their initiatives will be in great danger. On the other hand, social workers who use their research skills to document program effectiveness can use that information to help maintain current funding and apply for additional funding.

Financing

Another vital element of any policy or program is the method by which it is financed. Chapter 4 provided a detailed discussion of funding for social welfare programs, including the difference between private and public funding and funding of programs by different levels of government. You need to consider the sources of funding when you analyze a social policy or program so that you may determine its stability and adequacy. When funding is not ensured from year to year, the result can be chaos for staff and clients. Entitlements have the most year-to-year stability. However, as seen with the abolition of AFDC in 1996, even publicly funded entitlements can be eliminated. Public funding generally provides more stable and adequate funding than do other sources, but recent crises around the debt ceiling and the sequester illustrate the potential volatility of even these public funds. In particular, because private funding is dependent on voluntary giving, stability and adequacy will fluctuate depending on the givers.

Recall that certain publicly funded programs, such as the Social Security retirement program, are based on the insurance principle and require prior contributions. Other public programs, such as TANF, are funded through general revenue appropriations that specify how tax dollars are to be spent. Some public programs are funded totally through taxes collected at the federal level, others are funded solely with state revenues, and still others are funded with a combination of federal and state monies. In the case of the programs funded through the McKinney-Vento Homeless Assistance Act, federal funds are made available to augment state, local, and private funds. In the climate of devolution, even local governments (cities and counties) are providing significant funding for social services, including public health, school-based supports, mental health, and housing initiatives.

Programs can also be funded by out-of-pocket payments made by the people who receive the service. For example, a religious denomination or a for-profit company might institute a child care program that requires parents to pay for the service out of pocket. Clients also may pay privately for counseling or for some rehabilitation services.

When analyzing financing strategies, it is also important to consider how providers of services are reimbursed or paid, whether by public or private sources. If service providers are paid the same amount regardless of the outcome for clients, then they have less incentive to attain the policy goals. For this reason, the reimbursement system should support the policy goals. Again, social workers should focus on the outcome for their clients. The HEARTH Act of 2009 provides an example of how reimbursement policy can promote desired outcomes. Because the purpose of the HEARTH Act is to reduce homelessness, the legislation stipulates that the Department of Housing and Urban Development will provide financial incentives to community agencies that implement strategies proven to reduce homelessness. These strategies include programs to rapidly rehouse homeless families and permanent supportive housing programs for people who experience chronic homelessness. We will discuss the impact of reimbursement systems on policy and program effectiveness in more detail in coming chapters.

Cost-Effectiveness and Outcomes

The effectiveness of policy goals, benefits and services, eligibility rules, service delivery systems, and financing for existing policies and programs must be judged in relationship to outcomes for clients. However, whether policy analysis is done to justify continuing a program or policy or to inform development of new policies and programs, cost-effectiveness will also be a major concern. In evaluating cost-effectiveness, you will hopefully be able to call on someone skilled at doing fiscal analysis to help put together cost calculations. Drawing on your background in social work, you can bring a focus on benefits of positive outcomes for your clients to this analysis. In Chapter 6, we will examine specific techniques that can be used to determine cost-effectiveness and document client outcomes.

CONCLUSION

Each element of the policy and program analysis framework explained above needs to be examined in order to determine how it contributes to overall effectiveness. Cost-effectiveness and outcomes for clients should be evaluated for each element. Such evaluation is very useful in determining the merit of a policy or program and in convincing policy makers that the program should continue to receive funding and attention or should be modified.

You can utilize the insights gained from the framework for analysis and the discussion of needs determination and claims-making presented in this chapter to evaluate any social policy or program. Your analysis may identify areas in which policies and programs can be improved, and it may also demonstrate that certain policies result in negative outcomes for clients. For example, eligibility rules that limit TANF payments to five years can most certainly create hardships for children whose parents have not been able to find stable, long-term employment and may contribute to child hunger. Efforts to address child obesity may lead some to believe that child hunger is no longer a problem, rather than helping policy makers to understand the connections between food insecurity and obesity. As a professional social worker, you will be expected to be capable of judging the merits of existing policies and programs, using research to identify promising alternative approaches, and advocating for more effective policies.

CATCHING UP WITH THE POLICY GROUP

Now, it is time to check in with the policy group introduced in Chapter 1. Like you, they have been working to learn how to research their clients' needs and think about policies and programs designed to meet those needs.

Tiffany, Alejandro, Kelli, and Alice have been working together in their policy group for the past several weeks. Although there have been some bumps along the way, their group has gelled and they are working well together for the most part. Their current assignment is to identify a social problem and a specific target population affected by that problem. The group knew their next assignment, the development of an advocacy action plan detailing strategies the group would use to bring about policy change regarding their identified social problem, would build on this assignment. This assignment is proving to be the most difficult yet for the group because they all have diverse interests, and narrowing their focus to one topic is a challenge.

EXHIBIT 5.1

The Policy Group

Alejandro had worried about the group reaching an impasse, like it had in his past experience with small group work, so he was working hard to bring the group to a consensus. It seemed that most of the group members were interested in child welfare. In fact, during their last group meeting, Kelli discussed an article she read about kids who were getting free or reduced price breakfast and lunch meals at school through the federal Healthy, Hunger-Free Kids Act but were going hungry at night and over the weekends because their parents did not have enough money to feed them. This led to discussion about the millions of children who are affected by food insecurity/hunger each year. Tiffany talked about some of the kids she had worked with whose parents had recently become unemployed and now were home-less. There was little food available and the families had no place to prepare food. Tiffany felt that the problem of child hunger fit in with her interest in working with teens, since adolescents were also included in this category, and Alice was pretty open as long as it was something that was not too time-intensive.

Finally, after much debate and discussion, the group reached consensus and decided they would focus on child hunger. Alejandro wanted to make sure that the group kept up its momentum going into the next assignment so he worked with the other team members to identify individual tasks they would complete by their next meeting. It was Kelli who had begun to really energize the group. At her field place-ment, she had been asked to interview children who were at risk of being removed from their home while her field supervisor worked with the parents. The kids told her they were often hungry, and she knew they were struggling in school. She was seeing the results of food insecurity first hand. While she kept the specifics of her work confidential, her discussion of child hunger was now much more personal and powerful, and the other students also developed a deeper understanding of the problem. Kelli volunteered to do an Internet search on child hunger and gather some statistics about how many kids nationwide, and in what demographics, are affected by this problem. Alejandro said he would look into statistics at the state level. Due to her work at the free health clinic last year, Tiffany thought she would be able to identify some advocacy organizations that were involved with child hunger and could make some phone calls to try to network with some individuals at these organizations. Finally, Alice agreed to look into federal and state policies that addressed child hunger such as SNAP and the Healthy, Hunger-Free Kids Act (which includes the national lunch program and breakfast programs). She was especially interested in whether there was research demonstrating that these programs significantly reduced child hunger and, if so, at what cost. Each group member did independent research using reliable data sources that were as objective as possible and brought back their findings to the group. They knew they were expected to make sense of what they had learned, integrate their findings, and use that information to make decisions about engaging in policy practice to influence social policy development.

MAIN POINTS

- There are many ways of viewing social problems or needs. The way in which the problem or need is framed will greatly influence the policy solutions developed.

- Understanding how a problem is defined and documented, focusing on how values, ideologies, and self-interest influence policy, and researching what causal theories have been developed based on the definition of social problems, provide the foundation for effective policy analysis.

- Available research that either supports or refutes these causal theories should be carefully evaluated, and social workers may conduct their own research or policy evaluation, in order to determine the full scope of the policy's impact on client needs and goals.

- Strengths-based policy analysis asks questions that seek to identify the needs of people as well as their strengths, goals, and resources in order to guide future policy and program development.

- The goals, strengths, and resources of the people who are experiencing the problem or need (the target population) should be clearly reflected in the definition of need.

- A strengths-based, solutions focused approach to policy analysis should include asking client groups about their vision of appropriate solutions early in the needs analysis process.

- Claims-making is the process of promoting recognition of a social condition as deserving of action by policy makers. In addition to recognized need, there must be a successful claim made for societal responsibility and action to meet that need before social policy will be enacted.

- Claims can be based on rights, comparative disadvantage, utility, and appeals for social justice.

- A strengths-based policy and program analysis framework focusing on the following areas can help determine effectiveness: policy or program goals, benefits or services provided, eligibility rules, service delivery system, and financing.

- Each element of the policy and program analysis framework discussed in this chapter should be evaluated using reliable data sources, in terms of its relationship to positive outcomes for our clients.

EXERCISES

1. Immigration policy influences the Sanchez family in multiple ways. Examine how people interested in immigration reform are engaging in claims-making to get policies changed.
   a. On what basis do immigration reform advocates assert that policies need to change—human rights, comparative disadvantage, utility, or social justice? Do different advocacy organizations rely on different primary claims? (Your instructors can provide weblinks for many of these organizations. These links are available in the Weblinks and Teaching Tips accessible to them under Instructor's Resources on this text's website [www.routledgesw.com/policy]).
   b. Are members of the target group actively involved in this process? Give examples.
2. In Riverton as well as in your city or town, people who are homeless may differ in many ways. People experiencing homelessness include, among others:
   - former foster children;
   - people with mental illness and other disabilities;
   - veterans;
   - two-parent families with children;
   - single parents with children; and,
   - people with long histories of substance abuse.
     a. How do you think public attitudes about providing resources to each of these groups may differ?
     b. What information on these different groups might you present to help increase public support for caring for people who are homeless?

    c. How do services for each of these groups need to differ in Riverton?

    d. Some people who are homeless may fit into several of the categories listed above. For example, a homeless person may be a former foster child and veteran and have a long history of substance abuse. Because of former military service, there are benefits accorded only to veterans. Find out how benefits and services available to the groups listed above differ.

3. Consider the Carla Washburn case. Even though it is common to see grandparents raising grandchildren, social policies related to benefits often do not reflect this reality.

    a. Do a web search for "advocacy grandparents raising grandchildren" to find out about groups that are trying to get increased benefits and recognition for these grandparents. Note what action they are taking, whether they are focusing on strengths as well as needs, and how they are constructing their claims for increased benefits and recognition.

    b. Advocates for children and for elders, respectively, sometimes rely on claims that are perceived to advantage their target population, in comparison to another. How do such tactics fail when confronting complex situations involving interrelated populations, as when grandparents are raising their children? What kinds of values, and claims stemming from these values, could simultaneously advance the needs of older adults and children, in a context such as this?

    c. Review the information you have on Carla Washburn. How do you think you might interest her in helping to get increased recognition of the needs of grandparents raising grandchildren? Construct a short news story about the need for more attention to grandparents raising grandchildren and illustrate how you could use Carla Washburn's story in claims-making for these grandparents.

4. Go to the RAINN interactive case that focuses on an online service delivery system. Public social policies allow public funds to be used to provide this service. As explained in this chapter, the most important question to ask when evaluating the effectiveness of a service delivery system is: "Can this system deliver services or benefits in a cost-effective manner that achieves the desired outcomes for clients?" Given the information provided in the interactive case consider if this program is effective when evaluated using these criteria.

5. The website of the Special Supplemental Nutrition Program for Women, Infants, and Children (WIC) has a section that illustrates how research has been done to determine cost-effectiveness and outcomes for clients. Go to the site, navigate to the Research section, and then examine this material to get a first-hand look at policy and program evaluations.

6. Look at editorials and letters to the editor in newspapers. Start with recent issues and blogs associated with your local paper. However, you may have to cast a broader net to complete this exercise. Try to find examples of different terms for the same people or events being used to evoke various values in debating an

issue of concern to social workers. Are there references to "children at risk" or "juvenile delinquents in training"? Is there focus on vagrants or unemployed mothers and fathers? Are there some issues, and some populations, receiving very little attention in these forums? Why do you think this is so? Identify the values being evoked and the morality appeal that is being made. As a social worker, what words could you craft to evoke the values you believe should undergird the discussion?

CHAPTER 6

Social Policy Development: Research and Policy Practice

If you don't like the way the world is, you change it. You have an obligation to change it. You just do it one step at a time.

Marian Wright Edelman

While there is no guarantee that democracies will act rationally in formulating their social policies, it is also abundantly clear that they cannot even be expected to do so unless they are made aware of the full implications of the choices available to them.

Eveline M. Burns

Action indeed is the sole medium of expression for ethics.

Jane Addams

POLICY DEVELOPMENT MIGHT SEEM LIKE A MYSTERIOUS PROCESS, however, it is a process you can come to understand and even influence. Policy development is the process by which policies are created and implemented in order to meet an identified need. The purpose of policy practice is to influence this process. As we discussed in the previous chapter, policies can be designed to build on strengths and reflect the goals of the client group. You can play a role in designing or revising social policy. In fact, you are expected to do so. Ability to engage in research to understand not just your clients and their needs but also the effects of different policy approaches, in order to influence policy, is a key skill you will need to develop.

In this chapter, we first explore the process of policy development in detail, examining the different steps in that process. We then focus explicitly on the ways in which social workers can intervene in that process. Many of the ideas on policy practice we will discuss in this chapter were briefly introduced in Chapter 1. In addition, we will explore various ways that social workers engaged in policy practice can use the strengths principles discussed in the previous chapter to shape social policy. If you think a policy is serving your clients poorly, then you can help change it.

Effective social work involves a variety of skills, including individual counseling or therapy, coalition building, program development, and policy practice. Your work to help a specific client may require skills in relationship building and also policy practice. As a social worker, it is important to guard against focusing on only the psychological components of clients' pain and ignoring the political and economic factors that contribute to clients' problems. This is not an "either/or" proposition. Social workers have traditionally recognized that helping clients involves a tool kit of skills appropriate to both work with individuals and advocacy for policy reform (Middleman and Goldberg-Wood, 1990). In fact, it is often work with individual clients that makes social workers aware of the need for policy change and fuels passion for policy practice. This is one of the greatest assets that social workers, distinct from some other voices in the policy arena, bring to policy practice. When you do a dual assessment of your clients, that is, when you examine the political and economic, as well as the psychological factors that affect them, you will often see a pattern among your clients that points to the need for policy reform. You will begin to recognize the connections between clinical issues such as the number of "presenting problems" and unmet needs that stem from the lack of policy or from neglect of populations.

For example, as a social worker in schools, you may see increasing numbers of children who have problems in school and are homeless. You will likely be working with families around behavioral issues and providing referrals to help with rehousing. However, it is important to also work to see that policies contributing to the growing problem of homelessness are addressed, such as policies in the community that prioritize funds for homeless shelters over funds for rapid rehousing initiatives. You may also be able to help bring about changes within the school system and other institutions, in order to realize superior outcomes for your clients. You are on the front line and you can make sure what you see comes to the attention of policy makers. Policy makers need to know how much the numbers of homeless children are increasing and to recognize the impact of homelessness on school performance. School policies and programs may need to change so that there is an opportunity for children who are homeless to have access to a shower and clean clothes before starting their school day. Your community may need to develop policies and programs to promote rapid rehousing and prioritize families with children for rehousing. State and federal policies and programs also need to improve, not just in the area of homelessness, but also by addressing larger issues around job creation, family income supports and home financing.

You are not expected to take on all these policy issues. You are expected to consider how these issues influence your clients and to take action, alongside your clients, where you can. Although you obviously would not ask a family grappling with homelessness to focus their energies primarily on trying to change homelessness policy, it may be that as their situation stabilizes; they could contribute to reform efforts. Engaging in policy change can be a way for oppressed individuals to experience their own power, resulting not only in changes to policies and systems, but also to improvements in their individual well-being. It is important to recognize your clients' strengths and ask how they might contribute to efforts to bring about more just policies and programs. Although you will likely have a very full schedule completing your primary job responsibilities, as a social worker, you are expected to carve out some time for this kind of policy practice. You can also use your communication skills to push for policies and practices within your employing organization that facilitate your success in this critical area of social work responsibility. This chapter on policy practice will provide you with the tools necessary to shape policies that promote social justice for our clients.

STEPS IN POLICY DEVELOPMENT

We have already examined some of the steps in policy development in the context of policy analysis. The policy development process differs from the policy analysis process in that emphasis shifts from analyzing each element of an existing policy to actually engaging in the process of developing new policy or revising existing policy. However, an analysis of policy alternatives is part of the policy development process. Therefore, you can apply the ability to analyze need and existing policies, which you developed in Chapter 5, to understand policy development. In addition, sometimes social policy analysis will lead social workers to take a position that opposes any significant changes to existing policy, which can lead to using some of the same policy development skills to argue for preservation of the status quo. In periods of retrenchment at both the federal and state level such as we are now experiencing, this kind of policy practice is especially crucial if we are to retain the safety net programs upon which we all rely.

Quick Guide 4 provides a brief summary of how what you have learned thus far can be used in policy analysis and policy development. It can also guide you in doing the research necessary for effective policy practice. Some of the elements of the guide are explored in detail in this chapter. Quick Guides are designed so that they can be copied and kept where they can provide an easily accessible reminder of key steps in policy practice. Again, it is expected that policy practice will become a regular part of your daily work, and tools like these Quick Guides can be valuable aids as you approach your social work career.

QUICK GUIDE 4   Policy Analysis and Development Overview

This quick guide synthesizes key content on policy analysis and development. It provides a brief overview designed to remind you of key points to consider as you begin your policy practice.

Background/Context
- How do historical policy approaches to this social problem/need shape current policy?
- What was the cultural milieu at the time these approaches were taken? Is the current political and economic context the same or different?
- What were the group interests, and who were the key players involved in developing these historical policies?
- Is there any reason to think that historical approaches would work better or worse today?
- Did this historical policy approach build on the strengths of the target population?
- Alternatively, was it predicated on a pathology or deficit view of the people to be helped?
- How have definitions of the social problem/need and policy approaches changed over time?

Understanding the Social Problem/Need
- How is the problem or need defined and documented?
- How have values and self-interest shaped the definition and documentation?
- What causal theories have been developed based on the definition of social problems and what consequences are ascribed to the problem so defined?
- What is the evidence supporting these causal theories?
- How many people are affected and how?

Policy Analysis
- What are the policy or program goals and what is the logic link between the goals and positive outcomes for clients?
- What are the benefits or services provided?
- What are the eligibility rules?
- How are services/benefits delivered?
- How are services/benefits financed and reimbursed?
- What evidence is there that each element of the policy and program analysis framework examined above leads to positive outcomes for the target/client population, is cost effective, and sustainable?
- Is the policy politically, socially, and economically feasible?
- Are key social work values such as self-determination and social justice incorporated into the policy?
- How is the target/client population involved in evaluating the policy/program?
- What improvements are needed?

Policy Development
- Who is the target/client population and what specific need are you targeting?
- What are policy options and has the target population been involved in defining the need and policy options?
- What specific policy changes are being advocated and has the target population been involved in determining needed policy changes?
- How can a claim be made for the need for this policy change?
- What strategies will get the need for this policy change on the agenda of policy makers?
- What actions will be necessary to get this policy enacted and how can the target population be involved?
- Once implemented, how can you help ensure that the policy will be evaluated and improved based on client outcomes?

The list presented below provides a more detailed overview of the components of the policy development process in the Quick Guide. Each component includes information on how the strengths perspective can be integrated into that part of the policy development process. We will examine these components in greater detail to prepare you to engage in policy practice.

- **Define needs or social problems and strengths in partnership with clients.** The strengths perspective views definitions as negotiated, not fixed and imposed on others. Include the perspectives of the target group in defining goals and strengths as well as in identifying needs and structural barriers to meeting needs.

- **Document needs, strengths, and goals in partnership with clients.** Measure the amount of needs, the dimensions of structural barriers, and the clients' strengths and goals, including potential solutions.

- **Identify initial policy goals in partnership with clients.** Privilege the clients' goals; that is, seek out information on your clients' goals for themselves and give them careful consideration.

- **Engage in claims-making.** Claims-making is based on the right to self-determination and social justice necessary for people to meet their goals. Ideally potential client-generated goals/solutions are included.

- **Negotiate definition of policy goals.** Work with policy makers to ensure that they include the clients' goals when developing policy goals.

- **Legitimize policy goals with the public.** Building public support is key. Publicize information on the opportunities and resources necessary for people to meet their goals. Frame policy goals to align with key social values, and work to find common ground with important constituencies.

- **Formulate policy alternatives that meet established goals in partnership with clients.** Identify ways in which barriers to reaching goals are currently overcome by clients (strengths) and through programs (best practice). Formulate policy informed by consumer collaboration. In addition, assess workability at this stage. Evaluate the various elements of the proposed policy alternatives using the policy analysis framework presented in Chapter 5.

- **Develop, enact, and implement the policy or program in partnership with clients.** Policy and program design and implementation should be informed by consumer involvement.

- **Evaluate outcomes in partnership with clients.** Evaluation and assessment should emphasize client outcomes and client feedback to improve policy.

It might help you to grasp the importance of these steps, if we consider an example of a social policy developed without incorporating the elements of this process. A group of state legislators developed a policy proposal to require that all TANF recipients undergo regular drug testing in order to receive their benefits. However, they certainly did not discuss their proposed policy with welfare advocacy groups. In fact, they did not research who was on TANF in their state and did not realize that many grandparents raising grandchildren were receiving TANF. When advocates for grandparents raising grandchildren contacted the media and made it clear they found this proposed legislation unacceptable, it was defeated. These advocates asserted that grandparents who needed financial help when they were stepping up to care for their grandchildren, should not have to "pee in a cup" to get that help. The policy makers who proposed mandatory drug testing had little idea of the strengths or needs of TANF recipients such as these grandparents. They did not consider engaging them in the policy development process. The time and effort they spent on this failed legislation did nothing to improve the effectiveness of TANF and certainly did not improve outcomes for the target population.

Determining Need and Making Claims

Determining needs and making claims based on those needs form the foundation for the policy development process. Chapter 5 detailed ways in which needs were defined and claims made for existing policies. This chapter highlights what can be added when developing new social policy or reforming existing policy using the strengths perspective. Adopting a strengths-based approach enables policy makers to shift their focus from what has typically been done in the past to alternative strategies. One example of how to shift focus is to identify assets in the community to aid in policy development. Most impoverished communities have been the subject of numerous needs assessments that emphasize deficits, such as unemployment rates, low rates of homeownership, school dropout rates, and crime rates. However, their many assets, such as community associations, businesses, agencies, and community leaders, have not been assessed as carefully as their needs; neither have the myriad barriers that prevent members of the target group from meeting their needs and accomplishing their goals. For example, in low-income communities, access to banking services, including small business loans, is often limited. Assessing needs, strengths, and barriers provides information that supports a claim for assistance in overcoming barriers that other people might not face.

People engaging in needs assessment typically identify initial policy goals early in the needs assessment and claims-making processes because these individuals generally have some idea of the types of policies that they expect to champion. For example, if civic leaders have noted a lack of after-school activities and increasing gang membership, they may propose a policy to provide funding for after-school programs through the park and recreation departments. It is important to scrutinize policy goals from the beginning to ensure that they include the goals of the client

EXHIBIT 6.1

Social Work Students across the Country Regularly Engage in the Claims-Making Process on Behalf of Their Clients

A student at a university in the southwest worked to increase public awareness of the homelessness crisis in his state. He helped to organize a demonstration on the grounds of the state capitol where over *200 people camped overnight in tents or cardboard boxes.* He also helped to arrange a photo exhibit and presented information on homelessness at legislative committee meetings in support of a bill that *would provide $20 million for transitional housing.*

To learn more about social work students involved in policy practice, visit the website of Influencing State Policy.

group. In the case of the after-school program, asking the young people in the community directly about their needs—about preferred location and activities and involving them in the policy development process—will make it much more likely that any program that is implemented will be well attended. We will consider methods for making these assessments in the policy practice segment of this chapter.

Groups Involved in Needs Determination and Claims-Making   Major policies are rarely crafted quickly. Rather, they generally emerge from a process of development. Typically, there are a variety of provider groups, client groups, and advocacy groups who have identified needs, are engaging in claims-making, and are trying to provide direction for policy development. These groups may be operating independently and even in opposition to one another. Particular groups may have identified specific policy makers to champion their cause. For example, in the legislative arena, an advocacy group for people with developmental disabilities may be working closely with a senator who has a son who is developmentally disabled. Similarly, a service provider group that owns independent living facilities may have the ear of a legislator who formerly owned such facilities. If it is possible to get a number of groups or stakeholders to agree on a message and a policy goal, effectiveness can be amplified. Similarly, when it is possible to get even all the social work organizations in one state to focus their attention and provide a unified message on an issue, it is much more likely that issue will be addressed.

On the executive or agency side, a retired inspector of independent living facilities may now be lobbying on behalf of a client group with his former agency colleagues. These former agency colleagues will likely be involved in drafting any legislation that involves such facilities. There may also be researchers associated with national organizations such as the Child Welfare League of America (CWLA) or with universities that have conducted research on effective practices for people with developmental disabilities and are publicizing information on client needs and making recommendations for policy initiatives. When you examine research on policies and programs, be sure to scrutinize who did the research and who funded it. Consider whether this research is credible before incorporating it into your work, and be prepared to answer questions about the legitimacy of your data from those whose perspectives differ.

Legislators bring varying amounts of expertise on different subjects to policy making. For example, a legislator may be very familiar with transportation needs because of his career in the trucking business but might know little about social services. In such cases, legislators turn to people they know who possess expertise on the subject. However, they receive input on a huge variety of policy initiatives. Legislators are being pressed to enact agricultural policy, tax reform, water standards, educational reform, and many other initiatives of importance to their constituents. Pleas for increases in social services will have to vie with many competing claims for the legislator's attention. You and potentially your professors who do work in a specific policy arena can become involved in educating legislators. This is distinct from lobbying and is generally allowed in most job settings. You provide information to the legislator on upcoming legislation and let them know where they can find additional credible information. Of course, your contact will work best if this is not the first time your legislator has laid eyes on you. Go in and talk to your legislators or show up when they are making a presentation and make a point of introducing yourself so they know who you are and have formed a beginning relationship with you.

The Legislative Agenda Fundamentally, claims makers who want legislation enacted must compete to get on the legislative agenda. The term agenda, as used here, means "the list of subjects or problems to which government officials, and people outside of government closely associated with those officials, are paying some serious attention at any given time" (Kingdon, 2003, p. 3). Claims for attention from policy makers must compete with many other claims that may be more compelling. The policy practice section of this chapter contains a detailed discussion of methods for garnering policy makers' attention to your clients' needs and goals.

In many cases, the groups involved in claims-making described earlier might already be considering areas in which policy making is needed. They might even be in the process of drafting legislation. In a sense, these issues already are on the legislators' agenda. However, in order for the issue to progress to the point that a bill is introduced and acted upon, it somehow will need to move to what is termed the "decision agenda" (Kingdon, 2003). We will explore a real-life example of getting on the agenda later in the chapter.

A problem or need must press on the policy maker in some way in order to attract sufficient attention to move to the decision agenda. For example, if the media are covering a problem or need and advocating for change, then there may be pressure for change. Public opinion also influences the policy agenda. A crisis may help focus attention. For example, when the state's news media report that an older nursing home resident wandered away and died of exposure due to inadequate staff oversight, a public clamor for more stringent regulation of nursing facility staffing levels might arise. At this point, perceptions can be influenced by providing policy makers with information on the need for more adequate staffing. In fact, if specialists have accumulated research about the need and best practice, this may be the time that the information will be used.

Elections have an influence on which issues move to the decision-making agenda. For instance, a politician who promises to work to restrict access to abortion will press to get attention for reforming abortion regulations if elected. Similarly, constituents who contribute financially to a legislator's campaign or otherwise help the legislator get elected will generally receive greater attention to legislative issues they want on the agenda than other people or groups.

The process by which a policy issue moves to the decision-making agenda influences the resulting policy. For example, public outrage may prompt rapid action. However, if the public is convinced that an emergency exists, then policy changes to deal with the specific emergency may be enacted quickly without sufficient attention to underlying problems.

It should be clear by now that policy development is not a technical, step-by-step process. Rather, it tends to be messy and inexact. Policy development is very much influenced by the contexts which surround it—economically, politically, and socially—which is why this text began with consideration of the ways in which these forces have shaped social policy throughout our history. Many individuals and groups participate in the process. When input from these different groups converges at a time when policy makers are open to considering initiatives in that particular area, then policy can be developed or changed. The social work advocates, who over the long term will be most successful in influencing social policy, are those who learn to "read" this landscape and to adjust their policy practice responses accordingly.

Initial Steps in Policy Development: A Summary   To review and help you understand the policy development process, the components we have discussed thus far are listed below:

- Need must be determined. Information on strengths, needs, goals, and assets of the target group can also inform policy development. Initial policy goals are typically formulated during this stage.

- A claim for attention must be developed.

- Claims makers must get access to key policy makers.

- Pressure and direction for policy change from a sufficient number of key actors must converge to place the issue on the agenda.

- There must be a window of opportunity when other, more pressing policy issues are not higher on the decision agenda. At this point, if there is sufficient consensus, new policy will be made or current policy reformed.

Finally, remember that the policy development process is not linear. For example, a person who will become a claims maker may have access to a key policy maker before the claim is developed. In fact, that access might be the reason why that individual will be asked to help out. For example, family members of legislators and other elected officials frequently are asked to help promote education or conservation initiatives.

Crafting Policy Goals

Crafting policy goals includes negotiating what policy goals should be pursued with policy makers and legitimizing policy goals with the public. Once goals are determined, various policy alternatives that meet the established goals can be formulated and evaluated. The ideas of key actors about potential ways to meet needs and reach goals typically emerge as the need-identification and claims-making processes develop. Remember, key actors are those individuals and groups who hold significant, although by no means equal, power to influence policy making by virtue of their position, political influence, or expertise. They include elected officials, agency staff, advocacy groups, and researchers. Of course, the target group for the policy also should be recognized as having expertise by virtue of their lived experience. However, this expertise is often not acknowledged. The goals and ideas of clients are less likely to be heard unless advocates work to get attention for their perspectives. As a social worker, your efforts to develop policy goals that promote social justice should include attention to getting the voices of your clients heard.

Additionally, policy makers at the local, state, and national levels might be working on the same policy issues, largely unaware of initiatives under way at other levels. All of these groups may be defining policy goals very differently. These diverse ideas and definitions of policy goals may surface during the policy development process.

Achieving Consensus   The diverse goals of key actors must be melded into a sufficient consensus to get new policies enacted. This can be difficult. For example, groups pressing for more services for people with developmental disabilities may all agree on the general policy goal of more public support for these people. However, some factions might advocate more funds for independent living focused group homes, whereas other factions favor family-directed care available in the home.

Often, interviewing key actors and policy makers about their views of the problem and the particular policy options they are considering makes it possible to identify policy goals and options on which consensus may be reached. For example, when research companies are hired by states to help craft policies, they typically conduct extensive interviews with key actors early in the process. They particularly target stakeholders, those people who likely will experience either substantial gain or loss as a result of the policy change. Although tight budgets in many states are curtailing spending on research, advocacy groups can use some of these same techniques. People working to craft policy goals can perform a thorough literature review and become knowledgeable about potential goals and solutions, and they can also contact key stakeholders influential with legislators who may suggest solutions and then become invested in seeing a policy initiative implemented. This strategy may make passage of the policy much more likely. Although the major purpose of such interviews is to listen to stakeholders, these interviews can also be used to provide information about how members of the client group understand their needs and define their goals. My experience, and the experience of many seasoned policy makers I interviewed, is that policy proposals that actually get implemented usually incorporate a variety of ideas that one person or even a small group of people would not have developed. It is easier to craft policy goals and options around which consensus may develop when you are familiar with stakeholders' opinions and goals.

In addition, achieving consensus on policy goals is easier if the goals are general. For example, most policy makers would agree that it is important to have healthy babies. Conflict more commonly arrives at the point of determining the best ways in which to achieve that goal. For example, details such as the type and amount of assistance their mothers should receive will be more contentious. As we have discussed, self-interest, wealth and political power, values, and social movements can all influence policy goals. In addition, public opinion influences the passage of social policy. Although social policies are sometimes passed with little public attention, widespread public opposition to policy goals can help defeat a social policy. At times when obtaining widespread consensus might not be possible or realistic, amassing enough public support may be critical in getting policies approved or enacted. Groups attempting to stop health reform in 2009 worked very hard to stir up opposition, but advocacy groups and the media involved in the claims-making process helped to legitimize this policy goal with the public. As with many major social welfare reforms, large swathes of the public remain skeptical of health reform and additional work will be needed to increase public support as the policy making process, including regulatory development and implementation, continues.

Utilizing the Strengths Perspective   The strengths perspective mandates that efforts to develop public consensus and legitimize policy goals include assertive outreach to client groups, whose priorities for social policy development should be central to the process. For a review of the strengths perspective, go to the website of the Strengths Institute at the University of Kansas, School of Social Welfare (www.socwel.ku.edu). Social workers engaged in policy development have many options regarding the best ways in which to engage these client groups. Public hearings are often convened to get feedback on proposed policies and to lend legitimacy to the policies that are ultimately passed. Clients could provide feedback, but without support such as transportation and help in preparation, they might be unable to attend these hearings. The media may be open to presenting clients' perspectives on their needs and the most effective ways to help them meet those needs but often lack insight into these perspectives. Social workers can help clients make their voices heard by removing these barriers and by encouraging members of the media to get the whole story.

Values: Examining the Feasibility of Policy Alternatives

A great many potential solutions to problems may be vying for expression as policy goals and implementation strategies. It is much like a group making stew against a backdrop of social, economic, and political factors that are influencing the participants. To ensure that the resulting policies can actually address the policy goals and the targeted social problem, feasibility or workability of proposed solutions must be considered. People attempting to develop policies try to craft a workable solution and then convince policy makers to support it. Social work values can guide our examination of the workability of policy alternatives.

The following elements should be considered in determining whether a solution is workable.

- *Expected outcomes*. First and foremost, can the proposed solution realistically be expected to help the target population reach their goals and fulfill their needs? (Because of the power of unintended consequences, some proposed solutions could actually make things worse for the target group.)

- *Unintended Outcomes*. Under this component consider unintended outcomes such as whether the proposal, if enacted, could harm the environment, and decrease general public welfare. You should also take into account the opportunity cost, as pursuing any given approach will inevitably mean fewer resources available to consider alternative solutions.

- *Value base*. Are the values supported by this proposal consistent with social work values and the strengths perspective?

- *Level of risk*. Is the proposed solution low-risk? Is it likely to succeed? What is the probability of risking resources and leaving the target population worse off?

- *Ease of implementation*. How difficult would it be to develop an adequate and accessible benefit or service delivery system? How much would the existing service delivery system have to change in order to accommodate this policy change, as opposed to proposals that can largely build on the existing infrastructure?

- *Cost*. Can the policy be funded with existing resources or with grants that are likely to be secured? If a tax increase would be needed to fund the proposal, what is the likelihood it would be passed?

- *Flexibility.* Is the policy flexible enough to withstand environmental stressors like economic downturns, to provide some choice to members of the target group who will not all have exactly the same needs, and to address additional societal goals important to the citizenry?

- *Communicability.* Can the policy be easily communicated to policy makers, the public, and the target population? Is there likely to be considerable buy-in regarding the viability of this approach?

- *Likelihood of passage.* What is the likelihood that the policy will be passed? Are there sufficient numbers of policy makers, allies, and constituent groups that would support or could be persuaded to support its passage? How strong is the opposition?

Here is an example of how to use these criteria to consider a policy designed to improve the performance of low-income children in school and, ultimately, to increase their graduation rate. Parents and the larger community are united in supporting this goal. In addition, many members of the target group want this outcome. Social justice, equal opportunity, and concern for future prosperity are values that motivate interest in increasing high school graduation rates. Community activists therefore proposed a policy to provide full-day preschool programs at existing schools. Research indicates that if these programs are correctly implemented and made accessible, they will lead to higher graduation rates. Research further reveals that such programs are cost-effective and that state and federal funding as well as foundation money may be available. The proposal is low-risk in that many communities have already successfully implemented such programs. In addition, the preschool classes will be conducted at existing schools. Allowing each school the flexibility to decide how best to reach parents in its area, to respond to unique ethnic and cultural issues, and to help support the program will increase the likelihood of sustained success. Such an approach will address criteria concerned with *expected outcomes*, *value base*, *level of risk*, *costs*, and *ease of implementation*.

The concept of all-day preschool is easily communicated to parents and the media. Widespread parental support for the proposal makes its passage more likely. However, some taxpayers oppose any new school program that will increase property taxes. There is also some opposition from those who argue that the problem of low levels of high school graduation is an immediate one that should be addressed on a shorter time frame, instead of with long-term investments. Therefore, securing federal, state, or foundation support for the program will be crucial to obtaining the approval of the school board. This proposal meets the criteria of *communicability* and *likelihood of passage*, provided the always difficult issue of funding can be successfully negotiated. In coming to judgment, this proposal appears to be workable and one that social workers could support.

In contrast, a policy that does not fit the *values and strengths perspective* criteria is one that would require parents to attend parenting classes conducted by a trained social worker as a condition of allowing their children into the preschool program. The assumption behind such a policy is that low-income people are deficient parents. Clearly, this is not a strengths-based approach. In fact, voluntary rather than required participation for clients is typically a hallmark of strengths-based policy approaches. Therefore, offering voluntary parenting classes, based on parents' self-identified interests, and maximizing the opportunities for parents to become involved in their children's education and to advance their own educational goals, is very important and would be in keeping with the strengths perspective. These parents would be provided resources and opportunities to help their children to succeed that may have previously been unavailable to them. For example, they can be taught how to prepare for and participate effectively in parent–teacher conferences and school and community meetings. A voluntary policy that strongly supports parental involvement would be considered workable based on the criteria discussed above.

If a policy proposal does not fit these criteria, then it may be eliminated from consideration. In some cases, however, a policy proposal that is generally distasteful is presented to motivate decision makers to compromise and pass the preferred policy before the alternative policy gains momentum. For example, citizen groups might put forward a proposal to abolish free after-school programs for all junior high school students in a district in order to save tax dollars. However, the policy they actually favor is to require middle- and upper-income families to pay a fee for their children to use the service. Nevertheless, they propose abolishing the program in the hope that people who oppose any change in the program will believe the very existence of the program is threatened and consequently will be willing to compromise. It should be emphasized, though, that these tactics can reduce the ability of client groups to fully participate in policy development, as they might be uncomfortable advocating an approach they do not support, and as professional organizations are not always careful to include client groups in these kinds of strategy deliberations.

Finally, when examining the workability of policy alternatives, an approach should not be rejected because there is as yet no evidence it will work. An approach may be feasible, but untested. In fact, an original idea, particularly one emerging from the client group, could have great promise. It is more difficult to work out the details of piloting an untested approach, but it may be a much more effective strategy when the approach arises from people familiar with the nuances of the state or community's needs, strengths, goals, and resources. Some of our most cherished social policies today—Social Security, universal public education, Medicare—began as policy innovations that, over time, demonstrated the potential for significant positive outcomes.

Enacting and Implementing Policy

The next phase of the policy development process focuses on how policies get enacted and are subsequently implemented. Steps in this process will vary depending on who has been given authority to enact policy. Legislators at the state and federal levels are typically the policy makers we consider although, increasingly, social policy is also made at the local level, as city and county governments make decisions regarding education, health and mental health, and civil rights policies, in particular. In Chapter 4, we examined the steps necessary to pass legislation. However, the legislative branch is not the only branch that makes policy. As discussed in earlier chapters, the executive and judicial branches also make policy. The religious organization, corporation, or agency where you may be employed also makes many policies that govern your work and the ways in which clients interact with the agency.

The specific processes of determining need, making claims, and enacting policy will vary somewhat, depending on the setting, but the concepts are essentially the same. Need must be recognized and defined, claims-making must take place, and the issue must gain sufficient attention from policy makers to warrant action.

Generally, once a policy is approved, money must be appropriated to implement it. Many times, legislation has limited impact because the separate process of appropriating funds was not understood and successfully negotiated so that adequate funding was made available. The segment of this chapter that focuses on policy practice provides specific strategies to employ when pressing for policy enactment.

After a policy is enacted, agency staff will be charged with implementing the policy and/or establishing a program. It is at this stage that the details of who will be eligible, how the benefit or service will be delivered, and how service providers will be paid are worked out. If a state or federal agency is involved in implementing the policy, often a manual of rules and regulations—or procedures—is developed. Some local and private agencies also will codify their implementation plans in this way. If you are involved with a service agency, you can best understand the specifics of policy implementation by examining the written manuals as well as discussing the program with staff members. You also can research how the rules and regulations were written.

Legislation is seldom so specific that administrators know exactly what is to be done. For example, legislation may be passed giving a state agency the authority to license and regulate child care providers. However, the legislation might not specify the number of infants who can be cared for or the type of space that is appropriate. In such a case, a series of meetings with legislators, providers, and parents might be held to develop written rules and regulations. Many times, federal, state, and even local agencies may be required to engage in a rule-making process in which public input is gathered and must be considered. In other instances, a few staff people or perhaps only one staff person develops guidelines for implementation that might or might not be written. Some agencies have few, if any, written guidelines for implementing policies and programs.

Client groups can and should be part of the implementation process. Their input should be sought when rules are developed. Such participation promotes service delivery that is sensitive to the ethnic backgrounds of client groups. Often, clients can become service providers. Additionally, community agencies with which clients are already comfortable can be used to provide services.

Social Policy Research: Evaluating Policy Outcomes

Once enacted, programs developed to implement the policies should be evaluated, so that future policy development can focus on reforms if necessary and so that advocates are equipped with data about the efficacy of a given policy approach. Evaluation involves determining whether the goals of the policy were accomplished and the identified problems or needs were met or at least reduced. From a strengths perspective, clients should be part of the evaluation process, the evaluation should examine outcomes for clients, and, if possible, clients' views on the effectiveness of the program should be brought to the attention of the program administrators and policy makers. Further, it is important to be alert to potential interactions of the policy or programs with other policies and programs. For example, the success of a program promoting employment for low-income mothers can result in premature and disastrous loss of housing subsidies, as mothers' incomes rise above the eligibility threshold for housing assistance. Unless the interaction of these two programs is evaluated and steps are taken to integrate the two programs, clients are less likely to experience positive outcomes.

Evaluating policies and programs is a very important type of research for social workers. Even if you are not involved in actually conducting formal program evaluation research, examining the effectiveness of the policies and programs you will help implement is part of your professional practice. You can find examples of program and policy evaluations in academic journals, social work professional literature, think tanks, advocacy organizations and professional societies. When using information from advocacy organizations or think tanks affiliated with political parties or specific ideological viewpoints, be particularly vigilant in critically evaluating the information for possible bias. In addition, you can find out how the agencies where you may work evaluate policies and programs and become familiar with the results. One place to start in evaluating a program is by looking at whether the agency is actually implementing the policy as prescribed in written documents such as the policy manual. A student with a field placement in an agency working to make birth control more widely available evaluated her agency as being less effective because some thoroughly tested birth control devices could not be paid for by her agency. When reviewing the agency regulations, she found a birth control device that was being denied to low-income clients could actually be provided under agency regulations, and staff had simply never checked what was possible. Work to change policy and practice at the agency level when evaluation research points to areas needing improvement can be highly effective, but it also must be approached carefully because the stakes are high. Your position in the agency and your future chances to make a positive difference in clients' lives can be affected. You need to think through the potential impact of your activism. As a student, you should consult your field placement supervisor to determine how best to proceed.

Providing evaluative information to policy makers is a crucial component of policy development. When there is pressure for changing a policy, change is often made without knowledge of the results of evaluations of current programs. In fact, in some cases, evaluations might not have been completed because program staff did not think it was important or because resources to conduct an evaluation were never appropriated.

However, credible evaluations can help save effective programs and identify strategies for improving less effective programs. Unless policy and program evaluations are carefully conducted and the outcomes are used by professionals and publicized to policy makers, the development of more effective policies and programs will be hampered.

Although policy makers may try to anticipate outcomes, policies frequently generate unanticipated consequences, defined as unexpected events that result from the implementation of a policy. A policy can make things better for the general population but worse for the target group, or better or worse for some other groups (Ellis, 2003). For example, building a housing project for older adults with low incomes may involve tearing down existing housing that serves low-income families. In this case, the unanticipated consequence will be an increase in the number of homeless families. Of course, these consequences could have been foreseen if policy makers had developed outcome scenarios to try to determine displacement effects prior to implementing the policy. Other unanticipated consequences may include higher or lower costs than expected. Similarly, one policy or program could have an unintended effect on eligibility or effectiveness of other policies. For example, when a family receives a lump sum refund under the Earned Income Tax Credit program, they might have to spend it immediately or risk losing eligibility for programs such as Medicaid which have very low asset limits for eligibility. In order to deal with this negative program interaction, policy makers are now developing savings programs for low-income families that exempt a higher level of assets when eligibility is reassessed, so that families are able to weather emergencies such as unexpected car repair costs and perhaps even begin to save for other goals. Other states, in an effort to promote long-term economic security among those receiving public assistance, have eliminated asset tests entirely from programs such as the Supplemental Nutrition Assistance Program (SNAP) or Medicaid. Potential policy interactions should be carefully considered when thinking through policy options. However, no matter how carefully policy results are anticipated, there will likely be unexpected consequences. It is important to have contingency plans and to monitor implementation so that unanticipated outcomes can be discovered as early as possible and a plan for dealing with the unanticipated outcome can be formulated.

SOCIAL WORK POLICY PRACTICE AND THE ECOLOGICAL PERSPECTIVE

Having examined the various steps in the policy development process, we now address the question: What is the role of the social worker in this process? More to the point, what can your role be? Remember, the NASW *Code of Ethics* directs us to engage in policy practice in order to put our values into action. Analysis is necessary but not sufficient. Social workers are expected to take action to bring about policy changes that benefit their clients. Engaging in policy practice means making "efforts to influence the development, enactment, implementation, modification, or assessment of social policies, primarily to ensure social justice and equal access to basic social goods" (Barker, 2003, p. 330). People across the political spectrum can engage in efforts to change policy: liberals, conservatives, death penalty advocates, health care advocates and advocates of mercy killing and so on. Social workers can learn a great deal about the successful strategies and tactics used to shape policy from different political and professional perspectives.

However, this book focuses specifically on *social work* policy practice, that is, work to change social policy that influences your clients and your profession and that is informed by the *Code of Ethics* (Jansson, 2011). In the interest of brevity, I will simply use the term *policy practice* to refer to social work policy practice. This section will consider how social workers can help develop social policy, and it will examine how the ecological perspective can inform policy practice.

Although every social worker is directed by the *Code of Ethics* to engage in policy practice at some level, certain social workers have full-time policy practice jobs such as lobbying, serving as a legislative aide, working for think tanks and advocacy organizations, or rule making in public social service agencies. Others in public and private social service agencies may be designated to monitor legislation that affects their agencies and to testify at legislative committee hearings or mobilize supporters in support of, or opposition to, policy changes. Many social service agencies realize too late that they need to keep track of changes in relevant legislation if they are to stay in business. Some social workers believe that if they work to do good that is enough, and the rest will take care of itself. Unfortunately, many times there are people interested in cutting funding for social services willing to invest their time, money, and labor, and their efforts win the day.

Like most social workers, you will likely be providing direct service. You will have a very busy work life in addition to home and community responsibilities. As one person, what can you do? The next part of this chapter focuses on the options you have for becoming involved in policy practice. We will use the elements of policy development to identify places where you can help shape this process. You will be equipped with beginning tools you can use to influence social policy. When you see foster children shunted through multiple foster homes, or when you see old people die alone with inadequate care, then hopefully you will not feel powerless but, rather, passionate about carving out time for policy practice. You will also have some concrete ideas about how to proceed and how to integrate policy practice into the way in which you approach your work, instead of viewing it as an entirely separate endeavor.

The ecological perspective used in your practice classes provides insight into the policy practice process. The ecological perspective in social work focuses on the ways in which people and their environments influence, change, and shape each other (Germain, 1991). Social policies and programs are part of our ecology. Ecology is the set of relationships between people and their environment. Social workers are increasingly including wider environmental issues such as climate change and air pollution when they assess environmental factors influencing their clients and, certainly, there is ample evidence that individuals' experiences are deeply affected by such environmental forces as the economy, social structures, and the political context. Further, the ecological perspective directs attention to the risks and protective factors in the environment that either help or impede people's efforts to reach their goals. Social policies and programs can help your clients by providing needed benefits and services, or they can create barriers for your clients when, for example, they foster discrimination. The ecological perspective views the interaction between individuals and their different environments as a two-way exchange in which interactions are connected by complex feedback loops. Social workers can, therefore, use an ecological perspective to examine context and to understand the interactions and feedback mechanisms that connect clients and policies in order to shape effective policy.

The ecological perspective can help us discern why certain groups are disadvantaged in meeting their needs and how we may engage in policy practice to remove these barriers. Jim Taylor, a social work theorist, built on the ecological perspective in examining community factors and exploring the concept of "social niches." Social niches are "the environmental habitat of people including the resources they utilize and the people with which they associate" (Taylor, 1997). A housing development, school, or community center, and the people and resources associated with each of them, can all be components of social niches.

Taylor further distinguished between entrapping niches and enabling niches. People in entrapping niches face barriers that prevent them from fulfilling their needs. For example, they frequently have restricted access to people or resources outside their niche. Within entrapping niches, there are few economic resources and few chances to learn the skills and adopt the expectations that would facilitate escape. Entrapping niches are stigmatizing. For example, people in high-rise housing projects and homeless people living on the streets are caught in entrapping niches. Clearly, people in these niches have strengths, and their communities contain some resources. However, significant barriers to access to community resources are hallmarks of entrapping niches.

In contrast, people in enabling niches have resources readily available to help them meet their needs. Enabling niches provide resources, rewards, and incentives instead of barriers. For example, Kretzmann and McKnight (1993) have identified community assets such as excellent educational resources, interested adults, and vocational training programs. Communities that offer such assets are providing enabling niches for their young people. If you are unfamiliar with the work of Kretzmann and McKnight, visit the website of the Asset Based Community Development Institute (www.abcdinstitute.org) at Northwestern University (www. northwestern.edu/ipr) to learn more about their initiatives.

Taylor proposed that many social workers' clients are isolated in niches in society where very few empowering resources are available to them. These clients often have little money, work long hours, and spend any additional time they have taking care of their homes and families. Thus, they have little or no time or money for education or participation in religious or community groups. As a result, they do not come into contact with people, ideas, information, and opportunities that might help make them more effective at achieving the goals of an adequate income, education for themselves and their children, and perhaps even home ownership. Language and literacy barriers may be among the information barriers they face as are, sometimes, cultural divides and overt discrimination.

Transporting niches are places where people can get the help they need to move out of entrapping niches. Social work has sought to create transporting niches via settlement houses and community centers. On a micro level, supportive relationships with social work professionals can serve as transporting niches for individual clients. Social policies can provide funds and promote programs to create transporting niches.

By adopting a broader perspective on their clients' goals and the resources they need to meet them, social workers can help develop policy options that help to overcome barriers to accessing these resources. For example, they can promote policies to provide free language programs to low-income immigrants as well as low-interest loans and training for people who want to start small businesses. Community centers often house these programs and reach out to people in their community. Needs and goals may be understood in new ways and redefined as policy options are explored. For example, it is also possible to use a web-based approach to transport people to resources such as English language classes and small business training that are not readily available in their physical community. However, if we are to develop effective strategies, careful attention must be paid to the lack of access to online resources in many low-income communities.

The strengths perspective builds on the ecological approach. Reality is co-constructed, that is, people influence one another's views of reality. Positive expectations are created when you ask people, "What are your strengths and community resources, and how can they be developed?" Both these questions, and questions about need and problems, are important in formulating effective policy strategies.

POLICY RESEARCH AND PRACTICE: BASIC SKILLS AND TASKS

To help create a reality for ourselves and our clients that provides opportunities for self-determination and increased access to necessary resources, social workers need to develop a well-honed set of policy practice skills. These skills include the ability to conduct policy analysis, as presented in Chapter 5. You will also need to know how to conduct literature reviews, research demographic information on various target groups, and identify evidence-guided practices. Resources on the website accompanying this text can give you guidance if you feel that you need additional preparation to perform these tasks; ask your instructor to download these for you. For example, there is information on where to find specific data on client groups and information on how to evaluate the trustworthiness of websites. Beyond analytic and research skills, social workers need political skills, value-clarifying skills, and organizing skills in order to be effective policy practitioners (Jansson, 2003). Political skills enable social workers to understand and use power effectively. Value-clarifying skills help them to determine if the policy options under consideration are consistent with social work values and to frame policy alternatives in value terms that increase the likelihood of their acceptance. Finally, organizational skills assist social workers in negotiating consensus on policy and program directions.

In order to be an effective policy practitioner, you will need to use logic and research skills. You can also craft a more personal appeal that touches the emotions of decision makers by using personal stories that illustrate the need for policy change. The use of relationship, which is basic to social work practice, is also integral to policy practice. As you become engaged in policy practice, you will learn that people you are pressing for policy changes are often facing difficult budget constraints and are doing what they believe is best. If you can use your relationship skills to find common ground and to identify and build on existing strengths and community resources rather than create an "us versus them" mentality, you will be developing the networks necessary for effective policy practice. Your practice classes will help you build skills in these areas that you can use as you find opportunities to engage in policy practice. These skills are used in performing the following policy practice tasks:

- identifying the affected client population;
- examining your perspective;
- getting on the agenda;
- identifying policy options that include clients' perspectives;
- negotiating consensus on policy goals;
- helping to get policy enacted;
- evaluating policy based on client outcomes.

This list of tasks builds on Jansson's formulation of basic policy practice tasks (2011). We discuss each task, and the ways in which strengths perspective policy principles can be used to accomplish that task, below. The discussion particularly highlights Strengths Perspective Policy Principle 6, (see Chapter 5, Quick Guide 3), which states that the role of the social worker is not that of the expert who helps shape policy for hapless victims. Rather, it is that of collaborator and resource to help attract attention to the perspectives of the target group and to complement clients' efforts to advocate on their own behalf.

For the purpose of helping you understand the basics of how to engage in policy practice, the tasks are presented in linear order. In reality, however, you may be working on several tasks simultaneously and may, therefore, revisit each step while working on another element. For example, while conducting a literature review focusing on the needs of your target population, you may come upon interesting policy proposals as well as information useful for claims-making.

Additionally, I know many of you are already using web tools in your daily lives. Your instructor can provide you with a handout "Ten 'Old' Ideas for Using Technology in Macro Practice in New Ways" to help you use the web, including social media, to engage in policy practice. I hope that, with these suggestions as a starting point, you will become even more inventive and craft more effective uses for these tools in policy practice.

Identifying and Defining the Target Client Population

As you advance in your career, you will likely become very familiar with individuals who are affected by the policies you want to see changed. In order to consider policy change, it is important to clearly identify, define, and describe the characteristics of the target group in aggregate. For example, if you are interested in foster children, you need to be aware of the legal definitions specifying who is considered a foster child. You need to identify and define the group (Ellis, 2003, p. 24). How many members of the target population live in your town, state, and nation? What is their age, gender, and ethnicity? What is their socioeconomic status? How many have a physical or mental disability? What are their strengths? For example, if you were interested in reducing the number of placements foster children experience, it would be important to examine how gender, age, race, and disability levels upon entering the foster care system influence the number of placements experienced. The state agency in charge of foster care may be able to provide this information. You need to know the size and variation of the client population and receive direct input from its members.

Social workers should also attempt to document individual and community strengths and assets as well as the barriers confronting the affected client population. Identifying strengths can help in constructing solutions to seemingly unsolvable problems. Publications such as *Kids Count* and *Kansas Elder Count* provide some useful information on this subject at both the state and county levels (Annie E.

Casey Foundation, 2013; Center on Aging, 2002). Additionally, you can use sources reviewed in Chapter 5 to access these data. You can look at information on outcomes for children in your state at the website of the Annie E. Casey Foundation (www. aecf.org). Go to the current Kids Count Data Book and Data Center.

Often, members of the target group are already involved in political action. For example, there are groups of former foster children in some states actively engaged in foster care reform initiatives. Similar client groups have formed in a variety of policy arenas. As discussed previously, your community and state have many such organizations, which you can access by asking your professors, attending legislative hearings, consulting resource guides, and performing online research. However, sometimes there is no official state or local organization that is already active on behalf of a target group, or there may be a variety of fragmented organizations that have difficulty accessing policy makers and lack a unified message. There may be advocacy organizations engaging in policy practice on the community's behalf but without authentically collaborating with affected populations.

Certainly, in any group you will find diverse opinions. You can use your social work skills to help develop a shared vision of preferred reality. Basically, "developing a preferred reality" means helping your clients articulate what they want changed, a long-standing commitment of the social work profession. This is a solution-focused approach. Beyond listening, you can help create a preferred reality by identifying common ground between the views of clients and policy makers and by considering which policy change initiatives have the best chance of passing. Grand, sweeping changes may not be the place to start. Indeed, as a social worker who is not a member of the target group, you must carefully consider both the necessary efforts and the possible consequences for the target population before championing a high-risk policy change initiative.

Sometimes, members of the target group have faced so much oppression that they need help to expand their vision. Here, again, your social work skills will be useful. You can encourage them to think about their goals and demonstrate respect for their views. If you have developed policy research skills, you can also share information about what kinds of programs and services have helped people in similar circumstances in other areas.

To summarize, the following is a list of concrete, initial tasks that can help you identify the needs, strengths, and goals of the target population with which you are involved:

- Contact advocacy groups with client membership to get their perspectives.

- Conduct a literature review that includes newspaper articles and online sources as well as professional and academic literature.

- Note how various groups have portrayed the affected client group and characterized their problems.

- Ask social workers practicing with the affected client population to identify their clients' strengths, needs, and goals.

- Analyze demographics, identify location, and estimate the size of the target group.

- Help formulate an analysis of the client group's strengths, needs, and goals that incorporates their vision of preferred reality.

Once you and your clients have developed a preferred reality, you can provide support for that reality and help to craft a claim for policy makers' attention. The time you spend in becoming familiar with and documenting the needs, strengths, and goals of the client population will be invaluable in helping to craft a compelling message that gets their needs on the agenda. This information is also critical to developing effective policy options.

Examining Your Perspective

As you begin working with client groups, doing research, and continuing through your performance of other policy practice tasks, take time to examine your views on the policies being considered. As discussed in earlier chapters, the way in which a situation is viewed is significantly influenced by the viewer. This observation applies to you as a social worker. Therefore, it is important for you to examine your views and their effect on your policy practice. Ask yourself, "How did your family background shape your views? What education and experiences influenced your perspective?" After all, it is your perspective and passion that will motivate your policy practice.

Understanding your perspective will also help you identify potential allies. For example, if your perspectives have been influenced by membership in a church, faith-based groups are potential allies. The views of the client population should also have informed your perspective. If not, getting involved with advocacy groups that include members of the client group becomes even more important. At the same time, think about what is likely motivating the point of view of groups that may oppose you. Ideological and philosophical differences as well as the desire to play to a certain constituency should be considered. Do you know who is funding your opposition? Time spent doing online investigation as well as personal networking to gain these insights will help you craft more effective strategies for completing the rest of the steps.

Getting on the Agenda

We explored the process of setting an agenda in some depth earlier in the chapter. Here, we focus more specifically on how social workers can help clients get their issues onto the policy makers' decision agendas. Remember that policies and needs of all sorts are vying for policy makers' attention. Typically, interest in policy change develops gradually as need is recognized and claims are successfully made. Policy makers, whether in the agency or the legislature, become aware of the issue. At this point, we can say that the issue is on their agenda. Recall, however, that there is a separate decision agenda of issues where action will be taken and policy perhaps will change (Kingdon, 2003).

The example below illustrates the incremental process typical of efforts to get onto the agenda and then on to the decision agenda. You will note that not only the need but also a possible policy strategy was presented as part of the effort. After the example is presented, specific strategies you can use to get on the agenda are discussed.

Getting on the Agenda: A Real-Life Scenario   In one of my first jobs in a State Department of Human Services, I was asked to write up an idea I had read about, whereby parents of children with severe developmental disabilities would be eligible for special state-backed loans to buy homes on behalf of their children. This approach is strengths-based in that:

- it reflects the wishes of many people with severe developmental disabilities to remain in their communities;

- it meets their needs in non-segregated, normative ways; and,

- it builds on the strengths of families.

Because I was familiar with the work of local advocacy groups for people with developmental disabilities, I was aware that these groups supported these general policy goals. I managed to bring the idea to the attention of the head of my department by talking with her in the cafeteria before work. I wrote up the idea in June of that year, hoping it would be the subject of legislative decision making during the coming term, which began in the following January.

In September, I was congratulated because my concept paper would likely be incorporated into the "C" budget of the agency's legislative proposals. However, I subsequently discovered that the "C" budget was the agency's wish list and that it would probably be years before this particular initiative would be the subject of legislative decision making. A proposal moves from the "C" to the "B" budget and finally to the "A" budget only if there is sufficient money, political pressure, and time to move it to the top. Policies to develop home ownership loans finally were enacted primarily because of the work of clients' families, but I felt I had a small part in making it happen.

This example illustrates how social workers can carve out a little time for policy practice and use relationships, research, and writing skills to place an issue on the agenda. It also illustrates the importance of exercising patience, being in for the long haul, helping clients develop the power to move issues, and becoming savvy by means of experience.

Strategies for Utilizing the Strengths Approach   The strengths perspective asserts that clients' perspectives should be emphasized even at the point of getting on the agenda. How can you help ensure that policy makers understand clients' needs, strengths, and goals?

You can begin by collecting stories that illustrate capacity rather than incapacity. Create "story banks" of clients' struggles and successes that you can draw upon when you have a chance to talk to policy makers or influence public opinion. You may want to keep written notes so that your stories will be richer and can help policy makers understand the realities of people's lives. Of course, to protect client privacy, you must never make specific names and identifying information public. Even when using stories anonymously, you must have clients' permission to share them.

You can also find out if researchers are doing participatory action research in your area. In participatory action research, practitioners, researchers, and people in groups under study join together to conduct research with the purpose of contributing to social action. After obtaining written consent, researchers may engage people in the groups under study to tell their own stories. Your social work professors might already be doing this type of research.

When you are involved in research as well as in other interactions with clients, look carefully at the interpretation of the clients' situation that is reflected back to them. If the questions asked clearly indicate that the client is perceived as sick, isolated, and incapacitated, the power of such language influences how clients see themselves. If you become involved early in the research process, perhaps you can reframe the questions to focus on client strengths and capacities. Reformulating the questions might also change clients' responses. If you are not actually involved with the research, you can certainly find out what the researchers discovered. Community meetings, surveys, interviews, and focus groups involving members of the target population can also help you gather information on needs, strengths, and goals.

Think of yourself as a resource who can support the vision of the client group and bring new ideas and information to the policy development process. Ideally, as discussed in the previous section, you will have identified client organizations with which to collaborate. Such organizations often have local and state offices that would welcome your efforts. You can also conduct a literature search on the most effective practices for building on strengths and community resources with the client population you serve. Conferring with professional contacts, calling social workers and state agency staff, brainstorming with a group of colleagues, and conducting Internet searches also provides information that is not easily accessible to target group members. Additionally, you should consider approaches that have worked in other policy arenas. For example, if longitudinally monitoring and widely publicizing client outcomes for children, such as rising numbers in institutions, have helped reduce institutionalization, then policies to monitor and publicize rates for older adults may also result in decreased institutionalization.

You can also help develop and provide information to agency policy makers, the news media, and legislators. Watch for the window of opportunity that is created when media coverage increases around a crisis. Other, more predictable openings occur when policies or programs are up for renewal, routine evaluation reports are made, an election is impending, or budgets are being negotiated. You will need to use your assessment skills to evaluate your work environment and determine what is allowable if you want to remain employed. However, many agencies now understand the need for policy practice and would welcome your efforts if they are well thought out. You will likely not do all of the things discussed thus far to help get your clients' issues on the policy agenda, but you can choose to do something.

Working With Other Individuals and Groups It is also critical to locate and work with other people or advocacy groups as well as clients when you are engaged in claims-making for the purpose of getting on policy makers' agendas. Social work professors typically can help guide you to such groups, as can Internet searches and attending legislative committee hearings on the topic of interest. Be sure to find out if your state and local NASW chapters are currently working on this issue and consider joining forces with them. If you go to an advocacy group meeting and have some time and energy to give, you will most likely be very welcome. Below is a list of concrete, beginning tasks that can help with claims-making for the target population in whom you are interested.

- Identify members of the client population and other groups that would be willing to help with claims-making.

- If the target group has historically been oppressed, consider how a social justice claim could be made based on rights to equal treatment. Examine how claims have been made in the past for this and other groups and what approaches have been effective. Adapt them, if appropriate, to emphasize the strengths and contributions, as well as the needs, of the target population.

- Identify key actors who must be convinced of the merit of the claim and consider how the claim might need to be framed in order to garner their support.

- In collaboration with members of the target group as well as other key actors, develop a clear and easy-to-communicate statement that explains why policy makers should provide benefits or services to your target population.

- Begin to contact media and key actors so you can publicize the claim, and use social and alternative media channels to build relationships and promote your messages.

Identifying Policy Options that Include Client Perspectives

Your skills at gathering information as described above will be very useful when you are examining policy alternatives. You can employ the following strategies to iden-tify policy alternatives that build on clients' strengths and help access resources to meet the needs of the target population.

- List proposed policy options identified by client group members and other experts during the claims-making process. Consider which options are strengths-based. Determine whether any of these options are widely supported. If possible, brainstorm with people who may be your allies about how ideas might be combined and options crafted.

- Conduct a literature review and contact concerned national organizations to determine whether similar initiatives have been tried in other places. Consider what other states and agencies have tried. This should not only include legislation that has succeeded; it is also important to make note of failed attempts and to find out why they failed.

- Consider history. Much like the analysis you did in Chapter 2, you should determine whether conditions are the same or different in the current time and location when considering policy options similar to those tried in the past. Whole new policy ideas typically do not suddenly appear; rather, familiar elements may be recombined into a new structure. This is one of the reasons why a historical policy perspective is important.

Negotiating Policy Goals

Recall that, in the section on policy development, we discussed the role of key actors and the importance of clients' perspectives in negotiating policy goals. You can help gain attention to clients' perspectives and goals through the media and by facilitating client–legislator interaction. For example, social workers involved with older adults routinely invite legislators to speak at senior centers, and they provide transportation so that large groups of older adults can visit their legislators. Preparation for such meetings could emphasize how to focus the interaction on specific policy goals that clients support.

As a citizen and a constituent, you deserve access to your legislators. As a social worker, and most certainly as a student, you can request time from elected leaders or their staffs to hear their ideas concerning policy strategies that will meet your clients' needs and to share your clients' perspectives. Of course, you must always protect your clients' confidentiality. Armed with first-hand knowledge acquired from talking with clients and reviewing the professional literature on the subject, you will be ready to engage in a discussion from which both parties can learn a great deal. Such interactions will help you identify which strengths-based policy goals would likely receive legislative support. If you make certain to follow up with a "thank you" and additional information that may be helpful, you will establish a contact that allows you to provide and receive feedback. Every semester, I have students who successfully use this strategy to establish ongoing relationships with their legislators.

These strategies combine analytical and relationship-building skills; social workers are most effective in policy practice when they bring these complementary skills together. Finding ways to increase access to key actors is basic to effective policy practice. Of course, having access is not the same as having power. Contributions from key players and coalitions of voters can exert considerable power over legislative decisions. However, information can also help change people's minds. When attempting to influence policy, time spent in practicing the strategies discussed here will be very useful in helping you to develop information such as policy briefs that can be shared with legislators and other policy makers.

Helping to Get Policy Enacted

We have discussed how to identify policy options and achieve consensus on policy goals. We will now focus on how to determine which of the identified policy options you should support and try to get enacted. When you are considering new policies, it is crucial to think carefully about which options offer workable or feasible solutions. Look back at the criteria used to evaluate workability in the "Examining the Feasibility of Policy Alternatives" segment at the beginning of this chapter. These criteria can help you identify workable solutions. Further, you need to consider whether the policy can actually be implemented given the available time, talent, and funding. Social workers often champion policy options before giving much thought to these factors. Although it is important to dream on a grand scale, you should carefully consider the feasibility of your ideas before suggesting them to policy makers.

Considering Whether a New Law Is Needed   Many times, when social workers see a problem, there already is an applicable law, policy, or program in place that is ineffective because it is underfunded or incompetently implemented or monitored. In such cases, the appropriate policy change is not new legislation but, rather, increased funding or more easily enforced regulations. Keep in mind that when new laws are enacted, the effective portions of the previous law are often repealed. Try to determine which parts of the system work well and why. Are there minor policy or program enhancements that could bolster those parts? Policy practice focused solely on increasing funding for effective but underfunded programs is very important work. Although it is more glamorous to advocate an entirely new approach, when infrastructure and experience in administering a policy or program already exist, working for adequate funding can be the most effective approach.

In addition, funding regulations may be rewritten to create sanctions for ineffective implementation of a policy or program. When a program is sanctioned for ineffectiveness, funds can be withheld or fines can be levied. Conversely, incentives in the form of greater funding or other rewards can be offered for meeting or exceeding the specified outcomes.

Agency rules and regulations that specify how a program is to be administered can often be changed without passing new legislation. Modifying administrative and organizational behavior may help eliminate barriers to clients reaching their goals and thus enhance the effectiveness of social work practice. Policy advocacy might also be needed to ensure that staff charged with implementing the program are properly trained and have workloads conducive to effective practice. If agency rules or regulations do not require training and funds are not available to provide it, then little, if any, training may be provided. When program staff are not adequately trained, programs frequently do not work because they are inadequately implemented.

Using the Policy Analysis Framework In analyzing a proposed new policy that will result in new social programs, you should analyze each of the policy and program elements of the policy analysis framework detailed in Chapter 5. The elements are goals, benefits or services, eligibility rules, service delivery system, and financing. Each element should be examined for congruence with the strengths perspective. For example, policy options in terms of eligibility rules and type of service offered should be analyzed for capacity to increase access to resources that will allow clients to meet their goals in ways similar to those of other community members.

Consider the case in which eligibility rules for a service stipulate it will be provided only to people with disabilities who live in institutions or attend segregated special schools or adult achievement centers. The eligibility rule and the type of service or benefit provided entrap clients in a niche separate from the rest of the community and from other rich community resources. Such a policy is not strengths-based if it disregards the client's goal to remain a part of the larger community. Additionally, remember that the eligibility rules involve rationing. Policy advocacy can be aimed at ensuring that eligibility rules direct the majority of resources to people with the greatest need.

Going further, the service delivery system for policy or program implementation should build on existing resources rather than create separate, often redundant delivery systems. Social workers in public and private agencies frequently are involved in implementing the service delivery system for a new policy. For example, when foster care is privatized in a state, social workers in private agencies such as Catholic Charities or Lutheran Social Services could help develop agency policies that emphasize working closely with local churches and other community organizations in order to recruit more foster parents. Alternatively, they can develop agency policy to fund group homes. They can adopt a policy of referring children to the local mental health system, or they can develop specialized separate mental health services for foster children.

Social workers should analyze proposed financing of new legislation for adequacy and stability. Additionally, they should analyze the incentives created for providers by the way the service is reimbursed to ensure that there are no financial incentives to underserve clients or, conversely, to continue treating clients indefinitely without demonstrating progress toward goal achievement.

Analyzing Costs   An analysis of costs and benefits is a critical component of the research process whereby the feasibility of proposed legislation is examined. Preliminary budgets are often part of policy proposals. The budget analysts at the state legislative research office or a budget analyst in the agency that will administer proposed policies may be willing to provide information to help craft or evaluate a draft budget.

A cost–benefit analysis can be very complex. It is important to also draw attention to the costs to clients and to society of *not* implementing policies. Although policy makers certainly base decisions on more than cost, cost-effectiveness is an important element. There are many intangibles to which it is difficult to assign a value. Working with an expert to help perform the cost–benefit analysis or using already completed analyses as a starting point, is usually the preferred way to add such analysis to your arguments. If a bill dealing with the policy in which you have an interest has already been introduced, the state agency involved has likely been asked to generate a financial impact statement. If you contact the legislators who sponsored the bill, they may be able to tell you which agency official is responsible for examining the costs and benefits of a bill. The legislator or state agency staff may be able to give you a copy of the financial impact statement or fiscal note. Also, your state may provide fiscal notes for bills online. Agency staff may also be willing to talk with you about the assumptions they used to determine financial impact. You can use this information either to bolster or to refute cost–benefit claims made by other groups although, certainly, the official fiscal note may also be based on a particular ideology or perspective on proposed legislation, depending on the preferences of the administration charged with developing it.

You could also consider developing a family impact statement. Another potential way of helping to get legislation passed is to develop an impact statement that focuses on how the policy you are championing might help reduce health or economic disparities. Remember, it is important to highlight both costs and benefits.

You can also draw on research literature to bolster claims of potential cost-effectiveness. Returning to the preschool example, advocates interested in increasing access to preschool education in inner-city neighborhoods have pointed to research that indicates that at-risk children who attend high-quality preschool programs are less likely to be incarcerated as teens and adults (Bruner, 2002). If the relatively small cost per child of preschool education is compared to the $30,000 or more cost of incarcerating a juvenile offender per year, it is clear that the potential return on investment is quite high. Conversely, you can use this same sort of logic to calculate "the cost of failure," which can be thought of as the cost of not acting and thus making it much more likely that negative and very expensive consequences will occur (Bruner, 2002). Another good example of this calculation is contrasting the huge costs associated with premature births with the cost of making prenatal care for low-income mothers more widely available. Of course, not every child in the target group who misses out on service will experience high-cost negative outcomes. In using this strategy, it is important to guard against promoting the idea that, if not for a social program, negative outcomes for all potential recipients will result. This is neither accurate nor strengths-based. However, it is often possible to calculate the percentage and number who are likely to experience negative outcomes if nothing is done, and compare those aggregate costs to the aggregate costs of prevention or early intervention programs.

You can also use this approach to draw attention to greater costs to taxpayers if programs are cut back so intervention does not take place and, for example, a child goes into foster care or a correctional facility, or an older adult is admitted to a nursing home, runs out of money, and goes on Medicaid. The cost of institutionalization for a year has usually already been calculated and can be obtained from the state agency in charge of reimbursing institutions. Most agencies also have calculated an average cost per year for serving a client in the community. You then can compare the cost of social work intervention and service to maintain the client in the community, to the cost of institutionalization. The cost of providing services to a large number of people in the community is often much less and can be offset if the cost of just one person entering an institution is avoided. Step-down programs whereby intensive wrap-around services are offered to clients at high risk of institutionalization can often garner support by using this logic. Further, policies to implement evidence-based practice pilots on a wider scale can often be promoted if you can show their cost-effectiveness in this manner. However, all such analyses should also keep positive outcomes for these children and older adults at center stage. The value of a healthy child or an older adult's ability to remain in their home should not be reduced primarily to a dollar and cents calculation.

Evaluating Policy Based on Client Outcomes

Finally, it is important, even in the early stages of policy consideration, to think about how the effectiveness of the policy will be evaluated. If policy makers agree on outcomes they would like to see for clients after the policy is implemented, evaluation can then focus on these outcomes. If policy makers can be convinced to specify in the enabling legislation that evaluation will be based on outcomes for clients, then client-focused information will be made available to evaluate policy effectiveness and improve the policy.

For example, a student in one of my classes who had been a foster child worked with a child advocacy group to develop a policy proposal with the goal of increasing educational attainment for children who have been in foster care. They proposed legislation to guarantee funding for post-secondary education at a state college, community college, or county technical institute for former foster children. Because policy makers were concerned with the large numbers of former foster children who were entering homeless shelters as adults, they were interested in initiatives that might increase the ability of these individuals to become self-supporting.

Significantly, the specified goal—increased educational attainment for people who had been in foster care—could be tracked, and my student advocated that tracking be mandated in the initial legislation. Because the educational attainment of people who had grown up in foster care in previous years had been documented as part of the needs determination process, changes after the policy is implemented could be measured. Also, if this outcome is routinely tracked and monitored for people who have been in foster care, the impact of other changes in the foster care system and the magnitude of the change in educational outcomes can be monitored over time. It is important to think about outcome measures that include clients' goals as well as policy makers' goals early in the policy enactment process so that both sets of goals can be evaluated. In the case described above, policy makers were interested in improving educational achievement for former foster children, thereby decreasing their numbers in homeless shelters. These outcomes could all be monitored.

The failure to evaluate policies can contribute to ineffectiveness and even loss of service, because the outcomes of the prescribed intervention are not recorded and analyzed. For example, a policy may specify that juvenile offenders receive services in a group home. However, if the people who work with juvenile offenders placed in group homes fail to track recidivism rates (rates of repeat offenses) after leaving the group home, then policy makers cannot determine whether the program is effective or needs major revamping. Further, the social workers who staff the group home will not be able to defend the efficacy and cost-effectiveness of their work in the face of budget cuts that could ultimately result in closing the group home. In fact, I have witnessed just this scenario. Of course, savvy and client-centered social workers will monitor client outcomes regardless of whether such monitoring is required in order to avoid such a situation, and to ensure that programs are, indeed, achieving their outcome objectives for clients.

Policies may also have different effects on different social groups. Doing a policy impact analysis can help you understand these differences (Johnson, 2005). This type of analysis attempts to determine the consequences of policy interventions—before, during, and after their implementation—on the well-being of different social groups. There is usually a special focus on people in poverty and on other vulnerable groups. A policy impact analysis examines the distributional impact of policies across social groups, in terms of benefits or services received as well as harm done. Differences in impact based on gender, ethnicity, age, livelihood, and geographic location are typically identified. For example, a policy that specifies that applicants for service must apply online may speed up eligibility determination significantly for people who are computer literate, but it could greatly disadvantage people in rural areas without Internet access, older adults who might not use computers, or people in poverty. Work is under way to increase the amount and quality of policy impact analysis, at many levels of government. International organizations such as the United Nations are trying to encourage countries to engage in careful analysis of how public policy changes impact poverty, for example. Policies are often considered evidence-based policies before they have been tested with different social groups. This is problematic and it is important that you are aware that so-called evidence-based or best practice initiatives should not be implemented wholesale without attention to whether efficacy has been tested with the social group where it will be implemented. To learn more about policy impact analysis, particularly in the areas of poverty and social impact, go to the United Nations Development Programme Poverty Reduction website (www.undp.org/poverty), and search for Poverty and Social Impact Analysis. Read about the PSIA approach.

In order to analyze outcomes once a policy is enacted, we must know the condition of the target group prior to the intervention. This information is called base-line data. Ideally, information gathered in the need determination stage of policy development will provide baseline data; otherwise, these data will need to be gathered. Of course, if outcomes improve after the policy is implemented, it does not necessarily follow that the intervention or policy made the difference. There is a correlation rather than a causal link. You do know that the outcome improved after implementation of a policy change, but it will take more research to establish that the policy change actually caused the improved outcome. You need to be careful not to overstate the impact of the policy. Nonetheless, if more members of the client groups had a positive outcome after receiving services or benefits compared to members of the same groups in the baseline year, then policy makers will be interested in knowing that the policy change did not cause the situation to deteriorate and might have improved conditions. Further, remember the policy making process is typically iterative. That is, there will likely be repeated attempts to reform a specific policy and earlier information gathered on outcomes will be useful in incrementally improving the policy.

A PLACE TO START

Now it is time for you to put together the content provided in this chapter and consider how you can actually use it. This next segment of the chapter provides specific practical strategies for how you personally can become involved in policy practice. You may already be passionate about an area of social policy in which you want to get involved. Involvement with social work agencies often helps students focus on needed policy changes. Think critically about the social work agencies where you volunteer or do fieldwork. What policies govern their programs? How does funding drive the program? How is the program evaluated? Are outcomes for clients a component of the evaluation? Are evaluation results used to improve policy and program? If clients have grievances, does the agency give them a chance for a fair hearing? Examining the issues raised in these hearings might provide indicators of where policy is not working effectively. If clients do not have the opportunity for this kind of due process, there could be a need for policy advocacy so that they do have some recourse. Further, consider whether this is an agency where involvement in policy practice is supported and could potentially be a place you would want to work when you begin your social work career.

Focusing on one issue rather than taking up a whole host of issues at once will make it more likely you will be able to have an impact. You will also be more likely to bring about change if you join with a group already interested in advocacy rather than act alone. Further, if you get involved early in the change process, it is easier to have an impact than if you wait until most of the steps outlined in this chapter have been taken by others, and then voice your concerns.

If you have not already done so, a very good place to start is registering to vote and getting others to vote. Many young people took these steps in recent elections, and it made a great deal of difference. Obtain names, addresses, emails and phone numbers of the people who represent you at the city, county, state, and federal level. You will find they are easy to contact. They cannot effectively represent you and your clients if they do not have information on what is working and what needs improvement.

Seeking Support

If you are in field placement, ask your field instructor for guidance and ideas about where to start engaging in policy practice. Remember, policy practice is important at the agency level as well as at the legislative level. Rewriting the rules in an agency and helping to implement new policies and programs are forms of policy practice. For example, working to develop a pilot peer support program at a mental health center or addressing bullying at a public school by changing norms and instituting a more proactive bullying policy are good examples of agency-level policy practice that you may find less mystifying than congressional deliberations. Some students are encouraged to be leaders in agencies' pilot programs and may design a new tool or strategy and then find that this is adopted as policy for their agency. This is a critical form of policy practice because if the evaluation of a pilot shows it helped produce the desired outcomes, that information can be used to change agency policy or even used as evidence to change the state or federal policy approach. To find out more about policy practice involving a pilot peer support program, visit the website of the research office I direct, which is the Office of Aging and Long Term Care at the University of Kansas (www.oaltc.ku.edu). Read about the Pilot Mental Health Peer Support Program we developed with the Area Agencies on Aging.

Although policy practice at the agency level may seem less daunting initially, if you just give it a try, you might find yourself equally at home working for change at the legislative level. Indeed, the skills you practice, in setting agendas and building relationships and making claims, will help you in any policy practice venue, on any scale. Your agency may already have staff designated to follow legislation and talk to policy makers about needed changes. If so, see if you can work with them. If you are not yet in a field placement but have been a volunteer with an agency, agency staff may be willing to talk with you about the legislative policy changes they would like to see. Becoming a skilled policy practitioner means learning how to work effectively with agencies and other concerned groups to shape policies and programs

During your social work career, your policy practice work may include forming coalitions with clients and key constituent groups, finding or helping to elect supportive legislators, analyzing proposals, developing proposals, communicating ideas effectively, and advocating for policy enactment. You may become involved in efforts to take an issue to court. Some schools of social work offer joint degrees with their affiliated law schools. Seeking out people who were involved in these programs and enlisting the help of your local or national NASW chapter are starting places in evaluating the feasibility of a lawsuit. NASW also initiates or participates in development of legal briefs on selected social and practice issues. These briefs are called *amicus curiae* (friend of the court) briefs and may be available through your library under the topic of NASW Amicus Briefs.

Many NASW chapters also sponsor training programs to increase the political effectiveness of social workers; check out what local chapters are doing in your state. Nationally, NASW seeks to educate and mobilize social workers and other groups to press for a more just society. NASW publishes an excellent resource titled *Social Work Speaks*; it provides policy statements on a variety of social work issues, which can be used to guide social work political activism and policy advocacy (NASW, 2012e). NASW also has a political action arm called Political Action for Candidate Election (PACE). PACE endorses and contributes financially to candidates from any party who support the policy agenda of NASW.

We know that people are most familiar with policy issues that have a direct impact on them, their friends, and their families. If legislative bodies reflected the makeup of the voting public more closely, they would contain many more women, people of color, and people from low-income families. Such legislators might be more likely to vote for many of the policies that social workers champion. However, large numbers of eligible voters who could help elect such candidates are not registered to vote. In 2008, voter turnout among individuals with a household income of less than $20,000 was 55 percent. In 2010, only 40 percent of those whose family income was less than $50,000 turned out to vote (U.S. Census Bureau, 2010b). Given this lack of voter involvement, particularly among low-income citizens, there is a great need for political activism. **Political activism** is defined as actions taken for the purpose of influencing the outcome of elections or government decision making. Some students become so involved in political activism that they decide to run for political office. Exhibit 6.2 provides an example of a successful campaign waged by a social work student.

EXHIBIT 6.2 *Social Work Student Runs for Office*	Social work students in a Midwestern state were concerned about the growing numbers of teen pregnancies in the local high school where they were placed. For their project in a social policy class, they decided to develop an action plan and work to get more comprehensive sex education courses offered in high schools in their area as well as across the state. They met with high school and college students, including groups representing lesbian, gay, bisexual, transgender, and questioning (LGBTQ) students to learn about their experiences with sex education in high school and what changes they thought should be made. They developed informational programs including skits designed to increase public support for comprehensive sex education. They met with their local school board representatives as well as state legislators to advocate for comprehensive sex education. After working on this action plan, one of the students decided to run for a position on the school board. Many students and faculty supported her efforts. Her campaign was successful and she was elected to the school board.

Taking Action

When you are ready to take action, the task descriptions presented earlier in the chapter can guide your efforts. The tasks listed in each of those sections can help you develop steps for an action plan when you become involved in policy practice. You will need help and support from other groups, including the client population, to do what needs to be done. However, in most change efforts I have seen succeed, there have been a handful of determined people who persevere until the change occurs. Do not be discouraged if at first you attract only small numbers of people who are willing to help out. Even a few people who are actually willing to work on an issue can make a huge difference.

EXHIBIT 6.3 *Social Work Students can Successfully Advocate for Legislation that is Life-Changing for Their Clients*	Students at the University of Kansas were concerned about overrepresentation of minority youth in the Kansas juvenile justice system. They tracked a legislative bill that addressed this problem. Recognizing that the issue was not well understood, they devised an educational strategy that involved first developing relationships with legislators, state agency staff, and religious leaders and then making sure they had up-to-date information on the problem, possible solutions, and the need for this bill. The students successfully advocated for this bill, which was designed to reduce racial, geographic, and other biases in the juvenile justice system. They and fellow students celebrated a legislative victory when the bill was signed into law by the Governor.

An action plan is an important tool that details steps to take in planning and implementing your action strategy. A thoughtful plan can help make you aware of the potential influence of your actions and those of your group members. To learn more about developing an action plan, take time to explore the Sample Action Plan provided in Quick Guide 5 at the end of this chapter, and consider how it could be modified for an issue that you are passionate about.

Two principles guide my development of action plans.

- First, "keep it simple" (KIS) so that everyone understands what is to be done. Remember, the goal is to involve people from a variety of backgrounds, many of whom may not be as invested in your issue or your particular proposed strategy as you are, at least initially. If the plan is too long and detailed, "my eyes glaze over" (MEGO) will overtake group members, and they will lose interest.

- Second, if your group expends most of its energy in planning, there will not be any gas left in the tank to put the plan into action. As with detailed analysis of social problems, I have seen time and again that well-meaning groups admire the problem and start to plan but lose momentum before much is accomplished. Think realistically about how much time and effort group members have to give, and then contain the planning so that it does not use up most of their energy.

Integrating Other People Into Action Plans   A written action plan is very useful because it helps clarify strategy and assignment of responsibility. Also, if the action plan is developed as a group endeavor, that process can help create consensus about what needs to be done. Additionally, when other people are involved in drafting the action plan, they will also be more likely to work to implement it. However, instead of creating a comprehensive written action plan containing all the tasks we have covered thus far, a concise action plan can be developed, as illustrated in the Sample Action Plan (Quick Guide 5).

It is important to have a solid, carefully thought-out action plan and to make certain that everyone who is responsible for a task has agreed to do it, knows how to do it, is aware of the due date, has a copy of the plan, and expects to be held accountable. Your action plan can also include strategies for dealing with important stakeholders and gaining public support (Ellis, 2003). If possible, you can contemplate potential future developments, including unexpected opportunities and crises, so that you can plan for how you might respond in those events.

After developing the action plan, review it with people who have experience with change efforts in your chosen area. They often can identify misinformation and omissions, and they can offer constructive feedback. They may also join your effort or know other people who will. You will also have to monitor the action plan as it is implemented and modify it as needed. At the very least, you will need a list of tasks. You will also need to determine who will do what and in what order.

Focusing Your Efforts   Working from a strengths perspective, you could, for example, focus your policy practice efforts on simply increasing public awareness of a policy alternative that builds on the strengths and goals of service users. One approach would be to help your local newspaper or public radio station to develop a series of stories about innovative strengths-based policy alternatives, such as those that address the desperate need for affordable high-quality child care for single working mothers or for affordable home and community services for low-income elders. Today, almost all effective advocacy campaigns have some social media component. Small, grassroots efforts might use Twitter to collect petition signatures for a city council ordinance preventing discrimination against the LGBT community or write a blog to profile the stories of individuals experiencing homelessness in their community. For instance, the global anti-poverty organization, ONE, uses social media and cause marketing to raise awareness about the millions around the world who lack basic necessities, and to call on supporters to take action. A concerned mother used Facebook to start the organization One Million Moms for Gun Control, to press for stricter gun control legislation following several deadly mass shootings. In just over a month, more than 40,000 advocates "liked" the page. Additionally, many elected officials have Twitter accounts themselves, so you and other advocates can contact policy makers directly through the mini-blogging format. There likely are advocacy groups in your state that are already working on these issues where you could find people interested in collaborating with you. Initially, it is best to seek guidance from a seasoned policy practitioner to help prevent any breach of ethics concerning confidentiality and privacy. If you have begun to keep a story bank of clients' successes and struggles, as explained earlier, you will already have rich material to share. Media pieces may also contain contact phone numbers or email addresses of advocacy groups working on these issues, for people who want to get involved. Your action plan could include identifying interested reporters, convincing them of the merit of the stories, supplying information and perhaps speakers from the target group, and then evaluating the results of the effort. In today's social media environment, your ability to communicate directly with your potential allies does not depend on media outlets' willingness to cover you. Today, more than ever, you can create your own coverage and tell your own story.

When the work involved in making an impact seems overwhelming, break it down into small, manageable tasks. Take action where you can. Your skills will improve with practice, and other people will take notice because the ability to work effectively and persistently to bring about change is very valuable in a great variety of settings.

Interacting With Your Opposition   Expect to encounter opposition. Remember, there are groups in the policy stew who are committed to many different policy options. There may be groups whose goal is simply to block any and all initiatives. They are made up of people who feel they are best benefited by maintaining the status quo. You will need to learn how to work with people who share your concerns and deal with people who do not.

You need to become savvy about vested interests and people who espouse ideologies that are very different from your own. Consider how much power they have and what methods they used to acquire power. Strategies to counter these forces may include forming coalitions with clients and key constituent groups and finding or helping to elect supportive legislators. Realistically assessing the barriers to changing policy is important. You also will find key actors in government agencies and in the legislature who will be your allies. You may often also find common cause with people and groups who you initially identified as your opposition. Using a strengths perspective, you may find that goals such as having healthy children and protecting the frail are widely supported. Differences lie in opinions about what means are best to promote these goals. When necessary, your clinical social work skills may come in handy in crafting compromises. Compromise is okay. What is not okay is giving up in the face of opposition or sacrificing so much that your client group loses something essential.

Supporting Client Groups   Members of client groups may already possess well-developed political skills. If they do not, however, you can help connect them with advocacy training opportunities. Their involvement is key, but always temper effort to encourage their involvement with a careful assessment of the level of risk that such involvement represents for them. This assessment is particularly important when you are considering confrontational strategies, which may be necessary but also involve more risk. Because of this, you should exhaust low-risk strategies first and remember social workers' ethical obligations to gain clients' informed consent before involving them in any change effort, including policy practice.

Interacting With Policy Makers   When communicating with key stake holders such as legislators, it helps to prepare by doing research on their backgrounds and philosophies. Today, many legislators have their own websites. Perhaps they put out newsletters or use social media sites such as Twitter or Facebook. With just a little effort, you can learn their underlying philosophies and the areas in which they are active. As you examine the history of attempts to address needs in a particular area, pay attention to who has been involved in past initiatives. You know the importance of "starting where the client is" in practice. Similarly, "starting where policy makers are" and framing proposals to fit their ideas and approaches without compromising essential elements will likely generate more support. At the very least, a little research will help you avoid alienating a policy maker needlessly by, for example, beginning your interaction decrying "a bootstrap mentality" when the person you are talking to fancies himself a "self-made man." People who believe citizens should rely on themselves and pull themselves out of difficulty are very cautious about increasing spending on public welfare programs, but they might be convinced to support efforts that provide target populations with opportunities to improve their conditions, if framed as such.

Do not rely on technical information and logic alone to make your case. Consider normative affective strategies also. This means you should try to identify legislators who may be interested in an issue because of past involvement on a personal or professional level. For example, if a legislator has a disability or a family member with disabilities, she or he might take a greater interest in policies and programs for people with disabilities.

Package your ideas so that they are attractive to policy makers. A one-page brief is recommended because policy makers must deal with such a huge volume of issues that you need to get their attention and make major points as briefly as possible. Sometimes, an "incremental approach"—that is, an approach that presses for a small change to an existing program rather than radical change—is more appealing to policy makers. However, there are times when radical change is needed.

When you work as a change agent, staying focused on finding solutions may help achieve consensus about desired goals and outcomes. A solution-focused approach, much like the strengths approach, shifts emphasis from problems to goals, strengths, and resources. People are asked to envision their preferred future. This is sometimes called the "miracle question." They are then encouraged to begin to take steps in even small increments, toward creating this preferred future. Many times, people want the same positive outcomes but have different views about how to achieve them. Getting agreement on goals and outcomes is a crucial first step. Using this type of goal-focused and consensus-oriented approach may help dissenting legislators to actively engage in developing effective policies. You will note over and over that the same skills used in clinical practice with individuals, such as a solution-focused approach, can be adapted and used in policy practice. Further, policies and programs that promote wrap-around services for children with mental health issues might also be effective for older adults with chronic disease who are attempting to stay in the community. Helping with this sort of knowledge-transfer as well as with the integration of services so that one family will not be working with multiple case managers and agencies, is also policy practice.

Just as you can borrow ideas from other areas of social work practice to use when doing policy practice, you can also borrow innovative ideas from other states, and, in this increasingly global context, other countries. Innovation transfer and diffusion can help enhance and expand the tools available for policy practitioners. The web is a great source of information on innovative programs worldwide.

Policy change efforts undoubtedly are going on in your state, and you can help out with them. Start with one contact or one action. You may be surprised at the opportunities for policy practice that are readily available to you.

Facing Limits on Political Activism   Sometimes, social workers do not get involved in political activism because they believe it would violate the terms of their employment. In fact, limits on political activism in social service agencies are frequently misunderstood. For example, agencies may indicate that all sorts of political activism are prohibited under the Hatch Act (1939), a federal law that restricts the political activity of federal employees, District of Columbia government employees, and some state and local employees who are involved with federally funded programs. Private organizations whose activities are wholly financed by federal loans or grants are also covered by the Hatch Act. However, they may be able to use private funding to engage in advocacy work. Many states have adopted provisions similar to the Hatch Act for their employees. Further, some private non-profit organizations qualify for 501(c)3 tax-exempt status, allowing donors to receive tax privileges for their contributions. These organizations also must follow certain rules regarding political activism. However, there are a great many ways in which a social worker employed by public or private agencies can be politically active without violating the Hatch Act or rules governing tax-exempt status. Limitations under the Hatch Act are explained in detail on the federal government website of the U.S. Office of the Special Counsel (www.osc.gov). Go to the website, Bolder Advocacy, and search for Navigating the Rules, to find information on regulations applying to non-profit organizations (bolderadvocacy.org). There may be additional state or agency prohibitions against political activism in places where you will work. However, if you examine the written policy closely, you may find that it is not nearly as restrictive as agency personnel who have not actually taken time to examine the policy closely may believe. In an extension of their policy practice obligations, social workers whose policy activities are unduly proscribed by their employers can advocate for their professional right to engage in such practice by familiarizing themselves with the rules and explaining the importance of engagement to their employers.

CONCLUSION

This chapter provided an overview of the policy development process and of policy practice, examined your responsibility and opportunities to become involved, and suggested some beginning strategies. Research skills that are critical to effective policy practice were highlighted. Your social work practice and research classes will help you further develop skills that can be applied to influencing policy.

Additionally, there are many books that detail strategies and tactics to use in policy practice (Haynes and Mickelson, 2009; MacEachern, 1994; Schneider and Lester, 2001; Amidei, 2010). Some of these books are very specialized. For example, the focus may be entirely on how to use the Internet to build coalitions and get information to the people who need it. As you become engaged in social work practice with a specific client group, such as children in foster care or older adults with long-term care needs, chances to be involved in policy practice will abound if you are attuned to the opportunities and your obligation to be involved in influencing policy and programs.

MAIN POINTS

- Policy development is the process by which policies are created and implemented to meet identified need. Policies can also be developed that build on strengths and reflect the goals of the target group.

- Tasks in the policy development process include defining needs, social problems, and strengths; documenting needs, strengths, and goals; identifying initial policy goals; engaging in claims-making; crafting broadly supported policy goals; formulating policy alternatives that meet established goals; developing, enacting, and implementing the policy or program; and evaluating outcomes.

- Social, cultural, and community factors influence social policies.

- Policy practice "encompasses professional efforts to influence the development, enactment, implementation, modification, or assessment of social policies, primarily to ensure social justice and equal access to basic social goods" (Barker, 2003, p. 330).

- All social workers have a responsibility to be involved in some level of social work policy practice, as outlined in the NASW *Code of Ethics*. Involvement requires many skills, including policy analysis, political, value-clarifying, and organizational skills.

- Policy practice is informed by doing a dual assessment of clients, which includes an assessment of the specific policy issues that impact them and actively incorporates clients' perspectives and policy priorities.

- Policy practice tasks include understanding the target population, examining your perspective on the issue, getting on the agenda, identifying policy options that include the clients' perspectives, negotiating consensus on policy goals, getting the policy enacted, and evaluating the policy in terms of client outcomes. In order to complete many policy practice tasks, you will need to develop your skills in researching the needs of target populations, policy options, and current policies, and in evaluating outcomes of policies.

- Clinical social work skills, such as a solution-focused approach, can be adapted and used in policy practice. Social workers are most effective in policy practice when they bring their relational and analytical skills to these endeavors.

- Policy impact analysis, cost benefit analysis, and cost-effectiveness analysis are important tools for examining social policies.

- Policy practice is more than working to influence legislation. Rules and regulations created by the executive branch and private organizations, as well as opinions rendered by the judicial branch, all may limit or expand services and opportunities for our clients and can be influenced by effective policy practice.

- A written action plan can help guide policy practice. However, think realistically about how much time and effort your group has to give and avoid using all of the group's energy on planning.

- In periods of retrenchment at both the federal and state level such as we are now experiencing, it is critical that social workers engage in policy practice with the goal of retaining the safety net programs upon which we all rely.

- You can use the ideas presented in this chapter to become involved in policy practice in an area for which you have passion. Such policy practice will increase your chances to advance your clients' interests and fulfill your professional obligations as social workers called to advocate for clients.

THE POLICY GROUP TAKES ACTION

EXHIBIT 6.4

Policy Students at the State Capitol Building

QUICK GUIDE 5 Sample Action Plan – Narrative

In the last chapter Tiffany, Alejandro, Kelli, and Alice decided to focus on the social problem of child hunger. As you start to explore the policy group's development of an Action Plan (see Sample Action Plan template below), imagine you are part of the group. Consider how you would go about researching the problem of child hunger in your area—what organizations would you contact or what websites would you access? In order to complete the current assignment, development of an action plan outlining advocacy strategies to address this problem and then taking action, the group needs to find out more about child hunger and who is affected by this problem. They also want to find out about current policies and programs that address the problem of child hunger. To do this, the team members need to complete individual research assignments and share what they learn with the other team members.

Tiffany was given the task of finding out more about child hunger and what it means to be hungry in America. She had learned in class that it was important to determine how terms were to be defined and the problem constructed. She knew from her previous work at the free health clinic that child hunger was not just a problem in poor developing countries but she was not sure how the problem differed between countries. She found that in the U.S. it is very rare to see the obvious signs of severe food deprivation that are observed in other poorer countries (wasting, stunted growth, etc.), so the definition and signs of the problem were different in the U.S. The signs that a child is dealing with the issue of hunger in America are more indirect and difficult to identify (i.e. fatigue, headaches, difficulty concentrating, frequent illness, etc.). Consequently, rather than using hunger measures based on objective clinical symptoms used in other countries, alternative measures, such as self-report, have been developed to measure hunger here in the United States. Tiffany learned that the definition of hunger that has been used for approximately the past 20 years for policy and reporting purposes is a person not taking in a sufficient amount of food due to a shortage of finances or resources. Tiffany also discovered that many times hunger is placed in the broader context of food insecurity, which is the inability of families to obtain a sufficient amount of nutritious food to support a healthy life. In sum, she found that while hunger and food insecurity are harmful for all individuals, they can be especially damaging to the development of children's physical and mental health as well as their academic performance and future earnings potential. Once definitions and indicators of a problem are agreed upon, statistics can be gathered.

Kelli did an Internet search on child hunger statistics in the United States to determine how many children and their families in this country are affected by this problem. She was surprised by the statistics she found that said that over 50 million people in the U.S. dealt with food insecurity in 2011 and that almost 17 million of these individuals were children. Or, to put it another way, one out of five children are affected by hunger. The problem was much bigger than she thought and she discovered that households with children were more likely to be impacted by food insecurity than those without children. Also, families that were headed by single parents and African American and Hispanic households had higher than average rates of food insecurity. In approximately three-quarters of the states, 20 percent or more of children in 2010 lived in homes affected by food insecurity. She also found some great resources that provided state-by-state comparisons on food insecurity among children at the U.S. Department of Agriculture (USDA) and the Annie E. Casey Foundation websites.

Alejandro knew from his practicum at a junior high school in the city that child hunger and food insecurity affected many of the students at the school. When he talked with some of the teachers, they told him that over half of their students came to school hungry. He knew that food insecurity or hunger can cause significant disruption in a child's learning and negatively impact the development of their physical and mental health. Further, it could have detrimental long-term consequences on a child's future functioning. Alejandro knew that a majority of the kids in his school received free or reduced breakfast and lunch through the federally funded School Breakfast and National School Lunch program provided by the USDA and facilitated by local school districts. He also knew from his work with kids at the school and from conversations with faculty at the school that on weekends and in the summer many of these kids no longer had the two adequate, nutritious meals they received every school day. Alejandro believed the lack of adequate nutrition during the summer months could set these children up for failure once they returned to school again in the fall.

Finally, for her individual assignment Alice looked into other policies and programs that were in place to address child hunger and food insecurity here in the U.S. From her search she learned that there were some large food bank organizations (i.e. Harvesters) throughout the country that provided emergency food assistance to individuals—including children—struggling with food insecurity. She also found that many local churches and charitable organizations partner with Feeding America as part of their food bank network that provides assistance by establishing neighborhood food pantries. She knew from her previous work in social service organizations that the USDA funds the Supplemental Nutritional Assistance Program (SNAP), which provides financial assistance to those who meet income eligibility standards through an EBT card which can be used to purchase food related items at stores, and the National Breakfast and School Lunch Programs. She did not realize, however, that the USDA also funded the Summer Food Service Program which was enacted to address the summer months when kids are out of school and ensure that children in need are continuing to get a nutritious meal at least once a day during the break. Sadly, she found from her research that this summer food program is only reaching a small number of those children in need because there are not enough feeding sites (physical locations that work with community sponsors where the food is served to the children) throughout the country. Alice did some further digging and realized that there were no feeding sites for the Summer Food Service Program within a hundred mile radius of their location.

Based on what they found from their research into child hunger and insecurity and from seeing the experiences of children and their families who are dealing with this issue, Kelli, Tiffany, Alice, and Alejandro decide they would like to impact policy so that during the summer months children in their area will have access to at least one nutritious meal a day. They know that there is funding available through the USDA's Summer Food Service Program to provide summer meals to low-income children in their town but that up to this point no organization or agency has stepped forward to offer to serve as a feeding site for this program. The group decides to work with the community organization that oversees the parks and recreation activities in their town to enact an agency policy that establishes this organization as a feeding site for the Summer Food Service Program.

In their work, the policy group has come into contact with other groups interested in the area of child hunger and food insecurity that are engaging in advocacy efforts at the legislative level to protect SNAP and other programs to reduce food insecurity. The following action plan details the steps the policy group may take to accomplish the goal of implementing policy at the agency level by establishing a local summer service program feeding site. Some of the members of the policy group even carved out additional time to continue working with these advocacy organizations to bring about policy change at the macro level and used this action plan to assist with these efforts at the state legislature as well as at the federal level. In this action plan, we are assuming that the individuals in the policy group live in your community and state.

After reading through the process the policy group completed, what steps might you take to decrease the prevalence of this problem if the policy group meetings were taking place in your classroom? In other words, what strategies or action plan tasks do you think would work in your hometown to address the issue of food insecurity among children?

SAMPLE ACTION PLAN	ACTION PLAN TASKS TO ADDRESS IDENTIFIED PROBLEM	WHO WILL DO IT?	DATE DONE

	Months 1–2: Identifying the Target Population and Examining Your Perspective
	
	1. **Identify target population affected by identified problem**
	• Define the specific issue/social problem.
	• Contact state advocacy groups and use the Internet to determine who is affected; document the number affected and the demographic makeup of this population.
	• Consider what you know from your own practice experience about the strengths of the target group.
	
	2. **Do a literature search to research possible solutions**
	• Access articles on the Internet.
	• Investigate other states' efforts to determine differences and similarities in dealing with this issue.
	• Identify advocacy groups at the local, state, and national level with similar interests.
	
	3. **Examine your perspectives**
	• Why are you interested in this issue? What is the outcome you would like to see happen?
	• What is your motivation in advocating for change (identify your beliefs and values)?
	• Do you belong to civic or church groups that might share your interest in the topic?
	• If you are a student member of the NASW or school social work groups in your area, you may find likely allies in those groups.
	  – By identifying your interest in the issue, it might be possible to identify others with similar interests that will work with you to change policy.
	  – If so, develop a strategy or way to engage with these individuals/organizations—what is the most effective way to make contact.		

Months 2–3: Getting on the Agenda

1. **Talk to key actors about the issue**
   - Speak to advocacy groups about whether they are already working on the issue or interested in focusing on the issue. If not, ask if they are aware of other people or groups interested or knowledgeable about the issue and the best way to connect with these individuals or groups.

➤ **Legislative Advocacy:**
   - Visit your legislator's website (if applicable) to determine issues where s/he may have interests to see if there might be a link to your interest. For example, legislators who have rural areas in their district may be particularly concerned about your issue if you talk about effects on youth from rural areas.
   - Contact your state legislator. You can identify your legislator by visiting your state legislature's Web site, accessible from www.stateline.org.
     - Meeting with your legislator allows you to introduce yourself, share your position on the issue, and assess his/her interest in the topic. Remember to protect confidentiality of your clients when explaining the need for change. Be sure to thank your legislator for the visit.

➤ **Agency Advocacy:**
   - Seek support from colleagues by adding issue to team meetings.
   - Organize a worker-level working group to assess implications (financial, service delivery, community relationships).
   - Elicit support of line management by presenting positive implications for your (or staff's) work and discuss how to present to agency administration.
   - Based on discussion with staff and line management, determine most effective way to raise agency awareness and gain support of administration.

2. **Locate and engage with people who want to be involved with the identified issue**
   - Examples could include other students, service providers, members of the target population, an advocacy group, local NASW members, and a state legislator willing to sponsor a bill.
   - If focus is on legislative advocacy, call your state legislative hotline or make contact online. See which legislators are sponsoring bills in your area of interest. They may join you in contacting other legislators and trying to get this issue on the agenda.

3. **Try to get media coverage**
   - Write a letter to the editor of your local newspaper.
   - Call the local radio station to see if they will air a story on your issue. They are likely to be more interested if there is a personal "hook" for the story, so see if you can identify clients or service providers who are eager to tell their story. Again, remember that informed consent and confidentiality are essential ethical requirements of all social workers.

If you have time to take only the actions listed above, you have made a great start and have created a foundation for future involvement.

Months 3–4: Identifying Policy Options and Negotiating Consensus on Policy Goals

1. **Clarify the issue and discuss policy goals and solutions**
   - Work with like-minded advocates to ensure you have a clear statement that articulates reasons policy makers or agency administration should:
     - Support your recommendations rather than your opponents' position
     - Persuade their colleagues to support your suggested policy option/goals
     - Provide additional funding and regulatory authority if necessary.
   - Identify alternative solutions to addressing the issue. Think about the solutions in terms of goals, data collection for evidence-guided practices, eligibility rules, service delivery system, and financing.

2. **Negotiate consensus**
   - Meet with client advocacy groups to determine a mutually acceptable goal and solutions to addressing the issue in your state.
   - Develop a one-page information sheet about the issue and actions desired so that a consistent and concise message can be delivered to legislators.

Months 5–6: During Legislative Session—if applicable
1. **Tracking the legislative process**
   - Continue to speak with legislators and look for a legislator or legislative committee who will introduce and/or support the bill(s) you have outlined as essential to reform. As always, carefully protect identity of your clients. **Use composite examples that could not be linked to specific cases.** Don't be surprised if a bill is not introduced (or, even if introduced, fails to gain traction) during the first year.
   - Maintain contact with key actors or agency administrators. Attend meetings held by the advocacy group(s) working on similar issues.
   - Continue to increase public awareness of the issue through media efforts, community organizing, and research.

Months 7–8: Evaluating Your Efforts
1. **Evaluate campaign**
   - Even if the legislation you supported was not introduced or your plan was not implemented at the agency level, evaluate whether public awareness and support of the issue has increased. Did any legislators or agency administrators express interest in pursuing the policy in the next legislative session or at a later date?
   - If your legislation or policy/program was implemented, examine benefit utilization data as part of the evaluation of your initiatives. You can also use these data to increase community interest and awareness

around this issue, in addition to influencing the tenor of media coverage and/or any public opinion polling on the issue.

- Whether or not your outcome was achieved, review the steps you took in the process and determine which were the most and least effective and why.

2. **Use evaluation to think about strategies for next year.**

- **Strategies may include:**
  - Periodically meeting with interested legislators or agency administrators to encourage continued work on the issue.
  - Organizing a letter writing campaign encouraging those affected to write to their legislator to increase awareness of the need.
  - Staying in close contact with advocacy groups to strategize about how best to accomplish your goals.
  - Planning for the next legislative session (if applicable).
    - Continue to implement strategies to raise public awareness whether on a personal or professional basis.

3. **Keep copies of all your research and lists of contacts.**
   Issues have a way of coming up year after year. Particularly if an incident happens in your state that draws attention to this issue, you will want to be ready to provide information on possible ways to address the problem.

If legislators or agency administrators did work to get changes made, be sure to thank them.

EXERCISES

1. Go to the Riverton case at the text website (www.routledgesw.com/cases). What are the perceived needs and issues facing the Riverton community in regard to homelessness? Whose perspectives inform these perceptions?

a. What do you see as some of the strengths of the community?

b. Based on your review of the components of the Riverton case study, who are the key actors that you can identify to talk to about their concerns related to homelessness in Riverton and the possible underlying factors that are contributing to these concerns?

c. One of the resources on the website accompanying this text series is the Alvadora Neighborhood Association Meeting video. This meeting takes place in Riverton. You can view this video to see the process by which policy issues are introduced, considered, and decided upon in community meetings at the local level. You can also see some of the key stakeholders in Riverton. What factors do you think are motivating their actions in this meeting?

d. The city commission in Riverton is considering implementing an alcohol impact zone to deal with citizen complaints about people living at the homeless shelter. Use the Internet to learn about alcohol impact zones. Are you for or against implementation of this policy? Why? How does the NASW *Code of Ethics* inform your stance?

e. How do you think the problem of homelessness is being framed in Riverton? How do you think you might be able to reframe the discussion of homelessness so that there would be more attention paid to the root causes of homelessness such as lack of jobs and affordable housing?

f. Search online for information on strategies to reduce homelessness that communities like Riverton might consider. Identify three policy and/or program initiatives besides an alcohol impact zone that might work in Riverton. To what extent do these alternatives incorporate the strengths perspective? If these policy or program initiatives were implemented in Riverton, how could you involve the people who are homeless in evaluation of the initiative? Identify baseline information you would need to collect before the initiative was implemented and describe how you would evaluate the initiative.

g. Identify four strategies you might use to find common ground so that the community can begin to focus on needed policy and program reforms to reduce the number of people who are homeless in Riverton.

h. What have you learned from this case about policy practice that you might go out and apply in a real community?

2. Go to the Sanchez family case at the website for this text (www.routledgesw. com/policy). Your policy practice work with the Sanchez family needs to be guided by a dual assessment. Remember, a dual assessment is assessment of a client's strengths, needs, and resources to guide social work practice with the individual client, and assessment of the specific policy issues that impact your clients to help you consider what interventions requiring use of your policy practice skills are necessary. In completing the Exercises in Chapter 1, you did a dual assessment related to the Sanchez family. Consider the policy and program issues you identified in the course of the dual assessment. After identifying

specific policy and program issues, specify three steps you might take in the policy practice arena to help address these issues.

3. In order to make an effective case for changes in immigration policy, it can be helpful to involve families who experience the impact of current immigration policy in their daily lives.

   a. Who in the Sanchez family do you think might be willing to contribute ideas or even talk to legislators or the media about the need for immigration reform?

   b. Do you think it would be a good idea for them to become involved in advocacy work? Why, or why not? What do the NASW *Code of Ethics* and the strengths perspective, respectively, suggest about possible roles for members of the Sanchez family in this policy practice arena?

   c. If they do become involved, how could the chances the Sanchez family would experience negative consequences for their activism be reduced?

   d. What positive consequences might family members who engaged in activism experience?

   e. How would you go about first getting their permission, and then collecting their stories and getting their ideas to inform advocacy work for immigrants? What confidentiality requirements and other ethical issues should you consider before doing this?

   f. How would a social worker coming from a different cultural background from the Sanchez family need to approach this cultural difference in planning for effective policy practice?

4. Go to the Carla Washburn case at the website for this text (www.routledgesw. com/cases). In doing a dual assessment of Carla Washburn, you identify public home and community-based services provided through Area Agencies on Aging as critical programs that help older adults like Carla Washburn stay in the community. However, you are concerned these programs will be cut back during times of economic downturn.

   a. Go to the website of your local Area Agency on Aging to determine what services they offer that might be of help to Carla Washburn.

   b. Using online or print media resources, look for information about the impact of the current budget situation in your state on Area Agency on Aging and related services. How are these programs framed? How are the strengths and voices of the target population included (or not)?

   c. Contact an advocacy group for older adults in your state, such as the state chapter of the AARP or the Older Women's League (OWL) and find out what kind of advocacy work they are doing to promote expansion of these home- and community-based programs, or at least keep them from being drastically cut back.

5. Go to the RAINN case at the website for this text (www.routledgesw.com/cases). As more and more social services are offered online, new policy issues will need attention. Identify policy issues that are new or may be different when services

are offered online. Do you have ideas about how these issues may be best addressed? How do you think online services such as RAINN should be regulated? What types of agency policies could help to ensure that clients' needs are met within the context of this new service delivery model? If you were a social worker working with this effort, how might you make a case for the development of these policies?

6. Consider what you have learned about policy practice in this chapter as you develop your intervention plans for Brickville.

   a. What policies do you think the people in Brickville might identify as in need of change in their community?

   b. Which members of the Brickville community might be ready to take action to address ineffective policies that impact Brickville?

   c. Can you identify three possible steps you could take in using your policy practice skills in Brickville?

7. Go to www.socialworkersspeak.org. This website is part of the NASW effort to influence how social work issues and social policy are portrayed by the media. Look at the current topics. As outlined in this chapter, the media can have a significant influence on what policy issues get on the agenda of legislators and whether a successful claim can be made for public action on behalf of our clients. What issues are being discussed on this website? Do you think this discussion is helping to change policies on behalf of our clients? What improvements can you suggest to increase its effectiveness?

8. Identify the strengths that students, researchers, and practitioners can bring to the policy making process. Think about an area of policy practice where you have passion. What issues do you think are the most pressing and in need of your political involvement? It may be reducing rates of child abuse, making sure disabled older adults do not go hungry, or any of the many issues in need of advocacy. How might you get the groups identified above to become more involved in helping to improve policies in your area of interest? Suggest at least three specific strategies.

9. Given the policy practice interest area you identified in Question 8, should you focus your involvement in policy practice on federal or state-level policies? What are the benefits and drawbacks of each level (federal or state) of involvement?

Civil Rights

Once social change begins it cannot be reversed. You cannot un-educate the person that has learned to read. You cannot humiliate the person who feels pride. You cannot oppress the people who are not afraid anymore.

Cesar Chavez

We, the people, declare today that the most evident of truths—that all of us are created equal—is the star that guides us still, just as it guided our forebears through Seneca Falls and Selma and Stonewall . . .

President Barack Obama, Second Inaugural Address, January 21, 2013

Each time someone stands up for an ideal, or acts to improve the lot of others, or strikes out against injustice, he sends forth a tiny ripple of hope.

Robert F. Kennedy

S OCIAL WORK IS COMMITTED TO THE PROTECTION, PRESERVATION, and advancement of civil rights because civil rights are key to our work for social justice. Civil rights are legally enforceable protections that prevent arbitrary abuse by the state or other individuals. However, the rights taken for granted by citizens who are part of majority populations, for example, the right to vote, the right to fair treatment in employment, the right to live where desired, and the right to marry, are often denied to oppressed populations. This reality has driven oppressed groups and their allies to advocate for civil rights policies and their enforcement in order to eliminate discrimination and promote equality. In this chapter, we will examine major civil rights policies as well as some of the challenges still faced to secure civil rights for specific oppressed groups. The first section of the chapter offers a brief overview of the recent and current status of various oppressed groups, building on the historical base provided in Chapters 2 and 3. The second section focuses more narrowly on key laws and court rulings directed toward securing and expanding the basic rights of marginalized groups in the U.S.

One of the many benefits of being a social worker is getting to know people from diverse cultures and backgrounds. The NASW *Code of Ethics* specifically requires that social workers "act to expand choice and opportunity for all people, with special regard for vulnerable, disadvantaged, oppressed, and exploited people and groups" (NASW, 2008). Social workers embrace diversity and believe that a range of human characteristics—age, race, gender, ability level, sexual orientation—is normal and acceptable. These characteristics are not a valid basis for withholding basic societal benefits such as the right to an adequate education, housing, health care, employment, and social services. Yet, African Americans, American Indians, Hispanics or Latinos, Asian Americans, immigrants, women, people with disabilities, gay men and lesbians, people who are bisexual and transgender, and older adults all face threats to their civil rights, which contribute to the problems that bring them into contact with social workers. The capacity to help these clients reach their goals is either impeded or bolstered by the quality of the civil rights policies that protect them.

When you have completed this chapter, you will understand why it was necessary to enact legislation that has protected and increased people's civil rights. Moreover, you will be more aware of additional areas in which people are still being denied their basic rights. Your charge, then, as a social worker and someone who is committed to social justice, is to use what you learn to help improve conditions for members of oppressed groups throughout your social work career.

BACKGROUND AND HISTORY

Knowledge about diverse cultures and backgrounds is important in order to understand how policies and programs influence outcomes for members of these groups and how policies that work more effectively for these groups might be crafted. Taking an ecological approach helps us focus on the environmental barriers all groups face in meeting their needs and achieving their goals. The most obvious barrier encountered by disadvantaged groups is being underrepresented or not represented at all in the halls of the U.S. Congress, in our nation's courts, in most state legislatures, in executive positions in corporate America, and even in leadership positions in many social service agencies.

As explained in the policy practice section of Chapter 6, when people are making policy for target groups whom they perceive as unlike themselves—that is, the "other"—those policies likely will not adequately reflect the goals, strengths, and needs of the target group. In fact, many historical and current policies have erected barriers and promoted discrimination that increased the power and wealth of dominant groups. Members of oppressed groups may be subjected to racism, sexism, homophobia, ageism, and discrimination in employment, access to public benefits, physical and behavioral health care, housing, and even exercise of their democratic rights. Although race is an arbitrary classification of people, and the term is no longer widely used because it has little basis in human genetics or biology, racism clearly continues to influence interactions in our society. Racism is stereotyping and generalizing, usually negatively, about a group of people related by common descent or heredity often based on any or a combination of various physical features such as skin color or eye shape.

A key component of racial ideologies is that they connect physical characteristics with intellectual or behavioral traits such as intelligence and criminal behavior. Consequently, they tend to divide humanity into "superior" and "inferior" groups. This classification of people according to their perceived worth is manifest along other lines, as well. Sexism is discrimination based solely on gender. **Homophobia** is the fear of, and discrimination against, people who are gay, lesbian, transgender, or bisexual, on the basis of their sexual orientation or gender identity. Ageism is discrimination based on age, usually directed toward older adults, but often toward children as well.

Members of oppressed groups receive inequitable treatment in many areas. For example, they are frequently provided with poorer medical care and police protection. They lack equitable access to quality education and job opportunities, disparities that drive dramatic gaps in income and wealth between populations. Portrayals of their strengths and capacities are often hard to find in the media, and discrimination against them is often ignored or glossed over, or simply accepted as part of "the way things are." Indeed, some progress against the most overt forms of discrimination has led certain groups to argue that the U.S. does not face additional civil rights challenges, but social workers see otherwise in our daily practice. If you examine social and economic outcome indicators for various groups of Americans, you will see large differences for oppressed groups. For example, take a look at the national outcome indicators documented in *Kids Count Data Book*, a book published yearly by the Annie E. Casey Foundation that draws attention to the disparate outcomes for children from different ethnic groups across the U.S. *The Kids Count Data Book* can be found at the website of the Annie E. Casey Foundation (www.aecf.org). You will see that people of color have very high poverty rates. Other statistics, such as rates of suicide, incarceration, infant mortality, school dropout, and unemployment, may also be much higher for a given group. As we have seen, throughout history people often have attributed poorer outcomes to individual deficits of group members. If you still think individual failings and group characteristics, rather than societal barriers, are primarily to blame for these poor group outcomes, please challenge yourself to re-examine the realities of the lives of many members of these groups.

As policy analysts, you need to ask how social policies and programs contribute to these poorer outcomes and contribute to the systemic barriers that produce these clearly inequitable trends. Further, as policy practitioners, you need to work with oppressed groups to craft policies that more effectively help them fulfill needs and reach goals. Policies designed to ensure civil rights, as well as policies that institutionalize discrimination, need careful attention. Exhibit 7.1 lists a few of the most pressing negative outcomes for oppressed groups that can be addressed using policy practice skills. Perhaps one of these outcomes represents an issue for which you have passion enough to spark involvement.

OUTCOMES THAT NEED TO CHANGE

EXHIBIT 7.1

Focus on Outcomes

- **High rates of violence against women**. Every two minutes, somewhere in America, a person is sexually assaulted. One in six American women are victims of sexual assault, and one in 33 men. Every year approximately 207,754 individuals are victims of sexual assault. About 44 percent of rape victims are under age 18, and 80 percent are under 30. More than half of sexual assaults go unreported (Rape Abuse and Incest National Network, 2013 from U.S. Department of Justice data).

- **Large differences in educational attainment**. The percentage of Americans with a college degree varies greatly, with 52.4 percent of Asian Americans and 30.3 percent of white people having a college degree or more compared to 19.8 percent of the black population and 13.9 percent of Hispanics (U.S. Census Bureau from the 2012 Statistical Abstract).

- **Elevated dropout rates for Hispanics**. Of Hispanics aged 16–24, 13.6 percent dropped out of high school in 2011. This is compared to white individuals at 5 percent, black at 7.3 percent, and all races at 7.1 percent (U.S. Department of Education, 2013).

- **Many groups victimized by hate crimes**. For 2011, FBI hate crime data documented 6,222 hate crimes reported by 14,575 law enforcement agencies across the country. 47.4 percent of bias-motivated offenses were based on race, 19.2 percent on religion, 20.4 percent on sexual orientation, 12.2 percent on ethnicity, and 0.8 percent on disability (U.S. Department of Justice, 2013).

- **Elders as well as younger people with disabilities often institutionalized rather than having the choice of receiving long-term care services in the community**. The majority of public funds for long-term care continue to go to nursing facilities rather than home- and community-based services.

- **High rates of children of color living in communities with concentrated poverty**. African American children are the largest racial/ethnic group living in neighborhoods of concentrated poverty where 30 percent or more of the population is poor. African American children represent 27 percent of the population in high poverty areas, followed by American Indians at 24 percent, Hispanics at 19 percent, Asian/Pacific Islanders at 6 percent, and white Americans at 3 percent (Annie E. Casey Foundation using data from the Population Reference Bureau's analysis of data from the 2006–2010 American Community Survey).

- **Income disparities between men and women**. In 2011, the female to male earnings ratio based on full-time employment in the U.S. was 77 percent (U.S. Census, 2012—from the Income, Poverty, and Health Insurance Coverage in the United States 2011 population report).

- **High poverty rates for people with physical and mental disabilities**. For people aged 18–24 who have one or more disabilities, 28.8 percent are below the poverty level. That is, more than 4 million persons with a disability are living below the poverty level. Further, 18–64 year olds with a disability represented 16.3 percent of people in poverty compared to 7.7 percent of all individuals in this age group (U.S. Census Bureau, 2012—from the Income, Poverty, and Health Insurance Coverage in the United States 2011 population report).

- **Very high poverty rates for elderly women of color**. Hispanic and black women who lived alone experienced the highest rates of poverty among the elderly population at 40.8 percent and 30.7 percent, respectively (Administration on Aging based on U.S. Census data).

When examining civil rights, it is critical to consider not only equal rights but also policies that can help oppressed groups who have suffered structural discrimination for years, to surmount the effects of that prolonged discrimination. Structural discrimination refers to entrenched and long-lasting societal practices that favor one group over another based on group characteristics such as skin color. The concept of structural discrimination can be more easily understood by considering its effects for a group such as inner-city Mexican American girls. Take a moment to think back about the concepts related to empowering niches presented in Chapter 6. What are the barriers that keep assets such as adequate educational opportunities, access to well-paying jobs, health care, and adequate family income out of the inner-city area? Discrimination in hiring, lack of Latino physicians, and state school funding policies that negatively impact poor communities, are just a few of the reasons you and your classmates may list. When populations begin from very unequal starting points, policies that afford "equal opportunities" to each group can still result in highly unequal outcomes.

In examining policy options and strategies for decreasing discrimination, it is important to also consider the strengths and resources of oppressed groups. For example, voting rights for African Americans were secured in large part because church leaders in African American communities, where churches have traditionally been major community resources, mobilized and provided leadership. Similarly, as discussed in Chapter 3, Cesar Chavez, Dolores Huerta, and other Latino activists organized farm laborers to press for an end to discriminatory employment practices. If differences can be embraced and strengths recognized, then the need for people to relinquish their cultural roots and diverse backgrounds in order to be accepted in U.S. society might diminish. Instead, we can draw on these strengths to help create more equitable social policies and to enrich our overall society.

Social work students, like their clients, come from varied backgrounds. You might have grown up on stories of Cesar Chavez and his work to organize migrant workers. You also might be familiar with the historical images of "Whites Only" drinking water fountains and lunch counters, and you even might have memorized some of Dr. Martin Luther King, Jr.'s speeches. Conversely, you may have limited familiarity with the history of civil rights, and you may not have had much opportunity to consider how your own group memberships shape the advantages and disadvantages you experience. As a social worker, you cannot understand current civil rights debates if you do not know this history. If you need or want to learn more than what is covered in this chapter and the history chapters, your instructor can provide you with a list of web links to videos and other online resources. You can also see the faces of famous civil rights leaders and the places where they made history by visiting the website of the National Park Service (www.nps.gov) and searching for civil rights, women's rights, Mexican American rights, Native American rights, African American rights, and gay rights. Even better, you can make it a point to visit these historical sites in your area or when you travel. You may also want to talk with friends, family

EXHIBIT 7.2

Cesar Estrada Chavez and Dolores Huerta at the End of their Hunger Strike, 1968.

members, community leaders, or even clients whose life experiences can add to your understanding of our nation's struggles for civil rights and social justice.

CIVIL RIGHTS POLICIES IN THE UNITED STATES

The historical milestones in securing civil rights are integral parts of the history of U.S. social policy and, as such, have been discussed in earlier chapters. This section examines how these milestones have affected the current status of marginalized groups in this country. It focuses both on the progress that has been achieved and on the challenges that continue to confront us.

The foundation of civil rights protection in the U.S. is the Constitution, particularly the Bill of Rights. The Bill of Rights refers to the first ten amendments to the Constitution, which were ratified in 1791. Protection of basic civil rights under the U.S. Constitution, in many instances, is not confined to citizens. Rights reserved for citizens, such as the right to vote, or hold elective office, are spelled out in the Constitution. However, in most cases, the word "people" is used when specifying basic rights. These rights, then, apply equally to non-citizens who fall under U.S. jurisdiction. For example, the 14th Amendment to the U.S. Constitution states

> No state shall make or enforce any law which shall abridge the privileges or immunities of **citizens** of the U.S.; nor shall any state deprive any person of life, liberty, or property, without due process of law; nor deny to any **person** within its jurisdiction the equal protection of the laws.

Protections under the Bill of Rights include:

- Freedom of religion; freedom of speech; freedom of the press; the right to assemble (First Amendment).

- Freedom from "unreasonable searches and seizures" (Fourth Amendment).

- Protection against self-incrimination (Fifth Amendment).

- The right to "a speedy and public trial, by an impartial jury" (Sixth Amendment).

- Protection against excessive bail and "cruel and unusual punishments" (Eighth Amendment).

In addition, the civil rights of individuals and groups have been expanded on numerous occasions through subsequent amendments to the Constitution. For example, as shown in Chapter 2, the amendments approved during Reconstruction officially abolished slavery and extended voting rights and due process to the former slaves. Because we discussed the role of the Constitution with regard to civil rights in the history chapters, this chapter only briefly highlights particular amendments as they pertain to specific oppressed groups.

Disenfranchised Groups and Civil Rights

Many groups of U.S. citizens have faced discrimination. We have discussed the history of these groups. In this section, we will focus on the successes and shortcomings of efforts to enhance the civil rights of these groups. To do this, we must also examine the effects of social policies directed toward these groups.

African Americans   Chapters 2 and 3 trace the historical struggle for African American civil rights, from slavery, to Jim Crow, through the civil rights movement and the implementation of affirmative action. The landmark laws in this movement are the Civil Rights Act of 1964, which outlaws racial discrimination in employment and mandates equal access to public accommodations, and the Voting Rights Act of 1965. We will examine these laws in detail later in the chapter. Another key ruling is *Brown* vs. *Board of Education*, which declared school segregation to be unconstitutional. Achieving these legal victories, while requiring decades of struggle, proved easier than achieving real racial equity in the United States. Today, over 70 percent of young black children still go to schools where more than 50 percent of the students are from minority groups and almost half of white tudents go to schools where more than 90 percent of students are white.

EXHIBIT 7.3

Ruby Bridges (1960), the First Black Child to Attend an All-White Elementary School in the South.

EXHIBIT 7.4

Whitney M. Young

Whitney M. Young was born in Kentucky to a father who was the president of an all-black boarding high school and a mother who was the first African American Postmistress in Kentucky. Young earned an undergraduate degree in science and as a soldier in World War II he was trained in electrical engineering at MIT. After the war, Young earned his master's degree in social work and began volunteering at a local branch of the National Urban League. Young became president of the organization in 1961. While at the National Urban League, Young significantly increased both the number of employees in, and the annual budget of, the organization. Also, he urged major corporations to hire black workers for jobs that had been previously held by white employees. Because of his close relationships with influential business leaders, many in the African American community felt that Young had sold out to the white establishment. Young himself denied these accusations and instead focused on his belief that it was critical to work within the system to bring about change. When he felt it was called for, Young did take a strong stance on civil rights issues—such as when he assisted in organizing the March on Washington in 1963. Besides his position at the National Urban League, Young served at the President of the National Association of Social Workers from 1969 to 1971. While at NASW, he ensured that the organization focused on the major social and human rights issues that were facing the profession at the time, such as poverty, race reconciliation, and ending the Vietnam War. In 1971 Young died from a heart attack. Young is remembered as an influential civil rights leader who through his work was able to break down many of the barriers and inequalities facing African Americans.

Every man is our brother, and every man's burden is our own. Where poverty exists, all are poorer. Where hate flourishes, all are corrupted. Where injustice reins, all are unequal.

Source: Whitney M. Young

In addition, the unemployment rate for African American men is more than double that for white males (University of California-Berkley, 2012). Although the elections of Barack Obama in 2008 and 2012 marked a victory in the work to achieve equality for African Americans, the struggle is far from over.

We have also discussed the leadership roles of African Americans who were instrumental in shaping the civil rights movement. They blazed a trail that provided inspiration for other social movements focused on women's rights, disability rights, and rights for other minority groups. The events leading up to the passage of civil rights legislation, as well as the difficulties encountered in enforcing civil rights, make clear that it takes the long-term commitment of people who are passionate about civil rights to enact needed policies. Moreover, once policies are enacted, their proponents must continue to be vigilant to ensure that they are enforced. Leadership for civil rights efforts most often comes from members of the group experiencing discrimination. However, other groups are often motivated to join the struggle when they witness the harm done by discrimination and when there are specific appeals to our common values of freedom and opportunity. As discussed in previous chapters, economic, social, and historical factors contribute to support for discriminatory practices, and change does not happen without conflict. During these conflicts, the strengths of oppressed groups become clear. In fact, it is often through engaging in conflict that individuals and communities build their strengths. The African American community continues to provide leadership in the struggle for civil rights as well as other struggles for social justice. For more information on the history of African Americans' struggle for civil rights, visit the website of the National Association for the Advancement of Colored People (www.naacp.org and go to the Interactive Historical Timeline (http://www.naacp.org/pages/naacp-history).

Native Americans   Like African Americans, Native Americans were denied basic civil rights throughout most of the nation's history. Of central concern for many Native Americans is tribal sovereignty, which refers to the right of Indian peoples to govern themselves, determine tribal membership, regulate tribal business and domestic relations, and manage tribal property. Sovereignty implies a government-to-government relationship between the federal government and the tribes. However, as seen in Chapter 2, as far back as 1831, the Supreme Court ruled in *Cherokee Nation* vs. *Georgia* that Indian tribes are "domestic dependent nations" and, in effect, declared them to be wards of the federal government (Commager, 1958, p. 256). Subsequent government actions such as the Dawes Act of 1887 further undermined tribal sovereignty. In 1934, the Indian Reorganization Act gave tribes more autonomy in handling their own affairs. However, the termination policies instituted in the 1950s further eroded both tribal sovereignty and traditional cultural practices. To challenge these policies, groups such as the American Indian Movement (AIM) resorted to direct action, such as the occupation of Alcatraz and Wounded Knee. Other groups used the courts to press for the restoration of traditional land, water, and fishing rights. The Indian Self-Determination and Education Assistance Act of 1975 affirmed Native Americans' rights to be self-governing and to have greater autonomy and authority over federal programs for Indians.

Native Americans continue to fight for their civil rights, often on the basis of treaties and sovereignty rather than the U.S. Constitution. It is important to recognize that tribal sovereignty occurs within the economic and cultural contexts of the dominant culture in the U.S. Cultural issues that influence the ability to practice and pass on traditional religious beliefs, languages, and social practices without fear of discrimination are particularly important to many Native Americans. Their religious freedom has been compromised by denial of access to religious sites by the government, and their ability to worship through traditional means has been restricted. For example, the Supreme Court refused to prevent the government from building roads through forest lands that certain tribes considered sacred, even though one justice acknowledged that this construction "could have devastating effects on traditional Indian religious practices" (Postrel, 1988). During the last decade, Native American advocacy organizations have been specifically focusing on strengthening tribal advocacy before the U.S. Supreme Court and have developed the Tribal Supreme Court Project as part of the Tribal Sovereignty Protection Initiative. For more information on the struggle for Native American rights and relevant research, visit the website of the Native Americans Rights Fund (www.narf. org) and the website of the National Congress of American Indians Policy Research Center (www.ncaiprc.org).

Native Americans are also pressing for adequate funding to fully implement the Indian Child Welfare Act (ICWA) of 1978. This legislation is discussed in detail in Chapter 9. The ICWA mandates that tribes and tribal courts oversee decision making regarding Native American children who are facing out-of-home placement, thus making it more likely that their cultures will be preserved. However, lack of adequate federal funding makes such oversight very difficult for small tribes with limited resources. In 2008, the Fostering Connection to Success and Increasing Adoptions Act became law. This legislation made it possible for tribes to access additional federal funding to pay for foster and kinship care and to recruit and train caregivers. Native American leaders are working with tribes to implement more effective initiatives to increase the safety, sense of belonging, and well-being of their children. Battles over enforcement of the ICWA continue in the courts. To learn more about current initiatives to protect Native American children, go to the website of the National Indian Child Welfare Association (www.nicwa. org).

On reservations and in other urban and rural areas, Native Americans have suffered long-term bias and discrimination. Consequently, outcomes include disproportionately high rates of poverty, infant mortality, unemployment, and alcohol abuse in addition to low high-school completion rates. As the nation began to emerge from the recession in 2011, for example, Native Americans had an official unemployment rate more than twice the rate of non-Hispanic whites, and that joblessness is reported to be far higher in some areas, with more than half of Native Americans on reservations without jobs (U.S. Bureau of Labor Statistics, 2012b). Securing equal employment and educational opportunity is necessary if these outcomes are to change. Many tribes have opted to open casinos on their lands in order to use gambling as a source of income. However, prior to opening a casino, the tribe must obtain permission from the state government. This requirement has resulted in many legal disputes between tribes and states concerning tribal sovereignty.

Initiatives to reduce health disparities in tribal communities were bolstered by permanent reauthorization of the Indian Health Care Improvement Act (IHCIA) in 2010. The IHCIA authorizes health care services for American Indians and Alaska Natives through the Indian Health Service. This reauthorization was part of the Affordable Care Act which also created new programs to improve health outcomes in tribal communities.

Native American groups as well as other minority groups are also concerned about the "digital divide," the disparity in access to computers and the Internet between majority and minority groups. Lack of access to communication and information technology puts these groups at even greater risk of being unable to take advantage of educational and employment opportunities.

Hispanics/Latinos These largely interchangeable terms refer to the ethnic and cultural origin of people who come from Spanish-speaking countries. Chapters 2 and 3 traced the history of Mexican Americans—in the southwest. This group, as well as legal and undocumented migrant workers, has served as a source of indispensable yet inexpensive labor throughout much of U.S. history, particularly in the agricultural sector. As such, they live and work under difficult and often unhealthy conditions. In addition to Mexican Americans, immigrants and refugees from Spanish-speaking countries in Central and South America as well as Puerto Ricans, who are U.S. citizens, have experienced widespread discrimination and abuse even as they provided the labor that helped build this country. Today, immigration policy is a source of sharp debate in the U.S. political system. Some Americans are demanding that the government limit legal immigration and strengthen border patrols to prevent undocumented immigrants from entering the country, while immigrant rights organizations and immigrants themselves are pushing for policies that would recognize immigrants' economic and social contributions. These divides encompass many aspects of U.S. social policy, including the question of whether to provide educational and social services for undocumented immigrants and how to address future labor force needs. Recently, policies have even sought to restrict service eligibility of U.S. citizen children of immigrant parents; for example, some states have changed their calculation for SNAP (Supplemental Nutrition Assistance Program, or "Food Stamps") eligibility, making it more difficult for some children who are U.S. citizens to receive food aid, because of their parents' immigration status. These policy restrictions exacerbate social workers' concerns about the reluctance of Hispanic families with mixed immigration status to seek services to which family members are legally entitled. For example, a child born in the U.S. is entitled to health care if the family has a low income. However, the family may also contain an older sibling not born in the U.S., parents who are undocumented immigrants, or who are lawful permanent residents not yet eligible for public benefits. Fear of deportation, confusion about eligibility, or concerns about being labeled a "public charge" keeps them from getting health services for their child. Those non-citizens labeled a "public charge" can later be denied U.S. citizenship, a goal for most immigrants, for having depended on public assistance. Families are routinely split apart when parents are arrested and deported and must choose whether to leave a child who is a U.S. citizen here, or attempt to rebuild their lives in the country of origin, even though the children may have never lived there before or do not speak the language. Given the complexity of controlling immigration along the lengthy and sometimes sparsely populated Mexican border, the deep connections between Latinos in the U.S. and their family members in other countries, and the economic benefits that accrue to U.S. businesses that employ these immigrants, high levels of success in stemming illegal immigration are unlikely. In contrast, energy put into developing more responsive services, a workable process for supporting immigrants' aspirations of U.S. citizenship, a more targeted enforcement regimen, and access to education for people from diverse cultures can fuel economic growth. Work to get comprehensive immigration reform legislation through the Congress is ongoing.

As detailed above, the Hispanic community is very diverse, with distinctly different social and historical backgrounds. For example, Latinos living in New Mexico may have very different backgrounds and very different opportunities than do Cuban Americans living in Florida or Puerto Ricans in New York. Although the number of Hispanic Americans who are successful professionals, government leaders, and businesspeople is increasing, Hispanics continue to be over-represented among families with low incomes. Mexican Americans, particularly, continue to experience deficits in education which contribute to higher levels of poverty. Historically, some states with high concentrations of Latinos engaged in discriminatory practice such as segregated schools and channeling of Latino children into vocational schools or back into farm labor. Access to adequate education is particularly crucial, because although about 17 percent of the nation's total population is Hispanic, over 20 percent of U.S. children younger than five are Hispanic (U.S. Census Bureau, 2012h).

In recent decades, the Hispanic population in the U.S. has grown significantly. Hispanics now outnumber African Americans, and they are the largest ethnic group in the nation. According to Census Bureau projections, Hispanics will constitute 30 percent of the nation's population by 2050 (U.S. Census Bureau, 2009c). Because this population is growing so rapidly and because Latino voters were decisive factors in President Obama's 2008 and 2012 victories, these voters are now receiving attention from politicians with diverse agendas who are intent on winning their votes.

Around the country and in Washington DC, the numbers of Hispanic legislators and government officials are increasing. Thus, there is reason to hope that the power of an expanding number of Hispanic voters and elected officials will lead to the passage of policies to reduce discrimination. For more information on work to improve opportunities for Hispanic Americans, access the website of the National Council of La Raza (www.nclr.org).

Asian Americans   Asian Americans are people living in the U.S. who personally identify themselves as having Asian ancestry. There are over 17.3 million U.S. residents of Asian descent (U.S. Census Bureau, 2012b). Because Asia comprises myriad countries and regions, there are more than 20 Asian American subgroups in the U.S., and the Asian American population is very diverse. Although small in comparison to other ethnic groups in the U.S., its numbers and economic and political influence are growing. Asian Americans currently comprise approximately 5.6 percent of the U.S. population. Three of the largest Asian American groups are Chinese, Filipino, and Asian-Indian, followed by Koreans, Vietnamese, and Japanese. During the last decade, the Asian American population increased nearly 46 percent, the most of any group during that time period. Immigration was a major factor driving this rapid increase. After Spanish, Chinese is the most widely spoken non-English language in the U.S. (U.S. Census Bureau, 2012b). Discrimination is an experience that many Asian Americans share with other ethnic and racial minorities. For example, Chinese immigrants have experienced continuing exploitation in the workplace, from the early periods when they performed very dangerous work in building the nation's railways to the present time when newly arrived immigrants toil in urban sweatshops.

Japanese Americans experienced harsh discrimination during World War II. In particular, Japanese Americans living on the west coast, whom the government determined to be security risks, were incarcerated and sent to internment camps while their lands were confiscated. This policy was carried out even as family members were volunteering for and serving in the military. The internment of Japanese Americans demonstrates how concerns about safety and national security can lead to disregard for the civil rights of particular groups.

Because certain Asian Americans have worked hard to receive higher education and have secured good jobs, people sometimes assume that all Asian Americans are doing well. In fact, this stereotype often leads to the portrayal of Asian Americans as the "model minority." However, this image obscures the fact that Asian Americans experience discrimination and some groups have high rates of poverty. Asian American advocacy groups are working to dispel stereotypes and develop the necessary political influence to remove the remaining barriers to their full participation in society. Asian Americans also find common cause with other oppressed groups, where their policy interests align, as in the coalitions built with Latinos to push for immigration reform and humane treatment in immigration detention facilities. For more information about the history of Asian Americans and these advocacy groups, go to the websites of OCA National (www.ocanational.org), Japanese American

EXHIBIT 7.5

The Rise in the Asian American Population

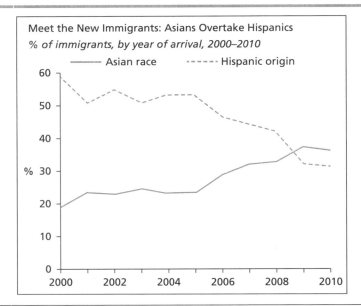

Meet the New Immigrants: Asians Overtake Hispanics

% of immigrants, by year of arrival, 2000–2010

Note: Based on total foreign-born population, including adults and children. Asians include mixed-race Asian population, regardless of Hispanic origin. Hispanics are of any race. The 2010 ACS includes only partial-year arrivals for 2010; arrivals for 2010 adjusted to full-year totals based on analsis of 2005-2009 ACS data on partial-year arrivals.

Source: Pew Research Center analysis of 2010 American Community Survey, Integrated Public Use Microdata Sample (IPUMS) files

PEW RESEARCH CENTER http://www.pewsocialtrends.org/2012/06/19/the-rise-of-asian-americans/

Citizens League (www.jacl.org), and the Southeast Asia Resource Action Center (www.searac.org).

Sexual Orientation and Gender Identity   The struggle for equal rights for people who are lesbian, gay, bisexual, transgender, or questioning (LGBTQ) has been part of the fabric of the struggle for human rights in the 20th and 21st centuries. Historically, millions of Americans regularly suffered discrimination based on sexual orientation, defined as "the tendency to experience erotic or romantic responses to men, women, or both, and the resulting sense of oneself" (NASW, 2003d). Discrimination based on sexual orientation and gender identity continues to create barriers to full social inclusion. Gender identity is a person's internal sense of his or her gender. Although many people's gender identity is congruent with their assigned natal sex, this is not the case for transgender people. Transgender is an umbrella term for people whose gender, gender identity, or expression of gender is in some way different from social norms for their assigned birth sex (NASW, 2009d).

Efforts to end discrimination against these groups in the United States are not new. Although the 1950s were a period of social isolation for gays and lesbians, the groundwork was being laid for the gay rights movement with the development of early gay and lesbian activist organizations such as the Mattachine Society and the Daughters of Bilitis. A major turning point in the struggle for gay rights was the Stonewall Riot of 1969. When New York police raided a gay bar in Greenwich Village and the patrons resisted, gay and lesbian groups around the country began to coalesce. Their activities and the new perspectives they advocated convinced several professional organizations to modify existing policies regarding sexual orientation. For example, in 1974, the American Psychiatric Association (APA) reversed its previous policy and removed homosexuality from its official list of mental disorders; homosexuality was defined instead as an alternative form of biopsychosocial development (Oltmanns and Emery, 1995). Although there has been progress, transgender people may still be required to obtain a diagnosis of "gender identity disorder" in order to receive transgender transition-related health services.

In 1977, the delegate assembly of the NASW passed a public policy statement that called on social workers to help eradicate homophobia. It further proposed that the NASW establish a National Task Force on Gay Rights to begin implementing this policy (Tice and Perkins, 2002). The National Committee on Lesbian, Gay, Bisexual and Transgender Issues (NCLGBTI) is now mandated by the NASW bylaws. The Committee reports on a regular basis to the NASW Board of Directors on matters of policy, and coordinates with the Program Committee on related activities.

It is important to also consider how heterosexual privilege is built into many facets of our society. Like male privilege and white privilege, because the dominant groups have written the social policies, those groups are favored in overt as well as covert ways. Privileges the dominant group takes for granted, such as the right to marry and to be able to show affection for one another in public without being subject to harassment or even violence, are still denied to same-sex couples in some states.

Advocates for LGBTQ rights continue to experience a combination of successes and reversals. They achieved a major victory in 1996 when the Supreme Court, in *Romer* vs. *Evans*, struck down an amendment to Colorado's Constitution that barred cities and localities from enacting laws protecting homosexuals against discrimination. Among the court's arguments was that the amendment violated the "equal protection of the laws" provision of the 14th Amendment (Dripps, 1996). Despite this ruling, however, discrimination in housing and employment remains widespread.

In 2003, the Supreme Court struck down sodomy laws, ruling that intimate consensual sexual conduct was part of the liberty protected by substantive due process under the 14th Amendment. In 2009, President Obama signed into law the Matthew Shepard and James Byrd, Jr. Hate Crimes Prevention Act, part of the National Defense Authorization Act. This legislation extends federal hate crimes law to include crimes motivated by a victim's gender, sexual orientation, gender identity, or disability. Inclusion of gender identity was a significant victory for advocates of people who are transgender.

LGBTQ youths are a particular concern to advocacy groups. These youths often face discrimination in their schools and communities as well as in their homes. They also have higher rates of homelessness and suicide. Repeated experiences of harmful discrimination and bullying can also place LGBTQ youths at increased risk of involvement with the juvenile courts and negatively influence the course of their delinquency case. Advocacy groups made up of attorneys and social workers as well as other concerned adults are working to improve outcomes for these children. For more information on advocacy work for LGBTQ youths involved in the juvenile justice system, go to the website of the National Center for Lesbian Rights (www. nclrights.org), and search for the Equity Project.

People in same-sex relationships in many states still do not have the right to make medical decisions for each other in medical emergencies, do not have rights of inheritance, and can be legally denied custody of their children and the opportunity to provide adoptive and foster care. LGBTQ people encounter barriers that often cause their needs for services, from housing to family counseling, to go largely unmet. Some states have passed domestic partnership legislation, which provides legal recognition or registration to unmarried couples, including same-sex couples. Certain states also extend some rights to same-sex civil unions. These laws do not provide the same entitlements and protections that marriage does in the state and federal systems. In 1996, Congress passed the Defense of Marriage Act (DOMA), which prohibited the recognition of same-sex marriages at the federal level and allowed states to ignore marriages of same-sex couples that are performed in other states. Many states still have statutes prohibiting same-sex marriage as well as constitutional amendments prohibiting same-sex marriages (National Conference of State Legislatures, 2013). Opponents also have called for a federal constitutional ban on same-sex marriages.

However, the policy tide seems to be turning in favor of marriage equality. In 2011, the Obama administration announced that it had concluded that DOMA is unconstitutional and that it would no longer defend DOMA in the courts. In 2012, a second Appeals court ruled that DOMA does violate the equal protection clause of the Constitution. As the legal case against DOMA continued, the law was defended only by attorneys representing members of Congress who oppose gay marriage. In 2013, the Supreme Court struck down Section 3 of DOMA. Section 3 limited the definition of marriage to marriages between a man and a woman for the purposes of federal benefits. The court ruled this was a violation of the U.S. Constitution's guarantee of equal protection under the law. The ruling was a great victory for same-sex couples and their children as well as for the many other people who fought long and hard for marriage equality. Now, legally married couples can claim the many federal benefits, rights and burdens conferred under current U.S. law. However, the full impact of this legislation will only be understood after regulations are developed that specify how federal rights and benefits will be extended to same-sex couples when it is the states, not the federal government, that dictate who is married.

A second Supreme Court case let stand a lower court ruling that California's Proposition 8 same-sex marriage ban was unconstitutional. However, the decision was based on procedural issues rather than addressing the rights of states to ban same-sex marriage. The Court took an incremental approach to this issue and that means that the state-by-state struggle to secure equal rights will continue.

Now that Proposition 8 is no longer in effect in California, it is legal for same-sex couples to marry in a growing number of states including New Jersey, Hawaii, Illinois, California, Massachusetts, Connecticut, Iowa, Vermont, Washington, Maine, New York, Maryland, Delaware, Minnesota, Rhode Island, and New Hampshire. Same-sex marriage is also legal in Washington DC. In some cases, state legislatures were persuaded to pass laws authorizing gay marriage, while measures in other states came as a result of court challenges or, in a few cases, after public referenda on the question. However, many states still have gay marriage bans through either laws or constitutional amendments or both.

Outside the U.S., same-sex marriage is legal in several countries including France, Canada, Norway, the Netherlands, Belgium, Spain, Uruguay, South Africa, Argentina, England, Wales and Sweden. The NASW is committed to full legal and social acceptance and recognition of lesbian, gay, bisexual, and transgender people (NASW, 2009d). Marriage equality has not been the only battle in the campaign for greater civil rights for LGBTQ individuals, however. In late 2010, the U.S. Senate passed a bill repealing the controversial "Don't Ask, Don't Tell" policy that required military servicemen and women to conceal their sexual identities. The policy officially ended when President Barack Obama signed the law in September 2011. The military provided further evidence of the corrosive effects of discrimination; in preparing to implement the inclusive new policy, military experts cited laudable service of LGBTQ soldiers and U.S. interests in attracting qualified candidates to the armed services. To learn more about the campaign for equal rights for LGBTQ Americans, go to the website of the Human Rights Campaign (www.hrc.org).

College students across the state of Washington took on an active role in the fight to uphold the state's marriage equality law during recent elections. Individuals who were opposed to same-sex marriage had succeeded in making the law a ballot issue. Student organizations formed Students United for Marriage (SUM), and along with the Washington United for Marriage coalition engaged in advocacy efforts to defend the existing law. SUM members, located at over two dozen universities and college campuses throughout the state, recruited volunteers, helped get individuals registered to vote and assisted in various get-out-the-vote activities. In the end these efforts proved to be successful as the same-sex marriage law was upheld by voters.

EXHIBIT 7.6

Students Work for Marriage Equality

Source: http://www.hrc.org/blog/entry/students-emerge-as-leaders-in-washington-marriage-fight

People with Disabilities   In 2010, the number of people with a disability in the United States reached 57,000,000, which is about 19 percent of the population not living in institutions (U.S. Census Bureau, 2012c). The advocacy efforts of people with disabilities and their families have changed the face of social policy in the education and employment sectors. The Education for All Handicapped Children Act of 1975 mandates free public education for all children with disabilities. Amendments passed in 1986 extend services to children with disabilities from birth through age five (Pollard, 1995). Other legislation such as the Mental Health Bill of Rights Act and the Developmentally Disabled Assistance and Bill of Rights expand protection and care for people with mental illness and developmental disabilities. However, these laws offer protection only in activities and programs involving the government (NASW, 2009b).

As discussed in Chapter 3, the Americans with Disabilities Act (ADA) of 1990 helped remove deterrents to full citizenship and inclusion for people with disabilities (Pollard, 1995). The ADA requires businesses and employers to make "reasonable accommodations" in order to allow people with disabilities the opportunity to perform job functions. This law has significantly increased the access of people with disabilities to needed resources. We will explore the ADA in depth in the section on major policies and programs. In 1999, the Supreme Court held in the landmark decision *Olmstead* vs. *L.C.* that Title II of the ADA requires states, whenever possible, to place qualified individuals with disabilities in community settings rather than in institutions. The Supreme Court called on the states to develop "comprehensive, effectively working plans" to provide services to people with disabilities in the most integrated settings possible. Additionally, Executive Order No. 13217, Community-Based Alternatives for Individuals with Disabilities, was signed on June 18, 2001. This initiative went beyond the Olmstead decision which mandated that the federal government be involved in quickly accomplishing the task set out for the states. It called on federal agencies to assist the states and also to examine their own policies and procedures to determine whether these policies presented barriers to community-based services. The attorney general and the secretary of the Department of Health and Human Services (USDHHS) were empowered to enforce the *Olmstead* decision. President Obama committed to more rigorously enforcing the Olmstead decision and to providing additional funding to states to aid in compliance. There is an ongoing struggle to get the Olmstead decision fully implemented at the state and federal level. The *Olmstead* decision supports the core social work value of self-determination and may lead to greater community integration for people with mental as well as physical disabilities. These efforts to ensure full inclusion of affected populations also provide inspiration for other campaigns for social justice and have led to important reforms within institutions throughout the social policy landscape, as efforts are made to fully integrate differently abled individuals as clients, workers, and leaders.

Like other groups facing discrimination, people with disabilities experience higher rates of poverty. Further, the number of people with disabilities will grow much larger as (1) the baby boom generation ages and (2) new medical advances make it possible to save people with injuries so serious that they would have died even a few years ago. Disability rights groups can be expected to continue to press their case legislatively as well as through the courts and grassroots, direct action. The combination of growth in the population with disabilities and the loudly voiced goal of the majority of people with disabilities to remain in the community will create fiscal and adaptive challenges for states and will require creative strategic planning to best use limited public resources.

People with mental illness have experienced both gains and setbacks in their pursuit of civil rights. Although people with mental illness have the right to refuse treatment, they may be committed involuntarily for treatment in a psychiatric hospital if they exhibit dangerous behavior or are incapable of self-care. However, once committed, they have the right to treatment. The legislative tenets of a client's right to treatment in the least restrictive community environment and to freedom from harm have been less well established (Marty and Chapin, 2000). One reason for this ambiguity is that the courts have been unwilling to protect the right to treatment outside of the institution when states cut back community-based options because of funding shortfalls. Deinstitutionalization of people with mental disabilities and the recognition of their right to refuse treatment help protect their civil rights. However, unless their right to treatment after they have re-entered the community is established and protected, they are in danger of struggling with mental illness without the needed supports or treatment. This danger has become ever more real as states have cut funding for home- and community-based services and for mental health centers in the face of large budget deficits. As states cut more than $1.5 billion in non-Medicaid funding for mental health services between 2009 and 2011, the National Alliance on Mental Illness called the strained nature of the mental health safety net a "crisis," with tragic consequences for individuals directly and indirectly affected by mental illness (NAMI, 2011). The consequences of inadequate treatment are becoming ever more evident as shamefully high numbers of people with untreated mental illness stack up in our prisons and homeless shelters.

One strategy to improve mental health treatment for people with health insurance is to push for both access and reimbursement for mental health services that are comparable to physical health benefits. Indeed, in 1996 the Mental Health Parity Act was passed. It required employers with more than 50 employees who offer health insurance to include mental health benefits comparable to physical health benefits. Additional laws and regulations to increase mental health parity have also been enacted in recent years including some new provisions under the Affordable Care Act, and are discussed in detail in Chapter 10. Adequate treatment for mental illness that goes beyond prescriptions for psychotropic medications will remain unavailable to many people with mental illness until there is parity in terms of equality of reimbursement as well as simplified access to services. The Bazelon Center for Mental Health and the

Law provides in-depth coverage of current civil rights issues for people with mental illness (www.bazelon.org).

Older Adults The 1964 Civil Rights Act did not prohibit discrimination on the basis of age. Three years later, however, the Age Discrimination in Employment Act (ADEA) prohibited employment discrimination against people between the ages of 40 and 70. Although this law protected workers within this age range, the cap on age allowed employers to enforce mandatory retirement and pursue other age-based discriminatory practices with employees and job applicants over the age of 70. In 1986, the ADEA was amended to eliminate the age cap. This revision abolished mandatory retirement for most employment and made age discrimination illegal for all employees 40 years and older (Equal Employment Opportunity Commission, 1999). In 1990, the Older Workers Benefit Protection Act (OWBPA) further amended the ADEA to specifically prohibit employers from denying benefits to older employees. Despite the numerous laws enacted to protect older workers and the increasing political and economic power of older Americans, alleged age-based discrimination is the fastest-growing source of litigation for unfair dismissal. Further, in the 2009 case *Gross* vs. *FBL Financial, Inc.*, the Supreme Court held that in an ADEA discrimination claim, the defendant employer does not have to prove that it would have taken the action regardless of the plaintiff's age, even when evidence is introduced showing that age was one motivating factor in its decision. Rather, the court held that the plaintiff/employee must prove by a "preponderance of the evidence" that age was the "but for" cause of the defendant's (employer's) demotion of the employee. By putting the burden of proof on the employee claiming discrimination, this ruling makes it more difficult for a worker to win an age discrimination case.

Compassionate ageism—the stereotypical belief that all older adults are frail and incapacitated—has led to the development of public and corporate policies that hinder older adults who are fit and capable, from fully participating in society. In fact, many older adults can and do continue to be employed as well as to contribute to their communities in varied and important ways. Some older adults in their 80s and 90s, and even at 100, are still in the workforce. Changes in the economy—particularly the recession's devastating effects on the retirement savings on some older workers—and changes in society—including the increasing number of older adults and new social expectations about active roles for people in later stages of life—have increased the number of older adults engaged in the workforce in some capacity. Contrary to widespread stereotypes, the older-adult population is quite diverse already in regard to workforce participation as well in many other arenas, and will become increasingly so. For example, the proportion of people age 60 and over who are from minority groups is expected to increase to 23.6 percent by 2030. LGBT individuals are more prominently represented among older populations than in previous generations, and there are wide gaps in the economic well-being of older adults, largely reflecting the economic inequities seen throughout the lifespan. Social policies must be adjusted to reflect this diversity.

Inadequate access to mental health care for older adults has long been an area of concern for social workers. Even though their need for mental health treatment has been well documented and research indicates that mental health treatment for older adults is effective, many mental health centers still see very few clients who are older adults in proportion to their numbers in the population. Ageism on the part of providers and reluctance on the part of older adults to seek help because of fear of stigma and possible institutionalization undoubtedly contribute to this problem, as do routine barriers such as lack of access to transportation or concern about out-of-pocket costs. Nonetheless, low reimbursement and lack of parity for mental health treatment in the Medicare program have also been major contributing factors. However, the passage of The Medicare Improvements for Patients and Providers Act of 2008 is designed to eliminate, over a six-year period, the discriminatory co-payment for outpatient mental health services (NASW, 2009c). This legislation was long sought by NASW, but continued advocacy will be necessary to secure access to adequate mental health care for older adults. Policy evolution in this area may have direct implications for social work students contemplating career options, too, as states consider incentives to encourage more qualified practitioners to focus on the mental health needs of older adults.

Abuse and neglect of vulnerable older adults in the home, community, and institution is a growing problem. There are still insufficient government oversight, unclear requirements and inadequate enforcement and funding for the protection of older adults. States continue to provide uneven enforcement of existing policies and many have yet to implement comprehensive services for older adults who are abused and neglected. These failures can be attributed in large part to societal attitudes about aging, changing divisions of responsibilities between families and the state, and the overall retreat of government from critical areas of obligation, discussed in earlier chapters regarding the influence of economics and politics on policy making.

Older adults also suffer discrimination when their right to self-determination in end-of-life decisions is abrogated. The Patient's Self-Determination Act of 1990 requires all hospitals participating in Medicare and Medicaid to inquire whether adult inpatients have advanced health care directives and to provide information on pertinent state laws and hospital policies. An advance directive is a document or statement produced by the patient specifying her or his choices for medical treatment—including no treatment. An advance directive can also be used to designate a person to make those choices should the patient be unable to do so. Although the 1990 law was intended to protect patients at the end of life, the lack of trained hospital staff who could effectively implement the policy has limited its effectiveness. Further, as a society, we have yet to effectively address the unacceptably high levels of untreated pain that many older adults experience at the end of life. This has been exacerbated by recent state efforts to restrict access to pain medication, which could be addicting; these safety precautions have had the unintended consequence of making it more difficult for individuals who rely on these sophisticated pharmaceuticals to adequately address their significant pain. Conflict surrounding assisted suicide continues to compromise the rights of patients, including older adults, to self-determination at end of life. We will examine policy initiatives to secure and protect the rights of older adults in these areas in Chapter 11. For more information on policy issues that impact older adults, visit the website of the AARP Research Center and the AARP Policy Institute (http://www.aarp.org/research/ppi/health-care/).

Women and Civil Rights   As we observed in reviewing the struggle for gender equality in Chapter 3, the fight for voting rights and for the rights to equity in education and athletics was long and difficult. Although women have made great gains in education and training and can enter many professions that were previously closed to them, the struggle against gender-based discrimination is not over. For example, women working full-time still earn only 82 percent of the salaries of full-time male workers, and the narrowing of this wage gap to this historic low in 2011 is due to declines in men's wages, not real advancements in women's economic standing (Institute for Women's Policy Research, 2012).

When gender equity in the U.S. is compared to that of other countries, it is clear that much more needs to be done. The Global Gender Gap Index developed by the World Economic Forum is a tool for comparing gender-based inequalities on economic, political, education and health-based criteria. In 2012 the U.S. ranked 22nd out of the 135 countries ranked (see the report at: www.weforum.org/reports/global-gender-gap-report-2012). The report also finds a correlation between national competitiveness and the gender gap, indicating that countries that are more successful in closing the gender gap are also better able to compete in the global marketplace. Discrimination against women is seen in all facets of U.S. society, including the highest levels of government. When Sonia Sotomayor and Elena Kagan were appointed to the Supreme Court during the Obama administration, the gender gap on the Supreme Court was reduced. There are now six men and three women on the Supreme Court.

Although the Equal Pay Act of 1963 prohibited wage discrimination on the basis of sex, there were many loopholes in this legislation and the gender gap in pay continued. The Pay Check Fairness Act, which includes the expectations that employers demonstrate that wage differentials between men and women with the same position who do the same work, stem from factors other than sex, and prohibits retaliation against people who ask about their employers' wage practices, has yet to pass in Congress even though it has been reintroduced 18 times. This Act is designed to close some of the loopholes in the Equal Pay Act. The case of Lilly Ledbetter, who sued Goodyear Tire and Rubber Company for discrimination based on sex, drew attention to the gender gap in pay. Concern about this case eventually led to passage of the Lilly Ledbetter Fair Pay Act of 2009. This legislation is examined in detail later in the chapter. However, much more work will be necessary if this gender gap is to be narrowed. Affirmative action has also helped women achieve gains in the workplace. However, as we shall see in the next section of this chapter, changes in affirmative action as well as other policies and programs have differential effects on women and men. In addition, the threats to affirmative action, legislatively and in the courts, could result in retreat from some of the advances women have made in recent years, especially in terms of access to employment opportunities.

Because women are more often the primary caregivers for children and elders, the lack of policies to adequately support people who work and care for dependents continues to place female workers at a disadvantage. This combination of factors contributes to the "feminization of poverty," that is, the disproportionately high number of women and their children who are living in poverty. Women's wages and earning potential are compromised by the lack of policy recognition of the value of their caregiving roles, and they are much more likely to be adversely financially affected by rising rates of divorce than are men. Moreover, women who have been poor all their lives face old age with inadequate retirement savings and pensions. The poverty rate for people age 65 and older decreases for men but increases slightly for women, compared to poverty rates in earlier life (Issa and Zedlewski, 2011). Finally, the current trend of dual-income families in the U.S. means that all family members, including men, suffer from lower wages paid to women. Low wages for women are a major cause of childhood poverty. For more information on the struggle for gender equity, go to the website of the National Organization for Women (www.now.org).

Women also continue to fight for the right to control their own bodies. After witnessing the battle over coverage of contraceptives under the Affordable Care Act, young women are learning once again that even their access to birth control is still a contentious public policy issue. Further, women are victims of domestic and sexual violence at rates much higher than men. Women are much more likely to report severe violence by an intimate partner, where they are beaten, shot, threatened with a gun, or choked. When women do use force with an intimate partner, it is often for self-defense. Women also suffer many more negative consequences as a result of violence by males than do men abused by women. Furthermore, the economic disadvantages women face make it more difficult to leave abusive relationships. Congressional action to provide a federal response to gender-related violence resulted in passage of the original Violence Against Women Act, enacted in 1994. An overview of this legislation in the context of its reauthorization in 2005, is provided later in this chapter. This legislation was reauthorized in 3013. For more information on violence against women and enforcement of the Violence Against Women Act, go to the Office on Violence Against Women at the U.S. Department of Justice website (www.justice.gov).

As seen in discussions of other areas of civil rights policy, sometimes changing societal attitudes can lead to a policy change, and sometimes changing laws can create the conditions that, ultimately, lead to different societal views. In regard to women's access to equitable opportunities throughout U.S. history, both of these

EXHIBIT 7.7

Lilly Ledbetter

Lilly Ledbetter was born Lilly McDaniel in 1938 and was raised in a small town in Alabama in a home that had no electricity or running water. Lilly and her husband Charles had two young children at home when Lilly applied for a job at Goodyear tire factory in 1979. She was one of the few women hired on as management at the factory. Lilly worked at the company for 19 years, even though she faced continuous sexual harassment and discrimination, and was near retirement when she received an anonymous note telling her that she was making much less than her male counterparts. Lilly had signed an agreement not to talk with co-workers about her pay, so she was unaware that she was being paid less than men in the same position. Once she became aware of the pay disparity she filed a sex discrimination lawsuit against Goodyear. Lilly's case went all the way to the U.S. Supreme Court and ultimately the court decided against Lilly. The Supreme Court ruled that she had waited too long to file her lawsuit, even though she had no knowledge of the pay discrepancy until this point. After the Supreme Court's ruling Lilly continued to lobby members of Congress and the president, Barack Obama, about the need for change in the law. Lilly's efforts culminated on January 29, 2009 when President Obama signed into law, as his first official piece of legislation, the Lilly Ledbetter Fair Pay Act of 2009.

interactions can be observed. In 2013, the U.S. military announced that the ban on women serving in active combat roles would be lifted, and women will have access to almost all of the military positions currently open to men. Women have ably demonstrated their combat-worthiness in past military engagements, including operations without a clear "front line," which tends to blur the lines between combat and non-combat roles. Concerns about women being drafted continue to be raised, but for the most part, this policy change was welcomed by Americans, including those serving in the military.

Lack of equity for women continues to result in negative outcomes for families and children. When we examine issues of poverty, housing, and lack of access to essential services such as health care and adequate education for children and families in later chapters, you will see this relationship illustrated time and again. If we are to effectively address these problems, civil rights issues related to gender and the intersection of age, ethnicity, and gender will need focused attention.

Affirmative Action

As discussed in Chapter 3, affirmative action evolved in the 1970s as advocates of equal opportunity became convinced that simply banning discrimination was insufficient to help marginalized groups overcome the effects of past discrimination. Affirmative action is often misunderstood and misrepresented. It is best understood as a tool for reducing discrimination in a broad spectrum of domains including, but not limited to, employment, education, and housing, (NASW, 2009b). The basic affirmative action strategies—proportional representation, numerical quotas, and set-asides for women and minorities—have been relatively successful in securing access to opportunities previously restricted largely to white males. Nevertheless, affirmative action has always been—and continues to be—highly controversial. Critics question the fairness and effectiveness of affirmative action, especially concerning its effects on white men. They frequently refer to affirmative action as reverse discrimination, defined as discrimination against the majority group arising from policies designed to overcome discrimination against minority groups. They have consistently challenged such policies and programs in the courts. In 1978, *The Regents of the University of California* vs. *Bakke* came before the Supreme Court. Allan Bakke, a white male, had been denied admission to the medical school, even though he had a higher grade point average than some minority candidates who were admitted. The court struck down the use of strict racial quotas in determining school admissions. Consequently, Bakke was admitted to the medical school. However, the ruling upheld the use of race as one determinant of admission to higher education. The *Bakke* decision fueled the reverse discrimination controversy.

In 2003, two major Supreme Court decisions essentially upheld the *Bakke* ruling. Both cases involved the University of Michigan. The university's College of Literature, Science, and the Arts had instituted an admissions system in which all candidates who received a rating of 100 points on a scale of 150 were accepted. In 1998, the college instituted an affirmative action program that automatically awarded 20 points to all Native American, African American, and Hispanic applicants. Two white students challenged this system as an exercise in reverse discrimination. In *Gratz* vs. *Bollinger*, the court upheld this challenge and declared the program unconstitutional. However, in *Grutter* vs. *Bollinger*, it ruled in favor of the law school's program, which considers race a factor in admissions but does not employ a strict numerical system (NASW, 2009b). Significantly, the court confirmed the argument of affirmative action proponents, that promoting racial and ethnic diversity on college campuses is a legitimate strategy for achieving social justice. In 2013 in the affirmative action admissions case, *Fisher* vs. *University of Texas* the Supreme Court took the *Grutter* and *Bakke decisions as given* for purposes of deciding this case *but did* reassert that consideration of race in admission policy must be "narrowly tailored." The justices sent the case back to the lower court, with the mandate to provide stricter scrutiny of the affirmative action plan of the University of Texas.

The Supreme Court has also placed greater restrictions on affirmative action policies concerning employment. In the 1995 case *Adarand Constructors* vs. *Peña*, the court invalidated a set-aside program established by the federal government that awarded special consideration to minority-owned construction firms. While affirmative action is designed in large part to create a more level playing field by remedying widespread patterns of past discrimination, the ruling specified that such an arrangement is legitimate only when the minority recipient could demonstrate that she or he had been the victim of clearly identified acts of discrimination in the past. It further mandated that all federal affirmative action programs be subjected to "strict scrutiny" (Weiss, 1997).

The federal government is able to influence state and local policies as well as businesses and corporations by requiring adherence to specific regulations and stipulations as a condition for receiving federal funds. The federal government used this power to require affirmative action to advance civil rights across the U.S. However, as discussed in previous chapters, we are now witnessing a return to more state control. Widespread discrimination under state rule in the 1960s spurred federal involvement in civil rights protection. The return to more state control could, therefore, lead to diminished support for civil rights.

Affirmative action will undoubtedly remain a controversial issue for the foreseeable future. As the representation of minorities in different fields has increased along with increasing diversity within the U.S. population, many people have come to believe that our society has reached a point at which we no longer need affirmative action. Further, some colleges and universities are now expanding efforts to promote diversity by providing additional financial support based on socioeconomic status rather than ethnicity, However, other groups still believe that persistent racial and ethnic gaps in educational attainment and economic security reveal that we still have a long way to go before we achieve equality and that affirmative action remains essential to this progress. The debate about whether disparities in outcomes are related primarily to race and ethnicity or low income and the lack of resource in low-income neighborhoods rages in this arena as well as in many other areas of concern to social work.

MAJOR POLICIES AND PROGRAMS

Our examination of the history of civil rights provided ample illustrations of social policies that served to deny rather than protect the civil rights of African Americans, Native Americans, Hispanics, Asian Americans, women, people with disabilities, gay men and lesbians, and older adults. Major policies and programs discussed below were implemented to protect civil rights, to eliminate discrimination, and to help repair the damage done by previous discriminatory policies. As such, they represent efforts to secure social justice for people of diverse backgrounds. Examining them in detail provides us with insight into what additional policies and programs are needed to achieve further progress in civil rights, as well as ways in which social workers can educate themselves in order to play roles in the successful defense of existing civil rights protections.

The Civil Rights Act of 1964

The Civil Rights Act of 1964 was an omnibus bill directed against the various forms of segregation and discrimination that characterized U.S. society—particularly in the southern states—in the 1960s. This landmark law attempted to decrease discrimination by:

- barring unequal application of voter registration requirements;

- outlawing segregation in hotels, restaurants, theaters, and other public accommodations;

- encouraging school desegregation and authorizing the U.S. attorney general to file lawsuits against schools that resisted integration;

- empowering federal agencies to withhold funds from programs that practiced segregation; and,

- creating the Equal Employment Opportunity Commission (EEOC) to oversee antidiscrimination efforts in employment.

Exhibit 7.8 summarizes the central features of the 1964 Civil Rights Act. I will use exhibits like this often in the rest of the chapters. They illustrate how to analyze policies and programs using the basic framework for analysis presented

EXHIBIT 7.8		
Civil Rights Act 1964	**Policy Goals**	To remove barriers to voter registration, end discrimination in public accommodations and programs receiving federal assistance, encourage school desegregation, and establish the Equal Employment Opportunity Commission to oversee anti-discrimination efforts in the workplace.
	Benefits or Services Provided	Enforcement of the right to register to vote; the right to use public accommodations such as hotels, restaurants, and theaters; desegregation of schools; and the right to obtain employment.
	Eligibility Rules	All people regardless of race, color, religion, or national origin. Employment protection also covers discrimination based on sex.
	Service Delivery System	Mandated places of public accommodation to remove barriers to use by desegregating facilities. Attorney General authorized to file suits to enforce rights.
	Financing	Federal general revenue used to fund enforcement agencies.

Source: Adapted from "Major features of the Civil Rights Act of 1964," by CongressLink, n.d. www.congresslink.org/civil/essay.html. Copyright 2004 Dirksen Congressional Center. Used with permission.

in earlier chapters. My intent is to help you quickly grasp the major components of social policies and programs and to also give you practice in using this simple framework so it will come automatically to mind when you are trying to understand a policy or program. Original laws/acts are typically summarized in these exhibits, and I discuss the later amendments in the text narrative. I do this because the original laws are the ones that illustrate the intent of the law and typically are good examples of the principles that undergird policy changes and initiatives. Further, they are usually simpler and allow you to easily grasp the basic elements of goals, benefits or services provided, eligibility rules, service delivery system, and financing. If you understand the fundamentals of the initial law, it is much easier to understand the reforms reflected in amendments and reauthorization.

The Civil Rights Restoration Act of 1987, which became law in spite of President Reagan's veto, amended the Civil Rights Act of 1964 by strengthening enforcement of nondiscrimination laws in private institutions that receive federal funds. The Civil Rights Act of 1991 further amended the 1964 law. This legislation was designed to address a series of Supreme Court decisions that rolled back support for employees who sued their employers for discrimination and is an example of how the branches of government interact in policy development. It strengthened and improved federal civil rights enforcement by mandating monetary damages in cases of intentional employment discrimination and by extending protection against employment discrimination to employees of Congress and some high-level political appointees. In addition, it extended civil rights legislation to include U.S. and U.S.-controlled employers operating abroad. Although the legislation broadened many aspects of civil rights law, it also included provisions prohibiting the use of quotas to increase representation of minority groups and it placed a cap on the damages paid in cases of intentional employment discrimination and unlawful harassment.

The Voting Rights Act of 1965

By 1965, escalating violence, televised accounts of the protest march from Selma to Montgomery, Alabama, where the marchers faced resistance from state troopers, and the murder of voting rights activists made it clear that stronger federal intervention was necessary to overcome state and local practices that disenfranchised African Americans. President Lyndon Johnson and many civil rights activists issued a call for strong voting rights legislation that resulted in the passage of the Voting Rights Act. This legislation temporarily suspended literacy tests, and it provided for the appointment of federal examiners with the power to approve election practices prior to their use and register qualified citizens to vote (U.S. Department of Justice, 2000). See Exhibit 7.9 for an overview of the specifics of the Voting Rights Act. Amendments to the Act in 1975 added protections from voting discrimination for groups whose native language is not English. In addition, the 24th Amendment to the U.S. Constitution had outlawed the use of poll taxes.

Policy Goals	To enforce the 15th Amendment to the Constitution granting all citizens an equal opportunity to vote.	**EXHIBIT 7.9**
Benefits or Services	Provide protection against the use of literacy tests or other election laws that denied or reduced voting rights.	*Voting Rights Act 1965*
Eligibility Rules	All citizens eligible to vote regardless of race or color.	
Service Delivery System	Federal examiners register voters and approve election law practices prior to their use. Attorney General directed to enforce the law and challenge discriminatory practices.	
Financing	Federal general revenue used to fund enforcement agencies.	

Source: From "Introduction to federal voting rights laws," by U.S. Department of Justice, 2000. www.usdoj.gov.

The effectiveness of the Voting Rights Act was evident within the first five years after its passage. From 1964 to 1968, the percentage of eligible black voters who were registered rose from 23 percent to 59 percent in the Deep South states of Alabama, Georgia, Louisiana, Mississippi, and South Carolina. As the number of registered black voters increased, so did the number of black elected officials. Prior to 1965, there were fewer than 100 black elected officials in the previously mentioned five states plus Virginia and North Carolina. By 1975, that number had risen to more than 1,000, primarily in county and municipal offices. Just one decade after the passage of legislation designed to increase the full representation of African Americans in the democratic process, one black man was serving in Congress, and 68 African Americans were state legislators (Hudson, 1998). In 2008 and 2012, the United States elected a black president.

In 2013, the Supreme Court struck down Arizona's Voter ID law. The justices ruled that Arizona's requirement that prospective voters submit proof of citizenship when registering, violates federal law. However, the 7–2 decision relied on the federal Motor Voter Act, not the Voting Rights Act, ruling that Arizona could not reject the federal voter registration form in favor of their own document requirements, but not ruling that requiring proof of citizenship is necessarily an undue infringement on voting rights. Immediately following the ruling, the architects of the Arizona Voter ID law announced plans to push the Federal Elections Commission to require proof of citizenship on the universal federal form.

The more consequential 2013 Supreme Court ruling for voting rights advocates was handed down in the *Shelby County* vs. *Holder* case. Central issues in this case were whether racial minorities continue to face barriers to voting in states with a history of discrimination and, further, whether these states should face particular scrutiny regarding their electoral rules. The justices, in a 5–4 decision, ruled Section 4 of the Voting Rights Act was unconstitutional. Section 4 specified a "coverage formula" to determine which states and local governments need to get approval before changing their voting laws. The court decided that nine states, mostly in the South, should no longer be required to receive advance federal approval to change their election laws. Now state voting restrictions will be subject to only "after the fact" litigation. This means the burden of proof will be on those alleging discrimination, instead of expecting states to demonstrate that their proposed changes will not deprive voters of their rights. While the court left open the possibility that Congress could craft new standards by which to determine which jurisdictions still warrant additional regulations, it is highly unlikely that Congress—which recently reauthorized the Voting Rights Act—would take on the politically charged issue of identifying which states and localities are engaged in racial discrimination in their elections. Without the substitution of new standards deemed constitutional, though, this core of the Voting Rights Act is effectively voided. The fight for voting rights will be more difficult as a consequence of this ruling.

The Education for All Handicapped Children Act of 1975

The Education for All Handicapped Children Act of 1975 mandated that all children with disabilities have available to them a free and appropriate public education. The law specified that education and related services should be designed to meet the unique needs of these children and would ensure that the rights of children with disabilities and their parents or guardians are protected. The Act also required that students with disabilities be "mainstreamed," that is, educated with peers without disabilities to the maximum extent appropriate. The federal government was to assist states and localities so they could provide for the education of all children with disabilities. Federal oversight to assess and assure the effectiveness of efforts to educate children with disabilities was also mandated. You can examine the details of this law in Exhibit 7.10.

In 1990, this statute was amended, and the title was changed to Individuals with Disabilities Education Act (IDEA). Additional amendments made in 1997 are commonly referred to as IDEA 97. This legislation was reauthorized in 2004 and called The Individuals with Disabilities Education Improvement Act of 2004. Although slated for reauthorization in 2011, reauthorization has been repeatedly delayed. IDEA secures the right of children to a "free and appropriate public education" by making federal funding for special education contingent upon compliance with IDEA. School districts are required to formulate an *individualized education plan* (IEP) for each student with disabilities and to provide education in the *least restrictive environment* (LRE). Inclusion—that is, the education of children with disabilities in the classroom with their peers—is required to the maximum extent possible. Although school districts continue to struggle to meet the mandates of this legislation, especially because, as is often the case with federal mandates, IDEA has never

Policy Goals	To provide free and appropriate public education to all children.	**EXHIBIT 7.10**
Benefits or Services	Special education and related services. Use of an Individualized Education Plan (IEP) for each eligible child. Education provided in the least restrictive environment.	*Education for All Handicapped Children Act 1975*
Eligibility Rules	Children ages 3–21 with disabilities.	
Service Delivery System	Public schools provide appropriate education. IEPs are prepared by multidisciplinary teams within the public schools and include input from the families and students.	
Financing	Federal funding provided to states to encourage public education of children with disabilities.	

Source: From "Education for All Handicapped Children Act of 1975." Pub. L. 94–142, s. 6.

been fully funded, children with disabilities now have a much greater chance of receiving an adequate public education than they did before the legislation was enacted. The implementation of IDEA has also led to new standards for teacher training and curriculum development that increase schools' ability to provide for the different learning styles of all students, another example of how ensuring the civil rights of a disadvantaged population has profound benefits for those not directly affected, too. For more information, visit the Individuals with Disabilities Education Act page at the U.S. Department of Education website (www.ed.gov).

The Americans with Disabilities Act of 1990

The Americans with Disabilities Act (ADA), which is summarized in Exhibit 7.11, illustrates how legislation can be formulated based on the goals of the target group and with their active participation in policy development. The ADA was designed to ensure full access to services and benefits for people with disabilities. The purposes of this Act are as follows:

- To provide a clear and comprehensive national mandate for the elimination of discrimination against individuals with disabilities.

- To provide clear, strong, consistent, enforceable standards addressing discrimination against individuals with disabilities.

- To ensure that the federal government plays a central role in enforcing the standards established in this Act on behalf of individuals with disabilities.

EXHIBIT 7.11 *Americans with Disabilities Act 1990*	**Policy Goals**	To eradicate discrimination directed toward people with disabilities, increase employment opportunities, and ensure equality of opportunity and access.
	Benefits or Services	Protection of right to equal opportunity in public accommodations, employment, transportation, state and local government services, and telecommunications.
	Eligibility Rules	People with a physical or mental impairment that limits one or more major life activities.
	Service Delivery System	Businesses and employers make and pay for reasonable accommodations. Department of Justice negotiates, mediates, and files suit in cases of discrimination unless employment related, in which case the Equal Employment Opportunity Commission handles the complaint.
	Financing	Federal general revenue used to fund enforcement agencies.

Source: From "ADA Homepage," by U.S. Department of Justice, 2004. www.ada.gov.

- To invoke the sweep of congressional authority, including the power to enforce the 14th Amendment and to regulate commerce, in order to address the major areas of day-to-day discrimination faced by people with disabilities (Americans with Disabilities Act of 1990).

To learn more about work to ensure rights for people with disabilities, go to the website of the National Disability Rights Network (www.ndrn.org) and ADA Watch (www.accessiblesociety.org/topics/ada/adawatchgroup.htm).

The principles of strengths-based policy development, as detailed in previous chapters, are clearly reflected in this policy. Over the last 30 years, society's view of people with disabilities has evolved from one in which they were segregated and devalued, to one in which they are active participants in our communities, with the decision-making capacity to control their own lives. There is a guiding principle in the disability community: "Nothing about us without us." In keeping with that principle, groups made up of people with disabilities and their families, including the independent living (IL) movement, worked to craft this legislation and were tireless in their efforts to secure passage of the ADA. The people who crafted this legislation clearly understood that disability is a social construct and, as such, is open to interpretation and modification (NASW, 2003e). Disability is no longer viewed as occurring solely in the individual but rather in the interface between personal capacity and environmental demands. Disability can thus be ameliorated by transforming the environment rather than by focusing primarily on what an individual is unable to do.

People with disabilities and their families worked hard to change the definition of the "problem of disability" from a focus on individual deficiencies to one that insisted that strengths, needs, and goals of people with disabilities be given center stage. The IL movement helped to create socio-political forces that reshaped policy makers' understanding of the nature of disability and resulting needs. It did so by shifting the approach to understanding need from considering disability as a problem to examining the environmental barriers that prevented people who were "differently able" from accessing needed resources. Professionals collaborated with the target group in crafting the legislation. Claims-making was based on appeals to social justice, equity, and the right to self-determination, all core social work values that reflect the strengths perspective. The focus was on civil rights for people with disabilities. For more information on the ADA and enforcement issues, go to the home page of the ADA at (www.ada.gov).

Since the bill became law, employment and educational outcomes for people with disabilities continue to be carefully monitored to ensure that the goals of the target group are being achieved. Although the ADA has not ended discrimination against people with disabilities and enforcement has been problematic, this legislative initiative provides a powerful example of how the strengths perspective can be reflected in crafting policy.

Some businesses and employers have challenged the need to comply with the ADA. Their reasons for resistance to making reasonable accommodations include fear of financial hardship and concern that people with disabilities create heightened liability risks both as employees and as customers. Courts have often sided with the defendant rather than the person with a disability. However, efforts to promote voluntary compliance, coupled with a willingness to pursue mandatory compliance through the courts, have resulted in increased access to many businesses and facilities that were previously inaccessible for many people with disabilities. The 2008 Amendments to the Americans with Disabilities Act (AADA), which broadened the definition of disability and the scope of coverage under the ADA, mitigated the effect of a series of Supreme Court decisions that interpreted the Americans with Disabilities Act of 1990 more narrowly.

The Reauthorization of Violence Against Women Act 2005 and 2013

The original Violence Against Women Act (VAWA), enacted in 1994, provided funding to increase investigation and prosecution of violent crimes against women, supported education and prevention programming, increased pre-trial detention of people accused of these crimes, imposed automatic and mandatory restitution requirements on those convicted, and allowed civil redress if prosecutors chose to leave cases unprosecuted. VAWA also created special provisions in U.S. immigration law to protect battered non-citizens, including allowing them to petition for their own permanent immigration status independent of abusive spouses. This legisla-

EXHIBIT 7.12 *Reauthorization of Violence Against Women Act 2005*		
Purpose	To fund direct services for sexual assault victims, screening for exposure to domestic and sexual violence and increase the enforcement of protections to immigrant victims. To create a health care initiative that trains health care professionals and medical students to recognize and identify domestic violence.
Benefits and Services provided	Provide services to people who have been victims of violent crimes.
Eligibility requirements	Person must be a victim of a violent crime for state/local providers to assist in mental or physical services.
Service Delivery System	Oversight rests with the Department of Justice with the responsibility for services granted to state and local level.
Financing	Funded by federal grants

Source: Adapted from information found in Congressional Research Service (2005). *Violence Against Women Act: History and Federal Funding.* Washington, DC: The Library of Congress.

tion begins to address the intersection of ethnicity, class, gender, and immigration status that increases risk for these women. These provisions were updated in 2000 by the Battered Immigrant Women's Protection Act of 2000, and legislation in 2005 reauthorized VAWA funding for fiscal years 2007–2011. The Reauthorization of Violence Against Women Act also amended and strengthened federal criminal law, strengthened protections for battered immigrants and victims of trafficking, and created new protections for victims in public housing. Exhibit 7.12 provides an overview of this legislation. VAWA was reauthorized in 2013 for another five years.

The Lilly Ledbetter Fair Pay Act 2009

Lilly Ledbetter worked for the Goodyear Tire and Rubber Company facility in Gadsden, Alabama, for almost 20 years. When she discovered that she was the lowest-paid supervisor of a group of 16, even though she was the most experienced, Ledbetter sued the company. A jury found that her employer had unlawfully discriminated against her based on sex. The Supreme Court rejected this ruling in a 5–4 decision on the basis that the lawsuit was not brought against Goodyear Tire and Rubber Company 180 days after the discrimination began, despite the fact that Ms. Ledbetter did not discover the pay discrepancy until many years later. Co-workers often do not know the pay grades for other employees at a company. In fact, many employers even prohibit employees from discussing their pay with each other, which makes it nearly impossible for co-workers to uncover pay discrimination.

To remedy this situation, Congress passed The Lilly Ledbetter Fair Pay Act in 2009. The Act makes clear that pay discrimination claims "accrue" whenever an employee receives a discriminatory paycheck. This law is also applicable when a discriminatory

		EXHIBIT 7.13
Policy goals	To ensure that victims of pay discrimination have an opportunity to file a claim and have legal discourse.	*The Lilly Ledbetter Fair Pay Act 2009*
Benefits and services	Guarantee and enforcement of the right to equal pay. No statute of limitations applies to this Act since each paycheck restarts the option for individuals to file a lawsuit	
Eligibility Rules	Person must demonstrate discrimination based on Title VII in regards to being paid less than other employees based on gender.	
Service Delivery System	Mandated the requirement for equal pay in the workforce. Attorney General authorized to file lawsuit to enforce the rights.	
Financing	Federal general revenue used to fund enforcement agencies.	

Source: Adapted from National Women's Law Center, (2009). *Lilly Ledbetter Fair Pay Act.* Washington, DC accessed at http://www.nwlc.org/fairpay/ledbetterfairpayact.html

pay decision or practice is adopted, when an employee becomes subject to the decision or practice, or when an employee is otherwise affected by the decision or practice. The legislation affects pay discrimination claims made on the basis of sex, race, national origin, age, religion, and disability. This Act was signed into law by President Obama shortly after he took office. Exhibit 7.13 provides an overview of this legislation.

The Matthew Shepard and James Byrd, Jr. Hate Crimes Prevention Act 2009

Matthew Shepherd and James Byrd, Jr. were both victims of hate crimes. Both were brutally murdered, but their murders were not considered hate crimes under the definition of federal hate crimes at the time of their murders. The Matthew Shepard and James Byrd, Jr. Hate Crimes Prevention Act of 2009 expanded the scope of the 1968 hate crimes legislation that applied to people attacked because of their race, religion, or national origin, to include crimes committed because of a person's gender, sexual orientation, gender identity, or disability. This legislation extends civil rights protection to the LGBTQ community, in particular. Exhibit 7.14 provides an overview of this legislation.

EXHIBIT 7.14 *Matthew Shepard and James Byrd, Jr. Hate Crimes Prevention Act (2009)*		
	Policy Goals	To make attacks based on sexual orientation, person's gender, sexual orientation, gender identity, or disability a federal hate crime.
	Benefits or Services	The federal government provides federal resources to state and local agencies to equip local officers with the tools they need to prosecute hate crimes. Grants are available to state and local law enforcement agencies that have incurred extraordinary expenses associated with the investigation and prosecution of hate crimes. Provides federal assistance for the investigation and prosecution of hate crimes committed against persons because of their gender, sexual orientation, gender identity, or disability.
	Eligibility Rules	Must be a victim of a hate crime based on gender, sexual orientation, gender identity or disability.
	Service Delivery System	State and local agencies investigate and prosecute hate crimes with federal assistance.
	Financing	Funded federally through the Department of Justice.

EVALUATING CIVIL RIGHTS POLICIES AND PROGRAMS

The following discussion acknowledges advances in securing civil rights and also examines work yet to be done. There is no question that the U.S. has made significant progress during the last 50 years toward protecting and enhancing the civil rights of many oppressed groups. Perhaps one of the most important changes has been an increased recognition of discrimination and a willingness to speak up and use a variety of strategies to end discriminatory practices. Groups that have experienced discrimination, including people of color, women, people with disabilities, and people discriminated against based on sexual orientation or gender identity, have demanded changes in social policies and programs and an end to unfair treatment. They have organized and, increasingly, they are finding common cause in each other's struggles, as in the recent alliances between LGBTQ and immigrant populations who both seek changes to immigration policy that would support the unity of same-sex couples, where one partner is not a U.S. citizen. The successes of disadvantaged groups in policy and, increasingly, in electing individuals to represent them, are reshaping the political and social landscapes in the United States. However, there is much more yet to be done. For example, people of color still experience discrimination, which results in the disproportionately negative educational, health, and employment outcomes discussed in this chapter. Because of de facto segregation—segregation caused by social practices, political acts, or economic circumstances, but not by actual laws—disproportionate numbers of people of color continue to live in inner-city and other isolated low-income neighborhoods with segregated and under-resourced schools, fewer essential services, and severely limited job opportunities.

Discrimination Based on Ethnicity and Gender

We have examined disparities in poverty rates, retirement programs, and employ-ment for women and people of color. A major reason why wages earned by women and people of color are lower than those of white males is that they are still disproportionately represented in the lowest-paying jobs, sometimes termed the secondary labor market. This tendency is referred to as occupational segregation. Employment in the secondary labor market also negatively influences the health of these groups because these jobs generally do not provide health insurance; some are, indeed, hazardous to workers' health, with high rates of work-related injuries and illnesses. For example, many child care, housekeeping, and public school para-professional positions provide low pay and few benefits. Although it is important to open up more job categories to women and people of color, it is also important to adequately compensate people who perform traditionally "female" work. To accom-plish this goal, we need to develop methods of determining the comparable worth of jobs and strategies for implementing comparable pay scales.

Harassment on the job is also a civil rights issue. Sexual harassment and harassment based on race and ethnicity create a hostile working environment and can limit employment longevity and promotion. Many people who encounter harassment on the job either put up with it or leave, both actions with significant potential psychological and economic consequences. Preventing harassment is key to equal access to employment and promotion. You can find more information on initiatives to protect civil liberties at the American Civil Liberties Union website (www.aclu.org).

Affirmative action, although successful in increasing access for groups previously excluded from many employment and educational opportunities, has certainly not leveled the playing field. For example, African Americans are still twice as likely as white people to be unemployed (U.S. Census Bureau, 2012m) and three times as likely to live in poverty (U.S. Census Bureau, 2012j). They are more than six times as likely to be incarcerated. Across generations, these disparities result in significant gaps in wealth and well-being. The economic recession's disproportionate impact on people of color has only intensified this inequity. Between 2005 and 2010, African American net worth fell by approximately 60 percent, such that median household net worth in 2010 was $130,600 for white people and only $15,500 for African Americans (Federal Reserve, 2012). Because so many opportunities in our country hinge on one's ability to finance them—education, access to health care, retirement security—this wealth gap translates to entrenched patterns of deep disadvantage for people of color.

Furthermore, for women of color, intersectionality highlights the fact that they belong to two groups that suffer discrimination. They experience racism differently than do men of color and they experience sexism differently than white women. They are often subject to more negative outcomes than other members of either group. For example, African American women earn less than African American men and white women. If these women have a disability or are not heterosexual, they may experience additional discrimination, illustrating how overlapping identities shape paths of opportunity and oppression in the U.S. The intersection of discrimination based on two or more characteristics needs to be acknowledged and analyzed in order to craft effective social policy to deal with multiple sources of discrimination.

Discrimination on the basis of sexual orientation and gender identity is still accepted social policy, and women's rights must constantly be defended. The need to make sure all children receive adequate basic education generates a great deal of discussion. However, the funding strategies to make adequate education a reality for all children have yet to materialize in many states; indeed, with reductions in state funding for public education and an increasing reliance on local property taxes as a funding source, greater inequities and inadequacies are likely.

Immigrants and undocumented workers are often blamed for many of our nation's woes, and efforts to restrict immigration have been a recurring theme in our history. Many states and localities continue to introduce initiatives requiring all residents to speak English only. Several states, beginning with Arizona, have introduced and, in some cases, passed, anti-immigrant legislation that seeks to criminalize the very existence of immigrants who lack permanent immigration authorization in the U.S., in an effort to induce them to "self-deport." Human rights violations and economic crises in other parts of the world contribute to the flow of refugees into our country. Therefore, we must reform our immigration and refugee policies in a way that (1) reaffirms the contributions immigrants have made to this country, (2) permits the U.S. to respond humanely to political refugees while still protecting national security, (3) celebrates linguistic and cultural diversity, and (4) supports the human rights of immigrants (NASW, 2012a). It is also important that fiscal relief be provided to states and communities that give services to large numbers of immigrants and refugees. Strengths-based immigration policy would recognize the tremendous current and potential future contributions of immigrants to the U.S., while making unification of immigrant families and protection of immigrants' human rights cornerstones of national policy. Some recent advances in immigration policy, such as the Obama administration's announcement of Deferred Action for Childhood Arrivals (DACA), inch closer to this approach. DACA provides protection from deportation and employment authorization for immigrant youth who came to the U.S. before they turned 16 and are either students or graduates from America's high schools. These students—commonly known as "Dreamers"—are strong advocates for further immigration reforms and possess many talents that are valuable to the U.S. Exhibit 7.15 provides an example of advocacy on behalf of immigrants.

Current Threats to Civil Rights and Human Rights

Given the ongoing war on terror and the accompanying climate of fear, people in this country who are Muslims or have family roots in the Middle East are at risk for increased discrimination. Following the September 11, 2001 terrorist attacks, Arab Americans especially, but not exclusively, have increasingly been targets of hate crimes and physical violence and have encountered discrimination on airlines, in employment, and at schools. There is continuing concern that The Uniting and

---

Social Work Students Advocate for Undocumented Immigrant Students

Social work students at a midwestern university were concerned about a bill introduced in the state legislature that would overturn the law allowing undocumented immigrant students to pay in-state tuition. For their class project these BSW students mobilized students from several other universities, and with the help of a film student, developed a video discussing the impact this bill would have on students and the community. They posted the video, You Don't Speak for Me, along with an online petition, on YouTube. The students then presented the signatures and comments from the petition, along with their verbal testimony, to the Senate committee assigned the bill. The bill passed in the House but died in the Senate committee.

EXHIBIT 7.15

Social Work Students Help Immigrants Become U.S. Citizens

Strengthening America by Providing Appropriate Tools Required to Intercept and Obstruct Terrorism Act of 2001 (USA Patriot Act; Public Law 107–56) is eroding civil liberties, particularly the right of due process.

The Patriot Act made it possible to authorize detention of undocumented immigrants on mere suspicion and use secret evidence in immigration proceedings that the immigrant can neither confront not rebut. At the same time, requirements for increased cooperation between federal, state, and local law enforcement agencies have also led to increased racial profiling and strained relationships between immigrants and their communities. In 2001, the Department of Homeland Security was created and in 2003, the Immigration and Naturalization Service was placed in that agency (and split into separate entities charged with enforcing border security (Immigration and Customs Enforcement, or ICE) and processing immigration paperwork (U.S. Citizenship and Immigration Services, or USCIS). Despite the work of advocates intent on getting the Patriot Act amended to provide meaningful privacy protections and judicial oversight of the government's surveillance power, the Patriot Act was extended in 2010 without amendment, indicating a continued emphasis on security over civil liberties. Revelations about extensive and intrusive cellphone and Internet databases being developed by the federal government has intensified the debates over security versus privacy and civil liberties. For further information about advocacy work to amend the Patriot Act and protect civil rights, visit the websites of the American-Arab Anti-Discrimination Committee (www.adc. org) and the American Civil Liberties Union (www.aclu.org).

Indeed, in previous periods when the U.S. has been gripped by fear, repression of people from a variety of backgrounds has escalated. For example, during the 1950s, when the U.S. public was very fearful of communism, Senator Joseph McCarthy (a Wisconsin Republican) spearheaded an infamous effort to stifle political dissent. McCarthy claimed that the State Department was composed of a large number of communists. He garnered widespread attention for his claims about the prevalence of communism in the government and raised suspicions about the alleged communist affiliations of prominent citizens. Many of these accusations later proved to be unfounded. Subsequent declassification of espionage records did indicate that some public employees were recruited as spies. However, harm to individuals wrongly accused, as well as the widespread fear of being labeled a communist for speaking out, was very damaging on an individual as well as societal level. A new term developed from this model of accusation and attack: "McCarthyism." Other such attacks, which often included inaccurate evidence and sensationalist tactics, are still referred to by this term. Given the current climate of fear in the U.S., social workers need to be alert to the possibility of the emergence of another era of McCarthyism that seeks to stifle dissent and scapegoat vulnerable populations and whistle blowers. During such periods, efforts to support the kind of speaking up and speaking out that is vital to securing and protecting civil rights for all citizens must be increased.

It is not only those who are seen as "enemies" from the outside, however, whose civil rights are threatened. Increasingly strict voting rights infringements, the burden of which fall disproportionately on low-income voters of color, are eroding some of our most fundamental civil rights protections and hollowing the democratic participation of underrepresented communities. In advance of the November 2012 presidential election, more than 15 states had passed legislation implementing one or more of the tactics described below; some of these measures are still pending the resolution of court cases challenging their constitutionality (ACLU, 2013):

- stringent voter identification requirements: these require individuals have the financial resources to either obtain suitable identification or navigate the process for obtaining one without charge; they have had the most significant impact on voting rights in the current context;

- proof of citizenship requirements;

- early voting restrictions;

- voter registration outreach restrictions;

- purge of voter rolls: apply purges to the voter rolls based on response to mailed notice, or lack of recent voting history; this can also require voters to register again under new and more restrictive, and potentially more costly, voter registration rules;

- restrictions on voter participation tools: limit or restrict tools used to facilitate participation by those with disabilities and those with difficulties getting to the polls on Election Day; access to information about where to vote may be unavailable for a voter who arrives at the wrong polling place.

NEXT STEPS

Given the history of civil rights struggles in the U.S. and some of the threats and challenges we face today, how are civil rights to be secured and protected for people of diverse backgrounds in our country? Clearly, social workers are called upon to advocate for equal rights for all citizens in the NASW *Code of Ethics*. Some people incorrectly believe that the strengths perspective is incompatible with conflict strategies to help oppressed groups. In fact, there is a close relationship between the strengths perspective and empowerment theory, which is rooted in conflict theory. Conflict theory focuses on how individuals and groups struggle to increase their power and maximize benefits, which in turn leads to political and social change. Strengths-based and empowerment-oriented interventions both focus on client and environmental strengths and strategies, including education (transfer of knowledge and skills, often among individuals in similar circumstances), self-help, social networks, advocacy, and social action, to help clients increase their power over their own lives. Both approaches strongly support client participation in all aspects of decision making that affect their lives. Moreover, both strategies seek egalitarian working relationships between social workers and their clients (Chapin and Cox, 2001).

Finally, commitment to social justice is an overarching value guiding both approaches. Work that identifies and bolsters the strengths of oppressed groups and helps them remove barriers to reaching their goals is at the heart of the strengths perspective; it also supports empowerment strategies. Conflict as well as consensus building may be necessary in collaborating with oppressed groups to achieve their goals. The strengths perspective provides tools for supporting the strengths of oppressed populations and for helping them acquire the necessary resources for successful civil rights initiatives. This text, which incorporates the strengths perspective, is designed to be an empowerment tool.

Social work's commitment to social justice encompasses work to protect human rights. Human rights include the universal right to an adequate standard of living that supports the health and well-being of families, and individuals' human rights, and are premised on the belief in the inherent dignity and inalienable rights of both female and male adults and children as members of the human family (NASW, 2012e). Our commitment to human rights can help guide policy practice with all of the diverse groups with whom we work. Using a human rights framework can help social workers to explore how the poverty and deprivation that many experience—in the U.S. and around the world—may be best understood as denials of essential rights, deserving remedies that include not just supportive services but also organizing and advocacy to address underlying conditions of injustice. To learn more about how social workers around the world are collaborating to secure human rights, go to the website of the International Federation of Social Workers (http://ifsw.org/), and then to Resources/Policies/Human Rights.

As detailed earlier in the chapter, many of the core civil rights protections guaranteed by the U.S. Constitution have been found by the courts to apply to citizens and non-citizens alike and so provide protection for undocumented immigrants. However, eligibility for publicly funded services and benefits is often reserved for citizens and legal residents. Increasingly, even people who are lawful permanent residents have seen their access to means-tested benefits attacked.

Social workers can encounter undocumented immigrants in a great many settings including health care, schools, mental health centers, and child welfare. They need to understand their special needs and have basic knowledge of immigration policy. NASW opposes "mandatory reporting of immigration status by health, mental health, social service, education, police, and other public service providers" (NASW, 2012a, p. 200). However, requiring social workers and other service providers to take on immigration enforcement functions has been proposed in states and municipalities around the country, with some policymakers threatening to hold providers criminally liable for "harboring" unauthorized immigrants if they fail to comply with these reporting obligations. The meeting of basic health, education and social service needs, particularly access to emergency services, for all people in the U.S., is necessary to maintain a healthy and civil society. For immigrant communities, this will require comprehensive immigration reform. The NASW continues to work to educate policy makers about needed immigration reform across the United States. (NASW, 2012a).

Reconsidering "Neutral" Policies

Social workers must analyze policies that, in theory, apply equally to all citizens so as to determine whether in practice they adversely affect people from diverse backgrounds. Policies apply to large categories of people, and individualizing policies to fit diverse needs is a complicated process. For example, low-income elders with disabilities are eligible to have their nursing home care paid for through Medicaid. Theoretically, Native Americans should have equal access to that benefit because providers of Medicaid benefits are prohibited from discriminating on the basis of race or ethnicity. However, nursing home policies often require certain types of beds and bed heights and certain dietary regimens. An elder raised in a traditional Native American culture may be more at ease in a bed at a lower level surrounded by sacred objects from home. In addition, the kind of food and food preparation provided in the nursing facility may be foreign to them and put them at risk of severe weight loss. When perceived from this perspective, nursing home policies that are not sensitive to racial and ethnic differences create barriers that limit access even though they appear neutral on the surface. Exploring this issue from a strengths perspective suggests alternative approaches. For example, nursing home regulations could incorporate traditional values of tribal caring, and Native American tribes could be provided with resources to design community-based, long-term care alternatives that reflect their lifestyle.

Another example of a seemingly neutral policy that disparately affects Hispanics as well as many other groups is the requirement to produce proof of citizenship, such as a birth certificate, in order to get benefits ranging from a driver's license to Medicaid. Hispanics, African Americans, Native Americans, people living in poverty, and the very old all are at greater risk of not having a U.S. birth certificate readily available. Further, because of the lack of access to health care, they may be more likely to have been born at home. For example, I recently worked with a 91-year-old veteran who had been told documentation of his 20-year history of military service was insufficient to allow him to renew the driver's license which he had held for 40 years in his home state. There were new laws requiring submission of a birth certificate before a license could be renewed. However, he was born at home, did not have a physician-attended birth, and never had a birth certificate. It was only now that he was being required to produce a birth certificate. He finally had to have his 94-year-old brother attest that he was present at his birth in Texas. This requirement to produce a birth certificate appears neutral because it applies to everyone. However, interested groups, including the Supreme Court, have acknowledged that these policies may impact some groups more than others, and that the burden is particularly onerous for those living in poverty. Hispanic and African American advocacy groups have been vocal in their opposition to these requirements. Elders are also negatively affected. It is clear how new requirements to produce a birth certificate to prove citizenship in a variety of arenas from registering to vote to getting a driver's license can erect barriers for many groups. Again, these policies could be modified to be less onerous to vulnerable groups. For example, alternative forms of documentation that prove individuals' identity and eligibility for benefits can be accepted, fees to request birth certificates can be lifted when the documents are required for essential activities of citizenship, and practices such as presumed eligibility, can provide continuous services while the verification is completed.

If you look carefully at the differential effects of policies, you undoubtedly will find many more examples. It is important to try to educate policy makers about cultural differences and to help craft more culturally sensitive policies. However, until people of color and other disadvantaged groups are much better represented among the ranks of policy makers, it will be difficult for policy makers to foresee the barriers, much less craft effective alternatives.

The Role of Social Workers

The NASW is committed to affirmative action and is working to increase diversity in the profession (NASW, 2012e). Attracting social workers from diverse backgrounds will prove helpful in identifying policies that do not work well for specific populations. Schools of social work continue to actively recruit students from diverse backgrounds and have also instituted curriculum policies to help sensitize their students to groups who have experienced historical discrimination.

Each new piece of proposed legislation needs to be scrutinized for differential negative effects on people of different backgrounds. Further, because legislation is typically quite broad, rules and regulations are written to determine how legislation will be implemented. Discriminatory rules and regulations can often be changed without creating new legislation. Social workers on the front line who are aware that certain policies perpetuate discrimination can help policy makers and administrators craft more effective rules and regulations. Typically, the more flexible the rules and regulations, the greater the opportunity for professionals to tailor services in ways better suited to people of diverse backgrounds. Although greater flexibility may also lead to abuse, it is impossible to legislate for all eventualities. Rather, allowing professionals latitude, creating incentives for compliance, and then closely monitoring for outcomes that indicate whether there is equal access to services, can be expected to reap more satisfactory results. Further, we have examined how discrimination is linked to poverty and therefore our efforts to increase and safeguard access to services will not insure that vulnerable groups actually get the services unless we also consider financial barriers. Lack of adequate mental health and substance abuse coverage by Medicare and Medicaid are examples of barriers that prevent many of the vulnerable groups we have discussed from getting needed services.

Our civil rights laws protect people who are members of protected classes, that is, people who are members of specified groups including men and women, on the basis of sex; any group that shares a common race, religion, color, or national origin; people over 40; and people with physical or mental disabilities. However, people are not protected from discrimination because they are poor or homeless or, in many cases, if they are gay or lesbian. Classism and heterosexism have yet to be challenged sufficiently to develop a body of law that adequately protects these groups. It is also necessary to more carefully examine how the intersection of ethnicity, class, gender, disability, and other characteristics that have been the basis for discrimination, affects people who are members of two or more of these groups, and to work to develop policy initiatives that address multiple forms of discrimination.

Further, many of our age discrimination policies protect older adults but do not protect children. For example, although older adults cannot be stripped of their basic right to self-determination without court action, we presume children are incapable of self-determination even in situations where it is evident that children clearly understand their situation and what is in their best interest. Social work advocacy for the groups listed above is needed if they are to receive adequate protection within an expanded framework of civil and human rights.

Social workers can also publicize information concerning progress toward equal opportunity in a form that most citizens can understand. For example, the National Urban League has developed the Equality Index, a statistical measurement of disparities that exist between black and white people in economics, education, health, housing, civic engagement, and social justice. A weighted index value of one is assigned to white people. An Equality Index value of less than one indicates that the group being compared is doing worse than white members of a category, whereas a value of one or more means the comparison group is doing as well as, or better, than the white group. The League's analysis indicates that the mean income of black workers is significantly less than that of their white counterparts. However, the service to country measure indicates higher rates of military service and civic participation among black as opposed to white Americans (National Urban League, 2012). Social workers need to help make their fellow citizens aware that inequality continues to be a problem in our society. You can find out more about this analysis and the Equality Index by visiting the National Urban League website (www.nul.org).

Because public as well as private monitoring of outcomes is necessary for laws to be effective, social workers can also advocate for more effective, comprehensive monitoring by federal and state agencies charged with enforcing civil rights legislation. These efforts should include demands for adequate funding for these agencies and the effective use of technology to foster greater transparency, so that individuals with civil rights concerns can monitor enforcement activities. Further, a huge impediment to progress in civil rights as well as in the social service arena is that legislation is passed and mandates are given, but funds to make the required changes are in very short supply.

To go further, social workers can think about how explicit attention to inclusiveness might shape policies and programs. This is in keeping with the idea of envisioning solutions discussed in earlier chapters. For example, what kinds of policies and programs could help achieve the goal of political representation in your state legislature that more closely mirrors the percentage of women or Latinos or Native Americans in your state?

Social workers and the social service systems in which they work often reflect the dominant culture in which they are immersed. Service delivery from diagnosis and assessment to financing, reimbursement, and general organization is shaped by this culture. At the same time, clients who come from different cultures have also been influenced by their backgrounds. Unfortunately, social workers are often ill-equipped to recognize and negotiate the cultural differences that can influence the effectiveness of services. If equal access to services tailored to diverse needs is to

---

QUICK GUIDE 6   Agency Analysis

Social workers need to continually monitor social service agency policies and practices to help reduce discrimination. You can do this by taking a close look at an agency with which you are familiar, and at outcomes for people involved with the agency. The questions below will give you a starting place in examining practices and identifying the appropriate outcomes to monitor for a particular agency.

- Does the agency serve a larger proportion of people from one ethnic group or gender than is found in the catchment or service area? If so, why?
- Does the agency typically contact the mother when working with a family?
- Where is the agency located? Location of service in itself can create access problems for certain groups.
- Is the agency accessible by people with physical disabilities?
- Who works in the agency? Does the gender and ethnic composition resemble that of the population served?
- Does the gender and ethnic composition of administrators and managers resemble that of the population served?
- Are staff who speak their language available to applicants and clients who do not speak English?
- Does the agency attempt to build on ethnic and cultural identities of clients or does it typically impose the identity of the staff?
- Does the agency acknowledge and serve the LGBTQ community, including same-sex couples and families?
- How do agency policies help to support or undermine positive outcomes for clients in the areas discussed above?
- What policies or practices contribute to or reduce experiences of discrimination on a personal level?

become a reality, then service providers must be trained to recognize and respond effectively to their clients' cultural backgrounds. Policies that promote diversity in service provider backgrounds are needed.

It is essential for professionals in service settings to be able to see their responsibility to be involved in policy practice clearly, and to call attention to policies that lead to unequal access; otherwise, such policies and practices will continue to put disadvantaged groups at even greater risk. Quick Guide 6 lists some questions that can help alert you to possible discrimination in social work settings where you practice. Consider these questions in relation to an agency with which you are familiar. If you conclude that access to service is unequal, then you can utilize the information contained in Chapter 6 to generate some ideas about how you might resolve this problem. The place to start is by personally challenging and rejecting racist, classist, ageist, sexist, or heterosexist attitudes and behavior in your own life. The person makes the social worker, which in turn informs a professional stance against oppression. The goal is to find ways to celebrate differences and to draw strength from diversity. Using a solution focused approach, in order for the agency you analyzed to be more inclusive, specifically, what would need to change in terms of policies, programs, and environment?

CONCLUSION

The U.S. is home to an array of cultures, races, and ethnicities. People of diverse backgrounds bring energy, optimism, global perspectives, and productive contributions to all areas of contemporary life. Social workers can help celebrate these differences and not allow them to be the basis for denying access to education, employment, health, or social services. We need to join together with other concerned groups to develop more cogent and effective policies and programs in order to ensure that these goals are realized in our society and communities (NASW, 2012e). The strengths perspective serves as a reminder that protecting the civil rights of disadvantaged individuals and groups is not only a moral imperative but also a matter of national prosperity, as we are enriched by the full participation and contribution of our country's great diversity.

CATCHING UP WITH THE POLICY GROUP

Now let us take a moment to check in with one of policy group members, Alejandro, as he navigates his way through his first social work job.

After graduation, Alejandro decided he really liked working in schools so he accepted a position as a school social worker at a high school in a small, rural community. Alejandro has recently begun working with a student named Saul who has disclosed that for the past several months a couple of other students

EXHIBIT 7.16

Policy Group Member Alejandro

in his school have been bullying him because of his sexual orientation. Saul states that these students have been making nasty comments to him at school and have posted denigrating messages about him on their Facebook pages. Saul says recently the bullying has started to become physical with some of these students pushing him when they walk by him in the hallway and saying things like, "Your kind needs to be taught a lesson." Saul says he has told some teachers about what has been going on and is sure that some have even seen incidents taking place, but nothing has been done to stop the bullying. Saul states it is getting to the point that he is afraid to even come to school anymore and he wishes there was a group at school for LGBTQ students to provide support and advice in protecting students' civil rights in situations like this one. Alejandro is familiar with his school's anti-bullying policy and knows that it prohibits bullying based on specific characteristics such as gender, ethnicity or race, and physical appearance but it does not include sexual orientation in this list of characteristics. Alejandro also knows that LGBTQ students are not protected under the state anti-bullying or discrimination laws. Alejandro is aware that many representatives in his state legislature have spoken out against gay rights and recently a school district in his state came under federal investigation for implementing policies that actually perpetuate bullying against LGBTQ students. One of these policies in another district mandated that teachers remain "neutral" in situations of anti-LGBTQ bullying so the kids are not provided with any assistance. Alejandro has connected Saul with community resources that will provide him with the support and assistance needed to deal with bullying, but he wants to do more to keep this kind of thing from happening to LGBTQ students in his school. Alejandro wants to revise his school's anti-bullying policy to include sexual orientation in the list of groups listed in the policy. He also feels that, based on conversations with some of the teachers, school staff need specific training on how to handle situations of bullying based on LGBTQ status.

Alejandro talked with the principal and she supports expanding the school's bullying policy to include sexual orientation. She was also in support of bringing someone in to provide training to teachers and staff but was concerned about the cost because there is no money in the budget for such an expense. The principal also told Alejandro that he would need to get the superintendent and school board's approval for the policy change. Alejandro set up time to speak at the next school board meeting but he is concerned about the negative reception he received when he informed them about the topic he would be addressing. He would like to put together a persuasive speech for the board but he is unsure of what information to include that would make an impact.

What organizations can Alejandro partner with who can provide him with the information needed to include in his speech for the board? What community organizations might Alejandro contact to provide training and education to staff at his school at a low cost? What are some steps Alejandro can take to bring about policy change at the state level? What challenges might Alejandro encounter as he moves forward with his efforts to expand the policy to include sexual orientation? What actions can he take to mitigate these challenges early on in the process?

What steps can Saul take to establish a LGBTQ group at his school? How can Alejandro assist him?

MAIN POINTS

- Civil rights are legally enforceable protections afforded to citizens for the purpose of preventing arbitrary abuse by the state or other individuals. Societal barriers to accessing equal rights for oppressed groups affect outcomes such as poverty, unemployment rates, and school dropout rates.

- The Constitution, including the Bill of Rights, is the foundation of civil rights protection in the U.S. Subsequent constitutional amendments, the Civil War, and civil rights movements of the 1950s and 1960s have helped secure additional rights for oppressed groups and ensure recognition of those rights by the majority population.

- The struggle of people of color to attain equal rights is central to the civil rights movement.

- Besides having to struggle to secure citizenship and individual civil rights, Native Americans have fought for tribal sovereignty in the U.S.

- Asians are the fastest growing immigrant group.

- Major legislation influencing the rights of people regardless of race, color, religion, and national origin includes the Civil Rights Act of 1964 as amended in 1987 and 1991 and the Voting Rights Act of 1965.

- The Education for All Handicapped Children Act of 1975 provides for free and appropriate public education for all children with disabilities. The Americans with Disabilities Act of 1990 mandates equal opportunity in applying for and securing access to jobs.

- Social policies that may appear to be neutral need to be carefully examined to ensure they do not, in fact, disadvantage women, people of color, and other diverse groups in our society.

- The Matthew Shepard and James Byrd, Jr. Hate Crimes Prevention Act of 2009 expands the scope of 1968 hate crimes legislation that applied to people attacked because of their race, religion or national origin, to hate crimes committed because of a person's gender, sexual orientation, gender identity, or disability.

- Core civil rights protections provided for in the Constitution extend to non-citizens in the U.S., except in cases where the Constitution specifies rights are reserved only for citizens. For a variety of reasons related to language barriers, cultural differences, xenophobic attitudes, and entrenched disadvantage, immigrant groups are especially vulnerable to civil rights violations.

- Religious leaders, particularly in the African American community, have often been instrumental in the fight for civil rights.

- Efforts to reduce discrimination based on sexual orientation have focused on employment, housing, education, and legal rights in marriage, as well as reduction of hate crimes.

- People with disabilities have fought for access to services, benefits, and non-institutionalized care. Civil rights for older adults have also been pressed in employment and end-of-life decisions.

- Women's rights initiatives have focused on suffrage, education, employment, domestic violence, reproductive freedom, and the still-unsuccessful push for the passage of the Equal Rights Amendment.

- Women in the U.S. have yet to achieve gender equity to the extent found in many other countries. Internationally, gender equity is positively related to economic productivity.

- Affirmative action is based on the idea that past and present discrimination warrants action to repair the damage done. It has been used as an effective tool for reducing discrimination, but it remains controversial.

- There is a continuing debate about whether disparities in educational outcomes, as well as outcomes in other areas, are related primarily to race and ethnicity or to low income and the lack of resources in low-income neighborhoods.

- Social workers have a commitment to social justice. By identifying the strengths of oppressed groups and removing barriers to goal attainment through conflict and consensus building, they can increase social justice.

- Significant strides have been made in the civil rights arena, but additional advocacy is needed to reduce the discrimination still present in U.S. society.

EXERCISES

1. The Sanchez family is a mixed-status family because some family members are citizens and some are not. Visit the website for the National Immigration Law Center for information about immigrants' eligibility for federal benefits.
   a. What difficulties can you identify that the family may encounter in navigating the eligibility requirements for:
      - Supplemental Nutrition Assistance Program (SNAP, formerly known as "Food Stamps");
      - Medicaid; and,
      - Social Security Disability?
   b. What agency or agencies might you contact in your state to learn about eligibility rules for non-citizens for state-funded benefits and services?
   c. What barriers not related to eligibility may discourage the family's use of benefits? Think about language differences, cultural distance, and the impact of "neutral" policies discussed in this chapter.
   d. If the Sanchez family lived in your state, what climate might they encounter? Has your state contemplated anti-immigrant legislation, such as laws that would require service providers to investigate immigrants' status?

    e. Can you suggest ways that a social worker, particularly one who is not a Latino or Latina, might help them navigate immigration laws and receive services? How would connecting the Sanchez family to services benefit their larger community?

2. Go the National Council of La Raza website, then to Issues and Programs, and examine the material under Civil Rights and Justice. Pick one of the policies covered under this heading and explain likely implications for the Sanchez family. Think about the discussion of policy practice from Chapters 5 and 6 and how you, as a social worker, might play a role in advocating for policy change in this area.

3. In Riverton, as well as in communities across the country, difficult issues related to rights and responsibilities of different groups of citizens must be confronted. The civil rights of people who are homeless are often violated, whether by endangering their right to vote, denying homeless children an equal right to education, exposing them to hate crimes, or attacking them with unjust laws that make it illegal for them to be homeless. Pick one of these ways in which the rights of people who are homeless are often violated. Visit the websites of groups that do advocacy work for the homeless, such as the National Council for the Homeless, to get ideas for how to help protect the rights of people who are homeless. As the social worker in the Riverton case vignette:

    a. Identify three strategies you could use to help protect the civil rights of Riverton citizens who are homeless if they are having their rights violated in one of these ways.

    b. Articulate the kinds of civil rights provisions on which you would rely.

    c. Discuss in small groups how communities can reconcile the civil right of the homeless with the concerns of the community, as articulated in the Riverton case vignette.

4. Carla Washburn receives a small pension from Social Security (OASDI). Although OASDI is available for all people regardless of race and gender, it is a seemingly neutral policy that, in reality, results in very different outcomes for different older adults.

    a. How do you think the fact that Carla Washburn is African American and a woman has influenced her ability to be financially secure in old age?

    b. What can social workers do, through practice and policy advocacy, to help level the playing field for older adults like Carla Washburn?

5. As you learned in your text, Native American tribes have pressed for a sovereign relationship with the federal government. Explain what is meant by a sovereign relationship and identify at least two implications for social policy based on your understanding of this relationship.

6. The issue of same-sex marriage has been heavily debated in many states recently. What is the current status of this debate in your state of residence? How is your state chapter of NASW involved in this debate?

CHAPTER 8

Income- and Asset-Based Social Policies and Programs

I am somehow less interested in the weight and convolutions of Einstein's brain than in the near certainty that people of equal talent have lived and died in cotton fields and sweatshops.

Stephen Jay Gould

Poverty does not belong in civilized human society. Its proper place is in a museum.

Muhammad Yunus, Banker to the Poor

The test of our progress is not whether we add more to the abundance of those who have much; it is whether we provide enough for those who have little.

Franklin D. Roosevelt

SOCIAL WORK STUDENTS IN THE UNITED STATES are seeing the effects of poverty on people who have struggled all their lives to keep their families housed and fed, as well as on people who were once solidly middle class. Programs that provide relief for people who have lost their jobs, cannot feed or clothe their children, or are not hired because of age or disability, are all straining to meet the needs of the swelling number of people applying for help. As more families fall into poverty, the ability of the family to fulfill the traditional role of primary institution in our society for support and socialization of children is further compromised. Moreover, the holes in our public safety net programs are becoming increasingly obvious as Americans who have lost their homes or given up hope of finding a job turn to homeless programs and food pantries to sustain their families. Although the chances of moving from a life of poverty to great wealth in the U.S. are very limited, moving from the middle class into poverty is often as simple as losing a job. For too many in the U.S., "economic mobility" primarily moves downward, while some families remain locked in disadvantage for generations. The recession and accompanying collapse of the housing market beginning in 2008 exposed the fragility of many households' economic well-being, but many individuals and families in poverty faced considerable threats to their health and security long before and well after the economic downturn officially ended.

Social workers practice with people of all income levels. However, throughout our profession's history and certainly today, many of our clients live in poverty. As discussed in the section on needs determination in Chapter 5, there can be many reasons a person has a low income, including loss of employment, physical and mental disabilities, lack of education, alcohol and drug abuse, discriminatory hiring practices, and lack of well-paying jobs in the community. Basically, people are poor because they lack the power to acquire resources to adequately meet their needs. Although there are many strategies for overcoming the barriers faced by people in poverty, the most immediate requirement is access to income that is adequate to acquire necessities such as food and shelter.

This chapter examines the major government policies and programs designed to reduce poverty. Its primary emphasis is on those policies and programs that provide cash to clients. However, because food stamps (now called the Supplemental Nutrition Assistance Program (SNAP)) and housing subsidies also directly help ameliorate the effects of poverty, we will analyze these policies and programs as well. In addition, because TANF, the major program that supports women and children who are living in poverty, also contains a large jobs program, this chapter also covers employment policy in the context of TANF. Other policies and programs that address the needs of people in poverty, notably Medicaid (which provides access to health care for many children and poor adults in the United States) are covered in other chapters. To help you understand the structure and functions of government anti-poverty policies and programs, we will also analyze official definitions of poverty, contrast universal with selective programs, and examine in greater detail some major asset-based policies currently advocated by social workers. As in previous chapters, we will use strengths perspective principles to analyze various income-support policies.

DEFINITIONS OF POVERTY

Poverty can be defined in a variety of ways. The focus can be on basic needs, capabilities, assets, or income. Using a basic needs perspective, poverty is seen as the lack of resources to fulfill basic human needs including food, health, and education. The capabilities perspective defines poverty as the absence of opportunities to achieve capabilities to be sheltered, well nourished, adequately clothed, healthy, and active in the community (Sen, 1999). When considering capabilities, the initial focus is on which groups have the capacity to secure opportunities for their families and communities to succeed, and what opportunities make this possible. Initiatives to increase access to these opportunities is in keeping with advancing support for a capacity building state which prioritizes public policies and programs that help families currently lacking these capacities, to build them.

When thinking about asset poverty, attention centers on lack of wealth such as homes, farms and businesses, stocks, savings accounts, and other financial assets;

why such large wealth disparities exist; and strategies to increase asset accumulation for low-income families. In this chapter, we will initially concentrate on income because this is the criterion used to determine eligibility in many anti-poverty, health and social service policies and programs in the U.S. Using an income perspective, people are considered poor if their income falls below a specific threshold. Experts who define poverty based on income frequently distinguish between absolute and relative poverty. Absolute poverty refers to a system whereby the government determines an objective income-level threshold or *poverty line*, which is used as a measure of who is poor. More specifically, the government calculates food, housing, and other basic needs in terms of the minimum level of income needed to survive. If an individual's or a family's income falls below the poverty line, then that individual or family is defined as poor. If, conversely, an individual has income even one dollar above that threshold, he or she would not be defined as officially "poor," even though his or her actual well-being may be practically indistinguishable from someone who is considered poor. Absolute measures of poverty typically are used when writing U.S. social policy dealing with eligibility for means-tested programs.

Poverty can also be defined in terms of a relative poverty threshold. Relative poverty is influenced heavily by societal standards that determine a threshold of income that allows people to afford what is generally considered to be an adequate standard of living at a given time in a society. For example, housing considered to be adequate by U.S. standards is different from housing considered adequate in developing countries. Likewise, what is considered a necessary material possession, and how much income is needed in order to secure it, varies from country to country and even among people within the U.S. For example, many Americans might not consider a television to be a necessity, but perhaps all Americans would define a refrigerator as a basic necessity. Obtaining adequate housing costs far more in some urban areas of the United States—especially on the coasts—than in rural areas in the Midwest, for example. One common measure for relative poverty is an income that is less than 50 percent of the median family income in a country or political subdivision. Median income is the income point at which half of the citizens have a higher income and half have a lower income. Most of the countries in Europe use the relative concept to measure official poverty levels. Comparison of poverty rates among developed countries is further complicated because of the differences in public benefit programs such as health care and housing subsidies that impact whether income is sufficient to cover basic needs. However, we do know that there is much greater income inequality in the U.S. than in most other developed countries. Income inequality is discussed in detail later in this chapter.

The Poverty Line/Poverty Threshold

The government uses an absolute income-level threshold, or poverty line, to determine who is poor. The poverty line has also been described as the *poverty index*, *poverty threshold*, or *poverty level*, depending on the context. Mollie Orshansky, a social science research analyst on the staff of the Social Security Administration, initially developed the official poverty threshold used by the U.S. government. Orshansky constructed this measure based on a survey of American households conducted in 1955. The results of this survey indicated that families of three or more members spent approximately one-third of their post-tax monthly income on food. Orshansky established the measurement of poverty by selecting the cheapest of four economy food plans developed by the Department of Agriculture and then multiplying the cost of that plan by three. Significantly, this food plan—referred to as the "Thrifty Food Plan"—outlined a nutritionally adequate diet for families under economic constraints or facing an emergency situation, but might not be adequate on a long-term basis for optimum nutrition and health (Fischer, 1992).

Currently, the U.S. Census Bureau is responsible for measuring poverty. In 2012, the poverty threshold for a family of four with two children under the age of 18 was $23,283, meaning that if a family's income was lower than this amount, the family was considered poor (U.S. Census Bureau, 2013b). This income level, which is adjusted yearly for inflation, is supposed to satisfy a family's minimal needs. In 2011, 46.2 million people in the U.S.—approximately 15 percent of the overall population—were living below this poverty line (U.S. Census Bureau, 2012e). This was the highest rate since 1993. Even though many social workers would consider this threshold very low, in terms of the actual income needed to secure a decent standard of living in their communities, many public means-tested programs such as Medicaid and TANF require clients to fall far below the poverty line in order to qualify for assistance. Calculations to determine who is poor are based on actual pre-tax income including financial assistance from the government such as Social Security and Supplemental Security Income (SSI). However, the poverty line does not consider non-cash benefits such as housing subsidies and SNAP, nor does it include a family's assets or liabilities adjustment, or adjustments for fixed or extraordinary expenses. Unlike earlier federal calculations of poverty levels that considered such factors as farm and non-farm residence and the gender of the family head, the current poverty line is adjusted only for family size and ages of family members. The poverty line also does not take into consideration the geographical location of families, except for those living in either Hawaii or Alaska (U.S. Census Bureau, 2012g). Consequently, it does not differentiate families in large urban areas from families living in small, rural communities where the cost of living may be lower. Additionally, people 65 and over are presumed to need less income and therefore have to be poorer to be considered below the poverty threshold, a fallacy we will discuss in detail in Chapter 11 on aging. A person younger than age 65 with income of $11,702 qualifies as poor, whereas a person who is 65 or older is poor at $10,788 annual income. Most analysts agree that the official poverty measures have many flaws. We will discuss initiatives to improve these measures in the segment, Alternative Policy Measures, below.

Poverty Guidelines

The poverty threshold is one method the federal government uses to measure poverty, though primarily for statistical purposes. In contrast, poverty guidelines represent different measures that are used to determine financial eligibility for various federal programs. One way that these guidelines differ from the poverty threshold is that they do not differentiate for age. The U.S. Department of Health and Human Services (USDHHS) publishes poverty guidelines in the *Federal Register*. In 2013, the poverty guideline for a family of four was $23,550 (USDHHS, 2013). The poverty guideline is adjusted using the annual average Consumer Price Index (CPI). Some of the programs that use the USDHHS poverty guidelines are SNAP, Head Start, and Children's Health Insurance Programs (CHIP). Many of these programs, in recognition of the inadequacy of the measure, allow individuals to qualify with incomes that exceed the poverty line by a specified percentage.

Alternative Poverty Measures

Poverty measures that only consider cash income when determining whether a family is poor but do not count non-cash benefits such as SNAP (food stamps) and refundable tax credits such as the Earned Income Tax Credit make it difficult to gauge the effect of these safety net programs on poverty (CBPP, 2013a). We will discuss these programs in detail in this chapter. Additionally, dramatic changes in household spending since the inception of the poverty measure, particularly given the increases in energy and health costs, make it difficult to argue that the current line accurately represents real economic hardship. Because of inadequacies in the official poverty measure, in the 1990s, a National Academy of Sciences (NAS) expert panel endorsed a more inclusive measure of poverty that incorporates tax benefits and non-cash benefits. The Census Bureau now issues poverty measures based on the NAS recommendations, as well as the "official" measure (Short, 2012). In 2011, the Bureau of Labor Statistics and U.S. Census Bureau jointly released a Supplemental Poverty Measure which, while not intended to replace the official measure as the criterion for benefit eligibility, does attempt to determine the extent to which incorporating expenses such as tax burdens, child care, and health insurance, as well as benefits such as subsidized housing and nutrition supports, alters poverty statistics in the U.S.

The utility of alternative measures when examining effectiveness of non-cash benefits in ameliorating poverty will be explored later in the chapter. However, there are political and practical concerns about shifting entirely to a new poverty measure, including ongoing difficulties in comparing poverty statistics from different time periods, as well as the hesitation of many policy makers to see poverty rates increase significantly as a result of using a new threshold. To find out more about poverty measures and who is poor, explore the website of the Institute for Research on Poverty (www.irp.wisc.edu).

INCOME-SUPPORT POLICIES AND PROGRAMS

Unlike many other developed countries, the U.S. does not have policies that guarantee a minimum income for each child or paid family leave for caregiving adults. Instead, we have enacted policies to provide a patchwork of income-support programs. Some of these programs require prior attachment to the workforce (that is, worker, spouse of worker, or child of worker) as a condition of eligibility. Other programs are available only to low-income citizens, or certain qualified resident immigrants, who meet some additional category of eligibility such as disability or having children in the family. Because income-support programs are so central to social work with people in poverty, Chapter 3 discussed the historical development of these policies and programs in detail.

Income-support programs are categorized as either universal or selective. Although all of these programs have eligibility requirements, *universal programs* are provided to eligible citizens regardless of income, whereas *selective programs* are typically means-tested and designed for people in poverty (Blau and Abramovitz, 2007). Some of the programs are entitlement programs, meaning that the government has a legal obligation to provide payments or benefits to all individuals who meet the eligibility requirements. Recall that we discussed entitlements in Chapter 4 in the context of mandatory versus discretionary spending and the federal budget. Mandatory spending at the federal level—which includes entitlement programs—is authorized by permanent laws, rather than by annual appropriation bills. Thus, it is more difficult for the federal government to eliminate or drastically reduce entitlements.

Some entitlement programs, such as unemployment insurance and Old-Age, Survivors, Disability and Health Insurance—which includes Medicare—are universal and require attachment to the workforce in order to qualify for benefits and services. Other entitlement programs, including SNAP, SSI, and the Earned Income Tax Credit (EITC) are selective and means-tested. Veterans' benefits are an entitlement based on prior military service.

Many of the programs that serve people in poverty are not entitlement programs. These programs include TANF, General Assistance, the Special Supplemental Nutrition Program for Women, Infants, and Children (WIC), the Elder Nutrition Program under the Older Americans Act, and public housing. People who apply and are eligible might not receive the benefits and services they need, depending on federal and state budgetary constraints.

In the following sections, we turn our attention to policies governing major programs that provide income support as well as housing and food assistance programs. We also examine housing, food, and jobs policies as they relate to TANF legislation.

UNIVERSAL PROGRAMS

In this section, we consider universal programs designed to provide income in the face of predictable age- and unpredictable work-related events that can cause people to be unable to continue to work. These programs also help stabilize the economy, because beneficiaries typically spend the income right away on necessities such as food, clothing, shelter, and health care.

Old-Age, Survivors, and Disability Insurance: How Young People Benefit

As presented in Chapter 3, the Social Security Act established several major income-support programs, including unemployment compensation and financial assistance for aged and blind individuals and dependent children. Nevertheless, as popularly used, the term *Social Security* generally refers to the program titled Old-Age, Survivors, and Disability Insurance (OASDI). OASDI was established to provide pensions to covered workers and their families when income is lost due to retirement, old age, or disability. It is important to remember that OASDI is an insurance program, not just simply a retirement program. The insurance function was expanded to include health insurance when Medicare was enacted in 1965. We will examine Medicare in greater detail in Chapter 10. Currently 94 percent of U.S. workers are covered by the Social Security system. Over 18 percent of the 314 million people in the U.S. receive OASDI benefits. In 2013, 58 million people were receiving a benefit from OASDI. OASDI has two parts. Workers who are retired, their families, and survivors of workers who have died receive monthly benefits under the Old-Age and Survivors Insurance (OASI) program. Workers who are disabled and their families receive monthly benefits under the Disability Insurance (DI) program. When examined separately, funding for the DI portion of the program is more problematic than for the program in its entirety. Exhibit 8.1 illustrates the increases in awards to retired and disabled workers. You can see that as the oldest of the baby boomers, people born between 1946 and 1964, began to reach retirement age, awards to retired workers rose. However, awards to disabled workers have increased proportionately more over the time period illustrated. This exhibit indicates that the annualized rate of increase is 1.6 percent for retired workers and 2.2 percent for disabled workers over the period from 1971 to 2011. The recent spike in disability benefits is due in part to the weak economy. Workers with disabilities who could, nonetheless, continue to work in less demanding jobs, applied for DIs when fewer such positions became available.

Clearly, OASDI provides insurance benefits to many people who are neither old nor retired workers. The Social Security Administration (SSA) oversees this insurance system. The future of the Social Security system and proposals to reform it, have emerged as a highly controversial political issue. We will consider these proposals later in this chapter.

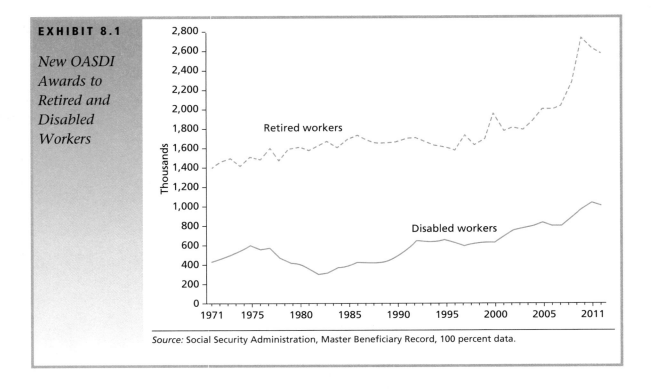

EXHIBIT 8.1

New OASDI Awards to Retired and Disabled Workers

Source: Social Security Administration, Master Beneficiary Record, 100 percent data.

Eligibility for OASDI benefits is dependent on age and work credits earned. For example, to be eligible for old-age retirement pensions, in general, a person has to complete 40 credits (10 years) of work. A covered worker can earn four credits each year by working for a certain amount of wages (Social Security Administration, 2013c). In 2013, a worker earned one credit for each $1,160 in earnings they had, up to a maximum of four credits per year. Eligibility for survivors' and disability benefits require fewer credits when death or disability occurs at a younger age. Once people earn the appropriate number of credits, they become eligible for early retirement benefits at age 62. Early retirees receive a lower monthly pension, for some up to 30 percent lower than if they waited to their full retirement age. People born before 1938 are eligible for full Social Security benefits at the age of 65. However, beginning in 2003, the age at which full benefits are payable increased in gradual steps from 65 to 67 (Social Security Administration, 2013d). People born after 1959 are not eligible to receive full benefits until the age of 67. Some experts advocate moving the age of eligibility for both early retirement and full retirement yet higher as life expectancy increases. Currently, if a person voluntarily elects to delay retirement until age 70, then her or his benefits increase for each month that OASDI payments are postponed. Benefit payments are made via direct deposit into a checking or savings account or through a debit card. In 2013, the average monthly

Social Security benefit for a retired worker was about $1,260; for a retired couple, it was approximately $2,048. Beneficiaries with disabilities received average monthly payments of $1,130; those with a spouse and one child received $1,919. A surviving spouse with two children averaged $2,592 (Social Security Administration, 2013e). There is no minimum amount that all eligible workers or their families must receive.

Over 1 in 4 of today's 20 year olds will become disabled before reaching 67, the current age at which they can begin to receive full retirement benefits. For the vast majority, the only long-term DIs they will ever have for themselves and their families is provided through OASDI. Disabled workers and their dependents account for about 20 percent of total benefits paid (Social Security Administration, 2013f).

Local SSA offices determine eligibility for benefits, and payments are processed through the U.S. Treasury Department. The administrative costs associated with providing OASDI are low. While people are in the labor force, their earnings are taxed to pay for Social Security benefits. Social Security payroll taxes are collected under the authority of the Federal Insurance Contributions Act (FICA). Payroll taxes are listed on pay receipts as FICA. Funds collected from people in the workforce are used to pay benefits to people who have already retired. When the government collects more taxes than are needed to pay benefits in a given year, the surplus is invested in U.S. Treasury Bond. As baby boomers joined the workforce, and women entered the workforce in unprecedented numbers, the surplus swelled. Indeed, that surplus is crucial to keeping the system solvent as the baby boomers retire and begin drawing benefits. However, in recent years cash flow into the fund has been less than expenditures for a variety of reasons. For example, large numbers of older workers lost jobs and took early retirement during the economic downturn in 2010. Other workers contributed less as their wages declined or they spent periods out of work during the recession. However, this does not mean the system is insolvent. Indeed, OASDI still has large surpluses.

There were about 3.2 workers for every OASDI beneficiary in 2008. In 2013 there were about 2.8 workers for every beneficiary. This ratio is expected to decline gradually to 2.1 by 2033, when most baby boomers have retired. However, because of projected gains in productivity per worker, the actual impact of the change in numbers of workers is not clear. Due in part to baby boomer retirement, the cost rate—measured by OASDI support costs as a percent of GDP—will rise rapidly from 2012 through 2030. Treasury will redeem trust fund assets in amounts that exceed interest earnings until exhaustion of trust fund reserves in 2033. It is important to understand that even after this date, tax income would still be sufficient to pay about three-quarters of scheduled benefits through 2086 (Social Security Administration, 2012g). Other variables could intervene to shift this timeline, including changes in immigration policy, changes in U.S. birthrates, economic cycles, OASDI policy changes, and long-term trends in lifespan and health. If you would like more detail on the current status of Social Security, go to the Social Security Administration website and search for The Annual Report of the Board of

Trustees of the Federal Old-Age and Survivors Insurance and Federal Disability Insurance Trust Funds.

Both employers and employees pay the FICA tax up to a certain maximum income. In 2013, employers and employees each paid 6.2 percent of an employee's gross income, for a total of 12.4 percent. FICA taxes are not deducted from income above the wage base. The wage base for 2013 is $113,700 (Social Security Administration, 2013h). Further, for 2011 and 2012, the Social Security payroll tax rate was reduced by two percentage points (from 12.4 percent to 10.4 percent). This is referred to as a "payroll tax holiday." The intent was to stimulate the economy. However, the funds not collected through insurance payments based on payroll meant that these dollars had to be replaced with federal tax dollars. This was a specific policy decision by Congress, as part of economic stimulus efforts, but there could be long-term effects for OASDI and those who depend on it. Key to the program's fiscal and political success is its structure as a social insurance program, where the government provides the institution through which individuals share the risks and rewards associated with participation in a capitalist economy. As the debate about OASDI reform continues, social workers should be wary of efforts to change its financing that would undermine this insurance principle.

Exhibit 8.2 summarizes information on OASDI using the policy and program analysis framework introduced in Chapter 5. The date shown in Exhibit 8.2 is the year in which the original legislation was passed. Although this and subsequent exhibits do not encompass all the details provided in the text and the web resources cited, they provide the basics in a format you can easily remember. For more detailed information on Social Security, go to the website for Social Security Online (www.ssa.gov).

Unemployment Insurance

Unemployment insurance serves two primary functions: (1) it ensures that unemployed workers receive minimal cash assistance, allowing them to meet basic needs

EXHIBIT 8.2 *Old Age, Survivors, and Disability Insurance (OASDI), 1935*		
Policy Goals	To protect workers and their families from loss of income due to retirement, disability, or death.	
Benefits or Services Provided	Monthly checks.	
Eligibility Rules	Determined by age, payment of payroll taxes, and disability.	
Service Delivery System	Social Security Administration offices determine eligibility, and funds are sent by check via U.S. mail or by electronic bank transfer.	
Financing	Payroll taxes paid by employees and their employers.	

such as housing, food, and clothing; and (2) it provides cash assistance during periods of high unemployment, which helps stabilize the economy. As such, unemployment insurance serves as both a stabilizing force in the larger economy and a protection for workers whose well-being is largely dependent on job opportunities over which they have little control. Approximately 97 percent of all permanent wage and salary workers are covered by unemployment insurance. In November 2012 more than 5.2 million unemployed workers received benefits (U.S. Department of Labor, 2012).

Eligibility for benefits is based on attachment to the labor force, which is determined by examining wages and weeks worked at the time of unemployment. Benefits are intended for people who are unemployed due to external circumstances and who will continue to actively seek work. Beneficiaries also must be able to work if an appropriate job becomes available.

Unemployment insurance is unique in that it is the only universal program created by individual states with federal oversight by the U.S. Department of Labor. Individual states have the opportunity to design the program's benefit structure and state tax structure. This arrangement causes variations across states in terms of eligibility and actual benefits. In 2012, the average state weekly unemployment benefit was approximately $300. However, the actual benefit a person receives varies greatly depending on the state and the worker's previous earnings. In all but three states, unemployment insurance is funded entirely by taxes on employers. The remaining three states tax employees as well. These taxes are collected by both the states and the federal government, and companies that comply with state requirements are eligible for substantial tax credits (U.S. Department of Labor, 2012). During periods of economic growth, taxes are collected and saved for times when larger numbers of workers become unemployed. Most states pay benefits for up to 26 weeks, with "extended benefits" funded jointly by states and federal sources during periods of high unemployment. You can get information on unemployment insurance at your state government website.

However, many Americans who are out of work do not qualify for unemployment insurance. They include part-time, temporary, and self-employed workers, as well as those who work in the informal economy. Additionally, although their eligibility for unemployment insurance has run out, many people still have not been able to find a job. In times of economic crisis and high unemployment, the federal government has stepped in to provide additional funding in order to protect and extend benefits in states with high unemployment. As a result of the American Recovery and Reinvestment Act passed by Congress in February 2009 some unemployed people in states with high unemployment rates could receive up to 99 weeks of benefits. Before the passage of the American Recovery and Reinvestment Act, the maximum number of weeks allowed was 26. Exhibit 8.3 summarizes the features of the unemployment insurance program. For the latest information on unemployment insurance, go to the U.S. Department of Labor website (www.dol.gov) and search for Unemployment Insurance.

EXHIBIT 8.3 *Unemployment Insurance, 1935*	**Policy Goals**	To provide income to meet basic needs for workers who have lost jobs and to stabilize the economy by encouraging spending.
	Benefits or Services Provided	Cash assistance for up to 26 weeks in most states. Extended benefits are available during high unemployment.
	Eligibility Rules	Workers must be unemployed due to no fault of their own and must meet requirements of wages earned and weeks worked in the past year. They also must be actively seeking work.
	Service Delivery System	State agencies determine eligibility for claims. Claims are filed weekly or biweekly until employment is secured.
	Financing	Funded primarily by taxes on employers.

Workers' Compensation

Workers' compensation was the first kind of social insurance program in the U.S. In 1908 the Congress enacted a workers' compensation program for federal employees. States also soon began enacting workers' compensation programs. This program—which, like unemployment insurance, is funded solely by employers—provides some protection for workers who are injured or killed at work, and also offers benefits to their families. In addition to paying for medical care to treat the injury or disability, workers' compensation provides cash assistance to ensure that people are not without income due to work-related injuries. Benefit levels vary from state to state. Most states pay recipients two-thirds of the worker's weekly earnings at the time of injury or death. The duration of payments depends on whether the disability is temporary or permanent. Survivors of deceased workers receive burial expenses and payments until they remarry, and children receive benefits until a certain age that is set by the state. The workers' compensation program can be very difficult for an injured worker to navigate. However, if benefits are not negotiated, the worker and the family could be left without adequate compensation. Social workers, attorneys specializing in workers' compensation claims, and other professionals might need to become involved in successfully pressing a claim.

The vast majority of the nation's wage and salary workers are covered by workers' compensation. In general, people are eligible for benefits regardless of fault or blame for the accident. The major exceptions to this rule are gross negligence, willful misconduct, and intoxication while working.

Private employers purchase policies through insurance companies, which distribute benefits following an injury or accident. These insurance companies are governed by state and federal statutes. In most cases, the program delivery system is organized by the state. Businesses pay premiums that are based on company size, level of risk to employees, and experience rating. The way claims are handled varies greatly from state to state. Workers who are encouraged to settle for lump-sum payments often find these funds do not equal their lost wages. Further, many workers experience long delays between the time of injury and the time benefits actually start. To find out more about worker's compensation in your state, go to the U.S. Department of Labor and search for Worker's Compensation. You will find a link to your state's workers' compensation board. Exhibit 8.4 summarizes the workers' compensation program.

Veterans' Benefits

Veterans' benefits include pensions to veterans with disabilities. Benefits are intended to restore veterans' capabilities to the greatest extent possible and to improve the quality of their lives and the lives of their families. Of the approximately 22.2 million veterans currently alive, approximately 3.5 million receive disability compensation and pensions (U.S. Department of Veterans' Affairs, 2013). In addition, almost one-quarter of the nation's population are potentially eligible for Veterans' Affairs (VA) benefits and services because they are family members or survivors of veterans (U.S. Department of Veterans' Affairs, 2009). Large numbers of individuals are newly eligible for these programs due to U.S. engagement in military conflict in the Middle East, in particular, and the need for social workers to serve these veterans and assist them in navigating available resources is increasing.

To be eligible for veterans' benefits, an individual must have been discharged from active military service. A veteran who received an honorable or general discharge from active military services is eligible for most benefits, but dishonorable discharge is likely to make a person ineligible. Disability compensation is paid for injury, disability, or death that occurred while the veteran was serving in the armed forces. The level of compensation payments for a veteran depends on the degree of disability, ranging from monthly payments of $129 to $2,816. In contrast, disability pensions are selective, means-tested benefits paid either to low-income veterans with a permanent and total disability that is not service-connected or to low-income

Policy Goals	To protect workers against the effects of occupational injuries or illnesses	**EXHIBIT 8.4**
Benefits or Services Provided	Cash and medical assistance.	*Workers' Compensation, 1908*
Eligibility Rules	Workers must be injured or killed on the job in accidents unrelated to intoxication, gross negligence, or willful misconduct.	
Service Delivery System	Programs are organized by states under federal legislation. Insurance companies receive claims and award benefits.	
Financing	Employers purchase policies from insurance companies.	

veterans age 65 or older regardless of physical condition (U.S. Department of Veterans' Affairs, 2013). Veterans' benefits are financed primarily through federal general revenues, with some co-payments made by military personnel, and are administered through the Compensation and Pension Service, a division of the Department of Veterans' Affairs (VA). The benefits and eligibility qualifications are too varied to be presented in a summary table. For additional information, do an online search for Department of Veterans' Affairs, Facts about the Department of Veterans' Affairs.

SELECTIVE PROGRAMS

Selective policies and programs that require a person to be impoverished as a condition of eligibility can be more clearly understood if you first think about who is considered poor in our society and why. In 2011, 16.1 million children (persons under 18) were growing up in poverty. The child poverty rate was 21.9 percent. This means one in five children in our country was growing up in poverty. Children living in female-headed families with no spouse present had a poverty rate of 47.6 percent, over four times the rate of children in married-couple families (10.9 percent). Child poverty varies greatly from state to state. In Mississippi, the state with the highest proportion of children in poverty, almost a third of children are poor. In New Mexico and Washington, DC, child poverty rates also near one-third. In ten states, childhood poverty rates are 25 percent or higher. The lowest childhood poverty rate (10 percent) was in New Hampshire (USDHHS, 2012b).

The poverty rate for all African Americans was 27.5 percent. The poverty rate for Hispanics was 25.3 percent. Women of color age 75 and over were at particularly high risk of poverty. The poverty rate for non-Hispanic white people was 9.8 percent. Overall, 6.6 percent of people, or 20.4 million people, lived in deep poverty. This means they had income below one-half the poverty threshold, meaning they had an income below about $11,500 for a family of four (USDHHS, 2012c).

As discussed above, although the recession has officially ended, longer-term trends mean that many Americans are not experiencing improvement in their economic status. Structural barriers such as educational deficits, mismatch of location of jobs and workers, lack of public transportation, and global relocation of jobs, makes it difficult for many in disadvantaged populations to experience real economic mobility. Looking at poverty statistics in the United States reveals clearly that while poverty is a more pervasive problem than many realize, some populations are at far greater risk of poverty than others.

Statistics on poverty show that women are hardest hit in every category. Many younger single women and older women are poor for some of the same reasons. They have spent most of their lives as unpaid caretakers; in addition, many poor women and people of color hold temporary or part-time jobs that are not covered by OASDI. Women faced discrimination in hiring in the past and continue to do so.

Although over 58 percent of working-age women are in the labor force, they still are disproportionately represented among those holding low-paying jobs with few benefits. Moreover, with so many women of all income and age levels now joining the workforce, there has been erosion in the beliefs that (1) caring for children is a full-time job for women; and (2) all low-income mothers, therefore, are worthy of government support in that role. There is no longer strong societal pressure for women to be at home full-time to take care of their children. However, the decision to stay at home to care for children is generally supported by the public when the family provides the income necessary to support the mother and children, or when the primary breadwinner had sufficient work history to qualify for OASDI prior to death or disability.

Now that public priorities have shifted, work requirements are a central component of TANF, even for single mothers with young children. However, analysis indicates these mothers work predominantly in low-paying jobs that do not provide benefits and therefore do not allow them to move out of poverty. In sum, then, the majority of the people who are poor are women and children for whom the usual sources of support, such as family and the labor market, have been, and continue to be, insufficient.

Temporary Assistance for Needy Families

Recall from Chapter 3 that the 1996 Personal Responsibility and Work Opportunity Reconciliation Act (PRWORA) replaced Aid to Families with Dependent Children (AFDC) with TANF. AFDC (originally ADC) was the federal cash public assistance program established as an entitlement under the Social Security Act. The 1996 TANF legislation eliminated the individual entitlement to cash assistance. Formerly, under the AFDC program, states were required to aid all families that met the state income requirements for eligibility. The federal government contributed at least half of the AFDC benefit costs, so federal welfare spending increased on an open-ended basis as AFDC caseloads rose. In contrast, TANF is a state-level block grant that empowers each state to determine when and under what circumstances it will provide cash assistance to families in poverty. States are no longer required to provide assistance to any individual or family (Committee on Ways and Means, 2000). States get a lump-sum payment that represents roughly what they received for AFDC and related services in 1994, and they have a "maintenance of effort" (MOE) requirement to continue to spend 75 percent to 80 percent of the amount they spent on AFDC and related services that year (Committee on Ways and Means, 2000). They also must meet some federal stipulations including work requirements and the cumulative five-year limit on cash assistance using federal funds. However, because of the block grant nature of TANF which gives states broad flexibility, there is no longer any federal protection for state cash assistance programs, and time limits in about one-third of the states are shorter than five years. Further, the TANF block grant is now an attractive revenue source for filling funding gaps for a variety of state programs. Cash benefits are now at least 20 percent below their 1996 levels in 34 states, after adjusting for inflation. This drop comes on top of much larger decreases in the previous quarter century, eroding TANF's ability to provide any real economic security for families in poverty. Two-thirds of the states reduced cash assistance benefit levels for poor families with children by over 40 percent in real terms between 1970 and 1996. Given persistent financial woes in many states these cuts could be followed by larger, more damaging changes in future years (Schott and Pavetti, 2011).

In 2011, total federal and state spending for TANF was $33.3 billion. Federal TANF funding was about $16.5 billion in block grants (Falk, 2013). The block grant is not adjusted for inflation or changes in caseload and so lost 30 percent of its value due to inflation between FY 1997 and FY 2012. The cash assistance portion of TANF was $9.6 billion; about half of what it was in 1996. Exhibit 8.5 shows how TANF dollars are spent. Because states now have great flexibility, they are free to use funds much more broadly than core welfare programs. As you can see, some states use a substantial portion of funding for these other services.

States have broad ability to set TANF eligibility requirements as well as to determine benefits and services. In 2011 there were about 1.9 million families, or 4,363,000 average monthly TANF recipients. The vast majority of TANF recipients are children. Cash benefits for a family of three with a single parent ranged from $170 a month in Mississippi to $923 a month in Alaska. Cash benefits are below 50 percent of the poverty line in all states and in the majority of states, they fall below *30 percent* of the poverty line. In fact, 14 states pay benefits that are below 20 percent of the poverty line (Finch and Schott, 2011). The cash benefit in those

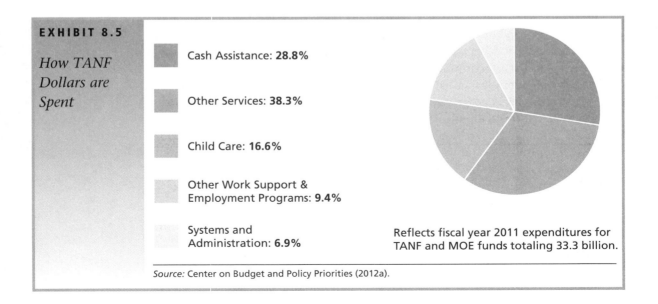

EXHIBIT 8.5

How TANF Dollars are Spent

Cash Assistance: **28.8%**

Other Services: **38.3%**

Child Care: **16.6%**

Other Work Support & Employment Programs: **9.4%**

Systems and Administration: **6.9%**

Reflects fiscal year 2011 expenditures for TANF and MOE funds totaling 33.3 billion.

Source: Center on Budget and Policy Priorities (2012a).

states is less than $300 a month (less than $3,600 a year) for a family of three. Yet deeper cuts are expected in many states in the coming years. Clearly, then, TANF payments are not nearly adequate to lift a family out of poverty, an analysis consistent with understanding of the goals of TANF, which include reducing welfare dependence and promoting marriage among poor single-parent families, but *not* reducing child poverty. To compare eligibility for TANF in your state with other states, visit the National Center for Children in Poverty website (www.nccp.org) and go to State Profiles. Find out what choices your state is making about TANF benefits. Some states have actually increased TANF benefits in response to the challenges facing families during the economic downturn. If your state is not one of them, find out why.

History and Development of TANF   The importance of historical, economic, social, and political contexts in shaping social policy is clearly illustrated by the debates leading up to the passage of the legislation that created TANF. Many of the themes that emerged during the welfare reform debate of the 1990s were not new. Ideological issues and concerns revolving around the morality of single motherhood, "deserving" versus "undeserving" poor people, and race have long historical roots, and we have examined them in previous chapters. Furthermore, under the previous AFDC program, low benefit levels meant that, historically, many recipients already engaged in paid labor, a fact obscured by the debate over work versus "dependence" (Abramovitz, 1996).

As the number of families receiving AFDC continued to rise in the 1970s, the focus increasingly shifted to moving recipients into paid work. However, with the greater participation of middle- and upper-income women in the workforce, strict work requirements, even for mothers with preschool children, gained much more political support in the 1990s. Although many women with young children of all income levels are working outside the home, proponents of work requirements overlook the crucial fact that—unlike TANF recipients, who are disproportionately single mothers—most mothers are not the sole breadwinners, homemakers, and caregivers in their families. Working outside the home and also being the only parent to handle child care and household tasks is a monumental undertaking, particularly if the parent lacks advanced educational preparation that would qualify her for the highly compensated employment that could afford her the opportunity to purchase additional supports. Children of working mothers can thrive if they have high-quality day care and plenty of parental involvement in their lives. However, TANF did not change the reality of the social context that shapes these families. Affordable high-quality day care for mothers on TANF continues to be in short supply, and when one person is working full-time and also doing all of the home chores, time for parental involvement is greatly reduced. These pressures have only been ratcheted up in the current economic downturn, as working mothers receiving TANF compete in the low-wage labor market with growing numbers of newly unemployed individuals, and as states and localities cut back further on necessary supports.

We know that poverty is a powerful predictor of all sorts of negative outcomes for children, from dropping out of school to poor physical and mental health to teenage pregnancy to juvenile crime. Children in families receiving TANF are still living in poverty, and the protective factors of high-quality day care—whether provided in a facility or by the mother—and time for parental involvement, are not adequately supported by current TANF policy. As you will see when we examine TANF goals in the next section, the need for improved day care if mothers are required to work outside the home is not explicitly addressed in the purpose statement.

TANF Goals   Section 401(a) of the Social Security Act states that the purpose of TANF is to give states more flexibility in operating a program that is intended to accomplish the following purposes:

- Provide assistance to needy families so that children may be cared for in their own homes or in the homes of relatives.

- End dependence on government benefits by promoting job preparation, work, and marriage for needy parents.

- Prevent and reduce the incidence of out-of-wedlock pregnancies.

- Encourage the formation and maintenance of two-parent families (Committee on Ways and Means, 2000).

Note that decreasing poverty and improving child well-being are not among these goals. Remember, the effectiveness of a policy should be evaluated based on stated goals. According to the strengths perspective, the goal of the target group not to live in poverty should be reflected in the policy goals statement. Were that the case, then reduction of poverty would be the central outcome on which the program's effectiveness would be judged. Instead, claims of success for TANF are centered on reduction of caseloads and increases in employment.

At the time the TANF legislation was passed, 4.4 million families were receiving cash public assistance (Committee on Ways and Means, 2000). The average monthly number of TANF families receiving cash benefits in December 2011 was 1.9 million (Falk, 2013). Thus, caseloads had been cut by more than half in this time period. Many supporters of TANF interpret this development as positive. Viewed from a different perspective, however, caseload declines in TANF have greatly exceeded declines in poverty, which means that a substantially smaller percentage of poor families now receives public income support.

At the same time, educational and workplace discrimination have prevented some people of color from getting jobs covered by OASDI and unemployment insurance, and, therefore, they are not eligible for those benefits. Because TANF may be the only income-support program for which these individuals qualify, insufficiencies in TANF create disproportionate hardships for these groups. Federal law stipulates that federal TANF dollars cannot be used for benefits or services for most legal immigrants until they have been Lawful Permanent Residents (LPR) for at least five years. Many of the children who are poor in our country have non-citizen parents who therefore cannot receive TANF benefits or services (CBPP, 2013a). Furthermore, use of any federal or state funds for undocumented immigrants is prohibited.

Family Formation Goals   As we have seen, one stated goal of TANF is to reduce the number of out-of-wedlock pregnancies and births by promoting marriage (Office of Family Assistance, 2009). In 2005, TANF was reauthorized with a renewed focus on work and on strengthening families through the promotion of responsible father-hood and healthy marriages. The TANF legislation gave states more flexibility to provide assistance to two-parent families. President Obama has taken a special interest in programs to promote responsible fatherhood. Programs designed to strengthen fatherhood and promote healthy marriage in families from an array of ethnic minority groups and families where parents are or have been incarcerated, were implemented and are being evaluated. A rigorous evaluation of one such program, Supporting Healthy Marriages, was published in 2012 (Hsueh et al., 2012). This evaluation can provide insight into the costs and benefits of a program designed to promote marriage. Supporting Healthy Marriage (SHM) is a skills-based relation-ship education program designed to help low-income married couples strengthen their relationships and result in more positive outcomes for parents and their chil-dren. From February 2007 to December 2009, 6,298 couples were recruited and were randomly assigned into one of two research groups. One group was offered SHM services. The other group was a control group and was not provided SHM services. The average SHM operating cost per couple was $9,100 annually. Although the SHM program produced a consistent pattern of small positive effects on multiple aspects of couples' relationships such as marital happiness and physical and psychological abuse, the program did not significantly affect whether couples stayed married at the 12-month follow-up point. There are plans to do further research to assess longer-term outcomes. As social workers, it is important to monitor outcomes for such programs, particularly at a time when TANF cash benefits are declining.

TANF Work Requirements and Sanctions   We have already seen that a major impetus for the creation of TANF came from pressure to push more aid recipients into the paid workforce. Not surprisingly, then, the PRWORA mandated that a specific percentage of families receiving TANF be involved in work activities and that this percentage rise over time. In 1997, the requirement was 25 percent; it increased to 50 percent in 2002. The Deficit Reduction Act of 2005 (DRA) which reauthorized TANF also increased work requirements (Administration for Children and Families, 2012). All states require recipients to be involved in work activities, which can include limited training and education activities directly related to work, within two years after they begin to receive assistance; many states impose immediate work requirements. Ninety percent of two-parent families must be engaged in work, typically for 35 hours per week (Pavetti, Finch, and Schott, 2013). States may choose to exempt parents with a child under the age of 12 months. State rules that allowed higher education to count as recipients' work activity have largely been replaced with an even more explicit work requirement, even as many parents find it more difficult to secure employment in the current labor market.

The PRWORA further requires states to reduce TANF cash benefits of adults who do not meet the work requirement. Most states impose "full-family sanctions" which mean benefits are terminated for the whole family if a parent does not meet the work requirements. Additionally, some states have chosen to eliminate SNAP and/or Medicaid benefits if the family head does not meet work requirements. The federal government will also reduce the amount of the block grant to any state in which the specified percentage of TANF recipients are not participating in work activities. As a partial balance to these requirements, states have the option of exempting up to 20 percent of families receiving TANF from the five-year time limit. Additionally, states may use their funds (but not federal monies) to continue assistance to families who have exceeded the limit. Exhibit 8.6 summarizes the major features of TANF.

The 1996 PRWORA legislation also combined welfare and employment policy so that a large portion of employment policy is now focused on welfare recipients. The 1997 Balanced Budget Act established welfare-to-work (WTW) grants as a component of the TANF Funding Work Incentive Program. The following year, the Workforce Investment Act required that a wide range of state programs, including WTW, employment services, unemployment insurance, vocational rehabilitation, adult education, and postsecondary vocational education, be brought together into a one-stop system. Of course, when the economy is shedding jobs and

EXHIBIT 8.6 *Temporary Assistance for Needy Families (TANF), 1996*	**Policy Goals**	To promote families by helping them care for children in their own home, supporting two-parent families, and discouraging out-of-wedlock pregnancies. To reduce dependency of needy families by focusing on job preparation, work, and marriage.
	Benefits or Services Provided	Monthly cash assistance. Services to promote work and reduce dependency.
	Eligibility Rules	Means-tested. Families with children must meet work requirements and not exceed time limit.
	Service Delivery System	State welfare agencies determine eligibility and administer payments to eligible families.
	Financing	Federal block grant given to each state, with states required to contribute additional funding.

unemployment is high, work opportunities for low-income families are much more difficult to find and sanctions for not meeting work goals make it even more difficult to meet basic needs during severe recessions. To find out about TANF and income inequality in your state, visit the website of Center on Budget and Policy Priorities (www.cbpp.org) and search for State Fact Sheets.

Non-Cash Programs That Assist Low-Income Families

A number of other programs help low-income families meet basic survival needs without providing direct cash assistance. These programs include SNAP, WIC, public housing, and the Tenant-Based Housing Assistance Program (Section 8). We discuss these selective programs only briefly here. However, information is available on websites where you may learn about these programs in more detail. You will likely encounter these programs as part of your practice and, indeed, being able to help your clients navigate the supports created by public policies is an essential social work skill.

SNAP The **Supplemental Nutrition Assistance Program, or SNAP** (formerly called the Food Stamp Program), was established to address hunger in the U.S. by helping low-income people to purchase nutritionally adequate food. In fiscal year 2011, SNAP assisted nearly 45 million people, about one in seven Americans. To be eligible for benefits, individuals or families must have monthly gross incomes that are less than 130 percent of the federal poverty guidelines and countable assets under $2,000. In FY 2012, the income limit was $2,422 a month for a family of four (USDA, 2012a). States can reduce or eliminate asset limits for SNAP and 36 states have eliminated the asset limit. For people who are eligible, SNAP is an entitlement. Indeed, this is why SNAP participation has risen significantly during the economic downturn; it is designed to grow with increases in poverty and need, unlike TANF.

Students Work to Decrease Hunger

Two students at the University of South Carolina took on an advocacy project to decrease hunger in their state. Goals were to increase awareness for those eligible for food stamps, create ways to decrease food stamp stigma and ensure no more cuts would be made to the state food stamp (SNAP) budget. For example, the students compiled research on hunger in South Carolina, and created and distributed a fact sheet to people around the capitol building entitled: Hunger in South Carolina. Educating legislators and the public about policy issues is a vital part of policy practice.

EXHIBIT 8.7

Students Challenge Stigma Related to Receiving Food Stamps (SNAP) and Advocate For No Reduction in Benefits

All public assistance recipients are eligible for SNAP, as are other people who meet the eligibility requirements (CBPP, 2013a).

Monthly allotments in the form of Electronic Benefit Transfer (EBT) cards are provided to eligible beneficiaries based on the Thrifty Food Plan (discussed at the beginning of the chapter). Recipients then use these cards to purchase specified food items in retail stores or, in some cases, farmers' markets or other outlets. The benefit formula is based on the assumption that families will spend 30 percent of their net income on food. The average SNAP household received about $278 a month in benefits in fiscal year 2012. The average recipient received about $133 a month (or about $1.48 per meal). Larger benefits are paid to very poor households than to households closer to the poverty line because they need more help affording an adequate diet (CBPP, 2013a).

SNAP is funded through general tax revenues. At the federal level, the Department of Agriculture administers the program through the Food and Nutrition Service, which has established certain eligibility, allotment, and benefit distribution guidelines. State- and local-level programs determine eligibility, allotments, and distribution of benefits within the parameters of the federal regulations. For more information on SNAP and other programs to reduce hunger, go to the Food Assistance Programs website at the U.S. Department of Agriculture (www.usda.gov).

The WIC Nutrition Program   The Special Supplemental Nutrition Program for Women, Infants, and Children (WIC) was established to help improve the health of low-income women, infants, and children up to age five who are nutritionally at risk for medically based or diet-based reasons. During FY 2011, the number of women, infants, and children receiving WIC benefits averaged almost 9 million per month. For FY 2012, Congress appropriated $6.618 billion for WIC (USDA, 2012b).

In order to be eligible for WIC, applicants must meet the following criteria:

- All recipients must have incomes at or below 185 percent of the poverty line and be determined to be nutritionally at risk by a health professional.

- Women are eligible if they are pregnant. After the baby is born, the mother receives benefits for one year if she breastfeeds and for six months if she does not. A woman need not be a single mother to be eligible.

- Infants are eligible for specifically designed benefits and services until their first birthday.

- Children are eligible for other WIC benefits until their fifth birthday.

WIC benefits include nutritious food, nutrition counseling and education, and referrals to health care and other social services when needed. To counteract the link between poverty and obesity, recipients now have access to a wider variety of healthy food choices, including fresh fruits and vegetables that were not covered earlier. In most states, WIC participants receive checks or vouchers to purchase the food in local retail stores. Some states already issue an electronic benefit card to participants and all states are required to implement WIC EBT statewide by October 1, 2020. WIC serves 53 percent of all infants born in the United States (USDA, 2012b).

WIC is funded by a federal grant appropriated by Congress, which may not be sufficient to cover all eligible women, infants, and children. WIC is not an entitlement program. Current estimates suggest that it serves fewer than 60 percent of eligible individuals in these categories. At the federal level, WIC, like SNAP, is administered by the Food and Nutrition Service. At the state and local levels, various agencies administer programs through locations such as state and county health departments, hospitals, community centers, schools, and Indian health facilities. Go to the WIC website at the U.S. Department of Agriculture (www.usda.gov) for the most up-to-date information on this program.

Public Housing Subsidized rental housing may be available to families, older adults, and people with disabilities who cannot afford to pay full rental costs in the private market. The goal of such programs is to provide safe, decent, affordable housing. Approximately 1.2 million households currently live in public housing. In addition, there is a long list of eligible people waiting for housing to become available (U.S. Department of Housing and Urban Development, 2013).

Income level is used to determine eligibility for public housing. Specifically, families and individuals are eligible if they earn less than 80 percent of the median income in the geographic area. Families, elders, and people with disabilities whose incomes are below 50 percent of the median income in the area receive preference (U.S. Department of Housing and Urban Development, 2013). Housing policies are therefore unique in that they define need in terms of relative poverty as measured in the person's geographic location. TANF and SSI recipients also meet the income limits for public housing, and they often need to live in public housing in order to survive on the small cash benefits they receive. Public housing is denied to people who have not exhibited good habits at other rental properties and have the potential to be detrimental to other tenants or the environment of the housing complexes. Individuals with drug-related convictions can also lose their eligibility for public housing, even long after their sentences have been served. A person or a family can continue to live in public housing until their income is assessed as high enough to afford housing in the private market, given that such housing is available in the private market in their area.

The public housing program is financed at the federal level through general revenues. The U.S. Department of Housing and Urban Development (HUD) provides federal funds to local housing offices, which actually manage the housing. These offices are in charge of collecting rent from tenants, enforcing leases, and maintaining the housing so that it continues to be safe and decent (U.S. Department of Housing and Urban Development, 2013). For more information on public housing, go to the website of the U.S. Department of Housing and Urban Development, Public Housing Program (www.hud.gov).

EXHIBIT 8.8

A Homeless Family

The Tenant-Based Housing Assistance Program This program has the same purpose as the public housing program: to provide low-income people with decent, safe, and affordable places to live. Instead of providing an actual apartment or home, the Housing Choice program uses a voucher system that permits eligible families to choose privately owned houses or apartments that meet program requirements and have reasonable rent that will be subsidized (U.S. Department of Housing and Urban Development, 2013).

People who apply for these vouchers and public housing recipients must meet the same income eligibility standards. Vouchers are limited, and families are placed on a waiting list when they apply. This program is financed through general revenues at the federal level. HUD provides the funds to local housing offices, which issue vouchers to families when their names come to the top of the waiting list. In addition to an inadequate supply of public housing and insufficient public funding for housing supports for low-income families, there is a huge gap between the number of low-income rentals available and the number of low-income families needing housing. This problem is contributing to rising rates of family homelessness.

Supplemental Security Income

Before Congress passed legislation creating the **Supplemental Security Income (SSI)** program in 1974, states had a patchwork of programs that provided assistance to people with limited or no income who were elderly or blind or had other disabilities. The federal legislation replaced this arrangement with a means-tested entitlement program that is uniform across the nation. In January 2013, almost 8.3 million Americans were receiving monthly SSI benefits, which amounted to approximately 2.31 percent of the overall population (Social Security Administration, 2013i). To receive SSI benefits, individuals must have very low incomes, including both cash and non-cash assistance. In addition, assets must be below $2,000 for individuals and $3,000 for a couple, excluding certain items such as a home, a car, and life insurance policies under $1,500 (Social Security Administration, 2013j). The last time the asset limits were updated was 1989. Other eligibility requirements are age (65 or older for age-based benefits), physical or mental disability that prevents work for at least one year, or blindness. Approximately 1.3 million U.S children (1.6 percent) receive SSI benefits. SSI provides monthly cash benefits to eligible people.

Benefits are not dependent on work history or marital status. The maximum monthly benefit in 2013 was $710 for individuals and $1,066 for couples when two individuals residing together were receiving SSI benefits (Social Security Administration, 2013j). The average monthly benefit was $526.00 as of January 2013 (Social Security Administration, 2013l). The SSA runs the SSI program through regional and district offices. SSA can contract with state or local agencies to administer the program. Some states also provide a state supplement to SSI. Although the SSA is in charge of both OASDI and SSI, they are very different programs. Recall that OASDI is an insurance program financed by Social Security insurance premiums/taxes collected under the FICA or the Self Employment Contributions Act (SECA), which are paid by workers and employers. These funds are not used to finance SSI. SSI is not insurance tied to work history. Rather, it is financed by general funds of the U.S. Treasury (personal income taxes, corporate and other taxes) (U.S. Social Security Administration, 2013k). Exhibit 8.9 summarizes the features of the federal SSI program.

Program Goals	To provide income assistance to the aged, blind individuals, and people with disabilities who have limited income and resources.	**EXHIBIT 8.9**
Benefits or Services Provided	Monthly check.	*Supplemental Security Income (SSI), 1974*
Eligibility Rules	Means-tested. Must be 65 or older, blind, or disabled.	
Service Delivery System	Social Security Administration offices administer the program, and funds are sent by check via U.S. mail or by electronic bank transfer.	
Financing	General tax revenue at the federal level.	

As discussed in earlier chapters, prior to the passage of the PRWORA in 1996, legal immigrants were eligible to receive SSI assistance from the federal government under the same eligibility rules as citizens. Currently, most immigrants in the U.S. are ineligible for most means-tested programs including SSI, TANF, and Medicaid until they obtain citizenship or reside in the U.S. as a Lawful Permanent Resident for five years. To find out more about eligibility for SSI, go to the Supplemental Security Income home page at the Social Security Administration website (www.ssa.gov).

General Assistance

General Assistance (GA) is provided to assist poor individuals and families who do not qualify for or are waiting for approval for federal programs such as SSI and TANF. GA programs provide minimal assistance and are generally a last resort for people in need. GA is administered by states, counties, and localities and is not funded or regulated by the federal government. Some states provide no GA, and the number of states providing this support has declined as states have cut income supports to reduce budget deficits. The states, counties, or localities administer the programs, determining both the benefits and the service delivery system. Many of the programs are called General Assistance, but some are referred to by a variety of names such as General Relief, Poor Relief, City Welfare, and General Public Assistance. Programs vary drastically in terms of the amounts and duration of bene-fits as well as eligibility rules. However, payments are generally low and may be as little as $100 a month. Payments take the form of cash or in-kind benefits such as food or clothing. In addition, some GA programs offer minimal medical assistance. Due to differences in reporting and in the types of GA programs offered by locali-ties, the number of recipients nationally is difficult to determine. Availability of GA is very limited. Because GA is financed from city and state coffers, and because of budget deficits at these levels of governments, capacity to fund General Assistance is drastically reduced at times of most need. Nevertheless, because GA can often be made available quickly to people in extreme poverty who do not qualify for other benefits, or are waiting for eligibility determination, it can be a lifesaver for very poor Americans. Exhibit 8.10 provides a policy analysis of GA.

EXHIBIT 8.10 *General Assistance (GA), 1935*		
	Program Goals	To help low-income people who are ineligible for federal assistance programs or waiting for approval meet their basic survival needs.
	Benefits or Services Provided	Temporary or long-term cash or in-kind assistance and medical care.
	Eligibility Rules	Means-tested. Eligibility varies but usually is reserved for people with very little or no income.
	Service Delivery System	States, counties, and localities determine eligibility and provide either cash or in-kind assistance.
	Financing	Funded entirely by the states, counties, and localities that admin-ister the programs.

The Earned Income Tax Credit

As discussed in Chapter 3, Congress enacted the EITC in 1975 in order to decrease the impact of Medicare and Social Security taxes that are deducted from the wages earned by low- and moderate-income families with children. The goal of EITC is to encourage people to work and to assist them in paying for expenses incurred because of work.

In 2012, more than 27 million workers received EITC refunds of almost $62 billion for the 2011 tax year. The EITC lifts more than 6 million people out of poverty each year and about half are children (IRS, 2013a). EITC has been described as the largest anti-poverty program in the U.S. Only citizens or permanent legal residents are eligible for the EITC. Benefits vary depending on the individual's or family's income level and number of children. Military and disability status are also considered. Combat pay and some disability benefits may be counted as earned income to qualify for EITC. In 2012, recipients with one child had to earn an income from work that was less than $36,920 ($42,130 for married, filing jointly). Recipients with three or more qualifying children had to earn a work income below $45,060 ($50,270 for married, filing jointly). Exhibit 8.11 illustrates the value of the EITC for families of different sizes at varying income levels

The EITC reduces taxes owed to the federal government and provides a refundable credit if the tax filer has already paid more than the amount owed with the credit. As illustrated in Exhibit 8.11, in 2012, the maximum credit was $5,891 (IRS, 2013a). However, the maximum credit for families with no children

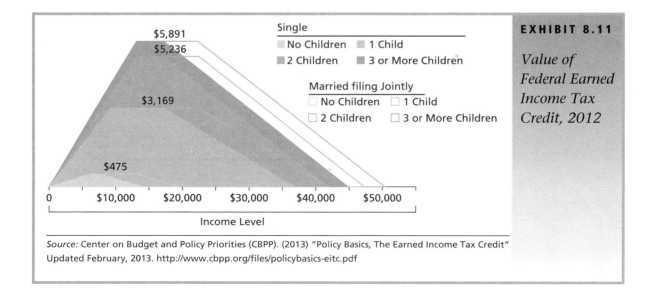

EXHIBIT 8.11

Value of Federal Earned Income Tax Credit, 2012

Source: Center on Budget and Policy Priorities (CBPP). (2013) "Policy Basics, The Earned Income Tax Credit" Updated February, 2013. http://www.cbpp.org/files/policybasics-eitc.pdf

was $475, revealing the extent to which the EITC is meant as an income support for working families. The benefit can be received in one lump-sum check at the end of the year, or it can be added to paychecks in smaller allotments throughout the year. Receiving a refund can affect eligibility for Medicaid, SSI, SNAP, or low-income housing if the recipient does not spend the refund within a certain time frame, which serves as a disincentive to savings for many low-income EITC recipients. TANF eligibility and benefits might be affected by the EITC, depending on the state.

To apply for the EITC, people must file a federal tax return with the IRS. The IRS administers the program and issues a refund to each recipient who is eligible for a refund. Due to this mechanism, administrative costs for EITC are low, as is the stigma associated with receipt. The program is financed by general revenue at the federal level. As a result of the benefit, fewer taxes are collected from individual tax returns. This reduces the general revenue funds available to the federal government.

EITC had eclipsed TANF as a means of support for people in poverty by 1994. EITC has been found to have a positive impact on the health and well-being of children. It leads to more hours worked and higher income as adults, which suggests that the immediate direct budget costs of the EITC are offset by public cost avoidance related to these improvements in health and well-being of children (CBPP, 2013b). Recent research also found that the EITC has helped improve employment and private health insurance rates, and children's health status as reported by mothers has also improved (Baughman, 2012). Steps were taken in 2009 to strengthen EITC through the American Recovery and Reinvestment Act, often referred to as the stimulus package. The amount larger families with three or more children can receive was raised. Research indicates these working families are more likely to be in poverty. Additionally, the marriage penalty was reduced for some families. In 2011, these two expansions together lifted an estimated 500,000 people out of poverty and reduced the severity of poverty for approximately 10 million more. Congress extended these improvements through 2017 under the American Taxpayer Relief Act, enacted in January 2013 (CBPP, 2013b). Twenty-four states have implemented their own EITC, usually calculated as a percentage of the federal EITC. In contrast, as explained earlier in this chapter, many states have continued to cut back TANF benefits, even though poverty rates have risen. However, as an income support for poor families, the EITC has been threatened by allegations of fraud and misuse, as well as by legislative attempts to cut state EITCs, in recent years. See Exhibit 8.12 for an analysis of the EITC.

EVALUATION OF INCOME-SUPPORT POLICIES AND PROGRAMS

We have examined a number of income-support policies and programs. The next section provides a more in-depth evaluation of two of the major programs, TANF

		EXHIBIT 8.12
Program Goals	To decrease the impact of payroll taxes on low-income families with children. To encourage non-workers to enter the workforce.	*Earned Income Tax Credit (EITC), 1975*
Benefits or Services Provided	Tax credit of up to $5,891 in tax year 2012. Credit can be used to reduce federal taxes owed or provide a cash refund.	
Eligibility Rules	In 2012, recipients with three or more qualifying children had to earn a work income below $45,060 ($50,270 for married, filing jointly); with two children their work income had to be less than $41,952 ($47,162 for married, filing jointly); with one child their work income had to be less than $36,920 ($42,130 for married, filing jointly); with no child their work income had to be less than $13,980 ($19,190 for married, filing jointly). Note, unemployment income does not count as earned income, but it may impact the amount of EITC based on the adjusted gross income.	
Service Delivery System	Recipients must file tax returns with the Internal Revenue Service, which refunds a check.	
Financing	Funded through general tax revenue and decreases the tax revenue collected by the federal government.	

Source: DeNavas-Walt, Proctor, and Smith (2012)

and OASDI, based on the strengths perspective and guided by the strengths policy principles articulated in earlier chapters. Recall that removing structural barriers to necessary resources is a key tenet of the strengths perspective. Therefore, policy and program goals and designs should focus on access, choice, and opportunities that lead to empowerment. In addition, the effectiveness of these programs should be judged not only on whether they achieve societal goals but also on whether they help clients achieve their goals.

Attention to the voices of client groups is essential to meaningful evaluation of TANF. The strengths perspective asserts that clients are experts on their own needs and goals and, therefore, should be consulted when policy is developed and evaluated. Welfare rights groups provide a variety of opinions. To view work that ensures the voices of welfare recipients and other low-income citizens are heard, access the website of Community Voices Heard. There are also other state welfare rights organizations. For another example, go to the website of Oregon TANF Alliance and read the stories of TANF recipients. Because these grassroots organizations typically are underfunded, their online presence varies. You can search on the web for organizations of low-income people working for welfare reform in your area. Some welfare rights groups are also part of the global struggle for human rights and provide links to information on the United Nations' Universal Declaration of Human Rights, the international standard for human rights (http://www.un.org/en/documents/udhr/index.shtml).

There are people who feel that rearing children should again be considered a full-time job worthy of public support. Caring for children is a socially and economically valuable activity, and there are costs when mothers and or/fathers no longer provide such care. As discussed earlier, low-income single parents face great challenges when they are required to be the sole breadwinners, homemakers, and caregivers. In contrast, middle-class women whose children already have many resources unavailable to children in low-income homes are often urged to stay at home "for the sake of their children."

However, given the realities of women in the workforce, welfare rights groups have also pointed to the desperate need for high-quality, low-cost child care for the more than one out of three working families with children who are low-income (below 200 percent of the poverty threshold). About 11 percent of working families were below the federal poverty threshold in 2011. More than 47.5 million adults and children, categorized as the working poor, struggle to get by.

Child care is also an important investment in all of our futures, because these children will be the people who will support and care for us in our old age. Without adequate care and education during their childhood, they will experience more negative outcomes including higher school dropout rates, reduced ability to find well-paying jobs, and higher incarceration rates. Adequate transportation is also crucial. A number of large corporations have made a commitment to locating new facilities only in cities that have adequate mass transportation so that more workers have access to these facilities. Transportation and high-quality child care are critical infrastructure investments that need to be in place to support low-income families in the labor force.

TANF and Poverty

A central, broadly shared goal of TANF clients is to move their families out of poverty. It is clear that the meager income provided through TANF will not end poverty. Indeed, the program is not designed to do so; rather, it is designed to lessen dependence on the public coffers. Research conducted prior to the economic downturn beginning in 2007 to evaluate the success of TANF, indicated that welfare caseloads went down and employment went up. Keep in mind, of course, that states can decrease their caseloads simply by changing their eligibility requirements. The decline in caseloads and increases in employment were due in part to the strong economy in the latter half of the 1990s and to changes in the EITC. Although child poverty rates for some groups dropped precipitously during the latter half of the 1990s, they then began to rise and are continuing to rise during the second decade of the 21st century. Currently one in five children is growing up in poverty. For children under age six, 24.5 percent, one in four, are growing up in poverty. In female single-parent households, for children under age six, more than half are growing up in poverty. The poverty rate for children under 18 is higher than those for adults aged 18 to 64 and adults aged 65 and older. The African American child poverty rate reached a low of 30.2 percent in 2001 and then rose to 37.4 percent in 2011. Similarly, the poverty rate for Hispanic or Latino children rose over 7 percent between the two time periods to 34.1 percent in 2011 (ASPE, 2012). Thirty-seven percent of American Indian children are poor; 14 percent of Asian children and 12.5 percent of white, non-Hispanic children live in poor families (Children's Defense Fund, 2012a). The large percentages of African American, American Indian, and Hispanic or Latino children now living in poverty are particularly troubling. The link between growing up in poverty and myriad negative outcomes for children is well documented. The impact of TANF on child well-being will have serious consequences for years to come and thus should be carefully monitored in evaluating TANF. Further, the outcomes of welfare leavers should be monitored by race and ethnicity to determine if discrimination either by welfare agencies or by employers is disproportionately disadvantaging people of color in meeting TANF requirements. Rigorous enforcement of antidiscrimination laws should accompany TANF work requirements if recipients are to move out of poverty.

There are families for whom finding employment is particularly challenging. These include families with physical and mental disabilities, substance abuse, low literacy, domestic violence, learning disabilities, or children with disabilities. TANF is largely failing these groups because they are not receiving employment assistance that addresses these barriers, and they are no longer being provided with a reliable safety net (Greenstein, 2013).

Average incomes among the poorest quintile of single mothers have actually fallen. Those who are leaving TANF for employment typically are finding jobs with wages that are below the poverty level. To compound this problem, they often do not receive employer benefits such as health care, and many of them fail to receive other public income supports for which they would be eligible, such as child care assistance and Medicaid or CHIP coverage. Many welfare rights groups endorse the living wage movement as a strategy for alleviating the problems associated with poverty-level wages. Living wage campaigns seek to pass local ordinances requiring private businesses that benefit from public money to pay their workers a living wage. A living wage is the income level necessary to live adequately within a given community. Generally speaking, each campaign defines this wage for its community. Many campaigns base the living wage calculation on the poverty guideline for a family of four. Using this formula, the standard living wage is approximately $10.00 an hour for employees who work a 40-hour week for 52 weeks. Some living wage proponents advocate for a living wage calculation tailored to housing costs in specific geographic areas. To get more information on this approach, go to the website of the Universal Living Wage Campaign (www.universallivingwage.org). You can also use the Living Wage Calculator developed by faculty at MIT to calculate the living wage in your community (livingwage.mit.edu).

Living wage movements also advocate for benefits such as health coverage and paid vacation. Living wage ordinances generally cover city and county service contractors and other employers who receive grants, loans, tax abatements, or other government support. However, the reality is that declining real wages for men and the shift in the economy towards more highly skilled information-based industries have meant that only the massive entry of women into the workforce has made it possible for many two-parent families to continue to have income levels similar to families in the 1970s. Families headed by single women are disproportionately living in poverty.

Devolution and Recessions

Recall from Chapter 2 that since the 1980s, an emphasis on devolution, whereby responsibility for social welfare was increasingly transferred from the federal government to the states, has reshaped many public programs. TANF is an example of a program in which much more control was shifted to the states. States were not required to provide uniform benefits or any benefits at all to low-income families, and they had much more latitude in how they could use their federal TANF block grants. In the last 16 years since TANF was enacted, national TANF caseloads have declined by 60 percent. Poverty rates also initially fell during the late 1990s as the economy boomed and unemployment rates dropped. However, as the economy began to falter in the early 2000s and the recession began in 2007, poverty rates rose and now are higher than they were in 1996, when TANF was enacted (Greenstein, 2013). Increases in deep poverty, which is household income at less than half of the federal poverty threshold, have been especially large. In the deep recession beginning in 2007, from which the U.S. has not yet fully recovered, TANF caseloads have decreased steeply in most states. Hard-pressed states, facing severe budget shortfalls during this period of high unemployment, do not have the money to address increasing need among their poorest families. Indeed, many states cut already-low TANF cash benefits still further, set yet more stringent TANF time limits or increased sanctions, and took other actions to keep caseloads from rising, or in some cases, even shrink them in the face of growing need.

Further, the block grant funding structure and caseload reduction credit actually provides states with an incentive to serve as few families as possible. Remember, states can reallocate the federal block grant to many different purposes. This creates a financial incentive to reduce cash assistance caseloads, even as unemployment and poverty in their state increase.

In contrast, the SNAP caseload, which remained a federal entitlement program and did not become a block grant to states, increased as poverty rates increased during the recession (see Exhibit 8.13). The number of individuals receiving SNAP in an average month grew from 26.3 million in 2007 to over 46 million in 2011 (CBPP, 2013a). Because the program is a federally funded entitlement, the additional benefits to cover newly eligible individuals were available automatically. Further, the program is uniform in all states and most low-income individuals are eligible, regardless of the state in which they live, so it is easier to swiftly deliver increased benefits to low-income families. Also, when low-income households receive these benefits, they are immediately spent and so create effective economic stimulus and directly improve families' lives. Many states have also eliminated assets tests for SNAP. Nonetheless, some elements of the program have created barriers to rapid responsiveness. Many legal immigrants are ineligible for the program for their first five years as LPRs although children are eligible no matter how long they have been in the U.S. (USDA, 2013). Also, since states normally pay half of the administrative costs, when they face budget crises they may cut staff needed to process new as well as existing cases and eliminate outreach dollars, further depressing the already-low participation rate among eligible households. Importantly, participation rates are especially low among working-poor families, indicating that these households may face barriers to learning about, applying for, and subsequently using these critical food resources.

On the other hand, TANF has been very slow to respond to the economic downturn. Although the much-touted federal block grant approach to meeting welfare needs that was basic to devolution gave states wide flexibility to develop and implement their own welfare programs, in times of economic crises we find, just as we did during the Great Depression, that most states are unable to meet their citizens' basic needs. In 1996, for every 100 families in poverty, 68 families received

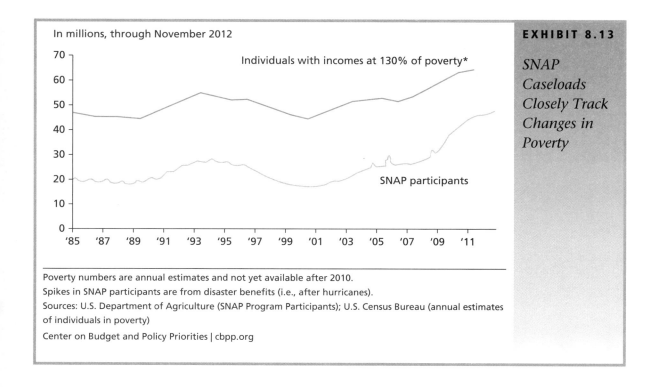

In millions, through November 2012

EXHIBIT 8.13

SNAP Caseloads Closely Track Changes in Poverty

Individuals with incomes at 130% of poverty*

SNAP participants

Poverty numbers are annual estimates and not yet available after 2010.

Spikes in SNAP participants are from disaster benefits (i.e., after hurricanes).

Sources: U.S. Department of Agriculture (SNAP Program Participants); U.S. Census Bureau (annual estimates of individuals in poverty)

Center on Budget and Policy Priorities | cbpp.org

TANF benefits. In 2011, with the country still reeling from the most serious economic downturn since the Great Depression, only 27 out of every 100 families in poverty received TANF. Disturbingly, some federal policy makers might be learning the wrong lessons from these divergent experiences. Today, there is continued pressure from some policy makers to change the SNAP program into a federal block grant to the states.

Because TANF is not a federal entitlement program (unlike its predecessor, AFDC), special federal emergency funds (Emergency Contingency Fund for State TANF Programs) were needed to help states, territories, and tribes meet TANF obligations (Pavetti and Rosenbaum, 2010). Five billion dollars in federal emergency funds, part of the American Recovery and Reinvestment Act, were appropriated for TANF, but legislation authorizing this funding was not passed until February 2009. This legislation also extended the Transitional Medical Assistance program for families leaving TANF through December 2010 and increased child care funding by $2 billion. This legislation has now expired. In 2012, Congress reduced overall federal TANF funding when it failed to fund the TANF Supplemental Grants, originally created by Congress as an integral part of TANF in 1996. These funds were provided to 17 states that had historically low welfare benefits, every year from then until last year. Overall, Federal Contingency Funds, which were designed to help states in times of difficulty, such as recession, were not effectively designed and have not functioned well (Schott, 2012).

Reforming TANF from a Strengths Perspective What changes in TANF policies and programs should be considered so as to effectively meet the needs and support the goals of low-income families? As discussed previously, welfare rights advocates argue that single parents receiving TANF should be given adequate support so they can provide necessary care for their children. Further, parents in the paid workforce should have access to high-quality child care, transportation, and training and education for jobs that pay a living wage. The strengths perspective also encourages us to carefully analyze the barriers that impede or prevent families from reaching the goal of self-support, including inadequate education, substance abuse, domestic violence, physical or mental illness, geographic location in areas of concentrated poverty with few employment opportunities, and the need to care for a chronically ill child. Significantly, families who are experiencing difficulties in meeting TANF work requirements often face many of these barriers simultaneously. Focusing on overcoming these barriers rather than primarily on enforcing work requirements would better serve these families.

The current emphasis on "work first" limits education and training options for TANF families. The "work first" emphasis can push women into traditionally low-paying, female-dominated occupations that frequently do not provide a living wage. In fact, TANF requirements can ensure low-wage employers a large workforce made up of women who do not have the qualifications that would enable them to leave for higher-paying jobs. Amending TANF requirements to enable women to enter educational and training programs can help them attain higher-paying jobs and move their families out of poverty. Analysis of TANF based on the strengths perspective clearly points to the need to restructure TANF policies to help women secure such jobs. Further, federal incentives and requirements need to be restructured so that TANF provides a more adequate safety net for children and families in times of high unemployment when securing a job becomes so much more difficult. Similarly, states need to focus their TANF funds on core functions such as more adequate cash benefits and more effective employment programs and supports, rather than diverting funds to other state government purposes.

Other needed reforms grounded in the strengths perspective and social work values include policies to protect a woman's choice of whether to marry or remain married, particularly for survivors of domestic violence. Additionally, policies to encourage parental involvement in the lives of their children, such as the option of working part-time outside the home or receiving work credits for involvement in school activities, may help mitigate the heightened risks of school failure, teen pregnancy, and delinquency that poor children face. Factors that discourage mothers and fathers from being more involved with their children, particularly in families headed by unmarried couples, need to be examined, and additional strategies to increase parental involvement should be crafted, based on that analysis.

Restoring the federal entitlement status of AFDC/TANF is one policy change that could help ensure that at least the basic survival needs of children in poor families are met. Receiving TANF is a survival strategy for women. They turn to TANF when other sources of support such as the family and the labor markets fail. Our nation's children should be provided with a safety net when other systems fail them.

Another strategy to reform TANF so that it reflects strengths principles is to reconsider the five-year time limit on receipt of federal funds. Families who do work may not earn enough money to survive without public income support even after five years. The five-year time limit fails to take into account the realities of caring for a family member with disabilities, domestic violence, economic recession, and low wages. If the five-year limit is not abolished, it needs to be modified to address these realities by stipulating that the clock may be stopped in such instances. For example, policies could be enacted specifying that periods when a parent must care full-time for a severely disabled family member will not be counted in calculating the five-year limit. Benefits also need to be restored for legal immigrants. NASW supports eliminating time limits and family caps. NASW also supports integrating welfare policies, housing, economic, child welfare, and mental health policies to create a comprehensive and holistic approach to eliminating or at least reducing poverty (NASW, 2012d).

Policies should be developed that meet the survival needs of poor families and support their efforts to move out of poverty. We need to build capacity. Investment of public monies in such strategies will mean that parents will be able to reach the goal of adequately caring for their children, even in the face of hardship. This outcome is much more important than reductions in caseloads for our nation's future. The responsiveness of TANF during economic downturns must be improved. TANF could be a critical part of our very thin safety net for families in poverty. However, it is currently structured in ways that make it very difficult to respond quickly. New performance measures and incentives are needed to encourage states to provide a more viable safety net for very poor families when it is needed most and to help improve employment outcomes long term (Schott, 2012). Because states had latitude in how they designed TANF programs and policies, there now is clear variation in the program from state to state. Comprehensive, systematic research comparing policies, programs, and outcomes between states that could inform further policy improvement is needed. While it is true that what works in one state will not necessarily work as well in another for a whole host of reasons, this natural experiment certainly merits investigation. Welfare reform continues to be a hotly contested topic and is a challenging but crucial arena for policy practice, especially as more families face economic hardship in a struggling economy.

One of the traditional strengths of our welfare programs in the U.S. is that we do have a safety net, though frayed, for families and children when the economy is in recession and the marketplace cannot provide jobs for a growing number of people. At a time when basic safety net programs such as EITC and SNAP as well as TANF are under attack, it is important that you be clear on the positive impact these programs do have on families struggling in poverty. Exhibit 8.14, from the nonprofit think tank Center on Budget and Policy Priorities, illustrates this impact. Alternative measures of poverty, developed by the NAS expert panel, discussed earlier in the chapter, were used to develop this exhibit. These alternative measures incorporate tax benefits and public non-cash benefits. This exhibit indicates that if the safety net had not existed in 2010, almost 29 percent of Americans would have been poor. That is almost twice the actual figure of about 15 percent.

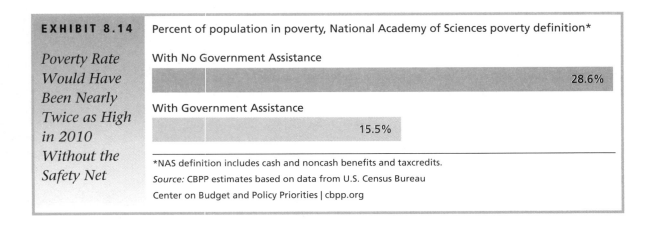

EXHIBIT 8.14

Poverty Rate Would Have Been Nearly Twice as High in 2010 Without the Safety Net

Percent of population in poverty, National Academy of Sciences poverty definition*

With No Government Assistance

28.6%

With Government Assistance

15.5%

*NAS definition includes cash and noncash benefits and taxcredits.

Source: CBPP estimates based on data from U.S. Census Bureau

Center on Budget and Policy Priorities | cbpp.org

States have authority over many key policies that govern basic safety net programs such as TANF and SNAP, as well as health programs that support low-income families including Medicaid and the CHIP. States can raise and, in some cases, even eliminate asset limits for these programs. When thinking about safety net programs from the strengths perspective, we know that assets such as a home or savings for education and retirement can help families escape from poverty long term. On the other hand, if people in poverty are sent the message that if they ever accumulate assets beyond a bare minimum, often as little as $2,000, the safety net programs they rely on when faced with joblessness, disability, or other crises will not be available to them, this can discourage efforts to move their family permanently out of poverty (Corporation for Enterprise Development, 2012). States that have eliminated asset limits for TANF and SNAP increase the possibility that families will not be dependent on safety net programs long term. The importance of policies that support asset accumulation for low-income families will be discussed in depth later in this chapter.

As state policies in the area of income support, as well as health care, diverge more and more, income inequality can be expected to grow even more in many states. If you want to go into more depth about income inequality, and examine ways you can present information on income inequality at different levels, including the state, I encourage you to use the web to learn more about the Lorenz Curve. A Lorenz Curve illustrates the degree of inequality in the distributions of two variables, and can be used to illustrate the extent to which income or assets are unequally distributed in any demographic unit (city, state, etc.) for which you have needed information. Such visual illustrations can be very useful in policy practice. There are many tools of this sort to help you engage in policy practice and you can easily discover them if you do a bit of sleuthing on the web.

OASDI from the Strengths Perspective

OASDI has been a great success story in lessening poverty for the people who are eligible for this program. Social Security currently has a $2.6 trillion surplus. The surplus is invested in U.S. Treasury Bonds which are considered one of the safest investments possible. These are not worthless IOUs as some critics have asserted. Social Security is funded by a separate payroll tax and was designed by law to never contribute to the federal deficit.

From a strengths perspective, any evaluation of OASDI should start by examining the opinions of the target group. Consumer groups such as the Older Women's League and the Gray Panthers provide insights about how OASDI has benefited generations of Americans as well as point out needed changes. They speak to the importance of OASDI in protecting workers and their families from loss of income due to retirement, disability, or death. The monthly check provides consumers with a choice of how best to meet their needs and the program's structure keeps administrative costs very low. Eligibility is determined by age, payment of payroll taxes, and disability, and beneficiaries do not have to submit to humiliating means tests. The Gray Panthers website provides recommendations for reforming OASDI under Know the Facts about Social Security.

Women and OASDI   If not for OASDI, more than half of women over 65 would be living in poverty. However, even with Social Security, older women are nearly twice as likely as older men to be poor. Because OASDI is employment-based and has its roots in the male-breadwinner family model, women have historically been disadvantaged by this system. Most women's retirement income is, in large part, determined by wages earned during their own or their spouses' current or past employment. Because older women have experienced gender inequality in educational and employment opportunities over a lifetime, they often enter old age with shorter, inconsistent, and lower-paid employment histories. OASDI does not provide a minimum benefit that takes into account part-time work as well as full-time work. Such a benefit policy would be particularly beneficial for women because they are more likely to work part-time or be out of the paid workforce to care for children or aging family members.

Although the policy of providing coverage for a spouse in the amount of half of the worker's earnings does partially recognize the role of the spouse in supporting the worker, this amount varies not by the contribution of the spouse but by the earnings of the worker. In addition, couples who divorce before their tenth anniversaries are not eligible for survivors' insurance. Further, when both spouses work outside the home, the couple may pay more taxes and receive lower yearly Social Security benefits at retirement than a one-earner couple with the same income.

Social Security credits are not earned for the unpaid labor necessary to care for children and older adults. Therefore, women, who have traditionally been expected to assume these duties, are disadvantaged initially by lack of payment for their work and at the time of retirement by lack of recognition of their contributions (Older Women's League, 2012). It is obvious that, given the role of caretaker and the insecurities of modern working life, many women will be unable to secure adequate retirement income based on their work record unless a method for providing Social Security credits for caregiving is devised. Visit the website of the Older Women's League (www.owl-national.org) to learn more about their Social Security reform proposals.

It is also important to acknowledge the crucial role OASDI plays in the lives of women so that the features particularly important for women are preserved in reform initiatives. These include: a progressive benefit formula that aids lower-income earners, who are disproportionately women; benefits for children and the parent who is their caregiver, when a working parent is disabled or dies prematurely; spousal and survivor benefits for married women, divorced women, and widows; a guaranteed lifetime benefit; and a full cost-of-living adjustment. The guaranteed lifetime benefit and full cost-of-living adjustment ensure that beneficiaries do not outlive their assets or see their income reduced by inflation, no matter how long they live. This is particularly important for women who, on average, live longer than men and are much poorer in old age. Because older adults' cost of living is actually often disproportionately high due to greater health care and long-term care expenses, the CPI used to calculate the cost-of-living adjustment is likely disadvantaging older adults. Indeed, many older adults tell us they have had to choose between having an adequate food budget and buying expensive medication their physician has prescribed so they can maintain their health. Now, policy makers are proposing using a chained CPI to reduce the cost-of-living adjustment even further in the coming years. This proposed change will only exacerbate the disproportionately high risk of poverty very old women and people of color currently face.

People of Color and OASDI   People who have experienced racial discrimination during their working lives also are less adequately served by a system that bases eligibility on amount of salary earned and time spent in covered jobs. Because benefits are earnings related, white, male, educated professionals who earn higher wages receive higher benefits. OASDI provides 90 percent or more of income for 55 percent of Hispanic and 49 percent of black older adults (CBPP, 2012b). Raising the retirement age still higher for OASDI is currently being considered by policy makers. The rationale is that people are living longer now than in 1935. While it is true that life expectancy is now longer, the primary reason is that many fewer people now die in childhood. In thinking about groups who do live longer, workers with higher incomes are often also long lived. Low-income workers and those in physically demanding jobs, disproportionately minority workers, generally have lower life expectancies. For example, African Americans and Native Americans have shorter life expectancies than white Americans, so raising the retirement age for full eligibility for old-age pensions beyond 67 reduces the likelihood that they will receive old-age pensions. In fact, some people argue that OASDI as currently configured is not as important for these groups because it is already less likely they will ever receive the old-age pensions benefits for which they have contributed. However, this argument overlooks the fact that workers of color receive disability and survivors' benefits. Because people of color are more likely to be employed in hazardous jobs and face significant health disparities, these benefits are especially important for them. For more information on this topic, go the website of the Urban Institute (www.urban.org) and review the many articles available under the heading, Retirement Policy.

Is OASDI Regressive or Progressive?   The Social Security tax is regressive because both high- and low-income employees pay at the same rate and, in 2010, the tax was not paid on income in excess of $113,700. However, distribution of benefits is progressive in that low-wage earners receive a proportionally higher rate of return. In this way, OASDI has a redistributive function that benefits citizens with low incomes or disabilities. Low government administrative costs, equaling less than one percent of each Social Security tax dollar collected, also benefit participants in the Social Security system.

How Solvent is OASDI?   The solvency of OASDI is perhaps the biggest issue in most citizens' minds. Some critics have warned that the system is in a state of "crisis" that requires immediate and drastic changes. In reality, as detailed earlier in the chapter, the program is solvent through 2033 (Social Security Administration, 2012). Moreover, even after that point, it could continue to pay a substantial proportion of benefits. Nevertheless, adjustments need to be made soon to the Social Security system so that more drastic changes will not be required later. The strain on the system is increasing as older adults choose early retirement at age 62 because they cannot find employment in the current sluggish economy and as payroll taxes decline with stagnant wages and a rising unemployment rate. Proposals for reforming the system include the following:

- raising the retirement age, although workers in physically demanding or stressful jobs, as well as those with other disabilities, may find it difficult to continue working longer;

- increasing the tax that workers and employers pay into the system;

- requiring that people with incomes above $113,700 continue to pay into the system;

- dedicating taxes on estates worth more than $3.5 million to Social Security; and

- mandating that all federal and state workers take part in the national retirement program.

Young people, concerned about the solvency of OASDI, have questioned whether Social Security benefits will be there for them. However, the fact is that the benefit is already there for them in the form of the disability and survivors' benefits that many young people currently receive. This insurance element of OASDI is often overlooked.

One highly controversial proposal for reforming Social Security is to privatize the system. However, with the decline in the stock market in the first years of this century and the economic meltdown later in the first decade, enthusiasm for privatization plans seems to have cooled. President George W. Bush's proposal to use Social Security funds to create private or personal accounts was opposed by many individuals and groups, including AARP. Under Bush's plan, younger workers who pay into OASDI could redirect a portion of their FICA taxes into private accounts where the money would be invested in various options. However, setting up and administering such a system would involve substantial costs. In addition, private accounts would divert funds from the current program, thus hastening the arrival of a solvency "crisis" within OASDI.

Although promoting strategies to help people with low incomes to save and accumulate assets is in keeping with the strengths perspective, doing so by reducing benefits guaranteed through our current, very modest, income-support programs could intensify the economic problems of future older adults. Social Security is a contract among generations, and as long as that contract is intact, relatively minor adjustments to payroll taxes, benefits, and eligibility rules can ensure solvency far into the future.

From the strengths perspective, OASDI provides consumer choice. It is non-stigmatizing and is a universal benefit. The program still enjoys public support despite well-funded efforts to undermine and dismantle it. Advocacy efforts designed to maintain and strengthen OASDI are sorely needed. You can start by simply getting your facts straight and speaking up when OASDI is discussed. If you want to do more, a quick web search will put you in touch with groups that are working on this issue. Indeed, as U.S. policy makers work to strengthen OASDI, social work advocates would do well to learn from the program's successes in reducing older adults' risk of poverty, compared to their economic status prior to its inception. A similar universal approach to protect all our nation's children could dramatically lessen the number of young people growing up in poverty.

ASSET-BASED POLICIES

We have discussed growing wealth inequality and its implications in previous chapters. Closer attention to asset accumulation, particularly for low-income, minority, and single-parent families, is necessary to understand the wealth gap and possible remedies. In a financial context, the term assets includes equity in a home, savings accounts, stocks and mutual funds, rental property, vehicles, and certificates of deposit (CDs). These assets can act as a storehouse for future consumption, but evidence suggests that asset accumulation may have psychological and behavioral effects, even beyond deferred consumption advantages. Assets can be a buffer against life crises such as unemployment and health emergencies. Financial assets also can be a means for acquiring less tangible assets such as an education. Assets are also a major vehicle for transferring wealth from generation to generation. Inequality in asset distribution in the U.S. is vastly greater than income inequality. Overall, the wealthiest 20 percent of people in the U.S. own over 85 percent of the nation's assets, whereas the bottom 40 percent—that is 120 million Americans—have about 0.3 percent (Wolff, 2012). Further, the wealth gap is growing in the U.S., even as constrained economic mobility makes it less likely that a given individual will move between the wealthier and less wealthy classes in society. This considerable inequality has prompted people to research differences in assets and to propose policies to increase the assets of people with low incomes. Further, helping people to accumulate assets, to save for homes, education, or other productive endeavors, may make it more possible to be secure economically over their lifetimes and across generations. Therefore, asset-based policies and programs focus on how to help people accumulate assets. These programs have been discussed briefly in other chapters, and the role social workers have played in formulating and implementing these policies has been highlighted.

Historically, there are some examples of public policies that helped many Americans accumulate life-changing assets. Two of these policies, discussed briefly in Chapters 2 and 3, are the Homestead Act of 1862, which increased the number of landowners in the U.S., and the 1944 GI Bill of Rights, which helped returning veterans purchase homes, start businesses, and attend college. Other asset-building policies focus primarily on the middle and upper classes in the form of provisions made through the tax system to encourage home ownership, college savings, and contributions to retirement accounts.

Michael Sherraden, a social worker, has been one of the primary advocates for a different approach to welfare policy that stresses the importance of asset accumulation as well as income support. In his book *Assets and the Poor: A New American Welfare Policy* (1991), he proposed that the U.S. needs a shift in paradigms from welfare benefits that focus exclusively on income maintenance to policies that would encourage and help low-income citizens obtain assets. He asserts that the bulk of welfare policy for low-income people focuses on providing a minimum level of income maintenance, that is on providing income that, due to necessity, must be spent on basic needs such as food and housing. Further, having assets may make you ineligible for these programs. The result is that these families might be able to fulfill their basic consumption needs but are maintained in poverty and, therefore, denied the advantages conferred by asset accumulation, including the ability to plan for the future. They are not able to accumulate assets that make it possible for them to weather emergencies and to create a base that could eventually lift them and their families out of poverty. Asset poverty is measured by examining the extent to which people have sufficient assets to continue to meet their basic needs during temporary hard times. Sherraden's emphasis on assets was meant to "complement" income assistance, not replace it. However asset-based policy can potentially also help prevent poverty, both in the short term, by helping to smooth over income losses, and longer-term, by enabling households to build greater economic security. Asset-based welfare policy strives to narrow the inequality in ownership of assets between the rich and the poor.

There is currently a large variety of policies and programs which help middle- and upper-class Americans accumulate assets. Indeed public expenditures on these programs are often pointed to in characterizing U.S. policies and programs as creating an upside-down welfare state where wealth is redistributed to people at the top of the income ladder, leaving the poor in dire straits. Asset-policy advocates are working to devise strategies that can help low-income families take advantage of policies such as home mortgage interest deductions and tax advantaged Individual Retirement Accounts (IRAs) that aid in asset accumulation. For example, Sherraden suggested establishing Individual Development Accounts (IDAs) that, in many ways, mirror IRAs, which are not utilized frequently by lower-income citizens. This means they cannot reap the considerable tax benefits—essentially functioning like public subsidies—conferred upon higher-income individuals. IDAs are savings accounts for poor people that are matched through public or private sources. Sherraden proposed that these IDAs be made available to all people in the future, with increased matched amounts and greater incentives available for people in poverty who choose to participate in the plan. Low-income people could invest monies from public benefits they receive as well as from income from work or other sources. These savings could be matched or augmented by contributions from the government, corporations, foundations, community groups, and individual donors (Sherraden, 2000). The goal of the IDA program is to help people in poverty accumulate wealth gradually as a long-term investment. People can use IDAs for education, job training, homeownership, operating a small business, or other development purposes.

IDAs benefit individuals by helping them to obtain needed resources to compete effectively in the economy. At the same time, they benefit society by encouraging people to save money for purposes that are in the public interest. Sherraden (2000) asserted that our nation has begun a paradigm shift to focusing on asset accumulation through the continued establishment and growth of asset-based programs for middle- and upper-income households, such as College Savings Plans (529s), IRAs, Roth IRAs, 401(k)s, and Medical Savings Accounts. These are all examples of policies that build on a strengths-based view of people as competent and able to set and reach goals and build economic security when public policies are structured to promote asset growth. However, poor families receive very few of the benefits financed with tax dollars focused on building an investment state in contrast to a welfare state. Asset-based policies such as IDAs can help change this imbalance.

Moreover, IDAs have gained support, bolstered by initial research statistics that attest to their ability to assist people living in poverty (Schreiner, Clancy, and Sherraden, 2002; Zhan, 2003). Findings of large-scale evaluations of these programs indicate that low-income people, even the very poor, can save. The savings were being used to make asset-building purchases such as homes and education. Further, participants reported increased feelings of short-term as well as long-term security, more hope for the future, greater self-confidence, and more ability to set and achieve goals (Corporation for Enterprise Development, 2009). Significantly, the federal government determined that IDAs cannot be considered as assets when eligibility for TANF, a means-tested program, is being established (Edwards and Mason, 2003). Some other states have similarly exempted assets held in IDAs during other eligibility determinations. IDA projects have been established across the country and many states have passed IDA legislation. For the most recent information on IDAs visit the Corporation for Enterprise Development at www.cfed.org.

Deindustrialization in the U.S. has brought about economic changes that have significantly altered employment patterns in the U.S. In the global economy as it is currently structured, poverty will persist, wages for low-skilled workers will likely continue to stagnate, and workers will be less likely to have steady employment over a lifetime. In this environment, having access to assets to fund more education and training, to weather downturns in the job market, or to start a small business, can potentially provide a path out of poverty. Programs to help people build assets as well as programs to make low-cost loans available to people who want to start a small business could potentially be very helpful. Indeed, we have international examples such as the Grameen Development Bank, founded in Bangladesh, to inform policy in this area. A peer lending strategy underlies the Grameen Bank's initiatives and has met with some success in extending micro-credit for small business development in very poor countries. However, there has recently been a higher rate of default on loans in some countries. Microfinance initiatives to help low-income people access the banking system and use financial services such as checking and savings accounts, as well as to get loans, are also meeting with some success in the United States as well as in other countries. You can learn more about microfinancing and peer lending by going to the websites of the Grameen Bank and the Grameen Foundation (www.grameenfoundation.org).

Bolstered by evidence that low-income individuals will, indeed, save with the right supports and incentives, and that the experience of accumulating assets may have deep and broad effects on individuals' well-being, in the U.S., researchers and policy makers continue to develop asset-based initiatives to help low-income families. One such initiative currently being expanded helps families and students save for college. Potentially these approaches can create more access to college education and also help to lessen student loan burden for future students. This and other asset-based initiatives will be further discussed as we turn our attention to proposals for fundamental reform.

Proposals for Fundamental Reform

In addition to proposing adjustments to existing programs, critics of U.S. policies designed to help people in need have proposed some fundamental reforms to the way in which support is provided. Currently, the economic downturn mandates continued focus on maintaining the frayed safety net provided by the programs discussed so far in this chapter. However, it is important to also consider other approaches to providing needed support for low-income families. Otherwise, disadvantaged populations will see little benefit from improvements in economic cycles, and future downturns will further imperil their economic security. Two notable proposals are the basic income grant and further expansion of asset-based, as opposed to income-based, programs.

Basic Income Grant   We have examined a number of income-support programs. Sometimes programs overlap, but more often there are huge gaps, and many people still live in dire poverty. Policy analysts have suggested replacing this patchwork system with a basic income grant (BIG). According to this plan, every family, regardless of income, would receive a uniform benefit. For high-income families, the benefit would be taxed at 50 percent. BIG payments to low-income families would go largely untaxed. However, like earlier proposals to create a minimum family income in this country, concerns about cost and work disincentives mitigate against establishment of a BIG for all citizens in the U.S. Such a program would clearly be costly.

The benefits, as well as cost avoidance due to reduction or elimination of other income-support programs, are complex to evaluate, and, therefore, the true cost–benefit of BIGs is difficult to predict. Further, the program might provide a work disincentive in that it could encourage people who currently earn less than the BIG grant to work fewer hours. The extent to which people, especially women with young children, would reduce their work time if this kind of program were instituted is unclear. However, such a program would make great strides in lifting families out of poverty and strengthening the social contract. To learn more about the BIG, go to the websites of the U.S. Basic Income Guarantee Network (www.usbig.net).

Asset-Based Reform   At this time, there are indications the welfare state may be undergoing a transformation. Increasingly, policy makers are trying to join the fundamental goal of providing economic and social protection of people who are poor and vulnerable with macroeconomic development goals. Ways to provide social protection and, at the same time, promote economic growth are being sought. Asset-based policies are part of this approach. For example, besides the asset-based approaches discussed earlier, Michael Sherraden as well as other advocates who are trying to attract attention to how low-income families can be helped to acquire assets, have long suggested a lump-sum payment from the federal government to children at birth. Significantly, most other developed countries provide some sort of children's allowance, viewing it as an investment not only in the child's future, but also in the nation's long-term economic prosperity. This payment could go into an IDA-type account that could later be used for education, health care, or other designated purposes. These accounts could provide a government match for low-income families who continued to save for their children's future. Further, research indicates that youth account ownership and savings predict college attendance, so a variation of this approach could be implemented to help low- and middle-income youth save for education in their own account (Elliott and Beverly, 2010). For more information on strategies to help young people save for college and avoid excess student loan debt, as well as research about why asset-based approaches may yield more positive educational outcomes for disadvantaged students, go to the Assets and Education Initiatives website (http://aedi.ku.edu).

A universal system of Child Development Accounts (CDAs) could motivate life-long savings accounts which would help American families move away from over-reliance on credit and serve as a cornerstone for a more productive and stable financial future (Adams and Scanlon, 2010). Importantly, such an approach would more closely parallel U.S. policy toward affluent young people, whose families receive incentives to accumulate financial and non-cash assets, in contrast to eligibility policies for means-tested programs, which mostly restrict low-income families' savings. Although nationwide implementation of child savings accounts is unlikely at this time in the U.S., asset-based policies have the potential to help some families escape poverty, if they are sufficiently funded. The federalist U.S. system is currently seeing policy innovations at the local and state government levels to test asset-based initiatives, and it is possible that positive outcomes from these efforts may spur federal advocacy towards CDAs. Importantly, however, CDAs, IDAs and other assets-based initiatives could complement, but not replace, public income-support programs. Peer lending and helping people with low incomes access financial services can support asset accumulation. However, they also shift our focus to the need for individual savings and financial services and away from the structural barriers, such as discrimination in employment, inferior educational institutions, and inadequate salaries and income supports that keep people in poverty. This shift in attention could decrease the likelihood that such barriers will be effectively addressed. Further, current federal and state funds to help low-income families meet survival needs are not adequate, and funneling those funds into asset-based programs, which may be more politically popular, could further erode an already badly frayed safety net for low-income families and their children. Nonetheless, it is clear that more pathways out of poverty must be charted to address growing income inequality and rates of poverty in the U.S. Developing, implementing, and evaluating additional ways to extend support for asset accumulation to moderate- and low-income families may help these families build a more economically secure future.

Poverty in the Global Context

We cannot leave a discussion of poverty without considering the face of poverty beyond the borders of the U.S. To measure the incidence and extent of poverty around the world, the United Nations uses a Multidimensional Poverty Index (MPI), which reflects acute deprivation in health, education, and standard of living. This expands on money-based measures by also taking into account factors including years of schooling, access to clean water, assets, and infant mortality. In the 109 countries included in the MPI Report, about 1.7 billion people—a third of their population—live in multidimensional poverty (United Nations, 2011). An estimated 1.3 billion people in those countries live on $1.25 a day or less. Social justice demands, as well as economic and security issues arising in the face of this level of global poverty, are propelling more young people, including social workers, into international careers focused on lessening global poverty. Young social workers who use a strengths approach bring to this work an understanding of the importance of developing interventions informed by the voices of the people experiencing poverty in these countries. To learn more about the MPI and U.N. initiatives to address global poverty and promote human development and well-being, go to http://hdr.undp.org.

Quick Guide 7 provides a brief description of major programs discussed in this chapter and information on how to help your clients apply for benefits. In this chapter and the subsequent three chapters on child welfare, health/mental health, and aging, we delve more deeply into the current policies and programs that provide the benefits and services on which your clients will rely. The Quick Guides at the end of these chapters will make it possible for you to quickly remind yourself how to help your clients access these programs. Indeed, as discussed earlier in the text, these efforts to help clients navigate social policies and the programs that stem from them, are critically important policy practice activities for social workers and a prime place where direct practice and policy study align.

QUICK GUIDE 7   Income- and Asset-Based Programs

Old-Age, Survivors, and Disability Insurance (OASDI)	Insurance program for workers who pay payroll taxes/insurance premiums into the Social Security Trust Fund based on earned income.
	The program pays retirement income depending on years of contribution. Monthly benefits are paid to those who are eligible including: workers, survivors (spouses and children) of deceased workers, and disabled workers when their work history qualifies. The cash assistance for disabled workers unable to work for at least one year excludes drug and alcohol addiction related disability.
	For more information and details on the application process, see: www.ssa.gov and socialsecuritydisability.ws/index.html
Temporary Assistance for Needy Families (TANF)	Monthly cash assistance for low-income families with children under 18 who qualify. Must be engaged in employment or work-related activities within two years. Requirements vary widely from state to state. For more information and details on the application process, see: benefit information on your state website and go to www.tanf-benefits.com

QUICK GUIDE 7   **Continued**

Supplemental Security Income (SSI)	Cash assistance for low-income adults and children with disabilities or sight impairment; must meet functional and income requirements. People 65 and older without disabilities who meet the financial limits are also eligible. For more information and details on the application process, see: www.ssa.gov/pgm/ssi.htm
Supplemental Nutrition Assistance Program (SNAP)	Food supplement program for qualifying low-income individuals and families; provides an income supplement, generally via an electronic transfer to a debit card. For more information and details on the application process, see: www. fns.usda.gov/snap
Women, Infants, and Children (WIC)	Food supplement program for qualifying low-income mothers and children intended to enhance health and wellness; limited to the purchase of certain foods. For more information and details on the application process, see: www. fns.usda.gov/wic
General Assistance (GA)	Short-term cash assistance for low-income adults who do not qualify for other assistance; available in some states/cities and often referred to as "general relief." Because this program varies greatly by state and locality, you will need to inquire locally about the program in your area. The Center for Budget and Policy Priorities provides some general information for each state at this web address: http://www.cbpp.org/cms/?fa=view&id=3603
Earned Income Tax Credit (EITC)	Tax credit issued for qualified income treated as withholding to be paid as a cash (refundable) tax benefit; the amount of credit depends on the number of qualifying children claimed for the benefit in the tax return along with other factors such as military service, disability, citizenship status, earned income, adjusted gross income, and residence. For more information on the application process, see: www.irs.gov/Individuals/EITC-Home-Page--It%E2%80%99s-easier-than-ever-to-find-out-if-you-qualify-for-EITC
Individual Development Account (IDA)	Funding for home, business, education, and other investments intended to help low-income savers attain financial stability. Find where programs are available at the following web address: cfed.org/programs/idas/directory_search/

CONCLUSION

Helping people to meet their basic needs for food, shelter, and income is the first step in effective social work practice. In psychology and human behavior courses, you have learned about the importance of tending to basic needs before expecting other therapeutic efforts to meet with success. As a social worker, you will likely come into contact with families who struggle constantly on very low incomes. It is incumbent on social workers to make certain their clients know about the benefits discussed in this chapter. Clients may also need help in filling out the often very complicated application forms, and in navigating the application process. Unfortunately, benefits frequently are inadequate and in short supply. Policy practice that is focused on expanding benefits and increasing access to eligible citizens is sorely needed. Social workers should also seek to inform public debate about the causes and consequences of poverty, the struggles facing individuals and families living with low incomes, and the inadequacy of our current poverty line for measuring the true scope of need in our communities. Further, more strategies to help low-income families escape from poverty should be developed and tested. Strong economic growth is not antithetical to policies and programs that offer social protection to our children so that they can grow up in good health, adequately nourished, and well educated. In fact, our economic future depends on having an educated, healthy, and engaged citizenry. More attention to asset-based policies and capacity building approaches may also help close the widening wealth gap in our country so that more Americans can look toward their futures with a foundation of economic security.

MAIN POINTS

- The government typically defines poverty in terms of a poverty threshold or *poverty line*, which was $23,283 for a family of four in 2012. People with incomes below the poverty line are considered poor.

- Poverty can also be defined in terms of relative poverty, whereby people are judged to be poor if they do not have sufficient resources to maintain a standard of living considered adequate in a given society at a particular time.

- The capabilities perspective defines poverty as the absence of opportunities to achieve capabilities to be sheltered, well nourished, adequately clothed, healthy, and active in the community.

- When considering capabilities, the initial focus is on which groups have the capacity to secure opportunities for their families and communities to succeed, and what opportunities make this possible. Initiatives to increase access to these opportunities is in keeping with advancing support for a capacity building state which prioritizes public policies and programs that help families, currently lacking these capacities, to build them.

- Recognition of the inadequacy of the current poverty threshold for measuring the incomes individuals and households truly need in order to afford a decent standard of living has led to calls for alternative measures that take into account the value of in-kind benefits available to some people in poverty, as well as the true cost of such necessities as housing and health care.

- Income-support programs can be categorized as universal or selective. Entitlement programs, which can be universal or selective, require benefits to be distributed to all people who meet the program criteria, regardless of total program cost.

- Universal income-support programs that are provided to eligible citizens regardless of income include Old-Age, Survivors, and Disability Insurance (OASDI); Unemployment Insurance; workers' compensation; and veterans' benefits.

- Key to the fiscal and political success of OASDI is its structure as a social insurance program, where the government provides the institution through which individuals share the risks and rewards associated with participation in a capitalist economy. As the debate about OASDI reform continues, social workers should be wary of efforts to change its financing that would undermine this insurance principle.

- Selective programs are means-tested and include TANF, the Food Stamp Program (SNAP), WIC, public housing, SSI, General Assistance, and EITC.

- TANF reflects changing attitudes about the role of women in society, as well as about our collective obligation to those experiencing financial challenges. Where parents in poverty used to receive a guaranteed cash grant to support their children, TANF today is a block grant that serves a declining percentage of poor families, provides only enough support to bring recipients to about half the official poverty line in most states, and uses strict sanctions and time limits to try to control the, mostly female, participants' lives.

- In contrast, the Supplemental Nutrition Assistance Program (SNAP) which has remained a primarily federal program that has not been converted into a block grant to the states, has grown significantly during the economic downturn. SNAP is designed to grow with increases in poverty and need.

- Especially in times of economic downturn, devolution can result in slow as well as inadequate responses to rising levels of poverty. This is compounded by shifts in some programs from entitlements to block grants, which further erode states' ability to meet growing need.

- Although badly frayed, our public safety net programs, such as SNAP, EITC, SSI, and TANF keep many people out of poverty and still others from falling even further into poverty, particularly during economic downturns.

- When evaluating the effectiveness of these policies and programs, strengths perspective principles emphasize examination of client goals and outcomes. Policy and program goals and design should focus on removing structural barriers and increasing access, choice, and opportunities that can lead to client empowerment. The effectiveness of the programs should be judged not only on whether they achieve societal goals but also on whether outcomes for clients are consistent with clients' own goals.

- Asset-based policies and programs are gaining support in the U.S. Individual Development Accounts (IDAs) have been instituted to assist families and individuals in saving for homes, education, and businesses in order to combat the inequality in asset distribution in the U.S.

- Advocates are also calling for the creation of Child Development Accounts to provide platforms and incentives for asset accumulation for low-income children, particularly given the potential for improved outcomes for those who grow up with the economic security an asset base can provide.

- Initiatives such as the Grameen Development Bank have experienced some success as models for peer lending for micro-enterprise internationally and may offer models for anti-poverty work in the U.S.

- Asset-based programs may complement, but should not replace, income-support programs.

- The Multidimensional Poverty Index (MPI), which expands on money-based measures by also taking into account factors including years of schooling, access to clean water, assets, and infant mortality, can be used to compare poverty rates globally.

EXERCISES

1. Go to the Sanchez family case at www.routledgesw.com/cases. Based on your knowledge of Sanchez family members, what benefits discussed in this chapter do you think Joey and Vicki might be eligible to receive?
   a. What further information would you need on Joey and Vicki Sanchez in order to more clearly determine eligibility? In crafting your answer, list the family member's name, programs for which she or he might be eligible, and additional information needed.
   b. How might the stigma attached to some means-tested programs impact this immigrant family, given their values and life experiences?
   c. Since the Sanchez family lives in a mostly immigrant community, how might policy changes in 1996 have affected the neighborhood's well-being? What policy reforms would positively impact families like these?
2. Go to the Riverton case at www.routledgesw.com/cases. It is often difficult to get benefits such as SSI or Veterans' Benefits for people who are homeless because they have no home address or bank account. If you were a social worker in Riverton, working with people who were homeless, how could you address this problem? What policy changes would you explore to aid other, similar clients?
3. Find out what other barriers people who are homeless encounter in applying for employment or benefits and services for which they are eligible. You can do this by using Internet resources and by talking to people who are homeless and the staff of programs that serve people who are homeless. Identify three barriers

they face, and suggest program or policy innovations that might help to overcome those barriers.

4. Go to the Washburn case at www.routledgesw.com/cases. Carla Washburn, like many grandparents today, raised her grandchild. Many grandparents raising grandchildren are struggling financially, which adds to the strains of this new role. Find out what benefits grandparents raising grandchildren can potentially receive in your state, and the eligibility requirement for grandparents. For example, do eligibility rules differ for grandparents applying for TANF, SNAP, WIC?

   a. If grandparents get TANF in your state, will they be required to return to work?

   b. What barriers do you think Carla Washburn would have faced if she had applied for these benefits?

   c. Grandparents raising grandchildren often live in poverty. Identify three policy or program changes that you believe are needed to help grandparents provide an adequate standard of living for their grandchildren and themselves.

   d. Some states are moving to require drug-testing for TANF recipients, a move which is diverting maintenance-of-effort funds and increasing the stigma experienced by low-income parents. How might such a policy impact the decision of someone like Carla Washburn to apply for cash assistance?

5. In this chapter we have discussed the growing wealth gap in this country. This disparity also manifests itself in disparities in capacity to purchase computers and smart phones with which to access online services. Typically, people without their own computers must access online services in public spaces. What problems can you see with the RAINN model of service delivery, which focuses on sexual abuse, for people without private access to the online service? As service delivery models evolve, what strategies could be used to make sure that people in poverty are not further disadvantaged by lack of access to such online services?

6. People who are already living in poverty when disaster strikes will be more vulnerable to natural disasters such as those experienced by the people in the Hudson City interactive case. What strategies would help human service agencies make sure these groups are prioritized for emergency evacuation and services? What policy changes might reduce their vulnerability, especially in areas at risk for future disasters?

7. If you do not already know people receiving TANF with whom you can talk, consider volunteering time at a community center in a low-income area, or perhaps in a child care center in that area. This experience will give you a chance to learn about the barriers to meeting basic needs faced by low-income families.

8. How could you become part of the effort in your area to promote a living wage? List the steps you would take.

9. Ask a member of your family who is age 65 or over what Social Security means for her or him. How would their lives be different without that income support?

10. Issues such as high-quality, low-cost child care; mass transit; and a living wage are likely issues that people in your community are already actively trying to push in the local and state policy arena. Find out how to join with other social workers and consumer groups to advocate for needed welfare reform by going to the website of your state chapter of NASW.

Policies and Programs for Children and Families

There can be no keener revelation of a society's soul than the way in which it treats its children.

Nelson Mandela

Children are the world's most valuable resources and its best hope for the future.
John F. Kennedy

Let us put our minds together and see what kind of life we can make for our children.
Sitting Bull

WHEN WE SEARCH FOR STRENGTHS AND RESOURCES in the family and community, our attention turns naturally to children. We know that children can thrive if they have adequate food, shelter, education, health care, and sufficient adult guidance. Many adults devote their lives to helping children build on their strengths, thus enhancing both the present and the future of our families and communities. Nevertheless, in the U.S., one in five children under age 18 is growing up in poverty (DeNavas-Walt, Proctor, and Smith, 2012). Poor children eat less nutritious meals, often live in unsafe homes, and are more likely to be victims of abuse and neglect. They are less healthy and less successful in school or attend inferior schools in disadvantaged neighborhoods, and they are three times more likely to die in childhood. Further, children who live in poverty face a significant chance of remaining in poverty throughout their lives. Forty-two percent of children whose families live in the bottom fifth of the income distribution will continue to remain in the bottom fifth once they become adults (Isaacs, 2007). Large health disparities are clear for children raised in poverty and for children of color, and these health differences, as well as other adverse events in childhood, may translate into increased disability and earlier deaths in adulthood. In addition, more than 400,000 children currently are in foster care (Children's Bureau, 2012). On a regular basis, several million children between the ages of 5 and 14 care for themselves without any adult supervision, creating a daily climate of risk. Suicide is the third leading cause of death among young people of 15 to 24 years of age. The first and second causes of death are accidents (primarily automobile) and homicide (CDC, 2010).

The statistics are even bleaker for children of color. To begin with, the infant mortality rate for African American children is 2.3 times the infant mortality rate of non-Hispanic white children (CDC, 2012). Further, 37.4 percent of African American children and 34.1 percent of Hispanic or Latino children are living in poverty (USDHHS, 2012b). The percentage of children of color who are removed from their homes and placed in foster care is disproportionately higher than would be expected given the percentage of children of color in the U.S. For example, 27 percent of children in foster care are African American, despite the fact that African Americans represent only 15.2 percent of all children in the U.S. under the age of 18 (U.S. Census Bureau, 2009b; USDHHS, 2012b).

Although our children represent our future, current policies and programs are failing to meet the needs of many of our youngest and most vulnerable Americans. In addition, it is clear that the future economic trajectory is one of increasing mandatory spending. According to the Urban Institute, federal spending will increase by 1 trillion dollars over the next ten years but spending on children will basically remain the same at the federal level. However, much of the funding for children's programs is at the state level and it comes in the form of education funding which often also includes child development programs. So, as in an increasing number of arenas, in some states, funding is increasing while in others, it is decreasing. Child development programs are particularly important for our future, and we are not investing sufficiently in those programs. Child welfare policies have developed primarily when the family and other systems that serve our children have failed. Unlike older adults, children are still primarily economically dependent on the family. These programs have been largely residual, and they have often focused on child saving rather than on strengthening families. That is, they have emphasized the child in danger, but supports such as adequate day care and family allowances that many other developed countries provide for all families are still not in place in the U.S. Thus, intervention is targeted to crisis situations rather than to providing vulnerable children and their families with the resources to avoid crisis. The result has been programs that are less effective in terms of both fiscal and human outcomes, with often-tragic consequences for children, families, and their communities. The United States, then, cannot be understood to truly have a "child welfare" policy, in terms of one that provides supports for the well-being of children generally, but, instead, a child risk response system, with children inevitably falling through the resulting cracks.

In Chapter 8, we discussed and critiqued the major programs designed to provide income support to children: EITC, TANF, and OASDI. We do not have children's allowances to help support all of our nation's children, and the policies and programs we do have leave many children to grow up in dire poverty.

Our lack of effective income-support programs is a grave risk factor for our children. Child hunger is increasing in the U.S. It is particularly severe on weekends and in the summer when many children do not have access to school meals. Chapter 8 explained in detail the need for additional, more adequate income-support programs and discussed needed changes in nutrition programs. In this chapter, we focus on policies and programs dealing with child protection, family preservation, permanency planning, adoption and foster care, and juvenile justice. Children in need of care are found in all of these systems. Additionally, children and families who are caught up in the juvenile justice system because a child has been charged with a crime are also often involved with other child welfare service providers. For example, the child may be in foster care, or the family may be receiving family preservation services. Finally, we will examine programs for children with special needs as well as child support enforcement policies. Of course, we have already covered a great deal of content elsewhere in this text relating directly and indirectly to children's well-being in the U.S. and will cover a great deal more in the coming chapters. For example, topics such as the health and mental health care systems, anti-poverty programs, and anti-discrimination regulations, which extend beyond the child population, are covered in other chapters. The challenges children face and the policies which attempt to respond to them overlap issue areas and cross jurisdictions; as a social worker, your efforts to help an individual child or a large group of children will necessarily require interfacing with policies in many sectors.

This chapter provides information that will help develop your understanding of child welfare and family policy and how they can be improved. Many social workers are employed in the child welfare system. Further, social workers in all settings will undoubtedly deal with issues of child welfare and thus need to be familiar with basic child welfare policies and programs. Therefore, this chapter also explores the steps necessary for crafting effective child welfare and family policy using the strengths perspective. By taking a strengths approach, we can develop policies and programs that enhance the ability of families to care for their children and reduce incidence of family dysfunction that puts children at risk.

HISTORY AND BACKGROUND OF PROGRAMS PROTECTING CHILDREN AND FAMILIES

Social workers have long been leaders in the field of child welfare. In contrast to fields such as health care and education where other professions dominate, the child welfare system has been primarily a social work domain since the beginning of the 20th century. As discussed in previous chapters, historical strategies for dealing with children in need of care included indenture, orphan trains, and large orphan asylums. In colonial times, children were subject to the same rules of criminal responsibility as adults, but reformers early on began to press for different treatment for children and youths. For example, Jane Addams and her colleagues from Hull House lobbied the Illinois state legislature for a separate juvenile court. As a result of their efforts, the first juvenile court opened in Cook County, Illinois, in 1899 (Allard and Young, 2002). This approach spread across the country, so that by 1925, all but two states had juvenile courts.

Most states did not pass laws to protect children from physical abuse by parents until the mid- to late 1800s. Even then, it took determined efforts by women's groups and other concerned citizens to convince legislators to pass such laws because children were viewed as the property of their parents. Widely publicized cases of severe abuse helped build public support for these laws, which allowed the courts to remove children in need of protection from their parents and place them in orphanages, asylums, and other families. However, the laws did not specify who was responsible for investigating child abuse and enforcing child protection statutes. Consequently, private societies were established to provide these services (Petr, 2004).

In 1875, the first Society for the Prevention of Cruelty to Children was founded in New York. Similar private societies subsequently were established across the U.S. These societies investigated cases of alleged child abuse and neglect, presented the cases in court, and advocated for legislation to safeguard children's welfare (Downs, Costin, and McFadden, 1996). You can review these legislative initiatives and the role of pioneer social workers in building our child welfare system at the Social Work History Station site hosted by the Boise State University website (www.social-workhistorystation.org). Because private societies dedicated to the protection of animals were much more organized than groups aiming to protect children during this period, private child protection societies modeled their programs and strategies on those of the animal protection societies.

As far back as 1935, Title IV-B, the Child Welfare Services Program of the Social Security Act, established the protection of children as a focus of public social service. Nevertheless, it was not until the powerful medical profession "rediscovered" child abuse in the 1960s that child maltreatment appeared on the policy agenda across the nation (Brissett-Chapman, 1995). The 1963 publication of a medical survey on "battered child syndrome" ignited public action. By presenting child abuse as a medical syndrome recognized by the medical profession, the 1963 report enhanced the validity of claims for the need for legislative intervention. By the mid-1960s, every state had passed legislation for the reporting of child abuse and the protection of children (Petr, 2004).

Currently, federal funds are provided to states and counties to help support child welfare services. Specifically, Title XX of the Social Security Act provides block grants for social services to states. In addition, Title IV-E provides reimbursement for a portion of the state's costs for foster care and adoption. Finally, Title IV-B provides grants to states for case management and prevention. The U.S. Children's Bureau, established in 1912, now oversees policies and funding affecting child welfare systems. The website of the U.S. Children's Bureau is a rich source of information about policies and programs for children (www.acf.hhs.gov).

CHILDREN AND FAMILIES TODAY

By examining the environment in which children are growing up, we can gain insight into why child welfare policies succeed or fail. Today, children are growing up in much smaller families than was the case during the baby boom of 1946–1964. In addition, children represent a smaller proportion of our population today than in 1960. In 2005, only 25 percent of the population was under the age of 18, compared with 36 percent in 1960. Moreover, this percentage decreased to approximately 24 percent by 2011 (U.S. Census Bureau, 2012d). This percentage is projected to remain relatively stable until 2050. However, this does not mean we have fewer children in the United States now. In fact, the population aged 18 and under today is larger than ever and the number is expected to continue to grow (U.S Census Bureau, 2012d).

Although the child population in the U.S. is expected to increase by 2050, the rate of this increase will be slower than for the population as a whole. In 2050 it is estimated that children will comprise 23 percent of the population compared to 25 percent in 2005 (Passel and Cohn, 2008). Consequently, there will be proportionally more adults to help support dependent children in the near future. However, it is unclear whether these adults will be willing or able to dedicate sufficient time and money to adequately nurture these children. Further, increases in the older-adult population during this period could mean that they also can be an added resource to help care for our children, though many of them will also need additional family and financial support.

EXHIBIT 9.1

Grandmother with Grandchild

Families have also become much more mobile. Many times, family members live far apart and, therefore, are less able to provide support and guidance to younger relatives. Further, the number of single-parent families increased to the point that in 2011, almost 25 million (35 percent) of U.S. children were living in single-parent homes and 41 percent (4 in 10) of all births were to unmarried women (Annie E. Casey Foundation, 2011b). Having two parents and many siblings does not ensure that children will receive the support they need, as those adults who grew up with abuse in two-parent homes and who often were hungry because there were so many mouths to feed, can attest. However, the absence of fathers, siblings, and grand-parents from the lives of children does mean that children have access to fewer of the resources that have traditionally supported them.

The percentage of U.S. children who are African American and Hispanic is also increasing. In 1980, 74 percent of children under age 18 were Caucasian, 15 percent were African American, 9 percent were Hispanic, and 2 percent were Asian/Pacific Islander. By 2005, the percentage of Caucasian children had dropped to 59 percent, the African American population had increased to 16 percent, the Hispanic population had more than doubled to 20 percent, and the Asian/Pacific Islander population had doubled to 5 percent (Passel and Cohn, 2008). Experts project that Hispanic children will increase to 35 percent of the child population by 2050. During this same period, the percentage of white, non-Hispanic children will decrease to 40 percent, while the percentage of African American children will be 14 percent. The number of U.S. children who are children of immigrants is also increasing. In fact the increase in the population of children under the age of

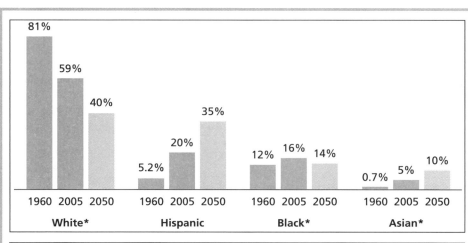

EXHIBIT 9.2

Changing Distribution of Children Aged 17 and Younger, 1960–2050

Note: All races modified and not Hispanic (*); American Indian/Alaska Native not shown. See "Methodology." Projections for 2050 indicated by light brown bars.

Source: Pew Research Center, 2008

http://www.pewhispanic.org/files/reports/85.pdf

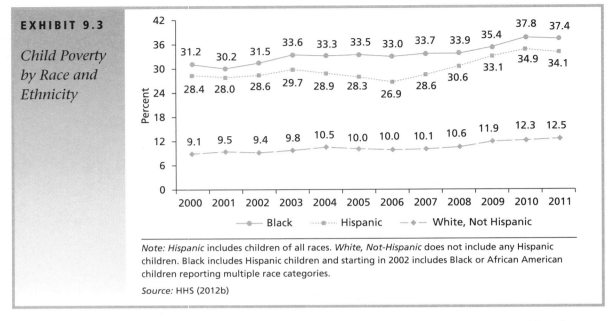

EXHIBIT 9.3

Child Poverty by Race and Ethnicity

Note: Hispanic includes children of all races. *White, Not-Hispanic* does not include any Hispanic children. Black includes Hispanic children and starting in 2002 includes Black or African American children reporting multiple race categories.

Source: HHS (2012b)

17 between now and 2050 will be due to new immigrants and children born to these individuals. Without this group there would actually be a decrease in the child population. In 2050 it is estimated that 34 percent of children will be immigrants or children of an immigrants compared to 23 percent in 2005 (Passel and Cohn, 2008). Exhibit 9.2 contrasts the distribution of children under age 18 in 2000 with the projected distribution for 2050. Children in these ethnic and racial groups experience particular risks, largely due to their disadvantaged position in society, as discussed in Chapter 7.

These numbers indicate that our nation's children are now more ethnically diverse, more likely to be growing up in single-parent homes, and more likely to have a smaller kinship network. Therefore, they may rely on new kinds of family and community support not based on the traditional biological definitions of families. Policies and practices that do not take into account these new realities are less likely to be effective.

Impact of Growing Poverty Rates on Child Welfare

Poverty can be extremely detrimental to children, especially in their early years. Research has found a strong relationship between poverty and child maltreatment with studies finding that that children from families with incomes below $15,000 were 22 times more likely to be victims of maltreatment compared to children with annual family incomes that exceeded $30,000. Children in poverty may be more vulnerable to certain types of maltreatment, such as neglect and physical abuse, and are at an increased risk for experiencing both short- and long-term negative outcomes (i.e. poor physical and mental health, unemployment, adult poverty, and victimization). This is especially troubling when one considers the poverty statistics for children in the U.S. As discussed in Chapter 8, currently 16.1 million children (under the age of 18), or one in five children, are growing up in poverty. For children under six years of age, one in four (24.5 percent) is living in poverty (U.S. Census Bureau, 2011). Additionally, race disparities exist in the rates of poverty among children, with 37.4 percent of African American children living in poverty in 2011 compared to 12.5 percent of white children (USDHHS, 2012b) (see prior Exhibit 9.3). Rates of poverty also vary by ethnicity: In 2011, 34.1 percent of Hispanic children were living in poverty.

The relationship between poverty and maltreatment is a complex one that must be interpreted carefully. It is important to note that child maltreatment occurs across all socioeconomic groups and the majority of parents living in poverty do not abuse or neglect their children. Further, although there is a correlation between poverty and maltreatment, this does not mean that poverty causes maltreatment. There are a number of theories as to why poverty is a leading predictor of maltreatment, such as the lack of access poor parents have to the resources needed to provide for their children. Another is that impoverished families may actually have maltreatment rates similar to those in parents in other socioeconomic groups, but they are more likely to be reported to Child Protective Services (CPS). With that being said, research has found that the interaction between poverty and other risk factors, such as substance abuse, depression, and social isolation, increases the risk for maltreatment. Further, stress has been found to be a risk factor for child maltreatment, and families dealing with economic hardship are experiencing significant stress in their daily lives. Due to the devastating impact poverty and economic crisis can have on vulnerable families, such as disproportionately high rates of child maltreatment, it is vital that we continue to invest in and expand our child welfare system to better provide for and strengthen these families.

The Child Welfare System

Child welfare policy has created a child welfare system. "The child welfare system is a group of services designed to promote the well-being of children by ensuring safety, achieving permanency, and strengthening families to care for their children successfully" (Child Welfare Information Gateway, 2012). Although the child welfare system is sometimes defined broadly to include services, such as Head Start, that are designed to be preventive, the core child welfare services are adoption service, foster care services, and services for families in which child abuse or neglect, sometimes called *child maltreatment*, is reported or suspected.

Federal law defines child maltreatment as "serious harm (neglect, physical abuse, sexual abuse, and emotional abuse or neglect) caused to children by parents or primary caregivers, such as extended family members or babysitters" (Child Abuse Prevention and Treatment Act, 1974). Neglect is the failure of caregivers to provide for basic needs such as nutrition, shelter, emotional care, and supervision. The largest category of maltreatment is neglect, which accounts for 78.5 percent of all incidences. In contrast, physical abuse accounts for 17.6 percent and sexual abuse for 9.1 percent (USDHHS, 2011b). Data on child maltreatment are reported by state CPS agencies. If a child is harmed by an acquaintance or a stranger, child welfare agencies generally do not intervene; law-enforcement agencies have exclusive responsibility for those cases. If the maltreatment is not investigated by the state CPS agency, it will not be included in the above statistics. Because reporting of child abuse and neglect tends to underrepresent actual incidence, particularly within some populations, it is likely that child maltreatment is an even larger problem in the U.S. than official statistics would suggest.

Child welfare systems are complex, and they vary from state to state. They are not one entity. Rather, public agencies (for example, departments of social services, child and family services) may contract with private child welfare agencies and community-based organizations to provide services to families. These services may include adoption, foster care, in-home ("family preservation") services, residential treatment, substance abuse treatment, parenting skills classes, mental health care, employment assistance, and financial or housing assistance. Because of the large role states play in the development of the child welfare system, children and families receive very different treatment in different states. To understand policies affecting children with whom you work, you will need to also become familiar with the policies and programs in your state. Part of the rationale for state jurisdiction is to keep control of such vital programs at a level of government closer to families, in the hope that they will better be able to respond to the unique needs of families in their communities. For social work advocates, that means that the chance of influencing child welfare policy should increase because policy makers are more accessible. Of course, the vast difference in wealth of states and ideological orientations towards welfare programs will influence the shape and scope of child welfare efforts. Interest in giving children an equal chance no matter the state where they were born fuels the push for more federal financing and oversight of child welfare. On the other hand, some states have been moving toward greater privatization of their child welfare services, which potentially creates even greater differences in treatment of children based on which private agency currently has the contract for providing services in a given section of the state. These trends can also complicate advocacy, as private entities might not respond to social workers in the same way as publicly accountable state or local governments.

State public and private child welfare agencies often provide services to children in the juvenile justice system as well as to children and families who seek out services on their own or who are referred by schools or other community organizations. Although the juvenile justice system typically is not considered part of the child welfare system, families in these two systems often face very similar problems. You will need to understand the policies and programs that structure each of these systems if you are to work effectively with children and families.

The Juvenile Justice System

Children and youths who are charged with crimes receive services through the juvenile justice system. The emphasis on rehabilitation within the juvenile justice system reflects the concept that young people are developmentally different from adults and, therefore, more amenable to treatment. Children and youths who come into the juvenile justice system may be experiencing mental illness, substance abuse, or have learning disabilities. They might have a history of abuse and of multiple placements in foster homes. Their backgrounds may be very similar to those of children in need of care who are receiving treatment through the child protection and foster care system. However, the juvenile justice system has been under criticism for years from people who feel that it often fails to rehabilitate youths.

Although the general public perception is that young people have become more crime-prone and dangerous than they were in years past, studies indicate that this is not the case (Sentencing Project, 1999). In the late 1980s, juvenile violent crime arrests grew until they reached their peak level in 1993. From 1994 to 2005, however, the number of arrests actually declined. By 2010, juvenile arrest rates for violent crimes had reached their lowest level since at least 1980 (Office of Juvenile Justice and Delinquency Prevention, 2011b).

Despite the fact that juveniles account for a small percentage of the overall arrest rate, over one million juveniles are still being arrested every year and, increasingly, are being tried as adults. In 1991, some 176,000 juveniles were tried as adults in criminal court (Sickmund, 1994). Today, that number exceeds 250,000 (National Juvenile Justice and Delinquency Prevention Coalition, 2013), despite the decline in arrests noted above. Research finds that more than half the states permit children aged 12 and under to be treated as adults for criminal justice purposes. In 22 states, plus the District of Columbia, children as young as seven can be prosecuted and tried in adult court where they will be subject to harsh adult sanctions, which can include mandatory sentences, long prison terms, and incarceration in adult prisons (Deitch, 2009). Significantly, many of the cases transferred to adult court are for non-violent drug or property offenses rather than for violent crimes.

Holding youthful offenders as adults has many serious consequences. For example, juveniles in adult prisons are more than 36 times more likely to commit suicide (Campaign for Youth Justice, 2007), and are at greater risk for sexual assault than any other population of inmates (National Prison Rape Elimination Commission, 2009). Moreover, after these youths are released, they are re-arrested sooner, more often, and for more serious offenses than are their counterparts who received treatment through the juvenile court system. NASW works to develop policies that recognize the fact that children and youths are developmentally different from adults and should be treated in ways that reflect these developmental differences (NASW, 2012b). Given effective intervention, children are less likely to progress through the system to adult crimes. Too many times in the juvenile justice system, appropriate treatment is not available when the child needs it, and youth and the larger society pay a significant price for this failed response.

Particularly troubling is the inequitable processing of African American youths through the system, such that they are overrepresented in both the juvenile justice system and adult prisons. In the U.S., black youths are over four times more likely and Hispanic youth twice as likely to be detained in a juvenile correctional facility as compared to white youth. Further, the majority of these youth are detained for non-violent offenses. In 2009, black youth were twice as likely to be arrested compared to white youth. During that same time, black youth accounted for 15.1 percent of the youth population but represented 31 percent of all juvenile arrests. The 2012 Supreme Court ruling that children cannot be given mandatory life sentences without the possibility of parole will potentially alter the sentences of 2,000 out of the 2,500 youth currently serving life sentences. Many of these youth will be minority youth as approximately 70 percent of young people sentenced to life imprisonment are youths of color (Children's Defense Fund, 2012b&c). Children and youth with special needs are also increasingly being incarcerated, particularly as gaps in mental health care make it more difficult for young people to access needed treatment. Further, the unique psychosocial needs of gay, lesbian, bisexual, and transgender adolescents in the juvenile justice system as well as in the child welfare system, are often overlooked. The negative outcomes for children in our correctional system and the racial disparities in incarceration rates indicate that this is an area where effective reform measures are badly needed. We will discuss some promising initiatives later in the chapter.

One sign that perhaps our society is ready to reconsider some of the most onerous policies that affect children is the March 2005 U.S. Supreme Court ruling *Roper* vs. *Simmons*, which abolished the death penalty for juvenile criminals. Before this change was made, the only countries that permitted the execution of offenders under the age of 18 were Iran, Nigeria, Saudi Arabia, and the U.S. Of these nations, the U.S. was responsible for 70 percent of all juvenile executions worldwide between the years 1998 and 2002 (Amnesty International, 2002). Additionally, in the past three years the Supreme Court has handed down rulings in several cases following its reasoning in *Roper* vs. *Simmons* that children are different from adults (National Juvenile Justice and Delinquency Prevention Coalition, 2013). For more information on the experiences of juveniles in adult criminal courts, visit the website of the Sentencing Project (www.sentencingproject.org).

MAJOR POLICIES AND PROGRAMS AFFECTING CHILD WELFARE AND JUVENILE JUSTICE

The following section examines major federal child welfare policies and programs as well as juvenile justice policies and legislation for children with special needs. As we explore these policies, you will observe that policy emphasis shifts back and forth

EXHIBIT 9.4

Adolescent Boys in a Juvenile Detention Facility.

between protecting children and preserving families. Similarly, ideological and societal shifts strongly influence the extent to which juvenile justice policy emphasizes rehabilitation at a given time. As you have learned, states have the primary responsibility for administering child welfare and juvenile justice programs. The quality and types of public services available for children and families vary greatly from state to state. In states hard hit by the economic downturn, child welfare services are being cut. Even basic elements such as hotlines to report child abuse are being downsized, such that callers might no longer reach a person to whom they can report their concerns. The service system is already fragmented and many times functions inadequately. Social workers in the child welfare system often do not have the tools they need to adequately perform their jobs, and high rates of worker turnover continue to negatively impact child welfare services. Given their first-hand knowledge of the impossibilities built into the system today, social workers are, therefore, uniquely positioned to advocate for changes in the child welfare system that will enhance their ability to appropriately serve children. Understanding the federal policies discussed below will help you to understand the basic parameters under which your state child welfare system operates, and to identify elements in need of reform.

The Child Abuse Prevention and Treatment Act

In 1974, the federal government became involved in child abuse prevention with the passage of the **Child Abuse Prevention and Treatment Act (CAPTA)** (Public Law 93–247). CAPTA established "minimum definitions that serve as a baseline for intervention" (NASW, 2012b). The law also provided states with federal funds to develop reporting systems for investigation of abuse and neglect. For state-by-state information on child abuse and neglect and information on a variety of child welfare policies, visit the Child Welfare Information Gateway homepage on the Department of Health and Human Services (USDHHS) website (www.childwelfare.gov). This site is maintained by the Children's Bureau of the U.S. Department of Health and Human Services and is an excellent source of the most up-to-date information on child abuse.

Congress has amended the CAPTA six times to reauthorize the program and to strengthen and expand programs centered on prevention and reporting. In 1978, it was amended to include provisions for comprehensive state adoption programs and it was further amended by the Keeping Children and Families Safe Act of 2003 (Public Law 108–36), which provided community-based grants for the prevention of child abuse and neglect. In November 2009, NASW submitted testimony to the House of Representatives calling for reauthorization and full funding of CAPTA to allow for the implementation of effective prevention strategies. The NASW testimony also stressed the need for more culturally appropriate services as well as initiatives to increase and retain professional child welfare workers. In December of 2010, The CAPTA Reauthorization Act of 2010 was signed into law. In addressing NASW's advocacy for the appropriate funding for CAPTA, the discretionary grant and basic state grant funding remained the same ($120 million) for fiscal year 2010 but will change to whatever sums "as may be necessary" for years 2011–2015. The law also promotes the coordination of services between CPS entities and domestic violence agencies and refines the prevention focus for the community-based child abuse prevention grants. Additionally, in line with the NASW recommendations, new reporting requirements include data collection on the number of CPS personnel, average caseloads, education and training requirements, demographic information and workload requirements, and the number of children referred for early intervention services under Individuals with Disabilities Education Act (IDEA) Part C (NASW, 2011). Exhibit 9.5 applies the policy analysis framework introduced in Chapter 5 to the CAPTA. These short summary descriptions are not intended to be comprehensive, but they can help you remember major elements of the basic policy and its intent.

Policy Goals	To strengthen the identification, reporting, and investigation of child maltreatment. To monitor research and publish information about child abuse and neglect.	**EXHIBIT 9.5** *Child Abuse Prevention and Treatment Act (CAPTA), 1974*
Benefits or Services Provided	Programs for reporting, investigating, treating, and preventing child abuse and neglect. National Center on Child Abuse and Neglect established as an information clearinghouse.	
Eligibility Rules	Children under age 18 at risk of or a victim of abuse or neglect.	
Service Delivery System	At the federal level, the Office on Child Abuse and Neglect in the Children's Bureau of DHHS administers the Act. State and local welfare agencies responsible for investigating and treating abuse and neglect implement the programs.	
Financing	Federal grant to the state based on population under age 18.	

The Juvenile Justice and Delinquency Prevention Act

Along with the CAPTA, in 1974 Congress also passed the **Juvenile Justice and Delinquency Prevention Act (JJDP Act)** (Public Law 93–415), which was last reauthorized in 2002. The goals of the original Act were to aid state and local governments in preventing and controlling juvenile delinquency and to improve the juvenile justice system. An additional important element was to protect juveniles from being inappropriately placed in the criminal justice system and from being harmed by exposure to adult inmates. This Act also emphasized the importance of community-based treatment for juvenile offenders.

The 2002 reauthorization of the JJDP Act requires states to develop and implement strategies to comply with four core protections for juveniles as a condition of receiving grants under the Act. The core protections are:

- reduction of the disproportionate number of juvenile minority-group members who come into contact with the juvenile justice system;

- separation of juveniles from adult offenders;

- removal of juveniles from adult jails; and,

- deinstitutionalization of juveniles who are status offenders, that is, who have committed crimes that would not be criminal if committed by an adult (Office of Juvenile Justice and Delinquency Prevention, 2002).

The Office of Juvenile Justice and Delinquency Prevention (OJJDP) in the U.S. Department of Justice works to achieve these goals. However, although the Act focused on rehabilitating youthful offenders, it did not provide sufficient resources to build an effective system. Further, federal funding to implement the JJDP Act declined 83 percent between 1999 and 2010 (National Juvenile Justice and Delinquency Prevention Coalition, 2013). State and local government will need much more funding if they are to develop juvenile justice systems that can achieve the goals of the Act. Currently reauthorization of the JJDP Act is six years overdue and child welfare advocates have been pressing for reauthorization for the past several years and have recently called on the Obama administration to forward a recommendation to Congress that they not only reauthorize, but strengthen the JJDP Act. A recent report from the National Juvenile Justice and Delinquency

EXHIBIT 9.6	**Policy Goals**	To prevent and control juvenile delinquency and improve the juvenile justice system.
Juvenile Justice and Delinquency Prevention (JJDP) Act, 1974	**Benefits or Services Provided**	Community-based treatment provided when appropriate to protect juveniles from unnecessary placement in the juvenile justice system and from harm incurred from exposure to adult inmates.
	Eligibility Rules	Juveniles adjudicated delinquent and at-risk children.
	Service Delivery System	Office of Juvenile Justice and Delinquency Prevention in the U.S. Department of Justice has oversight over state and local government actions taken to reach goals.
	Financing	Federal funds provided to state and local governments.

Prevention Coalition (2013) provides recommendations, which focus on five priority areas, for policy makers in order to reestablish an effective juvenile justice system. These areas include: restoration of federal leadership in and funding of juvenile justice policy; support and prioritize prevention, early intervention, and diversion strategies; ensure the safety and fairness of court involved youth, removal of youth from the adult criminal justice system; and support of youth re-entry into the community. Other proposed legislation includes prioritizing resources to actually implement requirements that homeless teenagers, runaways, truants, and other non-criminal youths not be moved into and socialized to the criminal justice system. It also provides for early mental health assessment, referral, and treatment of youth with mental health diagnoses/needs who come in contact with the juvenile justice system (American Bar Association, 2009). Exhibit 9.6 summarizes the features of the JJDP Act. For more information on juvenile justice legislation, visit the website of the Office of Juvenile Justice and Delinquency Prevention (www.ojjdp.gov/).

The Indian Child Welfare Act

Because the Indian Child Welfare Act is an excellent example of policy change guided by the client group, we have already examined the historical context for this legislation and discussed how it reflects strengths perspective principles. Here, we

EXHIBIT 9.7

Native American Child in Traditional Dress

briefly review the background of the Act in order to restate the conditions that propelled the passage of this unique piece of child welfare legislation. Recall that federal policy for Native Americans historically has emphasized forced acculturation. Religious conversion was pressed, and children were placed in boarding schools and other institutions and were systematically stripped of their native culture. Between 1969 and 1974, approximately 35 percent of Native American children were in foster homes and institutions (Matheson, 1996). Moreover, 85 percent of these placements were in non-Indian homes (American Academy of Child & Adolescent Psychiatry, 1975).

Native American leaders were determined to halt this cultural genocide. A number of tribes worked together to convince Congress to pass the **Indian Child Welfare Act (ICWA)** (Public Law 95–608) of 1978. The ICWA mandates that active efforts (compared to reasonable efforts mandated in other child welfare policy) be made to ensure that Native American children remain with their families, and it empowers tribes and tribal courts to oversee decision making regarding Native American children. Exhibit 9.8 applies the policy analysis framework to the ICWA. Currently there is a case before the Supreme Court that focuses on the intent and reach of ICWA. It concerns the right of a biological father with Indian heritage who gave up his parental rights and did not provide any financial support to the non-Native American mother, to object when the child was later put up for adoption with a white family. Depending on the decision, this case could have a significant impact on the interpretation and application of ICWA in future.

EXHIBIT 9.8 *Indian Child Welfare Act (ICWA), 1978*	**Policy Goals**	To protect the best interests of Native American children and families. To set minimum standards for removal and placement of Indian children and termination of parental rights. To recognize and strengthen the role of tribal government.
	Benefits or Services Provided	Endorses maintenance of Native American children with their families or placement in homes that reflect their culture. Tribes are actively involved in decision making.
	Eligibility Rules	All children who are members of federally recognized tribes, with membership determined by individual tribes.
	Service Delivery System	Tribal and urban Native American agencies have authority over state and federal courts to protect the best interests of their communities' children.
	Financing	Federal funds provided to tribal and urban Native American agencies.

Tribes vary greatly in their capacity to implement the ICWA. Unfortunately, federal funding for implementation has been insufficient for tribes with few resources. In order to implement the ICWA more fully, the federal government must provide adequate funding to establish Indian child and family services as well as more funding for training and monitoring. In addition, greater cooperation between states and tribes and increased employment and retention of Native American staff are essential if the ICWA is to achieve its goals. In order to accomplish the goals set out by ICWA, all involved parties—federal, state and tribes—must be willing to work together to reach a solution that protects the best interests of Native American children.

The Fostering Connection to Success and Increasing Adoptions Act was passed in 2008 to begin to address some of these problems. This legislation provides more federal financial support for tribal foster and kinship care, recruiting and training caregivers, and improving foster care and adoption services. In the past tribes could not access Title IV-E funds to administer their own foster care and adoption assistance programs unless they had an agreement with the state to access these funds. The Fostering Connection to Success and Increasing Adoptions Act now gives tribes the option of directly accessing and administering Title IV-E funds even if they do not have a tribal/state agreement. This will help to increase resources for Native American children and extend Title IV-E protections to more Native American children. This Act also allows tribes to access a share of their state's Chafee Foster Care Independence Program (CFCIP) funds in order to provide independent living services to tribal youth in the state (Children's Defense Fund, 2010). To learn more about current initiatives to protect American Indian children, go to the website of the National Indian Child Welfare Association (www.nicwa.org/).

Adoption Assistance and Child Welfare Act

Widely considered to be the most important piece of federal legislation to impact child welfare practice, the **Adoption Assistance and Child Welfare Act (AACWA)** of 1980 (Public Law 96–272) established family preservation as a major goal of the child welfare system. Before this law was enacted, extensive research had documented the impermanence of foster placement. In the 1960s and 1970s, the philosophies, financial incentives, and professional attitudes in state foster care systems emphasized "child saving" rather than "family saving" (Petr, 2004). Thousands of children grew up in foster care, with no permanent ties to any family. Because the system did not emphasize permanent relationships in biological and adoptive families, these children often grew up without the supports and family bonds that are considered important to healthy development.

The AACWA established financial incentives for states to emphasize permanency planning. In order to receive certain federal funding to help pay for their child welfare services, states are required to make a judicial determination that "reasonable efforts" were made to prevent unnecessary out-of-home placement

EXHIBIT 9.9 *Adoption Assistance and Child Welfare Act, 1980*	**Policy Goals**	To reduce the number of children in foster care for extended lengths of time through written permanency plans which emphasize family preservation, reunification, or adoption.
	Benefits or Services Provided	"Reasonable efforts" made to preserve the family. Establishment of a permanency plan for all children in the foster care system.
	Eligibility Rules	Children and families involved in investigation of and treatment for abuse and neglect.
	Service Delivery System	HHS is responsible for federal oversight. State and local agencies responsible for investigating and treating abuse and neglect, implement program changes. Periodic court reviews are conducted for each foster child case.
	Financing	Federal funds attached to incentives to reach goals.

(Petr, 2004). If such placements are found necessary, then states subsequently must make "reasonable efforts" to reunite the families. Unfortunately, the legislation did not define what constituted "reasonable efforts." State child welfare agencies thus varied widely in their efforts to increase permanency, and children continued to languish in foster care. Exhibit 9.9 summarizes the features of the AACWA.

Family Preservation and Support Services

Over the years, many states and counties have experimented with family preservation initiatives to prevent placement and support reunification. This work was reinforced by **Family Preservation and Support Services** provisions (Public Law 103–66), enacted as part of the Omnibus Budget Reconciliation Act of 1993.

The Family Preservation and Support Services provisions encourage the development of cohesive, community-based family preservation and support strategies that involve collaboration between child protection and child welfare workers and other service providers to implement family-centered interventions. The goals are to support the well-being of all family members and to enable parents to create safe, nurturing home environments. Federal funding is provided to the states, which establish the programs and services. Family support services may include activities such as support groups, home visits, and child care, with the purpose of increasing family strength and stability. Family preservation encompasses counseling or respite care as well as other interventions that help families who are at risk or in crisis to keep their children in their homes (Ahsan, 1996). Children and families at risk of abuse or neglect or in crisis are eligible for these services.

These provisions were reauthorized as the Promoting Safe and Stable Families (PSSF) program in 1997 and in 2006 as part of the Child and Family Services Improvement Act. The most recent reauthorization was in 2011 as part of the Child and Family Services Improvement and Innovation Act. This legislation reauthorized PSSF through the year 2016. This is one of the very few programs for which federal funds are made available to state child welfare services that focus on the prevention of child abuse and neglect as well as providing support and assistance to families after a substantiated claim of abuse or neglect has been determined. However, even under this program, families still must typically fall into crisis before services are rendered. Programs that provide supportive programming for families before a crisis develops are badly needed.

The Multi-Ethnic Placement Act

The intent of the **Multi-Ethnic Placement Act (MEPA)** of 1994 (Public Law 103–82) and the 1996 amendment, the Interethnic Adoption Provisions (MEPA-IEAP), is to remove barriers to permanency for children in the child protective system. Specific goals are:

- to eliminate discrimination based on race, color, or national origin of the child or the prospective parent;

- to shorten the time that children wait to be adopted; and,

- to facilitate the recruitment and retention of adoptive and foster care parents who can meet the distinctive needs of children awaiting placement (Hollinger, 1998).

The MEPA-IEAP prohibits states and other entities involved in foster care or adoption placements that receive federal financial assistance under Title IV-E, Title IV-B, or any other federal program from delaying or denying a child's foster care or adoptive placement because of the child's or the prospective parent's race, color, or national origin, or denying the opportunity to become a foster or adoptive parent for the same reasons. This Act also requires states to diligently recruit foster and adoptive parents who reflect the racial and ethnic diversity of the children in the state in need of foster and adoptive homes in order to remain eligible for federal assistance for their child welfare programs (Hollinger, 1998). Exhibit 9.10 summarizes the provisions of the MEPA-IEAP.

The MEPA-IEAP does not apply to children covered under the ICWA because of the unique political relationship between the Indian tribes and the federal government. In contrast to the ICWA, the MEPA-IEAP is designed to break down barriers to interracial adoption. However, the law does require increased efforts to recruit

EXHIBIT 9.10 *Multi-Ethnic Placement Act, 1994*	**Policy Goals**	To remove barriers to permanency by eliminating discrimination based on race, color, or national origin of the child or the prospective parent and reducing the waiting time before adoption.
	Benefits or Services Provided	Guidelines established for placement of children with prospective parents and recruitment and retention of adoptive and foster care parents.
	Eligibility Rules	All children in foster care awaiting adoption except for children covered under the Indian Child Welfare Act.
	Service Delivery System	State and local child protection agencies follow the federal guidelines in order to ensure funding for programs.
	Financing	Federal funds given to states.

and retain a multi-ethnic pool of prospective parents who reflect the racial and ethnic diversity of children in foster care.

Children of color, particularly African American children, were lingering dispro-portionately long in the system. Although the MEPA is designed to increase the number of homes available for same-race adoption while simultaneously removing barriers to cross-racial adoption, children of color still spend comparatively longer amounts of time in foster care before they are permanently placed. Even though agencies are increasing their efforts to recruit black families, some critics question whether this goal is realistic, given that black parents currently adopt foster children at a rate that is double their proportion in the population (Geen, 2003).

Although transracial adoptions have increased, in 2011, children of color comprised more than half of the children entering foster care and were overrepre-sented in foster care when compared to their numbers in the general population. Federal statistics for 2011 indicate 41 percent of the children waiting for families in the foster care system were white, 28 percent were black, and 21 percent were Hispanic (Annie E. Casey Foundation, 2011a). As the number of transracial adop-tions increases, the impact on children of color of being raised in white homes is still hotly debated. For example, since 1972 the National Association of Black Social Workers (NABSW) has taken a strong stance against transracial adoption and more recently has called for the repeal of the IEAP. For more information on NABSW's position on MEAP and transracial adoption visit their website at www.nabsw.org. Most research completed on transracial adoption indicates that the practice does not negatively affect the child's psychosocial and overall well-being. However, this research has been questioned on both theoretical and methodological grounds. For example, some studies indicate that minority children adopted into Caucasian families are prone to identify with the culture of their adopted families instead of their own races and cultures. This process can be problematic because identifying with one's own race and culture is correlated with fewer adjustment difficulties (Frasch and Brooks, 2003). For more detailed information on this legislation, see the Guide to the Multiethnic Placement Act of 1994 and the 1996 amendment, the Interethnic Adoption Provisions, available at the Children's Bureau website (www. acf.hhs.gov/programs/cb).

The Adoption and Safe Families Act

The **Adoption and Safe Families Act (ASFA)** of 1997 (Public Law 105–89) amended the Adoption Assistance and Child Welfare Act (AACWA) of 1980. The AACWA made reunification the primary goal for children who were removed from their homes. The law mandated that reasonable efforts be made to reunite the child and family, and it placed an 18-month time limit on foster care before termination of parental rights was initiated. Despite these stipulations, however, over 400,000 children were in foster care as of September 30, 2010 (USDHHS, 2011a).

In 1997, Congress enacted the ASFA, which placed more emphasis on child safety and was intended to increase adoptions. The ASFA provides that states are not required to make reasonable efforts to preserve or reunify families once a court has determined that (1) the parent subjected the child to "aggravated circumstances"; (2) the parent committed a felony assault that resulted in serious bodily injury to the child or another of the parent's children; (3) the parent is guilty of murder or voluntary manslaughter of another of her or his children, or abetted, aided, solicited, or conspired to commit such a crime; or (4) parental rights with another child had been terminated. ASFA further required that termination of parental rights be initiated for any child who had been out of the home for 15 of the prior 22 months (Wan, 1999). This change was intended to enable a quicker adoption process and thus to reduce the amount of time a child spends in limbo between foster care and either reunification or adoption. Between FY 2000 and FY 2010, the number of children in care measured at a point in time (September 30, 2000, and September 30, 2010) dropped from 552,000 in FY 2000 to 408,425 in FY 2010. Additionally, entries into and exits from foster care during those years decreased. However, between FY 2000 and FY 2010 the percentage of children who left the foster care system and were reunited with their families or placed in kinship care decreased. Forty-six percent of the children who left foster care in FY 2010 were in care for less than a year (USDHHS, 2011a).

When children are removed from the home, they become eligible for the benefits provided by ASFA. The intent of ASFA is to provide safe, stable, and permanent homes to these children in a timely manner. ASFA asserts that health and safety should be paramount in every decision made about children. The reasonable effort requirement for permanency planning was altered to provide for the "best interests of the child," given you accept the rationale that earlier and more forceful decisions about whether to reunify or adopt are in the child's best interest.

The Act further requires that permanency hearings be held within 12 months of the time when the child enters foster care. If reasonable efforts are not required, then the time frame is reduced to 30 days. Additionally, for children who have been in foster care for 15 of the prior 22 months, termination of parental rights must be initiated unless (1) a child is being cared for by a relative, (2) a compelling reason why termination would not be in the best interests of the child can be shown, or (3) the state has not provided the child's family with the necessary or timely services that would enable the child to return safely to the home.

In order to expedite the process of permanency, ASFA authorizes the use of concurrent planning, when appropriate. Concurrent planning provides states with the option of working on an alternative plan for the child even while it is attempting reunification (Adler, 2001). Despite all these changes, however, many children continue to remain in the foster care system longer than the policy intends. This is likely due to a combination of reasons. Many of the children that come into the system due to abuse or neglect present with complex needs. Currently, our child welfare system is not set up to address the social and emotional needs of these children and as a result it can be hard to find adoptive homes that have the capability and desire to adopt children with special needs. Further, the difficulty in finding adoptive homes for older children and the lack of adequate post adoption services may also contribute to the lengthy time many children spend in foster care.

ASFA is a federal program and is funded through federal dollars and some state matching grants. ASFA provides states with incentive payments for any increase in the number of adoptions over the number in a base year. It also provides an additional payment if children with special needs are adopted, and it makes health insurance available for children with special needs who cannot be adopted without such insurance. ASFA also removes geographic barriers to adoption by allowing children to be adopted outside the jurisdiction that is responsible for them (Adler, 2001).

ASFA services are delivered by a diverse group of professionals. The court system is involved in deciding the best interests of the child. Social workers and other professionals who provide case management and therapeutic services are responsible for planning treatment and for working with the courts to make recommendations for placing the child. Providing competent services for children in foster care clearly is critical. Nevertheless, in large part because of poor compensation for the stresses of the job, many staff who work with children are not properly trained.

ASFA was also designed to enhance state capacity and accountability. It provides additional funds to states to develop innovative new approaches. ASFA also provides funding for the USDHHS to make technical assistance available to states, communities, and courts. Furthermore, it requires states to submit an annual performance report to USDHHS. In turn, USDHHS is responsible for reporting each state's annual performance and for developing performance-based financial incentives for states (Adler, 2001). Finally, ASFA requires states to implement standards that ensure that

Policy Goals	To place emphasis on child safety and the best interests of children.	**EXHIBIT 9.11**
	To promote permanency for children in foster care and accelerate permanent placement.	*Adoption and Safe Families Act (ASFA), 1997*
	To increase accountability of the child welfare system.	
Benefits or Services Provided	Accelerates permanent placement by promoting adoption and shortening time limits for termination of parental rights.	
Eligibility Rules	Children are eligible when they are removed from their homes.	
Service Delivery System	Federal oversight of state and local child welfare agencies that implement mandated changes.	
	Court system decides the best interests of the child with recommendations from social workers and other professionals that provide case management and therapeutic services.	
Financing	Federal funding with some state matching funds.	
	Federal incentives given to states that have an increase in adoptions.	

children in foster care are provided with quality services that protect their health and safety (Adler, 2001). Exhibit 9.11 summarizes the major provisions of ASFA.

Independent Living Transition Services

Many children who are raised in foster care go on to lead full and happy lives as adults. However, children who grow up in foster care disproportionately experience negative outcomes in adulthood, such as homelessness, unemployment, poor health, and incarceration. The abrupt loss of financial and familial support that many foster care children experience when they turn 18 and are aged out of the foster care system leaves these young people ill-prepared for adulthood. In fact, most 18-year-olds are not independent. Rather, their families still provide a variety of emotional, financial, and skill-building supports. For instance, when young people rent their first apartments, parents often help them understand the terms of the leases, provide used furniture, perhaps even pay for the apartment and generally help with the transition to adulthood. Without these supports, former foster children have a harder time making this transition.

Concern that young people aging out of the foster care systems were not equipped to live on their own led Congress to authorize the Independent Living Program in 1986. Funding was provided for states to develop programs to help older foster youth make the transition to independence. The Chafee Foster Care Independent Living Act of 1999 (Public Law 106–109) provided further supports for aging-out adolescents transitioning to adulthood. More recently, additional financial support for these young people was included in the Fostering Connections to Success and Increasing Adoptions Act of 2008 (Public Law 110–351), which extends federal funding for youth in foster care to age 21 and requires that a caseworker must help the child complete a personal transition plan 90 days before they are set to exit the foster care system. This legislation also creates a federally subsidized guardianship program for kinship providers; mandates, expands and increases adoption incentives; and provides new funding to promote permanency.

Some states have experimented with privatizing foster care and adoption. As discussed in earlier chapters, *privatization* refers to the process whereby services formerly provided by the public sector are transferred to the private sector. The results of privatizing foster care and adoption have been mixed in terms of outcomes for children. In addition, privatized programs have not proved to be less expensive. The cost for foster care is high, and it continues to grow. We examine privatization and other strategies for improving the child welfare system in more detail later in the chapter.

The Child Support Enforcement Program

Many children living with only one of their biological parents do not receive adequate financial support from the noncustodial parent. Obviously, this has become a particularly critical missing link in addressing child poverty as increasing numbers of children grow up in single-parent households. The Child Support Enforcement (CSE) Program is designed to help remedy this situation. The CSE Program was established in 1975 as part of Title IV-D of the Social Security Act. At the federal level, the Office of Child Support Enforcement in the Administration for Children and Families (ACF) within USDHHS oversees child support enforcement. This federal, state, and local program provides the following services.

- establishing paternity;
- locating noncustodial parents;
- establishing child support obligations;
- collecting child support for families.

Currently, each state administers a child support program. In addition, Indian tribes may administer these programs. Different states place child support enforcement under the auspices of various agencies. In some states, the human services department is responsible for enforcement; in other states, the department of revenue performs this role. Additionally, many states (44 as of May 2012) contract with private agencies to provide certain components of the child support enforcement program. A parent with custody of a child who has a parent living outside the home may receive services through the CSE Program by applying to the agencies that administer the programs. Many families who are not receiving TANF use these services. However, for families receiving assistance through TANF, services are automatic. Part of the child support collected for these families is used to reimburse the federal and state governments for the TANF payments the family has received. Beginning in 2008, states were provided with incentives to pass through up to $100 a month of child support to TANF families with one child and up to $200 a month of child support to TANF families with two or more children (Wheaton and Sorenson, 2007). If states do pass through this money to TANF families, these families would be significantly benefited at relatively little cost to state governments. Child support payments for families not receiving TANF are sent directly to the families.

Although it was not technically a component of the CSE Program, the 1996 legislation that created TANF also improved the states' capacity to collect child support. The law established a national new-hire and wage-reporting system and instituted uniform interstate child support forms. It also provided funds to computerize statewide collection systems, and it authorized tough new penalties such as revoking driver's licenses for nonpayment of child support. Following these reforms, child support collection increased nationally to a record $27.3 billion in 2011 (USDHHS, 2012c). To find out more about CSE, visit the website of the Office of Child Support Enforcement (www.acf.hhs.gov/programs/css).

States and other service providers are also experimenting with programs designed to help noncustodial parents improve their ability to provide both financial and emotional support for their children. These programs help young unmarried parents find employment and improve their parenting skills. Because the service delivery system varies significantly from state to state and, in some cases, even among judicial districts, I have not provided a summary chart on CSE.

Legislation for Children With Special Educational Needs

Children who require special educational provisions because of a physical or mental disability are considered to have special educational needs. Legislation for children with special needs, such as the Education for All Handicapped Children Act of 1975 and its reauthorization, the IDEA of 1990, require states to provide education and services to meet these children's needs in the "least restrictive environment" (Briar-Lawson, Naccarato, and Drews, 2009). The IDEA was reauthorized in 2004 (Public Laws 108–446). Measures designed to hold the educational system more

QUICK GUIDE 8	Child Welfare and Juvenile Justice Programs
Child Abuse and Prevention Treatment Act (CAPTA)	Federal program that provides funding to states to develop systems and programs for reporting, investigating, treating, and preventing child abuse and neglect. Also established the National Center on Child Abuse and Neglect as an information clearinghouse. For more information on the services provided under this Act see: www. childwelfare.gov
Juvenile Justice and Delinquency Prevention Act (JJDP)	Assistance provided to states and local governments to address juvenile delinquency and improve the juvenile justice system. Focus on community-based treatment to avoid unnecessary entry in the juvenile justice system as well as protection for juveniles against exposure to adult inmates and jails. Oversight of the Act's provisions provided by the Office of Juvenile Justice and Delinquency Prevention in the U.S. Department of Justice. For more information on the services provided under this Act see: www.ojjdp.gov
Indian Child Welfare Act (ICWA)	Provides protection to all children who are members of federally tribes through the provision of minimum standards for the removal and placement of Native American children in the child welfare system. Mandates efforts be made to keep Native American children in their homes or place them in homes that reflect their culture. Establishes tribal authority over federal and state courts in the protection of Native American children. For more information on the services provided under this Act see: http://www. nicwa.org
Adoption Assistance and Child Welfare Act (AACWA)	Financial incentives provided to states to reduce the amount of time children spend in foster care by developing permanency plans for all children in the foster care system that emphasize family preservation, reunification, or adoption. Mandates that reasonable efforts must be made to keep children in the home or reunite children with their families. For more information see: www.childwelfare.gov
The Multi-Ethnic Placement Act (MEPA)	Funding provided to states to implement provisions focused on removing barriers to permanency for children in the child welfare system, except for those covered by ICWA. Looks to shorten time between entry into system and adoption by prohibiting child welfare agencies from denying placement or adoption based on race, color, or national origin of the child or prospective foster or adoptive parent. Requires that state child welfare agencies actively recruit and maintain foster and adoptive parents reflective of the racial and ethnic diversity of the children in their foster care system. For more information see: http://www.acf.hhs.gov
Adoption and Safe Families Act (ASFA)	Amended the Adoption Assistance and Child Welfare Act (AACWA) and is meant to ensure permanency and child safety through the promotion of adoption and acceleration of the termination of parental rights. Adoption promotion and support services are provided to foster children and adoptive families as well as coverage of health insurance for special needs children if necessary to ensure adoption. Additionally, adoption incentive payments are provided to states if yearly adoption numbers increase and for the adoption of special needs children. Services provided by various professionals, under federal oversight, including: social workers, case managers, other therapeutic professionals, and individuals in the court system. For more information see: http://www.childwelfare.gov

accountable for learning outcomes for children with disabilities are a major component of the reauthorization legislation. However, federal funding to help schools meet the new requirements has been inadequate.

Movements on behalf of children with special needs have helped draw attention to the importance of "most appropriate" placements and "least intrusive" interventions. Advocates have also promoted normalization for children with special needs. Normalization is a policy whereby schools endeavor to create an environment similar to that experienced by children without special needs. Parents and other advocates, including many educators and social workers, have lobbied tirelessly to implement policies that would allow children with special needs to receive inclusionary services in the public schools. Their work has reinforced the importance of these principles in child welfare services for all children. Some of the most innovative strategies involve wrap-around services which allow children with special needs to remain in the least restrictive environment, which is their own home and school. You can learn more about current work to improve conditions for children with special needs by visiting the Office of Special Education and Rehabilitative Services website at the website of the U.S. Department of Education (www.ed.gov).

Despite these advances in meeting the unique requirements of students with specific mental and physical needs, there are ongoing failures to promote their full strengths. An investigation by the Government Accountability Office (GAO) uncovered "hundreds of cases of alleged abuse and death" as a result of misuses of restraint and seclusion in public and private schools, and these interventions were disproportionately used on children with disabilities (Miller, 2010). Federal legislation has been proposed to prohibit elementary and secondary school personnel from managing any student by using chemical or mechanical restraint, physical restraint or escort that restricts breathing, or aversive behavioral intervention that compromises student health or safety, and requires staff to receive state-approved crisis intervention training (Miller, 2010). However, this legislation has not yet passed. Social workers in schools and other agencies regularly serve children with special educational needs. It is important that you become familiar with policies and programs targeted to these children, including their rights to appeal school and other policies that violate their civil and economic rights. For information specific to your state's programs, contact your State Department of Education.

EVALUATING POLICIES AND PROGRAMS FOR CHILDREN AND FAMILIES

The family is the foundation for the support of children. The application of strengths perspective policy principles when evaluating child welfare policies focuses attention on enhancing the family's capacity to support its children. Policies and programs need to be attuned to the ethnic, political, cultural, and economic contexts of families' lives. Further, they must provide additional resources to help families overcome barriers such as inadequate wages, lack of jobs, lack of training, and discrimination in the workforce, particularly given the connection between poverty and risk of child neglect. Families need assistance in obtaining access to knowledge and resources to address problems such as substance abuse and mental illness. Many parents and children who come into contact with the child welfare and juvenile justice systems may face co-occurring challenges. For instance, there may also be domestic violence and substance abuse problems in the family being served. Children and/or parents may have mental illnesses or chronic health conditions. Children with mental health issues who are in the foster care system are often given psychoactive medications at high rates, a problem which we discuss in more depth in Chapter 10. Yet other types of treatment such as the approach described below are often in short supply. The extent to which the child safety and permanency goals of child welfare policies and programs are met will be determined in large part by success in family capacity building. Family capacity building could include helping families to access needed treatment and developing occupational ladders for economically stressed families, whereby former clients who have been trained as adoption and foster support aides, parent aides, and reunification aides could deliver services. One particularly promising approach is Systems of Care (SOC). This is a philosophy of care that incorporates a strengths/needs-based (SNB) approach to child welfare practice. The goal is to provide safety, permanency, and well-being for each child in the state's child welfare programs. In order to achieve this outcome, SNB practices that involve collaboration between schools, families, and other social service agencies are integrated into child welfare programs and policies. Service systems are expected to work together. An additional goal is the integration of SNB practice within the broader systems reorganization efforts, such that children and their families have access to all departmental resources in order to achieve better outcomes for their lives. To learn more about how to apply the SOC philosophy in child welfare, go to the Child Welfare Information Gateway homepage at the website of the Department of Health and Human Services (www.childwelfare.gov).

As discussed in previous chapters, evaluating policies and programs using the strengths perspective involves seeking clients' input. Regarding child welfare, there are websites that provide parents' perspectives on child welfare policy, especially for children with special needs. For example, Family Voices, a national grassroots network of families and advocates for children with special needs, promotes the inclusion of all families as decision makers and supports partnerships between families and professionals. Family Voices makes available publications, funded in part by USDHHS, which describe mandates and strategies for involving families in developing and evaluating programs. You can learn more about the work of Family Voices at their website (www.familyvoices.org). In many states, child abuse prevention organizations work to strengthen families at risk and to help biological parents address challenges in order to reunify with children who have been removed from their homes. Often, these organizations can also promote systems reforms by lifting up the voices of biological and foster families and communicating these concerns to service providers and judicial decision makers. Teenage foster children who are transitioning from foster care are another particularly good source of information about needed change.

Strengths-based policy principles also stress involving service users in designing and delivering services. Families are defining themselves in new ways, and initiatives to identify and work with support networks that are not based on biological relationship can help bolster parents' capacities to care effectively for their children. Strengths-based approaches to reforming child welfare services include instituting policies that promote self-help and mutual assistance at the community level and investing in economic and occupational approaches that help families overcome the barriers that keep them in poverty. Strengths-based child welfare policy also recognizes the validity of different family forms, including same-sex parenting partners and multi-generational extended families.

Examining client outcomes is central to evaluation from a strengths perspective. However, because states vary widely in the statistics they keep and there is little coordination among systems, it is very difficult to develop a clear picture of outcomes for children in the child welfare and juvenile justice system on a national basis. Improving and standardizing state data systems are critical to enhancing our understanding of the success and failure of child welfare policy. (For more information on outcomes for children at the state and national levels, access the Kids Count Data Book on the Web.) Additionally, in order to promote social justice for children in the child welfare system, evaluation should track disparate outcomes for children of color and low-income children, for example, in order to identify patterns that suggest potential areas of needed systems reform.

In the next section, we will evaluate selected components of child protection and juvenile justice policy and consider next steps and necessary changes in the role of social workers in the child welfare system. We will also examine policy strategies to increase the effectiveness of social work within this system.

Students and Foster Care Youth Press for Transition Services

Students at the University of Washington-Tacoma were involved in a community project over two years mapping the system that serves youth who are "aging-out" of the fostercare system. They advocated for bills which would extend Medicaid coverage for all children leaving foster care from age 19 to age 21. Students organized a youth group to go to the Capitol for Youth Advocacy Day, became involved with a coalition, met with representatives, and empowered the youth to testify in front of the House and Senate with personal testimony. One student also had the opportunity to testify for the bill to extend Medicaid coverage in committee. The bill was passed and signed into law by the Governor. Many youths who were aging out of the system received health care until age 21 as a result of this work.

EXHIBIT 9.12

Student Advocates Target "Aging-out" Policy (Foster care)

Child Protection Policy From the Strengths Perspective

There are two different policy paradigms for child protection. One focuses on children's legal rights and views abusive parental behaviors as crimes requiring police-style investigation (Pelton, 1989). The second emphasizes social work-style investigation that focuses on assessing not only risk and safety but also the need for a range of interventions and services. Ineffective investigative practices and lawsuits have contributed to the development of litigation-oriented rather than social work operated child protection systems. However, research studies have indicated that providing biological parents with needed support can generate improved child welfare outcomes (Briar-Lawson et al., 2009). Given the multiple agencies that are often involved in these families' lives, it is clear there is a need for much greater service integration and tracking of outcomes across the mental health, domestic abuse, substance abuse, child welfare, and child protection systems in a way that focuses on families. The same children and families are often shuffled among these systems rather than receiving integrated, effective service. For example, it is estimated that more than half of all families involved with the child welfare system have substance abuse as a presenting problem. Yet few states have enacted policies that allow even drug-using pregnant mothers priority access to treatment beds for substance abuse, and long waits and expensive co-pays place quality treatment out of reach for many who need it.

Further, it is crucial that CPS function as an interrelated and integrated set of services that are part of a community-wide early prevention, intervention, and treatment system. Since the mid-1990s, there has been an increased focus on assessing family and community strengths as well as safety and risk. This focus needs to continue so that work with families becomes more strengths and empowerment based. We need policies that provide more flexibility in conducting investigations rather than adhering to a standardized, "one-size-fits-all" approach regardless of the specifics of the case. The use of a law-enforcement approach to investigating black families, given the discrimination that African American families have experienced within the law-enforcement system, the continued overrepresentation of African Americans in criminal justice, and the dearth of African American professionals to serve them, may be especially problematic. African American families are disproportionately represented in the child protection system due to a variety of systemic factors. Consequently, sensitivity to diversity is particularly important to successful child protection intervention. In some states, nonminority, non-poor children may be served more often in the mental health and disabilities system rather than in the child welfare system. For information on promising models for child welfare, go to the website, Positioning Public Child Welfare Guidance (www.ppcwg.org), which is a resource from the American Public Human Services Association.

Family Rights and Child Safety   As discussed earlier, the Adoption and Safe Families Act of 1997 (ASFA), which amended the Adoption Assistance and Child

Welfare Act (AACWA) of 1980, was enacted to place more emphasis on child safety and to increase the number of adoptions, thereby reducing the amount of time that children spend in the foster care system. Despite the passage of the ASFA, moving children out of the foster care system has proved to be difficult. Children are still lingering in the system, bouncing from one foster home to another. These children are not able to reap the benefits of living in a stable, healthy home environment.

The latest information from the Children's Bureau in the USDHHS, Administration for Children and Families (ACF), indicates that there has been a decrease in the number and rate of children who have suffered maltreatment in the last few years. Further, the 2011 rate was the lowest child victimization rate in five years. Additionally, the number of child fatalities has fluctuated over the past five years but reached its lowest rate in 2011. These data indicate an estimated 681,000 children were victims of child abuse and neglect in 2011, a rate of 9.1 per 1,000 children. Further, almost a fourth of the victims were younger than three years old, with children under one year old having the highest victimization rate of 21.2 per 1,000. More than three million reports of suspected child abuse and neglect were received in 2011, involving six million children nationwide (USDHHS, 2011b). Improved reporting systems and increased detection efforts, such as screening newborn infants for drug exposure and mothers for substance abuse, have helped to identify families that need services. However, poverty, inequality, and underemployment are also major contributors to family stressors that increase child abuse (Briar-Lawson et al., 2009), and these factors worsened during the recent economic recession. At the same time, traditional support systems provided by extended families, schools, and churches are no longer as available. Further research that examines risk factors for abuse and attempts to unravel the relationships among these contributing factors is clearly needed, as are investments in the functioning of our nation's families.

Policy changes in the ASFA allow for the rights of parents to be terminated more easily than was true under the AACWA. Advocates of these changes believed that this approach would enhance the potential for timely permanent placement. Critics contend, however, that the revised policies work against family reunification. Although cases move into permanency planning more quickly because of the ASFA, the 12-month timeline for a permanency hearing may not allow sufficient time for families to successfully work on their problems and get their children back. Consider, for example, that many children are removed from their homes owing to substance abuse issues. In fact, the majority of substantiated abuse and neglect cases are associated with drug abuse. A 12-month limit may not allow the parents enough time to rectify their situations to the point at which they can regain custody of their children. For example, one mother who was incarcerated found out her parental rights had been terminated when she saw her son being highlighted in an adoption promotion special. Further, inadequate financial assistance levels for families receiving TANF and the TANF time limits may make it less likely that parents can meet the time limits established under AFSA.

In order to promote permanency for children, we need to develop policies and programs that (1) provide support and services for families involved in kinship care, which means a child living with relatives without a parent present in the home, and (2) allow parents more time to regain some control over issues that are impeding them from being effective parents without severing ties to the biological family. Most kinship care placements are arranged privately without the involvement of a child welfare agency. Although there are a significant number of children placed in the care of the relative after a child welfare agency has become involved, only approximately half of these children are actually taken into state custody and placed into kinship foster care (Main, Macomber, and Geen, 2006). Kinship care placements have the benefit of keeping children within their family system and also negate the potential negative impact on children when they are placed with strangers. Further, kinship care can help children maintain a sense of family connection and more than likely allow them to have more frequent contact with their parents. It is important to note that although some research has indicated that kinship care is helpful in accomplishing the goal of getting children into a permanent home setting (George, 1990), it has also been found that kinship care can result in longer time frames before children are reunited with their families or moved into the adoption process (Zinn, 2009). Careful evaluation needs to be conducted on a case-by-case basis to determine if a kinship care placement is in the best interest of a child who comes into the child welfare system.

Family Reunification   High caseloads and financial disincentives work against family reunification. Most federal child welfare funding supports out-of-home rather than in-home services. In addition, the policies of many residential facilities do not support family reintegration. When facilities are located far from families, when family visits and phone calls are considered privileges rather than rights, and when no residential staff are responsible for working with families to facilitate discharge and reintegration into the community, family reintegration is less likely.

Gay, lesbian, bisexual, and transgender youths may have a particularly hard time in foster care. Due to hostility regarding their sexual orientation, many LGBTQ youth have been forced to leave foster care placements. Additionally, many face physical aggression and harassment in their group homes. Recently, the Administration on Children, Youth and Families located within the USDHHS awarded the L.A. Gay & Lesbian Center a 13.3 million dollar grant to create a model program that provides critical support to LGBTQ youth in the foster care system. The L.A. Gay & Lesbian Center is collaborating with others involved in the child welfare system to develop a comprehensive system of care that will protect the health and safety of LGBTQ foster youth. Once developed, this program can be replicated in other cities so that LGBTQ youth across the country are provided with the support needed to remain in a safe and stable foster care placement until adulthood (St. John, 2010).

Policy principles such as "reasonable efforts" in preventing out-of-home placement, the child's right to the least intrusive intervention and the least restrictive/most appropriate environment in placement, and emphasis on normalization, although laudable, are difficult to define and operationalize. Nevertheless, they promote a philosophy of child welfare intervention that is consistent with the strengths perspective in that they focus on child development and well-being as well as safety. As is the case in most policy arenas, there are many gray areas. However, these policy principles make it clear that extremes such as large, isolated children's institutions and foster care drift, which means that children spend years moving from one temporary placement to another, are no longer acceptable. When these principles are incorporated into law and enforced with financial sanctions and incentives, they help fortify the efforts of child welfare advocates who are petitioning hard-pressed state legislatures for additional funds and for reform of the child welfare system.

Many children in state custody have traditionally received services from private providers, such as church-affiliated non-profit group homes. Modifying the ways in which the state reimburses these private entities could promote more positive outcomes for children. Traditional reimbursement strategies that pay providers a set fee for each day children remain in out-of-home care create a financial disincentive for family reunification and effective permanency planning. Recognizing this problem, some states have begun paying for permanency and have instituted financial disincentives for allowing children to linger too long in foster care.

Teen Pregnancy As discussed previously, almost a half a million children are currently living in foster care in the U.S. and approximately 32 percent of these children are teenagers. Research has shown that youth in foster care are more likely to engage in risky behavior including engaging in more risky sexual behavior. Although the number of children born to teen mothers reached a record low in 2011, youth in foster care are much more likely to become pregnant than youth not involved in the child welfare system. In fact, compared to girls not in foster care, teen girls living in foster care are 2.5 times more likely to become pregnant by 19 and half of the young men aging out of foster care report getting someone pregnant compared to 19 percent of their peers outside the system (The National Campaign to Prevent Teen and Unplanned Pregnancy, 2009). These numbers are especially concerning when considering the risks to both the teen mother and their children. It has been found that many young parents who formerly lived in foster care were unemployed, convicted of a crime after leaving foster care, and a large number were on government assistance (Courtney, Hook, and Lee, 2009). Further, children of teen mothers are much more likely to be involved in the child welfare system. Teen mothers under 17 are 2.2 times more likely to have a child placed in foster care and twice as likely to have a reported case of abuse or neglect compared to those who have children after the age of 21 (Hoffman, 2006). One quarter of total public spending related to teen pregnancy is for child welfare costs related to teen

EXHIBIT 9.13

Teen Pregnancy

pregnancy for children in foster care (The National Campaign to Prevent Teen and Unplanned Pregnancy, 2011).

Clearly, addressing teen pregnancy prevention among youth in the child welfare system is a critical agenda item that needs more attention. Many agencies across the country are starting to address this issue through strategies such as: foster parent and case worker training; pregnancy prevention programming for teens and as part of independent living courses; and discussions during the development of an independent living plan. Further, in 2010 the federal government became involved in teen pregnancy prevention with the Obama's administration's Teen Pregnancy Prevention Initiative (TTPI). TTPI is a discretionary grant program overseen by the Centers for Disease Control (CDC) in partnership with the Office of Adolescent

Health. TTPI provides $105 million dollars in funding to various public and private entities for the development of age-appropriate evidence-based innovative community programs that focus on the reduction of teen pregnancy. Although this initiative has come under fire from groups who promote abstinence-only teen pregnancy prevention programs, it is crucial that initiatives such as these that provide youth with information on reproductive health, sex, sexually transmitted infections (STIs), and making informed decisions, continue to be funded. It is through these types of programs that youth are provided with the tools needed to care for themselves and plan for a productive future within their community.

Regardless of the type of strategy, in order to support the diverse needs of youth in the child welfare system, these efforts must look to engage a variety of key stakeholders with the goal of strengthening the safety net for those youth involved in the system. It is crucial that members of the child welfare system such as social workers, family and juvenile case judges, case managers, foster parents, and youth themselves, work together to influence the health outcomes of youth in care. These individuals can be involved in various ways including: providing adolescent sexual and reproductive training to foster parents and case workers; including family planning discussions and dialogue on contraception in transition plans when youth are transitioning out of foster care; providing evidence-based teen pregnancy prevention programs and services to youth in foster care; and addressing systemic barriers that lead to fragmented services and impose barriers to collaboration. All youth in foster care have the strengths and capabilities needed to overcome complex challenges and achieve their goals of independence and self-sufficiency. Policies and strategies need to be devised that provide the support and necessary services to teen parents, so that they can develop the foundation—educational as well as financial—and stability needed to be caring and effective parents to their children.

Privatization   As discussed earlier, the provision of child welfare services is becoming increasingly privatized. A privatized system relies much more heavily on market forces and competition to improve. Some private sector providers—particularly foster parents and church-affiliated group homes—traditionally have been part of the public child welfare system. However, for-profit providers are becoming more involved with the system. Even the jobs of adoption and foster care case managers and administrators, formerly located in the public sector, are being privatized.

A principal privatization strategy is for public entities to buy services for clients through purchase-of-service (POS) contracting rather than to provide services directly (Petr, 2004). The state then monitors and oversees the provision of services. In one form of privatization, POS vouchers are provided directly to recipients or their families. Modified managed care models, whereby private entities are paid a set amount per person to provide all needed services, have also been developed. Clearly, if there is not some sort of graduation of payment based on severity of need, agencies will have an incentive to "cream," that is to provide services to children with fewer needs. We will discuss managed care in more detail in Chapter 10 on health care.

Rigorous research is needed to evaluate the efficacy of these various privatization initiatives. Consistent with the strengths perspective, such research must carefully examine outcomes for clients as well as cost-effectiveness. At present, it is not clear how the profit motive will result in higher-quality services in the child welfare arena. Additionally, child welfare advocates have continually emphasized the need for more cooperation and integration among service providers. Again, it is unclear how a greater emphasis on competition will increase cooperation. Further, each time a private provider loses a contract to another provider, there are likely to be changes and disruptions for families and children receiving services. Given the disruptions children in this system have already experienced, it is hard to understand how building yet more disruptions and inconsistency into the system will be a positive change. Finally, evaluative research must examine the impact of privatization on child welfare workers. It is very difficult to recruit and retain skilled workers if the workplace does not provide adequate pay, benefits, and job stability. Because private agencies compete for contracts to provide services and may lose these contracts, job stability is reduced. Further, when cost is a driving factor, an agency that provides lower pay and fewer benefits for its workforce, and therefore offers services more cheaply, is more likely to win the contract.

Strategies for Supporting Families More Effectively   Children who are victims of child abuse sometimes have co-occurring issues of disability and mental illness. They may also be involved with the juvenile justice system. Thus, under traditional categorical approaches to policy and services, a family could be involved with as many as 15 workers from different agencies at one time. Regardless of which system children and their families enter, policies must ensure that they receive home- and community-based options whenever possible and that the services are tailored to their individual needs. Foster parents should be trained, and services should be delivered by professionals with expertise and appropriate professional training.

It is important that policies and adequate funding be in place to provide services at the point that the child has been reported as endangered and the family is in crisis. Respite and crisis nurseries and family capacity building initiatives all hold promise. One example of such an initiative, authorized by the Affordable Care Act, is the Maternal, Infant, and Early Childhood Home Visiting Program (MIECHV). MIECHV is administered by the Health Resources and Services Administration (HRSA) and the ACF, both of which are part of the USDHHS. The MIECHV program looks to facilitate collaboration between different levels of government (federal, state, local) in implementing effective home visiting programs. The program provides grant funds to states and jurisdictions for the implementation of innovative evidence-based home visiting programs or the expansion and improvement of existing programs. Programs funded through MIECHV provide voluntary home visiting services to pregnant women and women with children up to five years of age who fall within identified priority populations including: low-income families; families with parents who have a history of substance abuse or need substance abuse treatment; and families with a history of child abuse or neglect or past interaction with the child welfare system. This program works to improve the identification, provision, and coordination of services for at-risk communities and families who live within these communities by targeting a variety of participant outcomes including: prevention of child injuries, child abuse or maltreatment; and reduction in crime or domestic violence. For more information on this innovative program visit the Maternal and Child Health Bureau homepage on the USDHHS website (http://mchb.hrsa.gov).

School-based policies and programs that help families remain intact and keep children safe through wrap-around services have also been developed. Research on the effectiveness of such models continues. Rigorous study of various models will be necessary to determine which interventions are most effective in achieving specific outcomes with different types of families. It is particularly important to make sure models are tested with families that represent the ethnic diversity found in our communities. You can find out more about evidence-based practices to address child abuse and neglect at the website, Child Welfare Information Gateway.

Long-term models of counseling and support may be necessary for families in "perpetual crisis." Families coping with serious ongoing problems such as substance abuse, extreme poverty, and chronic unemployment will likely need more than short-term services if their children are to remain safely at home and not re-enter the foster care system. High rates of system re-entry after children are returned to their families indicate that these families continue to be vulnerable. Some advocates have endorsed long-term, low-cost support strategies such as self-help and mutual aid groups. As with other policy approaches, these programs must be evaluated to assess their effectiveness.

Finally, the promotion of child welfare requires government, community, and workplace policies that support workers in their roles as parents and build on the strengths of families and kinship networks. Examples of such policies are paid family leave at childbirth, flexible working hours, resources for caregivers, and on-site day care at the workplace. Preventive programs that improve outcomes for children, such as Head Start and home nursing visits for high-risk infants provide needed resources that help families build on their strengths and, ultimately, flourish. Programs that have been shown to be effective should be expanded. Advocates have further recommended that when new children enter either the child welfare or the juvenile justice system, their cases should be reviewed in order to determine which preventive services failed to reach them (Briar-Lawson et al., 2009). That information can then be used to develop new outreach approaches.

Juvenile Justice From the Strengths Perspective

Although studies of change in juvenile crime rates indicate otherwise, public perceptions of increasing juvenile crime have triggered a policy response in some states that emphasizes punishment and retribution, rather than building on the concept that young people are developmentally different from adults and, therefore, more amenable to treatment and rehabilitation. Not surprisingly, then, programs aimed at prevention and early intervention receive insufficient funding and attention.

Scholars in a variety of disciplines have found that the prevalence of juvenile delinquency is reduced when resources are directed towards effective prevention and intervention programs. An important element in prevention strategies is academic success. Schools should be mandated to educate children, rather than enforce zero tolerance policies that funnel children out of the school environment for non-criminal behavior and into the juvenile justice system. Research has found the zero tolerance policies in schools and stiffer criminal penalties are not effective in reducing juvenile delinquency or recidivism rates among youth. There are fewer employment opportunities for youth who are forced out of school and into the juvenile justice system and the prevalence of delinquent behavior among these youth is higher than for those youth who remain in school (Ryan, 2013). NASW has also weighed in on this issue, stating that social workers and social work agencies need to be proactive in establishing a dialogue among local school districts and school social workers that focuses on reducing suspensions and providing more effective services to children who have educational disabilities (NASW, 2012c).

While we can all agree that children deserve a safe and stable learning environment while at school, the majority of suspensions, expulsions, and arrests are for non-violent offenses. Further, removing children who are troubled from school without treatment does not solve the problem but, instead, leads to the creation of more troubled children. Dismantling the school to the prison pipeline created by zero tolerance policies, which leads to the criminalization of children, and implementing school disciplinary polices that provide more supportive responses and services and help at-risk youth achieve their educational potential, need to be key priorities in juvenile justice reform efforts (Children's Defense Fund, 2012a).

The social work profession has adopted a clear position in support of evidence-based policies and intervention programs. The NASW "Policy Statement on Juvenile Justice and Delinquency Prevention," issued in 2012, supports policy changes that would establish community-based care and alternate options such as small correctional and treatment facilities for troubled youth and their families. It also recommends equal treatment regardless of socioeconomic status or race/ethnicity to correct the biases that result in the disproportionate incarceration of indigent and minority youth. Disproportionality continues throughout the system and results in disproportionate minority contact with the system even though the reauthorization of the federal Juvenile Justice and Delinquency Prevention Act in 2002 required states to decrease this contact. Further, NASW also recommends cross-system collaboration between individuals in the child welfare and juvenile justice systems to provide interdisciplinary services that effectively and efficiently address the needs of the significant number of children in the child welfare system, with histories of abuse and neglect, who crossover into the juvenile justice system. NASW also recommends identifying the impact of early childhood trauma—such as abuse or neglect—through the use of evidence-based tools, and minimizing duplication of services. Culturally competent services should be provided, and the use of evidence-based services and interventions should be encouraged. Additionally, NASW recommends that professional social workers with case management, intake, interviewing, cultural competency, and counseling skills be hired to work with youth and families in the juvenile justice system (NASW, 2012c).

Assessment and treatment tailored to the individual youth in the home community are much more likely to be effective than are generalized treatment programs in large facilities far from home. Effective post-release plans and after-care programs are also important. Policies and funding that make such treatment approaches viable are needed. One initiative currently implemented in a few places around the country is the Mental Health Court, which is designed to improve effectiveness of interventions in cases involving youths with mental illnesses or developmental disabilities who break the law. Specific treatment programs, usually involving families, are implemented after the young person's court appearance. The goal is to reduce recidivism by addressing problems through treatment programs. This is an example of developing programs to more effectively integrate the systems serving our youth (National Center for Juvenile Justice and Mental Health, 2005).

The guiding principle of the Office of Juvenile Justice and Delinquency Prevention (Office of Juvenile Justice and Delinquency Prevention, 2011a) "to empower communities and engage youth and families" is based on the understanding that the strengths, experiences, and goals of these individuals provide a critical perspective that needs to be taken into consideration. Social workers can advocate across the nation for establishing and fully funding juvenile delinquency prevention programs, diversion programs, and early intervention programs that incorporate the recommendations of youth and their families. Some of these programs could be implemented through policy changes at the agency level. Others would require state or federal legislative action to increase funding or establish new policy. However, the first step in establishing these programs is to make practitioners and policy makers aware of cost-effective approaches that have been successful in reducing juvenile crime. As a social worker, you can be part of that effort. For more information on juvenile justice and on specific promising programs, visit the websites of the Office of Juvenile Justice and Delinquency Prevention (www.ncmhjj.com) and the Center for the Study and Prevention of Violence, Blueprints for Violence Prevention.

The Role of Social Workers in the Child Welfare System

Although social work has traditionally been the lead profession in the child welfare system, the recruitment and retention of professionally trained social workers in this area has been declining over the past decade. High caseloads, low pay, and increasing interest on the part of social work students in more clinically oriented careers have contributed to decreased involvement of social workers in the child welfare system. In addition, some states have attempted to save money by reclassifying public child welfare positions so that people without social work degrees can deliver these services. Other states have privatized their foster care and adoption systems. As we saw in Chapter 4, these kinds of funding decisions have a substantial impact on the services that clients receive and ultimately on the lives of our most vulnerable families and children.

The NASW has issued a policy statement asserting that (1) Social work staff should be employed in any human service organization that deal with and provide services to children and their families, (2) an undergraduate or graduate degree in social work should be required for the delivery and administration of public child welfare services (NASW, 2012a). Social workers need to help educate the public and policy makers about the importance of public child welfare services so that these services are adequately provided and supported.

CONCLUSION

Despite the high correlation of poverty with child abuse, neglect, and involvement with the juvenile justice system, symptom-focused problem remediation, rather than efforts to secure an adequate income base and increase access to jobs that pay a living wage, remain the major focus of work with the families of these children. Despite widespread recognition that successfully raising children in today's society is difficult, U.S. child welfare policy only intervenes at the point of crisis, rather than ensuring that families have access to supportive services before problems develop. Because families are the primary providers for children, policies that support and strengthen families in that role are basic to promoting child welfare. Social workers need to partner with families to advocate for policies that build on family strengths. Respect for diversity in families, including immigrant and gay and lesbian families, should be reinforced in policy.

Vulnerable children continue to be marginalized. Children in our society do not have basic rights such as the right to not be physically punished in schools and the right to participate in decision making about their own lives. Corporal punishment in schools is legal in 20 states and its use with students with disabilities is particularly troubling. We need to end corporal punishment in our schools and encourage children's participation in decision making about their future, which includes involving them in helping to shape policies and services. At the international level, the U.S. needs to ratify the United Nations Convention on the Rights of the Child. This human rights instrument spells out the economic, civil, political, social, and cultural rights of children. Countries that ratify it are bound by international law and compliance is monitored by the United Nations (UN). Of the UN members, only Somalia, Sudan, and the U.S. have not yet ratified this important international convention, and Somalia has signed this document, which is the step before ratification. There is concern in the U.S. that ratification could preempt national control over domestic policy and interfere with states' rights in the area of child welfare. Nonetheless, NASW continues to advocate for ratification of this critical convention designed to protect all children.

Policies that create or promote adequate family income supports, a living wage, educational and training opportunities for parents, affordable high-quality health care, child care, and housing, help to protect our nation's children and to empower families. Such policies enhance family functioning and lessen the need for intensive intervention to alleviate problems. To learn more about research findings and advocacy initiatives to help level the playing field and ensure opportunities for all children, visit the website of the Children's Defense Fund (www. childrensdefense.org). Further, the variety of service systems that become involved in children's lives, including mental health, schools, child welfare, and juvenile justice, need to work together to provide holistic support for vulnerable children and their families. The media can help develop a public perception of the strengths and needs of the family that promotes support for such policies. Social workers can provide media representatives with ideas for stories that reinforce these views and urge media groups to present them. Topics include grassroots community development efforts to create jobs and initiatives to provide innovative programs for families through the schools. Social workers can also help to empower clients to tell their stories and to advocate for their families within the systems with which they interact. As always, social workers must be careful not to jeopardize their clients' confidentiality.

Many public and private organizations are working to improve outcomes for children. Several major foundations have supported innovation in child welfare services. This type of public–private partnership could help craft more effective child welfare policies. You can learn about foundations promoting the welfare of children by visiting the websites of the Annie E. Casey Foundation, the Edna McConnell Clark Foundation, and the W. K. Kellogg Foundation.

CATCHING UP WITH THE POLICY GROUP

Now, let us catch up with Kelli from the policy group as she begins her social work career in child welfare.

Kelli has just started work at a child welfare agency where she is a case worker in the kinship (relative) foster care program. In working with her clients Kelli has noticed many of the relative foster families that children have been placed with are in the same financial situation as the parents whose home the children were removed from. Many times it seems to Kelli that children are being taken from one impoverished family and being placed into another. Further, the lack of services and lower foster care payments provided to relative foster care families perpetuates the cycle of poverty, rather than building families up and strengthening their ability to care for the children placed in their care. Recently Kelli began working with a Native American child who is eligible for services under ICWA. Kelli has noticed

EXHIBIT 9.14

Kelli

there are many services that are provided to families and foster families under ICWA that are not available to those clients and foster families that are not eligible for ICWA. She thinks that some of the services provided under ICWA would also benefit non-Native American families. Kelli feels that current state policies governing relative foster care need to be revised, or new policies implemented that provide more effective and necessary services and higher reimbursement rates to relative foster families, but is not sure what she can do to bring attention to this issue, or even how to begin to bring about the changes needed.

Thinking back to the sample action plan, what might be some beginning advocacy steps Kelli can take in regards to this situation (i.e. contacting your state legislator, partnering with other child welfare agencies/advocacy organizations/coworkers and involving the target population—relative foster care families—in the process)? Look up the guidelines for kinship care (federal, state, state NASW chapter) in your state. How are they different for children in general foster care as compared to ICWA foster care families? What changes could be made to these guidelines to better support foster care families and the children in their care?

MAIN POINTS

- Historically, child welfare policies emphasized child saving rather than family strengthening. Currently, there is ongoing tension between the family's right to preservation and the public's desire to protect children and keep them safe.

- The demographics of children in the U.S. have changed in the past 40 years. Children under age 18 represent a smaller proportion of the U.S. population, the racial composition is shifting with an increase in Hispanic children and a decrease in white non-Hispanic children, and more children are living in single-parent households. These trends will continue.

- Due to the devastating impact poverty and economic crisis can have on vulnerable families, it is imperative that we continue to invest in and expand our child welfare system to better provide for and strengthen these families.

- The child welfare system promotes child well-being by focusing on safety, permanency, and family support when providing adoption services and services for families with reports of suspected abuse and neglect.

- Child maltreatment is harm caused by parents or primary caregivers and includes neglect, physical abuse, sexual abuse, and emotional abuse or neglect.

- The first major federal social policy specifically intended to prevent child maltreatment was the Child Abuse Prevention and Treatment Act of 1974 (CAPTA). This Act emphasized the need for increased state efforts in reporting and investigating child abuse and neglect.

- The juvenile justice system was established to promote rehabilitation of young offenders. The Juvenile Justice and Delinquency Prevention Act of 1974 was passed to prevent and control juvenile delinquency and improve the juvenile justice system.

- Legislative policies that have influenced the child welfare system include efforts to ensure that Native American children remain with their families and tribal communities, prohibition of race consideration in placement decisions of non-Native American children, and emphasis on family preservation and reunification, which was later tempered by emphasis on safety and permanency.

- Foster children who age-out of the system at age 18 face many barriers to successful transition to adulthood because they lack many of the supports other young people receive to help them make this transition.

- The Fostering Connections to Success and Increasing Adoptions Act, 2008 (Public Law 110–351) extends federal funding for youth in foster care to the age of 21. This legislation also creates a federally subsidized guardianship program for kinship providers; mandates, expands and increases adoption incentives; and provides new funding to promote permanency and additional funding for tribal child welfare services.

- Legislation for children with special needs emphasizes the importance of meeting education needs in the least restrictive environment and normalization. These civil rights protections have reshaped American public education, where many students with special learning needs are now in mainstream classrooms.

- It is necessary to address teen pregnancy prevention among youth in the child welfare system. Policies and programs are needed that provide the support and services necessary for teen parents to build the foundation and stability that supports them in becoming caring and effective parents to their children.

- Schools must be mandated to educate children, rather than enforce zero tolerance policies that funnel children out of the school environment for non-criminal behavior and into the juvenile justice system. Resources should instead be funneled to school social workers, counselors, and other mental health providers to focus on positive behavioral interventions and the identification and treatment of problem behaviors.

- The social work profession has been the lead profession in child welfare, but the prevalence of social work professionals in public child welfare is decreasing. The NASW asserts that families have the right to the delivery and administration of public child welfare services by trained social workers.

- Despite the high correlation of poverty with child abuse, neglect, and involvement with the juvenile justice system, symptom-focused problem remediation remains the major focus of work with the families of these children. The strengths perspective urges greater focus on wrap-around services and family capacity building, including attention to increasing income and job opportunities.

EXERCISES

1. Consider the Sanchez family.
   a. What types of supports do you believe the Sanchez grandparents need in order to keep their grandson in kinship care?
   b. What policies and programs are needed to make that support possible?
   c. What kinds of child welfare services would support possible reunification of their grandchild with his birth mother?
   d. What considerations should guide child welfare social workers engaged with the Sanchez family, as they consider their recommendations regarding the future of Joey's placement?

2. In the Washburn case, could Carla Washburn be paid to be a foster care provider for her grandchild in your state?

   a. If so, what requirements would she have to meet?

   b. What do you think would be the benefits and drawbacks of pursuing this form of funding to help cover costs of raising grandchildren for grandparents?

3. Consider the Riverton case. Although we have very little information about homeless children in Riverton, their numbers are undoubtedly growing as more and more families face job loss and home foreclosure. What policies and programs are in place in your city or town to help children who are homeless? Are these services integrated with the child welfare system?

4. Use the Internet and talk with your professors and with providers in your area to identify evidence-guided practices to help children who are homeless. Which of these strategies would you recommend for implementation in Riverton? Why do you recommend these strategies for Riverton?

5. Reviewing the Hudson City case, think about how U.S. policy tries to prevent the negative impacts of natural disasters, instead of just responding once they happen. What would a similar approach look like in the arena of child welfare? How can social policy prevent crisis in families, instead of just dealing with the effects?

6. Both the Indian Child Welfare Act (ICWA) and the Multi-Ethnic Placement Act (MEPA) were passed to address civil rights issues that influence out-of-home placement of children. Yet they prescribe very different criteria to consider when deciding on appropriate out-of-home placements for children. How do you account for those differences?

7. Use the Internet and talk to your classmates and professors to learn about areas of child welfare policy and programs in need of reform in your state. Identify specific steps you and your classmates could take to improve child welfare policy in your state or community. What stops you from taking action? Brainstorm strategies for overcoming those barriers.

8. What are your state's laws about adoption rights for LGBT parents? Are same-sex partners encouraged to adopt together? Does the state recruit foster parents equitably, including outreach to same-sex families? What is the legislative history around this policy in your state?

9. Recently some state legislators have proposed that a family's welfare benefits (i.e. TANF) be cut by 30 percent if one or more of their children is doing poorly in school. What action or steps could you take if this type of initiative was proposed in your state or brought before your state legislature? Think about the agencies in your state with which you can partner to prevent this type of legislation from being implemented.

CHAPTER 10

Health and Mental Health
Policies and Programs

Health, including mental health, is fundamental to well-being.
Dorothy Kennedy (Community Organizer)

The health care market is not a market at all and most patients are powerless buyers.
Stephen Brill (adapted)

Of all the forms of inequality, injustice in health care is the most shocking and inhumane.
Martin Luther King, Jr.

THE U.S. HEALTH CARE SYSTEM NEEDS FUNDAMENTAL CHANGE. The high cost of health care is overburdening American families and is a key driver of federal debt. Further, lack of access to affordable health care continues to plague our system. In 2010, comprehensive health care reform legislation was passed and is now being incrementally implemented. When fully in place, many more Americans will have access to health insurance. This legislation also reduces the risk that those who already have insurance will lose it. However, policy reforms to effectively address major issues including high health care costs and disparities in health outcomes have yet to be enacted.

Health and mental health policy and programs influence social workers in all areas of practice, and a basic understanding of these policies and programs and further needed reform will be of major benefit at both the professional and personal levels.

Changes resulting from the passage of the final comprehensive health reform law, the Patient Protection and Affordable Care Act of 2010 (Public Law 111–148), as modified by the Health Care and Education Affordability Reconciliation Act (H.R. 4872), are highlighted in this chapter and we will explore their implications for social workers. In the remainder of this chapter, we will also refer to these Acts as the Affordable Care Act (ACA) or the 2010 health care reform legislation. As is true for much of social welfare policy, the details of some aspects of this legislation remain to

EXHIBIT 10.1

Patients and Health Care Workers

be worked out in regulations and policy implementation, which, for this reform, will happen over the next several years. Given the devolution of some health care policy to the state level, implementation of the ACA is complicated by ongoing negotiations between the federal and state governments, as well as the layers of complexity added by changing health technology and evolving demographics.

Because many of the factors that shape health care also shape mental health practice, this chapter begins with an overview and evaluation of health care policies and programs. We will also examine mental health policy in detail and discuss possible directions for improvement of health and mental health policies and programs. The information in this chapter reflects the latest information available at time of publication. Make sure to consult the Internet resources provided throughout the chapter to access the most current information. For the latest information on health care reform legislation, go to www.healthcare.gov.

HEALTH CARE IN THE UNITED STATES

Our health is determined by many factors including access to health care as well as the social and economic factors that influence opportunities to be healthy. Social determinants of health are "the circumstances, in which people are born, grow up, live, work, and age, as well as the systems put in place to deal with illness" (CDC, 2013). As has been illustrated throughout this text, these circumstance are shaped in large part by economics, social position, social policies, and politics. Social determinants of health have a large impact on health disparities, such as higher rates of infant mortality and markedly different life expectancies for different racial and ethnic groups. These factors also influence access to health care. Historically, in the U.S., health care has been rationed based on a person's ability to pay. In other words, health care has been treated as a commodity much like other commodities in the marketplace, such as cars and houses. Not surprisingly, then, people with money traditionally receive better health care. Our experience in the U.S. has illustrated that, if left unchecked, the market provides health care primarily only for those with the means to pay for it and the ability to navigate the market structures. Even those with the means to pay often cannot access needed information and lack the technical expertise or personal power to shop for the best care. The health care market in the U.S. is not really a market at all (Brill, 2013). It is not realistic to expect buyers (a.k.a. patients), especially when they are gravely ill or struggling with chronic conditions and significant social impairments to good health, to somehow acquire sufficient information to determine what tests they need, which hospital has the most reasonable charges for the tests, how to judge quality, and which doctor can oversee all this care most economically and competently. In fact, patients are often powerless buyers.

Significantly, most developed countries have chosen to treat health care not as a commodity but as a social utility. That is, basic health care is paid for publicly and is available to everyone as a right of citizenship. The recognition that people need to be healthy if they are to be productive citizens, and that untreated health problems can be dangerous to fellow citizens and corrosive to society, underpins this approach to health care. Further, many of these countries are very competitive in the global economy, and universal health care is viewed as an essential ingredient in building a productive workforce. Although these countries also ration care, this rationing is done in a variety of ways, which may include creating waiting lists for elective surgery, developing preferred protocols for dealing with specific conditions, and restricting referrals to specialists. After passing their form of comprehensive national health reform legislation, these nations have continued to work to improve their systems and to manage the ongoing tension between controlling costs and enhancing health care. As Reid concluded after examining the wide variety of approaches to health care internationally, it comes down to a moral question; most developed countries have answered the inherent moral question by deciding that all citizens should have basic health care (Reid, 2009).

For people who can afford health care, the advanced medical technology available in the U.S. is excellent. Many people in the U.S. receive adequate health care. However, even for those people who have insurance, the rationing of services by health maintenance organizations (HMOs), decreasing benefits, and spiraling costs have compromised the quality of health care they can afford. Just because you have health insurance, you are not guaranteed access to adequate health care. This issue of access to quality care will be very important as the people newly insured under the ACA attempt to access care in a system where health care providers are in short supply in many areas.

In the U.S., people who are insured receive their health insurance through either the private or the public (government) sector. Private health insurance includes employment-based insurance and direct-purchase insurance. Government health insurance includes Medicaid, Medicare, the Children's Health Insurance Program, and military health coverage. Some people have multiple forms of insurance. For instance, they may receive Medicare in conjunction with employment-based insurance, or they receive Medicaid and Medicare benefits simultaneously.

People who do not have either private or government health insurance fit into the category of "uninsured." Over 48.6 million people in the U.S., about 15.7 percent of the population, had no health insurance in 2011. Analysis of current health care statistics indicates that people in the U.S. with incomes below the poverty line are much more likely to have no health insurance at all. For example, children under 18 living in poverty were much more likely to be uninsured when compared to all children (Federal Interagency Forum on Child and Family Statistics, 2012). Health insurance coverage also varies substantially by race and ethnicity (DeNavas-Walt, Proctor, and Smith, 2012). For example, approximately 11 percent of white, non-Hispanic Americans were uninsured in 2011, compared to 19.5 percent of African Americans, 30.1 percent of Hispanics (any race), almost 25 percent of American Indians or Alaska Natives, and 16.8 percent of Asians. Of immigrants who are non-citizens, 45 percent were uninsured. Since 2000, the percentage uninsured has increased for all racial and ethnic groups. Social risk factors such as low income, English as a second language, and minority group membership are associated with decreased access to adequate health care and, ultimately, with poorer health outcomes and early death for many of the people whom social workers serve. These outcomes illustrate the power of social determinants of health. If you want the latest information on the uninsured or any of a wealth of other health-related statistics, visit the National Center for Health Statistics at www.cdc.gov/nchs/.

With the passage of the Patient Protection and Affordable Care Act of 2010 and the changes contained in the Health Care & Education Affordability Reconciliation Act, the U.S. joined the community of nations that ensure health care as a basic right for most of their people, rather than a privilege for some. While falling short of universal health care, this legislation is fundamentally changing many elements of our health care system. Some of the elements of health care reform took effect in 2010. However, other elements are to be phased in over four years. Provisions and effective dates are detailed later in the chapter.

Before health care reform legislation was passed in 2010, publicly supported health care was guaranteed without regard to income only for people age 65 and over and for people with certain disabilities who were eligible for Medicare. This means that some people 65 and over who were not eligible for Medicare, and most people younger than 65, did not qualify for publicly supported health care. Although many people receive health insurance as a benefit through their place of employment, many do not, and this system continues to erode. Between 2000 and 2012, the percentage of employers who offered health insurance fell from 68 percent to 61

EXHIBIT 10.2

Health Care Bill Passes in America

percent (KFF, 2013). Among those employers still offering health insurance, employee cost requirements continue to increase. This means that many middle-class Americans have seen their employer-provided health insurance disappear or become much more expensive. A major goal of the health reform legislation is to not only expand coverage to the uninsured but also to stabilize and strengthen our current employer-provided health insurance system. This objective has implications not only for individual access to health care but also for employer cost control and international competitiveness. Changes to help accomplish this include aiding small businesses in providing coverage for their employees and increasing competition for better prices. Passage of this law means that many more Americans will be guaranteed access to health insurance even if they are not old or impoverished.

The High Cost of Health Care

The federal Centers for Medicare and Medicaid Services (CMS) reported that U.S. health care spending grew 3.9 percent in 2011 and national health expenditures were $2.7 trillion or $8,680 per person and accounted for 17.9 percent of Gross Domestic Product (GDP) (CMS, 2012b). This was a sizeable increase from 2007 when per capita (person) health spending in the U.S. was $7,290, especially considering the economic downturn and resultant very small cost increases in most sectors of the economy between 2007 and 2011. U.S. per capita expenditures are far higher than other countries (Organization for Economic Co-operation and Development (OECD), 2012c).The latest data currently available which compare health care expenditures in the U.S. with other countries is for 2010. Health spending accounted for 17.6 percent of GDP in the U.S. in 2010 and was by far the highest among the most developed nations in the world. Following the U.S. were the Netherlands (at 12.0 percent of GDP), and France and Germany both at 11.6 percent of GDP. All three of these countries provide universal primary health care to their population. In comparing per person spending in 2010, the U.S. spent over twice as much as European countries such as France, Sweden, and the United Kingdom (OECD, 2012c). The OECD produces a wealth of international policy, program, and outcomes comparisons, and many of their resources are accessible at the OECD website (www.oecd.org).

However, even though the U.S. spends the most money on health care, some of our basic health outcomes are not as favorable as those of countries that spend much less. For example, the projected life expectancy at birth in the U.S. for children born in 2010 was 76 years for males and 81.1 years for females (OECD, 2012b). In contrast, children born in Japan in 2010 had a projected life expectancy at birth of 79.6 years for men and 86.4 years for women. Japan, Spain, and Switzerland were the three countries with the highest life expectancy (OECD, 2012c); they all provide universal primary health insurance and spent less on health care than the U.S. Similarly, infant mortality rates in the U.S. are among the highest for the industrialized countries. In 2011, the infant mortality rate in the U.S. was 6 per 1,000 infants. In contrast, infant mortality is the lowest in some of the Nordic countries including Iceland and Finland, and in Japan, with rates between 2.2 and 2.3 deaths per 1,000 live births (OECD, 2012b). Factors other than health care, such as rates of poverty, rates of smoking, obesity, exposure to environmental pollutants, unsafe work places, and lack of access to healthy food, also influence these outcomes. Although differences in definitions and how statistics are determined from country to country may account for some of the variation, it is clear that these health outcomes are not as positive for people in the U.S. as in many other countries. Additionally, we have fewer physicians per capita (2.4 per 1,000 people) than most developed countries, contributing to access problems, particularly in some rural and underserved communities. The same countries that provide universal health care also have, in many cases, more generous maternal leave policies, better income-support programs, stronger disease prevention policies, and a more vigorous labor protection system, all of which can also contribute to outcomes such as lower infant mortality and longer life expectancy. Further, in some countries, free health care for all citizens is provided directly through public clinics rather than using an insurance model where the government provides public insurance rather than direct health care. This approach can promote superior access by reducing the complexity of the system through which consumers are expected to access care.

Although spending on publicly funded health care in the U.S. accounts for only a portion of total health care spending, publicly funded health care costs are very hard to control. Unlike income-maintenance programs, for which the government can calculate the annual cost per person for Social Security retirement benefits or Supplemental Security Income (SSI) benefits, federal and state policy makers do not know how much health care an individual eligible for Medicaid, Medicare, or Children's Health Insurance Program (CHIP) will actually need. They also cannot know what costly but effective new medical technologies or medications may be developed in the coming year, or how the supply of health care providers may impact costs. Thus, predicting and controlling the costs of health care are very difficult for public policy makers, particularly when there are multiple private as well as public insurers. However, some countries such as Japan do a much better job of controlling health care costs. Like the U.S., Japan has a fee-for-service health care system in which there is unrestricted access to specialists and advanced medical technology is widely available. However, health care spending as a percent of GDP has increased at a much slower rate than in the U.S. This has been achieved, not by restricting access but, rather, by aggressively regulating health care prices for virtually all health care providers (Squires, 2012). There are a variety of approaches to controlling health care costs that can produce high-quality health care at markedly less cost than the current U.S. health care system.

Health care is one of the largest industries in the U.S. In 2011, health care provided 11.7 million jobs for wage and salary workers (KFF, 2012d). Furthermore, even greater growth is projected for the health care sector as the baby boom generation ages and needs more health care and the ACA is fully implemented. When we examine current public social policies and programs that support health care in the U.S., the interaction of demographics, economics, ideology and values, social movements, and history becomes evident. We have discussed these factors in detail in earlier chapters. In this section, we will examine some of them briefly as they specifically pertain to health care.

History and Background of Health Care Programs

Prior to the 20th century, the involvement of the federal government in health care was limited to care for military personnel and veterans. At the state level, all states had established some type of department of public health by 1909. In 1943, the Internal Revenue Service ruled that employees did not have to pay taxes on their employers' contributions to group health benefits. Because there were war-related wage controls at this time, companies needed to find ways other than salary increases to recruit and retain talent. This ruling made offering health benefits an attractive option. However, as discussed in Chapter 4, this tax break also represented a tax expenditure. The result was that the U.S. put tax dollars that would have been collected by the government into employer-based health insurance. This approach reflected the U.S.'s economic preference for private initiatives and its continued reliance on a workforce approach for the provision of non-stigmatized benefits. This policy preference has implications today, as individuals who experience unemployment, work part time, or work in marginalized industries are more likely to be uninsured.

Growing Federal Involvement in Health Care   In 1946, Congress passed the Hill–Burton Act, which provides public funds for hospital construction. In return, hospitals are to provide some free or reduced-charge care for indigent citizens (Division of Facilities Compliance and Recovery, 2010). In fact, concerns about reimbursement for the care that some hospitals were providing for people who could not pay has created a continuous impetus for legislation to provide federal funds to help impoverished families pay for health care. In addition, the need for a productive labor force and healthy recruits for the military, along with humanitarian concerns and fear of epidemics, contributed to growing support for a limited public entitlement to health care. Moreover, as longevity increased in the 20th century, a respected political constituency consisting of older adults grew in sufficient numbers to press successfully for policy change. This group helped get Social Security legislation passed in 1935. The exclusion of health care from the initial Social Security legislation illustrates the deep divisions and concerns about federal involvement in health care that, to an extent, were reflected in the 2010 debate. Older adults as well as labor unions and many other advocacy groups later helped press for the addition of Medicare (a program primarily for older adults) and Medicaid (a categorical program for people with very low incomes) in 1965. Recall that we discussed the genesis of these programs in Chapter 3.

Medicare, Medicaid, and Civil Rights   President Johnson signed Medicare into law in 1965. At that time, many hospitals in the U.S. were racially segregated. The new law specified that hospitals receiving federal Medicare dollars must be integrated. Advocates pressing for the end to racial discrimination in health care gained ground when the Social Security Administration (SSA) required hospitals applying for Medicare certification to prove they were not engaging in discrimination. This is an excellent example of how executive branch action can be used to implement new social policies that may be too contentious to get passed by the legislative branch. Initially there was strong resistance, but shortly after these Medicare regulations were implemented, the desegregation of the nation's hospitals was essentially complete. These Medicare regulations and the determination of SSA staff that they be enforced have been credited with integrating southern hospitals (Quadagno, 2000). This action created an historical precedent for using Medicare as a vehicle to expand civil rights for oppressed groups. A similar approach was used in April of 2010 when President Obama issued a memorandum on the subject, *Respecting the Rights of Hospital Patients to Receive Visitors and to Designate Surrogate Decision Makers for Medical Emergencies*. This memorandum required hospitals to give same-sex couples the right to be with a partner who is sick or dying. The memorandum applied to all hospitals that receive Medicare or Medicaid funding—nearly every hospital in the country. The memo also affirmed the rights of all patients to name anyone to be a surrogate decision maker, including a friend or a distant relative, and directed hospitals to follow patients' advance directives. This means that older adults' written directives concerning treatment they do and do not want at the end of life, which were not always followed in the past, will be more likely to be honored. The Department of Health and Human Services was directed to write the rules necessary to implement these requirements. Some experienced advocates said they had never thought of using Medicare and Medicaid funding as a tool to expand civil rights. Hopefully your familiarity with history and health care policy will mean you will be an advocate who *is* able to make those kinds of connections as you work for social justice. Although Medicaid and Medicare were important steps forward in securing health care for more people in the U.S., financing these programs in the face of rapidly rising costs continues to be a major challenge. So that you will more clearly understand options for controlling health care costs in these programs as well as in the new programs that are included in the health care reform legislation of 2010, in the next sections I will review some history and background on strategies that have been used thus far. I will also discuss incentives inherent in managed care and how they affect the health care delivery system, including social workers working as providers.

Background on Approaches to Health Care Finance and Cost Control Both Medicaid and Medicare were originally structured to be retrospective fee-for-service systems. In these systems, the government acts as insurer and reimburses private health care providers for services rendered. This approach is termed a retrospective payment system because the private provider submits a bill after services have been rendered and the insurer then reimburses the provider. This approach creates incentives to provide additional services while offering no incentives to control costs. In fact, it may lead to *overservice*, that is, performing tests or procedures that might not be necessary. Further, particularly in the field of mental health, providers may profit more if their clients do not improve or if the client is served in a more restrictive and more costly setting than they really need, such as a hospital or nursing facility. It is sometimes referred to as the "you spend it, we send it" approach to public health care financing. A reliance on this system resulted in the acceleration of health care costs, prompting the government as well as private insurers to experiment with a variety of cost control strategies. Many of these strategies involved prospective payment, in which insurers determine ahead of time the average cost for a procedure, such as an appendectomy or uncomplicated childbirth, in a previous year, add an inflation factor, and then prospectively (before treatment) set an amount they will reimburse the providers. For example, hospitals are reimbursed based on fixed rates for specific diagnoses or diagnosis-related groups (DRGs), regardless of the actual length of the hospital stay or the particular services provided to a specific person. If the hospital is able to complete treatment and discharge the patient in less than the average time and for less than average costs, they profit. However, the hospital must provide adequate care and patients can appeal premature discharge.

This same prospective approach may be used to determine the average annual costs, or perhaps the amount that would cover the costs, for 75 percent of healthy people in a certain age range. Public and private insurers can use such an approach to decide how much to pay a health maintenance organization (HMO) to care for each such person enrolled in its system for the year. HMOs offer comprehensive health care to enrolled members. Members, their employers, or the government prepay a fixed amount to enroll for a specified time, typically one year. Health care services are offered through designated providers who contract with the HMO. HMOs provide managed care.

HMOs assume responsibility for the health care services and the costs of care for their members. Under such a capitated approach, the HMO or managed care provider is expected to provide all elements of health care covered in the enrollee's contract in return for a fixed monthly or annual payment per person enrolled. The same basic techniques can be used to determine prospective payment amounts and institute prospective payment systems for various high-risk groups served through Medicare and Medicaid, such as older adults with disabilities or people with developmental disabilities or mental illness.

In contrast to the incentive for overservice inherent in the fee-for-service retrospective approach, the incentive in prospective payment systems is for *underservice*. Under managed care, the insurer controls the person's health care. If services can be provided more cheaply than the prospective payment rate, or avoided completely, then the provider makes a profit. The role of physicians in these systems is to act as gatekeepers, manage care more cost-effectively, and control access to costly specialists and services. Incentives and disincentives for physicians based on how they well they perform this role might be part of the managed care system. Managed care also typically involves administrative oversight to determine whether treatments recommended by physicians are necessary and should be approved. Further, managed care generally does not cover services provided outside the network of doctors under contract to the HMO.

Problems in access to service and quality of service can be expected to increase given these new incentives. To address these problems, statements of patient rights need to be developed and enforced. Some progress has been made in this area. For example, some states have passed laws that bar gag clauses in HMO contracts with health care providers. Gag clauses prohibit physicians from telling patients about expensive or alternative options not covered by their HMOs. The 2010 health care reform legislation also contains additional consumer protection.

Patients also need effective appeals processes. Additional public and private oversight and appeals procedures that are clear and easy to use can help protect patients. Further, the effectiveness of managed care approaches in holding down costs when examined in light of quality concerns and increased bureaucracy is certainly not clear-cut.

Further, financial incentives in managed care should be examined for how they do or do not reward preventive initiatives, particularly ones that consider the context of disease development, such as rates of smoking, obesity, or exposure to carcinogens for people in the managed care catchment areas. Financial incentives can be restructured when public funds are used to purchase health care from managed care entities. Incentivizing cost-effective preventive care can help hold down health care costs and increase health.

Yet another approach to restructuring incentives, *payment bundling*, is currently being examined. In this approach, hospitals and physicians are paid a lump sum for an episode of care (payments are "bundled"), rather than paid separately for each service provided. In the case of a knee replacement, for example, the payment would go to one entity, such as a hospital. The hospital would have to form a partnership with surgeons and rehabilitation providers and then divide the bundled payment so everyone gets a portion. Hopefully this would create the same incentives for all partners to provide services that would not result in additional hospitalizations or the need for more expensive care. Potentially, this integrated approach to services, particularly when coupled with attention to use of evidence-based practice and cost penalties for readmissions shortly following discharge, will help control medical costs and patients will receive higher quality and more coordinated services. It is vital that we identify and implement effective methods of controlling cost while improving quality.

Medical Savings Accounts (MSAs) are another health care innovation that has been promoted as a way to hold down costs. MSA strategies allow people who are self-employed or working for small businesses to place their own pre-tax money in an account that can then be used to pay for routine or long-term care. Additionally, some companies offer Flexible Spending Accounts which also allow employees to place their own pre-tax dollars in an account that can be used for health care, as yet another benefit in addition to adequate and affordable health insurance. Because an individual pays directly for health care with their own funds, he/she will presumably be more conscious of costs and more likely to shop for cheaper care. However, when an individual MSA is the only health benefit provided, the reality is that the insurance companies strike special deals with hospitals and providers and the individual will typically pay higher prices. Companies may use MSAs as an excuse to retreat from providing employer-based health care, leaving individuals vulnerable if health care costs exceed their savings. Further, such an approach could lead to a privatized insurance model for healthy and/or wealthy citizens, leaving lower-income and less healthy people in the traditional insurance pool to pay higher premiums. Because insurance premiums are based on the expected cost of taking care of the people in the insured pool or group, when healthy people leave the pool, average costs per person, and thus premiums, inevitably rise. This is also another example of risk-shifting from shared group risk to the individual.

Health Reform in the 1990s   A major initiative by the Clinton administration to institute national health care insurance failed in 1994. Nevertheless, some limited health care reforms were enacted during the 1990s. For example, the Health Insurance Portability and Accountability Act (HIPAA) of 1996 (Public Law 104–191) provides that workers must be able to continue purchasing their health insurance if they lose their jobs or change jobs. However, the cost is often prohibitively expensive, especially for someone unemployed. Other HIPAA provisions also address the privacy and security of health data. Additionally, Congress passed the Mental Health Parity Act in 1996, which was later strengthened and expanded by the Paul Wellstone and Pete Domenici Mental Health Parity and Addiction Equity Act of 2008. In 1997, the State Children's Health Insurance Program was created as part of the Balanced Budget Act of that year. We discuss these Acts in detail, later in this chapter.

2010 National Health Care Reform

Many presidents have tried to enact national health insurance. President Franklin D. Roosevelt attempted to include some kind of national health insurance program in Social Security in 1935. President Harry S. Truman championed a national health care insurance program. Every Democratic president and some Republican presidents since then have wanted to provide affordable coverage to more Americans. In 1965, the Medicare and Medicaid programs were enacted but still did not cover most Americans. When the ACA, as modified by the Health Care and Education Affordability Reconciliation Act, was signed into law in 2010, a task was accomplished that had eluded several past administrations. The passage of this law means that more Americans will receive health care even if they are not old or poor. Prior to passage of the ACA over 15 percent of the population had no insurance. After all provisions of the ACA are in effect, approximately 92 percent of the American population will have insurance. However, this law does not provide universal coverage (more than 30 million residents will still be uninsured), nor is there a "single-payer" plan in the law. A single-payer health care plan is one where the government pays for all health care and thereby is able to control costs. Coverage provided through the ACA is outlined in later sections of this chapter.

The 2012 Supreme Court Decision   Soon after it was signed into law, the constitutionality of the ACA was challenged in the Supreme Court. The subsequent ruling upheld the constitutionality of major parts of ACA, including the individual mandate requiring purchase of health insurance. However, the mandate for states to expand their Medicaid program to cover additional populations was struck down. This means that states now have the option of whether to implement the Medicaid expansion. Before the Supreme Court decision which struck down the Medicaid expansion mandate, it was projected that 94 percent of the American population would be insured but that figure has now dropped two percentage points (3 million fewer individuals will be covered). This also means that access to health care for low-income families will be very different depending on the state in which they live. However, all citizens, no matter what state they live in, will be paying the extra federal taxes to cover the cost in those states that decide to take part in the expansion. This state Medicaid expansion is entirely paid for by the federal government until 2016. After 2016, the federal cost share slowly drops until 2020 when the federal government will still be paying 90 percent of the costs of expansion and will continue to do so in subsequent years (KFF, 2012c).

Issues Left Unaddressed   Although this legislation is a giant step forward, there are many issues left unaddressed. Initially, the ACA contained provisions for long-term care insurance, termed Community Living Assistance Services and Supports (CLASS). However, it has already been determined that the long-term care component will not be implemented. This leaves both young and old vulnerable to the costs of long-term care and exposes the U.S. health care system, particularly Medicaid, to considerable liability. Many people do not realize that Medicare does not cover long-term care until faced with paying these extremely high costs out of pocket. Lack of affordable long-term care insurance leaves a gaping hole in our health care system which still must be addressed. Also, additional measures to control rising health care costs will still be needed, and approximately 8 percent of the population will still be uninsured after the ACA is fully implemented. Further, numerous social determinants of health are not addressed by the ACA. The ACA will not eliminate many of the factors that contribute to health disparities in our country, such as dangerous working conditions, unhealthy living quarters, unequal access to health care information, lack of sufficient numbers of competent providers in low-income

EXHIBIT 10.3

University of Kansas Social Work Students Press for Health Care Reform

areas, inadequate access to affordable healthy food, and few providers from minority groups. These issues will need to be addressed via employment policy, housing policy, and educational policy. As is the case in many social policy arenas, the effectiveness of policies in one area is greatly influenced by policies in other domains.

MAJOR HEALTH CARE POLICIES AND PROGRAMS

Major public health programs in the U.S. include Medicaid, Medicare, and the Children's Health Insurance Program (CHIP). In the next segment of this chapter, we discuss these programs as well as the policies that govern them. Among the specific topics we examine are differences in eligibility rules, service delivery systems, and financing. Of particular significance are the effects of these policies on the people who receive the benefits. Further, each of these programs been changed by the 2010 health care reform legislation as well as by the shifts in the health care system brought by changing expectations from consumers, evolving demographics, and emerging health needs. These changes are briefly identified as each policy and program is discussed. This chapter section ends with a more detailed discussion of the entire health care reform package and how it will be financed.

Medicaid

Title XIX of the Social Security Act established a program with the goal of providing health insurance and medical assistance to families with low incomes and few assets, and to certain individuals with disabilities. The program, known as Medicaid, was established in 1965 and is jointly funded by the federal and state governments. Medicaid, which is a means-tested program, is the largest program that provides medical and health-related services to America's poorest families and children. Medicaid accounts for about one-sixth of total health care spending in the country. Over 57 million low-income Americans receive Medicaid. Almost one-third of children receive Medicaid or the CHIP. Pregnant women who meet income guidelines can also receive Medicaid, and about four of every 10 births are paid for through Medicaid. There is evidence of significant positive outcomes resulting from Medicaid's provision of health care access to these vulnerable populations. Expansions of Medicaid eligibility for low-income children in the late 1980s and early 1990s led to a 5.1 percent reduction in childhood deaths. Also, expansions of Medicaid coverage for low-income pregnant women led to an 8.5 percent reduction in infant mortality, and a 7.8 percent reduction in the incidence of low birth weight (CBPP, 2013c).

Over half of Medicaid enrollees are children. However, roughly two-thirds of Medicaid spending is attributable to elderly and disabled beneficiaries, even though they make up just a quarter of all Medicaid enrollees. Medicaid is the largest single funding source in the U.S. for nursing homes and for facilities for people with developmental disabilities, paying for over 60 percent of nursing facility residents nationwide (KFF, 2012f). Many nursing home residents become impoverished because of the very high costs of nursing home care and thus become eligible for Medicaid in old age. This speaks to the need to address long-term care costs, as described above. Medicaid also helps shore up the gaps in Medicare for low-income older adults and is the largest single provider of medical care for people with Acquired Immune Deficiency Syndrome (AIDS). Exhibit 10.4 illustrates the percentage of Medicaid enrollees from each age group.

Older adults as well as younger people who would be eligible for Medicaid if they were in institutions can be served in the community via a Medicaid waiver. Waivers allow states to disregard certain requirements—for example, service must be provided in a Medicaid-certified facility—for people with severe disabilities. Waivers have made home- and community-based services available for some older adults and younger people with severe disabilities. Nevertheless, unlike nursing home care, these services are not an entitlement, and a number of states have long waiting lists.

Although Medicaid is supposed to make health care available to poor people, not all people who fall below the federal poverty level (FPL) have been eligible for Medicaid. Rather, recipients must meet specific eligibility criteria and many states set the income level for Medicaid far below the FPL. Moreover, many potentially eligible people either are unaware that they might be eligible or feel it would be too stigmatizing to admit they are impoverished in order to get help. Even when people do

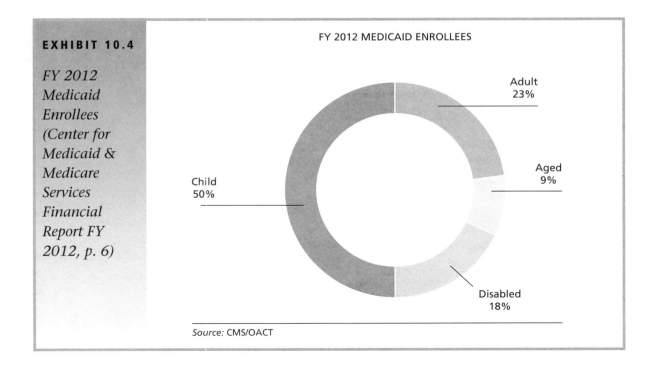

EXHIBIT 10.4

FY 2012 Medicaid Enrollees (Center for Medicaid & Medicare Services Financial Report FY 2012, p. 6)

FY 2012 MEDICAID ENROLLEES

Adult
23%

Aged
9%

Child
50%

Disabled
18%

Source: CMS/OACT

apply, they are often met with complex application forms and procedures, requirements to first spend through any savings they had accumulated, and long waits for eligibility determination. Despite these limitations, were it not for Medicaid, the number of uninsured people would be much higher. As people have lost their jobs and, therefore, health insurance during the economic downturn, Medicaid enrollment across the country has grown. Medicaid is an entitlement program, and it is this characteristic that enables Medicaid to grow, in order to cover more individuals during times of greater economic need. Because Medicaid costs are shared between states and the federal government, states also experienced spending growth. To buffer the effect of the economic crisis, enhanced federal assistance for state Medicaid programs was included in the $787 billion economic stimulus package enacted in February 2009 (CBO, 2009). However, the accelerated growth rate in Medicaid began to slow in 2011 and per beneficiary growth decreased in 2012 (USDHHS, 2012a).

Mandatory and Optional Coverage   Currently, to be eligible for federal funds, states are required to cover certain groups who meet financial criteria and also belong to one of Medicaid's categorically eligible groups: children; pregnant women; older adults (65+); adults with dependent children; and people with severe disabilities. States must provide Medicaid coverage for most individuals who receive federally assisted income-maintenance payments and for related groups that are not receiving cash payments. The following are examples of such groups:

- low-income families with children who meet eligibility criteria for State AFDC benefits that were in effect in 1996;
- SSI recipients;
- infants born to Medicaid-eligible pregnant women;
- recipients of adoption assistance and foster care under Title IV-E of the Social Security Act;
- children under the age of six and pregnant women with a family income below 133 percent of the FPL;
- children ages 16 to 19 with family incomes up to 100 percent of FPL.

States also have the option to provide Medicaid coverage for other "categorically needy" groups such as:

- infants up to the age of one and pregnant women not covered under the mandatory rules but whose family incomes are below 185 percent of the FPL (actual percentage to be set by each state);
- certain aged or blind adults or adults with disabilities who have incomes above those that require mandatory coverage but below the FPL;

- children under age 21 who meet income and resources requirements for TANF but who otherwise are not eligible for TANF;

- institutionalized individuals whose income and resources fall below specified limits;

- persons receiving care under home- and community-based services waivers;

- recipients of state supplementary payments.

States are required to cover the mandatory groups up to federal minimum income thresholds and are not allowed to cap enrollment or establish waiting lists. However, they do have some discretion in determining the groups that are eligible for Medicaid as well as the financial criteria for eligibility as outlined below. In addition, states have the option to implement a "medically needy" program. This option empowers states to extend Medicaid eligibility to additional qualified persons whose incomes are too high for them to be included under the mandatory or categorically needy groups. It allows these people to "spend down" to Medicaid eligibility by incurring medical and/or remedial care expenses, thereby reducing their incomes to a level below the maximum allowed by their states' Medicaid plans. Older adults and people with disabilities who need long-term care benefit from this option in many states. You can find detailed information on eligibility, covered services, and how to help clients access benefits by going to your state's official website and searching for Medicaid eligibility. Take a look at your state asset limits. In some states you cannot have more than $1,000 in total liquid assets in order to qualify for Medicaid. You can also find out if your state has reduced Medicaid coverage given current budget constraints.

Variations Among States   The standard Medicaid benefits provide specified groups of recipients with access to medical care, including long-term care in nursing facilities and institutions. Within broad federal guidelines, each of the states

- establishes its own eligibility standards;

- determines the type, amount, duration, and scope of services;

- sets the rate of payment for services; and,

- administers its own program.

Thus, the Medicaid program varies considerably from state to state as well as within each state over time. Each state designates an agency to administer its Medicaid program. Local branches of that agency typically determine eligibility. Social workers in hospitals and nursing facilities often assist medically needy people in applying for Medicaid, and some non-profit organizations have undertaken Medicaid and children's health insurance outreach efforts in an attempt to bring more eligible individuals into the coverage. Public and private providers are then paid for costs incurred for covered services. You can find out about how your state's health care spending for Medicaid and other public programs compares to that of other states by going to the Kaiser Family Foundation website (www.kff.org) and looking at State Health Facts. However, requirements will change in 2014, in ways that will likely affect states' program requirements and participation, and these changes will be detailed in the discussion of health care reform later on in the chapter.

The federal and state governments share the cost of Medicaid services via a matching formula that is adjusted annually. The federal matching rate, which is inversely related to a state's average per capita income level, can range from 50 percent to 74 percent. States are allowed to establish their own service reimbursement policies within federal guidelines. In FY 2012, Medicaid costs totaled $452.5 billion with the federal share accounting for $260.1 billion (CMS, 2012b). Some states also have their own state-funded programs to provide medical services to people not covered by Medicaid. See Exhibit 10.5 for a summary of Medicaid based on the basic policy analysis framework outlined earlier in this text.

Policy Goals	To provide health insurance to low-income people (includes people who are aged, disabled, blind, or members of families with dependent children) to improve access to medical and health care.	**EXHIBIT 10.5** *Medicaid, 1965*
Benefits or Services Provided	Health insurance for medical and health-related services. Pays for nursing facility care for low-income residents.	
Eligibility Rules	Low-income people with minimal assets that fall within the state's "categorically needy" groups.	
Service Delivery System	State development and administration under federal regulations. Federal oversight by the Centers for Medicaid and Medicare Services. Eligible recipients choose doctors or providers in the private or public sector who accept Medicaid to deliver the health services.	
Financing	Joint funding by the federal and state governments based on the state's average per capita income level.	

Medicaid and the PRWORA In 1996, the Personal Responsibility and Work Opportunity Reconciliation Act (PRWORA) decoupled Medicaid from public assistance and allowed states more latitude to expand Medicaid assistance to people in poverty who were not formerly covered. A new Medicaid coverage category for low-income families with children was established under Section 1931, which maintained the AFDC eligibility criteria that were in place in 1996. However, with the passage of the PRWORA, eligibility for Medicaid was separated from eligibility for income-support programs. As a result, Medicaid eligibility and termination were no longer automatically determined based on eligibility for cash assistance through TANF. Nevertheless, many families who were still eligible for Medicaid lost their benefits because they were ruled ineligible for cash assistance (Provost and Hughes, 2000). Families who receive TANF benefits are no longer guaranteed Medicaid, and states have the option of using one application for the two programs or using separate applications, which creates complications for applicants.

The PRWORA also changed Medicaid and SSI eligibility for legal immigrants. Immigrants who arrived after August 22, 1996, are ineligible for Medicaid and SSI benefits until they have resided in the country as a lawful permanent resident for five years, except in the case of emergency care (CMS, 2010). As the percentage of non-citizens in the U.S. grew particularly during the late 1990s, these restrictive eligibility rules contributed to increases in the uninsured population.

As a result of the PRWORA and a stronger economy, including lower rates of unemployment and fewer people living in poverty, Medicaid enrollment dropped from 31.5 million in 1996 to 27.9 million in 1999 (Provost and Hughes, 2000). Enrollment then increased drastically in the following years. This increase was fueled by the weak economy and by increased efforts in some states to enroll eligible people in Medicaid programs (Levit et al., 2004). Medicaid rolls rose even more quickly as a result of the recession that began in 2007 but the rate of growth began slowing in 2011. Beginning in 2014, Medicaid coverage is to be significantly expanded under the ACA in states that accept Medicaid expansion. Specific elements of this expansion are examined in a later segment of the chapter. However, for families receiving TANF as well as for other low-income families, the effect of the expansion will be that they will still be eligible for Medicaid until their income is at least 138 percent of poverty in states that accept Medicaid expansion. This means that people moving into low-paying jobs in those states will not lose their public health insurance right away. Medicaid's entitlement status allows it to play a countercyclical role in times of economic downturn. During economic slowdowns, Medicaid expenditures rise to cover some of the adults and children who lose their insurance coverage. Because of Medicaid's entitlement funding structure, federal funding levels automatically increase to match states' Medicaid expenditures. If Medicaid were capped and/or turned into a block grant, as some groups and members of Congress have urged, these increases would have been limited by predetermined federal funding caps or grant levels, thus adding to the economic woes of states faced with high unemployment and resulting loss of health insurance, and exacerbating the effects of a recession on vulnerable populations.

Medicaid and Managed Care   After Congress passed the 1997 Balanced Budget Act, states were no longer required to obtain waivers to enroll Medicaid recipients in managed care organizations. Now, more than two-thirds of the 70 million Medicaid beneficiaries are enrolled in managed care for at least a portion of their health services (CMS, 2012e). Unfortunately, managed care plans often have not had much experience with high-risk clients, who are disproportionately represented among the

Medicaid rolls. Medicaid clients who are high risk include very frail elders and developmentally disabled people with multiple physical health problems. Also, clients may have difficulty accessing and using the information they need for choosing plans. For these reasons, managed care plans might not be a good match for Medicaid recipients. Further, research focusing on the impact of Medicaid managed care on quality, cost, and access has found little indication that it has resulted in national savings (Sparer, 2012). A few states have had some success. They were likely to be states with relatively high reimbursement rates under fee-for-service, an issue that could have been addressed in ways other than moving to managed care. When turning to whether managed care improved access to care, the findings are again mixed. There is some indication that emergency department visits may be reduced, and more people had a usual source of care, but pregnant women were generally not better off. Quality of care has not been well studied even though states require performance measures for all managed care plans (Sparer, 2012). So, even though there is certainly no definitive research demonstrating the benefits of managed care, more states are shifting to managed care models. States are beginning to place their most vulnerable long-term care populations into managed care. Some states are hiring for-profit managed care organizations to provide Medicaid services while other states are using different strategies that involve long established non-profit community providers in providing managed care. Under either model, managed care is synonymous with privatization and, therefore, associated with government approaches to withdrawing from areas of public responsibility. Clearly the way that managed care is configured will likely influence outcomes achieved, and analysis to determine the effectiveness of managed care will need to take these differences into account.

Medicaid and Health Care Access   Medicaid provides health insurance for people who otherwise would likely have none. This policy is compatible with values such as social justice and adequacy to the extent that it provides some opportunity for oppressed groups to access health care. However, information about Medicaid eligibility needs to be made more accessible to a culturally diverse U.S. population, and service adequacy should attend to the specific needs of vulnerable populations, including those who live in underserved rural areas and those with particular and chronic health concerns.

Another problem associated with Medicaid is low reimbursement rates. Because of these low rates, many physicians are unwilling to serve Medicaid patients, thus limiting recipients' access to health care choices. Another limitation involves the eligibility requirements. Because people are required to "spend down" on health care until they are impoverished before they qualify for Medicaid, the eligibility requirements undermine people's strengths. If assets are accumulated, then benefits are lost. Medicaid also has relatively few mechanisms to ensure provision of quality care or to address the social determinants of health, although there are structures and incentives to address this included in the ACA. Thus, Medicaid clearly is ineffective in many ways, and it obviously does not provide health insurance to a large percentage of uninsured people. However, as detailed in the next segment of the chapter, Medicaid will be greatly expanded as part of the new health reform legislation. More low-income people including childless adults, many of them formerly uninsured, will now be covered. This category of the population was not formerly covered by Medicaid. In 2014, for residents in states that take part in Medicaid expansion, the program expanded to include individuals between the ages of 19 and 65 (parents and adults without dependent children) with incomes up to 138 percent of the FPL, based on modified adjusted gross income. This is an annual income of about $15,400 for one person and $30,675 for a family of four in 2012. You will note as you read about expansion of the ACA that some articles say eligibility is extended to 133 percent of FPL and others say 138 percent of FPL. This variation is because the first 5 percent of income is disregarded when determining eligibility (APHA, n.d.). This legislation also increases payments to primary care doctors who accept patients on Medicaid, in an effort to address the provider shortage in many communities.

Medicare

Medicare was created by Title XVIII of the Social Security Act. It is a national health insurance program designed primarily for people aged 65 or older. To be eligible, an individual must be a citizen or a permanent resident of the U.S. In addition, the person or his or her spouse must have worked for at least 10 years in Medicare covered employment. Younger people with disabilities who receive cash benefits for 24 months under the Social Security program and persons with end-stage renal disease (permanent kidney failure requiring dialysis or a kidney transplant) are also eligible for Medicare benefits. About 51 million older adults and people with disabilities receive Medicare. People can sign up for Medicare through their local Social Security office or online. Exhibit 10.6 summarizes the program's features.

EXHIBIT 10.6 *Medicare, 1965*		
	Policy Goals	To improve access to medical care by providing health insurance for eligible older adults and people with disabilities.
	Benefits or Services Provided	Health insurance. Part A covers hospital in-patient care. Part B covers doctor visits and outpatient hospital care. Limited prescription drug benefits.
	Eligibility Rules	People age 65, people with certain disabilities, or people with end-stage renal disease. Part A eligibility is linked to work history or additional payment of premiums.
	Service Delivery System	Federal administration by the Centers for Medicare and Medicaid Services. Recipients choose physicians or hospitals for care, and Medicare reimburses providers for the service.
	Financing	Part A is funded by payroll taxes. Part B is funded through premium payments from older adults and federal general revenue.

With the advent of managed care and the Medicare Part D prescription drug benefit, the Medicare system has become more difficult to navigate. You will find detailed information on eligibility, covered services, and how to help clients access benefits at the CMS (www.cms.gov) Medicare site.

As discussed in Chapter 8, the number of younger people who are now receiving Social Security benefits because of disability has grown substantially. These younger people with disabilities who receive cash benefits for 24 months under the Social Security program are also eligible for Medicare. The growth of this younger population has contributed to rising costs for Medicare. Exhibit 10.7 illustrates the growth in Medicare enrollment for both older adults and people with permanent disabilities between the 1960s and 2012.

It is often assumed that once a person is eligible for Medicare, spending on health care is no longer a major financial drain for that individual. In fact, typical Medicare beneficiaries spend nearly 15 percent of their household incomes on health care, as many prescription and physician co-pays fall to individual responsibility, and premiums often require cost-sharing. This is, on average, about three times the percentage non-Medicare households spend on health care. Almost 33 percent of Medicare enrollees have incomes below 150 percent of the federal poverty line and the health care burden on the near-poor and middle-income Medicare household is particularly heavy. These groups spend a higher percentage of household income on health care than Medicare households who are very low income and so are eligible for Medicaid (KFF, 2012e). Additionally, some older adults and

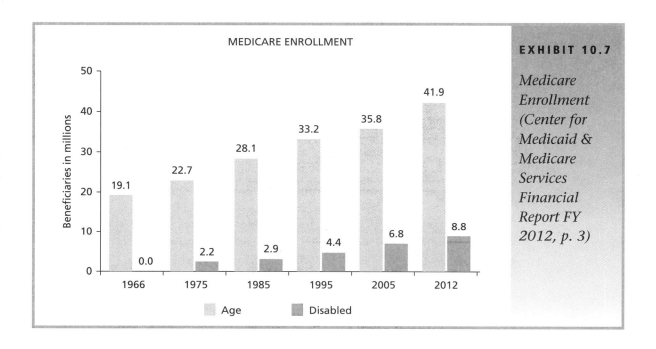

MEDICARE ENROLLMENT

EXHIBIT 10.7

Medicare Enrollment (Center for Medicaid & Medicare Services Financial Report FY 2012, p. 3)

individuals with disabilities might not access needed health care because of the imposition created by high out-of-pocket costs.

Uninsured rates among older Americans have dropped dramatically because of the availability of Medicare insurance. Medicare beneficiaries who have limited income and assets may get help paying for their out-of-pocket medical expenses from Medicaid. For people who are eligible for full Medicaid coverage, Medicaid supplements Medicare by providing services and supplies that are available under their state's Medicaid program. These people are termed "dual eligible," since they are simultaneously eligible for both major public insurance programs. Services that are covered by both programs will be paid first by Medicare and the difference by Medicaid, up to the state's limit. Compared to other Medicare beneficiaries, those dual eligible tend to be sicker and poorer. They are more likely to have Activities of Daily Living (ADL) and Instrumental Activities of Daily Living (IADL) limitations and chronic diseases. People who are dual eligible are among the most expensive for both Medicare and Medicaid, and efforts to provide more coordinated care and reduce unnecessary institutionalization in nursing facilities for this population could produce cost savings and increased care choices for this group. Medicaid disproportionately pays for non-acute/long-term care; Medicare for more than half of acute care for elders. The costs and futures of these two programs are thus linked.

Medicare focuses primarily on *acute* care, that is, short-term medical care, especially for serious disease or trauma. However, it also provides for rehabilitation of up to 100 days in a nursing facility. Contrary to what many older adults believe, Medicare does not pay for the long-term care needed for *chronic* conditions in a nursing facility, although it does pay for hospice benefits. These benefits have made end-of-life care more widely available for older adults who wish to forgo curative treatment and receive palliative care instead. The intent of the hospice is to improve the quality of care for dying patients and to reduce health care costs by decreasing the use of high-cost treatment options. Some services are not covered by any portion of Medicare. For example, certain other health care needs, such as eyeglasses, dentures and dental care, and hearing aids are not covered even though they obviously impact people's health. Additionally, Medicare does not provide transportation for medical appointments. Some people elect a Medicare Managed Care option, because certain of these programs will cover these necessary items. As detailed below, Medicare has four parts.

Medicare Part A, Hospital Insurance (HI) is paid for through payroll taxes. It is compulsory and helps cover the cost of inpatient hospital care, rehabilitation in skilled nursing facilities, some home health care, and hospice care. Each time patients are hospitalized during a new benefit period lasting 1 to 60 days, they must pay a $1,184 deductible. They also must pay additional charges if the hospitalization lasts beyond 60 days (USHSS, 2012a).

Medicare Part B is an optional program that enables people aged 65 and over to purchase medical care. Part B helps pay for outpatient hospital care, doctors' services, laboratory services, some mental health care, and certain other medical procedures not covered by Part A, such as occupational and physical therapy and some home health care. Certain preventive services are also covered, and the ACA strengthened these requirements, in an effort to improve health outcomes for older adults. Beneficiaries pay a monthly premium. In 2013 the base premium was $104 per month. Higher-income beneficiaries pay a higher monthly premium, which represents a larger percentage of the total cost of Part B. Beneficiaries also must pay substantial deductibles for most non-preventive services, despite some evidence that high out-of-pocket costs can influence individuals' utilization of needed health care. If people do not sign up for Part B insurance when they become eligible upon turning 65, they will pay a substantial penalty if they decide to purchase it in later years.

Older adults with Medicare Parts A and B coverage could still have to pay for nearly half of their acute care costs. These adults can purchase Medigap policies, which are designed to provide more comprehensive coverage, from private insurers. Because of the costs of Medicare Part B, gaps in Medicare coverage, and high deductibles, many elders cannot afford the health care they need. Nevertheless, Medicare has helped many older Americans access health care, and it has contributed to increasing longevity.

Managed care options such as HMOs, discussed below, are increasingly being relied upon to stem spiraling health care costs. As we have seen, however, mixed outcomes in terms of enhanced care and cost have fueled debate about the efficacy of this approach. Indeed, some HMOs are canceling coverage for older adults when Medicare reimbursement rates do not provide the profit margin they had anticipated. Some physicians who are not part of managed care systems are also refusing to take Medicare customers because of low reimbursement rates.

Medicare Part C, Medicare Advantage   The Balanced Budget Act of 1997 created Medicare Part C, renamed *Medicare Advantage* to replace the name *Medicare + Choice*. Medicare Advantage allows private companies to contract with Medicare to provide health coverage through managed care plans or private fee-for-service plans. People who receive both Medicare Part A and Part B are eligible to enroll in Medicare Advantage if there is a plan in their area. The private companies reduce out-of-pocket expenses and coordinate care. In addition, some plans pay for prescription medications (CMS, 2013a). However, this managed care approach has not been effective in reducing Medicare costs.

Medicare Part D   is optional and provides for prescription drugs. Congress passed the Medicare Prescription Drug, Improvement, and Modernization Act in 2003, which provides prescription drug coverage to more than 40 million Medicare beneficiaries. The Medicare prescription drug benefit is referred to as Part D. Previously, Medicare did not pay for prescription drugs administered outside the hospital, and due to ever-increasing costs and the growing efficacy of pharmaceutical management of health concerns, many older adults could not afford to buy the medications their doctors prescribed.

Consumer savings are estimated to be 10–25 percent off the retail price on many drugs. Medicare beneficiaries with low incomes may qualify for an additional credit to help pay for prescription drugs.

In 2012, the prescription drug benefit features of the basic benefit were:

- Monthly premium of about $30 depending on plan selected.

- $325 annual deductible.

- Medicare pays 75 percent of drug costs between the deductible and $2,970.

- Beneficiaries pay a much higher percent of costs between $2,830 and $4,750. This hole in coverage is termed the "donut hole." Under the ACA, the donut hole is reduced and completely phased out by 2020. This should make prescription drug coverage within Medicare not only less expensive for participants but also less confusing to navigate.

- Catastrophic protection after $4,700 total out-of-pocket expenses (CMS, 2013c).

Additional wording contained in the Part D legislation also improved payments to Medicare providers to ensure continued access to basic health care services for older adults and individuals with disabilities, especially those living in rural communities. Further, Medicare, rather than Medicaid, is now responsible for providing prescription drug coverage to dual eligible beneficiaries. Financial assistance with the Part D premium, deductible, and cost-sharing obligations is provided to Medicare beneficiaries with low incomes (CMS, 2013a). In 2013, beneficiaries who want to enroll in Part D have more than 20 stand-alone prescription drug plans to choose from in each state, along with many Medicare Advantage plans. Many older adults find it confusing to compare so many plans. However, competition and choice are hallmarks of this program and reflect the dominant approach in the U.S. health care system, where, as has been discussed, health care is considered a commodity to be purchased in the marketplace.

The Medicare prescription drug law is complex and has been widely debated. Nonetheless, Medicare Part D has cost significantly less than what was initially estimated. Part of the cost savings is because fewer people who were eligible for Medicare Part D actually took advantage of the benefit than was initially expected. Also, there has been an increase in the use of less expensive generic drugs. However, cost savings could be even greater than currently realized. The program has been widely criticized for not allowing Medicare to negotiate directly on behalf of all its beneficiaries, as the Veterans Administration does. Prescription drug costs are still rising at a much faster rate than incomes. Effective strategies for controlling the growth of health care costs, including prescription drugs, must be implemented if we are to have an effective, sustainable health care system.

Medicare Part D will remain adequately financed in the future because present law automatically provides government financing each year to meet the next year's expected costs within this entitlement. Expected government expenditures for 2013 are $60 billion (CBO, 2012).

The Centers for Medicare and Medicaid Services (CMS) is the federal agency that administers both Medicare and Medicaid. Medicare is federally funded, primarily through payroll taxes. Part A is financed through the Medicare Payroll Tax paid by both employers and employees. The premiums for Part B are supposed to cover 25 percent of its costs, with general tax revenues covering the rest. Significantly, Medicare is administered for a fraction of the cost of many private health insurance programs, revealing that concerns about fiscal sustainability of Medicare are more reflective of overall trends of rising health care costs, rather than to any particular features of Medicare itself.

In 2012, almost 51 million people were enrolled in one or both of Parts A and B of the Medicare program. After growing 6.1 percent in 2014, Medicare spending is projected to increase at an average annual rate of 6.8 percent for 2015 through 2021. This increase is due in part to enrollment growth as more baby boomers become eligible for Medicare. The Congressional Budget Office projects spending for Medicare in FY 2013 to be $592 billion (CBO, 2013a).

Assessing the future sustainability of Medicare as currently structured requires analyzing the state of the Medicare Trust Funds. Medicare's Hospital Insurance (HI) Trust Fund is currently paying out more than it receives in taxes and other dedicated revenues. The difference is made up by redeeming trust fund assets which include the Medicare insurance premiums that have been paid in previous years. Factors driving health care costs higher during this period include the rising cost of medical services, increases in utilization of services, and increases in intensity of services provided. There will also be continued strong growth in spending for home health care. Besides these factors which will increase the per person cost of health care, there will also be a large increase in numbers of people receiving Medicare because the baby boom generation (people born between 1946 and 1964) will become eligible for Medicare over the next two decades. Finally, the slower than expected economic growth during the recent recession reduced payroll tax contributions to the Funds, further straining Medicare's fiscal capacity. The projected date of HI Trust Fund exhaustion is 2024 (Social Security Administration, 2012). However, in 2024, dedicated revenues will still be sufficient to pay 87 percent of HI costs. The imbalance in the HI Trust Fund is an urgent concern which was part of the impetus for health care reform in 2010.

Projected Medicare costs are substantially lower than they otherwise would be because of provisions of the ACA (Board of Trustees, 2012). The new legislation includes a number of proposals to move away from the "à la carte" Medicare fee-for-service system and reduce costs for people receiving Medicare. The legislation reduces overpayments to private Medicare Advantage plans. It also improves chronic care and encourages doctors to collaborate and provide patient-centered care for the 80 percent of older Americans who have at least one chronic medical condition such as high blood pressure or diabetes. It provides new, free annual wellness visits and eliminates out-of-pocket co-payments for preventive benefits under Medicare, such as cancer and diabetes screenings. The health care reform legislation also improves Medicare payments for primary care, which will protect access to Medicare and encourages reimbursing health care providers on the basis of value, not volume.

In fact, Medicare costs are already slowing. Expenditures per beneficiary went up by just 0.4 percent in fiscal year 2012. This was markedly lower than the 3.4 percent increase in per capita GDP in 2012. In 2010 and 2011, per beneficiary Medicare growth was also slower than in past years. During the three-year period (2010–2012), per beneficiary spending increased an average of 1.9 percent annually, or more than 1 percentage point more slowly than the average annual growth of 3.2 percent in per capita GDP (Kronick and Po, 2013). However, further reform is needed and proposals for change will be discussed later in the chapter.

The Children's Health Insurance Program (CHIP)

Although Medicaid had made strides in enrolling children from low-income families, significant numbers of children remained uninsured. In fact, from 1988 to 1998, the percentage of the nation's children who had no health insurance grew from 13.1 percent to 15.4 percent. In order to help remedy this problem, the

EXHIBIT 10.8

CHIP has Improved Access to Health Care for Children

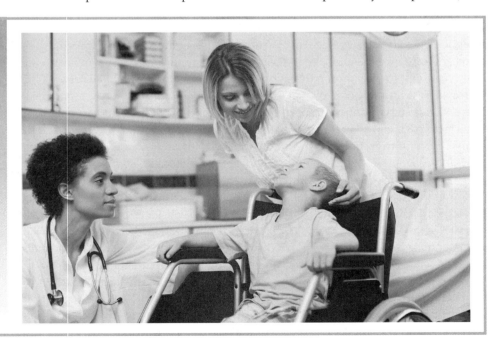

Balanced Budget Act of 1997 created a new children's health insurance program called the State Children's Health Insurance Program (SCHIP). The Act established SCHIP under Title XXI of the Social Security Act and made health insurance for children more widely available. This law authorizes states to offer health insurance for children up to age 19 who are not already insured. This program is state administered, and each state sets its own guidelines regarding eligibility and services. Eligibility rules are much more generous than are those for Medicaid, and working families without insurance may qualify. Services provided to children under this program are the same as services received by Medicaid recipients in each state.

In 2009, President Obama signed the Children's Health Insurance Program Reauthorization Act (CHIPRA) and SCHIP became CHIP. CHIPRA included a provision allowing children who are legal residents with permanent status to participate in CHIP without waiting the requisite five years. But states are not required to provide this coverage, and in today's recession, relatively few do. For more information on immigrants' eligibility for public benefits, visit the website of the National Immigration Law Center (www.nilc.org).

In recognition of the link between oral health and overall well-being, states are now required to include dental services in CHIP plans. CHIPRA also provides an

Purpose	The Children's Health Insurance Program Reauthorization Act (CHIPRA) renews and expands the Children's Health Insurance Program to increase the number of children with health insurance from roughly 7 million to 11 million.	**EXHIBIT 10.9** *Children's Health Insurance Programs Reauthorization Act (CHIPRA), 2009*
Benefits or Services	Covered services include doctors' visits, hospitalizations, emergency room visits, immunizations and dental care. CHIPRA also provides states with outreach funds and some demonstration funding for development of electronic records.	
Eligibility Rules	Uninsured children under the age of 19 whose family has a yearly income up to 300 percent of poverty depending on state guidelines. Reauthorization provides the opportunity for states to cover uninsured low-income pregnant women and children from legal immigrant families during the initial five years in this country.	
Service Delivery System	State administration. Federal oversight by the Centers for Medicaid and Medicare Services (CMS). Recipients choose a doctor or provider for health services.	
Financing	Jointly funded by federal and state governments. Federal funds are capped.	

Centers for Medicare & Medicaid Services. (2009). *Low Cost Health for Families & Children*. Baltimore, Maryland: http://www.cms.hhs.gov/LowCostHealthInsFamChild/

enhanced match for translation and interpretation services and includes $100 million in outreach grant funding. Exhibit 10.9 summarizes the features of CHIP.

As of January 2013, half of states (26, including DC) cover children in families with incomes up to at least 250 percent of the FPL. As is the case with Medicaid, the federal government matches state spending for CHIP. However, states receive a federal matching rate for CHIP that is higher than for Medicaid. Covered services include doctors' visits, hospitalizations, emergency room visits, immunizations, and dental care. CHIPRA also provides states with outreach funds and some demonstration funding for the development of electronic records. However, unlike Medicaid, which provides an individual entitlement such that if a child in a low-income family quali- fies she will get health coverage, federal CHIP funds are capped. Each state receives a capped allotment and when that allotment is gone, the federal government has no requirement to match funds for additional eligible children and the state has no obli- gation to serve them via CHIP. This constrains CHIP's ability to address gaps in health care coverage, particularly in times of rising need. In 2011, the CHIP provided health coverage to 8 million children. You will find a link to the CHIP program in your state at the federal government website, Insure Kids Now (www.insurekidsnow.gov).

The ACA also impacts CHIP. Entire families, including children, are now eligible for Medicaid if their income is below 138 percent of poverty in states that have accepted Medicaid expansion. So, in those states, some of the children formerly served by CHIP will now be insured through Medicaid. Given CHIP's nature as a capped funding stream, this shift of beneficiaries from CHIP to Medicaid may create more state capacity to serve more children whose incomes are just above 138 percent of poverty within CHIP. This is another way in which ACA expansion can contribute to health care access. Women and children currently covered under Medicaid will now be rescreened for CHIP in states that participate in Medicaid expansion. Changes to CHIP contained in the ACA include:

- maintenance of current income/eligibility level for children in Medicaid and CHIP until 2019;

- extension of CHIP funding through 2015 (CHIP benefit packages and cost-sharing rules under current law will not change during this period);

- a 23 percentage point increase in the CHIP match rate to states, up to a cap of 100 percent; and,

- addition of $40 million in federal funds to continue efforts to increase enrollment in CHIP and Medicaid (CMS, 2012d).

Quick Guide 9 provides a brief synopsis of Medicare, Medicaid, and CHIP. You might find this a valuable resource as you embark on your social work career and integrate policy practice into your work helping individuals to navigate these important health programs.

QUICK GUIDE 9   **Health and Mental Health Programs**

Medicaid Health insurance for medical and health-related services including nursing facility care, for low-income people. Eligibility varies from state to state. For more information and details on the appli-cation process, see: http://ssa-custhelp.ssa.gov/app/answers/detail/a_id/32/~/apply-for-medicaid, or go to your state Medicaid website.

Medicare Health insurance for older adults and people with disabilities. Eligibility is set at the federal level. Eligibility is based on attachment to the workforce and the program is financed in part by payroll taxes. For the latest information and details on the application process, see: http://www.socialsecurity.gov/medicareonly/.

State Children's Health Insurance Program (CHIP) Health insurance for children in families with too much income to qualify for Medicaid, but who cannot afford health insurance. Eligibility varies from state to state. It is administered at the state level, and supported by the federal government with expanded support under the Affordable Care Act of 2010. For current information about his program see: http://www.medicaid.gov/; select "CHIP State Plans."

The 2010 Patient Protection and Affordable Care Act

The ACA will fundamentally influence physical and mental health care for social workers and their clients. This health care reform initiative was endorsed by the American Medical Association and many health care providers and consumer groups and opposed by most insurance companies and every Republican in Congress.

Several elements of this legislation went into effect in 2010, while others will be phased in over several years. I summarize below some of the major provisions. However, because some of the rules and regulations that will determine more specif-ically just how this legislation will be implemented are yet to be written, you should seek out the newest information on this legislation as it is developed. To find out how health reform will affect health care in your state, visit the Families USA website and go to Health Coverage in the States: How Will Health Reform Help?

Major provisions of this legislation include the following.

- Beginning in 2010:

  - Insurance companies were no longer allowed to deny children coverage based on a pre-existing condition.

  - Insurance companies had to allow children to stay on their parent's insurance plans until the age of 26.

  - People denied insurance due to a pre-existing medical problem were provided with immediate access to high-risk insurance plans.

  - People on Medicare received a $250 rebate toward prescription drugs once their benefits ran out due to the donut hole currently encountered by people with high prescription costs. This hole in coverage will eventually be closed as health care reform is fully implemented.

- Insurance companies were prohibited from imposing lifetime dollar limits on essential benefits, like hospital stays.

- Funding was made available to expand the number of primary care doctors, nurses, and physician assistants in underserved areas.

- Beginning in 2011:

  - Medicare began providing free preventive care, which includes physical exams and exams to detect diseases such as diabetes and glaucoma, as well as certain vaccinations.

  - If insurers do not spend at least 80 percent of premium dollars on patient care and quality improvements, they have to provide a rebate to consumers.

- Beginning in 2012:

  - Incentives were created to encourage physicians to develop integrated health systems to better coordinate patient care and help improve quality of care.

  - Changes were implemented to standardize billing and require health plans to provide for secure, confidential electronic exchange of health information.

- Beginning in 2013:

  - Medicaid payments for primary care doctors were increased.

  - Open enrollment in the Healthcare Marketplace began in October 1, 2013. The Marketplace offers a choice of health plans that meets specified benefits and cost standards.

- Beginning in 2014:

  - Insurance companies will no longer be able to deny coverage to anyone with pre-existing conditions.

  - This legislation caps annual out-of-pocket spending for individuals and families to address the specter of bankruptcy from health costs.

  - Independent appeals panels will be created to contest health insurance decisions.

  - The uninsured and self-employed can purchase insurance through insurance exchanges with subsidies for individuals and families with income between 133 and 400 percent of the FPL. The exchanges will guarantee choices of quality, affordable insurance (at rates large groups get) if people lose their job, switch jobs, move or get sick. These policies must cover maternity leave and will have no gender rating. Gender rating typically results in women paying more for their insurance.

- Everyone is required to purchase health insurance or face a fine which for individuals is $95 a year, or up to 1 percent of income, whichever is greater. The penalty rises to $695, or 2.5 percent of income, by 2016. There are exceptions for low-income people and also based on religious beliefs.

- Tax credits are available for small businesses to make providing coverage more affordable.

- Funding for community health centers will be expanded.

- Coverage for mental and behavioral health needs in health care plans is improved.

- Funds to train primary care providers, including social workers, will be increased.

- In states that accept Medicaid expansion, nearly all U.S. citizens under 65 with family incomes up to 138 percent of the FPL qualify for Medicaid. This expansion will especially benefit childless adults and low-income parents who formerly did not qualify for Medicaid in most states. The federal government pays 100 percent of costs for covering newly eligible individuals through 2016 (no state cost-sharing). The federal match will then slowly be reduced until 2020 when the federal government will be paying 90 percent of these costs. For 2020 and in all the following years, the federal government will continue paying 90 percent of the costs for these beneficiaries.

- Funding is now available for pilots, demonstrations, and the creation of the Center for Medicare and Medicaid Innovation (CMI) to research cost containment approaches, prevention, medical homes, and other practices to improve service integration and patient outcomes.

- Beginning in 2015:

  - Employers with more than 50 employees must provide health insurance or pay a fine of $2,000 per worker each year if any worker receives federal subsidies to purchase health insurance. Fines are applied to the entire number of employees minus some allowances.

  - Physician payment will be tied to the quality of care they provide.

As detailed above, the ACA essentially provides Americans with a new health care bill of rights as well as many specific benefits (USDHHS, 2012a). However, besides the people with incomes below 138 percent of poverty who are not covered by current Medicaid income limits in states rejecting Medicaid expansion, an estimated 11 million undocumented immigrants will still be uninsured. Undocumented immigrants are ineligible for insurance subsidies and for Medicaid. These groups will continue to be uninsured as will people who are not otherwise covered and choose to pay the annual penalty. The IRS rules on who will actually pay this penalty provide a host of exemptions so that it is expected relatively few people will be subject to the penalty. The Congressional Budget Office projects that less than 2 percent of Americans will owe what is now being called a "shared responsibility payment" (CMS, 2013a).

In thinking through the impact of health care reform, some young people may overlook the substantial direct benefit that will accrue to them. In fact, young adults are among those who needed health reform the most. They are the most likely to be uninsured. Before the ACA was implemented, many were removed from their parents' health insurance before they had themselves secured coverage through a job. If they had pre-existing conditions, they could be turned down for insurance. Now more affordable insurance is available for them and, in states that have accepted Medicaid expansion, there are financial subsidies available for low-income young adults to help with the cost of health insurance.

Enforcement of the patient protections and corporate mandates included in the ACA will involve both federal and state agencies. Because many states have been reluctant to implement the provisions of the ACA, enforcement mechanisms could be slow to develop and patients in those states might find it more difficult to reap the benefits and protections provided by the ACA.

This health care reform legislation represents a change in the kind of risk-shifting discussed in previous chapters in relation to employment-based retirement pensions and proposed Social Security reforms where the individual has been expected to assume more risk. However, in the health care reform legislation, risk is shifting so that the federal and state governments are sharing more of the risk with the individual. Public assumption of more of this risk helps to build a healthy, productive workforce able to compete in a global economy with countries that do provide universal health care.

To find out how people in your state are being affected by health care reform and how the debate around Medicaid expansion and other aspects of ACA implementation is proceeding, go to the whitehouse.gov website and search for What Health Care Reform Means in Your State. You will also find timelines and other information at this website that will keep you up to date on health care reform and how it impacts you and your clients.

Affordable Care Act: Financing and Cost Control Issues   Funding for the 2010 health care reform initiative includes the following sources. Starting in 2012, the Medicare Payroll Tax was expanded to include unearned income. That is a 3.8 percent tax on investment income for families making more than $250,000 per year. Beginning in 2018, insurance companies will pay an excise tax on high-end

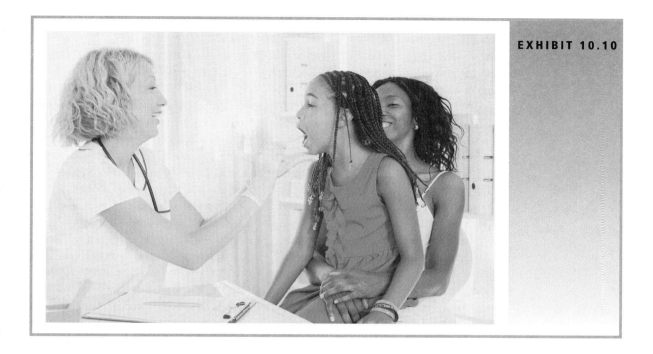

EXHIBIT 10.10

insurance plans worth over $27,500 for families. Dental and vision plans are exempt and will not be counted in the total cost of a family's plan. Payments to Medicare Advantage programs, a managed care approach to providing Medicare services, will be reduced. This managed care approach was found to increase rather than reduce Medicare costs. Revenue to finance health care reform also comes from industry fees and excise taxes, including a small excise tax on indoor tanning services (IRS, 2012). The revenue provisions in the bill and cost control elements are expected to bend the health care cost curve downward by putting pressure on health spending, closing unintended tax loopholes, and promoting tax compliance. It is expected that this legislation will lower health care costs over the long term.

However, because the U.S. did not choose to implement a single-payer style national health insurance like many other countries have, the federal government has much less leverage to control the amount by which private providers can increase their charges. Further, there is no "public option," which would have provided more competition for the private sector. A public option would have provided people with a government choice for buying health insurance. For example, people might have been able to buy insurance directly from the government, similar to what is provided to federal employees. Because these and other cost control features that could have potentially helped bring down costs were abandoned or weakened in order to get the legislation passed, cost control will need to be a high priority in future initiatives to improve our health care system. As was discussed in Chapter 6 on policy development, getting support for reform by passing legislation that establishes a commitment to meeting a need, in this case health care for all, is a crucial step and the original legislation can be amended or expanded in later years. Getting the initial stick in the ground, so to speak, is much more important than holding out for the perfect legislative initiative that will, in all likelihood, never be passed to become law.

When the ACA is fully phased in, most Americans will continue to be insured through their employer. However, the uninsured category will be much smaller because, although there is no public option, many more people will be eligible for public programs and/or able to afford to purchase insurance. Ninety-two percent of legal residents will be covered. According to Congressional Budget Office estimates, the current number of nonelderly people without health insurance coverage will drop by 14 million in 2014 and by about 30 million in the latter part of the decade, leaving 30 million nonelderly residents uninsured by 2022 (KFF, 2012b). By reducing the number of uninsured, this health care reform legislation is expected to reduce the hidden tax of about $1,000 per person that those with insurance now incur to cover the cost of the uninsured who rely on emergency rooms to get their care. Additionally, The ACA takes steps to change the current, largely fee-for-service health care system—which, as explained earlier, can lead to overuse and wasteful care—with a system of coordinated care. Such systems may reduce incentives for admission to hospital. The focus of health care coverage will shift, as well, toward a system that keeps people healthy.

The ACA also has some components that can help slow long-term growth in health care inflation. For example, the ACA created an Independent Payment Advisory Board (IPAB). The IPAB is an independent board of 15 physicians and health experts. Members are appointed by the president and approved by the Senate. If Medicare costs exceed a specified limit, the IPAB can make recommendations to Congress about how to reduce Medicare costs. Congress can either approve or reject these proposals. However, if Congress does not act, the proposals go into effect. The IPAB is prohibited from making recommendations that would ration care or shift costs to beneficiaries.

The ACA established an independent Patient-Centered Outcomes Research Institute (PCORI), which may help reduce health care inflation. This institute will help develop a research agenda for determining which health care treatments work better than others and disseminate this information broadly to practitioners and the public. Again, the intent is not to limit treatment or care; the law specifically prohibits that. Rather, the intent is to begin a national dialogue and hopefully develop some consensus about what works and what does not.

MAJOR MENTAL HEALTH POLICIES AND PROGRAMS

Mental health care has never received the same attention in public policy as physical health care. Many people in the U.S. do not understand that good mental health is essential to good physical health. Public funding for mental health care has historically been available primarily for people with severe psychiatric problems, and even then it was not adequate. Major barriers to caring for people with mental health problems include the stigma that surrounds mental illness, unfair treatment limitations and financial requirements that have historically been placed on mental health benefits in private insurance, and a fragmented mental health delivery system. Both Medicaid and Medicare provide funding for treatment for people with mental disorders, but there are many individuals who lack any insurance coverage. Further, mental health experts contend that the current system is focused on managing the disabilities associated with mental illness rather than on promoting recovery. Improving both mental health and physical health is integral to improving health care in the U.S. Because social workers provide most of the country's mental health services, we have a critical role in improving mental health policies and programs. By examining the barriers to adequate care for people with mental illness, reviewing the historical development of our current mental health/behavioral health system, and analyzing the major legislation that shapes the system, we will be able to identify the next steps that should be taken to improve mental health policy and programs.

Major mental disorders such as schizophrenia, depression, bipolar disorder, autism, and panic disorder are found worldwide, across racial and ethnic groups. Tragic and devastating disorders such as schizophrenia, depression and bipolar disorder, Alzheimer's disease, and the mental and behavioral disorders suffered by children, affect nearly one in five Americans in any year. Adults over age 18 who have been diagnosed with a major mental illness that results in functional impairment and substantially limits their ability to perform activities of daily living on a long-term basis are designated as having serious mental illness (SMI). This designation is used to determine eligibility for certain public programs.

Although African Americans, Hispanics or Latinos, American Indians, and Asian Americans are no less likely than whites to suffer from mental illness, they often do not get the help they need. For example, historically mental health services for African Americans were not widely available until 1965 when the state hospitals were desegregated. When members of minority groups do get access to treatment, the treatment may be substandard or too late. There is evidence that even diagnosis is affected by individuals' race or ethnicity. Barriers to adequate care that create these disparities include the large percentage of families in these groups who have historically lacked health insurance; treatment that is not tailored to people from different cultures or who speak different languages; lack of research specific to minorities; and lack of mental health services in isolated areas. Additionally, concerns about stigma and lack of physicians, particularly specialists, from these ethnic groups, negatively influence treatment. Because of these barriers, disparities in access to mental health services will persist even after the 2010 health reform legislation which will increase access, is fully implemented and, as a result, individuals' mental health and overall well-being will suffer. Work to eliminate these disparities must continue.

History and Background of Mental Health Programs

As discussed in Chapter 2, policies on mental health care have undergone major shifts. Prior to the 1800s, mentally ill people were cared for either at home or in almshouses. During the early 1800s, some small, privately funded hospitals were established that emphasized therapeutic rather than custodial care. However, they could serve only a tiny portion of the population with mental illness. During the mid-1800s, Dorothea Dix led a social movement to garner national attention for the plight of people with mental illness. She wanted the federal government to provide for institutions for these people. Although she was not successful in securing federal support, more than 30 state hospitals were established by the mid-1800s. The period witnessed a growing belief in the efficacy of treatment for people with mental illness. However, inadequate funding soon led to overcrowding and largely custodial care in some state institutions.

In the early 1900s, laws were passed in some states that made it legal to involuntarily sterilize people who were believed to be mentally ill, developmentally disabled or who had other disabilities that at the time were believed to be hereditary. In 1927, the Supreme Court upheld this practice in the case, *Buck* v. *Bell*. After this ruling, more states passed similar laws and ultimately, more than 65,000 people were involuntarily sterilized (National Council on Disability, 2012). People were being sterilized under these unjust laws up until the 1970s. Although research into many of the cases has been completed to show the people sterilized in fact had no hereditary deficiencies, this is beside the point. These laws were unjust no matter the capacity of the victims and illustrate how the push for equitable and appropriate treatment for those with mental illness is also a civil rights issue.

The mental hygiene movement, which emphasized community care, gained momentum after World War I, fueled by the recognition of the impact of mental health problems on soldiers. The federal government became involved in the delivery of mental health services to the general citizenry with the passage of the 1946 Mental Health Act, which established the National Institute of Mental Health. The National Institute of Mental Health (NIMH) is part of the National Institutes of Health (NIH) in the Department of Health and Human Services (USDHHS). NIMH is the federal agency that is primarily responsible for research on mental and behavioral disorders. Research conducted through this agency helps shape the nation's mental health policies and programs. You can learn about research currently being funded by visiting the National Institute of Mental Health website (www.nimh.nih.gov).

Community Mental Health and Deinstitutionalization Although interest in community mental health care grew in the 1950s, much of the treatment for people with SMI continued to be provided in state mental institutions. However, the development of medications that helped people with mental illness function outside of institutions, combined with growing awareness of deplorable conditions in some state institutions, led to the passage of the Mental Retardation and Community Mental Health Centers Construction Act of 1963 and the 1965 amendments. This landmark legislation, which we discuss in more detail in the following section on mental health policies and programs, provided communities with federal funds to construct community mental health centers, thereby providing outpatient services to people with SMI. However, the community mental health movement continued to suffer from underfunding. Although psychoactive drugs made transition to community living possible for many people, many of the psychoactive drugs prescribed have been found to have serious side effects. However, use of other types of therapy has often been discounted as too expensive and federal reimbursement policies continue to support widespread use of psychoactive drugs.

The deinstitutionalization movement swept through the states, propelled by hopes that community mental health treatment would be more cost-effective and humane. Deinstitutionalization refers to the policy of providing community-based services for people with disabilities who were formerly served in institutions. Thousands of people with mental illness left state institutions, new admissions to state institutions were strictly limited, and many state hospitals closed. Many of the people who were released were successfully reintegrated into communities. However, due to inadequate funding and services, large numbers of people received little or no mental health care. As a result, some people with mental illness have been rein-stitutionalized in prisons or nursing homes, while others are living in homeless shelters or on the streets. Some initiatives are under way to screen people in these settings for mental illness and, when necessary, refer them for treatment. However, detection and treatment of mental illness is certainly not a primary aim of these facilities. Therefore, they are unlikely to meet the treatment needs of people with mental illness who are reinstitutionalized in these settings.

Although inadequate funding continues to plague the community mental health movement, the two major federal health insurance programs, Medicaid and Medicare, do provide funding for some mental health services for eligible citizens. Medicaid pays for mental health care for people with mental illness who meet income and disability criteria. Medicare pays for certain kinds of mental health care for eligible people who are elderly, regardless of income, and for former workers who have been disabled for two years. Additionally, the Social Security Disability Insurance (SSDI) program provides cash assistance for former workers who have developed mental illness, although the criteria required to qualify for disability assistance with a mental, rather than a primarily physical, disability can make it difficult for individuals struggling with mental illness to receive these benefits. Finally, SSI provides cash assistance for people who have little or no income and meet stringent disability criteria.

In the late 1960s, many states revised their mental health codes to protect consumers' civil rights and to standardize criteria for involuntary hospitalization. In most cases, in order to be involuntarily hospitalized, a person must be found to be a current danger to herself or others or gravely disabled and incapable of self-care by reason of mental illness. The Mental Health Systems Act of 1980 contained a model bill of rights that states were expected to enact and enforce so as to protect the civil rights of people with mental illness. While the state can use civil commitment to compel certain people to accept inpatient commitment, nearly all states also have established measures to compel certain patients to follow outpatient treatment regimens. Courts can order Involuntary Outpatient Commitments (IOCs). Balancing protection of the civil rights of people who have mental disorders with safety concerns for them as well as others is a challenging policy issue and one with which social workers must constantly grapple. However, in many cases, no treatment is even available for people with mental disorders. Mental health centers have lacked sufficient funding, particularly as states have reduced spending on any discretionary items.

As part of the Reagan New Federalism initiative of the 1980s, several categorical programs for substance abuse and mental health were collapsed into a single Alcohol, Drug Abuse, and Mental Health block grant to states, and funding was cut by 20 percent (Monitz and Gorin, 2003). Although mental health care is still primarily the responsibility of the states, the State Comprehensive Mental Health Services Plan Act of 1986 encouraged a federal–state partnership in this area. This legislation allowed each state to use its block grant to expand community mental health services. I will discuss this law in greater detail later in the chapter.

As detailed in the Civil Rights chapter, a 1999 Supreme Court ruling, known as the Olmstead decision, required states, where possible, to provide services to qualified people with disabilities, including SMI, in the most integrated setting possible. Federal agencies were to assist the states to meet these requirements. However, although many state institutions have been closed, community-based services are still woefully underfunded in most states. The promise of the Olmstead decision has not become reality.

By 2000, the growing number of prisoners with mental illness in state and local correctional facilities helped to motivate the passage of America's Law Enforcement and Mental Health Project Act. This legislation included funds to set up mental health courts. Like the special drug courts, these courts are designed to deal with nonviolent offenders in ways that make it more likely they will receive treatment. Like many innovative programs that prove effective if adequately funded, funding for these special courts has been erratic.

Managed care approaches to providing mental health services have also been used to help control costs and coordinate services. Again, the results have been mixed. Although, theoretically, the incentive under managed care is to provide adequate and integrated care so that expensive hospitalizations are avoided, many times the incentive to provide less service has resulted in authorization of an unrealistically short number of treatment sessions to address the person's needs. Short-term psychopharmacology and 15-minute medication sessions with psychiatrists were seen as a way to hold down costs, even if other forms of intervention were best-suited for that particular individual and diagnosis. Although managed care systems certainly have not always delivered cost-effective integrated care, given the continued popularity of the basic approach, social workers need to help determine if there are ways that managed care concepts can be used to create a cost-effective mental health system and should advocate for systems reform within managed care, in order to best meet clients' needs.

The Substance Abuse and Mental Health Services Administration An agency within USDHHS, the Substance Abuse and Mental Health Services Administration (SAMHSA) was established in 1992. Its purpose is to improve the lives of people with or at risk of mental and substance abuse disorders. SAMHSA supports the development of policy, programs, and knowledge regarding mental health services and the prevention and treatment of substance abuse (Substance Abuse and Mental Health Services Administration, 2010). A priority area for SAMHSA is the estimated five million people in the U.S. who annually meet the criteria for both serious mental disorders and substance abuse, known as co-occurring conditions. Social workers have long been familiar with clients who self-medicate using a variety of addicting substances, including alcohol, tobacco, and drugs. When mental illness and substance abuse co-occur, treatment is further complicated. Since the advent of the War on Drugs in the 1970s, there has been more emphasis on law enforcement and less on substance abuse treatment. The combined effects of this emphasis on jailing people who use illegal drugs and closing mental hospitals has meant large numbers of people with mental illness are now incarcerated in correctional facilities. Many people with these co-occurring conditions are also homeless. Since 1981, most federal funding for substance abuse services has come in the form of block grants to states. Substance abuse funding is heavily reliant on state and local sources which are often inadequate. For more information about policies and treatment programs focused on this group, as well as information on mental health and substance abuse policies and programs in general, visit the SAMHSA website (www.samhsa.gov). Effective policies and programs that address the treatment, social service, and housing needs of people with these disorders are desperately needed, and social workers are well positioned to advocate for these investments.

Mental Health Parity and Increased Attention to Preparing Mental Health Professionals As has been detailed previously, mental health services have never been covered by public or private insurance systems to the same extent as have general health services. Most people with mental health conditions are not receiving the care they need. Advocates have long worked for parity, which means equivalent coverage between physical and mental health care. In 1996, the Mental Health Parity Act was passed, but opposition from insurance companies and employers resulted in legislation that was ineffective in achieving parity. In 2008, the Paul Wellstone and Pete Domenici Mental Health Parity and Addiction Equity Act was passed and closed some of the loopholes that had made the 1996 Mental Health Parity Act ineffective. The 2008 Act required parity in co-payments, deductibles, and out-of-pocket expenses. It also required parity in setting treatment limits. This legislation is discussed in more detail in the upcoming section on substance abuse.

The ACA also contains provisions to increase mental health parity. It has been estimated that the ACA, along with previous parity legislation, will expand mental health and substance use disorder benefits and parity protections for 62 million Americans (Bernio, Po, Skopec, and Glied, 2013). Beginning in 2014, the ACA improves access to quality health care that includes coverage for mental health and substance use disorder services. All individual and small group private market plans created after that date are required to cover mental health and substance use disorder services. They are part of the health care law's Essential Health Benefits (EHB) categories. Behavioral health benefits are covered at parity with other areas, such as medical and surgical benefits. Further, insurers can no longer deny anyone coverage because of a pre-existing behavioral health condition. The ACA also requires that new health plans cover recommended preventive benefits without cost-sharing. These preventive benefits include behavioral assessments for children and depression screening for adults and adolescents. However, there is still much more work to be done in achieving mental health parity.

As happened in the wake of World Wars I and II, mental health/behavioral health needs of returning soldiers from Iraq and Afghanistan are again requiring the nation to focus increased attention on preparing professionals to provide effective services. The number of soldiers with post traumatic stress disorders (PTSD) and increased rates of suicide have contributed to recognition of the need for expanded mental health services in the military. Social workers as well as other mental health professionals are being recruited and receiving educational stipends to practice on military bases and in veterans' hospitals. Social workers have long worked to establish policies and programs to ensure veterans receive adequate mental health care.

Growing Concerns Related to Children and Mental Health   In the wake of shrinking public revenues, funding for children's mental health services has been reduced at both the federal and state levels. As has been the case with adult mental health, there has been increased reliance on medication to treat children's mental health issues, even if social and behavioral interventions—instead of or in addition to pharmacology—would be most effective. The overuse of medication in the foster care system is of particular concern. A 2012 GAO report reviewed findings that foster children were prescribed psychotropic drugs at rates over three times higher than non-foster children. However, at the same time, it was reported that up to 30 percent of children in foster care who may have needed mental health services did not receive them during the time the research was completed (USGAO, 2012). Further, when comparing babies less than 1 year old, infants in foster care were nearly twice as likely to be prescribed a psychiatric drug than non-foster children. Some foster care children were taking as many as five of these medications. Costs for these medications were high. Although medication is clearly useful in treating mental health problems in children, its overuse, particularly in foster care, needs to be carefully monitored and alternative treatment options need to be expanded.

Mental Health Policies

We have discussed a variety of mental health legislative initiatives and programs. Two major federal mental health legislative milestones have been particularly important in shaping services nationwide. They are the Mental Retardation and Community Mental Health Centers Construction Act and the State Comprehensive Mental Health Services Plan Act.

The Mental Retardation and Community Mental Health Centers Construction Act Development of medication to control symptoms of people with chronic mental illness, the exposure of inhumane treatment of patients in some state mental hospitals, and the high expense of custodial care in these facilities led to the passage of the Mental Retardation and Community Mental Health Centers Construction Act of 1963 (Public Law 88–164) and the 1965 amendments. The goals of this legislation were to reduce the number of patients in state mental hospitals and to develop a system of community mental health centers that would provide services to the deinstitutionalized people. Federal funds were provided to the states through block grants. Funding, although inadequate, was to provide for the construction of community mental health centers where mental health services could be delivered locally by center staff.

Although the intent was to provide care for formerly institutionalized people in the least restrictive environment, in the community and with family, inadequate funding and staffing of formal services often created pressure on families to provide care beyond their means. Many people with chronic and severe mental illness were not adequately monitored, resulting in increased homelessness among people with mental illness. On the positive side, however, local access to mental health services did increase as a result of this legislation. See Exhibit 10.11 for a summary of the Act's provisions.

The 1975 amendments to the Community Mental Health Act, in combination with the Medicare provisions of the Social Security Amendments of 1965, also

Policy Goals	To reduce the number of patients in state mental hospitals. To develop a system of community mental health centers to provide services in the least restrictive environment.	**EXHIBIT 10.11**
Benefits or Services Provided	Community mental health services.	*Mental Retardation and Community Mental Health Centers Construction Act 1963, 1965*
Eligibility Rules	Formerly institutionalized people living in the community and community-dwelling people with mental illness and developmental disabilities.	
Service Delivery System	Community mental health centers provide local services.	
Financing	Federal block grant to the state.	

changed the availability of mental health services to older adults (Tice and Perkins, 1996b). Medicare provided the financial vehicle for at least limited access to mental health services for older adults.

The State Comprehensive Mental Health Services Plan Act   Although the federal government has never taken a major role in providing mental health services, Congress encouraged the federal–state partnership approach when it passed the State Comprehensive Mental Health Services Plan Act of 1986 (Public Law 99–660). This legislation authorized states to use federal block grants to expand community mental health services. Though the law permitted states greater flexibility in spending the federal block grants, the amount of money made available was not adequate to build an effective community mental health system. To compound this problem, states did not dedicate sufficient state funds to make comprehensive community-based mental health services a reality. At the federal level, the Substance Abuse and Mental Health Services Administration of USDHHS administers the block grants. At the same time, each state designates an agency to operate or oversee the statewide network of mental health services. Exhibit 10.12 summarizes the Act's provisions.

EXHIBIT 10.12 *State Comprehensive Mental Health Services Plan Act, 1986*		
Policy Goals	To provide support for community mental health services.
Benefits or Services Provided	Increased and expanded mental health services.
Eligibility Rules	People eligible for mental health services as defined by state.
Service Delivery System	State agency oversees network of mental health services.
Financing	Federal block grant to the state.

EVALUATING HEALTH AND MENTAL HEALTH POLICIES AND PROGRAMS

As we have seen throughout this chapter, U.S. health care policies have produced mixed results. Medicare, Medicaid, and CHIP provide health care for one in four Americans. Medicare enrollment has increased from 19 million beneficiaries in 1966 to over 50 million beneficiaries. Medicaid enrollment has increased from 10 million beneficiaries in 1967 to about 57 million beneficiaries (CMS, 2012b). Exhibit 10.13 illustrates this growth.

The health care reform legislation of 2010 expanded public programs such as Medicaid and CHIP. During the last decade such programs have successfully reduced

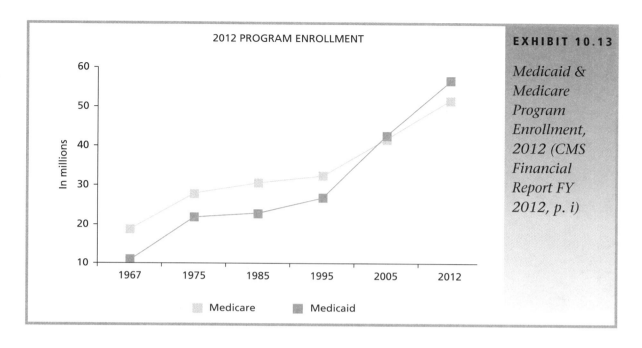

2012 PROGRAM ENROLLMENT

EXHIBIT 10.13

*Medicaid &
Medicare
Program
Enrollment,
2012 (CMS
Financial
Report FY
2012, p. i)*

the percentage of children without health insurance. The health reform legislation also extended coverage to a large group of formerly uninsured adults. However, this legislation is being phased in and people in some states will not be covered. Although it is expected that most people will continue to be insured through their employers, the new reality is that many people will no longer have stable lifelong employment with one employer or even in one field. Rather, many will have a series of employers, retrain for new careers as new arenas of employment expand and others decline, and perhaps be self-employed or unemployed for significant time periods. The 2010 health care reform legislation takes into account some of these new realities by moving somewhat away from the linkage between employment status and access to health care. It is important to make enrollment procedures in public insurance programs simpler so that people who lose their jobs can continue to have health insurance for their families.

Because many of the people who will now be eligible for public health insurance will be insured through Medicaid, the states who have accepted Medicaid expansion are bracing themselves for large influxes of people into their already strained Medicaid system. In fact, many states have been cutting their current Medicaid reimbursement rates, reducing outreach efforts, and curtailing benefits to optional populations because they have not had sufficient state funds to meet the federal match requirements due to the economic downturn. For example, although Medicaid rates paid to nursing homes for the care of Medicaid recipients are already lower than that paid by private pay residents, some states are cutting the Medicaid rates by an additional 10 percent. Further, when state revenues decrease, states often cut back on discretionary Medicaid spending, particularly for people with disabilities who are served in the community instead of in nursing facilities under Medicaid waiver programs. An additional concern is that expanding Medicaid will increase state Medicaid costs, even initially, in that more individuals who meet the "old" eligibility guidelines would "come out of the woodwork" because of the publicity and outreach related to implementation of the ACA. Of course, these people would have been eligible all along, but some states do not prioritize outreach. States would be responsible for paying the additional cost-sharing for these individuals, which would expand state liability for Medicaid spending. Nonetheless, the entitlement status of core Medicaid programs helps lessen hardship during economic downturn and, with the implementation of health care reform, many more people will be able to rely on Medicaid in states taking part in Medicaid expansion, particularly when they lose their jobs.

Under the new health care reform legislation, states will play a major part in determining what services people who are newly eligible for Medicaid will actually receive. Participating states will be able to choose to provide a minimum list of benefits to these new recipients. They will also be able to cut reimbursement levels for Medicaid services and implement other cost-sharing strategies such as co-pays for eligible recipients who are not impoverished. Thus, there will be great state variation in implementation of health care reform legislation, resulting costs, and health care outcomes for the citizens of the state.

It is also important to keep in mind that health care in many countries is not only paid for with public funds but also primarily provided at public medical centers run by the government. England and Sweden, as well as many other countries, are examples of such systems. In contrast, the U.S. has chosen to continue to expand public and private health insurance that is primarily used to pay for health care provided by the private sector. Exceptions to this general approach in the U.S. are military and Veteran's Administration hospitals where health care is both paid for and provided publicly. In thinking about how health care policy and programs can be structured, remember that expansion of public and private insurance is only one of the ways that many countries have successfully expanded access to needed health care. It has, like any policy system, distinct advantages and disadvantages, but U.S. policy makers have been, so far, unwilling to experiment with other models.

Challenges to the Medicare System

In this section, we address major challenges to the existing Medicare system. Although, as was detailed earlier, 2010 health care reform legislation does implement some Medicare cost controls, the steeply rising trajectory of health care costs will have to be bent more if the program is to remain solvent for future generations. The federal government insures large numbers of people and therefore has leverage in negotiating with the health care industry for better prices. However, historically, even this kind of government effort to control escalating health care costs has been limited. For example, the Medicare prescription drug legislation passed in 2003 prohibited Medicare from negotiating with drug companies for lower prices, even though the Veterans' Administration performs this service for veterans, and private health insurance companies do so for employer-based health plans. Consequently, each of the 50 million Medicare beneficiaries is in an individual buying group, and individual seniors lack the leverage to negotiate for lower prescription drug prices.

As medical costs continue to increase, the expenses involved in maintaining the Medicare system will also rise substantially. Options for containing the costs of Medicare generally fall into one of three categories: limiting services, raising the age of eligibility, and shifting costs to older adults by increasing out-of-pocket costs (Quadagno, 1999). These options will disproportionately affect low-income older adults, particularly women aged 75 and older, because of their relatively lower incomes in old age. Remember that, unlike Social Security, in which costs per beneficiary are determined by law and can be known, Medicare costs are determined in large part by the type and amount of health care received by beneficiaries and the costs of providing it (Binstock, 1999). Costs could also be controlled by further limiting reimbursement rates for health care providers and products such as prescription drugs and medical equipment. However, as discussed above, there has been reluctance to implement such policies. Further, Medicare health care provider rates are already so low that in some areas it is difficult to find doctors who are willing to accept new Medicare patients. However, reimbursement limits on hospitals have not been found to result in similar access issues. The ACA does reduce reimbursements to hospitals and to certain other providers, but not to physicians.

The ACA also contains incentives for providers of Medicare services to establish "affordable care organizations." Providers taking part in these organizations will agree to be held accountable for improving the health care for individuals as well as for improving the health of populations. At the same time they will be expected to reduce the rate of growth in health care spending (CMS, 2011).

Although Medicare costs have grown rapidly, health care costs in the private sector have grown even more quickly. In fact, Medicare is widely lauded for its cost effectiveness. To bring the U.S. deficit under control, health care costs in both the public and private sectors will need to be addressed. We will discuss the future of Medicare in greater detail in the next chapter, which focuses on older adults.

Ageism in the Medicare Health Care Cost Debate Means of controlling health care costs, particularly in the face of technological advances in health care that are effective but also very expensive, will pose significant challenges as health care is extended to a larger population. These issues will become more serious when costs increase as the baby boom generation retires. The Social Security and Medicare Board of Trustees project that Medicare costs will grow substantially from approximately 3.7 percent of GDP in 2011 to 5.7 percent of GDP by 2035, and will increase gradually thereafter to about 6.7 percent of GDP by 2086 (The Board of Trustees, 2012). Methods of controlling health care costs will need more serious national debate and action, sooner rather than later, so that Medicare can continue to be provided to people who depend on it.

EXHIBIT 10.14

Medicare Makes Health Care Affordable for Many Older Adults

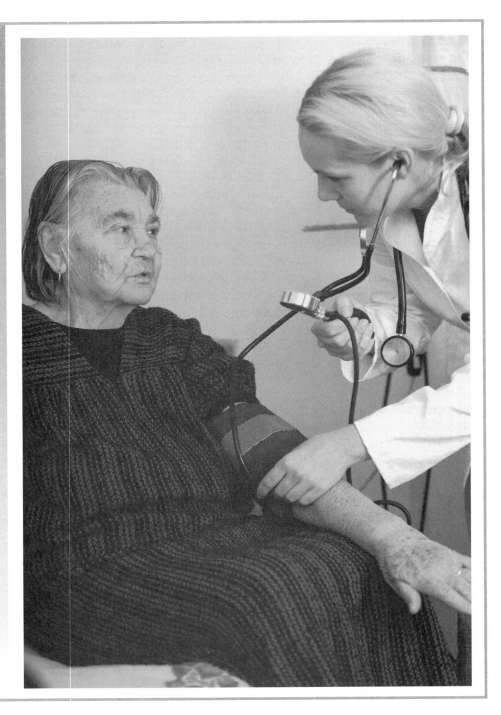

However, as we evaluate options for controlling health care costs, it is crucial to guard against the stereotyping and blaming that often lead to discrimination against people when discussing treatment and treatment costs. For example, during the health care reform debate, the "unplugging granny" metaphor was used as short-hand for what people thought they knew about how people on Medicare were draining the public health care coffers. This metaphor conjured up images of hospitals full of very old Americans kept alive on ventilators. As pointed out by Kingsley, it also feeds the caricature of the elderly population as disabled, of no use, and a burden on the rest of society (2010). This is an example of ageism which is characterized by negative stereotypes, and this kind of stereotyping can lead to discriminatory actions such as reduction in medical services. The "plugging in the elderly" discussion is demeaning and, furthermore, research indicates it has no relation to reality. In line with the International Code of Diagnoses and Procedures, "plugging in" refers to "intubation and ventilation." Dr. Kingsley had access to the latest database of hospital admissions and discharges in the U.S. (approximately eight million or 20 percent random sample of 2007 cases), to look at this procedure by ten-year age categories. His findings are:

- The age category of the largest proportion of patients on ventilators in 2007 was 0 through 9 (18 percent).

- Only 3 percent of ventilator patients were 90+.

- The 80 through 89 age group contained only 12.4 percent of patients on ventilators.

- A smaller proportion of patients on ventilators were in the 80 through 89 and 90+ age range than in the 50 through 59 (13.7 percent), 60 through 69 (16.4 percent), and the 70 through 79 (17.5 percent) age ranges.

- Further examination of the very expensive ventilator costs ($126,000+) by ten-year age categories indicates that 29 percent are incurred by patients under the age of ten while only 2.1 percent are incurred by patients 90+, and 10.3 percent are incurred by patients 80 through 89.

Kingsley indicated that the point of presenting these findings is not to shift blame from an older to a younger age group. Rather, his goal is to encourage us to stop blaming patients in *any* age group for increasing health care costs. Babies should not be blamed for health care costs, nor should the elderly. Patients of any age are deserving of the care they need (Kingsley, 2010).

Substance Abuse, Pandemics, and the Health Care System

U.S. health care policies have been particularly deficient in two areas: treatment of substance abuse and response to pandemics. Regarding substance abuse, the federal government has not been sufficiently supportive of policies and programs to provide treatment through medical and mental health interventions. We cannot ignore the fact that 60 percent of people with mental health conditions and nearly 90 percent of people with substance use disorders do not receive the care they need. That is why the ACA is so important to mental health. The health care law, along with previous parity legislation, will expand mental health and substance use disorder benefits and parity protections for 62 million Americans.

SAMHSA has also done work to build a more effective and culturally aware approach to substance abuse. This agency has also worked to promote more effective integrated treatment of people with dual diagnoses of both mental illness and substance abuse. However, most federal legislation reflects the belief that use and abuse of drugs should be controlled primarily through law enforcement and punishment. For example, the Anti-Drug Abuse Act of 1988 focuses on control strategies rather than treatment. When the Paul Wellstone and Pete Domenici Mental Health Parity and Addiction Equity Act of 2008 was fully implemented in 2011, it was hoped that treatment would become more widely available. However, definitive research to document the effect and cost implications of this law has yet to be completed. This law requires employer-sponsored health insurance plans to provide coverage for addiction and mental illness at a level consistent with other health conditions; however, this requirement only affects employers who have chosen to cover these kinds of treatment at all, and only applies to employers with more than 50 employees. Further, there is a trigger provision that goes into effect if costs rise too dramatically in the first year. The trigger provision gives the company plan a one-year exemption. Nonetheless, this parity legislation, combined with the increased access to health insurance provided under the health reform legislation passed in 2010, means more people suffering from addiction will be able to get treatment. Policies dealing with substance abuse are particularly important for social workers who provide services to clients who abuse alcohol and drugs. Minority group members who abuse drugs are much more likely to end up in prison than are members of more privileged populations who also have substance abuse challenges. Further, when effective treatment options are unavailable, those addicted, their children and their entire families suffer serious negative consequences. Substance abuse is not just a criminal justice issue. It is also a family issue and a public health issue. For the latest information on federal drug abuse policy, go to the website of the Office of National Drug Control Policy (www.white-housedrugpolicy.gov). Be sure to take a look at the *National Drug Control Strategy*, the president's plan to reduce drug use and its consequences. These plans are updated yearly.

Pandemics are epidemics that occur across large geographic regions. Two well-known examples are Acquired Immune Deficiency Syndrome (AIDS) and Human Immunodeficiency Virus (HIV). Since the 1980s, these pandemics have presented major challenges to our health care system, and the federal government often has been slow to respond. In fact, the Ryan White Comprehensive AIDS Resources

Emergency (CARE) Act of 1990 is the only major federal policy implemented as a direct response to AIDS/HIV in our country. Passed after years of work by advocacy groups, this legislation authorized federal funds for health care services for people who have AIDS or are HIV-positive. This legislation was reauthorized in 2006 and, in 2009, President Obama signed legislation which extends the Ryan White Care Act for an additional four years. For more information on the CARE Act of 1990, go to the website of the Health Resources and Services Administration (HRSA) (www.hrsa.gov), Health and Human Services HIV/AIDS Bureau (HAB). Additionally the White House has issued a National *HIV/AIDS Strategy for the United States*, which is available at http://www.cdc.gov/hiv/policies/nhas.html.

Because AIDS/HIV patients were initially perceived to be members of marginalized groups, particularly gay men and intravenous drug users, social values that held these people responsible for their illness interfered with mounting a timely and effective public health response. The devastating effects of pandemics such as AIDS/HIV make it increasingly clear that U.S. health policy makers must pay close attention to the influence of global health conditions. The H1N1 flu epidemic in 2009 provided yet another clear illustration of growing global interdependency in the health arena and of the economic impact of pandemics. The flu moved rapidly across borders, and international cooperation was necessary to control its spread. Economic consequences were felt around the world as worker productivity decreased in the wake of the flu pandemic.

Social Work Education and Health Care Reform   The Health Care and Education Affordability Reconciliation Act, which was part of health care reform, also includes education provisions that make it easier for social work students to complete an affordable education. It mandates increased funding for Pell Grants and increased the federal maximum Pell Grant Award. This legislation also includes geriatric and behavioral health training grants and loan repayment funding for behavioral health providers, including social workers. This legislation was a victory for social workers, who have long been advocating for funds to help students become social workers so the health and mental health needs of Americans can more adequately be met. However, there is still more to be done if we are to close the gap between the number of social workers being educated and future need in the health care field, particularly in the area of aging services. To find out more about how this legislation can help you, and other students more generally, afford college, go to whitehouse.gov and search for the Health Care and Education Reconciliation Act.

Next Steps for Promoting More Effective Health and Mental Health Policies

Universal access to both health and mental health services is vital to well-being. The NASW has long backed a universal approach to ensuring provision of health care. While the health care reform legislation of 2010 helped to close the gap in insurance availability for low-income people, there is much more to be done. We do not yet have a universal system that covers all people in the U.S.

Given the long-held preference in the U.S. for public–private partnerships and the already established system of private health insurance provided through the workplace, it is not surprising that this health care reform legislation incorporates both public and private insurance strategies. However, because no single entity is acting as the universal insurer, there is not a single payer. So, avoiding increases in health care costs by negotiating with health care providers and pharmaceutical companies based on buying power of a universal insurer is not possible. Therefore, it will be hard to control rapidly rising health care costs with this approach to extending coverage to people without insurance. Further, analysts on the right see even this blend of public and private insurance as a government "takeover" of health care.

Nonetheless, for an expanded system to be cost-effective, the U.S. will have to implement more policies to contain rising costs, which means further limiting profits in the powerful health care industry. Under Medicare and Medicaid, most health care is provided privately but reimbursed publicly, with the federal government acting as insurer. It is far too costly for the federal government to simply pay whatever providers decide to charge. As discussed earlier, possible strategies are to implement prospective setting of payment rates and to use the power of the huge buying group to negotiate lower prices. Further, we need to reduce the substantial costs associated with the multiple insurance companies that now oversee health care. Additionally, it is important to design payment systems such that service providers do not have large financial incentives to either provide or withhold treatment. Rather, providers should base treatment decisions solely on the best interests of the patient (NASW, 2012a).

As Steven Brill has pointed out, when health care reform is debated, the focus has been primarily on *who will pay?* But, we have largely ignored the question, *are prices too high?* (2013). We should expect our policy makers to scrutinize all parts of the health care systems, including hospitals and pharmaceutical companies, to identify cost savings and then to take steps to control these costs. Given ongoing congressional efforts to stem the U.S. deficit, health care cost controls are particularly important since rising health care costs could squeeze out federal spending in other critical areas, including education and housing and other concerns of social workers. You can ask your congressional representatives to take these steps.

Medicare Reform

Turning to Medicare, it is critical that Medicare be maintained as a defined benefit rather than shifting to a defined contribution approach. In the latter approach, Medicare would allocate a set amount for each older adult, to be used to purchase health care. Once the older adult spent that money, the federal government would have no further responsibility for her or his health care, regardless of the amount of care she or he needs. This could lead to serious gaps in access for those without the resources to cover the differences in costs. Another reform proposal which involves risk-shifting to older adults is the use of a voucher system. Beneficiaries would receive a premium support, or voucher, to buy private health care coverage or traditional Medicare. This is promoted as a way to increase competition and thus control costs. However, the reality is that most Medicare beneficiaries are not in a position, particularly when they are ill, to do comparison shopping. Further, the value of the voucher would likely not keep pace with actual health care inflation and gradually more of the costs of health care will be shifted to individuals receiving Medicare. These ideas for reform which shifts risks to individuals will likely resurface again and again and it is critical that you have some familiarity with them so you can speak up when they are proposed.

Mental Health Care

In the area of mental health, the NASW has vigorously supported full parity of mental health coverage with other health care coverage in public as well as private health insurance systems. Social workers have advocated long and hard for mental health and substance abuse parity. Social workers have also voiced concerns about how these insurance systems define mental illness for reimbursement purposes. Mental health policies that provide funding for services specify the definition of mental illness and the basis upon which diagnoses should be made. *The Diagnostic and Statistical Manual of Mental Disorders*, 5th Edition (*DSM-5*) is the latest edition of this manual, which is widely used to classify mental disorders in the U.S. (American Psychiatric Association, 2013). Social workers have participated in heated debates about the need to view mental illness and mental health in biopsychosocial terms rather than focusing so heavily on a neurobiological approach. Definitions and classifications contained in mental health policies would need to be revised if services based on broader definitions of mental health and illness were to be reimbursed through public programs. Visit the website of the National Alliance on Mental Illness (www.nami.org) to learn more about mental health advocacy initiatives.

Further, we need to develop policies that support health and mental health training for people from a variety of racial and ethnic backgrounds in order to enhance the provision of culturally competent services. Additional ways of promoting more culturally competent health care include boosting research specific to minorities, tailoring treatment to those from different cultures who speak different languages, integrating mental health care with primary medical care, and increasing mental health services in isolated areas. Essential social work services should be available in both mental health and health care settings. The expertise of social workers should be recognized. Social work services should be reimbursed at rates comparable to those of other professions. NASW also advocates for all health settings to employ master's level and baccalaureate level social workers from accredited schools of social work who are licenced or certified at the appropriate level.

EXHIBIT 10.15 *Students Fight for Mental Health Funding*	Forty-five social work students at a university in the northeast created and implemented a social action plan to combat potential state budget cuts to mental health funding. The students testified in front of legislative committees, compiled data on financial burdens facing local mental health facilities, generated alternative options for budget cuts, and worked to get increased media coverage of mental health allocations. The students' efforts, as well as those of other advocacy groups, helped to restore more than 27 million dollars for mental health funding.

Strategies to Promote Recovery, Diversity, and Health Mental health experts working from the strengths perspective advocate for mental health policies that concentrate on promoting recovery and building resilience (Saleebey, 2013). People with SMI often need housing and employment support. Policies should promote full community participation instead of institutionalization, homelessness, and long-term disability. The efforts of people with mental illness to find work should be supported rather than discouraged by negative sanctions such as loss of public benefits. Policies that promote employment of people who have been mentally ill as providers of mental health services should be expanded. For people with mental illness who are in correctional facilities and homeless shelters, policies supporting detection and treatment are critical. The right to treatment as well as the right to refuse treatment should be protected. People with co-occurring conditions, such as mental illness and substance abuse, need integrated services that address both conditions.

Social Workers and Health Care Reform

Social workers have long advocated for health care reforms and celebrated the passage of the ACA in 2010. Although it does not provide universal health care, the 2010 health care reform legislation will dramatically increase access to these services. However, there is much more work to be done. At both the federal and the state levels, rules and regulations will need to be developed in order to implement this legislation (Gorin, 2010). Remember, states make the choices about whether and how they develop the Medicaid expansion made possible under this legislation. In states that choose to expand Medicaid, coverage for some groups and services is mandated, but the legislation also contains options and incentives to expand coverage further which states may or may not decide to pursue. Go to the website of the Kaiser Family Foundation and browse their resources on health care reform to learn more about the options your state may or may not decide to implement. The way that rules and regulations are developed at the state level for both mandatory and optional insurance coverage in your state will have great impact on your clients.

EXHIBIT 10.16

*Students
Advocate for
Medicaid
Expansion*

Social work students at a large university in a state where the governor was undecided on whether to accept Medicaid expansion under the ACA, organized an online campaign to educate voters about the number of uninsured who would be eligible if the state accepted Medicaid expansion, and how expansion would benefit everyone in the state by improving health care, job creation, and creating healthier and more financially stable families. They also initiated an online petition that was sent to the governor, took part in a rally held at the state capitol to support Medicaid expansion, and recruited other faculty and students to join them.

You and your classmates can influence this process if you become informed and then apply the policy practice skills outlined in Chapter 6. This is an extremely important time for involvement of social workers.

It is also crucial that social workers help educate people about the benefits available to them, to encourage states to implement provisions of the ACA which benefit our clients, and to help see provisions that protect patients' rights to health care are enforced. Most immediately, social workers need to understand when and how to sign up clients now eligible for services under the ACA. However, signing up is only the first step. We must also continue to work to ensure that there are an adequate number of service providers and that they are delivering accessible, culturally appropriate services to our clients. These provider shortages are particularly acute in rural areas and, to a lesser extent, in underserved urban communities, as well.

Social workers in hospitals, nursing homes, and other health care settings are directly involved in determining eligibility for public health insurance programs as well as in helping to sort out private insurance problems. Social workers in all settings need to know which public programs are available and how to help their clients determine if they are eligible. They also need to understand mechanisms for patient protection within public and private insurance programs such as the right to due process and the right to appeal insurance companies' decisions. Clients may be unfamiliar with their rights and might need help in negotiating the appeals system.

Social workers can also continue to oppose efforts to turn Medicaid into a block grant to states. It is important to continue to work to create increased access to health care if a more equitable system is to develop. Equal access to mental health and substance abuse care, regardless of employment status, is of particular importance to social workers who often are providers of these services. Social workers can help to see that parity laws are enforced by helping clients take action when services are unfairly limited and denied (NASW, 2012d). They also need to work to ensure that mental health services are covered in publicly and privately provided health care plans as the ACA is fully implemented.

Look at the information provided in this chapter and the multitude of Internet resources included, think for yourself, and then speak up when health care reform is discussed. Many people have misperceptions about health reform. You can provide them with information you have learned in this text and from trusted sources on the web that will help them become more knowledgeable. You can also relay the experiences of your clients, including those who lack insurance and struggle to access needed care. Not only will you be helping develop an informed public consensus about this legislation, you will also be helping people learn how they or their family could benefit from the legislation, and how they can gain access to needed health and mental health care. The more conversant you become with this legislation, the more effective you will be in helping your clients become eligible for health insurance. To find out more about social work and health care reform, go to the NASW website and look at the publications available under the "health" topic.

It is also important to keep in mind that, as the experience of other countries has demonstrated, making health care more widely available will not, by itself, create equality in health outcomes. The influential Whitehall Studies of lifespan inequality and health care, conducted in the United Kingdom, found that structural issues of hierarchy and locus of control, along with other dimensions of social class, have a profound and enduring effect on health status and outcomes. This is true even when access to health care services becomes more universal (Marmot and Brunner, 2005). The Whitehall Studies' researchers found a steep inverse association between social class and mortality from a wide variety of diseases. This research involved British civil servants, none of whom was poor in the absolute sense. However, researchers found there was a social gradient in mortality running from the bottom to the top of society. The more senior people in the employment hierarchy lived longer, as compared to those in lower employment grades. In discussing the implications of their studies, the researchers indicated that when attempting to understand differences in health care outcomes, more attention needs to be paid to social environment and the consequences of income inequality. This research lends further support to the importance of social determinants of health discussed earlier in the chapter. Other studies of health care outcomes also draw attention to these factors (Blank and Burau, 2010). Certainly this is seen in the U.S., where individuals who experience racism, economic oppression, and other marginalization suffer disproportionately on a variety of health indicators, including exposure to toxins, risk of obesity and chronic disease, and injury leading to early disability.

There are many additional areas where social workers can play an important part in changing health care policies. For example, although the social work literature has critiqued the medical model, which focuses narrowly on the diagnosis and treatment of illness and pathology by medical experts, it is not enough simply to critique current policies and practice. Rather, promoting health and wellness instead of focusing narrowly on treating illness is central to the strengths perspective. Policies are needed to support new approaches that are not based on pathology and deficits.

A Health Model   Using the strengths perspective, Weick, a prominent social work scholar, has proposed a health model based on a biopsychosocial approach. In contrast to the medical model, Weick's health model urges us to focus on the multiple influences that affect health and health care. Living in unsafe neighborhoods with few health care facilities, dangerous working conditions, and inadequate nutrition are examples of such influences. Weick points out how the environment determines people's health.

The goal of Weick's model is to empower people. Work based on this model encourages holistic approaches that include prevention as well as strategies for maintaining or regaining good health. These strategies emphasize the capacity of people to improve their own health. This model is not about shifting responsibility for health to individuals themselves, but, instead, taking a broader view of what contributes to health outcomes. The intent is to expand our thinking beyond health care and increase focus on health. Weick's approach encourages practitioners to identify and challenge economic and cultural barriers to health and health care. It also urges them to advocate for policies that promote assertive outreach and for programs that provide clients with essential health-related information (Saleebey, 2013; Weick, 1986).

Such approaches also reduce the stigma attached to receiving mental health services because they present the act of seeking out services to maintain or regain mental health as a strength. Mental health initiatives based on the health model would be designed to reinforce the positive steps citizens can take to maintain their mental health, as well as the benefits of doing so. For example, schools and the broader community could be encouraged to do more to promote strategies for preventing mental health problems and seeking formal treatment if necessary. The initiatives currently under way to encourage positive health habits during pregnancy, reduce obesity, and increase immunization rates for children, provide ideas for developing and implementing such strategies.

A health perspective guides us to consider how we can establish policies that create an environment in which people have the maximum chance for good health and can develop their strengths more fully. For example, addressing environmental issues, such as exposure to air and water pollution, that have a negative impact on health will help improve the health of many people. Social workers need to be alert to the negative health effects of environmental pollution, particularly in low-income neighborhoods and tribal communities. Similarly, policies that increase access to healthy food and opportunities to safely walk and get exercise in a neighborhood, are vital to reduce obesity and other health problems.

Social workers in the mental health field have worked for years to enact policies that support recovery for people with serious and persistent mental illness (Saleebey, 2013). The focus has been on resilience and strengths rather than on disability and deficits. This work illustrates how the strengths perspective can be used in crafting health policy. Employing a health perspective will help you see new possibilities for improving health care in the U.S.

CONCLUSION

Health and mental health policies in our country have created a system in which some people who can afford health care get excellent care, but many other people do not have even basic health care. We have a legacy of neglect of health and mental health care for members of racial and ethnic minority groups. With the implementation of the 2010 ACA, many barriers to health care access will be addressed, but it is naive to expect that health care disparities and differences in health outcomes will disappear. Economic, occupational, social, and environmental policies also influence the state of our health, and the health implications of these policies must be carefully considered if longevity and quality of life are to be maintained. Faced with an aging population and attendant increases in both acute and chronic health care needs, it is critical that we find ways to control health care costs, promote wellness, and ensure adequate health care for people across their life spans. In the final two chapters of this book, we first examine policies and programs for older adults and then turn our attention to strategies for dealing with future policy dilemmas. The health care policy basics covered in this chapter provide the foundation for thinking about how we may begin to address future challenges, including those posed by greater longevity and rapidly increasing health care costs.

CATCHING UP WITH THE POLICY GROUP

Now let us catch up with Alice as she begins working as a hospital social worker.

Alice was delighted when she was hired to do hospital social work. She knew that when family members were hospitalized, the stress could be significant. However, she realized there were opportunities for connecting families to extra supports they might not have known about, that could help them after discharge from the hospital. In her work as a discharge planner, she is called to talk to new teen moms who lack support. She makes sure the teens know about programs such as WIC and TANF and the community nursery and, more specifically, know how to access the services provided by these programs. However, her position does not allow her to visit these new mothers in their homes and she often does not see them again unless their baby is very ill or injured seriously enough to require hospitalization. She remembered reading about a program in her policy class that provided funds for voluntary follow-up home visits for mothers and their children (see discussion of the Maternal, Infant, and Early Childhood Home Visiting Program in Chapter 9). She wants to see such a program started in her community, so she has set about making it happen. She talked to her supervisor at the hospital who had not heard of the program. Alice then used the Internet to learn more about the program and how it was funded. She also got in touch with colleagues in the county public health office who worked with mothers and infants. Now she is not sure what her next step is and what she should do next to go about getting this program implemented in her community.

EXHIBIT 10.17

Alice

Think back about what you learned in Chapter 6. What do you think Alice should do next? Can you think of things she might have done differently? How might she get young moms involved in advocating for a home visiting program? What assessment and analysis might have helped her to determine whether a home visiting program was the best way to support these clients, and, then, to make the case for this investment? What do you think her next steps might be as she implements an action plan to create new policies and programs and improve the lives of new mothers and their babies?

MAIN POINTS

- Social determinants of health are "the circumstances, in which people are born, grow up, live, work, and age, as well as the systems put in place to deal with illness" (CDC, 2013). These circumstances also influence access to health care.

- Prior to passage of the Affordable Care Act (ACA), over 15 percent of the American population was uninsured. When the ACA is fully implemented, the percentage of people without insurance is projected to be less than 8 percent.

- Most people with insurance are insured through their employers. The U.S. has the highest per person expenditure for health care, but many health outcomes are not as positive as those in countries that spend far less.

- Medicaid provides health insurance to low-income people who fall within the state guidelines for "categorically needy." Medicaid is jointly funded by federal and state governments.

- Medicare provides health insurance for eligible people over age 65, people with certain disabilities, and people with end-stage renal disease. Medicare is administered at the federal level, funded by payroll taxes (Part A) and premium payments and the federal general fund (Part B). The Medicare Prescription Drug Act was passed in 2003 and provides limited coverage for prescription drugs.

- Medicare was used as a vehicle to expand civil rights by requiring hospitals receiving Medicare to be integrated in the 1960s, and again in 2010 by requiring hospitals receiving Medicare and Medicaid to give same-sex couples the right to be with a partner who is sick or dying.

- The State Children's Health Insurance Program, now called CHIP, was established in 1997 to increase the number of children insured in the U.S. Children under the age of 19 are eligible for this insurance program.

- Cost containment efforts in U.S. health care have resulted in diagnosis-related groups (DRGs) and the introduction of managed care providers to both public and private insurance systems. The incentive for underservice in managed care makes necessary increased attention to protecting patients' rights to adequate treatment.

- While falling short of universal health care, The Patient Protection and Affordable Care Act of 2010, as modified by the Health Care and Education Affordability Reconciliation Act (ACA) will expand coverage to an estimated 30 million people when fully phased in. This legislation includes major changes to Medicaid and Medicare.

- Health care costs will continue to rise in the U.S. and effective cost containment strategies must be identified and implemented in order to build an adequate, sustainable health care system.

- To address these concerns, the 2010 health care reforms also include funding for pilots, demonstrations, and the creation of the Center for Medicare and Medicaid Innovation (CMI) to research cost containment approaches, prevention, medical homes, and other practices to improve service integration and patient outcomes.

- Major mental disorders are experienced by one in five people in the U.S. These disorders often go untreated owing to barriers such as a fragmented mental health delivery system, inadequate funding, stigma attached to service utilization, and lack of cultural competence.

- Deinstitutionalization refers to the policy of providing community-based services for people with disabilities who were formerly served in institutions. The Mental Retardation and Community Mental Health Centers Construction Act and the State Comprehensive Mental Health Services Plan Act were two major pieces of legislation that contributed to the deinstitutionalization of people with mental illness.

- Lack of adequate funding to build an effective community mental health service system has resulted in the reinstitutionalization of many people with mental illness in our correctional system where mental health services are often lacking.

- Overuse of psychotropic medications, particularly with children in foster care, has been repeatedly documented, but alternative mental health treatment approaches are often still not accessible or affordable.

- In 2008, the Paul Wellstone and Pete Domenici Mental Health Parity and Addiction Equity Act was passed and closed some of the loopholes that had made the 1996 Mental Health Parity Act ineffective. The 2008 Act required parity in co-payments, deductibles, and out-of-pocket expenses. It also required parity in setting treatment limits.

- Social workers need to be involved in educating people about the ACA, ensuring that rules and regulations developed in their state are equitable, helping people to get the health benefits for which they are now eligible, and ensuring that the patients' rights afforded by the legislation are enforced.

- Promotion of health and wellness rather than a narrow focus on treatment of illness is central to the strengths perspective. The challenge is to develop policies that create an environment in which people have the maximum chance for good health and can develop their strengths more fully.

EXERCISES

1. Go to the Sanchez family case on the website for this text. Do you think Joey, the Sanchez family grandchild, would qualify for CHIP in your state?
   a. How would you determine if he was eligible?
   b. What other members of the family do you think might qualify for the major health care programs discussed in this chapter?

c. How might having health insurance make a difference in the lives of the Sanchez family? What other barriers to securing health care might they encounter, even with insurance coverage?

2. We know that health outcomes for Latinos/Hispanic Americans are not as positive as for the majority population. Problems related to service access help to create these health outcome disparities. What strategies for overcoming problems in accessing health care for Hispanic families such as the Sanchez family might prove effective in reducing health outcome disparities?

3. Go to the Carla Washburn case on the website for this text. Carla Washburn receives Medicare. During the debate on health care reform, many older adults expressed fear their Medicare benefits would be reduced. In fact, in 2010, older adults at Tea Party rallies opposing the new legislation often stated they were against the ACA because it will harm Medicare. Look back in this chapter and do some further research on how Medicare benefits will change as a result of health care reform.

   a. How would you explain those changes to Carla Washburn or to older adults in your family who may be afraid that Medicare will be weakened as a result of health care reform?

   b. As detailed in the vignette, Carla Washburn interacts with a variety of people and community agencies in her community. Which of these people and/or agencies do you think might do outreach to older adults like Carla to help them more clearly understand the impact of health care reform? How do you think organizations working to increase support for health care reform could work with community agencies to help build more widespread understanding of the new health care reform initiatives?

4. Go to the Riverton case on the website for this text. Health care reform will potentially expand access to Medicaid for the homeless people in Riverton. Contact the staff of your local homeless shelter or, better yet, do some volunteer work there, and find out how homeless people currently get their health care needs met. Ask if there are plans to help get homeless people on Medicaid if they become eligible in your state due to Medicaid expansion.

   a. Take the knowledge you gather and identify what agencies in Riverton would be the logical ones to help homeless people access medical care.

   b. What do you think will be some of the barriers to getting homeless people signed up and participating in health care plans?

   c. What are some strategies for overcoming these barriers?

   d. Some researchers have reported that as many as 80 percent of people they studied who were homeless have serious mental health, drug abuse, and/or alcoholism problems. What policy and program modifications related to screening, outreach, and treatment do you think homeless shelters and providers of treatment would need to implement in order to get effective treatment for homeless people with these conditions?

5. What types of mental health resources will be needed across a community like Hudson City, following a disaster?
   a. How could a strong mental health service system prior to a disaster position a community to recover more quickly?
   b. If you were a social worker working with uninsured people in Hudson City, what might be some of your concerns regarding their access to health care?
6. Online treatment alternatives such as the one illustrated in the RAINN case are increasingly being developed to treat mental health concerns. What questions do you think should be considered before new public funds for health care are made available for online treatment alternatives? How can innovations in treatment modalities improve outcomes and contain costs? What considerations regarding access to treatment, especially for vulnerable populations, need to be emphasized in such service shifts?
7. The legacy of oppression of Native Americans has produced conditions that have led to public health outcomes that are poorer for Native Americans than for the general population. Identify at least three policy changes at the federal, state, or local level that could help to equalize conditions between poorer Native American communities and their more affluent non-native counterparts.
8. Indian Health Services has a very high rate of professional staff turnover on many reservations and this contributes to poor health care outcomes. What strategies, including policy changes, can you suggest to increase the quality of health care staff and reduce the rate of health care staff turnover in these communities? How might some of the new initiatives in the 2010 health care reform address these needs?
9. As discussed in this chapter, research has indicated that inequities in health care service as well as outcomes persist even when access to health care services becomes more universal. Identify four possible reasons these inequities persist and suggest policy and program changes social workers could champion that would help reduce inequity.
10. Participate in one of the many health care promotion activities currently being implemented, such as outreach to young pregnant women who are not receiving prenatal care, initiatives to get children outdoors and exercising, smoking prevention or cessation efforts with teenagers or adults. Write up a brief summary of what was done and what was learned from the experience. Be sure to discuss how greater access to services under health care reform will or will not impact these health issues, what more needs to be done, and the potential role of social workers in dealing with these health issues.
11. Pick a group such as children, refugees, or older adults. Figure out how you would help clients in this group determine the publicly financed health care services for which they would be eligible.
   a. How could they find out if they qualified for these services?
   b. What web resources are available and trustworthy to help them?

12. Choose a social work agency where you think you might like to work. Find out if they provide health insurance to entry level workers. Is the cost affordable? Are dependents covered? If you have worked previously, how do these health care benefits compare to what you received with previous jobs? What factors do you think account for the differences?

13. Consider how the 2010 health care reform legislation will directly impact you. For example, will you be able to stay on your parents' insurance longer? How will your ability to get college grants and loans, and pay off student loans be affected? If you have a pre-existing condition, a disability, or lose your job, how will you be affected? How can you use your own story to help others understand the impact of this legislation? What does this suggest for the importance of stories in raising awareness and building support for key social policy changes?

CHAPTER 11

Policies and Programs
for Older Adults

Age is an opportunity, no less than youth itself.

Henry Wadsworth Longfellow

Our childhood and youth in large part determine whether our old age is the winter of life, or the harvest.

Author Unknown

We reject the belief that America must choose between caring for the generation that built this country and investing in the generation that will build its future.

Barack Obama

W E ARE BOMBARDED DAILY with messages about the role older adults play in our society. Many of these messages depict older people as dependent, debilitated, idle, and a driver of federal debt. Again, you will need to think for yourself. Hopefully, you know a variety of older adults and have experienced firsthand how they have and continue to contribute to society, so you can counter negative stereotypes. If not, consider ways to increase the age diversity in your social circle. As pointed out in earlier chapters, the strengths perspective is premised on the importance of being attuned to the voices of diverse groups. This chapter will help you understand both the opportunities and challenges faced by older adults and the policies and programs that serve them. These policies and programs are very likely also benefiting you today, and will be vital to your own old age. Furthermore, in fundamental ways, the well-being of the entire society is connected to how well our policy structures support older adults in our communities.

Do you think old age begins when the invitation to join AARP arrives to mark your 50th birthday? Or, does it begin at 60 when you become eligible for services through the Older American Act? Perhaps it is 65, the age most people become eligible for Medicare, or 67, when most young people today can now expect to become eligible for full Social Security retirement benefits.

EXHIBIT 11.1

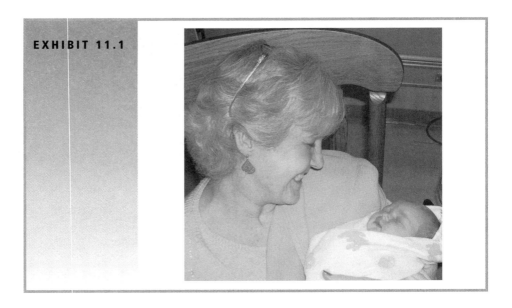

A study by the Pew Research Center reported that people aged 18 to 29 who were surveyed believed that the average person becomes old when they turn 60. Middle-aged respondents said the age was closer to 70, and people aged 65 and over responded that the average person becomes old at 74 (Pew Research Center, 2009).

EXHIBIT 11.2

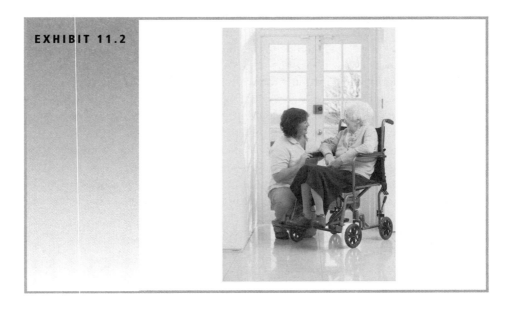

EXHIBIT 11.3

Especially because life expectancy continues to increase, depending on the definition of "old" being used, people may be categorized as old for over a third, and for some people, over half of their lives. Clearly, an age category that can include people from 50 to 120, a range of 70 years, will contain adults with needs and capacities that are extremely diverse.

Policy responding to older-adult populations in the U.S. should be flexible and robust enough to meet the needs of this diverse aging population, providing for their current needs, building on their strengths, and laying a strong foundation for the future. Attaining the age of 65, 75, and increasingly even 100 is a testament to the strengths of older adults. The rewards of survival should not be poverty and loneliness or premature institutionalization in a nursing facility. Rather, we need to develop public social policies that support older adults in their quest to age well. To understand the issues associated with aging from the strengths perspective, we need to broaden our focus from the deficits and problems associated with aging and consider the resources necessary to age well. Further, because older adults have all had a life time of experience, a solution focused approach to policies and programs whereby the service users are asked to propose workable strategies, is one that is particularly applicable when developing services and supports for older adults.

EXHIBIT 11.4

Kahana and Kahana, prominent scholars in the aging field, define aging well as a "comprehensive and holistic process in which older adults adapt self and the environment to respond actively to the challenges of aging" (1996). Aging well becomes possible when we minimize the negative effects of losses that are often associated with aging—such as those of some physical and mental capacity, employment, and loved ones—and maximize the benefits that accompany a long life, such as a large network of family and friends, the wisdom acquired through years of surmounting obstacles, and accumulated assets. An emphasis on social integration, social engagement, social networks and the social environment in defining what it means to age well is also supported by the ecological perspective, which recognizes the influence of relationships and transactions among the older adult, other individuals, and the older adult's social and physical environments. In addition, the use of the strengths perspective in work with older adults can help refocus our understanding of this stage of life (Nelson-Becker, Chapin, and Fast, 2013). Although the period of older adulthood, as well as all other stages of life, certainly requires adaptation, the strengths perspective emphasizes the new goals and resources that can have a transformative effect on the last stage of life. When people do not assume that older adults want to retire and rest, but rather create opportunities for them to continue to set their own goals and participate in the life of the community, then older adults will be able to use the diversity of goals and resources they possess to create and pursue their own visions of aging well and, in the process, positively influence their communities. For example, an older adult receiving a public or private pension may now have the time and resources to work part-time for the city parks and recreation department planting and tending flowers in the city park or coaching children's sports teams. Doing these things may have been a long-term goal or something they want to do that utilizes their resources and skills without the added pressure of a full-time job. If policies permit the hiring of part-time workers, and age discrimination is not allowed, older adults can take part in meaningful, productive activities far into advanced age. We need policies that support older adults who not only want to work because it is personally fulfilling but also those who must work at least part-time out of economic necessity. Many older adults have been hard hit by the economic downturn and need to work, but may not want, or be able, to work full-time. Resources such as an adequate public transportation system can support paid work as well as other activities older adults find meaningful, such as spending time with friends and family and building relationships with younger relatives. Carefully crafted public social policies can help older adults overcome barriers in the social environment that limit autonomy and pose risks to financial and health security. The focus on person in environment that is the hallmark of social work places social workers in a key position to press for such policies and programs.

This chapter provides an overview of key policy issues that currently influence older adults. The many changes in policy and programs for older adults resulting from the passage of the Affordable Care Act (ACA) in 2010 are also discussed in this chapter. These include changes in the area of elder justice that have important implications for social workers. In this chapter, we will examine and evaluate major policies and programs and explore policy strategies that promote economic security, adequate health care, and social engagement, toward the goal of supporting "aging well."

HISTORY AND BACKGROUND

Prior to the 20th century, most people worked as long as they possibly could and then depended primarily on their families to support them. As you learned in Chapter 2, as far back as the Middle Ages, some guilds and other private organizations developed mutual aid and insurance programs to help their members when they could not work. However, such supports were not available to most people. Poorhouses were the last refuge for older adults who could not work, did not have assets, and had no families who were willing or able to care for them. Keep in mind, however, that in those days, life expectancy was shorter, families typically had more children, and children generally stayed in the same communities as their parents and grandparents. Consequently, there were proportionately fewer elders in need of financial support and health care in relation to the number of children and grandchildren in the community who were available to provide care. Further, most women did not work outside the home and, therefore, were available to care for elders, although the strains of this uncompensated caregiving impacted women's financial, physical, and mental well-being throughout history.

Policy and Program Responses

Before 1870, the majority of U.S. workers were employed on farms. However, in the late 19th and early 20th centuries, industrialization spread rapidly, families became much more mobile, and life expectancy increased. Proportionately fewer people worked as independent farmers, tradesmen, and artisans engaged in family enterprises. Although the traditional supports for people in old age were disappearing at the same time that longevity was increasing, social programs to meet their needs were slow to develop. Private charities, community organizations, and local governments did provide some relief for destitute and disabled older adults. However, prior to the 1930s, there were few public social programs for older adults. In the following sections, we discuss the early public and private retirement programs that were available in the 1800s. We also examine a variety of federal social policies and programs for older adults that were developed beginning in the 1930s.

Private Retirement Programs   In the U.S., the American Express Company established the first private pension plan in 1875. Within a short time, some banking, utility, railroad, and manufacturing companies also started offering pensions to their employees (Pension Benefit Guaranty Corporation, 2009). Most of the early pension plans provided defined benefit plans. Defined benefit plans pay a specific amount every month if the retired person has worked the required number of years. These early plans were funded entirely by employers (Pension Benefit Guaranty Corporation, 2009). However, only a fraction of U.S. employees worked in jobs covered by such plans.

Public Retirement Programs   Recall from our discussion in Chapter 2 that large numbers of veterans, as well as widows and families of veterans, received military pensions after the Civil War. By the early 1900s, many states and municipalities had established retirement programs for their employees. In addition, by that time, many European nations had developed publicly supported retirement systems for the general citizenry. For example, in 1899, Chancellor Otto von Bismarck established a state retirement system in Germany that provided benefits for retired workers aged 65 and older.

During the first half of the 20th century, the idea that people should leave the workforce at a certain age and then be subsidized in their retirement through public benefits gained wider support. Industrialization, advances in medicine, and the problem of surplus labor, particularly during economic downturns, contributed to an environment in which retirement policy could be enacted. In the U.S., the Great Depression was a particularly hard time for older people. Many elders lost their homes, farms, and life savings. Often, children moved away to pursue opportunities in other parts of the country and, therefore, could not be counted on to support their parents. Further, jobs were in short supply, which increased public support for policies to get older adults out of the workforce.

Given these conditions, social movements such as the Townsend Movement and the Ham and Eggs Movement gained momentum and exerted strong political pressure on the federal government to enact old age insurance (Axinn and Stern, 2001). Like the Townsend Movement, which we discussed previously, the Ham and Eggs Movement endorsed pensions for unemployed older adults. Specifically, it pressed for weekly pensions for unemployed Californians aged 50 and older. The movement's rallying cry was "$30 every Thursday," reflecting a commitment to providing a subsistence level of support for older adults out of the workforce (Social Security Administration, 2007). Although some of the policy initiatives this group supported were based on dubious economics, this was the first time in U.S. history that elders organized as a voting bloc to support legislation. It was this confluence of ideology, economics, history, and social movements that made possible the enactment of watershed legislation such as the Social Security Act of 1935, which established Old-Age, Survivors, and Disability Insurance (OASDI). If you would like to learn more about the Townsend Movement, the Ham and Eggs Movement, and other social movements in support of public pensions, go to the website of the Social Security Administration (www.ssa.gov), search for History, and then choose Historical Background and Development.

Policies to Provide Health Care and Support Social Engagement   The other major public programs that aid older adults were established 30 years later. With the passage of Medicare, Medicaid, and the Older Americans Act, 1965 was a banner year for legislation for older adults. As discussed in the previous chapter, Medicare is the health insurance program for older adults and people with disabilities, and Medicaid is a means-tested program for people who have low incomes. Medicare provides eligible older adults with coverage for inpatient hospital care. Optional Medicare coverage for outpatient hospital care and doctors' services can be purchased for an additional premium. Medicaid is the primary payment source for nursing facility care. Many older adults become eligible for Medicaid after they impoverish themselves by paying for long-term care because that care is so costly. Expenditures for OASDI, Medicare, and Medicaid make up the bulk of federal spending directed to older adults. Because access to health care is an essential component of aging well, social workers must be familiar with the resources Medicaid and Medicare provide to older adults and how elders can navigate these programs to secure the health care they need. Information in Chapter 10 provided that foundational knowledge.

Congress also passed the Older Americans Act (OAA) in 1965. This law was designed to improve the coordination of planning and programs for older adults and to support their efforts to remain in the community even when they needed long-term care. However, it has never been adequately funded. We discuss the OAA and its subsequent amendments in the following section on major policies and programs. With the passage of OASDI, Medicare, Medicaid, and the OAA, the nation had established policies to address economic security, health care, and social engagement, three crucial arenas where public support for older adults is needed.

Changes to Job-Specific Pension Programs Some employment positions in both the public and private sectors offer job-specific pensions. The number of people with job-specific pensions increased markedly among private sector workers between 1950 and 1980. However, in the 1980s, this trend reversed itself and many companies have now eliminated or cut back on their pension programs and switched from defined benefit pension plans to defined contribution plans (Munnell, Aubry, and Muldoon, 2008). A defined contribution plan is one where employers contribute a certain amount to a retirement account that the employee then invests in company-approved fund options. Unlike defined benefit plans, defined contribution plans do not guarantee a specific amount of retirement income. Employees are also less likely to participate in defined contribution plans, where participation is often voluntary, than the mandatory defined benefit plans they replace. And employees in defined contribution plans are more vulnerable to fluctuations in the market that may diminish their asset holdings than are those with defined benefit plans. Further, less than half of the people who have job-specific pension programs have worked a sufficient number of years to be fully vested in their plans and hence entitled to their pensions, and few private pensions provide a replacement rate of income that is adequate for retirement. Finally, most job-specific pension plans do not provide cost-of-living increases. The first comprehensive effort to regulate the private pension system was the Employee Retirement Income Security Act (ERISA), enacted in 1974. ERISA covers health as well as pension benefits in qualified plans. We examine ERISA in more detail in "Major Policies and Programs" later in this chapter. Collectively, these differences between defined benefit and defined contribution retirement plans suggest that the latter are inferior in terms of helping older adults to secure a financially sound retirement.

Pensions at Risk In the last three decades we have seen a large shift in responsibility for protecting Americans from a range of risks including retirement. Jacob Hacker chronicles these changes in his 2006 book: *The Great Risk-Shift: The Assault on Jobs, Families, Health Care, and Retirement.* Hacker points out that after several decades in which employers and the government assumed new responsibilities for protecting Americans against a range of risks including incapacity to work due to disability/advanced age, this has changed in many arenas. Conservative interests have pressed to reverse this trend and to focus policy and programs instead on promoting individual responsibility and the so-called ownership society. In the area of retirement income, we have already discussed the accelerated rate at which private employers are shifting from defined pension plans, where the company was responsible for paying retirement benefits for as long as the retiree lived, to one where the company made defined pension contributions (often only if the employee was contributing him/herself, as well), but the employee was responsible for investing them and providing for their own retirement. During the first decade of the 21st century, President Bush attempted to retool Social Security, the nation's largest public pension system and biggest defined benefit pension plan, so that it would also contain elements of a defined contribution plan. These proposals to partially privatize Social Security would have also promoted yet more shifting of risk. In this instance, the shift was from the federal government to individual citizens. Bush proposed that a portion of the workers' FICA taxes would be diverted into private accounts in the workers' names, which the worker could then invest, with the potential for market gains and losses. Bush's initiatives to privatize Social Security did not succeed. Nonetheless, workers have seen their retirement security further erode during the economic downturns of the last decade because of the risk-shifting among private employers who have replaced defined benefit plans with defined contribution plans, such as 401(k)s; the sustained periods of unemployment experienced by many workers; and the increased volatility of the labor market, which tends to sever employees' connections from company-sponsored retirement plans. This shift has had immediate negative effects on older workers. Workers who were relying on defined contribution plans to fund their retirement have realized that their investments can quickly evaporate in times of economic downturn.

SSI for Older Adults   In 1974, the Social Security Act was again amended to create the Supplemental Security Income (SSI) program. As explained in Chapter 8, SSI provides income to older adults as well as to other people in poverty. Unlike OASDI, SSI benefits are not dependent on work history or marital status. It is a means-tested public benefit, not a social insurance program. In April 2013, 1,173,000 older adults received both a benefit through OASDI and SSI. This means that their benefit from OASDI was so low that they were still in extreme poverty and therefore qualified for SSI. Additionally, approximately 919,000 older adults received only SSI, meaning that they or their spouse did not work for a sufficient amount of time in a job where they contributed to the OASDI, an insurance program, and they were also in extreme poverty. Payments to older adults 65 and older made up approximately 25 percent of all SSI payments and the average monthly benefit was $423.00 (Social Security Administration, 2013a). Women are the majority of beneficiaries for old age assistance under SSI, largely because of inequities they experience within OASDI and the labor market as a whole.

The National Institute on Aging   In 1974, the National Institute on Aging (NIA) was established at the federal level to conduct research and provide training related to the aging process and the problems and diseases associated with an aging population. The NIA's research initiatives focus on improving the health and well-being of older adults in the U.S. For example, the NIA has been given primary responsibility for research involving Alzheimer's disease. If a cure or even more effective treatment for this devastating disease could be found, health care savings as well as improvement in the lives of older adults and their caregivers would be profound. You can learn more about the NIA's current and past research initiatives by browsing their website (www.nia.nih.gov).

Mental Health Services   The 1975 amendments to the Community Mental Health Act, in combination with Medicare and Medicaid, made it possible for a greater number of older adults to receive mental health services (Tice and Perkins, 1996b). In addition, funds provided by the OAA and services made available through some senior centers and community mental health centers helped increase availability of mental health care for older adults. However, inadequate access to mental health services for older adults continues for several reasons, including:

- inadequate training of mental health providers to meet the specific needs of older adults;

- reluctance on the part of many community mental health centers to perform outreach;

- lack of parity in mental health reimbursement;

- overriding needs of many elders for basic resources such as clothes, food, and shelter;

- cultural barriers;

- misinformation about the efficacy of mental health treatment for older adults; and

- elders' negative stereotypes about receiving mental health services.

Suicide rates among older adults, particularly for men, are a serious concern. The suicide rate for people 65 and over remains high. Older adults face many losses including loss of family, jobs, and health that can create the risk of mental health problems. The loss of expected investment income during the recent economic crisis has added to their economic woes. But mental health needs are not only a consequence of challenges facing older adults; they are also a cause of system-wide concerns in aging policy. Depression and anxiety have been linked to higher rates of nursing home placement. Treatment of mental health concerns in older adults can be very effective, but as yet there have not been sufficient services to meet the mental health needs of older adults in the community or in nursing facilities. However, mental health parity legislation, discussed in the last chapter, should provide some help for older adults in need of mental health services.

Mandatory Retirement   In 1986, an amendment to the Age Discrimination in Employment Act of 1967 abolished mandatory retirement for most jobs. This legislation was discussed in detail under the topic of age discrimination in Chapter 7. However, ageism continues to create barriers to economic security and well-being for many older adults. While older adults in most employment arenas no longer face mandatory retirement, unemployment rates reached record highs for men and women 55 and older in the face of the economic downturn that began in 2007.

Further, after losing their jobs, older adults spent more time out of work than did younger people.

Long-Term Care   Although many older adults will never need formal long-term care (LTC), all are at risk of requiring it. LTC includes many types of medical and social services for people with disabilities or chronic illness. Remember that it is Medicaid rather than Medicare that pays for most formal LTC and that people must be in poverty before they become eligible for Medicaid. Although a chronic physical or mental disability that necessitates LTC assistance may occur at any age, the older we become, the more likely it is that such a disability will develop or worsen. LTC assistance takes many forms and is provided in many settings, including nursing homes, assisted living facilities, and private homes. LTC also includes home care services and unpaid care from caregivers (Fox-Grage, Folkemer, Burwell, and Horahan, 2001). One component of LTC, home- and community-based services, typically is defined as services and supports that assist individuals to continue to live within their homes or a community setting. Personal care, assistance with chores, nutritional programs, night support, and transportation are examples of community-based services (Kane, Kane, and Ladd, 1998).

Before the 1980s, the primary option for formal LTC services was nursing facility care. However, in 1981, the Medicaid Home and Community-Based Services (HCBS) Waiver program was established as part of the Social Security Act. Before the passage of this legislation, Medicaid LTC benefits were limited to home health and personal care services and to institutional facilities such as hospitals, nursing facilities, and intermediate care facilities for persons with mental retardation (ICF/MR). However, the HCBS program now gives states the authority to waive certain Medicaid regulations—for example, living in a nursing facility—in order for Medicaid to cover LTC costs if the recipient requires nursing facility care and has a very low income, and to offer additional services not otherwise available through their Medicaid programs, for individuals meeting strict eligibility criteria.

The Medicaid HCBS waiver program recognizes that many people at risk of being institutionalized in these facilities can be served in their homes and communities at a cost that is no higher than that of institutional care. However, Medicaid is means-tested, so people who do not have low incomes currently have few sources to help them pay for home- and community-based services or nursing facility care. If private-pay individuals are admitted to nursing facilities, the costs are so high that they often become impoverished. At that point, they become eligible for Medicaid at a cost much higher to the taxpayer than the cost of home- and community-based services.

Despite the appeal of home- and community-based services for many older adults, nursing facilities are a mainstay of the LTC system. In fact, the vast majority of public spending for LTC still goes to nursing homes. Although there is a constant push for more home- and community-based alternatives, nursing facilities will continue to provide both rehabilitative and LTC to many older adults. Social workers who are employed in nursing facilities see firsthand the challenges these institutions face and the critical role that they play as a part of the nation's LTC system. The Nursing Home Reform Act, which was part of the Omnibus Budget Reconciliation Act of 1987, provided for reform in the areas of nurse's aide training, survey and certification procedures, pre-admission screening, and annual reviews for people with mental illness. It also mandated that nursing facility residents have access to ombudsmen when they require protection and advocacy services. Efforts to reform nursing home care in both the legislative and the agency policy and program arenas continue. Any discussion of LTC policy would be incomplete without careful attention to the role of family caregivers in providing informal (unpaid) LTC services. Most older adults in need of LTC depend completely on family members and friends to provide that care. Policies and programs needed to support family caregivers are detailed later in the chapter.

Prescription Drug Policy   In 2003, Congress passed the Medicare Prescription Drug, Improvement, and Modernization Act. This legislation has helped many older adults buy needed prescriptions. Specific policy changes that are making this legislation more effective will be discussed in detail later in the chapter. The provisions of the new Medicare prescription drug benefit are complicated, and older adults and their families often have difficulty understanding what is and is not covered. However, the State Health Insurance Assistance Programs (SHIP) can help older adults as well as social workers understand publicly funded health care policies and programs. SHIP is a national program created as part of the Omnibus Budget Reconciliation Act of 1990. The Act authorized the Centers for Medicaid and Medicare to make grants to the states to provide Medicare recipients and their families with free counseling and assistance on a wide range of Medicare, Medicaid, and Medigap matters. This program relies heavily on trained volunteers. To find out where older adults in your state can get this help, go to Find a State SHIP at the website of the National SHIP Resource Center (www.shiptalk.org).

Shortage of Gerontologically Trained Professionals   With the aging of the baby boomer generation, there will be a growing shortage of physicians, nurses, social workers, and other health professionals who have gerontological expertise. A variety of federal, state, and foundation initiatives have been implemented to help close this gap. One particularly notable long-term foundation initiative that has yielded very positive results is that of the Hartford Foundation. You can find out more about grants available to increase the number of geriatrically trained social workers as well as other professionals at the website of the John A. Hartford Foundation.

Provisions of the new health care reform law will also increase the availability of physicians for Medicaid and Medicare by providing incentives for doctors to go into the primary care field. This includes providing grants to medical schools to recruit and train students who will practice medicine in rural communities. There are also incentives for training nurses, social workers, and other medical providers as well as loan forgiveness programs to defray the cost of professional education. Primary care doctors who treat Medicare patients receive an extra 10 percent bonus from 2011 to 2016. Paperwork for doctors who treat Medicare and Medicaid patients is also to be reduced.

The Influence of Demographics

During the last 60 years, advances in medicine, technology, and public health policy have contributed to increased life expectancy. With some exceptions, most notably the baby boom, a period of increased births after World War II, fertility rates have also declined. These developments are resulting in the aging of the U.S. population. The demographics of the older-adult population are changing as well, paralleling our diversifying society. In 1950, the life expectancy of Americans was 68.2 years at birth, compared to 78.7 in 2011 (Hoyert and Xu, 2012). Today, there are over 43.14 million adults aged 65 or older in the U.S. and they make up about 13.5 percent of the population (U.S. Census Bureau, 2012f). That number is expected to reach 72.1 million and be 19.3 percent of the population by 2030 (Hoyert and Xu, 2012). However, the forecasted rate of increase is slowing as the baby boomers achieve old age (Administration on Aging, 2010). In addition, elders who are gay, lesbian, transgender, or bisexual; people with developmental disabilities; adults living alone; immigrants and refugees; and older people in prisons will also constitute a larger part of the older-adult population. Although the number of children in our society will not decline, the ratio of children to older adults will decrease markedly.

In order to understand the impact of longer life expectancies on programs for older adults, it is important to also look at life expectancy for people who live to be 65, because this is the subset who use the programs. Life expectancies at both age 65 and age 85 have increased. Under current mortality conditions, people who survive to age 65 can expect to live an average of 19.2 more years, nearly five years longer than people aged 65 in 1960. In 2009, the life expectancy of people who survive to age 85 was 7 years for women and 5.9 years for men.

Life expectancy varies by race, but the difference decreases with age. In 2009, life expectancy at birth was 4.3 years higher for white people than for black people. At age 65, white people can expect to live an average of 1.3 years longer than black people. Among those who survive to age 85, however, the life expectancy among black people is slightly higher (6.8 years) than for white people (6.6 years).

Life expectancy at age 65 in the U.S. is lower than that of many other industrialized nations. In 2009, women aged 65 in Japan could expect to live on average 3.7 years longer than women in the U.S. (Federal Interagency Forum on Aging-Related Statistics, 2012).

Among older adults, people 85 and older are the fastest-growing age group (Administration on Aging, 2010). Over half of older adults 85+ have no disabilities (Butler, 2008), while others have various functional limitations. This diversity in needs even among the very old should be recognized.

If you would like to calculate your life expectancy based on your age today, you can do so by going to the Life Expectancy Calculator available at the Social Security Administration website. (http://www.ssa.gov/planners/lifeexpectancy.htm). Consider what sorts of supports and policies you will need as you age into your eighties because you are likely to live that long and perhaps even longer.

Exhibit 11.5 shows how the demographics of our country have changed between 1900 and 2000. Note that in Exhibit 11.5 the population in 1900 resembles a pyramid. There were many children and comparatively fewer adults. This is similar to what you see in many developing nations today. Now, take a look at 1950. By 1950 the baby boom which began in 1946 and continued to 1964 was just beginning, so the under-five age group was markedly larger than the cohort of children born in the 1930s and the cohort born in the early 1940s. By 2000, people born during the baby boom were in their middle years. The oldest were in their fifties, and the youngest were in their thirties. You can see there is a great bulge in the population in those age groups.

Now look at Exhibit 11.6 which shows the population in 2012 with projections for 2060. The chart is changing shape and is no longer a pyramid. Although there are more children being born, there are also more people living to adulthood, and the population aged 65 and over is becoming larger. It is predicted that by 2056 the number of children 18 and under will be outnumbered for the first time by

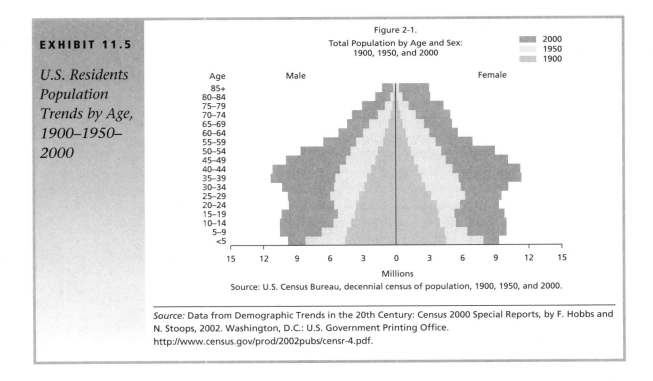

EXHIBIT 11.5

U.S. Residents Population Trends by Age, 1900–1950– 2000

Figure 2-1.
Total Population by Age and Sex:
1900, 1950, and 2000

2000
1950
1900

Source: U.S. Census Bureau, decennial census of population, 1900, 1950, and 2000.

Source: Data from Demographic Trends in the 20th Century: Census 2000 Special Reports, by F. Hobbs and N. Stoops, 2002. Washington, D.C.: U.S. Government Printing Office. http://www.census.gov/prod/2002pubs/censr-4.pdf.

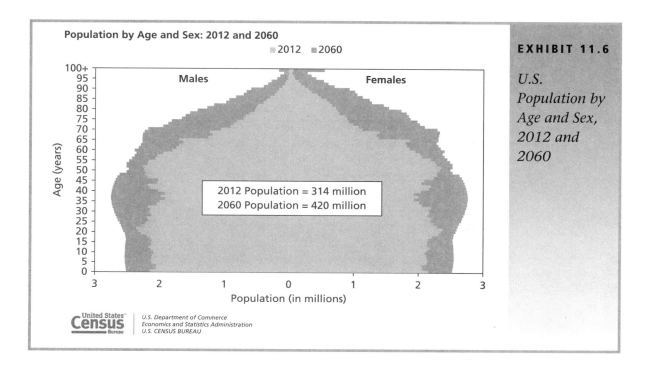

EXHIBIT 11.6

U.S. Population by Age and Sex, 2012 and 2060

those 65 years and older (Ortman, 2013). However, more babies were born in the U.S. in 2007 than any other year in the nation's history and although, more recently, birth rates have slowed, it is clear that characterizing the aging of the baby boom as the "Pig in the Python," because the population pyramid bulged as that generation passed through, left the incorrect impression that we would be dealing with much smaller cohorts of older adults in the future. In fact, if you look closely at the U.S population trends in 2060, shown in Exhibit 11.6, you will see that large cohorts of older adults continue to be expected from now into the future. In fact, the Millennial Generation, born between 1980 and 2000 is larger than the baby boom generation and, of course, can be expected to live even longer, given improvements in health care and technology that translate into reduced mortality. Therefore, our society will continue to contain large numbers of older adults long after the baby boomers, the youngest of whom will be in their late nineties in 2060, are gone.

These charts also indicate that women outnumber men in the older-adult population. This disparity becomes even more pronounced after age 85 with women making up 71 percent of the population; when you consider people who are aged 100 and over, 85 percent of these centenarians are women. Furthermore, the percentage of older adults (65 plus) who are members of minority groups (other than white alone and not of Hispanic origin) will increase from 19.85 percent of all who are 65 and older in 2010 to 40.5 percent by 2050. Specifically, it is projected that African Americans will represent 11.2 percent, and Hispanic older adults will represent 19.8 percent of the elder population, Asian Americans will represent almost 8.4 percent, Native Americans will represent 0.7 percent, non-Hispanic Native Hawaiian and Pacific Islander elders will represent 0.2 percent, and non-Hispanic persons 65 and older of two or more races will represent 1.2 percent of the elder population in 2050 (U.S. Census Bureau, 2008). By way of comparison, the percentage of minority children under age 18 in the U.S. is projected to be greater than the percentage that is single-race non-Hispanic white by the time of the 2020 census (U.S. Census Bureau, 2012f). The percentage of young people from minority groups will continue to be much larger, then, than the percentage of these groups in the elder population. As a result, a growing cohort of younger people from minority groups will be called on to care for an elder population that will be predominantly white. Becoming familiar with the changes depicted here will help you understand and anticipate the trends and challenges our society will face in the coming years.

Exhibit 11.6 also reflects 2012 Census Bureau projections indicating the U.S. will grow more slowly over the coming decades compared to projections released as late as 2009. These new projections are based on the 2010 Census. These projections indicate that the population aged 65 and older is projected to more than double, from 43.1 million in 2012 to 92.0 million in 2060. The number of the oldest old is projected to more than triple to 18.2 million by 2060 compared to 5.9 million now. However, they would still represent only 4.3 percent of the total population (U.S. Census Bureau, 2012f). Further, by 2060, the term "oldest old" will probably be reserved for people 100 and over, mirroring expected changes in societal perceptions of age, as well. Hopefully, as the Census Bureau does for other populations, researchers will reach the point where they report out statistics for older adults in 10-year increments as the size of that group increases, so that the great diversity in older adults is not further masked by putting people whose age differs so markedly into one group when analysis is done.

By 2060, the U.S. will be a plurality nation, that is, the non-Hispanic white population will remain the largest single group, but no group will be in the majority (U.S. Census Bureau, 2012l). Further, by 2060, it is projected that just over one in five U.S. residents will be 65 and over, compared to approximately one in seven today. However, recent work by the Max Planck Institute for Demographic Research (2013) in Germany indicates that the U.S. Census Bureau, as well as groups projecting population growth in other countries, may have miscalculated the future birth rate because women are now delaying more births into their thirties and forties rather than forgoing motherhood, and the method currently used for projecting birth rates does not capture that change. As younger cohorts of women are followed through their entire reproductive years, these changes and their implications are becoming clearer, and therefore projections will undoubtedly be modified in the coming years. If birth rates are, in fact, markedly higher than now projected, this will impact estimates of the percentage but not the number of older adults in the future and the accuracy of this and other exhibits that estimate the size and shape of our future population. In the final chapter of this text, I help you understand in more depth what influences future forecasts and how they can best be used in your work to shape policy and programs.

Demographics have a very powerful effect on our lives, including the size of the workforce, the need for health care, the demand for LTC, and societal attitudes. For example, although proportionately more families are caring for older adults than ever before and will undoubtedly continue to do so, in future generations there will be proportionately fewer children to provide informal care and more adults needing care. Thus, we can expect that the need for formal care will increase. Proposed solutions to LTC problems based on the belief that today's families have somehow deserted their older members and must be pressed harder to care for them are flawed. Demographics are far different today, and relying still more heavily on their families to provide LTC is not a workable solution for many older adults with disabilities.

Poverty and Aging in the Community   Coupled with these trends is the growing emphasis on helping people age in the community. Aging in the community means that an older adult with disabilities is able to maintain residence in his/her community rather than enter a nursing facility. If older adults are to age in place, issues of poverty and inequities in service delivery, especially in rural communities, will need to be addressed. In 2012, the official poverty rate for adults age 65 and older was 8.7 percent, which was lower than the overall poverty rate of 15 percent (USDHHS, 2012b). About 3.6 million older people live below the poverty line using this official method of calculating poverty. However, the Census Bureau also issued a new poverty supplemental measure that factors in living expenses and taxpayer-provided benefits. This measure includes medical expenses that the official formula leaves out (Short, 2012). Older adults have more medical expenses including Medicare premiums, deductibles, and medication costs and, therefore, this modified measure might be a more accurate representation of older adults' financial status. Using this measure, it was found that poverty was disproportionately affecting people 65 and older. For this population, the poverty rate was about 15.1 percent, or almost double the 8.7 percent rate found using the official formula. As described in Chapter 8, older women and people of color are at much greater risk of experiencing poverty. Further, proportionately more of the older-adult population was classified as "near poor," meaning that their incomes fell between the poverty level and 125 percent of this level, than in the overall population. Poverty rates increase with age and so those 85 and older, particularly women, have higher rates of poverty than does the entire population 65 and over. Importantly, poverty statistics for older adults are evidence of the potential for public policy to positively affect individual and group well-being. Were it not for Social Security, the official poverty rate for older adults would top 43 percent (CBPP, 2012b).

Further, the federal poverty threshold for adults aged 65 years and older is lower than that for younger adults. The estimate for the threshold for 2012 is $11,011 vs. $11,945 for those under 65. In other words, people aged 65 and older must have lower incomes than younger people to be considered impoverished (U.S. Census Bureau, 2013b). This disparity reflects the assumption that older people spend less money on food and other necessities. Remember, the poverty level is formulated by multiplying the monthly food expense by three. Therefore, when an age group is projected to consume a smaller amount of food, its poverty level is lowered. The major problem with this formula is that older people spend proportionately more money than younger people on housing and transportation, as well as health care (Hooyman and Kiyak, 2002). There is also little evidence that they spend less on food. In fact, many have special dietary needs related to chronic conditions such as diabetes and hypertension and may be less able to prepare complicated meals, thus increasing food costs. If the same standard were used for older adults as for the rest of the population, then, the poverty rate for older adults would be higher. When considering poverty among older adults from an international perspective, research in 2007 that compared the economic status of older adults in the U.S. to other major industrialized nations, indicated that the U.S. has the highest rate of poverty (Sierminska, Brandolini, and Smeeding, 2007).

Voting Patterns of Older Adults   Although older adults are a minority of eligible voters, they have very high rates of voting and voter registration. For this reason, their political power influences some policy makers to consider their needs. However, because the elder population is very heterogeneous and diverse in ways that may also influence how they look at social policy addressing their needs and those of younger generations, it is naive to expect they will all vote as a bloc or support entirely the same legislative agenda.

MAJOR POLICIES AND PROGRAMS

OASDI, SSI, Medicare, and Medicaid have been examined in detail in other chapters. Later in this chapter, we will discuss these policies and programs in terms of the overall implications the aging of the baby boomers has for public policy. Here, we consider two other major policies that influence the lives of older adults, the Older Americans Act of 1965 and the Employee Retirement Income Security Act of 1974.

The Older Americans Act

Congress passed the Older Americans Act (OAA) (Public Law 89–73) in 1965 to reduce the fragmentation in public services for older adults and generate additional resources to assist them. The OAA created the Administration on Aging (AOA), a federal agency housed in the Department of Health and Human Services (USDHHS, formerly Health, Education, and Welfare) that coordinates the implementation of the Act and heightens awareness of aging concerns. In 2012 the AOA became part of the newly created federal Administration for Community Living (ACL). The ACL is part of the USDHHS. ACL brings together into a single entity the AOA, the Office on Disability, and the Administration on Developmental Disabilities. The ACL works with states, tribes, community providers, businesses, non-profit organizations, universities, and families to help people of all ages with disabilities to continue to live in their homes and be full participants in their communities. This change has been criticized for taking attention away from older adults in general and focusing more narrowly on those with disabilities. Although many older adults have serious disabilities, many do not, but still face significant barriers, such as discrimination in the workplace, lack of inclusion in community planning and services, and little support for charting new roles that contribute to society when they are no longer parents or workers. Narrowing attention to the physical challenges of aging at just the point that the baby boomers (people born between 1946 and 1964) begin to swell the ranks of older adults could create yet another barrier to aging well.

In addition to creating the AOA, the OAA also made grants available to states for community planning and programs as well as for research, demonstration, and training initiatives in aging. In 1972, the OAA was expanded to include a national nutrition program for older adults. In 1973, the OAA Comprehensive Services Amendments established local Area Agencies on Aging (AAAs). They also created an employment program for older adults with low incomes. In addition, the amendments provided grants to local community agencies for multipurpose senior centers as well as to AAAs, responsible for identifying local needs, planning, and funding services. These services help promote social engagement and enhance independent living. Beginning in 2003, the AOA has been working with the Centers for Medicare and Medicaid Services (CMS) to develop Aging and Disability Resource Centers (ADRCs) across the country to integrate aging and disability services. The intent is that the ACL and the ADRCs can bring about a stronger focus on community inclusion both for older adults and people with disabilities.

The OAA provides monies for services such as case management, in-home services such as limited personal care, nursing services, chore services, and legal assistance. The OAA also funds senior centers, meal programs, and supportive services such as transportation. In addition, it supports health promotion and disease prevention activities, services targeted to low-income elders, and advocacy initiatives such as the LTC ombudsman program. The Older Americans Act Amendments of 2000 created the National Family Caregiver Support Program, which helps sustain caregivers and guards against social isolation. These amendments also extended the programs established by the OAA. State agencies provide oversight for local AAAs. In turn, these agencies either deliver services themselves or contract with private agencies to do so.

The OAA is financed at the federal level by general tax revenues. Programs funded through the OAA are not entitlements. Consequently, money for these programs often runs out, leaving eligible applicants without needed services. The original intent was that OAA-funded services would be available to people 60 years of age and older, regardless of income. However, due to inadequate funding, services have to be directed to people who are most in need. State agencies and AAAs conduct outreach to attempt to serve more low-income minority elders and elders located in rural settings, which creates tension between a universal approach and targeted services. Politically, elders who are very poor vote less than do middle- and upper-income elders. Therefore, political support for the OAA and for AAAs is bolstered by continuing to provide support for a broad swath of elders. Additionally, many older people who hover just above the poverty line and therefore are not in the low-income target group, still cannot afford the services they need. AAAs try to serve these people as well, when sufficient funds are available. However, because funding to fully implement the OAA is inadequate, many older people who need these services have not been able to obtain them. State and local monies are often used to provide additional funding, which results in wide variation in the availability of services from state to state and community to community. Although the OAA was to be reauthorized in 2011, it was still awaiting reauthorization when this text went to press. Work to reauthorize the OAA represents an opportunity for people interested in having input into this process to make their voices heard. Your local AAA can provide you with information on how to get involved in advocating for passage. See Exhibit 11.7 for a summary of the OAA.

EXHIBIT 11.7 *Older Americans Act, 1965*	**Policy Goals**	To create a comprehensive, coordinated service network for older adults.
	Benefits or Services Provided	Planning and coordination as well as services. Access services including transportation, outreach, case management and in-home services, supportive services, legal assistance, and congregate and home delivered meals. National Family Caregiver Support Program.
	Eligibility Rules	Age 60 and over. Priority is given to low-income minority elders and older adults living in rural areas.
	Service Delivery System	The federal Administration on Aging coordinates overall implementation. State agencies oversee local Area Agencies on Aging, which deliver services directly or through contracts with private agencies.
	Financing	Federally funded by general revenue taxes.

Source: Adapted from Administration on Aging (2004).

The Employee Retirement Income Security Act

The first comprehensive effort to regulate the private pension system was the Employee Retirement Income Security Act (ERISA) (Public Law 93–406), enacted in

1974. The ERISA defines how long a person can be required to work before becoming eligible to participate in a private pension plan, to accumulate benefits, and to be vested, that is, to have a non-forfeitable right to those benefits. It also requires plan sponsors to provide adequate funding for the plan. In addition, it guarantees payment of certain benefits if an insured plan is terminated. In such cases, benefits are paid through a federally chartered corporation, the Pension Benefit Guaranty Corporation (PBGC). The Labor Department's Employee Benefits Security Administration, together with the Internal Revenue Service (IRS), administers the ERISA.

The PBGC insures certain defined benefit pension plans by guaranteeing benefits up to specified legal limits, which means that some workers will not get their full pensions if their company underfunds their pension program and PBGC becomes involved. The PBGC does not receive tax funds. Rather, income is generated through insurance premiums paid by employers, through investments, and through assets recovered from terminated plans. Weaknesses in some of the pension plans that the PBGC insures have fueled concerns about the corporation's capacity to fund promised benefits. See Exhibit 11.8 for a summary of the Act.

The Pension Protection Act of 2006 modified ERISA and required that employers significantly increase the funding for defined benefit plans. The Act contained a number of additional improvements such as increasing limits for contributions to IRAs and 401(k)s. It also made permanent the Saver's Credit, which is a tax credit for retirement savings that benefits people with low to moderate incomes. However, it did not reverse the trend of "risk-shifting" which leaves so many older adults

Policy Goals	To regulate the private pension system by setting minimum standards and providing limited pension guarantees.	**EXHIBIT 11.8**
Benefits or Services Provided	Established minimum standards for participation, vesting, benefit accrual, and funding in qualified programs. Ensures payments to employees who have met the time requirements for nonforfeiture.	*Employee Retirement Income Security Act, 1974*
Eligibility Rules	Participants in employer-provided defined benefit pension plans covered by the Act who meet time requirements for full participation in the plan.	
Service Delivery System	Benefits paid through the Pension Benefit Guaranty Corporation (PBGC). Federal oversight by the Labor Department's Employee Benefits Security Administration and the Internal Revenue Service.	
Financing	The PBGC is funded by insurance premiums paid by employers, investments, and recovered assets from terminated plans.	

Source: Adapted from U.S. Department of Labor (n.d.)

vulnerable to uncertain economic futures. Further, the economic downturn that began in 2007 resulted in yet larger increases in plan underfunding. PBGC estimated its exposure to underfunded plans "reasonably possible to terminate" at $168 billion in 2009, an increase from $47 billion in 2008 (PBGC, 2010). The recent economic downturn has increased uncertainty about solvency of pension plans. This means even workers who have defined benefit retirement plans have become less secure. The 2012 PBGC report forecasts continued deterioration of the financial position of multi-employer pension plans which are collectively bargained by labor unions. Single-employer plans, which are available from individual employers, are in comparatively better shape. For the latest information on this subject visit the website of the PBGC (www.pbgc.gov).

No CLASS: The Loss of the Long-Term Care Provisions of the Affordable Care Act

Paying for LTC has long been a major concern for older adults. Indeed, many young people become disabled and need LTC. When originally passed in 2010, the Community Living Assistance Services and Supports (CLASS) provisions of the 2010 health care reform legislation created a voluntary national insurance program to provide cash benefits to people with serious disabilities. However, the Obama administration withdrew support from CLASS because of concerns that, without substantial changes, the insurance premiums would be far too expensive for most buyers, as well as projections indicating the program would be financially unsustainable. In 2013, as part of a budget deal, CLASS was repealed and a new national commission to develop a plan for better financing and delivery of LTC services was authorized. Currently both old and young people in need of LTC are regularly impoverished by the high costs involved. Advocacy groups will continue to monitor the work of the commission and advocate for legislation to increase access to LTC and make it affordable.

Elder Justice Act and the Patient Safety and Abuse Prevention Act

Other provisions of the 2010 health care reform legislation that are of particular importance for older adults include the Elder Justice Act and the Patient Safety and Abuse Prevention Act. The main provisions of the Elder Justice Act include funding for Adult Protective Services, grants to support the Long-Term Care Ombudsman Program, and the establishment of an Elder Justice Coordinating Council. The Patient Safety and Abuse Prevention Act requires criminal background checks for persons seeking employment in nursing facilities and other LTC facilities. Increased funding to prevent elder abuse is badly needed. Elder abuse takes many forms—physical, emotional, sexual abuse; financial exploitation; neglect (either self-neglect or by a caretaker); and abandonment. A survey of 38 states by the National Adult Protective Services Association (NAPSA) indicated that caseloads at Adult Protective

EXHIBIT 11.9

Advocates for Children and Elders Join Forces

Field instructors and former students in a Midwestern state continue to use the policy practice skills and networks forged in the MSW program to improve the lives of older adults. The call centers for reporting child and adult abuse in their state were consolidated due to budget cuts. When workers at their agencies called to report abuse to the two remaining call centers in the state, often no one answered and they were asked to leave a message. This was difficult for service providers, but a much more daunting barrier for citizens who wanted to report abuse. After doing research, talking to each other and to their supervisors in various agencies, and attending a county coalition on aging meeting where they brought up this problem, they were ready to take further action. They brainstormed with the coalition how best to proceed. They then contacted the Silver Haired Legislature (a legislative advocacy group made up of older adults) and the AARP chapter in their state, shared what they had learned, and asked if these organizations would be interested in advocating to improve this dysfunctional system. They also got media coverage for the problem and contacted a legislator who is an advocate for older adults as well as children to help build an intergenerational coalition that could press for additional funding in this area critical to the safety of both children and older adults.

Services agencies (APS), which investigate reported cases of elder abuse, increased by 24 percent in 2009 (Ramnarace, 2010). Yet state agency funding was cut by an average of 14 percent. Provisions in this legislation pertaining to adult protective services were to provide funding for more caseworkers nationwide. This legislation also requires criminal background checks for persons seeking employment in nursing facilities and other LTC facilities. However, funding for this legislation has been very slow in coming. Remember, it is one thing to get legislation passed, but the victory is hollow if advocates do not continue to push for necessary funding for implementation. This is not only an elder justice issue, but also a women's issue. The vast majority of abuse happens to women, and older women are particularly vulnerable and underserved. Domestic violence shelters typically focus their services on younger women. So, when adequate funding for services for older women with chronic illnesses at risk of abuse and neglect in their home is lacking, these women may find themselves unjustly and unnecessarily institutionalized in a nursing facility. For more information on policies and programs to combat elder abuse, go to the website of the National Center on Elder Abuse at the AOA (www.ncea.aoa.gov).

EVALUATING POLICIES AND PROGRAMS FOR OLDER ADULTS

The remaining sections of this chapter focus on evaluating current policies and identifying needed policy changes in the areas of economic security, health care, and social engagement. We will begin by examining the social context in which people in our society grow old. This process will help us identify the strengths, needs, and differences of older adults, which should be considered when evaluating current policy and considering possible reforms. The resources of older adults and the supports they need are most clearly understood in the context of their lifecycle. Older adults who were poor all of their lives, who were denied educational and employment opportunities, and who received inadequate health care, bring that legacy of poverty and discrimination to their later years. Thus, older women and people of color are much more likely to be poor in old age, just as they were more likely to be poor earlier in life. Similarly, strong ties to family, friends, church, and community, created and nurtured over a lifetime, may continue to provide older adults with needed support. Moreover, diversity in life experiences greatly influences the lives of older adults. People who have led very different lives and have had access to varying types and amounts of resources will bring these differences to old age. Age is not the great equalizer. Therefore, any agenda charted must take these individual differences into account.

When we consider needed policy reforms for older adults, we must be careful not to equate strengths with independence. Rather, we should focus more on interdependence among different generations. Indeed, the historic importance of older adults as grandparents providing help to both children and grandchildren creates a base for interdependence later on when grandparents are in need of help. One generation provides reciprocal care for another. These systems of interdependence can be a vital source of support when elders are in need of increased care due to chronic illnesses. Discussing this interdependence, particularly the contributions that older adults can and often do make, helps us reframe relationships by emphasizing their reciprocal nature. For example, older women are the repositories of rich historical memories of their families and communities. Local AAAs can help elders find intergenerational programs in which young and old people work together to build historical records of their communities. Our society needs to develop more programs and policies that build links and promote interdependence among generations while highlighting the competencies of both young and old people.

Focusing on reciprocity in relationships will become increasingly important during the next 20–30 years because of changes in family structures and the needs of older adults. Currently, informal sources of support are the backbone of the U.S. system of caring for older adults. This reality will not change in the foreseeable future. Therefore, we will need policies and programs such as elder care at work, increased respite care, and training to improve caregivers' abilities.

Although informal caregivers will continue to be the major source of care for elders, owing to lower birth rates and increasing divorce rates, fewer family members are able to provide adequate support. Additionally, many middle-aged people are caring for small children and aging parents at the same time. These adults are known as the *sandwich generation*. As informal support becomes less available, formal support will increasingly be necessary to meet the needs of older adults. This trend will have the greatest impact on low-income older adults who do not have the resources to pay for caregiving, placing increased demands on publicly funded social services. Keeping in mind the insights concerning the social environment of older adults discussed in this section, we will now consider policy issues in the areas of economic security, health care, and social engagement.

Economic Security

The provisions of OASDI, the mainstay of economic security for older adults in this country, were discussed in detail in previous chapters. Popularly known as Social Security, this program is often described as one leg of the three-legged stool that supports retirement. The other two legs are private savings and job-specific pension programs. However, both private savings and job-specific pensions are in short supply among many of the older adults whom social workers serve. In addition, even when older adults have these additional sources of income, they are often inadequate to sustain them if they do not also receive Social Security and Medicare benefits. Many adults who retire become "unretired" when they realize that the combined income from Social Security, job-related pensions, and private savings is not sufficient to sustain them. As longevity increases, more people will want and need to continue working and already some people are continuing to be employed well into their nineties. Now people refer to a four-legged stool that supports people in old age rather than in retirement, and the fourth leg is work. Of course, returning to work is possible only when severe disabilities, which are more common in old age and disproportionately affect members of racial and ethnic minorities, have not taken their toll, and when jobs are available and extended to older adults in a non-discriminatory manner. Exhibit 11.10 presents the income source for older adults by income quintiles. This means the population is divided into fifths based on income. People in the first quintile have the lowest incomes. For them as well as for people in the next two quintiles, Social Security is their major income source. As previously discussed, this exhibit also illustrates disparities in other sources of income such as assets and pensions.

Income Source	1st Quintile	2nd Quintile	3rd Quintile	4th Quintile	5th Quintile
Social Security	84.3	83.3	65.7	43.5	17.3
Pensions	2.9	6.9	15.9	25.8	19.1
Asset Income	1.8	2.6	5.4	7.8	16.1
Earnings	2.4	4.1	9.6	19.4	44.9
Public Assistance	7.0	1.6	0.5	0.2	0.1
Other	1.6	1.4	2.8	3.3	2.4

Source: Adapted from Federal Interagency Forum on Aging-Related Statistics (2012).

EXHIBIT 11.10

Percent of Income by Income Source for Adults Aged 65 Years or Older by Income Quintiles, 2010

Major insurance programs such as OASDI and Medicare not only improve people's well-being, they are also political tools that help secure loyalty to the state, and sometimes, to a political party. Americans are wary of attempts to cut back these benefits. Similarly, now that many people, particularly in the middle class, are depending on the stock market to build their retirement savings in guaranteed contribution pension systems, they are very concerned about stock market regulation. Tighter regulation of the stock market was not popular when it was thought it would cut into profits and thus reduce retirement income. However, as it became obvious in 2008 and 2009 that these profits could all evaporate, support for government regulation increased. As the stock market began to recover, however, interest in regulation waned.

The precipitous decline in the stock market and the ballooning deficit following the invasion of Iraq during the George W. Bush administration that markedly worsened with the economic downturn beginning in 2007, caused many older adults to reconsider the wisdom of relying heavily on the private sector to finance their retirement. As older adults watched their private savings dwindle and, in some cases, their employer pensions collapse, the fragility of the "three-legged stool" in its current formulation became evident. Many continued working, but many also lost their jobs and were unable to find new ones. In 2011, the labor participation rate for women age 65–69 was approximately 27 percent and 37 percent for men (Federal Interagency Forum on Aging-Related Statistics, 2012). This is an increase from the 1990s. However, if improvements in the economy and the stock market continue, rates of retirement, particularly for people well past 65, are expected to accelerate. Nonetheless, without Social Security, almost half of older adults would live in poverty after retiring. For minority elders, Social Security is even more vital. Thus, support for preserving Social Security is high among older adults but also among younger people (Pew Research Center, 2011). Young people understand Social Security provides the only guaranteed source of income in retirement many of them will ever have, and they also value the security of knowing that their parents and grandparents have adequate and stable income.

In addition, cutting back Social Security will not reduce the current federal deficit. Although this reality is seldom portrayed in the media, because Social Security is financed through a dedicated payroll tax, none of the federal deficit has ever been caused by Social Security. In fact, Social Security is a creditor, not a debtor, of the federal government.

Given the shakiness of the sources of support for older adults other than OASDI, policy makers will be under significant pressure to decide how to keep OASDI financially solvent for the long term. The aging of the baby boomers and longer life expectancy will add to these pressures. Policy alternatives include cutting benefits, raising taxes, limiting eligibility, or some combination of all three. Each of these alternatives will increase the burden on some group of citizens. For example, cutting benefits will most negatively impact low-income older adults, particularly very old women. Many people receive small benefits, and even the maximum monthly benefit is $2,513 per month for those who retire at full retirement age, which until

2019 is 66 years (Social Security Administration, 2012). However, raising taxes on retirement benefits for higher-income older adults could generate additional revenues without destroying the universal, insurance-based approach to public pensions, although it could erode some political support for OASDI as it shifts closer to a means-tested program. Of course, payroll taxes (FICA) could also be increased, and high-income taxpayers could be required to pay FICA on all earned income. Another option is to raise the age at which an individual becomes eligible for full benefits to 68, 69, or even 70. Additionally, the age when people can receive reduced benefits, often referred to as taking early retirement, could be raised beyond 62. Such an approach, however, would further penalize people of color, who have shorter life expectancies, as well as those who need to leave the job market in order to serve as informal caregivers or because they are experiencing disabilities but have not yet qualified for disability assistance. You can go to the AARP website, and use the Strengthen Social Security Tool to determine how you would close the Social Security funding gap. You can adjust the benefits people receive and/or the contributions they make while working, and see how that impacts future solvency and the benefits you and your clients will rely on in old age.

As explained in Chapter 8, relatively minor adjustments can keep OASDI solvent well beyond the current 2033 projection if they are enacted soon (Social Security Administration, 2012). However, the longer that reform is delayed, the greater the changes that will be necessary. The key to the future solvency of OASDI is continued economic growth averaging 3 percent or more in the coming years. Gross Domestic Product (GDP) is the output of goods and services produced by labor and property in the U.S. Considering the sluggish GDP growth rate experienced since 2008, it is clear that a 3 percent growth rate will be a challenge in some years. Further, policies to help boost GDP must be carefully considered in light of environmental concerns. Boosting production without regard to environmental degradation will have serious negative impact on the well-being of all age groups and ultimately impair productivity.

Some experts have proposed that the best strategy for improving the economic status of older adults with very low incomes is through changes in the SSI, a federal income supplement program, not a federal insurance program (Browne, 1998). For example, raising SSI benefits to 110 percent of the federal poverty line (FPL) and lowering the age of eligibility from 65 to 62 would help a great many older adults escape dire poverty. However, remember that because of inadequacies in the way that poverty is measured, people at 110 percent of FPL will still have very low incomes. Additionally, there are trade-offs associated with relying on means-tested programs instead of social insurance, including vulnerability of program funding in economic downturns or periods of budget-cutting and the stigma associated with relying on public assistance.

Because their rates of poverty are higher, and their life expectancy is longer, older women are more likely to outlive their sources of income and to experience dire poverty in old age. However, many older adults who probably are eligible for

SSI never apply for it. Therefore, social workers should make certain that older adults are informed about SSI and are aware that they can receive assistance in filling out the complicated application form. Along with the reforms discussed above, the barriers to accessing benefits under the current policy, such as complex forms and insufficient staffing, need to be addressed. To find out more about eligibility for SSI, go to the Supplemental Security Income website at the Social Security Administration (www.ssa.gov). More low-income older adults also need to be informed about SNAP, the Low-Income Housing Energy Assistance Program (LIHEAP), and programs such as Low Income Subsidies for Medicare. Many elders who struggle in poverty do not know about these programs for which they are eligible and/or do not know how to access them. More outreach to eligible older adults is needed, but one way policy makers may control costs is by cutting funding for outreach, thereby likely limiting access for people who need it most.

Finally, older adults who are able to work should be allowed to do so. To assist older workers, we can enact policies that support their access to employment. One such policy is phased retirement, in which an individual reduces the number of hours she or he works during the years leading up to retirement. Other initiatives include creating more part-time positions and strictly enforcing laws that prohibit age discrimination in hiring and layoffs. Indeed, we are now seeing a much greater emphasis by researchers on productive aging, including involvement in paid work and volunteering. However, a productivity focus must be carefully evaluated because of its potential for further devaluing severely disabled older adults or those whose accumulated life strains make engaging extensively in productive activities difficult. In contrast, discussions of aging well can clearly encompass the needs as well as contributions of all older adults.

The 21st century will be unique in that four or five generations of many families will be alive at the same time. Therefore, we need to evaluate all policies and proposals carefully for their intergenerational impact. Overemphasis on the negative economic impact of population aging threatens to create conflict between young and old. For example, increasing public expenditures on health care and income support for elders that outpace spending on programs for children could be used as evidence of inequitable treatment of young people. Critics may then propose cutbacks in spending on elders as a "remedy" to this alleged injustice. Clearly, the fundamental importance of intergenerational solidarity needs to be underscored in policy decisions. Social workers, who take a perspective that looks at entire families and communities, can contribute positively to this framing of policy issues.

Significantly, the moral obligation of one generation to another can be combined with enlightened self-interest in crafting policies that support the multigenerational families of the future. Policies to support grandparents as caregivers for grandchildren need to be improved. Intergenerational approaches, such as foster grandparents, in which the contributions of elders are clear, help build mutual respect and recognize the older adult's traditional role in fostering alliances among generations. In 2011, the first of the baby boomers turned 65; by 2031, they will begin turning 85. As this large cohort of older adults becomes frailer, we will need to have effective policies and programs in place to deal with these issues. However, between now and 2030 we do have a window of opportunity for planning and reform because the cohort of children born during the Great Depression that began in 1929 is comparatively smaller than previous cohorts. Thus, the ranks of the oldest old (85+) who are much more likely to need all forms of care, including LTC, will not begin to swell until 2030. Additionally, remember that all baby boomers will not turn 65 or 85 at once. Rather, the last of the baby boomers will not reach these markers for an additional 18 years. Further, many baby boomers and their children are eager to participate in planning and implementing policy changes.

Health Care

Rising health care costs create a heavy burden for all of us. Many older adults have very high health care expenses even when receiving Medicare because they still must pay deductibles, co-pays, costs for additional insurance, and health care expenses that are not covered by Medicare. However, it is in the area of LTC that older adults are most vulnerable. Although private LTC insurance is touted as a private initiative that helps older adults meet these needs, only a small proportion of older adults will be able to afford to pay the premiums over the course of the many years before they actually need the service. Although only 4 percent of people aged 65 and over reside in nursing facilities, the percentage increases sharply for people aged 85 and over. Even though aging should not be equated with disability, disabilities do increase with age. The average age of nursing facility residents is well over 80. As discussed in previous chapters, Medicaid is the public program that currently pays for the majority of LTC. However, Medicaid is available only to people with very low incomes and few financial assets. Middle-income and low-income elders rapidly become impoverished by high LTC costs; in 2012, a private room cost an average of $90,500 annually, according to a 2012 survey by MetLife. A semi-private room cost more than $81,000 per year (2012). Further, although spouses remaining in the community no longer have to completely impoverish themselves before getting help will nursing home bills, as was the case prior to 1988, they still must "spend down" income, typically to 150 percent of FPL in order for their disabled husband or wife to be eligible for Medicaid LTC services.

To maximize both quality of life and cost effectiveness, there needs to be much more emphasis on home- and community-based support. Alliances between disability rights groups and the aging community allow for freer exchange of ideas and can potentially result in a stronger LTC service system and more home- and community-based options for all people with disabilities. However, sometimes the needs of older adults can be missed when services are examined without regard to age. For example, when state spending on people with disabilities is examined by age on a per person basis, instead of aggregated, it often becomes clear that much less is being spent on a per case basis on disabled people aged 65 and over. Further, many older adults with comparatively much less costly needs for service remain in nursing facilities because caring for them in the community has not been prioritized by the state. Research has shown that these older adults can receive care in the community at less cost. Contrary to the view that once they begin to receive publicly financed LTC services, older adults remain on these services the rest of their lives, research has indicated that many older adults rely on public community-based LTC services in the community for a limited period of time. Use often follows an acute care episode such as a stroke or a broken hip. Then the older adults may stop using these services and remain in the community for an extended period of time, perhaps even until death (Chapin, Baca, Macmillan, Rachlin, and Zimmerman, 2009). However, if that person had remained in the nursing home beyond the period of rehabilitation, public Medicaid costs for their care would have been much higher and could well have continued for the rest of their lives. Therefore, programs and policies to make sure the nursing home does not become a permanent home at public expense for older adults who want to return to the community and are able to do so, need to be prioritized.

For people who must have care in a nursing home, the culture change movement is working to radically transform the nursing home environment. The intent is to make the physical and organizational structures of nursing facilities less institutional. For more information on culture change in nursing facilities, go to the website of the Pioneer Network. Cost-effective public policies that support more integration of the nursing facility into the life of the community and create a more homelike environment should be supported, particularly as they can improve outcomes for older adults who remain in institutions and those who transition back to community living. Additionally, higher minimum standards for nursing staff are needed in order to improve the quality of care provided in nursing facilities, even with the recognition that this will raise costs.

Even though the rehabilitative role of nursing facilities and the growing availability of community-based alternatives are transforming the LTC system, the system is still not balanced because a disproportionate amount of public LTC expenditures go to nursing home care. Further, short-sighted cutbacks to home- and community-based services resulting from current state budget shortfalls will increase state LTC costs overall as people no longer have any choice but to enter nursing facilities. There is no doubt that home- and community-based services can be more cost-effective than nursing facility care for some of the residents of nursing facilities. Moreover, the majority of older adults prefer to remain in their communities even when they have disabilities requiring LTC. We can develop strategies to provide home- and community-based LTC services more cost-effectively. Additionally, housing options such as assisted living and supported housing can help older adults remain in the community. However, while less expensive than nursing homes, these options may be more expensive than helping older adults remain in their own homes. Comparative costs and the preferences of older adults must be carefully considered before sinking more of our very limited public LTC dollars into expensive housing options.

Some states have implemented Medicaid consumer-directed services and cash and counseling models that give consumers who are disabled the option of directing their own care. While consumers have more freedom of choice with these options, they are also assuming more responsibility, and it is again important to be mindful of the potential for risk-shifting. The concern is that focus will shift from funding the service consumer's need, to giving them a capped amount which may or may not cover needed services. For more information on consumer-directed options, go to the Cash and Counseling website (www.cashandcounseling.org).

In order to minimize the number of older adults who are too disabled to care for themselves, policies and programs to eliminate health care disparities and promote healthy lifestyles will need to be strengthened. Mental health is key to these kinds of initiatives. Remember from the discussion of mental health earlier in the chapter that depression among older adults has been linked to higher rates of institutionalization and higher health care costs. So, policies and programs to address mental health needs that older adults can afford, are vital to helping them remain in the community and to reducing health care costs, including LTC. Exhibit 11.11 illustrates the percentage of the older-adult population who have clinical depression.

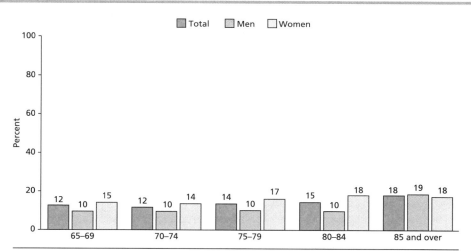

EXHIBIT 11.11

Percentage of People Age 65 and Over with Clinically Relevant Depressive Symptoms, by Age Group and Sex, 2008

Notes: The definition of "clinically relevant depressive symptoms" is four or more symptoms out of a list of eight depressive symptoms from an abbreviated version of the Center of Epidemiological Studies Depression Scale (CES-D) adapted by the Health and Retirement Study (HRS). The CES-D scale is a measure of depressive symptoms and is not to be used as a diagnosis of clinical depression. A detailed explanation concerning the "four or more symptoms" cut off can be found in the following documentation: http://hrsonline.isrumich.edu/docs/userg/dr-005.pdf.
Proportions are based on weighted data using the preliminary respondent weight from HRS 2008. Reference population: These data refer to the civilian noninstitutionalized population.

Source: Health and Retirement Study.
This table originally appeared as Indicator 19 Depressive symptoms, in Federal Interagency Forum on Aging-Related Statistics (2012).

Depression in older adults is *not* a normal part of aging. The National Institute of Health reports that research indicates most older adults are satisfied with their lives, even though they have more physical ailments (2011). The issue is that when older adults do suffer from depression, they often are reluctant to talk about it and may feel stigma and fear that they could be institutionalized. The current health care system exacerbates these barriers; primary care physicians often overlook depression in older adults and mental health treatment is often inaccessible and unaffordable. Further, many mental health centers have no aging specialist and do little to reach out to older adults. So, mental health issues in older adults often continue to go untreated or to be treated only with medication. Some progress was made in making mental health services for older adults more affordable when the Medicare Improvement for Patients and Providers Act was passed in 2008. This Act reduces co-pays incrementally for Medicare's outpatient mental health services beginning in 2010. However, as discussed earlier, gerontologically trained clinicians to provide these services are in very short supply in many areas of the country.

End-of-life Planning   Finally, any evaluation of policies that will support adequate health care for older adults must address the end-of-life planning that is necessary if elders are to live out their lives free of unnecessary pain. Older adults often are not adequately treated for pain. Policies are needed to ensure that older adults with the cognitive ability to do so retain power over life's end so that humane and compassionate end-of-life care is provided. Policies to help improve end-of-life care both in nursing facilities and in the community are needed. The majority of older people in the U.S. die outside their homes, in nursing homes or hospitals. One option that has become available to Medicare beneficiaries is hospice care. To find out more about eligibility for Medicare hospice benefits, go to the U.S. Government Medicare website and search for hospice (www.medicare.gov). Hospice care is an approach to end-of-life care that focuses on comfort and alleviation of pain rather than treatment of a terminal illness. Although hospice care is available to Medicare and Medicaid beneficiaries and many adults who carry private insurance, it is used in only a small percentage of deaths in the U.S. To learn more about hospice care, go to the website of the International Association for Hospice and Palliative Care (www.hospicecare.com).

The right to self-determination needs to be protected at the end of life. Although it is not always honored, all people in the U.S. have the right to make known their wishes for end-of-life care by signing two basic documents: (1) a living will that states the desired treatment, and (2) a durable power of attorney for health care decisions, which allows a person to designate an individual to make those decisions once she or he can no longer do so. Finally, policies and programs need to be designed so that they take into account cultural differences in end-of-life preferences. Here, as in many other arenas, these preferences need to be assessed and respected. The responsibility of hospitals to follow patients' wishes regarding end-of-life care was reaffirmed in 2010 when President Obama issued the memorandum, *Respecting the Rights of Hospital Patients to Receive Visitors and to Designate Surrogate Decision Makers for Medical Emergencies*, which directed hospitals to follow patients' advance directives.

A few states have already passed assisted dying legislation. These laws make it possible for adult residents who are mentally competent and terminally ill to make a voluntary request and then obtain a prescription medication that will hasten their death. In 2013, Vermont joined Washington and Oregon to become the third state to allow such an option. There are Death with Dignity campaigns being launched in many other states. To find out more about this issue, you can visit the website of the Death with Dignity National Center. You will want to consider the ethical dimensions of this issue, including individuals' right to self-determination and the importance of sending strengths-based messages about the potential for fulfilling life even with terminal illness.

Social Engagement

Positive social engagement is a key element of aging well. On the other hand, social isolation is a risk factor for deteriorating physical and mental health status, and it increases the chances of nursing facility placement for older adults. Social engagement—including opportunities to make choices in how and when to participate, to build relationships, set goals, and work to attain them—is integral to aging well. We can gain insight into the kinds of policies that are needed to support aging well by examining research that can inform effective policy initiatives in this area. Research on aging well has helped refocus theories of aging so that the emphasis has moved from disengagement and decline to integrating the positive and negative aspects of biopsychosocial aging, thereby providing a more balanced view of aging (Nelson-Becker, Chapin, and Fast, 2013; Baltes and Baltes, 1990; Kahana and Kahana, 1996).

These developments call attention to the roles of older adults as key participants in their own processes of aging well based on their competencies, resilience, and life experiences. For example, many women in old age are confronted with the task of taking control of their lives for the first time. Historically, women's strengths and their capacity to control their own lives have not been valued. Nevertheless, due to economic or personal circumstances such as death of spouse or divorce in later life, women may be abruptly faced with the need to assume control of their lives. Social workers and other professionals who come into contact with these women during such transition periods need to be aware of helpful community resources and ready to provide encouragement. Supporting older women in this transition affirms their capacity for self-determination. Women who are so supported may be less likely to allow family members or health care professionals to assume control for them in the future. Although more emphasis on interdependence might be necessary, only older adults can fully understand their interests, hopes, and desires for aging well. Clearly stated and well-publicized policies to protect the right of older adults to self-determination can help change their expectations as well as those of professionals and caregivers.

Preserving the capacity of elders for self-determination is critical to aging well even when their life conditions may necessitate more emphasis on interdependence. Significantly, self-determination and interdependence are not mutually exclusive. Rather, there is room for self-determination in all social interactions and relationships. For example, an elder could choose to turn to her or his family for advice and care. The family may recommend that the elder consider a nursing facility. However, the elder can still be given a choice to the extent that her or his cognitive abilities allow.

Social exchange theory also helps us understand the importance of social engagement in the lives of older adults (Dowd, 1980). This theory uses the economic metaphor of *exchange* to explain social interaction among older adults. In general, people develop social relationships because they find them to be mutually rewarding. However, aging often involves decreasing social, political, and economic power due to changes in the person's economic, psychological, and employment status. Unfortunately, as social resources are lost, so is the capacity to engage in mutually rewarding social interactions. At the same time, however, people who have engaged in lifelong caregiving may be able to draw upon additional resources and receive care from those they cared for who feel the need to reciprocate. They have built social capital and created a strong social network.

Theoretical work on social exchange theory sheds light on the relationship between social resources and social engagement. Viewed from this perspective, the loneliness and social isolation of many older adults cannot be adequately addressed unless we develop strategies for overcoming barriers to social resources such as economic security, adequate transportation, and meaningful roles that allow elders to continue contributing to the community. In addition to the loss of social resources, social engagement can be restricted by the widespread cultural belief that women are less valuable than men and that older people are less valuable than younger people. Sexism and ageism continue to be barriers to policies and practices that could support aging well.

Recent nursing home research has begun to shed light on the capacity of even older adults in nursing homes to be civically engaged when given the opportunity (Leedahl, 2013). If policies and programs emphasize the importance, and support the efforts, of families and community organizations to help older adults stay active in their communities, social isolation can clearly be lessened. For example, older adults with serious disabilities can still be out and about in the community with help. They might use telephone- and web-based strategies to help with community outreach for any number of causes. By expanding our imaginations beyond coming to nursing homes and providing assistance to residents, we can use the strengths approach to help residents find ways to increase social engagement. Such initiatives can help prevent social isolation, increase interaction between generations, and improve our communities.

To summarize, we know the older adult population of the future will be larger, older, and more diverse than it is today. If older adults are to have the opportunity to age well, then social policies will need to recognize and honor this diversity and plan to fully embrace the strengths and capacities that people bring to later life. Policies that address economic security, health care, and opportunities for social engagement will need to be continually evaluated for differences in effectiveness across these diverse groups.

NEXT STEPS

Although many people are now living longer, this is not the case for some groups. For example, a recent study in the journal, *Health Affairs*, reported declining life expectancy for women in about 43 percent of the nation's counties (Olshansky et al., 2012). Many of these counties were in rural and low-income areas. It has been theorized that this decrease is related to higher smoking rates, obesity, and less education, but many experts indicate we do not know why. We do know that life expectancy is influenced by education level and racial group membership. The *Health Affairs* journal report recommends policy development that implements educational enhancements at young, middle and older ages for people of all races (Olshansky et al., 2012). In fact, issues such as lack of access to healthy food choices in low-income areas, which leads to obesity in children as well as older adults, must be tackled to increase the number of older adults who experience a healthy old age and also to control health care costs. There is no guarantee that the generations entering older adulthood in the future will live longer than the previous generations. In fact, environmental degradation, unchecked health disparities, and lifestyle choices could shorten life expectancy for some members of future generations. In contrast, health promotion and disease prevention services could not only increase life expectancy but also extend healthy life expectancy, the primary objective of most of us. Meeting the information needs of older adults about health and other services requires particularly careful planning. Technological prowess is increasing among older adults, and this will continue as people who have experienced the computer revolution in their workplaces become older adults. Further, many people now over 65 are regularly spending time on Facebook and YouTube. However, many do not, and the very old (85+) are even less likely to use online resources to get information. Therefore, making sure that the information they need is available through the media and social networks that they do use is critical. Staff in physicians' offices, churches, and senior centers can be vital sources of information for older adults if they are kept fully informed of changes in policies and programs. Information provided online will not reach many older adults unless younger people in their social networks recognize their information needs and give them the information. At the same time, efforts to increase access to computers in senior housing, nursing homes, senior centers, and in libraries should be prioritized so that older adults can build their skills and get needed information directly and easily. An added benefit is that older adults often enjoy using the computers to play video games and have the opportunity to play them with their grandchildren. Use of the interactive elements of the Internet to combat social isolation in older adults can potentially offer an avenue for relationship-building even when older adults have lost mobility.

Gerontologists have posited that older adults are now entering a "third age," defined as a new societal structure, construct, or life stage that is an outgrowth of retirement policies made available through pensions and Social Security income (Fahey, 1996). These retirement years are theoretically an economically secure, mature stage of life with opportunities for travel, further education, and different work possibilities. However, older adults are increasingly delaying retirement because the economic downturn has depleted their retirement savings, and thus, will not experience as many years of retirement. Although increased life expectancy and adequate retirement income result in more time for leisure and involvement in activities for some older adults, there is also increased chance of loss and disability. Further, our culture has not yet adapted to the reality that many elders are now experiencing prolonged health and productive lives. Therefore, older adults must find meaning and validation without the reassurance of existing societal norms.

Social work has both the value base and the skill set necessary to assist older adults in celebrating the third age. Social work values commit us to working with vulnerable and underserved populations as well as to providing support for client self-determination. Given social work's holistic approach and its focus on the biopsychosocial and spiritual aspects of individuals in their environment, social workers are well positioned to support policies and programs that allow older adults to remain socially engaged as they undergo different biological, social, psychological, and spiritual changes. Barriers that prevent healthy older adults from participating fully in the workforce, such as lack of public transportation, inflexible work schedules, and age discrimination, need to be eliminated. These changes, as well as many of the other changes that will make communities more livable for older adults, will also improve the quality of life for people of all ages. When older adults become disabled, they need prompt access to home- and community-based services so that they are not needlessly institutionalized. We need to create models of care that support the strengths of older adults and preserve their right to self-determination.

Many theories of aging well are used to describe older adults' adaptation and coping based on stress models. For example, Baltes and Baltes (1990) describe aging well in terms of selective optimization with compensation. That is, older adults cope and adapt to changing physical and cognitive limitations by concentrating on high-priority areas. It is important for researchers and policy makers to think in terms of the *process* of aging well instead of the physical and psychological outcomes of aging. Focusing on aging well will help them understand how older adults minimize losses through adaptation and will enable them to develop policies and programs that support this process (Chiriboga, 1996). Further, the strengths perspective helps us recognize the potential for older adults to set new goals and transcend losses in pursuing new life goals. Our understanding of the aging process is changing rapidly and social workers need to keep abreast of these changes so that their practice with older adults reflects these new discoveries.

Developing a Strengths-Based Agenda

How, then, can we chart a policy agenda for the new millennium that helps build on the strengths and resources of older adults so that the years after 65, 85, or even 100, are good years to be alive? Social workers engaged in policy practice can help develop and implement a strengths-based agenda. Strengths perspective policy principles point to the importance of engaging the target group in developing and implementing new policies, determining how best to build on strengths and overcome barriers to implementation, garnering resources, and evaluating outcomes. In order to craft new policies that support aging well for a diverse population of older adults today and in the future, it is important to engage adults and their families across economic and racial groups in defining common interests. Efforts to find consensus must be initiated and supported. For example, information on options for Social Security reform that focuses on potential common interests needs to be widely disseminated and discussed. Strategies to mobilize older people from diverse backgrounds in support of needed policy change must be developed. Younger people also need to understand that public support for older adults enables them to use their resources for themselves and their children rather than taking their parents into their homes as many earlier generations did. If they get involved now, then supportive programs will be in place for them when they become older adults.

Heightening intergenerational conflict is the most destructive course in preparing our future agenda. It is a false dichotomy. If we are lucky, all of us, including young people, will one day be old. Women and children are not impoverished because older adults receive Social Security. Children growing up in poverty disproportionately live in single-parent homes headed by women. These women often receive lower wages than men. Lower wages provide inadequate support for these young families and will contribute to inadequate income in old age because they inhibit savings and contributions to pension funds. Low income throughout the life span is linked to early death and increased chronic and acute disease. Therefore, policies that diminish the rates of poverty among young people will reduce their health problems in old age. As noted at the beginning of this chapter, a person's childhood and youth greatly influence health and welfare in old age. Initiatives such as living wage campaigns and expanded affordable job training programs can help address poverty for all ages and are key to people aging well.

Further, increased access to health care for younger people that is made possible by the 2010 health reform legislation will have great impact on future older adults.

Although some scholars from social work and other disciplines continue to emphasize the disparity between spending on children's programs and programs that primarily benefit older adults as though that will somehow increase willingness to invest in children, their arguments typically overlook vital points. First, comparisons of spending on children and older adults often focus on federal spending and ignore state and local spending. As has been discussed earlier in the text in relation to international comparisons of social welfare spending, state and local spending is a significant part of the social welfare expenditure picture in the U.S., and when all public spending is not part of the calculation, a distorted picture results. For example, most investment in children's development in the U.S. comes in the form of spending at the state and local levels on public education. Second, any comparison of growth in spending needs to consider per capita (per person) spending rather than aggregate spending. As you have learned, the older-adult population is rapidly increasing now while the child population is more stable. Further, children comprise an age group made up of people 18 and under while the older-adult age group is comprised of people 65 and over, which covers 50 years. Also, benefits such as the Earned Income Tax Credit and the Child Tax Credit which are designed to lessen the financial burden on families with children are not added in when determining whether these families are in poverty. If you look at per capita spending on children at all levels of government and factor in these benefits, spending on children has in fact grown in recent years. Finally, the growth in spending on older adults is in large part due to uncontrolled growth in health care costs. It is no surprise that in general, children use less health care than older adults, but here the focus should be on finding ways to control health care costs while ensuring effective care for all generations.

International research on poverty does not find evidence of a tradeoff between childhood and elder poverty. In fact, they typically move in concert. There is little indication of a crowding out effect where spending on either children or elders leads to less spending on the other groups (Brady, 2009). Rather, poverty in both groups is often closely related to overall poverty and countries willing and able to spend on one group typically also have progressive policies to help the other. Instead of spending time trying to determine which age group of people in poverty is being disproportionately benefited, the focus needs to be on how to counter the political influence of those who believe that the role of government should be limited to providing for defense and public safety, and little else. Coalitions need to be built to help reverse the further redistribution of wealth away from low- and middle-income families so that both children and older adults will be more secure.

Groups such as the Older Women's League (OWL), as well as groups formed specifically to advocate for Social Security and Medicare rights, are working to forge coalitions among generations. You can learn more about some of these efforts at the website of the Medicare Rights Center. Generations United is a politically active group that is also working to promote intergenerational policies (you can view proposals for policy reforms supported by older adults at the OWL and Generations United websites). Many programs have been established to promote intergenerational connections that are beneficial to all participants. Two examples are the Experience Corps and Connecting Generations. Both of these organizations have extensive websites where you can learn more about their initiatives.

In Chapter 10, we considered the importance of policies and programs that promote good health. Policies and programs that address smoking cessation, weight loss, and exercise can help younger adults prepare for a healthier old age and can

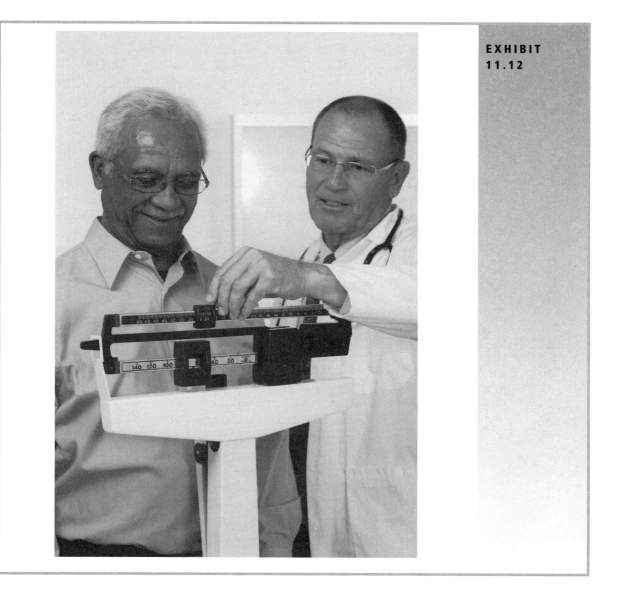

EXHIBIT 11.12

help older adults prevent the onset of disabilities. Senior centers as well as other community agencies could be much more proactive in getting older adults involved in health and wellness programs.

Creating Needed Infrastructure

In the area of social engagement, efforts are under way at the local, state, and federal levels to create the infrastructure necessary for continued social engagement for older adults with disabilities. For example, communities are now beginning to design age-sensitive community infrastructures so that older adults with impaired mobility can have easy access to places such as churches, restaurants, and public buildings where they have traditionally engaged in social interaction. In some communities, universal housing codes that enhance accessibility in residential construction are receiving greater support. In addition, policies are being passed that require all new construction to conform to these codes. These policies not only support social engagement but also social integration and inclusion for people regardless of age or disability. The emphasis is on interacting with the mainstream community and ensuring that people gain full access to the opportunities, rights and services available to the members of the mainstream.

AAAs and state aging agencies continue to implement promising initiatives such as the National Family Caregiver Support Program, which trains and supports caregivers at all stages of the caregiving experience and also seeks to lessen their social isolation. To find out more, visit the website of the National Family Caregiver Support Program. As the baby boom becomes the elder boom, policies to help caregivers will become even more important. Because men are now living longer, they will increasingly be available to care for their spouses. However, they will need support in assuming a role with which they may be very unfamiliar. In addition, support for caregivers must be increased. For example, we must develop strategies to more equitably recognize the contributions of younger unpaid caregivers in public pension systems. Caregivers are most often women and women are much more likely to be impoverished in old age than are men. Further, when lack of economic resources needed to access community-based LTC services combines with other sources of caregiver burden, the result can be that an older adult is placed in a nursing facility prematurely. This is especially problematic for people with low and moderate incomes who are not poor enough to qualify for Medicaid LTC services in the community but who will quickly become impoverished and qualify for Medicaid once they are in the nursing facility. Finally, we need to develop and implement individualized caregiver assessment tools that help us to identify the unique needs of caregivers who may be young or older, male or female, and come from increasingly diverse backgrounds.

Other state agencies are also beginning to realize that preparing for the elder boom is not the job of only the aging agencies. For example, state transportation departments are beginning to test the visibility of road-sign paint with 65-year-old drivers rather than 25-year-old men so that older adults can continue driving safely and thus enhance social engagement. Overall, state transportation agencies have long been involved in providing services to older adults, and they are now giving increased attention to policies in that arena. As discussed above, social workers can also weigh in on congressional debate around reauthorization of the OAA. As in other areas of social policy, social workers need to get involved in policy advocacy.

Finally, it is essential that we challenge cultural biases that devalue older adults. For example, we need to focus greater attention on the capacities rather than the deficits of older adults. This century will provide ample opportunities for social workers who have been educated to join with older adults from a variety of backgrounds to help create effective policy. It is clear that supporting older people's strengths so that they can remain an active and contributing part of the community, rather than narrowly focusing on traditional services, will be an important component of planning for the elder boom. Advocacy for policies that allow older social workers flexibility in their work schedule and opportunities to keep contributing professionally even after retirement is a place to begin. Flexibility in policies to accommodate the diversity among older adults, and caution in creating entitlements so expensive that resentment mounts among younger citizens, will be integral to effective planning. Social work values of self-determination and social justice which are also basic to policy practice from the strengths approach can guide development of needed policies and programs.

CONCLUSION

Reciprocity between young and old people provides the mutual support on which both groups rely. Policies need to ensure that the generations continue to live in harmony. Exaggerating the economic impact of population aging threatens the intergenerational social contract. Positive social engagement among older adults and between young and old people is vital to a continued sense of responsibility and reciprocity. Framing the needs of older adults as competing with the needs of younger people fosters conflict. Alternatively, policies may be crafted to invest in intergenerational approaches that more effectively meet need across the life span.

In the areas of economic security and health care, children have been primarily served through means-tested public assistance programs while older adults are primarily served through social insurance programs. Investing in universal income support and health care systems for our children as well as for older adults will help ensure the future for all citizens. A thriving economy is vital to adequately support young as well as older citizens, and healthy children who are well cared for are crucial to economic growth and to securing our future. However, when economic growth is emphasized without adequate attention to environmental concerns, the well-being of all age groups is jeopardized. Further, we need to develop effective strategies to control health care costs including LTC costs without compromising quality, and the American public will need to find the will to insist such strategies be implemented.

With the growth in the older population in the U.S., more older adults than ever before have the possibility of aging well. The challenge is to craft policies that are equitable and acceptable to young and old alike. Older disabled adults who can no longer work are particularly vulnerable and in need of advocacy by social workers committed to social justice for all. The social work profession has the necessary value base and practice orientation to lead efforts to craft effective policies and provide services for older adults. At least 75 percent of social workers are likely to practice with older adults and their families in some capacity (CSWE, 2010). However, the already large gap in the number of social workers with the education in gerontology needed to serve the older-adult population, is becoming ever wider. Armed with your knowledge about the policy context in which today's older adults struggle or thrive, you can play a critical role in charting social policy for our nation's future, and your own.

CATCHING UP WITH THE POLICY GROUP

Now let us check in with Tiffany, the fourth member of the policy group. Tiffany had planned to work with children, but along the way her plans changed.

EXHIBIT 11.13

Tiffany

Tiffany decided to take a job at the local AAA after she graduated. She knew that these agencies had been created by the OAA, and in her state, AAA's provided case management to older adults and support services to caregivers. She had grown up a long distance away from her grandparents and had actually never spent much time in the company of older adults. However, the AAA was convenient to where she lived and the position was open when she needed a job. She was surprised to find some of her clients shared her off-beat sense of humor and many of them were quick to tell her their life stories, although some of her clients were very closed off. For many of them, their modest Social Security retirement was their major source of income. Although most of her clients were not depressed, she did regularly see people who showed many signs of depression. She would encourage them to seek help at the local mental health center but the cost of co-pays for treatment was a deterrent. Further, the lack of public transportation in her largely suburban community made getting to the mental health center challenging, and many of her clients had serious disabilities that made it even harder to travel. She knew that mental health treatment had been found to be effective with older adults, but she also knew that they did not receive services at the mental health center at nearly the rate that younger adults did.

She decided to talk to her colleagues and her supervisor at the AAA. Some of them reported the same pattern, so her supervisor suggested inviting over a therapist at the mental health center to talk about their services and ways of improving access. During the meeting, Tiffany explained how when she did a dual assessment of her clients and looked for patterns of challenges that might stem from policy barriers, it was clear that many older adults faced significant barriers to receiving needed mental health services. She and other workers gave specific examples such as lack of transportation to the mental health centers and worry over co-pays. The speaker from the mental health center passed out information on how provisions of the Affordable Care Act increased access to mental health services and would help with co-pays for many of the AAA's low-income clients. He also had pamphlets that addressed issues of stigma surrounding mental health services and provided information on mental health resources in their area. Finally, he said the state legislature was considering a bill that would provide funding for mental health aging specialists in mental health centers statewide. These mental health specialists would also be able to provide in-home mental health treatment in some cases. Because Tiffany had been in contact with her local legislator for an assignment in her policy class, she provided information to her colleagues on how to contact their legislators. They also began to urge their friends and family to get behind this legislation. If Tiffany and her co-workers want to do more, what other steps could you suggest? If the legislation passes, how could she help make sure that funds are appropriated to actually implement the legislation? If the legislation is implemented, what sort of evaluation should be done to make sure that there is outcome data when budget cuts come and the aging specialist positions need to be defended?

MAIN POINTS

- Policies and programs for older adults should not focus primarily on disability and deficits but, rather, promote aging well. Aging well is the process of minimizing the negative effects of losses associated with aging by adapting to the challenges and maximizing the benefits of long life.

- The use of the strengths perspective in work with older adults can help refocus our understanding of this stage of life. The strengths perspective emphasizes the new goals and resources that can have a transformative effect on the last stage of life.

- Economic security, health care, and social engagement are three critical areas addressed in the passage of key legislation for older adults. Major public policies and programs affecting older adults in these dimensions include OASDI, Medicare, Medicaid, and the OAA.

- Long-term care (LTC) refers to medical and social services provided to people with disabilities or chronic illnesses. LTC occurs in many settings and includes nursing homes, assisted living, unpaid care by informal caregivers, and home- and community-based services. Informal unpaid caregivers still provide the majority of LTC, although this reliance on informal supports is strained, due to changes in demographics, family composition, and the economy.

- Policy makers, researchers, and consumers can work together to develop effective strategies to control health care costs including LTC costs without compromising quality. The American public will need to find the will to insist such strategies be implemented if we are to have adequate health care in the future.

- The OAA was enacted to support planning and coordinate services for older adults through the provision of access services, in-home services, legal assistance, senior centers, meal programs, and supportive services.

- Older adults are living longer today and comprise a larger percentage of the entire population than previous cohorts of older adults. The first cohort of baby boomers (people born between 1946 and 1964), reached the age of 65 in 2011, and the baby boom generation will continue to greatly impact the policy arena as the U.S. decides how to meet the needs of a larger and more diverse aging population.

- The Employee Retirement Income Security Act (ERISA), passed in 1974, was the first federal legislation to regulate the private pension system. The Act set minimum standards for participation, vesting, funding, and benefit accrual in qualified job-specific pensions. ERISA established the Pension

Benefit Guaranty Corporation to insure certain defined benefit pension plans.

- Economic security of older adults is generally augmented by public insurance programs such as OASDI retirement benefits, SSI benefits, or private sources such as job-specific pensions, and private savings. As the "three-legged" stool of retirement security has shifted more risk to individuals, there are more chances for vulnerable individuals to experience deprivation.

- Long-term financial solvency of the OASDI needs to be the focus of present political decisions. Making changes now, such as increasing payroll taxes and the taxable income limit, decreasing benefits, or increasing the age of eligibility for retirement benefits, will enable the program to provide full benefits beyond 2033.

- Increasing Supplemental Security Income benefits for older adults in poverty is a promising option for addressing the needs of low-income seniors. SSI is a federal income supplement program, not a federal insurance program.

- The current push in LTC is for community tenure with the establishment of home- and community-based services, use of nursing homes for short-term rehabilitation stays, and hospice services that assist people in dying at home.

- Policy reforms are needed to remove barriers to productive work for older adults. This will help promote both financial security and social engagement, but such attention to productivity must be carefully planned lest it contribute to marginalizing older adults whose physical or other limitations prevent such work.

- Alliances between disability rights groups and the aging community can potentially result in a stronger LTC service system for all people with disabilities. However, sometimes the needs of older adults can be missed when services for all groups are examined without regard to age.

- The CLASS provisions of the 2010 health care reform legislation that established a voluntary national insurance program to provide cash benefits to pay for LTC for people with long-term disabilities, have been repealed. This means there is still a gaping hole in health care protection which threatens to impoverish many Americans when a family member becomes disabled and needs LTC.

- Future policy initiatives should take into account outcomes across the life span. Promoting intergenerational programs and policies is preferable to fostering conflict between older adults and younger adults and children.

- Arguments about inequitable spending on children when compared to older adults often overlook state and local spending on children, and focus on aggregate rather than per person spending. Also uncontrolled health care spending that negatively affects all age groups, is a major driver of projected increases in spending on older adults because older adults need more health care than do children.

- There is a large and growing need for social workers with the education in gerontology necessary to serve older adults.

- Strengths perspective policy principles and solution focused approaches can be used in charting a policy agenda informed by the needs and goals of an increasingly diverse older adult population as well as those of younger generations.

EXERCISES

1. Go to the Sanchez case available at www.routledgesw.com. Think about what you have learned about the family and institutional supports that are available to the Sanchez family.
   a. How do you think the needs of Hector and Celia Sanchez might differ from those of the majority community as they age?
   b. How do you think the family and community supports may differ?
   c. What sorts of policy and programs changes do you think would be necessary to increase involvement of Hispanic elders in senior center activities such as meals programs and recreational programs?
2. Go to the Washburn case available at www.routledgesw.com. In implementing the strengths perspective in social policy analysis, the focus is on giving voice to clients. Although you cannot talk to Mrs. Washburn, imagine yourself in her situation and try to answer these questions from her perspective.
   a. What might Mrs. Washburn voice as her needs and concerns?
   b. What might Mrs. Washburn say are her goals for "aging well"?
   c. What do you think Mrs. Washburn, as a stakeholder, would like to see implemented in the area of additional social policies and programs? Identify three things.
   d. How can social workers use strengths perspective principles to engage older adults in efforts to bring about more just policies?
3. What strengths identified in Carla Washburn's community might potentially be built on when attempting to ameliorate some of the needs of elders as well as others in the community?
4. In this chapter you have learned about policies and programs not available to younger people that can help provide additional support for homeless older adults in Riverton.

a. Identify these policies and programs.

b. Sometimes homeless older adults who are disabled are admitted to nursing facilities because social service workers feel that at least they will have food and shelter.

- What are the pros and cons of such a service strategy?
- Do you think it is in the best interest of the older adult?
- Do you think it is cost-effective?
- Can you think of a more effective strategy?

5. In small groups, discuss the policy implications of the demographic changes this country will undergo between now and 2030.

a. List three positive aspects of these demographic changes and explore how policies could be enacted to build on these positive aspects.

b. List three negative aspects of these changes and explore what policies may be needed to lessen negative outcomes.

6. Older adults and people with disabilities are often not consulted when a community such as Hudson City does disaster planning, although they may experience specific risks in such a disaster.

a. What steps would need to be taken to change this fact and who would need to take them?

b. See if you can find out if the needs of older adults and people with disabilities have been considered and these groups have been involved in disaster planning in your city. If not, list some strategies that might help get these groups included.

7. Medicaid agencies in some states are putting more and more resources for older adults online.

a. Is this happening in your state?

b. Do most low-income disabled elders in your state have a computer and know how to use it?

c. What steps need to be taken to ensure that older adults and not just the professionals that work with them have access to resources important to their health and well-being?

8. Visit your local senior center. Find out how the center is funded. Who is eligible for services and what services are provided?

a. How old is the average participant?

b. Do you think the senior center will need to change if it is to attract the baby boomers as they age?

c. What policy and program changes would you suggest?

d. What opportunities for intergenerational programming do you see? Are there any intergenerational aspects to programming currently?

e. Is the senior center involved in any policy advocacy, around the reauthorization of the OAA or other important legislation? How do they engage older adults in these efforts?

9. How can the stories that social workers, in their role as activist clinicians, hear from older adults in direct practice settings be used to advocate for more effective policies for our clients?

   a. Identify three specific steps social workers could take to make this link.

   b. What are some cautions to consider when using clients' stories to inform policy?

10. Visit the Administration for Community Living website and read more about the OAA. Do the programs and policies outlined by the OAA support a strengths-based approach to programs for older adults? What changes might you want to see in the OAA as it is reauthorized?

11. As has been highlighted in this text, it is challenging for people to make effective policy for groups they perceive as the "other," that is, groups of people they perceive as very different from themselves with very different problems. Although, if we are lucky, all of us will be old someday, many young people have great difficulty imagining themselves as old and certainly view older adults as the "other."

    a. What strategies do you think might be effective in helping young people better understand the strengths as well as problems of older adults?

    b. What steps would you take to build this level of understanding more widely in our society so there would be broader backing for policies that support older adults' strengths?

CHAPTER 12

The Future

An image of the future is at the base of all choice oriented behavior. We need a vision of the future that energizes our journey.

Author Unknown

If we are worried about the future, then we must look today at the upbringing of children.

Gordon B. Hinckley

The arc of the moral universe is long, but it bends towards justice.

Martin Luther King, Jr.

The future does not just happen. When you act on your vision and hopes, you shape the future.

Rosemary K. Chapin

THIS CHAPTER FOCUSES ON THE FUTURE. Because no one has an accurate crystal ball, it might seem unwise to try to foretell the future, especially in these uncertain times. However, beliefs about the future are central to all the actions we take. For example, when rainy weather is forecast, we grab an umbrella. Similarly, when we hear a friend is having a party on Saturday, we get ready for fun. An interest in prediction and control fuels our attention to the future. People who choose social work as a career generally do so because they want their life's work to be meaningful and rewarding, and they believe that social work will provide those benefits. Because policy and programs are enacted to influence the future, you will need to be attuned to what people are predicting about future conditions in order to engage in effective policy practice. As Macarov (1991) has pointed out, without forecasting there is no freedom of decision.

This chapter, however, is not only about what people are predicting about the future. It also identifies strategies for understanding why certain forecasts are made, and for interpreting potential future scenarios with an eye toward impacting future outcomes. We are all inundated with dire warnings—our economic system is teetering on the brink of collapse, our natural environment is damaged beyond repair—and with, alternatively, suspiciously euphoric predictions about the bright future that awaits—technology will solve our problems. Somehow, we have to make sense of all this, chart a course for ourselves, and decide how best to help our clients. However, there are tools to aid you. We will examine a set of guidelines for analyzing forecasts that will help you make sense of the myriad and often conflicting forecasts you will be asked to consider in the coming years. After examining these guidelines, we will explore major trends that are expected to influence future social policy. Finally, you will be challenged to use this information to develop the foresight that can help improve policies and, ultimately, future outcomes for your clients. You can draw on the strengths-focused approach to policy development and the solution focused strategies you have learned to move from challenges to goals. You can employ the tools for empowerment you now have, to help increase support for capacity building approaches which are highlighted throughout this chapter. As you have learned, in this text the capacity building approach refers to policies and programs that focus on strengthening the skills, competencies and abilities of people and communities and on helping them secure the resources and supports needed for full economic and social inclusion.

FUTURE FORECASTS

Forecasts can be more clearly understood if we consider the motivations of the groups that make the forecasts, the social environment in which the forecasts are made, and the assumptions on which the forecasts are based. Guidelines for exploring factors that shape forecasts are presented below. As you become familiar with these guidelines and begin to use them to analyze forecasts you encounter in the public media, you will be better able to identify which forecasts are not credible and which ones should be heeded.

Guidelines for Understanding Future Forecasts

Take a look at Quick Guide 10. It provides a set of guidelines you can use to understand why forecasts are made, whether they will be accurate, and how they might influence future actions, including policy making. These guidelines are based on recent analysis of the effect and accuracy of forecasts made by social workers early in the 20th century. Elements of the guidelines are discussed in detail below.

Analyze the Purpose   When you examine assertions about the future, consider first the background of the person or group making the forecast, including the reasons

QUICK GUIDE 10	**Understanding Future Forecasts**

Use this guide to understand why forecasts are made, whether they will be accurate, and how they might influence future actions, including policy making.

1. Analyze the purpose.
   - Social mobilization: encourage groups of people to take action and be prepared for the future being forecast;
   - System replacement;
   - Enhancement of a specific professional group; and,
   - Collective learning and adaptation.

2. Assess the underlying assumptions and credibility of source information.
3. Consider the influence of current socioeconomic conditions.
4. Do not expect the numbers to speak for themselves.
5. Assess the extent to which surprise events were anticipated.

why this person or group is trying to forecast the future. What is the purpose of this forecast? Among the reasons people make forecasts are the following:

- social mobilization;

- system replacement;

- enhancement of a specific professional group; and,

- collective learning and adaptation.

Social mobilization refers to efforts aimed at encouraging large groups of people to take action and prepare themselves for the future that is being forecast. People pressing for system replacement are trying to demonstrate that unless a system is fundamentally changed or replaced, it will be unable to deal adequately with future conditions. People who believe conditions in the future will make their specific professional group larger or more important will want to publicize that forecast in order to enhance their group. People also make forecasts in order to foster collective learning and adaptation so that groups and society at large are not taken by surprise but, rather, can learn and adapt to the coming conditions.

For example, one claim about the future is that the number of jobs for social workers will grow by about 14 percent (to 811,700) between 2010 and 2020 (U.S. Bureau of Labor Statistics, 2012a). The need for gerontological social workers is predicted to increase particularly quickly. When considering the purpose of these forecasts related to increased demand for gerontological social workers, we need to keep in mind that there will be large increases in the number of older adults because of the aging of the baby boomers, a topic discussed in Chapter 11. Therefore, if social work education does not change so as to prepare more social workers to work with older adults, the profession will not be able to provide the necessary services to those who need them. To avoid such a situation, social work educators are being called upon to modify the educational system. This example illustrates three purposes of claims about the future: system replacement, social mobilization, and professional enhancement. People who are already involved in gerontological social work are particularly interested in publicizing this future need in order to garner increased attention to, and resources for, gerontological social work and the aging population with whom they work. Thus, their profession will be enhanced. Clearly, the goals of collective learning and adaptation also motivate the forecasts. By making the need for gerontological social workers well known, those who do so hope the forecasts will lead to adaptation to fill the need.

To orient yourself to the competing claims about the future and to sharpen your ability to evaluate various projections, try to find forecasts about the future in the popular press and on the web. Investigate the backgrounds of the people making these forecasts and consider which of the reasons listed above might have motivated them. Ask yourself, "What is the purpose of this forecast?" A favorite example of mine of a forecast we have already exposed as unlikely to come true is "Social Security will not be there for seniors in the future." As discussed in previous chapters, the Social Security Trust Fund is solvent through 2033. In addition, it can remain solvent well beyond that point if we make certain adjustments in benefits and contributions. Consider what purposes people may have for forecasting the collapse of Social Security. Another prediction that does not appear to be accurate is one commonly heard in the 1990s about increased computer usage by young people in the future leading to much more social isolation. Instead, social networking sites abound and young people are connecting with other young people with similar interests around the world.

Purpose biases such forecasts. Such bias is inevitable. Throughout this text, we have explored many examples of how reality is constructed based on people's points of view. A forecast is such a construction, except that it deals with a possible future reality. Awareness of bias can augment your understanding of the forecast.

Assess Underlying Assumptions and the Credibility of Source Information   After you have analyzed the purposes of the forecasts, carefully consider the sources used to generate them. You should analyze sources for credibility in much the same way that you examine sources appropriate for reference in professional writing.

One prominent example of a credible source on which many forecasts are based is U.S. Census Bureau population projections and estimates. The term population projection refers to the number of people who are expected to be in a given group in a specific year. An example is the number of women in the U.S. who will be age 40 and older in 2030. Population projections are based on a number of underlying assumptions. Demographers who make population projections start with a set of characteristics of interest in a population for a base year (usually a census year). They then apply different assumptions about the amount, direction, and rate of change that could be experienced by that population in ensuing years. For example, to create a population projection of the number of women over 40 in 2030, demographers could begin with the number of women over 20 in 2010 (a base census year) and then apply assumptions about how many women would either die or migrate in or out of the country over the next 20 years.

The U.S. Census Bureau uses a cohort-component method for developing projections. This method follows each cohort of people of the same age across time. It bases population projections on assumptions about trends in the following areas: (a) mortality—the rate of death for each age group, generally considered separately for men and women; (b) fertility—the rate of births, generally considered separately by age group and race; and (c) net migration—the balance of people entering and leaving a population. For example, when developing projections of the size of the U.S. population for the year 2030, based on data from the 2010 census, the calculation can be thought of as:

2030 population = 2010 population + (births – deaths) + (net migration) + error.

Events such as epidemics, widespread crop failures, global economic crises, and wars obviously influence the actual rate of births, deaths, and net migration. For this reason, the agency creates a range of projections. Each range is based on different sets of assumptions regarding birth, death, and net migration. Basic assumptions are sometimes in error. For example, in 2013 researchers at the Max Planck Institute for Demographic Research in Germany asserted that assumptions used in estimating future fertility rate by the U.S. Census Bureau as well as in other countries, were based on a flawed methodology that did not capture the changing pattern of more women delaying childbearing into their late thirties and forties.

However, when people develop forecasts, they add yet more assumptions based on various factors that we examine below. What you need to remember is that forecasts are built on layers of assumptions. There is nothing inherently wrong with this; in fact, most policy analyses are based on a series of assumptions. However, it is vital that you take time to examine the assumptions made before accepting a forecast as likely to be an accurate portrayal of the future.

Consider the influence of current socioeconomic conditions, which can influence the assumptions on which forecasts are based. For example, if the economy is in a slump and political efforts are under way to cut social services in order to reduce taxes, the cuts will be easier to justify if people assume that most children in the future will be much better educated and more economically secure than most of us were in our childhood. Forecasts can then be developed that make that point and create that impression. Additionally, current economic constraints may be fueling a push to view future generations of older people as healthy and capable of self-support rather than in need of more public support. In fact, in gerontological research, there is a heightened focus on productive aging now. In contrast, during the Great Depression, when jobs were scarce and policy makers wanted elders out of the labor force, elders were labeled as unable to keep up with the demands of a mechanized workplace. However, just a few years later, when World War II created demand for older adults in the workforce, they were expected to (and in fact did) perform very well in industrialized settings.

Even though people may try to persuade you to the contrary, numbers do not speak for themselves. They must be interpreted. An obvious example is calculating the number of people aged 65 and older and then assuming that it represents the number of people incapable of working for the purpose of forecasting dependency. Public policy designed to create opportunity for younger workers and support people in retirement underpins this association. In fact, many people aged 65 and older can and do work. In addition, advances in health care and changing attitudes in the workplace will undoubtedly make it possible for many older adults to do so.

Similarly, while advocates of reduced immigration levels use the total number of foreign-born individuals in the U.S. today to argue for further restrictions, based on the idea that continued future immigration at the current rate would be disastrous for U.S. society, the reality is that a larger percentage of the U.S. population was foreign-born in 1890 (15 percent) than in 2010 (12.4 percent), and certainly history does not suggest that this earlier immigration was detrimental to the country (U.S. Census Bureau, 2010a). Clearly, then, we can emphasize or downplay different interpretations of population projections depending on the future we want to portray. We can reframe discussions of future public costs associated with retirement to focus on issues of choice, the availability of work, the capacity to work, and the willingness of taxpayers to support people in retirement rather than on the numbers of people who are over 65 and therefore assumed to be dependent. Similarly, we can talk about high levels of immigration as a problem to be addressed or as an enduring part of our national fabric and a testament to the allure of the U.S. as a land of opportunity.

Numbers can only be understood within a context that accounts for the many variables that will affect those numbers' impact. Because numbers can be manipulated, social workers need to be attuned to the origins of forecasts as well as the role of social work values in interpreting them. As illustrated above, language can be used to recast societal change as threats or opportunities. Social workers can engage in re-languaging discussions of the future. For example, instead of allowing discussion of the aging of our society to be framed as a "coming tsunami," the discussion can be reframed to celebrate the advances in society that have made a longer life expectancy possible and to focus on how our society can benefit if older adults are supported in their efforts to age well, as outlined in the previous chapter.

A final consideration is the extent to which the person making the forecast acknowledges and discusses surprise events that could influence the forecast's accuracy. For example, the events of September 11, 2001 helped fuel an economic downturn and contributed to the U.S. decision to invade Iraq. The economic downturn beginning in 2007 in the wake of the banking crisis also unexpectedly changed our economic outlook, although certainly there is considerable evidence that this particular event could have been anticipated more than it was. These events significantly affected the accuracy of earlier forecasts about economic trends in the U.S. during the first decade of the 21st century. Similarly, the baby boom dramatically influenced the accuracy of earlier population projections for 1980 and 2000.

Although nobody can anticipate and consider all future scenarios, the most likely so-called unforeseen events should be anticipated to the extent possible. Possible future breakthroughs in disease prevention are particularly relevant in considering future public social welfare costs and burdens. Current approaches exist for factoring in some of these possibilities. For example, demographers and policy makers attempting to anticipate future costs for Medicare and Medicaid create alternative scenarios based on possible events that will affect future costs of prescriptions and rates of disability. They consider the possible impact of such factors as more stringent anti-smoking campaigns, greater participation in exercise programs by baby boomers, and possible advances in the treatment of Alzheimer's disease or cancer when developing forecasts of rates of disability, use of medications and, ultimately, Medicaid and Medicare expenditures. In the same way, planners in the private sector also consider the likelihood that such alternative scenarios will come to pass when they make decisions regarding future investments in long-term care (LTC) facilities. Savvy planners in all areas of the economy make similar calculations.

Medical advances, biological warfare, climate change, natural disasters, and major economic downturns are examples of surprise events that can have a great impact on the accuracy of future forecasts. Worldwide flu pandemics that particularly threaten young people provide yet another example of such a "surprise event," as do increasingly violent natural disasters that many scientists believe are related to global climate change. Even if authors do not alert readers that such surprise events may dramatically change the accuracy of their projections, it is incumbent on readers to consider that possibility.

The most accurate forecasts include alternative scenarios that account for the likelihood of at least some "unlikely" events: dramatic breakthroughs in disease control, natural disasters, terrorist attacks, economic crises, or global conflict. Take a moment to think about what surprise events you have seen in your lifetime, what unlikely events you can imagine, and how they might affect future forecasts.

Thinking About the Future Using a Values-Based Lens: The Strengths Approach

The guidelines discussed above can help us analyze the accuracy and utility of a forecast. However, social workers interested in promoting a strengths approach when considering future social policy initiatives need to conduct additional analysis. From a strengths perspective, forecasts should always be evaluated to gauge whether they are based on a deficit view of the population being discussed. For example, not very long ago, a common prediction was that people with severe disabilities would spend their lives in institutions and certainly would not join the workforce. This forecast was based on the assumption that this population was totally dependent on other people.

It is also important to consider the amount of attention given to the current cohort about whom the forecast is being made. Significantly, some forecasts made earlier in the 20th century concerning the social service needs of older adults today failed to take into account the racial and ethnic diversity in the population of children who would become today's elders. When you examine current forecasts, look carefully for similar oversights. For example, people who make forecasts about the future needs of Hispanics or Latinos must pay attention to the life conditions, strengths, and goals of Hispanic families today, including the diversity within this population. If they do so, then they will not overlook such vital information as the rate of entry of Hispanic women into the full-time workforce. This information is an important factor in forecasting the need for formal care of dependent family members and the range of possibilities for future birth rates. Similarly, lack of attention to the goals and preferences of people in their forties today will impair our ability to forecast needed resources and social services in 2030 and beyond, when that cohort will be over 65.

Engaging and paying close attention to specific service users is a central tenet of the strengths perspective. However, although citizen involvement is considered an important component in crafting effective social policy from a strengths perspective, it is only one component. Clearly, there is more to be done. We turn now to additional elements that provide guidance in understanding forecasts and crafting future social policies that reflect the strengths perspective.

Values rooted in the NASW *Code of Ethics* underpin the strengths approach. We are experiencing unprecedented structural change and accompanying uncertainty about the future. Professional values, such as commitment to social justice and the reduction of inequity, offer an anchor that social work professionals can use when considering future policies and programs. Social workers must carefully consider the interplay of professional values, demographics, societal goals, and political realities when they evaluate future scenarios. For example, social service professionals might favor spending more money on children and less on older adults because children experience higher poverty rates. This policy is in keeping with a longstanding commitment to social justice and, therefore, generational equity. However, as we discussed earlier, forecasts to support such policy changes must be carefully crafted, lest we lend unwitting support to those who would dismantle all federal entitlement programs regardless of which age groups they target. The well-being of all generations is interlocked, and future social policies need to be crafted with attention to their intergenerational effects.

Finally, the strengths perspective is based on the insight that our understanding of conditions and events is socially constructed. Social constructions of conditions influence future social policy responses and thus, future realities. To the extent that action or inaction by persons with knowledge of the forecasts can shape the future, forecasts have the capacity to become self-fulfilling prophecies. Indeed, basic to many forecasts is a desire to ultimately improve future conditions. An important component of understanding forecasting is the effort to foresee how specific forecasts, added to the weight of other forecasts, may influence the resources and services available to our clients. Forecasts that do not take into account the diverse and fluid needs of future generations may compound the problems of providing necessary resources and services.

Forecasts can be made that reflect a strengths perspective view of population cohorts and of institutions. Because forecasts can become self-fulfilling prophecies, forecasts rooted in fact, which also reflect a belief in the infinite potential of human beings and avoid pitting groups against each other, can inform social policies that build a foundation for a just and prosperous future. If you would like a detailed look at the work of futurists—that is, people who study and predict the future based in part on current trends—you can go to the websites of the Rand Pardee Center (Study of the Future), the Institute for the Future, and the World Future Society.

FACTORS THAT WILL SHAPE FUTURE SOCIAL POLICIES

Armed with these insights into understanding future forecasts, we turn now to major factors that will most likely influence future social policy: increasing racial and ethnic diversity, medical and technological changes, and globalization and depletion of natural resources. In this section, we will analyze these factors and consider what their influence on policy might be, as well as potential responses for social workers.

Population Growth

In 2012, the U.S. population exceeded 314 million (U.S. Census Bureau, 2013a) and the world population exceeded 6.8 billion (U.S. Census Bureau, 2011). Further, the U.S. Census Bureau projects that by 2050, the U.S. population will exceed 399 million (U.S. Census Bureau, 2013c) and the world population will exceed 9 billion (U.S. Census Bureau, 2011). As illustrated in Exhibit 12.1, the world population grew from 3 billion in 1959 to 6 billion by 1999. Thus, the population of the earth doubled in just 40 years. The Census Bureau's latest projections suggest that world population growth will continue in the 21st century, but at a slower rate. The world population is expected to increase from 6 billion in 1999 to 9 billion by 2044. This is an increase of 50 percent and is expected to take 45 years. In terms of population growth rate, the peak period occurred in 1962 and 1963 when the annual growth rate was 2.2 percent. The growth rate in 2010 was approximately 1 percent and is projected to be 0.45 percent for 2050, less than a quarter of the highest growth rate. Possible reasons for decreased population growth rates identified by researchers include: increased access to education for women, greater availability of

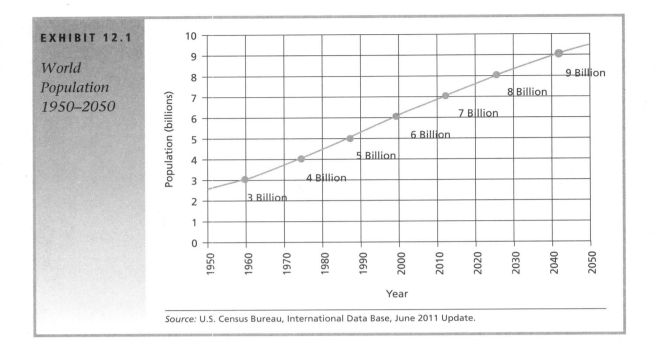

EXHIBIT 12.1

World Population 1950–2050

Source: U.S. Census Bureau, International Data Base, June 2011 Update.

contraceptives, growing expectation that children will survive to adulthood, lack of adequate supports such as affordable day care for working women, and an increase in the number of deaths due to aging of the population. Of course, cataclysmic disasters and worldwide economic depressions can also influence population growth rates.

The two major factors driving population growth in a country are fertility and net immigration. The crude birth rate—that is, the rate of births per 1,000 people— is predicted to decrease in the U.S. until 2026 because a comparatively smaller percentage of women will be in their childbearing years. However, the total number of births each year in the 21st century could exceed the highest annual number of births ever achieved in the U.S. because a larger overall number (as opposed to percentage) of women will be in their childbearing years. Since 2008, there has been a decrease in both numbers of births and birth rates. Although reasons for these declines are not yet understood, they may be due to the economic slowdown and delayed patterns of childbirth. Experts predict that there will be more than 5 million births each year in the U.S. by 2034, compared to approximately 3.9 million births between July 1, 2011 and July 1, 2012 (Cohn, 2012). The composition of the population is changing as well. The percentage of children is expected to remain stable around 24 percent through 2030, while the percentage of older adults is expected to grow to 19 percent by that date, still less than the percentage of children in the population (U.S. Census Bureau, 2009a).

Net immigration accounts for 40 percent of current U.S. population growth. Similarly to the global population trends discussed above, despite these large population increases, the actual *rate* of U.S. population growth is projected to decrease. The amount of decrease depends on the amount of immigration assumed in the forecast. This decline will be due primarily to the aging of the population, which will lead to a large increase in the number of deaths. The future population will be older than is currently the case. In 2010, the median age of the population was 37.2 years. By 2050, it is projected to increase to 39 years (U.S. Census Bureau, 2012l). Visit the U.S. Census Bureau website (www.census.gov) to obtain the latest statistics on world population, U.S. population (go to Population Clock), and the population of your state.

Increasing Diversity in the U.S.

In previous chapters we have discussed increasing diversity among children and older adults. In this chapter, we will examine implications for future social policy of increasing ethnic and racial diversity across the life span in the U.S. Exhibit 12.2 illustrates the increase in the proportion of the population that is of Hispanic origin of any race, as well as of certain other groups, between 2012 and 2060.The drop in the percentage who are white alone and non-Hispanic white alone, is also illustrated. While the non-Hispanic white population will remain the largest single group numerically, no group will make up a majority by the middle of this century (U.S. Census Bureau, 2012i).

Of course, while more than half of Hispanics are native-born U.S. citizens, growth in the Hispanic population in the U.S. is significantly influenced by immigration laws which, in turn, have historically reflected both labor needs in the U.S. and the prejudices of some of our citizens, resulting in ambivalent and, at times, dysfunctional policy responses. Immigration rates provide a good example of the interconnection in different forecasts, as well. For example, growth in the Hispanic population, which has a younger median age than, in particular, non-Hispanic whites, is a significant factor in keeping Social Security solvent. Similarly, Hispanics play important roles in the current and future economies of the U.S., including helping to meet the need for more workers in the growing health care and dependent care sectors. And immigrants of all national origins contribute to the vibrant diversity of the U.S., a defining cultural feature that will continue to shape our political and social systems in the future.

To summarize, in the future, a larger proportion of the U.S. population will be of African American, Hispanic, Asian and Pacific Islander, and American Indian, Eskimo, and Aleut origin. Additionally, increasing numbers will trace their ancestry to two or more of these groups as well as to whites. Examining population projections helps us sketch a broad outline of a future that will clearly require public social policies that meet the needs, and build on the strengths, of a population that will be larger, older, and more diverse.

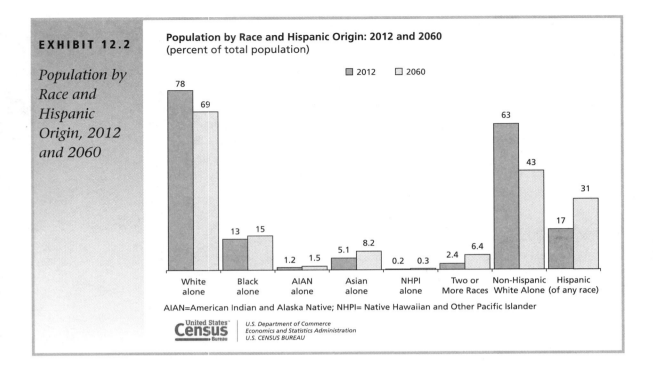

EXHIBIT 12.2

Population by Race and Hispanic Origin, 2012 and 2060

Population by Race and Hispanic Origin: 2012 and 2060
(percent of total population)

AIAN=American Indian and Alaska Native; NHPI= Native Hawaiian and Other Pacific Islander

U.S. Department of Commerce
Economics and Statistics Administration
U.S. CENSUS BUREAU

Medical and Technological Changes

Medical advances have contributed to a major increase in life expectancy in the U.S. In fact, according to current forecasts, by 2030, there will be more than 72.8 million older adults in the U.S. Of this population, 168,000 Americans will be centenarians (100 years of age or older), compared with 78,000 in 2015 (U.S. Census Bureau, 2012e). Applications derived from genetic research could lead to major changes in the areas of reproduction, organ replacement, and treatment of what are now devastating diseases, leading not only to increases in life expectancy but dramatic changes in disability rates, as well (Gore, 2013).

New medical advances provide more alternatives for controlling reproduction and fertility, but they also create opportunities for exploitation. Poor women in particular may be vulnerable to having their bodies used in order to provide children for childless people, through coerced surrogacy or more experimental procedures. Children may struggle to gain access to their own genetic and parentage information when conceived using reproductive technology. Breakthroughs in genetic research may create life-saving opportunities for people suffering from a variety of diseases. However, they also will create a host of ethical dilemmas for people who will have a greater range of choices to consider but still must make decisions in the face of great uncertainty and risk. Social workers will likely be at the center of many of these controversies, helping clients to navigate options and make medical decisions, but also pushing policy makers and health care providers to prioritize the values of self-determination, respect for the dignity and worth of all people, and the primacy of client concerns.

Advances in information technology have transformed the ways that many people in the U.S. communicate, access information and education, investigate medical options, and conduct business. Electronically mediated communication technologies change the ways in which social workers provide services, educate practitioners, manage agencies, influence policy, and conduct research and evaluation (NASW, 2009a). These technologies make practice possible on a global scale. We can now work more easily with all sizes of systems, across boundaries of physical distance. Online therapy, use of cellphone applications and social media for community as well as national political organizing, and the ability to rapidly access ideas for policy alternatives from across the globe via computerized databases, are but a few of the numerous possibilities created by these new technologies. For example, cellphone applications have been developed to help people struggling with mental or physical illnesses chart symptoms over the day and provide suggestions for addressing them. These applications can also be used by a clinician to review the client's week, detect patterns, and work with the client to develop more effective responses. Policy practitioners can send and receive video, audio, and text instantaneously, update colleagues to alert them to legislative initiatives being debated, get their input, and call for immediate action from an entire network of advocates.

Technology may also play an increasing role when the social worker is serving as first-contact person and can call on knowledge-based software for triage questioning, possibly augmented by a remote consultation with a specialist. This can be particularly valuable in reaching underserved communities and populations in rural areas. Contemplating the potentially transformative force of these trends in technology requires considering how multiple levels of forecasts work in tandem, as the increasing penetration of these technologies within U.S. society is aided by the coming of age of the large millennial generation of technologically savvy young people. The technologies they foster simultaneously can be used to transform the lives of frail elders and active baby boomers. However, advances in technology provide not only opportunities but also challenges. Issues of privacy and confidentiality are becoming more critical as increasing amounts of personal health and income information are being stored in computer databases. Unauthorized use of data and hackers compromise privacy and increasingly fluid lines between client and practitioner can blur boundaries.

In addition, people in poverty, those in some isolated areas, and people who face cultural, linguistic, and disability-based barriers often lack access to computers and/or to high-speed Internet, which limits their ability to participate in a computerized society. While there is some evidence that mobile technologies are helping to shrink this digital divide, it persists, and it will limit the opportunities of less-affluent people to find employment, receive adequate health care, communicate with powerful entities, and even receive a thorough education.

Globalization and Environmental Degradation

From our inception, U.S. social policy has been influenced by conditions in other countries. Immigrants and indentured servants fleeing adverse conditions in their home countries streamed into what was to become the U.S. As chronicled in Chapters 2 and 3, many U.S. social policies and programs have international origins. The English Poor Laws shaped public policy in the colonies, and their influence can be seen even today. The Settlement House Movement and the Social Security Act also trace their roots to Europe. Today, we are seeing growing international economic, political, and social integration of the world's nations as globalization increases.

As discussed in Chapter 4, globalization affects not only economic but also political and social conditions in the U.S. and around the world. Globalization has created opportunities for economic development and has led to increasing interdependency and closer relations among people from different countries. At the same time, however, both U.S. and international workers are competing for jobs that may be transient as employers find workers in other countries who will work for lower wages, accept unsafe working conditions, and expect even fewer benefits. Child labor is a particular concern. Further, the lack of government enforcement of pollution and safety standards in some countries attracts businesses that hope to make a profit at the expense of both the citizenry and the environment. Social welfare systems are being restructured in the U.S. and in many other countries with the stated goal of making the economy more competitive. However, policies that cut back social services and education in order to reduce taxes often overlook the fact that a healthy and well-educated citizenry is essential to economic competitiveness.

Additionally, as people from very different cultures and religious backgrounds come into close and constant contact, religious conflicts are becoming more visible and are consuming valuable resources that could be used for positive purposes. People in many parts of the world have yet to find ways of accommodating diversity by peaceful means. Global competition for natural resources also fuels violent confrontation. This competition is expected to increase as the world population grows, natural resources are depleted, and globalization becomes even more widespread. Concerns about environmental degradation and depletion of natural resources cast a shadow over our future. Although social work has always emphasized person-in-environment, the social environment has been our major concern. Consequently, we have paid much less attention to the influence of the natural environment on human development, even though environmental degradation affects all types of social work practice. For example, children exposed to high levels of mercury and lead experience higher rates of developmental disabilities. Similarly, poor air quality contributes to severe respiratory problems for many children and adults, and high levels of pesticides and toxins have been linked to life-threatening health problems. People living in poverty in both inner-city and rural areas are more likely to be victimized by unsafe environmental practices.

Major disasters in other parts of the world such as volcano eruptions and earthquakes as well as disasters in the U.S. such as Hurricane Katrina, Super Storm Sandy, and the massive Gulf oil spill of 2010 also shape future social policy. For example, in the wake of Hurricane Katrina, the need for policies requiring specific disaster plans for people with disabilities became clear. Migration of displaced workers from areas where disasters have occurred requires emergency response programs and also has much larger and longer-lasting policy implications for the places to which they migrate. Globalization clearly impacts social conditions and the social policy options that attempt to address them. In this globalized context, there is evidence of convergence, growing similarity between countries in challenges faced and policies enacted over time. Sources of policy convergence include borrowing of policy ideas from other countries, such as the U.S. did in crafting the Social Security Act. Instantaneous transnational communication now makes possible the rapid sharing of ideas. Similar policies in different countries can also develop independently in response to parallel domestic problems or pressures such as reforms of retirement policies in the face of a growing elder population, or restrictions on immigration as wars, disasters, and increasing poverty in other countries increase flows of people. Sometimes similar policies are developed to promote international harmonization so that businesses can operate under similar policies from country to country. International economic competition can also promote policy convergence, as can international legal constraints. While there are tremendous opportunities to learn from other nations, effective policy must take into account the cultural context of the country. Wholesale adoption of policies or practices that are promoted as evidence-based practice or policies is inappropriate unless they have been examined in a variety of cultural contexts. Labeling policies and practices as "best practice" is problematic unless they have been tested in a culturally inclusive way. A policy or program that works well in one country, or for that matter with the majority population in the same country, will not necessarily be effective in another country or with different populations within a country. Furthermore, it may be impossible to get a law enacted to establish that policy, given different political milieus in various countries, or to administer it, given differences in organizational structures and capacities.

U.S. social policy is also influenced indirectly by other nations' social conditions and policy responses. Disasters arising from unregulated corporate misdeeds in one country can cause the price of seafood and oil to rise around the world. The world faces threats that cannot be contained by any one nation. They include:

- depletion of resources such as clean water, forests, biodiversity;

- spread of infectious disease, particularly given population mobility and cuts to health infrastructure;

- spillover effects from internal conflicts;

- climate change and its impact on agriculture, health, and economic growth; and,

- health consequences from increased pollution.

These challenges have widespread potential ramifications. We are already seeing global conflict over scarce resources; increased threat of disease and poverty; increased costs as nations try to deal with the consequences of environmental degradation; and migration, as people flee devastated areas. However, we are also seeing transnational grassroots organizations forming to begin to address these issues. For instance, indigenous groups from the U.S. and Canada are joining together to oppose threats to tribal water resources affected by policies across borders. You can go to the website of the Indigenous Environmental Network to find out about such initiatives. Labor organizations have united displaced workers in the U.S. with the laborers in Central America who now work for the same company, so that they can collectively insist upon fair labor practices and stronger environmental protections.

Global social and economic trends are directly related to migrants' reasons for leaving their countries of origin. They include high levels of poverty and unemployment in their home countries, decimation of agricultural land, austerity imposed by economic agreements, displacement due to war, and oppressive policies. Some people also become victims of human trafficking and are subsequently exploited in cities and towns across the U.S. Increasingly, social service agencies are being called on to provide services for these survivors when they are uncovered by staff of criminal justice, domestic violence, and child welfare agencies. Federal, state, and local initiatives have been developed and are attempting to address these often hidden, and, thus, inadequately addressed problems. For more information on funding for initiatives to deal with human trafficking and slavery in the U.S., go to the website of the Office for Victims of Crime (OVC) (www.ojp.usdoj.gov/ovc), at the U.S. Department of Justice and search for Human Trafficking.

EXHIBIT 12.3 *Students in Midwest Increase Awareness of Global Human Trafficking*	MSW students in a social policy class at a major Midwestern university decided to work to increase awareness of the impact of global human trafficking on their city, and to press for more services to help people from around the globe who were victims of human trafficking in their area. They researched the trafficking problem and found local groups to partner with who were attempting to confront this issue. In partnership with these groups, they urged local newspapers and TV stations to do stories on the subject, and they contacted their U.S. Senators and Representatives to ask them to allocate additional funding to provide services for victims of human trafficking. They also helped survivors of human trafficking to tell their stories to legislators. Media coverage and legislator awareness of human trafficking problems increased as a result of their policy practice work.

As more middle-class Americans regularly travel abroad, interface electronically across national borders, and share life events such as the global financial meltdown, a new view of our interconnectedness and potential for learning from each other may be emerging. We are increasingly learning from a global pool of knowledge. For example, innovative approaches to care for preterm babies such as Kangaroo Care first developed in Colombia, South America, and the melding of day care and preschool policy currently taking place in some northern European countries have informed children's policy in the U.S. Kangaroo Care emphasizes constant skin-to-skin contact between baby and mother or father and has been shown to improve outcomes for frail preterm newborns. See pictures and learn about the policies that make Kangaroo Care possible at the website of the March of Dimes (www. marchofdimes.com, search for "Kangaroo Care"). Similarly, the U.S.'s broad-based approach to higher education has informed international education policy. Many of the challenges, as well as opportunities, that will shape our future can best be addressed through international cooperation. However, Americans will have to come together to create a consensus that supports tackling common problems at an international level.

The State of the Future Index

One tool to help us consider the future from an international perspective is the State of the Future Index (SOFI), a measure of the 10-year outlook for the future. The SOFI is constructed with key variables and forecasts which, in the aggregate, provide insight about the future. The SOFI is designed to show direction and intensity of change in the outlook and to identify responsible factors. The SOFI can be constructed at both the global and national levels. This index was developed in 2000 and updated in 2012 as part of the Millennium Project of the World Federation of United Nations Associations.

Variables which were part of the computation of the 2012 SOFI include (The Millennium Project, 2012):

1.   Population with access to improved water sources (% of national population)

2.   Literacy rate (% above 15)

3.   School enrollment, secondary (% gross)

4.   Poverty headcount ratio at $1.25 a day (% world population)

5.   Total greenhouse gas emissions (106 kt)

6.   Unemployment, total (% of world labor force)

7.   Energy efficiency (GDP/energy)

8.   Population growth (annual %)

9.   People killed and injured in terrorist attacks

10.   Electricity production from renewable sources (% production)

11.   Prevalence of undernourishment

12.   Freedom rights (Country Score) (1= most free to 7 least)

13.   Ecological footprint/Biocapacity ratio

14.   GDP per capita (constant 2000 US$)

15.   Voter turnout (% voting population)

16.   Physicians (per 1,000 people)

17.   Internet users (per 1,000 people)

18.   Infant mortality (deaths per 1,000 births)

19.   Forest lands (% of national land area)

20.   Life expectancy at birth (years)

21.   Seats held by women in national parliament (% of members)

22.   Economic income inequality (share of top 1%)

23.   Prevalence of HIV (% of population age 15 and 49)

The danger in combining many variables into a single index number is that detail is lost; progress in one area can be obscured by declines in another. Variables also differ in importance. The apparent precision of attaching numbers and creating an index may give the mistaken impression of accuracy. However, this approach does provide a way of thinking about the relationship among variables in systems. For example, if a policy is enacted that increases enrollment in secondary education for girls and boys, do you also see a future change in poverty rates, unemployment, or infant mortality? It can also help in thinking through the impact of proposed policy changes, and in making nation-to-nation comparisons. You can find more information on SOFI by searching the web for Millennium Project State of the Future Index.

FUTURE POLICY DIRECTIONS

As we have seen, demographic trends, medical and technological advances, and the economic, environmental, and social changes that accompany increasing globalization will likely influence future social policies. This text has provided numerous examples of how, in the wake of earlier changes, the government became involved in creating social policies to protect the public at large as well as to protect people deprived of their civil rights. We have also examined instances in which policy making was designed to help quell unrest and preserve the interests of capitalism during periods of rapid change. Compassion as well as greed has motivated the creation of social policy. In fact, a variety of changes and motivations may propel the passage of a single piece of legislation. Undoubtedly, these factors will also drive future social policy.

Ideology—the beliefs that guide a group—will also continue to shape social policy in the future. The belief that government contributes to the creation of social problems is often contrasted with the belief that government has a responsibility to act as an ameliorating force in a capitalist society and to promote equality of opportunity. Conservatives are characterized as typically holding the former opinion, while liberals or progressives are associated with the latter. However, the examination of social policies and programs in this text has provided ample examples of policies that made problems worse as well as policies that improved social conditions. Armed with the knowledge that government can both help and harm the citizenry and that the forces discussed above will most likely continue to exert great influence on social policy, we can now consider what future social policy directions would more effectively support social work's dual mission of enhancing well-being and meeting basic needs. This section brings together many of the policy and program initiatives discussed in earlier chapters to provide you with a composite picture of promising strategies.

Diversity and the Work-Based Safety Net

Given that U.S. public social policies have consistently emphasized individualism, personal responsibility, and the work ethic, particularly for people in poverty, we probably can expect that future policies will also emphasize attachment to the workforce. Thus, if a safety net is to survive, it will quite likely be work-based. However, advocates of a work-based safety net have not adequately considered whether the supply of jobs that provide a living wage in the U.S. is sufficient to support this approach. They also need to ask whether there will be sufficient jobs in the future in the wake of increased mechanization, robotics, and outsourcing.

Nonetheless, unless the public sentiment that propelled the latest welfare reform efforts changes radically in the years to come, future welfare policies will continue to promote work outside the home, even for low-income mothers with very young children and those with other barriers to employment. Workplace policies that provide the support necessary for mothers to succeed in their dual roles of parent and employee will be vital, then, to the well-being of their families and children and of society. Generous family leave and flexible work schedules will be crucial. However, these policy changes will not be sufficient because the U.S., like many other industrialized countries, is experiencing rapid population aging, lower birth rates, and rising rates of labor force participation by women. This means that in our country as well as in many others, women will be less available to provide care for family members and so care for children and for older adults who are disabled will have to be provided in different ways. If women are to work, they will need access to either publicly or privately funded high-quality day care in the workplace. Providing high-quality day care and universal preschool are the kind of policies that also are capacity building. This kind of investment in early childhood development can help close the educational gap between low-income children and their peers and result in increased opportunities for economic success. These kinds of policies are ones that are also likely to appeal to middle-income families. It will be critical to craft policy initiatives in various arenas that promote social justice and can also garner support from the middle class. Middle-class Americans have seen their homes lose value, health care become unaffordable, and their children shoulder huge loan debt in order to go to college. It is no accident that action on these issues was part of President Obama's reform efforts.

As our population becomes more diverse, so will our workforce, necessitating new products and services, as well as policies. Further, the first wave of the millennial generation, born between 1982 and 2003 and increasingly claiming multiracial/multiethnic identities, has now entered the workforce. Some scholars believe that this generation will be much less concerned about issues of race and ethnicity (Winograd and Hais, 2008) and may not be as likely to block policy reform on the basis that people ethnically or racially different from themselves might be disproportionately benefited. They may be more communitarian and interested in developing an opportunity state which focuses on capacity building as opposed to a welfare state or an enabling state. They are definitely into use of social media to create community and to increase political momentum and are credited with playing a significant part in the re-election of President Obama. On the other hand, the fact that coming generations will be more racially and ethnically diverse is being reported with alarm by other groups interested in arousing people to enact policies to limit immigration and services to minority groups such as translation of application forms into other languages.

In addition, even as jobs that pay a living wage for people without specialized training disappear in our country, immigrants from less stable or affluent countries are seeking entry into the U.S. Development of coherent and effective immigration policies that promote social justice must be given high priority. Policies that will help stabilize, or at least not exacerbate, conditions in these sending countries are also needed. Clearly, denying health care and education to people who are living in our country is not capacity building and, in fact, endangers community health and safety.

In other countries, such as the United Kingdom, the social safety net is being cut back as economic woes increase and countries are faced with mounting debt. Although our social safety net is much less developed than in many of these countries, nonetheless we can expect increased attacks on our safety net programs. The argument that public programs which provide for older adults, people with disabilities, workers who lose their jobs, and children are not only the morally right path to take but also help to strengthen our economy and provide counter-cyclical support in times of economic downturn will need to be strongly and strategically made if we are to protect these investments. Indeed, the kind of grassroots, web savvy organizing that marked Obama's successful presidential campaigns will be necessary in order to build widespread understanding and support for health care reform and other social safety net programs. Further, these programs can be reconfigured with attention to capacity building. For example, many people with disabilities and older adults would welcome opportunities for job retraining and help finding jobs rather than simply being declared eligible for cash benefits. Such emphasis on strengths and capacity could also potentially reduce the length or level of dependency on public benefits.

Wages, Jobs, and Retirement   Improving women's wages is central to reducing childhood poverty. Women's economic development through micro-enterprises and Individual Development Accounts may help them become entrepreneurs. Because workers are increasingly being expected to assume responsibility for investment of their guaranteed contribution retirement programs at work, access to comprehensive and clear financial education will be crucial, particularly for women and people of color who have traditionally had more limited experience with investing. Public social policies need to be designed and funded so that they benefit women and people of color to the same extent that they benefit men. Further, for both men and women, living wage initiatives are critical. Families where members are working full time should be able to earn a wage sufficient to adequately house, feed, and clothe their family.

Globalization has led to reduced job permanency. Therefore, we need to develop initiatives to help workers transition between jobs. Moreover, as jobs become more transient, the right of workers to transfer retirement benefits from one job to another becomes ever more important. Further, because of increases in immigration, services developed should take into account the needs of people for whom English is a second language.

A new paradigm is developing whereby retirement is considered a process marked by successive decisions, in contrast to the traditional conception of retirement as a single and irreversible event. People may retire from one job and then very shortly re-enter the ranks of non-retired people as they begin new careers. In fact, more companies and individuals are beginning to embrace alternatives to the "40 years of 40-hour work weeks until retirement" conception of work life. As we saw in Chapter 11, such alternatives include part-time positions, job sharing, and phased retirement. Clearly, we need to design policies that support this kind of workplace flexibility while protecting health and retirement benefits. Such policies will also benefit younger men and women who are trying to juggle the responsibilities of work and dependent care when both parents are in the workforce. Currently, the non-portability of pensions and the lack of benefits for part-time work impede the development of alternative work patterns. We will need to craft future employment and retirement policy with careful attention to the needs of both younger workers and workers who are nearing retirement. Further, given the increasing numbers of people who will work in multiple countries over a lifetime, there is a need for global steps to assure stability for retirement security, work, and health care. Transferability of health care and retirement benefits between countries would be of great benefit to these international workers. Developing such policies does not require creation of a world government; rather, what is needed is world governance which builds on the core idea that countries can benefit by cooperating with certain common rules.

Supporting the Intergenerational Family In addition to the reforms proposed above, the intergenerational nature of the family needs to be recognized in the workplace. We need to develop supports for workers who also care for frail elders. Support of these kinds of family-friendly policies in both the public and the private sector will also help employed people provide adequate care for their children and elderly family members. To support this generation of caregivers, we will need policies that provide for family medical leave, adult day care, and flexible time. We also need to find more ways to recognize and honor caring work. Finally, we need to devise methods of compensating unpaid care work, particularly with regard to earning retirement credits. Further, the voices of intergenerational families from diverse ethnic backgrounds must be heard in the development of employment and family policies. Social workers will need to press policy makers and encourage families to make these connections. The impact of future policies on diverse intergenerational families will need careful consideration. Without attention to these issues, policies will inadvertently undercut the functioning and development of the diverse families of the future.

In another family-related development, the sandwich generation will decline as the baby boomers become the generation needing care and their smaller numbers of offspring become the sandwich generation. Members of this smaller sandwich generation will struggle to care for both their children and for elders who become frailer as they live longer and longer. Social workers need to engage older adults, their children, and their grandchildren in developing a vision around which we can develop workable policies and programs that respond to increasing diversity and the coming elder boom. Simplistic approaches and characterizations will not suffice. Rather, policies must be crafted based on a complex and diverse vision not only of the older people of 2030 but also of their children and grandchildren. The challenge is to help develop policies that maximize the advantages of an aging society.

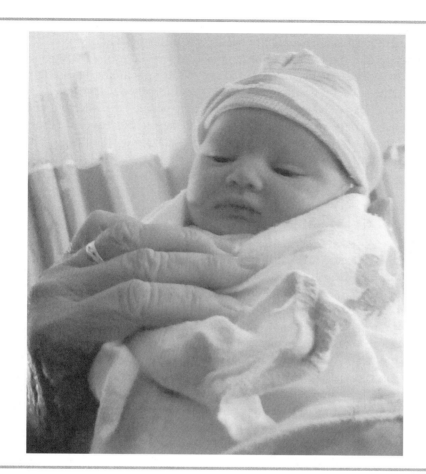

EXHIBIT 12.4

Newborn Baby Girl in Grandfather's Hands

Health

Advances in medical technology have enabled us to map our genes and prolong life artificially and have created additional options for reproduction. Ethical dilemmas surrounding the human impact of these advances are the purview of social workers. Genetic mapping holds the promise of making possible precision medicine whereby treatment is tailored based on your genetic profile. At the same time, there is tremendous potential for discrimination based on knowledge of increased risk of needing costly medical treatment. The Genetic Information Non-Discrimination Act of 2008 offers some protection for Americans from discrimination based on their genetic information in both health insurance and employment. The Affordable Care Act also strengthens this protection.

Recall from earlier chapters that the U.S. as well as other countries has a shameful history of forced sterilization based on often inaccurate assessments of potential for producing unhealthy offspring. However, forced sterilization is no less just if based on accurate genetic testing, Emerging pressures for cost control and the rationing of health care may tempt health care institutions and insurers to press for sterilization and the use of end-of-life practices that control costs. Socioeconomic factors will differentially influence access to care, including end-of-life care for clients who have limited ability to pay. Additionally, social workers will need to advocate for policies that allow competent people to make informed health care choices. These policies should also address patients' need to be thoroughly informed about options and consequences. Finally, they should protect patients from coercion.

Climate Justice

In addition to the issues we have just considered, our health also depends on the state of our physical environment. For example, low-income people may live in areas where policies to control pollution are not adequate or are not properly enforced. Consequently, social workers should be alert to cases of "environmental discrimination," such as locating polluting factories and waste-disposal facilities disproportionately in low-income neighborhoods. In our role as activist clinicians, it is important to consider environmental factors when assessing clients' needs and planning interventions that may include challenging the policies that are damaging clients' physical environment. Social workers need to be attentive to the unequal burdens on vulnerable populations created by climate change and work for climate justice.

One important factor that contributes to environmental degradation is over-population. In the area of global population growth, NASW supports:

> The fundamental right of each individual throughout the world to manage his or her fertility and to have access to a full range of effective family planning and repro-ductive health services regardless of the individual's income, marital status, age, race, ethnicity, gender, sexual orientation, national origin, or residence.
>
> (NASW, 2012e, p. 133)

Although the profession supports individual rights in access to family planning and reproductive health care services, it will continue to oppose forced sterilization and all non-voluntary birth control policies.

Not only does the natural environment affect our health and welfare, but social welfare policies can affect the environment. For instance, housing and transporta-tion policies designed to help low-income people may create further environmental problems if they encourage urban sprawl and travel by automobile rather than mass transportation. Social workers appreciate the importance of "person/environmental fit" in the helping process. Policies that will help maintain a healthy environment are critical to attaining and maintaining an adequate quality of life for both our clients and ourselves. Policy solutions will need to be crafted with a clear focus on sustainability. That is, we need policies that will improve conditions today without compromising our prospects for the future.

Policies to protect the environment will be effective only if the public agencies charged with enforcing them are adequately funded. Additionally, in terms of protecting the future health of our clients on a very concrete level, social workers should make sure that their agencies have policies in place to help their clients in case of disasters. This kind of future planning is critical. Social work agencies can also work to be more environmentally responsible in purchasing, travel, and other decisions, in order to both reduce the profession's environmental footprint and model sustainability.

Information Technology and Privacy

Advances in information technology improve communication and may ease record keeping. New, innovative ways of providing services via the Internet will likely multiply in the future. Social workers can now practice globally and create communities of activists via social media. However, the growing use of computer networks to store and share client information constitutes a threat to confidentiality, particularly when police authorities and the courts demand access to records. The Health Insurance Portability and Accountability Act of 1996 (HIPAA) helps to protect patient privacy. However, it is also sometimes used as an excuse to not figure out how to share information in ways that can benefit clients. According to the U.S. Department of Health and Human Services (USDHHS, 2013), the official federal hub for all HIPAA issues:

> The HIPAA Privacy Rule provides federal protections for personal health information held by covered entities and gives patients an array of rights with respect to that information. At the same time, the Privacy Rule is balanced so that it permits the disclosure of personal health information needed for patient care and other important purposes.

Interpretations of HIPAA can vary widely from agency to agency. If you are being told that sharing of information that would clearly benefit clients is forbidden by HIPAA, consider whether there is a way to get a second opinion. If your agency is simply misinformed, the problem may be easily solved by getting a more accurate interpretation. However, use your social work skills to determine who and what other factors may be motivating the current agency interpretation. As in any advocacy effort, you then need to evaluate risks and benefits before proceeding with a change strategy. Clearly, filling out the same assessment time after time at different agencies is a drain on clients and results in providers potentially making treatment decisions based on conflicting information and without knowledge of interventions being implemented by other providers. However, confidentiality and patient privacy must also be guarded. Therefore, we need to become savvy about ethical and legal issues related to information technology. In addition, we must research how to use information technology effectively. Finally, we need to advocate for policies that protect clients' privacy when new technology is implemented. The NASW *Code of Ethics* should guide decisions about collecting, storing, retrieving, and sharing electronic client data. Future advances in the capacity to share client information electronically in order to better coordinate care can benefit our clients if systems can be designed that safeguard the data.

Social workers also need to promote policies that reduce the digital divide that disadvantages many of our clients. Otherwise, groups with little access to modern and widely used information technologies will fall further behind in the competition to secure resources and opportunities. For example, people in need who do not own a computer and do not have funds to pay for Internet access will become even more disadvantaged as public agencies transition more and more to an online application process and shrink availability of in-person application sites.

The Influence of Pluralism on Future Social Policy

The U.S. is said to have a pluralistic system of government. As discussed in Chapter 4, in the context of social policy development, *pluralism* refers to a system whereby a variety of interest groups compete to help shape social policies and provide resulting social services. As diversity increases in a society, the variety of interest groups competing to influence the policy process can be expected to multiply. Therefore, pluralism in future social policy and program development will likely increase. Because enacting and implementing major new public social policies typically requires coalitions of a variety of interest groups, policy changes tend to be incremental. Forces that resist change and forces that propel change create checks and balances on each other.

Although most change is incremental, transformative policy changes sometimes do occur, often in response to surprise events. A prominent example is the creation of the Office of Homeland Security in 2001 in the wake of the September 11, 2001 terrorist attacks. Another example is the health care reform legislation that contained many incremental changes but also had transformative elements in that it greatly extended availability of health care in states that opt for Medicaid expansion. The intended and unintended consequences of future transformative changes need to be scrutinized with particular care because the outcomes of such major changes are difficult to foresee and may have negative as well as positive impacts on client populations.

Privatization

Although the radical right can be expected to continue to argue for the abolition of government social programs, particularly those that do not primarily benefit wealthy individuals and corporations, government will continue to be the primary source of funds for social programs. Public and private agencies will likely continue to provide publicly funded social services. Privatization is often sold as a tool for balancing budgets. The state sets an amount that it will pay for a specific service, and the contractor is obligated to provide the service for that amount. However, if the private contractor is unable to provide the necessary services for the set price, state officials do not relish the prospect of having nursing facility residents and children in private foster care deposited on the capitol steps. This is also a core issue when managed care provided by private contractors is used to provide health care for Medicaid clients. Consequently, the state often ends up pumping additional appropriations into private coffers. Also, as more private providers, particularly non-profit voluntary and religious organizations, become increasingly dependent on public funding to function effectively, a very powerful constituency of middle-class voters who are staff members of those organizations may demand additional funding.

For all these reasons, privatized social services will very likely cost more—rather than less—than services provided directly through the government. Privatization can also be more costly because tax dollars often flow into for-profit private initiatives without the same structural checks and balances that exist in government agencies. For example, if government employees "blow the whistle" to expose unsafe or illegal practices, their positions may be protected, especially if they are in classified government positions where job requirements and conditions under which they can be dismissed are clearly laid out. In contrast, in private corporations, if complaints surface and the contract is lost, the employee's job disappears. For this reason, employees in private firms may be less likely to report waste and corruption. Finally, privatization often involves declassifying the jobs of direct care providers. As a result, social work education is no longer a requirement for these positions. Consequently, client protection based on adherence to professional ethics is weakened.

Clearly, then, government will increasingly have the role of ensuring that services provided by the private sector are adequate. Even when services are privatized, the state will still be responsible for monitoring inputs and ensuring outcomes. Privatization creates additional layers of service oversight. In addition, it often reduces the wages, qualifications, and career ladder for direct service providers because cutting labor costs is vital to making a profit. Privatization shifts the focus of government involvement toward oversight, while it increases the responsibilities of the private sector to deliver services.

Privatization and decentralization of service provision also can be expected to lead to even greater service fragmentation. Service fragmentation means that many organizations will be providing services with less overall coordination or attention to overlapping services and gaps. For example, many churches and other charitable organizations are establishing food pantries and other services in a piece-meal fashion in order to serve the needs of low-income families who no longer receive public welfare.

Despite all of these complications, pluralism, as reflected in public–private partnerships, now sustains non-profit organizations and a commercial welfare industry. Further, privately provided services are often more acceptable to the significant number of people who believe in less government. It is unlikely, then, that we will return to public provision of services even if privatized services do not prove to be more cost-effective or produce more positive outcomes for clients. Therefore, for the foreseeable future, policy makers will focus on making privatized approaches work.

If future public–private partnerships are to work to the benefit of their clients, social workers who understand both the limitations and the potential of such partnerships need to work to ensure adequate public funding and oversight. If the future brings yet more policy initiatives to increase privatization, it will be even more vital to compare the costs of publicly provided services with the costs of privatized services. Policies sold on the basis of cost-effectiveness should be monitored to see if they actually reduce costs. Following the money is always a good idea in understanding and evaluating policies and programs.

Reconsidering Core Values

Although cost-effectiveness is often at the center of the debate about future policy initiatives, value choices also influence the design and oversight of social policy and programs. Work and financial independence are highly valued in our society, as are family care for dependent members and personal freedom to direct one's course in life. Reciprocity is also a core value. Building on these values, U.S. social welfare policy may be viewed from a perspective that focuses on well-being and social responsibility rather than simply on the lessening of deficits such as poverty or even on material well-being (Morris, 2002). For example, a greater focus on well-being could lead to improvements in SNAP, the food stamp program, so that it is more focused on promoting good health rather than just providing food assistance that is barely adequate. A public social policy and program infrastructure could be developed that provides more chances for all citizens to have access to basic food, housing, and health care and enables them to pursue a range of opportunities in a healthy environment. This is the essence of capacity building, which has been discussed in different contexts throughout this text. Indeed, measuring and promoting quality of life should also be receiving increased attention as we consider ways to stabilize our economy and increase GDP. When only GDP is considered when evaluating how our economy is currently doing, factors that threaten our future, such as environmental degradation and lack of investment in health and education can be ignored.

Economic efficiency and social justice may be complementary (Morris, 2002). People whose basic needs are met and who have multiple options to enhance their well-being are more likely to fuel economic growth. If policy makers become convinced that tax cuts for wealthy people and spending cuts for low-income people actually impede economic growth, they will be more likely to support socially just policies. One strategy for promoting a more just society is to encourage social capital formation. It includes developing a healthy, well-educated workforce and increased support for the developmental approach to enacting public social welfare policies and programs that bolster economic and community development (Midgley, Tracey, and Livermore, 2000). Policies and programs that focus on enhancing the capacity of people in need to participate in the productive economy rather than rely on social services might receive support from a wider spectrum of voters. Supported employment for people with disabilities, job-training programs for unemployed workers, Child Development Accounts that equip all children for future economic security, and Individual Development Accounts that enable low-income people to accumulate assets are examples of initiatives that reflect a developmental approach. These initiatives generally include incentives rather than requirements for participation.

Using a developmental, capacity building approach, the government redistributes wealth through education, income transfer, asset incentives, and job creation. It also enforces antidiscrimination laws in order to ensure that more people can compete effectively for the benefits of the economy. However, there will never be equality of opportunity because of the individual differences people bring to the competition. People in the target population who are more likely to succeed without new initiatives will also likely be the ones who benefit most from these initiatives. Helping people who are most likely to succeed is not a bad idea. Certainly, many people who have benefited from policies and programs that emphasize a developmental, capacity building approach would not actually have succeeded without those opportunities, and the overall society has been strengthened as a result. Promising examples of the developmental approach include universal and progressive savings programs beginning at birth. Dr. Michael Sherraden, a social worker, has been a major proponent of such programs. His work on assets has influenced policy development in the U.S., Taiwan, Canada, Indonesia, the United Kingdom, and other countries. For example, in some countries, all newborns have been given an account at birth, with a larger initial deposit into the accounts of children in low-income families. To find out more about these promising approaches, read about the Global Assets Project at the website of the Center for Social Development at Washington University in St. Louis (csd.wustl.edu). However, all policy proposals should be carefully evaluated in terms of potential for risk-shifting from government or employers to the individual. Conversely, assumption of greater risk by the government in certain basic areas such as health care can help create a more productive workforce.

Although attention to capacity building is vital, and a developmental approach has great potential, it will not eliminate the need for public income support and social service programs because many people still will not be able to take advantage of educational and job opportunities. Further, because initiatives that reflect a developmental approach are typically oversold so as to gain support and may take decades to demonstrate their full potential, disappointment often ensues when public costs are not quickly and significantly reduced after these initiatives are enacted. Nevertheless, the emphasis on reciprocal obligation, the importance of work, and saving that is central to the developmental approach is consistent with the dominant ideologies in the country today. Significantly, ideology often takes precedence over data—even data on costs and expenditures—in the public arena.

Using the Electoral Process

As in the past, future social policy will be shaped by electoral realities and changing public pressures. Throughout this chapter, we have outlined policy approaches more attuned to the future economic, demographic, and cultural environment that could be expected to contribute to a more equitable future. The key to a more equitable future is participation by people who believe in such a vision of the future. Social workers adhere to the *Code of Ethics*, which supports that vision. Social workers need to participate much more effectively in electoral politics in order to make the vision a reality. The NASW has developed a series of policy statements outlining the organization's support for a wide variety of needed policy changes. These statements are contained in *Social Work Speaks*, a publication frequently referenced in this text. If these policies are to be implemented, then more social workers must engage in electoral politics and help elect candidates—including social workers themselves—who will support needed changes. In the future, the profession must give increased attention and support to the work of the NASW's Political Action for Candidate Election (PACE) as well as other strategies to influence national and state policies. If you are interested in learning more about policy practice and involvement in policy deliberation by social workers, visit the website of the Social Work Policy Institute at www.socialworkpolicy.org.

On a more immediate level, you can register to vote and encourage your friends to vote. Bring up issues of social justice and engage in debate. See if you can integrate information on voter registration into your organization's client intake process. Think about running for office. Contact your elected officials regularly to share your concerns about future policy directions. Consider doing some policy related research for your local legislator. For example, an MSW student who is concerned with increasing voter turnout is researching the possibility of reducing the voting age to 16. Such policies have already been adopted in other countries and could also make it possible to conduct much more meaningful voter education in high schools in the future.

Try to find an issue or a candidate that arouses your passion. If you do get involved, try not to lose heart when a policy you endorse is enacted but does not produce all of the outcomes you had hoped for. Remember what you learned in the sections on history and policy development in this text, and consider how discouraging those struggles must have been for advocates of abolition and women's suffrage and full civil rights for people of color. Ask yourself, "What in my life actually does work out just as I had planned?" Your answer will probably be, "Very little." In fact, the impulse to oversimplify challenges and identify a single, "fix-all" approach fuels the unrealistic expectation that one policy will change human behavior, reduce structural barriers, and solve all our troubles, and can spur the disengagement of the very voices most needed in the policy arena. Social work practice, at its core, relies on the use of skills and relationships to effect significant changes that improve people's lives. Social policy advocacy is another arena in which to manifest this mission. Your education and value base help to equip you to shape social policy currents which will, in turn, create a more supportive context for your work with clients.

Your voice and your work are important. Your efforts will be even more effective if you band together with other like-minded professionals and work with citizens' groups to make your voices heard. Many students today are skilled at using social media. As the election of Obama illustrated, use of social media to develop citizen activists can be a powerful tool for reform. Think about the online networks of which you are a part. How can you mobilize them for social change?

THE STRENGTHS PERSPECTIVE IN A NEW ERA

Social work has historically developed as a response to local needs. Similarly, the strengths perspective originally developed as an approach to meeting mental health needs of people with serious and persistent mental illness in one state. However, as could be expected after considering the ramifications of global convergence, social workers are finding problems around the world to be more alike than different. Social work is committed to promoting the general welfare of society, from local to global levels. Technology and economic integration reduce "distance" between countries and promote collective problem-solving. Our best chance to address today's serious challenges comes from this cooperation.

Social workers are in a unique position because their professional education has traditionally emphasized person-in-environment and included at least some focus on ways to influence community systems. Social workers can use these skills to lay the foundation for a more strengths-focused approach to social policy development. Effective social work practice requires "searching the environment for forces that enhance or suppress human possibilities and life chances and attending to those through community building, resource development, and acquisition (Saleebey, 2013, p. 295). Doing this work in a way that emphasizes client self-determination, responsibility, and possibility is at the heart of the strengths approach. Asking the people who are our service users what solutions they suggest can uncover new ideas and potentially energize their involvement in the change process, much as has been seen when using solution focused therapy. By creating opportunities for policy makers to listen to service users from the beginning of the policy development process, and by explicitly focusing on outcomes important to this population, social workers can help policy makers obtain the information necessary to craft future strengths-based policy and to engage in a more strengths-based policy process.

Social workers can help shape our image of the future and implement needed policy changes by becoming involved in electoral politics, publishing articles in professional journals and the popular press, using social media to identify and coordinate groups of activists, and by helping to organize and participating in formal and informal local, state, national, and international forums. The involvement of social workers who are attuned to the strengths of all people in the global village and who are committed to social justice and skilled in policy practice is critical today. The ethics statements of the International Federation of Social Workers can help to guide our practice in the global context. You can learn more about work to establish international standards for ethical social work at the website of the International Federation of Social Workers (www.ifsw.org; go to Statement of Ethical Principles).

Turning to the U.S., we need effective policy responses to major changes, including our aging and diversifying population and the growing wealth gap. As has been chronicled in this text, public social policies do not develop out of thin air. Rather, in a pluralistic society such as ours, people come together to champion a variety of interests and cobble together legislation which has sufficient support to pass. Hopefully, if social workers armed with policy practice skills and an understanding of the strengths perspective are involved, the voices of the population the policy targets will be clearly heard during this legislative process.

However, if a policy is to be effective, there is much more work to be done after legislation is passed. Social polices succeed or fail in large part at the implementation stage. The health care reform legislation of 2010 is a good example to consider. Social workers should not wait to be told what this law will mean for their clients. Rules and regulations, many of them made at the state level, will determine this legislation's impact. Social workers may be able to influence this rule-making process if they find out who will be responsible for the process in their state and begin to interact with them, mobilize groups of affected individuals, and prepare effective arguments to advance their agendas. If your state has not elected to be part of Medicaid expansion, you need to advocate for health care for low-income people in your state that is equal to the care received in states that have agreed to Medicaid expansion. It is particularly important to monitor the effects of that decision on your clients and to compare those outcomes to similar groups in other states where Medicaid has been expanded. For example, how has that decision influenced health outcomes for children and adults? What percentage of women receive inadequate prenatal care? Have rates of untreated mental illness increased? Also, consider the budgetary impact. Your state is not capacity building in the health care arena to the extent other states are and that has real impact not only on families with low incomes but also on all families, regardless of income, that receive health care in your state.

After Affordable Care Act rules are made and programs implemented, many people will be confused about the new policies and programs. There will be a great need for community education and outreach, especially to traditionally hard-to-reach groups, including those for whom English is a second language, isolated rural populations, people with low educational attainment, and some minority groups. Social work students could be very helpful in the area of community outreach. In fact, the advocacy work of students chronicled in this text has included many examples of students developing educational materials and going into the community to help people become aware of benefits for which they are eligible, and, in the process, shaping the official implementation practices for such policies. Such student initiatives provide invaluable experience in learning how to overcome stigma and work across cultures. Additionally, students can look at what kinds of mechanisms their agencies have so that clients can give feedback on how a policy is working or not, and consider how it can be improved. Health care reform is a mammoth undertaking. Policies and programs probably will not work smoothly at first. They will need reworking, and hopefully our clients' voices will be integral to making the policies and programs more effective. It is not acceptable to just decry a policy as ineffective or lament the perpetuation of social injustice. Large public programs can bring great benefits. However, they also can be unresponsive, and people, particularly those who are living in poverty, many times do not have the option to vote with their feet and go elsewhere. The challenge is to develop the mechanisms that can help make these programs more responsive to our clients' needs.

You also should realize that major policy reforms such as the 2010 health care legislation will be contested for years. Just as initial passage was hard fought, groups who fear this legislation may portend a new social contract where more of the risks we all face are addressed via public insurance strategies rather than individually, can be expected to continue to raise objections during the implementation phase. Indeed, many groups will point to problems with this legislation, and their critique can lead to important improvements. Additionally, experience from the 1960s and 1970s indicates that when advocates successfully organize and mobilize clients and they sign up for services for which they are legally entitled, the number of recipients and thus costs increase, and there may be a backlash. Advocacy on behalf of families eligible for AFDC during these periods was not just about increasing the utilization rate for these services among eligible populations, but about enhancing the power of low-income Americans, and that can make people in power feel threatened. These efforts may have helped fuel the backlash that resulted in punitive TANF reforms in the 1990s. So, do not be surprised or discouraged by opposition. Rather, prepare for it and use the tools you learned in this class to help address backlash, protect current effective policies and programs that are increasingly under attack, and continue to press for a more just social contract. You are our future. Hard-headed realism as well as idealism will be needed in order to engage in effective advocacy.

CONCLUSION

An image of the future is at the base of all choice-oriented behavior. We need an image of a future worth going to, a future that can be embraced and enjoyed, not decried. We also need some guidance on how to get there. The synthesis of careful data analysis, citizen involvement, and professional values enables us to help sketch an image of the future that energizes our efforts to craft effective policy and programs. With your clients, it is not only the lived past but the anticipated future that will motivate their actions. Think how you can listen to your clients and interact in a way in which their hopes for the future are supported and they might even be engaged in crafting more effective policies and programs. The social work profession has deep roots in movements to bring about social change. Since the beginning of the profession, social workers have been instruments of social control as well as social assistance. Undoubtedly, social workers will continue, as a profession, to fulfill both of these important functions. You can also strive to fulfill social work's central mission of enhancing well-being and meeting basic needs. As a policy practitioner, you can be a change leader. As a social work student, there are multiple ways for you to develop and demonstrate skills in change leadership, starting with your field placements. For example, you can make sure that taking part in collaborative efforts to identify and implement needed changes in your agency and in the community is part of your field placement plan. Armed with beginning skills in policy practice and, hopefully, inspired to bring all your intelligence and creativity to bear on the big challenges we currently face, you can help develop and implement policies and programs that work for our clients. Be sure to take time to celebrate even the small victories you achieve. Celebration of strengths and of attaining goals is central to the strengths approach to policy practice. I wish you well in this exciting work to create a better future for our clients and ourselves.

MAIN POINTS

- A framework for understanding future forecasts draws attention to the following components: purpose, underlying assumptions and credibility of source, influence of current socioeconomic conditions, interpretation of the numbers or data, and anticipation of surprise events.

- When thinking about the future from the strengths perspective, the following points should be considered. First, life conditions, strengths, and goals of the current cohorts for which predictions are being made should be taken into account. Second, social constructions of conditions influence future social policy responses and future realities. Third, the social work *Code of Ethics* can help anchor our thinking about future policies and their potential impacts.

- The number of people in the U.S. is expected to increase in the next 50 years because of fertility rates and net immigration. Yet the rate of population growth will decrease, owing to the greater age of the population and subsequent number of deaths as well as declining birth rates.

- As the population grows it will become more ethnically diverse, with the percentage of white non-Hispanics decreasing and the Hispanic-origin population increasing most rapidly.

- In addition to increases in population and diversity, other factors such as medical advances, changes in information technology, globalization, and environmental degradation and depletion of natural resources, will shape the future of the U.S. and the profession of social work.

- Given current U.S. values, it is expected that future public social policy will continue to emphasize attachment to the workforce, but this raises the specter of gaps in supports as people's relationships to their jobs change.

- Global efforts will be necessary to assure stability in the areas of retirement security, work, and health care for an increasingly mobile workforce whose members may be employed in a variety of countries during their careers.

- Future health care policy reforms are needed to increase access to adequate health services, including the opportunity for competent people to make informed choices about health care.

- Environmental discrimination and the impact of policies on the natural environment need to be more carefully considered.

- Pluralism can be expected to increase as the diversity of the population increases.

- Privatization of publicly funded social services needs to be carefully evaluated in terms of both benefits and limitations so that funding and oversight can be tailored to deliver adequate services.

- Future policies will likely focus on both cost-effectiveness and value choices. It is possible to develop public social policies that are economically efficient and also promote social justice.

- Social workers need to participate effectively in electoral politics in order to implement policies consistent with their ethics that promote the well-being of individuals and meet basic needs. This can be done by voting, organizing, debating, running for office, campaigning, lobbying, and conducting policy-related research.

- The use of social media to develop citizen activists can be a powerful tool for policy reform.

- Social workers need to take an active role in the implementation and evaluation of the Affordable Care Act and make sure the voices of their clients are heard when outcomes are examined.

- Major policy reforms such as the 2010 health care legislation are also often contended during the implementation phase. Backlash can also be expected, and social workers should prepare for it.

- Convergence refers to the growing similarity of countries in challenges faced and policies enacted over time.

- Technological advances have created new tools for social work practice and made it easier to collaborate with people from other countries, and to identify promising policy initiatives. However, the cultural context of countries can profoundly influence policy effectiveness.

- We need to help develop a vision of the future that energizes our journey.

EXERCISES

1. Consider the Sanchez family. The Sanchez family is personally experiencing the impact of current immigration policy. Go to the Reform Immigration for America website and examine the latest immigration policy reforms being proposed. If comprehensive immigration reform legislation is passed, what would be the impact on the Sanchez family? What roles might the Sanchez family play in pushing for positive immigration policy, and how could you support them, as their social worker?

2. In Riverton, the economic downturn continues to take its toll and increase the ranks of the homeless. Homelessness exists in wealthy Western nations as well as in poor countries. Various governments and cultures attend to this worldwide problem differently. Considering what you know about global convergence, do a web search to find out how different governments and cultures define, prioritize, and attend to this worldwide problem.
   a. How does the problem of homelessness differ in wealthy versus developing countries?
   b. What can we learn from other countries about policies and programs that would help in addressing homelessness in Riverton?
   c. What cautions would we need to consider in trying to adopt, in Riverton, policies used to address homelessness in other countries?

3. Consider what you have learned about Carla Washburn and her community. What strategies and community resources could be used to help build future intergenerational cooperation in crafting policies and programs in her town?

4. First, imagine it is 10 years from now and write down a personal goal you hope you will have achieved. Second, write down a goal of a change in social policy you think can be achieved in the next 10 years. Be ready to discuss your social policy ideas in class.

5. What do you think are the benefits and drawbacks of having 16-year-olds vote? Do you think that change would increase voter participation? Do you think we might have more future policies that address the needs of children if younger people could vote? Are you for or against such a policy change? Why?

6. The RAINN case provides an example of how more social services may be offered in the future. Think about the clients with whom you work or clients served in an agency with which you are familiar. How could they be served using online resources? What barriers will they face as more and more services are provided online? What strategies could help these people receive the service and benefits they need in the face of these changes?

7. As we look to the future, climate experts believe that we will face more frequent and more severe natural disasters, due to climate change. As you face this future:

   a. What preparation should communities undertake?

   b. What disaster-related policies would have helped citizens of Hudson City prior to the disaster? How should such disaster prevention and relief policies take into account the disparate experiences of marginalized populations?

   c. Pick a social service agency in your community and find out how it has prepared for disasters. What policies are in place to make sure clients are safe and continue to get vital services and benefits?

   d. What additional plans and policies should the agency consider putting in place? Go to http://www.fema.gov/plan-prepare-mitigate for ideas.

8. Think of your practicum agency, a social work agency where you have volunteered, or another organization that provides services to target populations. How well prepared is this organization, in your assessment, for the changes in population diversity and aging discussed in this chapter? What changes might they need to make to improve their chances of accommodating these shifts?

References

Abramovitz, M. (1996). *Regulating the lives of women: Social welfare policy from colonial times to the present* (rev. ed.). Boston, MA: South End Press.

ACLU. (2013). Let people vote. Available at: http://www.aclu.org/let-people-vote-removing-restrictions-and-barriers-voting-america.

Adams, D., & Scanlon, E. (2010, September). Lessons from SEED, a national demonstration of child development accounts. Available at: http://csd.wustl.edu/Publications/Documents/SEEDSynthesis_Final.pdf.

Adarand Constructors vs. Peña. 515 U.S.C. 200 (1995). Available at: http://caselaw.lp.findlaw.com/scripts/getcase.pl?court=us&vol=000&invol=v10252.

Adler, L. (2001). The meaning of permanence: A critical analysis of the Adoption and Safe Families Act of 1997. *President and Fellows of Harvard College Harvard Journal on Legislation*, *38*(1).

Administration for Children and Families. (ACF). (2012, March 15). TANF work requirements and state strategies to fulfill them. Available at: http://www.acf.hhs.gov/programs/opre/resource/tanf-work-requirements-and-state-strategies-to-fulfill-them.

Administration on Aging. (2004). A layman's guide to the Older Americans Act. Available at: www.aoa.gov.

Administration on Aging. (2010, June 23). Projected future growth of the older population. Available at: http://www.aoa.gov/AoARoot/Aging_Statistics/future_growth/future_growth.aspx.

Ahsan, N. (1996). The Family Preservation and Support Services Programs. *The Future of Children*, *6*(3), 157–160.

Allard, P., & Young, M. C. (2002). Prosecuting juveniles in adult court: The practitioner's perspective. *Journal of Forensic Psychology Practice*, *2*(2), 65–78.

American Academy of Child & Adolescent Psychiatry. (1975). Policy Statement: Placement of American Indian children. Available at: http://www.aacap.org/cs/root/policy_statements/placement_of_american_indian_children.

American Bar Association. (2009). *Criminal justice improvements: Juvenile Justice and Delinquency Prevention Act*. Available at: http://www.abanet.org/poladv/priorities/juvjustice/

American Psychiatric Association. (2013). *The Diagnostic and Statistical Manual of Mental Disorders (DSM-5)* (5th ed.). Arlington, VA: American Psychiatric Publishing.

American Public Health Association (APHA). (n.d.). Medicaid expansion. Available at: http://www.apha.org/advocacy/Health+Reform/ACAbasics/medicaid.htm.

Americans with Disabilities Act of 1990, Pub. L. No. 101–336,104 Stat. 328. Available at: http://www.ada.gov/pubs/ada.htm.

Amidei, N. (2010). *So you want to make a difference: Advocacy is the key* (16th ed.). CreateSpace Independent Publishing Platform.

Amnesty International. (2002). United States of America. Indecent and internationally illegal: The death penalty against juvenile offenders. Available: www.amnestyusa.org/abolish/reports/amr51_144_2002.pdf.

Anderson, B. W. (1986). *Understanding the Old Testament* (4th ed.). Englewood Cliffs, NJ: Prentice Hall.

Annie E. Casey Foundation. (AECF). (2009). 2009 Kids Count Data Book: A national and state-by-state effort to track the status of children in the United States. Available at: http://www.aecf.org/MajorInitiatives/KIDSCOUNT.aspx.

Annie E. Casey Foundation. (AECF). (2011a). Data across states: Children in foster care by race or Hispanic origin (percent)—2011. Available at: http://datacenter.kidscount.org/data/acrossstates/Rankings.aspx?loct=2&by=a&order=a&ind=6246&dtm=12993&ch=a&tf=867.

Annie E. Casey Foundation. (AECF). (2011b). Data across states: Children in single parent families. Available at: http://datacenter.kidscount.org/data/acrossstates/Rankings.aspx?loct=2&by=a&order=a&ind=106&dtm=430&tf=867.

Annie E. Casey Foundation. (AECF). (2013). *Kids Count Data Books: A national and state-by-state effort to track the status of children in the United States.* Under 'Publications and Resources' Available at: http://www.aecf.org/MajorInitiatives/KIDSCOUNT.aspx.

Assistant Secretary for Planning and Evaluation. (ASPE). (2012, September 12). Information on poverty and income statistics: A summary of 2012 Current Population Survey data. Available at: http://aspe.hhs.gov/hsp/12/povertyandincomeest/ib.shtml.

Axinn, J., & Stern, M. J. (2001). *Social welfare: A history of the American response to need* (5th ed.). Boston, MA: Allyn & Bacon.

Baltes, P. B., & Baltes, M. M. (1990). Psychological perspectives on successful aging: The model of selective optimization with compensation. In P. B. Baltes & M. M. Baltes (Eds.), *Successful aging: Perspectives from the behavioral sciences* (pp. 1–34). Cambridge: Cambridge University Press.

Banerjee, M. (2002). Voicing realities and recommending reform in PRWORA. *Social Work, 47*(3), 315–358.

Barker, R. (1999). *Milestones in the development of social work and social welfare.* Washington, DC: NASW Press.

Barker, R. L. (2003). *The social work dictionary* (5th ed., p. 357). Washington, DC: NASW Press.

Basch, N. (1998). Family values and 19th-century American politics. *Reviews in American History, 26*(4), 687–692.

Baughman, R. A. (2012). The effects of state EITC expansion on children's health. The Carsey Institute at the Scholars' Repository, paper 168. Available from: http://scholars.unh.edu/carsey/168.

Bell, W. (1987). *Contemporary social welfare* (2nd ed.). Michigan: Macmillan.

Bernio, K., Po, R., Skopec, L., & Glied, S. (2013, February 20). ASPE issue brief: Affordable Care Act expands mental health and substance use disorder benefits and federal parity protections for 62 million Americans. Available at: http://aspe.hhs.gov/health/reports/2013/mental/rb_mental.cfm.

Bernstein, I. (1996). *Guns or butter: The presidency of Lyndon Johnson.* New York: Oxford University Press.

Binstock, R. (1999). Challenges to United States policies on aging in the new millennium. *Hallym International Journal on Aging, 1*(1), 3–13.

Blank, R., & Burau, V. (2010). *Comparative health policy* (3rd ed.). New York: Palgrave Macmillan.

Blau, J., & Abramovitz, M. (2007). *The dynamics of social welfare policy* (2nd ed.). New York: Oxford University Press.

Brady, D. (2009). *Rich democracies, poor people: How politics explains poverty.* New York: Oxford University Press.

Briar-Lawson, K., Naccarato, T., & Drews, J. (2009). Child and family welfare policies and services. In J. Midgley & M. Livermore (Eds.), *The handbook of social policy* (2nd ed.) (pp. 315–335). Thousand Oaks, CA: Sage Publications.

Brill, S. (2013, March 4). Bitter pill: Why medical bills are killing us. *Time, 181*, 16–55.

Brissett-Chapman, S. (1995). Child abuse and neglect: Direct practice. In R. L. Edwards & J. G. Hopps (Eds.), *Encyclopedia of social work* (19th ed., pp. 353–366). Alexandria, VA: National Association of Social Workers.

Brown vs. Board of Education of Topeka, 347 U.S. 483 (1954). Available at: http://caselaw.lp.findlaw.com/scripts/getcase.pl?court=us&vol=347&invol=483.

Browne, C. (1998). *Women, feminism, and aging.* New York: Springer.

Bruner, C. (2002). *A stitch in time: Calculating the costs of school un-readiness,* Washington, DC: The Finance Project.

Burns, E. (1965). Where welfare falls short. *The Public Interest, 1,* 1–138.

Burns, E. M. (1956). *Social security and public policy.* New York: McGraw-Hill.

Butler, R. (2008). *The longevity revolution: The benefits and challenges of living a long life.* New York: Perseus Books Group.

California vs. Bakke, 483 U.S. 265 (1978). Available at: http://caselaw.lp.findlaw.com/cgi-bin/getcase.pl?court=us&vol=438&invol=265.

Campaign for Youth Justice. (2007). *Jailing juveniles: The dangers of incarcerating youth in adult jails in America.* Washington, DC: Campaign for Youth Justice. Available at: www.campaignforyouthjustice.org.

Cannon, J. (Ed.). (1997). *The Oxford companion to British history.* New York: Oxford University Press.

Carlton-LaNey, I. (1999). African American social work pioneers' response to need. *Social Work, 44*(4), 311–321.

Center on Aging. (2002). *Kansas elder count.* New York: Milbank Memorial Fund.

Center on Budget and Policy Priorities. (CBPP). (2003). *Number of Americans without health insurance rose in 2002.* Washington, DC: Author.

Center on Budget and Policy Priorities. (CBPP). (2009a). *Policy basics: Where do our federal tax dollars go?*

Center on Budget and Public Priorities. (CBPP). (2009b). *Policy basics: The Earned Income Tax Credit.* Washington, DC.

Center on Budget and Policy Priorities. (CBPP). (2012, November 6). *Policy basics: Top ten facts about Social Security.* Available at: http://www.cbpp.org/cms/index.cfm?fa=view&id=3261.

Center on Budget and Policy Priorities. (CBPP). (2013a, March 28). Chart book: SNAP helps struggling families put food on the table. Available at: http://www.cbpp.org/cms/index.cfm?fa=view&id=3744.

Center on Budget and Policy Priorities. (CBPP). (2013b, February 1). Policy basics: The Earned Income Tax Credit. Available at: http://www.cbpp.org/files/policybasics-eitc.pdf.

Center on Budget and Policy Priorities. (CBPP). (2013c). Policy basics: Introduction to Medicaid. Available at: http://www.cbpp.org/cms/index.cfm?fa=view&id=2223.

Centers for Disease Control. (CDC). (2012). Infant mortality statistics from the 2008 period linked birth/infant death data set. National Vital Statistics Reports. Available at: http://www.cdc.gov/nchs/data/nvsr/nvsr60/nvsr60_05.pdf.

Centers for Disease Control. (CDC). (2013). Social determinants of health. Available at: http://www.cdc.gov/socialdeterminants/.

Centers for Disease Control and Prevention. (CDCP). (2009). Changing patterns of non-marital childbearing in the United States: Data brief #18. Hyattsville, MD: National Center for Health Statistics.

Centers for Medicare & Medicaid Services. (CMS). (2008). 2008 Medicaid Managed Care Enrollment Report. Available at: http://www.cms.gov/MedicaidDataSourcesGenInfo/04_MdManCrEnrllRep.asp.

Centers for Medicare & Medicaid Services. (CMS). (2009). Medicare Trustees report. Available at: http://www.cms.hhs.gov/ReportsTrustFunds/.

Centers for Medicare & Medicaid Services. (CMS). (2010). The Mental Health Parity and Addiction Equity Act. Available at: http://www.cms.gov/HealthInsReformforConsume/04_TheMentalHealth ParityAct.asp.

Centers for Medicare & Medicaid Services. (CMS). (2011, March 31). Accountable care organizations: Improving care coordination for people with Medicare. Available at: http://www.healthcare.gov/news/factsheets/2011/03/accountablecare03312011a.html.

Centers for Medicare & Medicaid Services. (CMS). (2012a). 2012 Actuarial report on the financial outlook for Medicaid. Available at: http://medicaid.gov/Medicaid-CHIP-Program-Information/By-Topics/Financing-and-Reimbursement/Downloads/medicaid-actuarial-report-2012.pdf.

Centers for Medicare & Medicaid Services. (CMS). (2012b, November 15). CMS financial report, fiscal year 2012. Available at: http://www.cms.gov/Research-Statistics-Data-and-Systems/Statistics-Trends-and-Reports/CFOReport/Downloads/2012_CMS_Financial_Report.pdf.

Centers for Medicare & Medicaid Services (CMS). (2012c). CHIP data in the Medicaid Statistical Information System (MSIS). Available at: http://www.cms.gov/Research-Statistics-Data-and-Systems/Computer-Data-and-Systems/MedicaidDataSourcesGenInfo/Downloads/MAX_IB12_CHIPData.pdf.

Centers for Medicare & Medicaid Services (CMS). (2012d). Children's Health Insurance Program. Available at: http://www.medicaid.gov/medicaid-chip-program-information/by-topics/childrens-health-insurance-program-chip/childrens-health-insurance-program-chip.html.

Centers for Medicare & Medicaid Services (CMS). (2012e). CHIP data in the Medicaid Statistical Information System (MSIS). Available at: http://www.cms.gov/Research-Statistics-Data-and-Systems/Statistics-Trends-and-Reports/NationalHealthExpendData/downloads/highlights.pdf.

Centers for Medicare & Medicaid Services. (CMS). (2013a). Your Medicare coverage. Available at: http://www.medicare.gov/coverage/your-medicare-coverage.html.

Centers for Medicare & Medicaid Services. (CMS). (2013b). Fact sheet: Individual shared responsibility for health insurance coverage and minimum coverage proposed rules. Available at: http://www.cms.gov/apps/media/press/factsheet.asp?Counter=4511&intNumPerPage=10&checkDate=&checkKey=&srchType=1&numDays=3500&srchOpt=0&srchData=&keywordType=All&chkNewsType=6&intPage=&showAll=&pYear=&year=&desc=&cboOrder.

Centers for Medicare & Medicaid Services. (CMS). (2013c). Social determinants of health. Available at: http://www.cdc.gov/socialdeterminants/.

Chambers, D. E. (2000). *Social policy and social programs: A method for the practical public policy analyst* (3rd ed.). Boston, MA: Allyn & Bacon.

Chambers, D., & Wedel, K. (2009). *Social policy and social programs: A method for the practical public policy analyst* (5th ed.). Needham Heights, MA: Allyn & Bacon/Pearson.

Chambers, D., & Bonk, J. F. (2012). Social policy and social programs: A method for the practical public policy analyst (6th ed.). Boston, MA: Allyn & Bacon/Pearson.

Chapin, R. (1995). Social policy development: The strengths perspective. *Social Work, 40*(4), 506–514.

Chapin, R., Baca, B., Macmillan, K., Rachlin, R., & Zimmerman, M. (2009). Residential outcomes for nursing facility applicants who have been diverted: Where are they five years later? *The Gerontologist, 49*(1), 46–56.

Chapin, R., & Cox, E. (2001). Changing the paradigm: Strengths-based and empowerment-oriented social work with frail elders. *Journal of Gerontological Social Work, 6*(3/4), 165–180.

Chapin, R., Nelson-Becker, H., & Macmillan, K. (2006). Strengths based and solution focused approaches to practice with older adults. In B. Berkman and S. D'Ambruso (Eds.), *The Oxford handbook of social work in aging*. New York: Oxford University Press.

Cherokee Nation vs. Georgi, 30 U.S. 1 (1831). Available at: http://caselaw.lp.findlaw.com/scripts/getcase.pl?court=us&vol=30&invol=\.

Child Abuse Prevention and Treatment Act, 42 U.S.C. 5106 § (1974).

Child Welfare Information Gateway. (2009). *Foster care statistics*. Available at: http://www.childwelfare.gov/pubs/factsheets/foster.cfm#two.

Child Welfare Information Gateway. (2010). *Adoption by family type: Transracial/transcultural families*. Available at: http://www.childwelfare.gov/adoption/adoptive/transracial.cfm.

Child Welfare Information Gateway. (2012). *How the child welfare system works*. Washington, DC: U.S. Department of Health and Human Services, Children's Bureau.

Children's Bureau. (2012). *Frequently asked questions*. Available at: http://www.acf.hhs.gov/programs/cb/resource/foster-care-faq8.

Children's Defense Fund. (2010). Fostering Connections to Success and Increasing Adoptions Act summary.

Available at: http://www.childrensdefense.org/child-research-data-publications/data/FCSIAA-detailed-summary.pdf.

Children's Defense Fund. (2012a). *The state of America's children, 2012 handbook*. Washington, DC: The Children's Defense Fund.

Children's Defense Fund. (2012b). *Portrait of inequality 2012: Black children in America*. Washington, DC: The Children's Defense Fund. Available at www.childrensdefense.org.

Children's Defense Fund. (2012c). *Portrait of inequality 2012: Hispanic children in America*. Washington, DC: The Children's Defense Fund. Available at www.childrensdefense.org.

Chiriboga, D. A. (1996). Comments on conceptual and empirical advances in understanding aging well through proactive adaptation. In V. L. Bengtson (Ed.), *Adulthood and aging: Research on continuities and discontinuities* (pp. 41–45). New York: Springer.

Clark, P., & Slack, P. (1976). *English towns in transition: 1500–1700*. New York: Oxford University Press.

Claxton, M., & Hansen, R. (2004). Working poor suffer under Bush tax cuts. *The Detroit News*.

Cohn, D. (2012, December 14). Census Bureau lowers U.S. growth forecast, mainly due to reduced immigration and births. Available at: http://www.pewsocialtrends.org/2012/12/14/census-bureau-lowers-u-s-growth-forecast-mainly-due-to-reduced-immigration-and-births/.

Coll, B. (1972). Public assistance in the United States: Colonial times to 1860. In E. W. Martin (Ed.), *Comparative development in social welfare* (pp. 128–158). London: Allen & Unwin.

Commager, H. (Ed.). (1958). *Documents of American history* (6th ed.) (p. 256). New York: Appleton-Century-Crofts.

Committee on Ways and Means. (2000). *2000 green book*. U.S. House of Representatives. Washington, DC: U.S. Government Printing Office.

Congressional Budget Office. (CBO). (2009). An analysis of the President's budgetary proposals for fiscal year. Available at: http://www.cbo.gov/ftpdocs/102xx/doc10296/06-16-AnalysisPresBudget_forWeb.pdf.

Congressional Budget Office. (CBO). (2010). Cost estimates for health care legislation. Available at: http://www.cbo.gov/ftpdocs/113xx/doc11379/Manager'sAmendmenttoReconciliationProposal.pdf.

Congressional Budget Office. (CBO). (2012, July). Estimates for the insurance coverage provisions of the Affordable Care Act updated for the recent Supreme Court decision. Available at: http://cbo.gov/sites/default/files/cbofiles/attachments/43472-07-24-2012-CoverageEstimates.pdf.

Congressional Budget Office. (CBO). (2013a, February). The budget and economic outlook: Fiscal years 2013–2023. Available at: https://www.cbo.gov/sites/default/files/cbofiles/attachments/43907-BudgetOutlook.pdf.

Congressional Budget Office. (CBO). (2013b). CBO's February 2013 Medicare baseline. Available at: http://www.cbo.gov/sites/default/files/cbofiles/attachments/43894_Medicare2.pdf.

Corporation for Enterprise Development. (CFED). (2009). American dream demonstration. Available at: http://cfed.org/assets/pdfs/American_Dream_Demonstration.pdf.

Corporation for Enterprise Development. (CFED). (2012). Growing number of Americans can't cover basic expenses if job loss or other emergency strikes. Available at: http://cfed.org/newsroom/pr/growing_number_of_americans_cant_cover_basic_expenses_if_job_loss_or_other_emergency_strikes/.

Council on Social Work Education. (CSWE). (2010). *Strengthening the impact of social work to improve the quality of life for older adults & their families: A blueprint for the new millennium*. Alexandria, VA: Council on Social Work Education.

Courtney, M., Hook, J. L., & Lee, J. S. (2009). *Distinct subgroups of former foster youth during young adulthood: Implications for policy and practice*. Chicago, IL: Chapin Hall Center for Children at the University of Chicago.

Davis, A. (1984). *Spearheads for reform*. New Brunswick, NJ: Rutgers University Press.

Day, P. (2000). Social policy from colonial times to the Civil War. In J. Midgley, M. Tracy, & M. Livermore (Eds.), *The handbook of social policy* (pp. 85–96). Thousand Oaks, CA: Sage Publications.

Day, P. (2009). *A new history of social welfare* (6th ed.). Boston, MA: Pearson.

Deitch, M. (2009). *From time-out to hard time: Young children in the adult criminal justice system.* Austin, TX: LBJ School of Public Affairs, University of Texas.

DeLoria, P. J. (1993). The twentieth century and beyond. In B. Ballantine & I. Ballantine (Eds.), *The Native Americans: An illustrated history* (pp. 384–465). Atlanta, GA: Turner Publishing.

DeNavas-Walt, C., Proctor, B., & Mills, R. (2004). *Income, poverty, and health insurance coverage in the United States: 2003* (pp. 60–226). Washington, DC: U.S. Bureau of the Census.

DeNavas-Walt, C., Proctor, B. D., & Smith, J. C. (2012). *U.S. Census Bureau, current population reports, income, poverty, and health insurance coverage in the United States: 2011.* Washington, DC: U.S. Government Printing Office. Available at: http:// www.census.gov/prod/2012pubs/p60-243.pdf.

DeWitt, L. (2003). *Brief history.* Social Security Administration Historian's Office. Available at: www.ssa.gov/history/briefhistory3.html.

Division of Facilities Compliance and Recovery. (2010). *The Hill-Burton Free Care Program.* Available at: http://www.hrsa.gov/hillburton/compliance-recovery.htm.

Dobelstein, A. W. (2003). *Social welfare: Policy and analysis* (3rd ed.). Pacific Grove, CA: Brooks/Cole.

Dowd, J. (1980). Aging as exchange: A preface to theory. In J. Quadagno (Ed.), *Aging, the individual, and society* (pp. 103–121). New York: St. Martin's Press.

Downs, S. W., Costin, L. B., & McFadden, E. J. (1996). *Child welfare and family services: Policies and practice.* White Plains, NY: Longman.

Dred Scott vs. Sandford, 60 U.S. 393 (1857). 60 U.S. 393 (How.) Available at: http://caselaw.lp.findlaw.com/ scripts/getcase.pl?court=us&vol=6&invol=393.

Drew, E. (1996). *Showdown: The struggle between the Gingrich Congress and the Clinton White House.* New York: Simon & Schuster.

Dripps, D. A. (1996). A new era for gay rights? *Trial 32*(9), 18–21. Retrieved October 3, 2004, from proquest. umi.com.

Education for All Handicapped Children Act of 1975, Pub. L. 94–142, S. 6. Available at: asclepius.com/ angel/special.html.

Edwards, K., & Mason, L. M. (2003). *State policy trends for individual development accounts in the United States: 1993–2003.* St. Louis, MO: Center for Social Development.

Elk vs. Wilkins, 112 U.S. 94 (1884). Retrieved May 18, 2010 Available at: http://supreme.justia.com/ us/112/94/case.html.

Elliott, W., & Beverly, S. (2010, January). CSD Publication No. 10-04. *The role of savings and wealth in reducing "wilt" between expectations and college attendance.* St. Louis, MO: George Warren Brown School of Social Work. Available at: http:// csd.wustl.edu/Publications/Documents/RB10-04. pdf.

Ellis, R. (2003). *Impacting social policy: A practitioner's guide to analysis and action.* Pacific Grove, CA: Thomson/Brooks Cole.

Encyclopedia of Social Work. (2008). 20th Edition, National Association of Social Workers and Oxford University Press.

Equal Employment Opportunity Commission. (1999). Milestones in the history of the U.S. Equal Employment Opportunity Commission. Available at: http://www.eeoc.gov/eeoc/history/35th/ milestones/ index.html.

Equal Rights Amendment. (2013). ERA Task Force, National Council of Women's Organizations. Available at: http://www.equalrightsamendment. org/.

Esping-Andersen, G. (2002). *Why we need a new welfare state.* New York: Oxford University Press.

Fahey, C. (1996). Social work education and the field of aging. *The Gerontologist, 36*(1), 36–41.

Falk, G. (2013, January 22). The Temporary Assistance for Needy Families (TANF) block grant: Responses to frequently asked questions. Available at: http:// www.fas.org/sgp/crs/misc/RL32760.pdf.

Faragher, J. (1990). *The encyclopedia of colonial and revolutionary America.* New York: Facts on File.

Federal Interagency Forum on Aging-Related Statistics (2012). *Older Americans 2012: Key indicators of well-*

being. Washington, DC: U.S. Government Printing Office.

Federal Interagency Forum on Child and Family Statistics. (2012). America's children in brief: Key national indicators of well-being 2012. Available at: http://childstats.gov/pdf/ac2012/ac_12.pdf.

Federal Reserve (2012). *Changes in U.S. family finances from 2007–2010: Evidence from the survey of consumer finances*. Available at: http://www.federalreserve.gov/pubs/bulletin/2012/pdf/scf12.pdf.

Finch, I., & Schott, L. (2011, November 21). TANF benefits fell further in 2011 and are worth much less than in 1996 in most states. Available at: http://www.cbpp.org/cms/?fa=view&id=3625.

Fischer, G. (1992). The development and history of the poverty thresholds. *Social Security Bulletin*, 55(4), 3–14.

Food and Nutrition Service. (2009). Available at: http://www.fns.usda.gov.

Fox-Grage, W., Folkemer, D., Burwell, B., & Horahan, K. (2001). *Community-based long-term care*. Forum for State Health Policy Leadership. Denver, CO: National Conference of State Legislatures.

Frasch, K. M., & Brooks, D. (2003). Normative development in transracial adoptive families: An integration of the literature and implications for the construction of a theoretical framework. *Families in Society: The Journal of Contemporary Human Services*, 84(2), 201–212.

Fukui, S., Goscha, R., Rapp, C., Mabry, A., Liddy, P., & Marty, D. (2012). Strengths model case management fidelity scores and client outcomes. *Psychiatric Services*, 63, 708–710.

Geen, R. (2003). Who will adopt the foster care children left behind? *Caring for Children, Brief No. 2*. Available at: http://www.urban.org/publications/310809.html.

Geertz, C. (1973). *The interpretation of cultures*. New York: Basic Books.

George, R. (1990). The reunification process in substitute care. *Social Service Review*, 64(3), 22–457.

Gergen, K. (1999). *An invitation to social construction*. Thousand Oaks, CA: Sage Publications.

Germain, C. (1991). *Human behavior in the social environment: An ecological view*. New York: Columbia University Press.

Gilbert, N. (2002). *Transformation of the welfare state: The silent surrender of public responsibility*. New York: Oxford University Press.

Gilbert, N., Specht, H., & Terrell, P. (1998). *Dimensions of social welfare policy* (4th ed.). Needham Heights, MA: Allyn & Bacon.

Gilbert, N., & Terrell, P. (2001). *Dimensions of social welfare policy* (5th ed.). Boston, MA: Allyn & Bacon.

Gilbert, N., & Terrell, P. (2009). *Dimensions of social welfare policy* (7th ed.). Boston, MA: Allyn & Bacon.

Gist, J. (2007). *Spending entitlements and tax entitlements*. Washington, DC: AARP Public Policy Institute.

Goldstein, A. (2004). Bush signs Unborn Victims Act: Federal law establishes 2 crimes against pregnant women. *The Washington Post*, p. A4. Retrieved September 30, 2004, from proquest.umi.com.

Gordon, L. (1998). How welfare became a dirty word. *New Global Development: Journal of International and Comparative Social Welfare*, 14, 1–14.

Gore, A. (2013). *The future: Six drivers of global change*. Random House: New York.

Gorin, S. H. (2010). The Patient Protection and Affordable Care Act, cost control, and the battle for health care reform. *Health & Social Work*, 35(3), 163–166.

Gratz vs. Bollinger. 539 U.S. 244 (2003). Available at: http://caselaw.lp.findlaw.com/scripts/getcase.pl?court=us&vol=000&invol=02-516.

Greenhouse, L. (2003, June 24). Justices back affirmative action by 5 to 4, but wider vote bans a racial point system. *The New York Times*, p. A1. Retrieved October 3, 2004, from proquest.umi.com.

Greenstein, R. (2013, February 6). Commentary: How effective is the safety net? Available at: http://www.cbpp.org/cms/index.cfm?fa=view&id=3898.

Gross vs. FBL Financial, Inc., 557 U.S. (2009). Available at: http://caselaw.lp.findlaw.com/cgi-bin/getcase.pl?court=us&navby=case&vol=000&invol=08-441.

Grutter vs. Bollinger. 539 U.S. 306 (2003). Available at: http://caselaw.lp.findlaw.com/scripts/getcase.pl?court=us&vol=000&invol=02-241.

Gustafson, C. (2012). FY 2012 PBGC Exposure Report. Pension Benefit Guaranty Corporation. Available at: http://www.pbgc.gov/documents/2012-exposure-report.pdf.

Hacker, J. (2002). *The divided welfare state*. New York: Cambridge University Press.

Hacker, J. (2006). *The great risk-shift: The assault on jobs, families, health care, and retirement*. New York: Oxford University Press.

Haynes, K. S., & Mickelson, J. S. (2009). *Affecting change: Social workers in the political arena* (7th ed.). Boston, MA: Allyn & Bacon.

Hays, E. M. (1989). *Prayers for the planetary pilgrim*. Leavenworth, KS: Forest of Peace Publishing.

Healthy Marriage and Responsible Fatherhood Grant Programs: Institute for Research on Poverty. (2010). Who is poor? Available at: http://www.irp.wisc.edu/faqs/faq3.htm.

HEARTH Act, 42 U.S.C. §1143 2009P.L. 111–22 Cite McKinney-Vento Homeless Assistance Act, 42 U.S.C. § 11301 et seq. (1987).

Hine, R., & Faragher, J. (2000). *The American West: A new interpretive history*. New Haven, CT: Yale University Press.

Hoffman, S. D. (2006). *By the numbers: The public costs of adolescent childbearing*. Washington, DC: National Campaign to Prevent Teen Pregnancy.

Hofstadter, R. (1963). *The Progressive Movement, 1900–1915*. Englewood Cliffs, NJ: Prentice-Hall.

Hollinger, J. (1998). *A guide to the Multiethnic Placement Act of 1994 as amended by the Interethnic Adoption Provisions of 1996*. Washington, DC: American Bar Association Center on Children and the Law, National Resource Center on Legal and Court Issues.

Hooyman, N. R. (1994). Diversity and populations at risk: Women. In F. G. Reamer (Ed.), *The foundations of social work knowledge* (pp. 309–345). New York: Columbia University Press.

Hooyman, N. R., & Kiyak, H. A. (2002). *Social gerontology: A multidisciplinary perspective* (6th ed.). Boston, MA: Allyn & Bacon.

House Budget Committee. Democratic Caucus. (2005). *Summary and analysis of the president's fiscal year 2006 budget*. Retrieved February 15, 2005, from www.house.gov/budget_democrats/analyses/FY06budget_analysis.pdf.

Hoyert, D. L., & Xu, J. (2012, October 10). Deaths: Preliminary data for 2011. *National Vital Statistics Reports, 61*(6). Available at: http://www.cdc.gov/nchs/data/nvsr/nvsr61/nvsr61_06.pdf.

Hsueh, J., Alderson, D. P., Lundquist, E., Michalopoulos, C., Gubits, D., David Fein, D., & Knox, V. (2012). OPRE Report 2012–11. *The supporting healthy marriage evaluation: Early impacts on low-income families*. Washington, DC: Office of Planning, Research and Evaluation, Administration for Children and Families, U.S. Department of Health and Human Services.

Hudson, D. M. (1998). *Along racial lines: Consequences of the 1965 Voting Rights Act*. New York: Peter Lang.

Hymowitz, C., & Weissman, M. (1980). *A history of women in America*. New York: Bantam Books.

Institute for Research on Poverty (IRP). (2009). Who is Poor? Is poverty different for different groups in the population? Available at: http://www.irp.wisc.edu/faqs/faq3.htm.

Institute for Research on Poverty (IRP). (2011). What are the poverty thresholds and poverty guidelines? Available at: http://www.irp.wisc.edu/faqs/faq1.htm#thresholds.

Institute for Women's Policy Research. (March 2012). *The gender pay gap: 2011*. Washington, DC: Author.

Internal Revenue Service. (IRS). (2012). Affordable Care Act tax provisions. Available at: http://www.irs.gov/uac/Affordable-Care-Act-Tax-Provisions.

Internal Revenue Service. (IRS). (2013a). *EITC fast facts*. Available at: http://www.eitc.irs.gov/ptoolkit/basicmaterials/ff/.

Internal Revenue Service. (IRS). (2013b). *Publication 596 (2012), Earned Income Credit (EIC)*. Available at: http://www.irs.gov/publications/p596/index.html.

Isaacs, J. B. (2007). *Economic mobility of families across generations*. Washington, DC: Brookings Institution, Economic Mobility Project.

Isaacs, J., Toran, K., Hahn, H., Fortuny, K., & Steuerle, C. E. (2012). *Urban Institute, kids' share 2012: Report on federal expenditures on children through 2011.* Washington, DC: Urban Institute. Available at: www.urban.org.

Issa, P., & Zedlewski, S. R. (2011). Poverty among older Americans: 2009. Washington, DC: The Urban Institute. Available at: http://www.urban.org/UploadedPDF/412296-Poverty-Among-Older-Americans.pdf.

Jansson, B. (2003). *Becoming an effective policy advocate* (4th ed.). Pacific Grove, CA: Thomson/Brooks Cole.

Jansson, B. S. (2011). *Becoming an effective policy advocate: From policy practice to social justice* (6th ed.). Belmont, CA: Brooks/Cole.

Johnson, R. (2005). A taxonomy of measurement objectives for policy impact analysis. *Policy Studies Journal, 2*(3), 201–208.

Kahana, E., & Kahana, B. (1996). Conceptual and empirical advances in understanding aging well through proactive adaptation. In V. L. Bengtson (Ed.), *Adulthood and aging: Research on continuities and discontinuities* (pp. 18–40). New York: Springer.

Kaiser Family Foundation. (KFF). (2012a, August 1). A Guide to the Supreme Court's decision on the ACA's Medicaid expansion. Available at: http://kff.org/health-reform/issue-brief/a-guide-to-the-supreme-courts-decision/.

Kaiser Family Foundation. (KFF). (2012b, September 11). Employer health benefits survey. Available at: http://kff.org/private-insurance/report/employer-health-benefits-2012-annual-survey/.

Kaiser Family Foundation. (KFF). (2012c, May 1). Five key questions about Medicaid and its role in state/federal budgets and health reform. Available at: http://kff.org/health-reform/report/five-key-questions-about-medicaid-and-its/.

Kaiser Family Foundation. (KFF). (2012d). Medicare policy: Health care on a budget: The financial burden of health spending by Medicare households. Available at: http://www.kff.org/medicare/upload/8171-02.pdf.

Kaiser Family Foundation. (KFF). (2012e, November 14). Medicare spending and financing fact sheet. Available at: http://kff.org/health-reform/fact-sheet/medicare-spending-and-financing-fact-sheet/.

Kaiser Family Foundation. (KFF). (2012f). State health facts. Available at: http://www.statehealthfacts.org/comparemaptable.jsp?ind=612&cat=4.

Kaiser Family Foundation. (KFF). (2012g). Total health care employment. Available at: http://kff.org/other/state-indicator/total-health-care-employment/.

Kaiser Family Foundation. (KFF). (2012h). U.S. global health policy. Available at: http://www.global-healthfacts.org/data/topic/map.aspx?ind=91.

Kaiser Family Foundation. (KFF). (2013, March 4). The Medicaid program at a glance. Available at: http://kff.org/medicaid/fact-sheet/the-medicaid-program-at-a-glance-update/.

Kane, R., Kane, R., & Ladd, R. (1998). *The heart of long-term care.* New York: Oxford University Press.

Kansas Action for Children. (2001). *The Kansas child welfare system: Where are we? Where should we be going?* Topeka: Author.

Katz, M. (2008). *The price of citizenship.* Philadelphia, PA: University of Pennsylvania Press.

Kenney, C. (1981). New look to grants. *Boston Globe,* p. 1. Retrieved October 2, 2004, from proquest.umi.com.

Keynes, J. M. (1936). *The general theory of employment, interest and money.* New Delhi: Atlantic.

Kingdon, J. (2003). *Agendas, alternative, and public policies,* (2nd ed., p. 3). New York: Addison-Wesley Educational Publishers.

Kingsley, D. (2010). *Ageism in the health care debate.* Lawrence, KS: Douglas County Coalition on Aging.

Klees, B. S., Wolfe, C. J., & Curtis, C. A. (2012, December 31). Brief summaries of Medicare & Medicaid. Available at: http://www.cms.gov/Research-Statistics-Data-and-Systems/Statistics-Trends-and-Reports/MedicareProgramRatesStats/Downloads/MedicareMedicaidSummaries2012.pdf.

Knappman, E., Christianson, S., & Paddock, L. (Eds.). (2002). *Great American trials* (2nd ed., Vols. 1–2). Detroit: Gale Group.

Kretzmann, J., & McKnight, J. (1993). *Building communities from the inside out: A path toward finding and mobilizing a community's assets*. Evanston, IL: Institute for Policy Research, Northwestern University.

Kronick, R., & Po, R. (2013, January 7). Growth in Medicare spending per beneficiary continues to hit historic lows. Available at: http://aspe.hhs.gov/health/reports/2013/medicarespendinggrowth/ib.cfm.

Kutler, S. I. (Ed.). (2003). *Dictionary of American history* (3rd ed., Vols. 1–10). New York: Charles Scribner's Sons.

Leedahl, S. N. (2013). Older adults in nursing homes: Assessing relationships between multiple constructs of social integration, facility characteristics, and health. (Unpublished doctoral dissertation). The University of Kansas.

Levit, K., Smith, C., Cowan, C., Sensenig, A., Catlin, A., & The Health Accounts Team. (2004). Health spending rebound continues in 2002. *Health Affairs*, 23(1), 147–159.

Link, A., & Catton, W. (1967). *American epoch: A history of the United States since the 1890s*. Vol. 1: 1897–1920. (3rd ed.). New York: Alfred A. Knopf.

Loeske, D. (1995). Writing rights: The "homeless mentally ill" and involuntary hospitalization. In J. Best (Ed.), *Images of issues* (pp. 261–286). New York: Aldine De Gruyter.

Lowe, T. B. (2006). Nineteenth century review of mental health care for African Americans: A legacy of service and policy barriers. *Journal of Sociology & Social Welfare*, 33(4), 29–51.

Macarov, D. (1991). *Certain change: Social work practice in the future*. Silver Spring, MD: NASW.

Macartney, S. (2011). *U.S. Census Bureau, child poverty in the United States 2009 and 2010: Selected race groups and Hispanic origin*: American Community Survey Briefs. Available at: http://www.census.gov/prod/2011pubs/acsbr10-05.pdf.

MacEachern, D. (1994). *Enough is enough: A hellraiser's guide to community activism*. New York: Avon Books.

Main, R., Macomber, J., & Geen, R. (2006). *Trends in Service Receipt: Children in kinship care gaining ground*. Washington, DC: The Urban Institute. Available at: www.urban.org.

Marmot, M., & Brunner, E. (2005). Cohort profile: The Whitehall II study. *International Journal of Epidemiology*, 34(2), 251–256.

Marshall, T. H. (1950). *Citizenship and social class, and other essays*. Cambridge, UK: Cambridge University Press.

Martin, J. A., Hamilton, B. E., Ventura, S. J., Osterman, J. K., Wilson, E. C., Mathews, T. J., & Division of Vital Statistics. (2012, August 28). Births: Final data for 2010. *National Vital Statistics Reports*, 61(1). Available at: http://www.cdc.gov/nchs/data/nvsr/nvsr61/nvsr61_01.pdf.

Marty, D., & Chapin, R. (2000). The legislative tenets of client's right to treatment in the least restrictive environment and freedom from harm: Implications for community providers. *Community Mental Health Journal*, 36(6), 545–556.

Matheson, L. (1996). The politics of the Indian Child Welfare Act. *Social Work*, 41(2), 232–235.

Max Planck Institute for Demographic Research. (2013, March 21). Lifetime fertility on the rise. Available at: http://www.mpg.de/7042238/Demography.

McInnis-Dittrich, K. (1994). *Integrating social welfare policy and social work practice*. Pacific Grove, CA: Brooks/Cole.

McKinney-Vento Homeless Assistance Act, 42 U.S.C. § 11301 *et seq*. (1987).

McPhail, B. A. (2003). A Feminist Policy Analysis Framework: Through a Gendered Lens. *The Social Policy Journal* 2(3), pp. 39–61.

Met Life Mature Market Institute. (2012, November). Market survey of long-term care costs: The 2012 MetLife Market survey of nursing home, assisted living, adult day services, and home care costs. Available at: https://www.metlife.com/assets/cao/mmi/publications/studies/2012/studies/mmi-2012-market-survey-long-term-care-costs.pdf.

Middleman, R., & Goldberg-Wood, G. (1990). *Skills for direct practice in social work*. New York: Columbia University Press.

Midgley, J. (2009). Social development and social work: Towards global dialogue. In H. G. Homfeldt & C.

Reutlinger (Eds.), *Sociale Arbeit und Sociale Entwicklung* (pp. 12–24). Scheiner Verlag.

Midgley, J. (2012a). Development. In L. M. Healy & R. Link (Eds.), *Handbook on international social welfare* (pp. 24–29). New York: Oxford University Press.

Midgley, J. (2012b). The institutional approach to social policy. In J. Midgley, M. Tracy, & M. Livermore (Eds.), *The handbook of social policy* (pp. 365–375). Thousand Oaks, CA: Sage Publications.

Midgley, J., & Sherraden, M. (2009). The social development perspective in social policy. In J. Midgley & M. Livermore (Eds.), *The handbook of social policy* (2nd ed., pp. 279–294). Thousand Oaks, CA: Sage Publications, Inc.

Midgley, J., Tracey, M., & Livermore, M. (Eds.). (2000). The future of social policy. In *The handbook of social policy* (pp. 493–502). Thousand Oaks, CA: Sage Publications.

Mildred, J. (2003). Claimsmakers in the child sexual abuse "wars": Who are they and what do they want? *Journal of Social Work*, 48(4), 492–503.

Millenium Project. (2012). State of the Future Index (SOFI). Available at: http://www.millenium-project.org/millenium/SOFI.html.

Miller, K. (2010). *Myth vs. fact: Keeping All Students Safe Act.* Available at: http://edlabor.house.gov/blog/2010/02/myth-vs-fact-preventing-harmfu.shtml.

Monitz, C., & Gorin, S. (2003). *Health and heath care policy: A social work perspective.* Boston, MA: Allyn & Bacon.

Morris, P. M. (2002). The capabilities perspective: A framework for social justice. *Families in Society, The Journal of Contemporary Human Services*, 83(3), 365–373.

Moynihan, D. P. (1973). *The politics of a guaranteed income: The Nixon administration and the family assistance plan.* New York: Vintage Books.

Munnell, A., Aubry, J., & Muldoon, D. (2008). The financial crisis and private defined benefit plans. Center for Retirement Research at Boston College. Available at: http://crr.bc.edu/images/stories/Briefs/ib_8–18.pdf.

Nabokov, P. (1993). Long threads. In B. Ballantine & I. Ballantine (Eds.), *Native Americans: An illustrated history* (pp. 301–383). Atlanta, GA: Turner Publishing.

Nash, G. B., Jeffrey, R. J., Howe, J. R., Frederick, P. J., Davis, A. D., & Winkler, A. M. (2004). *The American people: Creating a nation and a society* (6th ed.). New York: Pearson/Longman.

National Alliance on Mental Illness. (March 2011). *State mental health cuts: A national crisis.* Washington, DC: Author.

National Alliance to End Homelessness. (2009). *HEARTH Act section-by-section analysis.* Available at: http://www.endhomelessness.org/content/article/detail/2385.

National Association of Social Workers. (NASW). (1973). *Standards for social service manpower* (p. 4). Washington, DC: NASW Press.

National Association of Social Workers. (NASW). (2003a). Lesbian, gay, and bisexual issues. In *Social work speaks: National Association of Social Workers policy statements, 2003–2006* (6th ed., pp. 224–235). Washington, DC: NASW Press.

National Association of Social Workers. (NASW). (2003b). People with disabilities. In *Social work speaks: National Association of Social Workers policy statements, 2003–2006* (6th ed., pp. 270–275). Washington, DC: NASW Press.

National Association of Social Workers. (NASW). (2008). *Code of ethics.* Washington, DC: NASW. Available at: http://www.naswdc.org.

National Association of Social Workers. (NASW). (2009a). Health care policy. In *Social work speaks: National Association of Social Workers policy statements, 2009–2012* (8th ed., pp. 167–176). Washington, DC: NASW Press.

National Association of Social Workers. (NASW). (2009b). Affirmative action. In *Social work speaks: National Association of Social Workers policy statements, 2009–2012* (8th ed., pp. 22–28). Washington, DC: NASW Press.

National Association of Social Workers. (NASW). (2009c). Aging and wellness. In *Social work speaks: National Association of Social Workers policy statements, 2009–2012* (8th ed., pp. 14–19). Washington, DC: NASW Press.

National Association of Social Workers. (NASW). (2009d). Lesbian, gay, and bisexual issues. In *Social work speaks: National Association of Social Workers policy statements, 2009–2012* (8th ed., pp. 218–223). Washington, DC: NASW Press.

National Association of Social Workers. (NASW). (2011). Social work blog, CAPTA Reauthorization Bill signed into law. Available at: http://www.socialworkblog.org/advocacy/2011/01/news-from-the-hill-january-2011.

National Association of Social Workers. (NASW). (2012a). Building on progressive priorities: Sustaining our nation's safety net. Available at: http://www.naswdc.org/advocacy/2012%20NASW%20Obama%20Document.pdf.

National Association of Social Workers. (NASW). (2012b). Child abuse and neglect. In *Social work speaks: National Association of Social Workers policy statements, 2012–2014* (9th ed., pp. 43–49). Washington, DC: NASW Press.

National Association of Social Workers. (NASW). (2012c). Juvenile justice and delinquency prevention. In *Social work speaks: National Association of Social Workers policy statements, 2012–2014* (9th ed., pp. 209–214). Washington, DC: NASW Press.

National Association of Social Workers. (NASW). (2012d). Mental health. In *Social work speaks: National Association of Social Workers policy statements, 2012–2014* (9th ed., pp. 230–235). Washington, DC: NASW Press.

National Association of Social Workers. (NASW). (2012e). *Social Work Speaks: National Association of Social Workers policy statements 2012–2014* (9th ed.). Washington, DC: NASW Press.

National Center on Elder Abuse. (2003). *Fact sheet*. Available at: http://www.ncea.aoa.gov/ncearoot/main_site/Library/Statistics_Research/Abuse_Statistics/Statistics_At_Glance.aspx.

National Center for Juvenile Justice and Mental Health. (2005). *Mental health courts*. Available at: http://www.ncmhjj.com/resource_kit/pdfs/Diversion/Readings/JuvenileMentalHealthCourts.pdf.

National Conference of State Legislatures. (2013) Available at http://www.ncsl.org/issues-research/human-services/same-sex-marriage-overview.aspx.

National Council on Disability. (2012, September 27). Rocking the cradle: Ensuring the rights of parents with disabilities and their children. Available at: http://www.ncd.gov/publications/2012/Sep272012/.

National Institute of Health. (2011, April). Senior health: Depression. Available at: https://nihseniorhealth.gov/depression/aboutdepression/01.html.

National Juvenile Justice and Delinquency Prevention Coalition. (2013). Promoting safe communities: Recommendations for the administration. Opportunities for juvenile justice & delinquency prevention reform. Available at: http://promote-safecommunities.org/images/pdfs/NJJDPC_RecstoCongress_03122013_web.pdf.

National Prison Rape Commission. (2009, June). National prison rape elimination commission report. Available at: http://www.campaignforyouthjustice.org/documents/CFYJNR_JailingJuveniles.pdf.

National Urban League. (2012). *The state of Black America 2012*. New York: National Urban League.

National WIC Association. (2009). WIC for a healthier America. Available at: http://www.nwica.org/?q=advocacy/6.

Nelson-Becker, H., Chapin, R., & Fast, B. (2013). The strengths model with older adults: Critical practice components. In D. Saleebey (Ed.), *The strengths perspective in social work practice*. White Plains, NY: Longman.

O'Connor, J. (1973). *The fiscal crisis of the state*. New York: Saint Martin's Press.

Office of Family Assistance. (2009). *Fact sheet*. Washington, DC: Author. Available at www.acf.hhs.gov/opa/fact_sheets/tanf_factsheet.html.

Office of Juvenile Justice and Delinquency Prevention. (2002). Guidance manual for monitoring facilities under the JJDP Act. Available at: http://dcj.state.co.us/oajja/ComplianceMonitoring/OJJDPGuidanceManualMonitoringFacilities.pdf.

Office of Juvenile Justice and Delinquency Prevention. (2011a). Final plan for Fiscal Year 2011. Available at: http://www.gpo.gov/fdsys/pkg/FR-2011-07-08/html/2011-17186.htm.

Office of Juvenile Justice and Delinquency Prevention. (2011b). *Statistical briefing book: Juvenile arrest rate.* Washington, DC: U.S. Department of Justice. Retrieved on April 14, 2014 from: http://www.ojjdp.gov/ojstatbb/crime/JAR_Display.asp?ID=qa05201.

Office of Management and Budget. (2005). Overview of the president's 2006 Budget. Available at: http://www.whitehouse.gov/omb/rewrite/budget/fy2006/overview.html.

Office of Management and Budget. (2013). Table 1.3—Summary of receipts, outlays, and surpluses or deficits (–) in current dollars, constant (FY 2005) dollars, and as percentages of GDP: 1940–2018. Available at: http://www.whitehouse.gov/omb/budget/historicals.

Oko, J. (2006). Evaluating alternative approaches to social work: A critical review of the strengths perspective. *Families in Society*, *87*(4), 601–611.

Older Women's League. (OWL). (2012). Available at: http://www.owl-national.org/.

Olmstead vs. L. C. 527 U.S. 581 (1999). Available at: http://caselaw.lp.findlaw.com/scripts/getcase.pl?court=us&vol=000&invol=98–536.

Olsen, K. (1999). *Daily life in 18th-century England.* Westport, CT: Greenwood Press.

Olshansky, S. J., Antonucci, T., Berkman, L., Binstock, R. H., Boersch-Supan, A., Cacioppo, J. T., et al. (2012). Differences in life expectancy due to race and educational differences are widening, and many may not catch up. *Health Affairs*, *31*, 1803–1813. doi:10.1377/hlthaff.2011.0746.

Oltmanns, T. F., & Emery, R. E. (1995). *Abnormal psychology.* Englewood Cliffs, NJ: Prentice Hall.

Organisation for Economic Co-operation and Development. (OECD). (2008). *OECD Factbook 2009.* Paris: The OECD Database.

Organisation for Economic Co-operation and Development. (OECD). (2009). OECD health data 2009: How does the United States compare? Available at: http://www.oecd.org/dataoecd/46/2/38980580.pdf.

Organisation for Economic Co-operation and Development. (OECD). (2012a, August 12). Infant mortality. Available at: http://www.oecd.org/els/family/CO1.1%20Infant%20mortality%20-%20updated%20081212.pdf.

Organisation for Economic Co-operation and Development. (OECD). (2012b, October 30). Life expectancy at birth, females [Data file]. Available at: http://www.oecd-ilibrary.org/social-issues-migration-health/life-expectancy-at-birth-females_20758480-table6.

Organisation for Economic Co-operation and Development. (OECD). (2012c). OECD health data 2012: How does the United States compare? Available at: http://www.oecd.org/unitedstates/BriefingNoteUSA2012.pdf.

Organisation for Economic Co-operation and Development. (OECD). (2013). *OECD Factbook 2013: Economic, Environmental and Social Statistics.* Available at: http://www.oecd-ilibrary.org/economics/oecd-factbook-2013_factbook-2013-en.

Ortman, J. M. (2013, February 7). U.S. population projections: 2012 to 2060. Presentation for the FFC/GW Brown Bag Seminar Series in Forecasting. Washington, DC. Available at: http://www.gwu.edu/~forcpgm/Ortman.pdf.

Passel, J. S., & Cohn, D. (2008). Pew Research Center, U.S. population projections: 2005–2050. Available at: www.pewresearch.org.

Patterson, J. T. (1996). *Great expectations: The United States, 1945–1974.* New York: Oxford University Press.

Pavetti, L. (2013). *Testimony on the impact of the recession and the Recovery Act on social safety net programs before the House Budget Committee.* Washington, DC: Center on Budget and Public Priorities.

Pavetti, L., & Rosenbaum, D. (2010). *Creating a safety net that works when the economy doesn't: The role of the Food Stamp and TANF Programs.* Washington, DC: Center on Budget and Public Priorities.

Pavetti, L., Finch, I., & Schott, L. (2013, March 1). TANF emerging from the downturn a weaker safety net. Available at: http://www.cbpp.org/cms/?fa=view&id=3915.

Pear, R. (2005, February 8). Subject to Bush's knife: Aid for food and heating. *New York Times*, p. A22.

Pelton, L. H. (1989). *For reasons of poverty: A critical analysis of the public child welfare system in the United States.* New York: Praeger.

Pension Benefit Guaranty Corporation (PBGC). (2009). *History of Pension Benefit Guaranty Corporation.* Available at: http://www.pbgc.gov/about/who-we-are/pg/history-of-pbgc.html.

Pension Benefit Guaranty Corporation (PBGC). (2010). Strategic plan: 2011–2016. Available at: http://www.pbgc.gov/docs/2011–2016strategicplan.pdf.

Petr, C. G. (2004). *Social work with children and their families: Pragmatic foundations* (2nd ed.). New York: Oxford University Press.

Pew Research Center. (2009). Growing old in America: Expectations vs. reality. Available at: http://www.pewsocialtrends.org/2009/06/29/growing-old-in-america-expectations-vs-reality/.

Pew Research Center. (2011, July 7). GOP divided over benefit reductions: Public wants changes in entitlements, not changes in benefits. Available at: http://www.people-press.org/files/legacy-pdf/7-7-11%20Entitlements%20Release.pdf.

Piven, F. F., & Cloward, R. A. (1971). *Regulating the poor: The functions of public welfare.* New York: Pantheon.

Plessy vs. Ferguson, 163 U.S. 537 (1896). Available at: http://caselaw.lp.findlaw.com/scripts/getcase.pl?court=us&vol=163&invol=537.

Pollard, W. L. (1995). Civil rights. In R. L. Edwards & J. G. Hopps (Eds.), *Encyclopedia of social work* (19th ed., pp. 494–502). New York: NASW Press.

Popple, P. (1995). Social work profession: History. In R. L. Edwards & J. G. Hopps (Eds.), *Encyclopedia of social work* (19th ed., pp. 2282–2292). Washington, DC: NASW Press.

Popple, P. R., & Leighninger, L. (2004). *The policy-based profession: An introduction to social welfare policy analysis for social workers* (3rd ed.). Boston, MA: Allyn & Bacon.

Postrel, V. I. (1988, May 20). Religious rights: A matter of property. *Wall Street Journal*, p. 1. Retrieved October 3, 2004.

Provine, D. (2007). *Unequal under law: Race in the war on drugs.* Chicago, IL: University of Chicago Press.

Provost, C., & Hughes, P. (2000). Medicaid: 35 years of service. *Health Care Financing Review, 22*(1), 141–174.

Quadagno, J. (1999). *Aging and the life course: An introduction to social gerontology.* Boston, MA: McGraw-Hill.

Quadagno, J. (2000). Promoting civil rights through the welfare state: How Medicare integrated southern hospitals. *Social Problems, 47*(1), 68–69.

Quigley, W. (1996a). Five hundred years of English Poor Laws, 1349–1834: Regulating the working and nonworking poor. *Akron Law Review, 30*(1), 73–128.

Quigley, W. (1996b). Work or starve: Regulation of the poor in colonial America. *University of San Francisco Law Review, 31*, 35–83.

Ramnarace, C. (2010, March 25). Congress passes Elder Justice Act. AARP Bulletin. Available at: http://www.aarp.org/politics-society/advocacy/info-03-2010/congress_passes_elder_justice_act.html.

Rapp, C., Pettus, C., & Goscha, R. (2006). Principles of strengths-based policy. *Journal of Policy Practice, 5*(4), 3–18.

Rappaport, J., Davidson, W., Wilson, M., & Mitchell, A. (1975). Alternatives to blaming the victim or the environment: Our places to stand have not moved the earth. *American Psychologist, 30*(4), 525–528.

Reid, P. N. (1995). Social welfare history. In R. L. Edwards & J. G. Hopps (Eds.), *Encyclopedia of social work* (19th ed., pp. 2006–2225). Washington, DC: NASW Press.

Reid, T. R. (2009). *The healing of America: A global quest for better, cheaper and fairer healthcare.* New York: Penguin Press.

Reisch, M. (2000). Social policy and the Great Society. In J. Midgley, M. Tracy, & M. Livermore (Eds.), *The handbook of social policy* (pp. 127–142). Thousand Oaks, CA: Sage Publications.

Richmond, M. (1917). *Social diagnosis.* New York: Russell Sage Foundation.

Roberts, P. C. (1988). Supply-side economics—Theory and results. *Public Interest, 93* (Fall), 16ff. Retrieved September 21, 2004, from http://www.nationalaffairs.com/public_interest/detail/supply-side-economicstheory-and-results.

Romer vs. Evans U.S. C 517 U.S. 620. (1996). Available at: http://caselaw.lp.findlaw.com.cgi-bin/getcase.pl?court=us&vol=000&invol=u10179.

Rowse, A. L. (1950). *The England of Elizabeth.* New York: Macmillan.

Ryan, L. (2013). No more delays Mr. President: Appoint the nation's next Juvenile Justice Chief. Available at: http://jjie.org/no-more-delays-mr-president-appoint-nations-next-juvenile-justice-chief/.

Saleebey, D. (2013). *The strengths perspective in social work practice* (6th ed.). Boston, MA: Pearson.

Saleebey, D. (Ed.). (1992). Introduction: Power in the people. In *The strengths perspective in social work practice* (pp. 3–17). New York: Longman.

Schick, A. (with LoStracco, F.). (2000). *The federal budget: Politics, policy, process* (rev. ed.). Washington, DC: Brookings Institution Press.

Schneider, R., & Lester, L. (2001). *Social work advocates: A new framework for action*. Belmont, CA: Wadsworth.

Schott, L., & Pavetti, L. (2011, October 3). *Many States Cutting TANF Budgets Harshly Despite High Unemployment and Unprecedented Need*. Available at: http://www.cbpp.org/files/5-19-11tanf.pdf.

Schott, L. (2012, December 4). Policy basics: An introduction to TANF. Available at: http://www.cbpp.org/cms/?fa=view&id=936.

Schreiner, M., Clancy, M., & Sherraden, M. (2002). Saving performance in the American Dream Demonstration: A national demonstration of individual development accounts. St. Louis, MO: Center for Social Development. Available at: http://gwbweb. wustl.edu/csd/Publications/2002/ADDreport2002.pdf.

Segal, C., & Stineback, D. (1977). *Puritans, Indians, and manifest destiny*. New York: Putnam.

Sen, A. (1999). *Development as freedom*. New York: Anchor.

Sentencing Project. (1999). Critical choices: New options in juvenile crime policy. Available at: http://www.sentencingproject.org/doc/publications/sl_criticalchoices.pdf.

Sherraden, M. (1991). *Assets and the poor: A new American welfare policy*. Armonk, NY: M. E. Sharpe.

Sherraden, M. (2000). From research to policy: Lessons from Individual Development Accounts. *Journal of Consumer Affairs*, *34*(2), 159–181.

Sherraden, M. S., & Ansong, D. (2013). Conceptual development of the CYFI Model of Children and Youth as Economic Citizens (CSD Research Report 1303). St. Louis, MO: Washington University, Center for Social Development. Available at: http://csd.wustl.edu/Publications/Documents/RR13-03.pdf.

Sherraden, M. S., Slosar, B., & Sherraden, M. (2002). Innovation in social policy: Collaborative policy advocacy. *Social Work*, *47*(3), 209–223.

Short, K. (2012, November). The Research supplemental poverty measure: 2011. Available at: http://www.census.gov/prod/2012pubs/p60-244.pdf.

Sickmund, M. (1994). *OJJDP update on statistics: How juveniles get to criminal court*. Washington, DC: Office of Juvenile Justice and Delinquency Prevention.

Sierminska, E., Brandolini, A., & Smeeding, T. (2007). Cross-national comparison of income and wealth status in retirement: First results from the Luxembourg Wealth Study (LWS), Center for Retirement Research. Boston, MA: Boston College.

Singman, J. (1995). *Daily life in Elizabethan England*. Westport, CT: Greenwood Press.

Skocpol, T. (1993). America's first social security system: The expansion of benefits for Civil War veterans. *Political Science Quarterly*, *108*(1), 85–116.

Social Security Administration. (2007). A brief history of social security. SSA Publication No. 21-059. Retrieved October 2, 2004, from www.ssa.gov.

Social Security Administration. (2009). Annual Statistical Supplement, 2009. Workers' Compensation Program Description and Legislative History. Available at: www.socialsecurity.gov/policy/docs/statcomps/supplement/2009/workerscomp.html.

Social Security Administration. (2012, April 25). The 2012 Annual Report of the Board of Trustees of the Federal Old-Age and Survivors Insurance and Federal Disability Insurance Trust Funds. Available at: http://www.ssa.gov/oact/tr/2012/index.html.

Social Security Administration. (2013a). Monthly Statistical Snapshot, April 2013. Available at: http://www.ssa.gov/policy/docs/quickfacts/stat_snapshot/.

Social Security Administration. (2013b). Maximum retirement benefit. Available at: http://ssa-custhelp.ssa.gov/app/answers/detail/a_id/5/~/maximum-social-security-retirement-benefit.

Social Security Administration. (2013c). Number of Credits to be eligible for Social Security retirement benefits. Available at: http://ssa-custhelp.ssa.gov/app/answers/detail/a_id/356/kw/Eligibility%20for%20OASDI%20benefits.

Social Security Administration. (2013d). Retirement planner: Benefits by year of birth. Available at: http://www.socialsecurity.gov/retire2/agereduction.htm.

Social Security Administration. (2013e). The average monthly social security benefit for a retired worker. Available at: http://ssa-custhelp.ssa.gov/app/answers/detail/a_id/13/~/average-monthly-social-security-benefit-for-a-retired-worker.

Social Security Administration. (2013f). Fact Sheet – Social Security. Available at: http://www.ssa.gov/pressoffice/basicfact.htm.

Social Security Administration. (2013g). Status of the Social Security and Medicare Programs, Office of the Chief Actuary, 2013 Trust Report. Available at: http://www.ssa.gov/oact/trsum/.

Social Security Administration. (2013h). OASDI and SSI program rates & limits, 2013. Available at: http://www.socialsecurity.gov/policy/docs/quickfacts/prog_highlights/index.html.

Social Security Administration. (2013i). Monthly statistical snapshot, June 2013 [Data set]. Available at: http://www.ssa.gov/policy/docs/quickfacts/stat_snapshot/.

Social Security Administration. (2013j). Understanding Supplemental Security Income. Available from: http://www.ssa.gov/ssi/text-understanding-ssi.htm.

Social Security Administration. (2013k). SSI federal payment amounts for 2013. Available at: http://www.ssa.gov/oact/cola/SSI.html.

Social Security Administration. (2013l). SSI monthly statistics, May, 2013. Available at: http://www.socialsecurity.gov/policy/docs/statcomps/ssi_monthly/.

Spano, R. (2000). Creating the context for the analysis of social policies: Understanding the historical context. In D. Chambers, *Social policy and social programs: A method for the practical public policy analyst* (pp. 31–45). Boston, MA: Allyn & Bacon.

Sparer, M. (2012, September). Medicaid managed care: Costs, access, and quality of care. Available at: http://www.rwjf.org/content/dam/farm/reports/reports/2012/rwjf401106.

Squires, D. (2012). *Explaining high health care spending in the United States: An international comparison of supply, utilization, prices, and quality.* New York: The Commonwealth Fund.

St. John, S. (2010). Landmark $13.3 million grant to fund L.A. Gay & Lesbian Center's development of model program to serve LGBTQ foster youth. Available at: http://laglc.convio.net/site/News2?page–ewsArticle&id=13263.

Stevenson, R. W. (2005, February 8). President offers budget proposal with broad cuts. *New York Times.*

Substance Abuse and Mental Health Services Administration. (2010). *About SAMSHA.* Available at: www.samhsa.gov/about.

Swatos, W. (Ed.). (1998). *Encyclopedia of religion and society.* Walnut Creek, CA: AltaMira Press.

Taylor, J. (1997). Niches and practice: Extending the ecological perspective. In D. Saleebey (Ed.). *The strengths perspective in social work practice* (2nd ed., pp. 217–227). New York: Longman.

The Board of Trustees, Federal Hospital Insurance and Federal Supplementary Medical Insurance Trust Funds. (2012, April 23). 2012 Annual report of the Board of Trustees of the Federal Hospital Insurance and Federal Supplementary Medical Insurance Trust Funds. Available at: http://www.cms.gov/Research-Statistics-Data-and-Systems/Statistics-Trends-and-Reports/ReportsTrustFunds/downloads/tr2012.pdf.

The Board of Trustees, Federal Old-Age and Survivors Insurance and Federal Disability Insurance Trust Funds. (2012, April 25). The 2012 Annual report of the Board of Trustees of the Federal Old-Age and Survivors Insurance and Federal Disability Insurance Trust Funds. Available at: http://www.ssa.gov/oact/tr/2012/tr2012.pdf.

The Millennium Project. (2012). State of the Future Index (SOFI). Available at: http://www.millennium-project.org/millennium/SOFI.html.

The National Campaign to Prevent Teen and Unplanned Pregnancy. (2009). *Fast facts: Reproductive health outcomes among youth who have ever lived in foster care*. Washington, DC: The National Campaign to Prevent Teen and Unplanned Pregnancy. Retrieved on April 14, 2013, from http://www. TheNationalCampaign.org/resources/pdf/FastFacts_ FosterCare_Reproductive_Outcomes.pdf.

The National Campaign to Prevent Teen and Unplanned Pregnancy. (2011). *Counting it up: The public costs of teen childbearing: Key data*. Washington, DC: The National Campaign to Prevent Teen Pregnancy. Retrieved on April 14, 2013, from http://www.thenationalcampaign.org/ costs/pdf/counting-it-up/key-data.pdf.

Tice, C. J., & Perkins, K. (1996a). *Faces of social policy: A strengths perspective*. Pacific Grove, CA: Wadsworth Publishing.

Tice, C., & Perkins, K. (1996b). *Mental health issues and aging*. Pacific Grove, CA: Brooks/Cole.

Tice, C., & Perkins, K. (2002). *The faces of social policy: A strengths perspective*. Pacific Grove, CA: Wadsworth Group, Brooks/Cole.

Title IX Education Amendments. (1972). 20 U.S.C. Section 1681–1688. Available at www.dol.gov/ oasam/regs/statutes/titleix.htm.

Titmuss, R. M. (1974). *Social policy: An introduction*. New York: Pantheon Books.

Towle, C. (1945/1987). *Common human needs*. Silver Spring, MD: National Association of Social Workers. (Original work published 1945.)

Trattner, W. (1999). *From poor law to welfare state: A history of social welfare in America* (6th ed.). New York: The Free Press.

U.S. Bureau of Labor Statistics, U.S. Department of Labor. (2012a, March 29). Occupational outlook handbook: Social workers, 2012–13 edition. Available at: http://www.bls.gov/ooh/community-and-social-service/social-workers.htm.

U.S. Bureau of Labor Statistics (2012b, September 5). Racial and ethnic characteristics of the U.S. labor force, 2011. Available at: http://www.bls.gov/ opub/ted/2012/ted_20120905.htm.

U.S. Census Bureau. (1996). *Population projections of the United States by age, sex, race, and Hispanic origin: 1995 to 2050*. Current Population Reports, P25–1130. Washington, DC: U.S. Government Printing Office.

U.S. Census Bureau. (2008). NP2008_D1: Projected population by single year of age, sex, race, and Hispanic origin for the United States: July 1, 2000 to July 1, 2050. http://www.aoa.gov/AoARoot/ Aging_Statistics/future_growth/future_growth. aspx#hispanic.

U.S. Census Bureau. (2009a). 2009 National Population Projects (Supplemental). Available at: http://www. census.gov/population/www/projections/ 2009projections.html.

U.S. Census Bureau. (2009b). *Poverty thresholds by size of family and number of children*. Washington, DC: U.S. Government Printing Office. Available at: http://www.census.gov/hhes/www/poverty/ threshld.html.

U.S. Census Bureau. (2009c). National characteristics data. Table 4: Annual estimates of the Black or African American alone resident population by sex and age for the United States: April 1, 2000 to July 1, 2008; Table 2: Annual estimates of the resident population by sex and selected age groups for the United States: April 1, 2000 to July 1, 2008; Table 3. White alone or in combination population by age and sex: 2008.

U.S. Census Bureau. (2010). Current population survey. Available at: http://www.census.gov/cps/.

U.S. Census Bureau. (2011, June). International database, world population: 1950–2050. Available at: http://www.census.gov/population/international/ data/idb/worldpopgraph.php.

U.S. Census Bureau. (2012a). American fact finder. 2012 population estimates. Estimates of the components of resident population change: April 1, 2010 to July 1, 2012. Available at: http://fact-finder2.census.gov/faces/tableservices/jsf/pages/ productview.xhtml?pid=PEP_2012_ PEPTCOMP&prodType=table.

U.S. Census Bureau. (2012b). American profiles. Available at: http://www.census.gov/newsroom/ releases/archives/facts_for_features_special_ editions/cb12-ff09.html.

U.S. Census Bureau. (2012c). Americans with disabilities: 2010. Available at: http://www.census.gov/ prod/2012pubs/p70-131.pdf.

U.S. Census Bureau. (2012d). Child population: Number of children (in millions) ages 0–17 in the United States by age, 1950–2011 and projected 2012–2050; Available at: http://www.childstats.gov/americaschildren/tables/pop1.asp.

U.S. Census Bureau. (2012e). Current Population Survey (CPS), 2012 Annual Social and Economic Supplement (ASEC). Available at: http://www.census.gov/hhes/www/poverty/about/overview/index.html.

U.S. Census Bureau. (2012f). Estimates of the components of resident population change: April 1, 2010 to July 1, 2012. Available at: http://factfinder2.census.gov/faces/tableservices/jsf/pages/productview.xhtml?pid=PEP_2012_PEPAGESEX&prodType=table.

U.S. Census Bureau. (2012g). How the Census Bureau measures poverty; social, economic, and housing statistics division: Poverty. Available at: http://www.census.gov/hhes/www/poverty/about/overview/measure.html.

U.S. Census Bureau. (2012h). Most children younger than age 1 are minorities, Census Bureau reports. Available at: http://www.census.gov/popest/.

U.S. Census Bureau. (2012i). 2012 national population projections: Summary tables—Table 1. Available at: http://www.census.gov/population/projections/data/national/2012/summarytables.html.

U.S. Census Bureau. (2012j). Race Table 13. Poverty status of the population by sex and age, for Black alone and White alone, not Hispanic: 2010. Available at: http://www.census.gov/population/race/data/ppl-ba11.html.

U.S. Census Bureau. (2012k). The 2012 statistical abstract: The national data book. Population: Native and foreign-born populations by selected characteristics. Available at: http://www.census.gov/compendia/statab/cats/population/native_and_foreign-born_populations.html.

U.S. Census Bureau. (2012l, December 12). U.S. Census Bureau projections show a slower growing, older, more diverse nation a half century from now. Available at: https://www.census.gov/newsroom/releases/archives/population/cb12-243.html.

U.S. Census Bureau (2012m). The 2012 statistical abstract: Table 627. Unemployed and unemployment rates by educational attainment, sex, race, and Hispanic origin: 2000 to 2010. Available at: http://www.census.gov/compendia/statab/2012/tables/12s0627.pdf.

U.S. Census Bureau. (2013a). Monthly population estimates for the United States: April 1, 2010 to December 1, 2013. Available at: http://factfinder2.census.gov/faces/tableservices/jsf/pages/productview.xhtml?pid=PEP_2012_PEPMONTHN&prodType=table.

U.S. Census Bureau. (2013b). Poverty Thresholds [Data file]. Available from: http://www.census.gov/hhes/www/poverty/data/threshld/index.html.

U.S. Census Bureau. (2013c). Table 1. Projections of the population and components of change for the United States: 2015 to 2060. Available at: http://www.census.gov/population/projections/data/national/2012/summarytables.html.

U.S. Census Bureau. (2013d). World Population: Available at: http://www.census.gov/population/international/data/idb/worldpopgraph.php.

U.S. Department of Agriculture (USDA). (2012a, April). Building a healthy America: A profile of the Supplemental Nutrition Assistance Program. Available at: http://www.fns.usda.gov/ORA/menu/Published/SNAP/FILES/Other/BuildingHealthyAmerica.pdf.

U.S. Department of Agriculture (USDA). (2012b, December). WIC—The Special Supplemental Nutrition Program for women, infants and children. Available at: http://www.fns.usda.gov/wic/WIC-Fact-Sheet.pdf.

U.S. Department of Agriculture (USDA). (2013) SNAP: Non-citizen eligibility. Available at: http://www.fns.usda.gov/snap/mobile/eligibility/non-citizen-eligibility.html.

U.S. Department of Health and Human Services (USDHHS). (2011a). The AFCARS Report. Available at: http://www.acf.hhs.gov/sites/default/files/cb/afcarsreport19.pdf.

U.S. Department of Health and Human Services (USDHHS). (2011b). Children's Bureau, child maltreatment report, 2011. Available at: http://www.acf.hhs.gov/programs/cb/resource/child-maltreatment-2011.

U.S. Department of Health and Human Services (USDHHS). (2012a). Actuarial Report on the financial outlook for Medicaid. Available at: http://www.medicaid.gov/Medicaid-CHIP-Program-Information/By-Topics/Financing-and-Reimbursement/Downloads/medicaid-actuarial-report-2012.pdf.

U.S. Department of Health and Human Services (USDHHS). (2012b). Information on poverty and income statistics: A summary of 2012 current population survey data. Available at: http://aspe.hhs.gov/hsp/12/povertyandincomeest/ib.shtml.

U.S. Department of Health and Human Services (USDHHS). (2012c). Office of child support and enforcement, FY 2011 preliminary report. Available at: http://www.acf.hhs.gov/programs/css.

U.S. Department of Health and Human Services (USDHHS). (2013). Understanding health information privacy. Available at: http://www.hhs.gov/ocr/privacy/hipaa/understanding/index.html.

U.S. Department of Health, the Office of Minority Health. (2012, September 17). American Indian/Alaska Native profile. Available at: http://minorityhealth.hhs.gov/templates/browse.aspx?lvl=2&lvlid=52.

U.S. Department of Health, U.S. Department of the Interior, & U.S. Department of Justice. (2011). Indian alcohol and substance abuse memorandum of agreement. Available at: http://www.justice.gov/tribal/docs/tloa-iasa-memo-aug2011.pdf.

U.S. Department of Housing and Urban Development. (2013, May 3). HUD's Public Housing Program. Available at: http://portal.hud.gov/hudportal/HUD?src=/topics/rental_assistance/phprog.

U.S. Department of Justice. (2000). Introduction to federal voting rights laws. Available at: www.usdoj.gov/crt/voting/intro/intro_b.htm.

U.S. Department of Justice. (2011). Indian alcohol and substance abuse: Memorandum of agreement between U.S. Department of Health and Human Services, U.S. Department of the Interior, and U.S. Department of Justice. Available at: http://www.justice.gov/tribal/docs/tloa-iasa-memo-aug2011.pdf.

U.S. Department of Labor. (n.d.). Frequently asked questions about pension plans and ERISA. Available at: www.dol.gov.

U.S. Department of Labor. (2012, December 10). Unemployment insurance. Available at: http://workforcesecurity.doleta.gov/unemploy/uitax-topic.asp.

U.S. Department of the Treasury. (2013). The debt to the penny and who holds it. Available at: http://www.treasurydirect.gov/NP/debt/current.

U.S. Department of Veterans' Affairs. (2009). Facts about the Department of Veterans' Affairs. Available at: http://www1.va.gov/OPA/fact/docs/vafacts.pdf.

U.S. Department of Veterans' Affairs. (2013). Compensation. Available at: http://www.benefits.va.gov/COMPENSATION/index.asp.

U.S. Government Accountability Office (GAO). (2012). Concerns remain about appropriate services for children in Medicaid and foster care. Available at: http://www.gao.gov/assets/660/650716.pdf.

United Nations. (2011). Multidimensional Poverty Index (MPI). Available at: http://hdr.undp.org/en/statistics/mpi/.

University of California-Berkley. (2012). Black employment and unemployment. Retrieved from: http://laborcenter.berkeley.edu/blackworkers/monthly/bwreport_2012-09-07_52.pdf.

Van de Water, P. N., & Sherman, A. (2012, October 16). Social Security keeps 21 million Americans out of poverty: A state-by-state analysis. Available at: http://www.cbpp.org/cms/?fa=view&id=3851.

Waldfogel, J. (2000). Economic dimensions of social welfare policy. In J. Midgley, M. Tracy, & M. Livermore (Eds.), *The handbook of social policy* (pp. 27–40). Thousand Oaks, CA: Sage Publications.

Wan, L. (1999). Parents killing parents: Creating a presumption of unfitness. *Albany Law Review*, *63*(1), 333–359.

Weick, A. (1986). The philosophical context of a health model of social work. *Social Casework*, *67*(9), 551–559.

Weimer, D., & Vining, A. R. (1999). *Policy analysis: Concepts and practice* (3rd ed.). Upper Saddle River, NJ: Prentice Hall.

Weiss, R. J. (1997). *"We want jobs": A history of affirmative action*. New York: Garland Press.

Wheaton, L., & Sorenson, E. (2007). The potential impact of increasing child support payments to TANF families, Brief 5, the Urban Institute. Available at: http://www.urban.org/UploadedPDF/411595_child_support.pdf.

Wilensky, H. L., & Lebeaux, C. N. (1965). *Industrial society and social welfare: The impact of industrialization on the supply and organization of social welfare services in the United States*. New York: The Free Press.

Winograd, M., & Hais, M. (2008). *Millennial makeover: MySpace, YouTube, and the future of American politics*. New Jersey: Rutgers University Press.

Wolff, E. N. (2012). *The asset price meltdown and the wealth of the middle class*. New York: New York University.

Zerbe, R., & McCurdy, H. (2000). The end of market failure. *Regulation, 23*(2), 10–14.

Zhan, M. (2003). *Saving outcomes of single mothers in Individual Development Accounts*. St. Louis, MO: Center for Social Development.

Zinn, A. (2009). Foster family characteristics, kinship, and permanence. *Social Services Review, 83*, 185–219.

Credits

Exhibit 1.2 : Source: Adapted from "Social policy development: The strengths perspective," by R. Chapin, 40, 4, pp. 506–514. Copyright © 1995 National Association or Social Workers, Inc.

Quick Guide 1: Source: Adapted from "Social policy development: The strengths perspective," by R. Chapin. Social Work, 40, 4, pp. 506–514. Copyright © 1995 by National Association of Social Workers, Inc. Used with permission of NASW. Based on the work of Chambers, 2000; Gilbert and Terrell, 1998; and Tice & Perkins, 2002.

Exhibit 2.1: Courtesy of Roger Evans

Exhibit 2.3: Reference: The Social Welfare History Project; retrieved from http://www.socialwelfare-history.com/organizations/childrens-aid-society-of-new-york/

Exhibit 2.4: Reference: E. Franklin Frazier. (2000). Howard University, Social Work Library. Retrieved Nov 14, 2012 from http://www.howard.edu/library/social_work_library/Franklin_Frazier.htm

Exhibit 3.2: Source: Library of Congress, George Grantham Bain Collection

Exhibit 3.3: Source: Library of Congress, Harris & Ewing Collection

Exhibit 3.4: Source: Library of Congress, Harris & Ewing Collection

Exhibit 3.5 Howard J Miller produced for Westinghouse for the War Production Coordinating Committee, NARA Still Pictures Branch. © Corbis. Used with Permission.

Exhibit 3.6: Gene Herrick, Photographer, February 22, 1956, © Associated Press

Exhibit 3.7: September 24, 1965, Delano, CA, Grape Strike, Dolores Huerta, © Paul Richards Harvey Richards Media Archive

Exhibit 3.8: Reference: Indian child welfare act is her legacy. (1998). NASW NEWS Retrieved Nov 13, 2012 from http://www.socialworkers.org/profession/centennial/manning.htm

Exhibit 3.10: The Center on Budget and Policy Priorities: www.cbpp.org

Exhibit 4.1: © Albert Duce, used by creative commons attribution license. References: http://www.wsws.org/en/articles/2010/03/whit-m25.html; http://www.huffingtonpost.com/2011/03/23/detroit-decline_n_813696.html#218521; http://www.treehugger.com/culture/detroit-all-its-faded-and-decayed-glory.html

Exhibit 4.2: Source: Congressional Budget Office, Washington DC: U.S. Government Printing Office. Note: Percentages may not total 100 due to rounding.

Exhibit 4.3: Source: The Budget and Economic Outlook: Fiscal Years 2012 to 2022. Congressional Budget Office. 2012. Washington DC; US Government Printing Office. http://www.cbo.gov/publication/42905

Exhibit 4.4: © Center on Budget and Policy Priorities: www.cbpp.org

Exhibit 4.5: Source: Tax Policy Center, http://decision evidence.com/2012/09/yes-mrs-calabash-redistribution-is-occurring-from-the-bottom-up. Posted September 22, 2012 by Michael Morrison; Title: "Yes, Mrs. Calabash, Redistribution is Occuring: From the Bottom Up"

Exhibit 4.6: © Center on Budget and Policy Priorities: www.cbpp.org

Exhibit 4.7: © Center on Budget and Policy Priorities: www.cbpp.org

Exhibit 4.8: Source: "OECD Factbook 2009" Organisation for Economic Co-operations and Development. The OECD Database. Paris: OECD. www.oecd.org.

Exhibit 7.2: Cesar Estrada Chavez and Dolores Huerta at End of Hunger Strike, 1968 © William James Warren

Exhibit 7.3: 1960 © Assocated Press

Exhibit 7.4: Library of Congress via New York World-Telegram and the Sun staff, John Bottega photographer, 1963

Exhibit 7.7: Courtesy of Lily Ledbetter

Exhibit 7.8: Source: Cartoon Source: Copyright © 2003 Mike Keefe. All rights reserved. Used with permission of Cagle Cartoons. www.caglecartoons.com

Exhibit 7.9: Source: Adapted from "Major features of the Civil Rights Act of 1964," by CongressLink, n.d. www.congresslink.org/civil/essay.html. Copyright 2004 Dirksen Congressional Center. Used with permission.

Exhibit 7.10: Source: From "Introduction to federal voting rights laws," by U.S. Department of Justice, 2000. www.usdoj.gov.

Exhibit 7.11: Source: From "Education for All Handicapped Children Act of 1975." Pub. L. 94–142, s. 6.

Exhibit 7.12: Source: From "ADA Homepage," by U.S. Department of Justice, 2004. www.ada.gov.

Exhibit 7.13: Source: Adapted from information found in Congressional Research Service. (2005). Violence Against Women Act: History and Federal Funding. Washington, D.C.: The Library of Congress

Exhibit 7.14: Source: Adapted from National Women's Law Center. (2009). Lilly Ledbetter Fair Pay Act. Washington, D.C. accessed at http://www.nwlc.org/fairpay/ledbetterfairpayact.html

Exhibit 8.1: Source: Social Security Administration, Master Beneficiary Record, 100 percent data.

Exhibit 8.5: Source: Center on Budget and Policy Priorities (2012) Policy Basics: An Introduction to TANF; Available at: http://www.cbpp.org/cms/?fa=view&id=936

Exhibit 8.8: © Steve Jacobs

Exhibit 8.11: Center on Budget and Policy Priorities (CBPP). Web address for chart: http://www.cbpp.org/files/policybasics-eitc.pdf

Exhibit 8.12: Source: DeNavas-Walt, Carmen, Bernadette D. Proctor, and Jessica C. Smith, U.S. Census Bureau, Current Population Reports, P60-243, Income, Poverty, and Health Insurance Coverage in the United States: 2011, U.S. Government Printing Office, Washington, DC,

2012. Available at: http://www.census.gov/prod/2012pubs/p60-243.pdf

Exhibit 8.13: Reference: Center on Budget and Policy Priorities (2013) Chart Book: SNAP Helps Struggling Families Put Food On The Table, Available at: http://www.cbpp.org/cms/index.cfm?fa=view&id=3744

Exhibit 9.2: Source: http://www.pewhispanic.org/files/reports/85.pdf

Exhibit 9.3: Source: HHS 2012 – ASPE report. Available: http://aspe.hhs.gov/hsp/12/povertyandincomeest/ib.shtml

Exhibit 9.4: © Children's Defense Fund

Exhibit 9.7: © Sergei Bachlakov

Exhibit 9.13: © Monkey Business Images

Exhibit 10.1: © ranplett

Exhibit 10.8: © Slobodan Vasic

Exhibit 10.10: © Miodrag Gajic

Exhibit 10.14: © Slobodan Vasic

Exhibit 10.15: © Miodrag Gajic

Exhibit 11.2: © Administration on aging

Exhibit 11.3: © Catherine Yeulet

Exhibit 11.5: Source: Data from Demographic Trends in the 20th Century: Census 2000 Special Reports, by F. Hobbs & N. Stoops, 2002. Washington, D.C.: U.S. Government Printing Office. http://www.census.gov/prod/2002pubs/censr-4.pdf.

Exhibit 11.6: Source: United States Census Bureau

Exhibit 11.7: Source: Adapted from "A layman's guide to the Older Americans Act," by Administration on Aging, 2004. www.aoa.gov.

Exhibit 11.8: Source: Adapted from "Frequently asked questions about pension plans and ERISA," by U.S. Department of Labor, n.d. www.dol.gov.

Exhibit 11.10: Source: Adapted from Federal Interagency Forum on Aging-Related Statistics (2012)

Exhibit 11.11: Source: Health and Retirement Study. This table originally appeared as Indicator 19 Depressive Symptoms, in Federal Interagency Forum on Aging-Related Statistics (2012). Older Americans 2012: Key Indicators of Well-Being. Federal Interagency Forum on Aging-Related Statistics. Washington, DC: U.S. Government Printing Office

Exhibit 12.1: Source: U.S. Census Bureau, International Data Base, June 2011 Update

Exhibit 12.2: Source: United States Census Bureau

able-bodied poor 38, 87
abolitionist movement 45–6
abortion: and cultural conservatives 136; gag rule 101, 106; legalization of 90; rights/G. W. Bush 106–7
absolute poverty refers to a measure of who is poor whereby the government determines an objective income level threshold or *poverty line*, 309
abuse *see also* child abuse; child maltreatment; child protection; neglect: elders/older adults 148, 275, 490, 491; physical 363, 368; prevention 148, 373, 490; reporting systems 372; sexual 369
academic success, and juvenile delinquency 398
access: and Affordable Care Act 458, 462; to college education 350; equal/to public accommodations 79; to health care/and employment 449; health care/Medicaid 425–6; immigrants to services 131; to key actors 228; to mental health services 441, 446, 478
accidents, children in poverty 361
accreditation standards, CSWE 6
acculturation, forced 376
Acquired Immune Deficiency Syndrome (AIDS) 420, 454–5
action planning, policy practice 237–8
action plans: advocacy 194; affirmative 93, 280; getting back into workforce 131; policy practice 236–8, 243; sample 244–6; social 458
activism: and altruism 180; and G. H. W. Bush 99; Native Americans 90, 91; political 235–6, 240–1, 546; potential impact of 216; and social media 541, 548; students 235–6; working class 163
activist role, federal government 76
activists: African American civil rights 78; anti-slavery 46; citizen 547, 551; clinicians 7; social workers as 540; women 59, 64; women's rights 89
Activities of Daily Living (ADL) limitations 428
Act of Congress 1871 46
Act of Settlement of 1662 39, 42

acute care, Medicare 428
Adams, Abigail 43
Adams, John 43
adaptation, and forecasts 519
Adarand Constructors vs. *Peña* 280
Addams, Jane 55, 56, 60, 68, 363
addiction *see* substance abuse
adequacy refers to the ability of social welfare programs to address and sufficiently meet the needs of the general public, of income/social programs 154, 155–6
Administration for Children and Families (ACF) 384
Administration for Community Living (ACL) 486–7
Administration for Children and Families (ACF) 391
Administration on Aging (AOA) 486–7
Administration on Children, Youth and Families 392
Administration on Developmental Disabilities 487
adolescents, transition to adulthood 384
adoption: improving 377; incentives to states 382; interracial 379; Native American children 92; numbers of 391; permanency/concurrent planning 392; policies to increase 381; privatization 384; provided by religious organizations 105; Social Security Act 1935 363; and special/complex needs 382; state programs 372; transracial 380
Adoption and Safe Families Act (ASFA) 1997 amended the Adoption Assistance and Child Welfare Act (AACWA) of 1980 to emphasize child safety and the best interests of children and to promote permanency, 381–3, 386, 390–1
Adoption Assistance and Child Welfare Act (AACWA) 1980 is federal legislation that established permanency planning as a major goal of the child welfare system through family reunification, family preservation, and adoption, 377–8, 381, 386, 391

Adult Protective Services 490–1

advance directive is a document or statement by patients specifying choices for medical treatment or designating a person to make those choices should the patient be unable to do so, 275, 414, 501

advocacy: Asian American groups 267; assessing risks/benefits 541; on behalf of immigrants 293; child and adult abuse 491; children with special needs 388; civil rights 79; and discrimination 305; groups/working with 226; for homeless people 181; for LGBTQ youths 270; Native American organizations 264; and people with disabilities 272; policy 229; and policy practice 7–8; and public recognition of social problems 169; and social media 238; social policy 547; and social workers 201; of students 236, 327, 389, 459, 549; training for clients 239

affirmative action is a general term that refers to policies and programs designed to compensate for discrimination against marginalized groups such as women and people of color, 93–4, 279–81, 305; challenging/G. W. Bush 106–7; and education 94; and employment 93; failure of 292; and Supreme Court 99, 112, 280; threats to 277

Affordable Care Act 2010 417–19 see also Patient Protection and Affordable Care Act 2010; and CHIP 434; contraception 68, 129; cost of 151; and discrimination in health care 539; evaluation of 551; mental health parity 446; and Obama 111, 117; resistance to 110; rules 548; and tribal communities 265

affordable care organizations 451

African Americans: in child protection system 390; children in foster care 361, 380; children in population 365; children in poverty 257, 336–7, 367; civil rights 50, 77–80, 261–3; discrimination 51, 261–3; education 122; elected positions/seats in Congress 50–1; employment 51; incarceration 292; inequitable treatment of/juvenile justice system 370; and Jim Crow laws 51, 76, 78–9; life expectancies of 345; mental health services 441; mothers claiming AFDC 83; net worth/recession 292; organizations of 59; post Reconstruction 51; poverty 51, 292, 320; and racism 56; rights of 45, 51; and Settlement House Movement 55; suffrage to male 50; treatment/after Civil War 50; treatment of/Independence to civil war 45–6; unemployment 263, 292

age discrimination 299

Age Discrimination in Employment Act (ADEA) 274, 478

ageism is discrimination based on age, usually directed towards older adults, but often towards children as well, 256; compassionate 274; and mandatory retirement 478; in Medicare 451–3; and oppressed groups 255; policies/practices 502

agency analysis 300

agency-level policy practice 234

agendas, getting on 223–6

age-sensitive community infrastructures 508

aging see also aging well: and poverty 485–6; productive 496; U.S. population 481, 527

Aging and Disability Resource Centers (ADRCs) 487

aging in the community means that an older adult with disabilities is able to maintain residence in the community rather than enter a nursing facility, 485–6

aging in place means that an older adult with disabilities is able to maintain residence in the community rather than enter a nursing facility, 485

aging well is a "comprehensive and holistic process in which older adults adapt self and the environment to respond actively to the challenges of aging" (Kahana & Kahana, 1996): barriers to 487; defined 472–3; policies to support 510, 512; and social engagement 501, 502; and social policy 471; supporting 505; theories of 504–5

agrarian economy, Early Middle Ages 36

agricultural economy 126

agricultural sector, Hispanics/Latinos 265

agricultural workers, wages of 80

agriculture, decline of/Middle Ages (Eng.) 37

aid: to control unrest 86; during Great Depression 70; mutual aid 35

Aid to Dependent Children (ADC) 73

Aid to Families with Dependent Children (AFDC) 73, 83, 97, 100, 101, 321

Alabama, protest march/Selma to Montgomery 283

Alaskan Natives: health care 265; poverty 93

Alcatraz Island, occupation of/Native Americans 91, 263

Alcohol, Drug Abuse, and Mental Health block grant 444

alien nations, Indian tribes as 50

Alito, Samuel 106

alliances, LGBTQ/immigrant populations 291

almshouses were institutions for poor people supported by private funds, and they were reserved for the "worthy poor," particularly elders, 39, 42

altruism: and activism 180; institutionalizing 128

Alzheimer's disease 477

Amendments to the Americans with Disabilities Act (AADA) 2008 288
American Association of Social Workers (AASW) 71
American Express Company 474
American Indian Movement (AIM) 91, 263
American Indians, child poverty rate 337 *see also* Native Americans
American Psychiatric Association (APA) 269
American Recovery and Reinvestment Act 2009 317, 334, 340
American Red Cross 67
American Revolution, social welfare policy 43–4
Americans with Disabilities Act (ADA) 1990 10, 100, 117, 272, 286–7, 305
American Taxpayer Relief Act 2013 334
America's Law Enforcement and Mental Health Project Act 2000 444
amicus curiae briefs 235
analysis: social problem 9; of strengths/resources 9
analytical skills, of social workers 220, 228
Annie E. Casey Foundation 163, 256
anti-bullying laws, and LGBTQ students 303
anti-discrimination laws 62, 337
anti-discrimination policies, children/older adults 299
Anti-Drug Abuse Act 1988 454
anti-poverty policy, moral reform as 54
anti-poverty programs 75, 82–3, 84, 86, 87
anxiety, and older adults 478
appeals processes, patients 415, 459
appropriation bills 140
Arab Americans, discrimination 293
Area Agencies on Aging (AAAs) 487, 492, 508, 511
Area Redevelopment Act 1961 82
Arizona, voter I.D. laws 284
Asian Americans: child poverty rate 337; civil rights 267–8; as model minority 267; population 268
assessment(s): dual assessment 7, 23, 201, 242, 511; environmental factors 540
asset accumulation, low-income families 343, 347, 347–8, 349, 350, 351, 352
asset-based approaches, poverty 102
asset-based policies 347–54, 356
asset-based reform 351–2
asset-building policies 348
asset inequality 121
asset limits, negative outcomes of 343
asset poverty 308–9, 348
assets: and eligibility/Medicaid 422; and eligibility requirements 348; to fund education/training 350; term 347

Assets and the Poor: A New American Welfare Policy 348
asset tests: and economic insecurity 190, 216; SNAP 327, 339; SSI program 331
assimilation, of Native Americans 91
assisted dying legislation 501
assumptions: and claims-making 183–5; and forecasts 520–3
attorney, durable power of 500
autonomy, supporting client's 21
awareness raising 238

baby boomers 113, 143, 313, 431, 451, 481, 483, 496, 512, 538
Bakke, Allan 279–80
Balanced Budget Act 1997 326, 424, 429, 433
Baltes, P. B. and Baltes, M. M. 504
base-line data: data collected to understand the condition of the target group prior to an intervention, 233
basic income grant (BIG) 351
basic needs, meeting/institutional approaches 125
basic needs perspective, poverty 308
battered child syndrome 363 *see also* child abuse
Battered Immigrant Women's Protection Act 2000 289
begging, Middle Ages 37, 38
behavioral health benefits 446
behavior, choice-oriented 549
beliefs: causes of poverty 170; own/and policy practice 223; traditional/conservative 136
Benefit Guaranty Corporation 513
benefits: barriers to access 496; cash/TANF 322; eligibility requirements 459; lack of/part-time workers 537; and Lawful Permanent Residents (LPR) 325; and legal immigrants 101, 341; linked to obligations 131; means-tested 89; non-cash and poverty 311; policy analysis of 189–90; and proof of citizenship 297; reduced/under G. W. Bush 105; retired workers 315; and stigmatization 189; time-limited benefits/unemployed people 131; and undocumented immigrants 296; and work requirements 87, 89, 131, 551; younger disabled people 427
best practice, rolling out of 233
bicameral legislature 139
Biden, Joe 120
Bill of Rights 1791 44, 260
biopsychosocial approach, health model 461

birth certificates, and eligibility rules 297
birth control: Affordable Care Act 2010 129, 277; non-voluntary 540
birth control clinics 69
birth rates: falling/Caucasian Americans 113; to single mothers 104, 365
Bismark, Otto von 474
black communities, self-help organizations 45
black families, and child welfare system 390
black power 86
black separatism 86
blame, patients for health care costs 453
block grants are funds made available by the federal government where much of the decision-making authority about how the money is to be spent is allocated to the states (Kenney, 1981), 97; community mental health services 448; federal support in form of 146; mental health centers 447; substance abuse services 445; TANF 322 326, 338, 356
Brace, Charles Loring 52, 53
Bracero Program 80
Bridges, Ruby 261
Brill, Steven 456
Brown vs. Board of Education of Topeka 77, 122, 261
Buck v. Bell 442
Buddhism, and social welfare 31
budget cuts, and economic recession 146
budget deficits 89
budgets: federal 142, 164; federal/state 139–40
bullying, LGBTQ students 302–3
Bureau of Indian Affairs (BIA) 46, 91, 92
Bureau of Public Assistance 11
Bureau of Public Assistance of the Social Security Board 70
Bush, George H. W. 96, 99–100
Bush, George W. 103, 104–7, 150–1, 346, 476–7, 494
business interests, and taxation 146

California, and same-sex marriage 112, 271
campaign funding, and policy agenda 208
Canon Law 37
capabilities perspective, poverty 308, 355
capacity building approach 75, 164; families 388, 396, 404, 536; Obama 107; and people/infrastructure 115; and safety net programs 537; social policy 129, 544; TANF 341; wealth redistribution 545
capacity building state focuses on strengthening the skills, competencies, and abilities of people and communities and on helping them secure the resources and support needed for full economic and social inclusion, 103, 107, 109, 130–3, 164, 308, 355
capacity, illustrating 225
capitalism: industrial 127; laissez-faire 33; maintenance of capitalism hypothesis 127–8; Progressive Era 58; and social inequality 135; and social policy 121; and social welfare policies 113, 131; welfare 128
capitated approach is a strategy for providing health care under which an HMO or managed care provider is expected to provide all elements of health care covered in the enrollee's contract in return for a fixed monthly or annual payment per person enrolled, 415
CAPTA Reauthorization Act 2010 372
caregivers: family/long-term care 480; grandparents as 496; informal 492; intergenerational 496; recognizing younger 508; supporting 538; women/and work requirements 535–6; women as 277, 508
care, informal 485, 492
caretaker grants 73
caring: for children 321, 336; for children/older adults 344; compensation for 538
Carmichael, Stokely 86
Carter, Jimmy 89, 136
case review, child welfare/social justice system 397
case-to-cause 7
casework, as field within social working 56
casework services, to displaced veterans/families 67–8
cash benefits, TANF 322
casino income, Native Americans tribes 265
categorical grants are funds made available by the federal government which strictly regulated what programs the funds could be used for and stipulated how the monies could be spent for specific programs such as community development services, mental health, alcohol and drug abuse, social services and maternal and child health services, 97
Catholic immigrants, discrimination against 53
Catt, Carrie Chapman 68
causal theories: and research 196; social problems 180–2
cause marketing 238
causes, common 291
cellphone applications, and use of in mental/physical illness 529
Census Bureau 311, 520, 521
centenarians are people who are age 100 and over, 483

Center for Medicare and Medicaid Innovation (CMI) is the federal agency that administers both Medicare and Medicaid, 437

Centers for Disease Control (CDC) 394

Centers for Medicare and Medicaid Services (CMS) 410, 431–2, 464, 487

Chafee Foster Care Independence Program (CFCIP) funds 377

Chafee Foster Care Independent Living Act 1999 384

Chambers, D. E. 186

change: and African American social workers 56; and economic crises 11; incremental/radical 240; process/client involvement 7; successful 236; transformative 542

change agents 240

charitable contributions 148

charity: and Christianity 32; informed by science 54, 55; as religious duty 32; and stigmatization 32; views of 29

Charity Organization Society (COS) 54

charting for dollars 161

Chavez, Cesar 80, 258, 259

Cherokee nation 46

Cherokee Nation vs. *Georgia* 46, 50, 90, 263

child abuse *see also* child maltreatment; child protection; neglect: battered child syndrome 363; and drug abuse 392; funding of 148; and poverty 404; prevention 148, 372–3; rates of 391; reporting systems 391; risk factors 391; and social policy 3–4; and stress 367, 391

Child Abuse Prevention and Treatment Act (CAPTA) 1974 is the legislation that provided federal funds to states to develop reporting systems for investigations of abuse and neglect, 88, 372–3, 373, 386, 403

Child and Family Services Improvement Act 2006 379

Child and Family Services Improvement and Innovation Act 2011 379

child care: as community strength 13; lack of/and poverty 102; lack of funding for 98; need for 536; and TANF 323, 324; and women in workforce 336

Child Development Accounts (CDAs) 352, 357, 545

child development programs 361

child/family allowance 87

childhood deaths, reduction of/and Medicaid 419

child hunger 195–6, 244–5, 362

child labor 61

child maltreatment is serious harm (neglect, physical abuse, sexual abuse, and emotional abuse or neglect) caused to children by parents or primary caregivers, such as extended family members or babysitters (Child Abuse Prevention and Treatment Act, 1974): *see also* child abuse; child protection; neglect: defined 367; numbers suffering 391; and poverty 366–7, 367; and stress 367; term 403

Child Nutrition Act 4, 7

child population, U.S. 364

child poverty *see* poverty

child poverty rate 158, 320, 336

child protection *see also* child abuse; child maltreatment; neglect: African Americans in system 390; federal government responsibility for 58; history/background 363; laws 61; national standard for 88; policy paradigms 390; policy/strengths perspective 390–7

Child Protective Services (CPS) 367

children *see also* child abuse: as able-bodied poor 87; anti-discrimination policies 299; bearing brunt of cuts 146; in care 381; child fatalities 391; claims on behalf of 183; of color/foster care 380; of color/ health disparities 360; of color/raised in white homes 380; criminalization of 398; demographics 403; with disability/institutionalization 257; with disability/restraint and exclusion 387; educational disabilities 398; educational gap 536; and EITC 334; and families today 364–70; in foster care 360–1; foster care/mental health issues 388; foster care/ negative outcomes 383; foster children/challenges facing 4; health care 102, 109; health/education and class divisions 132; health insurance 433; laws/ working conditions 59; lump-sum payments at birth 351; marginalization of vulnerable 400; and Medicaid 419; and mental illness 388, 446; Native American/initiatives to protect 264; Native American/removed from families 92; outcomes for/ ethnic group 256; poverty 73, 96, 113, 122, 279, 337, 360–1; poverty/race disparities 366; programs to support 59; reunification with families 381, 382, 388, 392, 403; self-determination 299; services to 131; and social welfare system 4–5; special needs 388, 404; as TANF recipients 322; of teen mothers 393; uninsured 432, 449; use of psychotropic medications 465; as worthy poor 52

Children's Aid Society (CAS) 52, 53

Children's Bureau 391

Children's Health Insurance Program 109, 432–4

Children's Health Insurance Program Reauthorization Act (CHIPRA) 433

children's programs 361, 362–4

Child-Saving Movement 52–3, 63
child savings accounts 352
child saving v. family saving 377
child support, collecting 387
child-support enforcement legislation 122
Child Support Enforcement Program (CSE) 384–5
child support programs, states 387
child welfare: and growing poverty 366–7; initiatives 52, 60–1, 88; Native Americans 91; outcomes 390; policies 361, 364, 389, 402; services 361, 368, 370, 372, 395
child welfare system "The child welfare system is a group of services designed to promote the wellbeing of children by ensuring safety, achieving permanency, and strengthening families to successfully care for their children" (National Clearinghouse on Child Abuse and Neglect, 2003), 367–8; case review 397; and family preservation 377; and social justice 389; social workers role 399; and social work profession 362; and substance abuse 390
child welfare workers, impact of privatization on 396
Chinese language 267
choice-oriented behavior 549
Christianity, and social welfare 32
chronic conditions, and Medicare 428, 432
cities, 19c. growth of 48
citizen activists 547, 551
citizens: engaged 113; responsibility of 130
citizenship: and communitarians 137; denial of 266; and eligibility for benefits 131; proof of 297; and social rights 128; and voting 284
Citizens United vs. *Federal Election Commission* 110
civic engagement, older adults 502
Civilian Conservation Corps (CCC) 70
civil liberties: and Patriot Act 294; v. security 294
civil rights 254, 303; African Americans 50, 77–80, 261–3; background/history of 255–60; black/coalitions with white liberal groups 77; federal/state responsibility for 280; gay rights demonstrations 99; under G. W. Bush 105; Hispanic Americans struggle for 80–1; Hispanics/Latinos 265–7; and immigrants 305; laws 79–80; laws/protected classes 299; LGBTQ community 268–71; and Medicare/Medicaid 413, 464; monitoring enforcement 299; movement 78, 305; Native Americans 90–3, 263–5; in New Nation 43–4; next steps 295–301; non-citizens 305; older adults 274–6, 304; people with disabilities 272–4, 304; people with mental illness 273, 444; policies/programs 260–1, 291–6; protests 78; and religious

leaders 304; struggle 59, 77–80; threats to 293–5; violent opposition/to advocates 79; and women 89, 276–9
Civil Rights Act 1964 79, 93, 98, 261, 274, 281–3
Civil Rights Act 1991 99, 282
Civil Rights Restoration Act 1987 281–2
Civil War: and aftermath 50–2; and pensions 474
Civil Works Administration (CWA) 70
claims: and social justice 182–3; workers' compensation 318–19
claims-making is work done by concerned individuals and groups to make the case to policy makers, key actors, and the public at large that resources should be allocated to meet a recognized need, 13–14, 182–5, 197; bases for 183; groups involved in/policy development 206–7; involving target population 184; and legislative agenda 207; and morality 183; and policy development 204, 205–9; publicizing 226; and students 206; working with others 226
CLASS *see* Community Living Assistance Services and Supports (CLASS)
class: and health/education of children 132; and health status/outcomes 460; middle/and policy initiatives 536; middle/and unemployment 536; and poverty 307; and tax entitlements 153–4
classic conservatives, laissez-faire economics 134, 135, 136
classism 299
Clayton Antitrust Act 1914 58
client groups: the population that is the primary focus of a social policy or program—the terms "service users" and "target group" also refer to the population, *see also* client(s); service users: supporting/policy practice 239; term 3
client involvement *see also* consumer involvement: change process 7; claims-making 13; decision making 296; evaluation of TANF 335; identifying policy options 227; implementation of policy 214–15; policy change 201; policy development 15; policy evaluation 215; in resource allocation 162
client–legislator interaction, facilitating 227
client outcomes *see* outcomes
client(s): expanding role of 12–13; problems/deficits of 11, 14; strengths/goals of 14, 20; strengths/resources of 11; term 3
clients' perspectives 12; incorporating/in policy analysis 188–9; policy development 14; policy goals 227–8
climate change 111, 114, 160, 532

climate justice 540–1
clinicians, activist 7
Clinton, Bill 100–1, 417
Cloward, Richard 86
Code of Ethics (2008): core values 5–6; and diversity 254–5; and equal rights 295; and future social policy 550; and mission of social work 3; and policy practice 19, 217; sharing electronic client data 542; strengths approach 524; and vision of future 546
coercion, protecting patients from 540
Coit, Stanton 55
collective approach, Native American religions 31–2
College Savings Plans 349
colonial era, social welfare policy 41–3
Common Human Needs 10–11, 70
common human needs 73
communicability, of policy alternatives 212
communication, electronic 529
communism, fear of 294
communitarians advance a political philosophy that seeks a middle ground between liberal and conservative traditions and emphasizes responsibility to community, 137
community action programs (CAPs) 84
community assets, as enabling niches 219
community-based care: juvenile offenders 398; long-term care 513; Medicaid waivers 420
community health centers, funding 437
community(ies): aging in the 485–6; cost of maintaining clients in 231; identifying strengths of 205; maintaining disabled people in 272; and social media 536; and social welfare 137; strengths/resources of 189
community inclusion, older adults/disabled people 487
Community Living Assistance Services and Supports (CLASS) 418, 490, 513
Community Mental Health Act 1975 amendments 447, 478
community mental health care 442–5
community mental health centers 82, 98, 447
community mental health movement 443
community mental health services 448, 465
community strength, child care as 13
community systems, influencing 547
compassionate ageism 274
compassion, natural/Confusianism 31
competitiveness, national/and gender gap 276
complex needs, and foster care/adoption 382

compromising 239
computers, access to 504, 542 *see also* Internet
concurrent planning provides states with the option of working on an alternative plan for children receiving protective services even while it is attempting reunification (Adler, 2001), 382
confidentiality: of clients 225, 227, 401; and technology 529, 541
conflict: conflict theory 295; intergenerational 114, 496, 505; over resources 532; resolution/and policy practice 13
confrontational strategies 239
Confusianism, and social welfare 31
Congress 139, 140
Congressional Budget Office 431
Connecting Generations 507
consensus building, and policy practice 13
consensus-oriented approaches 240
consent, of clients/change efforts 239
conservative agenda, implementing 96–7
conservative movement, and role of state 108
conservative politics 95, 134, 135–7
constitutionalism, and classic conservatives 136
Constitution, the 43–4; 13th Amendment 50; 14th Amendment 50, 50–1, 77, 78, 269, 287; 15th Amendment 50, 80; 16th Amendment 59; 18th Amendment 64, 67; 19th Amendment 59, 67, 68; 24th Amendment 80, 283; amendments to 44; Bill of Rights 1791 260; and civil rights protection 305; and general welfare 130; Reconstruction Amendments 50
consumer-directed services, Medicaid 499
consumer involvement, policy/program design 204 *see also* client involvement
consumer protection, federal responsibility for 58
consumer-side economics 133–4
contraception: advice/transition plans 395; Affordable Care Act 2010 129; and health insurance plans 68
Contract with America 101–2
convergence is the growing similarity of countries in challenges faced and policies enacted over time, 531, 547, 552
co-occurring conditions 445
core values *see also* values: reconsidering 544–6; self-determination 6, 14, 529; social-justice 6; social work 5–6, 173, 504
corporal punishment 400
corporate policy makers, and economic status 159

corporations: investing in human capital/social welfare 136; lack of trust in 123; limiting size/power of 58; power of 159, 182; tax breaks 151, 182
cost-benefit analysis 230, 242
cost-effectiveness, analyzing 192, 193–4, 230–1, 242
cost-of-living adjustment (COLA) 89
cost(s): analyzing 230–1; control/health care 414–16, 464, 509; control/Patient Protection and Affordable Care Act 2010 438–40; of failure/analysing 231; health care 145, 410–12, 414–16, 431–2, 450, 451, 456, 464, 509, 512; of means testing 190; Medicaid 423; Medicare 432, 440; of not implementing policies 230; of policy alternatives 211; prescription drugs 430, 451; privatized social services 543; publicly provided/privatized services 544; to taxpayers/analyzing 231; of wars 111, 144, 145; of welfare rolls 83, 86
Council on Social Work Education (CSWE): establishment of 77; standards 6
counseling, long-term 397
courses, for/about African Americans 58
court system 139
creative thinking skills 120
crime: 16th C. (Eng) 38; hate crimes 257, 269, 290, 293, 304; juvenile 369, 397
criminalization of children 398
criminal justice system, children in adult 375
crises, effects of see economic crises
crisis: families in perpetual 397; as opportunity for change 226
crisis intervention: families 361; training 387
crisis nurseries 396
critical thinking skills 19
Crow, Jim 51, 76, 78–9
cultural conservatives 136
cultural contexts, of practice/policies 531
cultural differences: and effectiveness of services 300; end-of-life preferences 500
cultural genocide 376
culturally competent services 399, 457
culture change movement, nursing homes 498
culture(s): of clients 300; culturally competent services 399, 457; and Native Americans 91, 92, 264–5, 376; very early 35
custodial care, people with mental illness 442
cuts, home-and community-based services 498

Daughters of Bilitis 269
Dawes Act 1887 46–7, 90, 263
death penalty, juvenile criminals 370
deaths, premature/and poverty 360
Death with Dignity campaigns 501
debt, of America 111, 145, 147, 164
decision agenda 207
decision making, client involvement 296
de facto segregation refers to segregation caused due to social practices, political acts or economic circumstances but not by actual laws. For example, disproportionate numbers of people of color continue to live in inner-city and other isolated low-income neighborhoods with segregated schools and severely limited job opportunities, 291
Defense of Marriage Act (DOMA) 112, 270
defense spending 100, 105, 184
Deferred Action for Childhood Arrivals (DACA) 293
deficit, following Iraq 494
Deficit Reduction Act (DRA) 2005 325
deficits approach 174, 175
defined benefit/defined contribution approach, Medicare 456
defined benefit plans are pension plans under which the retiree is paid a specific amount every month if the retired person has worked the required number of years, 474, 476, 477, 489
defined contribution plans are pension plans whereby employers contribute a certain amount to a retirement account that the employee can then invest in company-approved fund options. Unlike defined benefit plans, defined contribution plans do not guarantee a specific amount of retirement income, 149, 476, 477
defining target client population, policy practice 221–3
deindustrialization is the process whereby less skilled manufacturing jobs have moved to countries where wages are lower, 131, 350
deinstitutionalization refers to the policy of providing community-based services for people with disabilities who were formerly served in institutions, 443, 465; of juvenile offenders 374; people with mental illness 82, 98, 124, 273, 442–5, 447
demand, for services 1
demand-side: economics 133–4
demand-side economics 133–4
democratic ideals, reform to return to 58

Democratic Leadership Council (DLC) 100
Democratic Party, and bill of rights 44
democratic political system 43
democratic representation, underrepresented
communities 295
democratic socialism is a system of political/
economic thought which posits that because
capitalism is predicated on the pursuit of individual
self-interest and profit, it inevitably increases social
inequality and therefore cannot be relied on to
advance the public good in a democracy 134–5
Democrats, New 100
demogrant is a uniform payment to certain categories
of persons identified only by demographic (usually
age) characteristics, 88
demographics *see also* population: analyzing 223; and
forecasts 520–1; influence of 481–5
dental services, CHIP 433
Department of Agriculture 328
Department of Health and Human Services (USDHHS)
see U.S. Department of Health and Human Services
(USDHH)
Department of Homeland Security 110, 294
Department of Housing and Urban Development
(HUD) 176, 193, 329
Department of Labor 60
Department of Veterans' Affairs (VA) 320
dependent child, defined 73
deportation 110, 266; self-deport 293
depression, older adults 478, 499
deprivation, as denial of human rights 296
deserving poor 38
destitution, as indicator of individual deficits 73
Detroit, deindustrialization 131–2
developing a preferred reality 222–3
developmental approach 545–6
developmental disabilities, Medicaid funding 419
Developmentally Disabled Assistance, and Bill of
Rights 272
devolution: federal government to states 95; and
funding 193; health care policy 407; New
Federalism/OBRA and 97–100; and poverty 356; and
recessions/TANF 338–40; of services 150, 193; social
service programming 146
Dhammapada, the 31
dharma 31
diagnoses, and reimbursement 161
diagnosis-related groups (DRGs) 414, 464
Diagnostic and Statistical Manual of Mental Disorders,
5th Edition (DSM-5) 457

difference, celebrating 301
differential outcomes, information on 179
digital divide 265, 529, 542
direct action 78, 91
direct public welfare expenditure 149
disabilities: access laws 122; and child poverty 360;
children/corporal punishment 400; and civil rights
272–4, 304; and community inclusion 487;
disability insurance benefits 73; disability pensions
319–20; disability rights groups 273; disabled
workers 313; disaster plans for people with 531;
education of children 285–6; and employment 100,
545; and family leave 100; future rates of 315; under
G. H. W. Bush 97, 100; and institutionalization 257;
mainstream education for 285; and Medicaid 420;
and medical v. social needs 180; and Medicare/
Medicaid 101; numbers of people with 272; and
OASDI 346; older adults/aging in the community
485; pensions 319; people with 10; and poverty
257, 272; restricting access to benefits 97; veterans
319
Disability Insurance (DI) program 313
disadvantaged groups: lack of representation of 255;
resources available to 11
disasters, major 531, 541
discharge planners 462
discretionary spending refers to all the spending
authorized by the 13 appropriation bills that are
passed each year by Congress and signed by the
president. It includes funding for national defense,
transportation, educational and social programs
such as Head Start, and agriculture, 140, 143, 145,
150, 164, 312
discrimination: and advocacy 305; and affirmative
action 93–4, 279–81; African Americans 51–2,
261–3; age 299; Arab Americans 293; Asian
Americans 267–8; based on ethnicity/gender 291–3;
against Catholic immigrants 53; employment 51,
79, 98, 99, 100, 168, 258; environmental 540, 551;
gender-based 82, 90, 276, 291–3; Hispanic
Americans 80; Hispanics/Latinos 81, 265–7; and the
Holocaust 75; against immigrants 47–8; intersection
of 292; Japanese Americans 267; legal/skin color 77;
LGBTQ community 268–71, 303 *see also* and sexual
orientation; mothers' pensions 60; Muslims 293;
Native Americans 263–5; older adults 274–6, 478,
496; oppressed groups 256; people of color 291;
people with disabilities 100, 272–4, 287; policies
promoting 255; racial/ethnic 62; racial/in health
care 413; reverse 93, 279; in schools 90; and sexual

orientation 99, 290, 292, 304 *see also* LGBTQ community; in social work settings 301; and strengths perspective 11; structural 258; wages 289; women 276–9

disenfranchised groups: African Americans/civil rights 261–3; Asian Americans/civil rights 267–8; and civil rights 261; Hispanics and Latinos/civil rights 265–7; LGBTQ community 268–71; Native Americans/civil rights 263–5; older adults 274–6; people with disabilities 272–4; women 276–9

diversity: and child protection interventions 390; increasing in U.S. 527–8; population 551; respect for 6; and work-based safety net 535–7

divorce: rates 104; and women 279

divorcees, survivors' insurance 344

Dix, Dorothea 49, 442

doctors: incentives to go into primary care 480, 481; and Medicare patients 451

documenting: problems/needs 175–9, 196; strengths 221

domestic dependent nations, Indian Tribes as 263

domestic partnership legislation provides legal recognition or registration of committed lesbian and gay relations, 270

domestic violence: claim of 182; shelters/older women 491

Don't Ask, Don't Tell policy 271

Douglass, Frederick 45

Dreamers 293

Dred Scott vs. *Sandford* (1857) 45

driving, older adults 508–9

dropout rates, Hispanics 257

drug abuse, and child abuse/neglect 392

drug-related convictions, and public housing 329

dual assessment 7, 23, 201, 242, 511

dual diagnoses, mental health/substance abuse 454

dual eligibility, Medicaid/Medicare 428, 430

dual-income families 279

due process, erosion of 294

durable power of attorney 500

Early Childhood Home Visiting Program 396, 462

Early Middle Ages, feudal system 36

Earned Income Tax Credit (EITC) 88, 142, 333–4, 335, 354

ecological perspective in social work focuses on the ways in which people and their environment influence, change, and shape each other (Germain, 1991): aging well 472; civil rights 255; policy practice 217–19

ecology is the study of relationships between people and their environment, 218

economic aid, to control unrest 86

Economic and Social Conscience hypotheses 129–30

economic competitiveness 530

economic consequences, flu pandemic 455

economic context of social policy focuses on the production, distribution, and use of income, wealth and resources, 120, 163

economic crises: effects of 11; and election of Obama 107; and forecasts 522–3; and G. W. Bush 107; and social welfare 151

economic development, of women 537

economic downturn: and devolution of responsibility/social programs 146; effects of 11; and federal spending 144; and Medicaid 421; and Medicaid expansion 449–50; and not-for-profit sector 148; and older adults 473, 478–9, 494; and privatization 105; and reforms 108; and retirement 504; and September 11 522; and solvency of pension plans 490; supporting poor families 60; and TANF 342

economic efficiency focuses on three interrelated issues: (1) the probable impact of the intervention on the overall economy, (2) the relative merits of spending on one social program rather than another, and (3) the ways in which the incentives and/or disincentives created by the program will likely influence individual behavior, 124, 544

economic growth: dealing with slowing 135; and environmental concerns 509; and solvency of OASDI 495

economic instability, and federal deficit/national debt 147

economic mobility 320

Economic Opportunity Act 1964 84

economic recession, and budget cuts 146

economic recovery, and Obama 108

economics: consumer-side/demand-side 133–4; Keynesian 96; laissez-faire 135

economic schools of thought 133–4

economic security: and low-income families 216; older adults 493–7, 512, 513

economic status, and corporate policy makers 159

economic trends, forecasting 522–3

economy: agricultural 126; and definition of social problems 184; dependence on immigrants 113; and entry to World War II 74; and GDP 544; and Hispanic workers 527; industrial to service/

informational 103; and social welfare policies 129; of social work agencies 161–2; stablilization of/fiscal policy 133

education *see also* training: access to college 350; affirmative action 94; attainment/foster children 232; differences in attainment 232, 257; disabled children 285–6; as financial asset 347; funding 292; improving performance/low-income children 212–13; inequalities 146; lack of/and poverty 44; and Mexican Americans 266; and poor children of color 122; public/and capitalism 127; saving for 351; separate but equal policy 122; of social workers 457; social work/health care reforms 455; standards for social work 76–7; and workforce 131

educational gap, low-income children 536

Education Amendments 1972 90

Education for All Handicapped Children Act 1975 272, 285–6, 305, 385

education options, TANF families 340

effectiveness: policies/programs 191–2, 215, 356; of policy 231–3; of services/and cultural differences 300; of services/and social policy 3; of social work/ strengths perspective 22

elder abuse *see* abuse

Elder Justice Act 490–1

Elder Justice Coordinating Council 490

elders *see also* older adults: claims on behalf of 183; with disability/institutionalization 257; families unable to support 72; future/predominantly white 484; organizing as a voting block 475; and social insurance programs 114; stereotypes 453

elected officials: black 284; Twitter accounts 238

elections, and policy agenda 208

electoral politics, social worker involvement 546, 548, 551

electoral process, using 546–7

Electronic Benefit Transfer (EBT) cards 328

electronic records, CHIPRA 434

eligibility requirements: and assets 348; benefits 459; and birth certificates 297–8; and immigration status 265; income-support programs/policies 312; and judicial decisions 191; Medicaid 420, 423, 425; Medicare 426–7; OASDI 314, 343; policy analysis 190–1; programs 131; public housing 329; and residual programs 126; SCHIP 433; SNAP 327, 328, 339; SSI program 331; TANF 194, 321, 322, 349; and undocumented immigrants 296; unemployment insurance 317; veterans' benefits 319; WIC nutrition program 329

Eliot, Martha 70

elites: and capitalism 127; and marketplace economy 121; social control by 35, 255; and social welfare 30

Elk vs. *Wilkins* 50

Emancipation Proclamation 50

emergencies, and inability to accumulate assets 343

Emergency Contingency Fund for State TANF Programs 340

emergency funds, special federal 340

Employee Benefits Security Administration 489

employee pensions 474

Employee Retirement Income Security Act (ERISA) 1974 enacted in 1974, is federal legislation designed to regulate the private pension system, 476, 488–90, 512–13

employer-provided health insurance 409–10, 412, 437

employment *see also* unemployment; work: and access to health care 449; affirmative action 93; African Americans 51; and benefits 131; discrimination 51, 79, 80, 98, 99, 100, 168, 258; green jobs 108; job creation 108, 109; and mental illness 458; older adults 473, 487, 493, 494, 496, 504, 513; people with disability 100, 101, 545; and transportation 336; women 99

empowerment is the process of working to help client groups build skills that can lead to achieving more power over their lives, 461

empowerment-based helping strategies 14

empowerment theory 295

enabling niches are environments that have resources readily available to help them meet their needs, 218–19

enabling state is one where public benefits are provided to citizens in order to help them be more productive workers and citizens, 113, 130–3

end-of-life care 275–6, 428, 500–1

energy reform 107

English colonies, social welfare in 41–2

English Poor Laws 36–40, 87

entitlement program is a government program for which all citizens who meet the eligibility requirements legally qualify, 140, 192, 355; Medicaid as 421, 424, 450

entrapping niches are environments with barriers that prevent people from filling their needs. For example, they frequently have restricted access to people or resources outside their niche, 218

environmental: discrimination 540, 551

environmental concerns: and economic growth 509; and health 461; and social policy 114

environmental degradation 530–3; and economic growth 135; and life expectancy 503; and over-population 540
environmental disasters 123, 160, 164
environmental discrimination 540, 551
environment(s): physical/and health 540; strengths of 9; sustainable 160
epidemics, Middle Ages 37
Equal Employment Opportunity Commission (EEOC) 98, 281
equality *see also* inequality(ies): marriage 271; of opportunity 545; Progressive Era 59; and selective programs 126
Equality Index 299
equal opportunities 89, 98
Equal Pay Act 1963 82, 276
equal protection under law: and DOMA 270; and same-sex marriage 112
Equal Rights Amendment (ERA) 1972 68, 89
equal treatment claims, and social justice 226
equity requires that all people be treated equally or fairly: and eligibility rules 190; gender 277, 305; horizontal/vertical 124; principle of 124
Esping-Andersen, G. 129–30
Essential Health Benefits (EHB) 446
ethical dilemmas: genetic research 528; and medical technology 539
ethnicity, and discrimination 291–3
eugenics 75
Europe: retirement systems 474; welfare states 130
evaluation: ACA/social workers role 551; child protection policy 390–7; civil rights policies/programs 291–6; family reunification 392–3; family rights/child safety 390–1; of income-support programs/policies 334–47; of initiatives 163; juvenile justice system 397–9; mental health policies/programs 448–50; OASDI 343–7; policies/programs 188, 197; policies/programs for children and families 387–400; policies/programs for older adults 491–503; policy/based on client outcomes 231–3; of policy effectiveness 17; policy outcomes 215–16; privatization initiatives/child welfare services 395; research 196, 207; service delivery systems 17; of social policy 15, 173; of TANF 335, 336–8; teen pregnancy policies 393–5; value of 216
evidence-based initiatives, rolling out of 233
Examining the Feasibility of Policy Alternatives 228
excise taxes 439

exclusion 11
executions, of juveniles 370
executive branch: and change 111, 413; role of 138, 214
Executive Order No. 13217, Community-Based Alternatives for Individuals with Disabilities 2001 272
executive orders, under Obama 111–12
expenditure: social/categories of 156; U.S./other countries 156–8
Experience Corps 507
experience, personal/and social policy 8
experts, defining reality 172
exploitation: Hispanic Americans 80; and reproduction technology 528; workplace/Chinese immigrants 267
external factors, and need 11

Facebook 132, 238, 239
faith-based initiatives 105, 136 *see also* religious institutions
Family and Medical Leave Act (FMLA) 1993 100
family assistance experiments 87–8
Family Assistance Plan (FAP) 87–8
family formation goals, TANF 325
family-friendly policies 538
family(ies): changes in configuration of 104; intergenerational 538; mobility of 365; multigenerational 496; and poverty 103–5
family impact statements 230
family leave 100, 535
family planning/birth control clinics 68, 69
family preservation, and child welfare system 377, 378, 403
Family Preservation and Support Services 378–9
family reunification 381, 382, 392–3, 403
family saving, v. child saving 377
family support: maternalistic 60; strategies/evaluating 396
Family Support Act 1988 98
family violence, social construction of 171–2
Family Voices 388
fatherhood, responsible 325
fear, climate of 293, 294
federal assistance, American Revolution 44
federal assistance to states, OBRA 97
federal budgets 139–40, 142, 164
Federal Contingency Funds 340
federal debt 110, 164

federal deficit 115; and economic instability 147; under G. W. Bush 144, 145; under Reagan 96; and Social Security 494

federal government: activist role 76; involvement in social welfare 59; lack of responsibility for social reform 52; Progressive Era 58; responsibility for welfare 95, 101, 117; responsibility/protecting interests 147

Federal Insurance Contributions Act (FICA) 141, 315, 316, 495

federal poverty line (FPL), and SSI benefits 495 *see also* poverty line

federal poverty thresholds, older adults 485–6

federal programs, core 150

Federal Register 311

federal spending 142–5

feedback, client/policy development 204

fee-for-service systems provide payment for specific services rendered, 414

female work 291

Feminine Mystique, The 89

feminization of poverty refers to the disproportionately high number of women and their children who are living in poverty, 279

fertility rates 481, 521, 526

fetus, rights of 106

feudal system, Early Middle Ages 36

finance, health care 414–16

financial crisis 123, 164

financial impact statements 230

financial support, for disabled veterans and families of 44

financing: analysis of 192–3; Patient Protection and Affordable Care Act 2010 438–40

Finland 131

fiscal policy is policy designed to regulate the economy by increasing or decreasing spending, interest rates, and taxes in response to economic conditions: and stabilization of economy 133

Fisher vs. *University of Texas* 112, 280

five-year limit, TANF 341

Flexible Spending Accounts, health care 416

flu epidemic, economic consequences 455

Food and Nutrition Service 328, 329

food bank organizations 245

food costs, older adults 486

food insecurity 194, 195, 244–5

Food Stamp Act 1964 85

Food Stamp Act 1977 89

Food Stamp Program is a government program established to address hunger in the United States by helping low-income people to purchase nutritionally adequate food, 97, 101, 265 *see also* Supplemental Nutrition Assistance Program (SNAP)

Force Acts 1870-1871 50

forced acculturation 376

Ford, Gerald 88, 89

forecasts 518–25

foster care: African American children 361, 380; aging out of 384; children in 360; children of color 380; entries/exits 381; improving 377; initiatives 232; kinship 392, 401–2, 403; LGBTQ youth 392; moving children out of 391; Native American children 92, 376; negative outcomes of 383; overuse of medication 446, 465; permanency/concurrent planning 382, 392; privatization 384; problems of 377; provided by religious organizations 105; reform initiatives 222; Social Security Act 1935 363; standards for 382–3; and teen pregnancy 393; youths in/sexual behavior 393

foster children, challenges facing 4

Fostering Connections to Success and Increasing Adoptions Act 2008 264, 377, 384, 403

framework for policy analysis 185–94

frameworks, for policy development 15–17

Frazier, Franklin 57, 58

Freedmen's Bureau 51

free-trade agreements, and liberalism 136

Friedan, Betty 89

Friedman, Milton 134

friendly visitors 56

friend of the court briefs 235

full-family sanctions, TANF 326

funding: campaign/and policy agenda 208; child abuse/neglect 372; community health centers 437; cuts 1, 273; education 292; federal/ASFA 382; federal/child welfare services 379; under G. H. W. Bush 97; health care *see* health care; ICWA 376–7; impact of funding strategies 139–49; linked to outcomes 193; long-term care 498; Medicaid 423; mental health services 98, 273, 441, 443, 444; and OAA 487–8; Patient Protection and Affordable Care Act 438–40; and policy enactment 214; policy practice focussed on 228; public/private 97, 192–3; public/provision of services 148; public sector casework 94; under Reagan 95–6; regulations as sanctions/incentives 229; and religiously affiliated nursing facilities 35; Social Security 343; of social work agencies 161; state/children's programs 361; strategies/benefits and drawbacks of 148–9; TANF 340; Title IV-E funds 377; WIC nutrition program 329

Funding Work Incentive Program, TANF 326

future forecasts 518–25, 550

future, image of 549–50

gag rules 101, 106, 415

gay rights demonstrations 99

gay rights movement 269

gender, and discrimination 82, 89–90, 276, 291–3

gender equity, U.S. 276, 305

gender identity 15, 173, 268, 269, 290, 292, 304

gender-related violence 277

General Assistance (GA) consists of programs provided by some state and local government to assist poor individuals and families who do not qualify for or are waiting for approval for federal programs such as SSI and TANF, 332, 354

general tax revenue is revenue not dedicated automatically for functions such as road maintenance or paying for specific services or benefits but can be used for general purposes, 140, 141, 144, 328, 331, 335, 431, 487

General Theory of Employment, Interest, and Money, The 133

general welfare, and the Constitution 130

Generations United 506–7

generation to generation transfer of wealth 347

generic drugs 430

Genetic Information Non-Discrimination Act 2008 539

genetic mapping 539

genetic research, ethical dilemmas 528

genocide, cultural 376

geography, and poverty 310

Germany, retirement system 474

gerontology, social workers educated in 480–1, 510, 514, 519–20

GI Bill of Rights 1944 75, 117, 348

Gilbert, N. 113

Gingrich, Newt 101

Global Assets Project 545

global competition, for natural resources 530

global competitiveness, and taxation 158

global economy, and poverty 350

Global Gender Gap Index 276

globalization refers to the international economic, political, and social integration of the world's nations, 530–3; ramifications of 158–60, 164, 537; term 158

global poverty 350, 352

goal orientation, strengths-based approaches 174

goals: clients/policy development 204, 205; crafting policy 209–11; goal-focussed approaches 240; legislative support for 228; locating 187; manifest/latent 187–8; negotiating policy 227–8; policy/analysis of 186–9; policy/public support for 204

government: Native American mistrust of 47; pluralistic 542; Progressive Era 57; provision of social welfare/desirable outcomes 128–9; reform of urban 58; role of/under Obama 107; and social justice 113; three branches of 138–9, 214; views of 66

Government Accountability Office (GAO) 387

government health insurance 409

government intervention, impetus for 123

government spending, as redistributive process 143

graduation rates, improving/low-income children 212–13

Grameen Development Bank 350, 357

Grand Old Party (GOP) 46

grandparents, as caregivers 496

grants: Alcohol, Drug Abuse, and Mental Health block grant 444; basic income grant (BIG) 351; block grants 146, 321, 326, 356, 445, 447; categorical/block 97; child protection/case management and prevention 363; community mental health services 448; mental health centers 448; OAA 487; outreach/CHIPRA 434; Pell Grants 455; prevention child abuse 372; social work education 455; substance abuse treatment 445; welfare-to-work (WTW) 326; WIC funding 329

Gratz vs. *Bollinger* 280

Gray Panthers 343

Great Depression: effects of 116; expanding welfare state in 67–76; and federal role/social welfare 184; and Keynesian economics 134; mothers' pensions 60; and older adults 474; and social policy 70

Great Risk-Shift: The Assault on Jobs, Families, Health Care, and Retirement, The 476

Great Society, the 83–5

Greek society, social welfare 33

green jobs 108

Green Party works to create a sustainable world where nature and human society coexist in harmony. In the area of social welfare, it advocates social justice, non-violence, personal and global responsibility, and respect for diversity, 137

Greenspan, Alan 107

gross domestic product (GDP) is the total monetary value of all goods and services produced by labor and property in a country annually, 140; and economy 544; and growth 495; spent on healthcare 411; spent on social welfare 149
Gross vs. *FBL Financial, Inc.* 274
growth: economic/social policy as engine of 129; and GDP 495
Grutter vs. *Bollinger* 280
guaranteed annual income plan 89
guardianship program, kinship providers 384, 403
Guilds 37
gun control legislation 110

H1N1 flu epidemic 455
Hacker, J. 95, 476
Ham and Eggs Movement 475
harassment: on the job 292; sexual 292
Harrington, Michael 82
Hartford Foundation 480
Hatch Act (1939) 241
hate crimes 257, 269, 290, 293, 304
Hayes, Rutherford B. 51
Head Start 84, 85, 367, 397
health *see also* health care; health disparities: child/ and EITC 334; and environmental issues 461; future policy directions 539–40; and globalization 159; of Native Americans 47; people in secondary labor market 291; and physical environment 540; and pollution 461, 532, 540
Health Affairs 503
health benefits programs 94 *see also* Medicaid; Medicare
health care *see also* health; health care system: access to 415, 506; Alaskan Natives 265; benefits/global workers 538; capitated approach 415; children 102, 109; and coercion 540; as commodity/social utility 408; costs 145, 410–12, 414–16, 431, 451, 453, 456, 464, 509, 512 *see also* spending; denial to African Americans 45; ethical dilemmas 539; federal government involvement 413; finance 109, 414–16; Hispanic/Latino children 266; household spend/ Medicare 427; and immigration 108–10; industry 412; lack of/and poverty 44; limited public entitlement 413; major policies/programs 419; Medicaid *see* Medicaid; Medicare *see* Medicare; older adults 497–501, 512; overservice/underservice 414, 415; oversight 415; policies for older people 475; preventative initiatives 416; public/and capitalism 127; quality of 408; racial discrimination in 413;

rationing of 408; spending 151, 411, 412, 419, 464 *see also* costs; and workforce 408; younger people 506
Health Care and Education Affordability Reconciliation Act (H.R. 4872) 109, 406, 409, 417, 455, 464
health care inflation 440
health care legislation, contesting of 549, 552
Healthcare Marketplace 436
health care programs, history/background 412–17
health care reform 406; 1990s 416–17; 2010 109, 417–19; client's voices in 549; under Clinton 101; impact of 438; implementation of/state variations 450; legislation 109, 432, 448–50, 455; under Obama 107, 109, 117, 138; and social work education 455; and social workers 458–60; and young adults 438
health care system 407–19; and pandemics 454–5; and substance abuse 453–4
health disparities: children in poverty 360; and life expectancy 503; and social determinants of health 407–8; tribal communities 265
health/economic indicators, Hispanic/Latino population 81
health indicators 157–8
health insurance *see also* Medicaid; Medicare: access to 406; and adequate health care 408; children 433; employer-provided 409–10, 412, 437; government health insurance 409; long-term care insurance 418; and pre-existing conditions 435, 436, 438; premiums 416; private health insurance 409; public option 439; requirement 437; role of social workers 459; single-payer health care plan 417; uninsured people 409, 417, 424, 428, 432, 438, 440, 449, 463
Health Insurance Portability and Accountability Act (HIPAA) 1996 provided that workers must be able to continue purchasing their health insurance if they lose their jobs or change jobs (NASW, 2003a), 417, 541
health maintenance organizations (HMOs) provide health care for each person enrolled in its system for the year in return for an amount per person decided upon in advance by public or private insurers, 408, 415
health model 461
health outcomes 411, 464
health policies/programs, promoting effectiveness 455–6
health promotion, and life expectancy 503

Health Resources and Services Administration (HRSA) 396

Health Security Act 101

Healthy, Hunger-Free Kids Act 195

HEARTH Act 2009 176–9, 180–1, 187, 190, 193

Height, Dorothy I. 78

Helping Families Save Their Home Act 176

helping strategies, empowerment-based 14

heterosexism 299

heterosexual privilege 269

Hill–Burton Act is federal legislation passed in 1946 that provided public funds for hospital construction and in return, hospitals were to provide some free or reduced charge care for indigent citizens (Division of Facilities Compliance and Recovery, 2003), 413

Hispanics *see also* Latinos: child poverty rate 337; children in population 365; dropout rates 257; Hispanic population 527, 551; poverty 81, 320; as public charges 266; struggle for civil rights 80–1; treatment of/Independence to civil war 47; youths in juvenile justice system 370

history, and current social policy 34–6

Holocaust, effects of 75

home and community based services (HCBS) are defined as services and supports that assist individuals to continue to live within their home or a community setting. Personal care, assistance with chores, nutritional programs, night support, and transportation are examples of community-based services (Kane, Kane, & Ladd, 1998): and disabled people 257, 420; and families 396–7; funding 273; importance of 497–9; and long-term care 479, 512, 513; and Medicaid 85; older adults 1, 504; waivers 420, 422

home-based services, Medicaid waivers 420

Homeless Assistance Act 180

Homeless Emergency Assistance and Rapid Transition to Housing (HEARTH) Act *see* HEARTH Act

homelessness *see also* HEARTH Act 2009; Helping Families Save Their Home Act: causes of 177; and co-occurring conditions 445; defined 177–8; LGBTQ youths 270; mentally ill people 273, 443, 447; as national problem 176; preventing 181; problems in addressing 179; rapid rehousing 181, 193; and school performance 201; size of homeless population 178; strengths perspective 9; teenagers 1

homeless people initiative, San Francisco 191

home sharing initiative 18

Homestead Act 1862 51–2, 348

home visiting programs 396, 462

homophobia is the fear of, and discrimination against, people who are gay, lesbian, transgender, or bisexual, on the basis of their sexual orientation or gender identity, 256

homosexuality, as mental disorder/biopsychosocial development 269–70

Hopkins, Harry 70, 71

horizontal equity focuses on the equal distribution of resources to people irrespective of factors such as ethnicity, location, socioeconomic status (SES), or age, 124

hospice benefits 428

hospice care is an approach to end-of-life care that focuses on comfort and alleviating pain rather than treating a terminal illness, 41, 428, 500

hospitalization, involuntary 443

hospitals: for the mentally ill 48–9, 442; military and Veteran's Administration 450

hospital social workers 462

household inequality 103, 104

households, single-parent 104

houses of correction, workhouses as 42

housing: high-rise public 174; and older adults 486; public 229–30; racial/class segregation in 77; rapid rehousing 181, 193

housing insecurity 181

housing market, collapse of 307

Huerta, Dolores 81, 258, 259

Hull House 55, 363

human capital refers to the productive capacity of citizens which can be enhanced through programs such as education, health care, and job training that make people more productive and thereby increase national wealth, 133, 134, 160

Human Immunodeficiency Virus (HIV) 454–5

humanitarian impulse hypotheses 128

human labor, and workhouses 42

human rights 293–5, 296 *see also* right(s)

human trafficking 532

hunger: children 195–6, 244–5, 362; definition of 244; measuring U.S. 244

Hurricane Katrina 531

identifying target client population 221–3

ideology: and policy 535; and social movements 180

immigrants *see also* immigration: access to services 131; alliance with LGBTQ community 291; ambivalence towards 34; battered 289; and benefits

101, 325, 339, 341; children of 366; civil rights violations 305; discrimination against 47–8; during Independence to civil war 45; Irish 48; and means-tested programs 331; Medicaid/SSI eligibility 424; new 62; and Patriot Act 294; policy towards workers 80; prejudice against 62; Progressive Era 58; Public Health Service 44; rights of 293; targeting of Catholic 53; undocumented 265, 296, 325, 438; uninsured 424, 438

immigration *see also* immigrants: anti-immigrant legislation 293; enforcement and social workers 296; and ethnic composition of U.S. 112–13; and forecasts 522; and health care 108–10; legislation curtailing 62; policies/and social justice 536; policy 265, 293; and population growth 526, 527; post civil war 52; reform 110, 111, 117, 138, 266, 297; status/and service eligibility 265; system under Obama 109

Immigration and Customs Enforcement (ICE) 294

Immigration and Naturalization Service 294

implementation of policy 211, 213–15, 548

incarceration *see also* prisons: African Americans 292; juveniles in adult prisons 369; minority groups/substance abuse 454; people with mental illness 445

incentives: for providers/new legislation 230; for working 131

inclusion refers to offering education services to children with disabilities in the regular classrooms where other children are educated, 285

income *see also* income inequality; income-support programs/policies: adequacy of 154, 155–6; black workers 299; decline in/under G. W. Bush 107; distribution 154, 155; sources/older adults 493

income-based programs 353–4

income inequality 103 *see also* income; income-support programs/policies; consequences of 460; and elites 121; growth of 155, 343; under G. W. Bush 103; reducing 154; women/men 257

income perspective, poverty 309

income-support programs/policies 312, 355 *see also* TANF; and CDAs/IDAs 352; evaluation of 334–47; lack of/effect on children 362; residual approach 129

incremental approaches, change 240

indentured servitude 42–3

independence, work/financial 544

independent living (IL) movement 287

Independent Living Program 384

Independent Living Transition services 383–4

Independent Payment Advisory Board (IPAB) 440

Indian Appropriation Act 1851 46

Indian Child Welfare Act (ICWA) 1978 is the federal legislation that mandates active efforts be made to ensure that Native American children remain with their families, and that empowers tribes and tribal courts to oversee decision making regarding Native American children, 92, 264, 375–7, 386, 402

Indian Health Care Improvement Act (IHCIA) 2010 265

Indian Health Service 265

Indian Removal Act 1830 46

Indian removal policy 46

Indian Reorganization Act 1934 90, 263

Indian Self-Determination and Education Assistance Act 1975 264

Indian tribes *see also* Native Americans: as alien nations 50; child support programs 387; as domestic dependent nations 263

indicators, health and welfare 157–8

indigenous groups, transnational 532

Individual Development Accounts (IDAs) 349–50, 354, 356, 537, 545

individualism, and liberalism 43

individualized education plan (IEP) 285

individual pathology 97

individual responsibility 95

Individual Retirement Accounts (IRAs) 102, 349

Individuals with Disabilities Education Act (IDEA) 285–6, 373, 385

Individuals with Disabilities Education Improvement Act 2004 285

industrial capitalism, and social welfare 127–8

industrialization: and older adults 474; and unwillingness to help others 128; and the welfare state 127

industrialization movement 37

industrialization-welfare hypothesis 127

inequalities: household 104

inequality(ies): asset 121, 347; and capitalism 135; education 146; household 103; income 103, 121, 154, 155, 257, 343, 460; increasing 103; lifespan 460; marketplace economy 121; and oppressed groups 256; between rich and poor 36

infant mortality 108–9; African Americans 361; children of color 361; Hispanic/Latino population 81; and Medicaid 419; U.S. rates 157–8, 411

infectious diseases 531

inflation, health care 440

influence, of corporations 159

informal care 485, 492

information: child abuse 372; on differential outcomes 179; and forecasts 520–3; and Internet 225; needs/older adults 503–4; for policy makers 216; sharing/and HIPAA 541

information technology *see also* computers; Internet: advances in 529; ethical/legal issues 541–2; lack of access to/Native Americans 265; and privacy 541–2

infrastructure(s): age-sensitive community 508; creating needed 508–9; investing in 108

initiatives, evaluation of 163

injustice, combating 3

innovation transfer 240

institutional approaches: public relief 41–2; social welfare 125, 129

institutional barriers, regulatory policy 122

institutionalization *see also* deinstitutionalization: cost of 231; older adults/needless 504; people with disability 257; people with mental illness 124

institutions: local government provision of 48; Native American children in 376; public/19c. growth of 48; state mental health 49

Instrumental Activities of Daily Living (IADL) limitations 428

insurance, and pre-existing conditions 435, 436, 438

insurance companies, lobbying by 105

insurance coverage, by race/ethnicity 409

insurance models 130

insurance programs, as political tools 494

insurance, single-payer health care system 109

integration, social 508

interdependence, and self-determination 502

interests: protecting/women and minorities 147; vested 239

Interethnic Adoption Provisions (MEPA-IEAP) 379

intergenerational, caregivers 496

intergenerational conflict 114, 496, 505

intergenerational families, supporting 538

intergenerational interdependence 492

intergenerational policies/programs 492, 506–7, 513, 524

intergenerational reciprocity 509

intergenerational social contract 509

intergenerational solidarity 496

intermarriage, laws 80

Internal Revenue Service (IRS) 88, 489

International Committee on Planned Parenthood 69

International Federation of Social Workers 548

International Planned Parenthood Federation 69

Internet: building coalitions 241; and low-income families 219, 542; and older adults 503; and service provision 541; and social isolation 504, 520

Internet resources 221, 225, 226

internment, Japanese Americans 75, 267

interpretation services, CHIPRA 434

intersectionality 79, 292

intubation/ventilation 453

investment, in human capital 133, 134, 160

involuntary hospitalization 443

Involuntary Outpatient Commitments (IOCs) 444

involuntary sterilization 442, 539, 540

involvement: client/in change process 7; students/ developing services 17–18; of target groups/social policy 173

Irish Immigrants, discrimination against 48

Islam, and social welfare 30–1

Jackson, Andrew 46

Jannson, B. S. 221

Japanese Americans, internment 75, 267

Japan, health care 412

Jefferson, Thomas 44

Jim Crow laws 51, 76, 78–9

Job Corps 84

job creation 108, 109

jobs, future policy directions 537–8 *see also* work

Job-Specific Pension Programs 476

job training programs 87, 545

Johnson, Lyndon 82, 83, 283, 413

Judaism, and social welfare 30

judicial branch is the division of government comprising the court system. Both the federal and state judiciaries include a supreme court, a court of appeals, and district courts, 139, 214

judicial decisions, and eligibility rules 191

judiciary, generating social policy/limitations of 77

justice, climate 540–1

juvenile crime 369, 397

juvenile delinquency: and academic success 398; and zero tolerance policies 398

Juvenile Justice and Delinquency Prevention Act is the federal legislation originally designed to aid state and local governments in their work to prevent and control juvenile delinquency the juvenile justice system: 1974 373–5, 386, 403; 2002 398

juvenile justice system is the system through which children and youth charged with crimes receive services, 369–70; black youths in 370; case review

397; effective 375; evaluation 397–9; Hispanic youths in 370; inequitable treatment of African Americans 370; juvenile courts 363; minority youth in 236; post-release plans/after-care 399; punishment and retribution/treatment 397; and rehabilitation 369, 398
juvenile offenders: in adult prisons 370, 374; death penalty 370; deinstitutionalization of 374; executions 370; rape of 369; status offenders 374; tried as adults 369

Kahana, E. and Kahana B. 472
Kangaroo Care 533
Kansas Elder Count 221
Keating-Owen Child Labor Act 1916 61
Keeping Children and Families Safe Act 2003 372
Kelley, Florence 55, 60
Kennedy, John F. 78, 81, 82
Keynesian economics, also referred to as demand-side or consumer-side economics, is based on the writings of John Maynard Keynes. It is an economic school that supports government intervention such as public welfare programs to help to stimulate and regulate the economy, 96, 133–4
Keynes, John Maynard 70
Kids Count 163, 221
Kids Count Data Book 256
King, Martin Luther Jr. 78, 86
King, Rodney 99
Kingsley, D. 453
kinship care/foster care 392, 401–2, 403
knowledge-based software, triage 529
knowledge, global pool of 533
Koran (Qur'an), the 30–1
Kretzmann, J. and McKnight, J. 219
Ku Klux Klan 50, 64

labor: cheap farm 80, 265; child 61; as commodity 131
labor organizations, transnational 532
labor unions, and social benefits 129
L.A. Gay & Lesbian Center 392
La Huelga 80
laissez-faire capitalism 33
laissez-faire economy refers to an economy with minimal or no government regulation of economic activities: traditional conservatives 134, 135, 136
Lakota people, activism by 91
land: appropriation of Native American's 45, 46, 47, 51–2; ownership/and Native Americans 90

language, and re-languaging discussions 522
latent goals are goals that are not typically publicized because it would be difficult to achieve a consensus to support these goals or the goals that would not be considered socially acceptable, 187–8
Latinos *see also* Hispanics: poverty 81, 337; as public charges 266; treatment of/Independence to civil war 47
law enforcement, and substance abuse 445
Lawful Permanent Residents (LPR) 102, 325
law(s) *see also* legislation: antidiscrimination 62, 337; child protection 61; civil rights laws 79–80; intermarriage 80; is a new one needed? 228–9; voter identification laws 80, 281, 284, 295; working conditions 59
leadership roles, African Americans 262, 263
learning, and forecasts 519
least restrictive environment (LRE) 285, 385, 393
Ledbetter, Lilly 276, 278
Ledbetter vs. *Goodyear Tire & Rubber Co.* 106
legislation *see also* law(s): Act of Congress 1871 46; Act of Settlement of 1662 39, 42; Adoption and Safe Families Act (ASFA) 1997 381–3, 382, 391; Adoption Assistance and Child Welfare Act (AACWA) 1980 377–8, 381, 391; Affordable Care Act 2010 68, 110, 111, 117, 129, 151, 265, 277, 417–19, 434, 446, 539, 548, 551 *see also* Patient Protection and Affordable Care Act 2010; Age Discrimination in Employment Act (ADEA) 274, 478; Amendments to the Americans with Disabilities Act (AADA) 2008 288; American Recovery and Reinvestment Act 2009 317, 334, 340; Americans with Disabilities Act (ADA) 1990 10, 100, 117, 272, 286–7, 305; American Taxpayer Relief Act 2013 334; America's Law Enforcement and Mental Health Project Act 2000 444; Anti-Drug Abuse Act 1988 454; anti-immigrant 293; Area Redevelopment Act 1961 82; assisted dying 501; Balanced Budget Act 1997 326, 424, 429, 433; Battered Immigrant Women's Protection Act 2000 289; Bill of Rights 1791 44, 260; CAPTA Reauthorization Act 2010 372; Chafee Foster Care Independent Living Act 1999 384; Child Abuse Prevention and Treatment Act (CAPTA) 1974 88, 372–3, 373, 386, 403; Child and Family Services Improvement Act 2006 379; Child and Family Services Improvement and Innovation Act 2011 379; Child Nutrition Act 4, 7; Children's Health Insurance Program Reauthorization Act (CHIPRA) 433; children with special needs 385, 387; Civil

Rights Act 1964 79, 93, 98, 261, 274, 281–3; Civil
Rights Act 1991 99, 282; Civil Rights Restoration
Act 1987 281–2; Clayton Antitrust Act 1914 58;
Community Mental Health Act 1975 amendments
447, 478; curtailing immigration 62; Dawes Act
1887 46–7, 90, 263; Defense of Marriage Act
(DOMA) 112, 270; Deficit Reduction Act (DRA)
2005 325; domestic partnership 270; Economic
Opportunity Act 1964 84; Education Amendments
1972 90; Education for All Handicapped Children
Act 1975 272, 285–6, 305, 385; Elder Justice Act
490–1; Employee Retirement Income Security Act
(ERISA) 1974 476, 488–90, 512–13; English Poor
Laws 36–40; Equal Pay Act 1963 82, 276; Equal
Rights Amendment (ERA) 1972 68; Executive Order
No. 13217, Community-Based Alternatives for
Individuals with Disabilities 2001 272; Family and
Medical Leave Act (FMLA) 1993 100; Family Support
Act 1988 98; Federal Insurance Contributions Act
(FICA) 141, 315, 316, 495; Food Stamp Act 1964 85;
Food Stamp Act 1977 89; Force Acts 1870-1871 50;
Fostering Connections to Success and Increasing
Adoptions Act 2008 264, 377, 384, 403; Genetic
Information Non-Discrimination Act 2008 539; GI
Bill of Rights 1944 75–6, 117, 348; Hatch Act (1939)
241; Health Care and Education Affordability
Reconciliation Act (H.R. 4872) 109, 406, 409, 417,
455, 464; health care reform 2010 109, 448–50;
Health Insurance Portability and Accountability Act
(HIPAA) 1996 417, 541; Health Security Act 101;
Healthy, Hunger-Free Kids Act 195; HEARTH Act
2009 176–9, 180–1, 187, 190, 193; Helping Families
Save Their Home Act 176; Hill–Burton Act 413;
Homeless Assistance Act 180; Homestead Act 1862
51–2, 348; Indian Appropriation Act 1851 46;
Indian Child Welfare Act (ICWA) 1978 92, 264,
375–7, 386, 402; Indian Health Care Improvement
Act (IHCIA) 2010 265; Indian Removal Act 1830 46;
Indian Reorganization Act 1934 90, 263; Indian
Self-Determination and Education Assistance Act
1975 264; Individuals with Disabilities Education
Act (IDEA) 285–6, 373, 385; Individuals with
Disabilities Education Improvement Act 2004 285;
Interethnic Adoption Provisions (MEPA-IEAP) 379;
Jim Crow laws 51, 76, 78–9; Juvenile Justice and
Delinquency Prevention Act 1974 373–5, 386, 403;
Juvenile Justice and Delinquency Prevention Act
2002 398; Keating-Owen Child Labor Act 1916 61;
Keeping Children and Families Safe Act 2003 372;
Lilly Ledbetter Fair Pay Act 2009 106, 276, 289–90;

Matthew Shepard and James Byrd, Jr. Hate Crimes
Prevention Act 2009 269, 290, 305; McKinney-
Vento Homeless Assistance Act 175–6, 177, 183,
188, 189–90, 193; Meat Inspection Act (1906) 59;
Medicare Improvements for Patients and Providers
Act 2008 275, 500; Medicare Prescription Drug,
Improvement and Modernization Act 2003 430,
480; Mental Health Act 1946 76, 81; Mental Health
Bill of Rights Act 272–3; Mental Health Parity Act
1996 417, 445, 465; Mental Health Systems Act
1980 443–4; Mental Retardation and Community
Mental Health Centers Construction Act 1963 and
1965 443, 447–8, 465; Mental Retardation Facilities
and Community Mental Health Centers
Construction Act 1963 81; Motor Voter Act 111,
284; Multi-Ethnic Placement Act (MEPA) 1994
379–81, 386; National Defense Authorization Act
269; National Labor Relations Act 1935 74; new/
financing of 230; Nursing Home Reform Act 480;
Older Americans Act (OAA) 1965 85, 475, 478,
486–8, 512; Older Workers Benefit Protection Act
(OWBPA) 274; Omnibus Budget Reconciliation Act
1990 480; Omnibus Budget Reconciliation Act 1993
378, 480; Omnibus Budget Reconciliation Act
(OBRA) 1981 97; Patient Protection and Affordable
Care Act 2010 109, 406, 409, 435–8, 464; Patient
Safety and Abuse Prevention Act 490–1; Patient's
Self-Determination Act 1990 275; Patriot Act 294;
Paul Wellstone and Pete Domenici Mental Health
Parity and Addiction Equity Act 2008 417, 445, 454,
465; Pay Check Fairness Act 276; Pension Protection
Act 2006 489; Personal Responsibility and Work
Opportunity Reconciliation Act (PRWORA) 1996
101, 117, 321, 325, 326, 423–4; Poor Law 1536 38;
Poor Law 1601 38–9; Progressive Era 62; Pure Food
and Drug Act (1906) 59; Recovery Act 151; role of
social workers in scrutinizing 298; Ryan White
Comprehensive AIDS Resources Emergency (CARE)
Act 1990 454–5; Servicemen's Readjustment Act
1944 75; Social Security Act 1935 70, 72–3, 82, 101,
113, 129, 184, 324, 363, 419, 426; Social Service
Amendments 1974 83, 89; State Children's Health
Insurance Program (CHIP) 433, 435, 464; State
Children's Health Insurance Program (SCHIP) 102;
State Comprehensive Mental Health Services Plan
Act 1986 444, 448, 465; Stewart B. McKinney
Homeless Assistance Act see McKinney-Vento
Homeless Assistance Act; strengths perspective 129;
Supplemental Security Income (SSI) program 88;
Ticket to Work and Work Incentives Improvement

Act 1999 101; Uniting and Strengthening America by Providing Appropriate Tools Required to Intercept and Obstruct Terrorism Act of 2001 *see* Patriot Act; Violence Against Women Act 1994 277; Violence Against Women Act 2005 and 2013 reauthorizations 288–9; Volstead Act 1919 61–2; Voting Rights Act 1965 80, 111, 261, 283–4; Workforce Investment Act 326

legislative agenda, and claims-making 207

legislative branch is the division of government charged with passing legislation. At the federal level and in most states, it consists of two chambers, the House of Representatives and the Senate, 138–9, 214

legislative level policy practice 235

legislators: African American 284; educating 207; Hispanic 267; providing information to 226

lesbian, gay, bisexual, transgender, and questioning (LGBTQ) *see* LGBTQ

LGBTQ bullying 302–3

LGBTQ community: alliances with immigrant populations 291; civil rights 268–71; and social services/faith based communities 35; youths/problems of 270

LGBTQ legislation 290

LGBTQ youth: foster care 392; homelessness 270; in juvenile justice system 370

liberal consensus, under Reagan 136

liberal construct 43

liberalism is a political philosophy that endorses individual freedom and advocates government intervention to ensure an adequate minimum living condition for all people, 134

liberals: political philosophy 135–7; traditional 136

libertarians advance a political philosophy that posits government grows at the expense of individual freedom and advocates absolute and unrestricted liberty, 137

liberty, commitment to 46

licensure laws, state specific 94

licensure, of social workers 94

life expectancies: increasing 471; low-income areas 503; of low-income workers 345; and medical advances 528–9; and prevention 503; racial/ethnic groups 408; U.S. 411, 481; women 503

life span: inequality 460; meeting needs across 509; outcomes across 513; poverty 505

life style choices, and life expectancy 503

likelihood of passage, and policy alternatives 212

Lilly Ledbetter Fair Pay Act 2009 106, 276, 278, 289–90

Lincoln, Abraham 46, 50

literacy tests, voting rights 283

literature reviews 222, 225, 227, 230

litigation, age based discrimination 274

litigation-oriented child protection services 390

living wage is the income level that advocates calculate is necessary to live adequately within a given community, 337, 537

living wills 500

loan repayment funding, social work education 455

loans: low-cost/business start-up 350; peer lending strategy 350, 352

local approaches, provision of food/housing 160

local government, and social welfare 48, 137

local policy making 214

local responsibility is a principle which mandates that each locality should be responsible for helping only its own residents, 39, 101

loneliness 502

long-term care: community-based care 513; costs 420; funding 498; informal care 480; insurance 418; managed care 425; and Medicaid 479, 497, 508; and Medicare 418, 479; older adults 479–80, 497, 512

Long-Term Care Ombudsman Program 490

Lorenz Curve 343

Los Angeles, race riots 99

losses, negative effects of/older people 472, 478

Lowell, Josephine Shaw 54

low-income areas, life expectancies 503

low-income communities, lack of access to online resources 219

low-income families: access to computers 529, 542; asset accumulation 343, 347, 347–8, 350, 351, 352; children/and Medicaid 419; children/improving school performance 212–13; under Clinton 102; and economic security 216; Hispanics/Latinos 266; and Medicaid 418, 423–4; non-cash programs 327–30; savings 349, 350; tax entitlements 154

Low-Income Housing Energy Assistance Program (LIHEAP) 496

low-income neighborhoods, and polluting factories 540

low-income older adults, and Medicare 451

low-income people: fear of power of 549; under Reagan 95

Low Income Subsidies for Medicare 496

low-income workers, life expectancies of 345

lump-sum payments at birth 351

Macarov, D. 517
maintenance of capitalism hypothesis 127–8
maintenance of effort (MOE) requirement 321
Malcolm X 86
Malthus, Thomas 54
maltreatment *see* child maltreatment
managed care is a health care system under which
the insurer controls the person's health care, and
health care providers agree to accept a set fee per
treatment or a flat rate per patient, 415; and cost
containment 464; effectiveness of 416; HMO
provision of 415, 429; and Medicaid 424–5, 543;
and Medicare 427, 428, 429, 439; mental health
services 444–5; modified models 395; and
physicians reimbursement 429; private contractors
543; privatization of 543; and underservice 464
mandatory spending is government spending directed
toward individuals and institutions that are legally
entitled to it, 140, 142, 144, 145, 150, 151, 312, 361
manifest goals are the publicly stated goals,
Manpower Development Training Act (MDTA),
187–8
Manning, Leah Katherine Hicks 92
Manpower Development Training Act (MDTA) 82
marginalized people, and economic crises 11
market failure is a "circumstance in which the
pursuit of private interest does not lead to an
efficient use of society's resources or a fair
distribution of society's goods" (Weimer & Vining,
1999, p.41), 123
marketplace economy means that citizens exchange
goods and services, typically by working for a
salary, 121
markets, open/liberalism 136
marriage equality 271
marriage incentives, TANF 129, 341
marriage penalty, and EITC 334
marriage rates 104
Marshall and Titmuss hypotheses 128–9
Marshall, John 46
Marshall, T. H. 128
Maternal, Infant, and Early Childhood Home Visiting
Program (MIECHV) 396
maternalistic approaches 59–60
Mattachine Society 269
Matthew Shepard and James Byrd, Jr. Hate Crimes
Prevention Act 2009 269, 290, 305
Max Planck Institute for Demographic Research 484, 521
McCarthyism 294
McCarthy, Joseph 294

McKinney-Vento Homeless Assistance Act 175–6, 177,
183, 188, 189–90, 193
meaning, social construction of 171
means-testing for financial need: benefits 89; cost of
190; disability pensions 321–2; income-support
programs/policies 312; Medicaid 419; mothers'
pensions 60; public assistance programs 73;
selective programs 356; SSI program 331; and
stigmatization 190
Meat Inspection Act (1906) 59
media: and clients' perspective 227; and policy agenda
207; providing information to 226; publicizing
claims 226; working with 211, 401
Medicaid is a health care program for certain
categories of people with very low incomes that is
jointly funded by the federal and state
governments, 84–5, 419–26; and baby boomers 143;
consumer-directed services 499; costs 423; and
disabled people 101, 419–20; enrollment 424,
448–9; expansion of 109, 110, 417–18, 425, 437,
438, 449, 548; federal responsibility for 97; funded
acute care 191; guidelines 94, 464; and health care
access 425–6; history/background 413; and long-
term care 479, 497, 508; and managed care 424–5,
543; mandatory/optional coverage 421–2; means-
testing 419; medically needy program 422; mental
health treatment 441, 443; nursing home care 297,
419, 449; and older adults 190, 475; outcomes 419;
and pregnant women 419; private nursing home
industry 97; and PRWORA 423–4; quality of 425;
and religiously affiliated nursing facilities 35; state
variations 422–3; summary 435; and TANF 424;
waivers 450; work requirements 326
Medicaid Home and Community-Based Services
(HCBS) Waiver program 479
medical advances, and life expectancies 528–9
medical centers, public 450
medical expenses, older adults 485
medically needy program, Medicaid 422
medical model 8, 56, 460
Medical Savings Accounts allow people who are self-
employed or working for small businesses to place
their own pretax money in an account that can
then be used to pay for routine or long-term care
(NASW 2003a), 349, 416
medical technology, and ethical dilemmas 539
Medicare is a national government health insurance
program for people 65 or older who are eligible for
Social Security and for certain categories of younger
people with disabilities. Medicare focuses primarily

on acute care and provides little coverage for long-term care, 84–5, 426–31; administration costs 431; ageism in 451–3; and baby boomers 144; challenges to 450–3; and civil rights 416–17, 464; contributions 141; cost control 450; cost-effectiveness of 451; costs 431, 440; defined benefit/defined contribution approach 456; and disabled people 101; eligibility 409, 464; enrollment 427, 431, 448–9; expansion of 458; history/background 413; hospice benefits 500; Hospital Insurance Trust Fund 145, 428, 431; and long-term care 418, 479; managed care 428, 439; mental health treatment 275, 441, 443, 447; and national debt 145; and older adults 184, 429, 475, 497; and payroll taxes 428, 431; prescription drugs 429–31, 450–1, 480; preventative initiatives 436; under Reagan 95; reform 456–7; as single-payer system 109; summary 435; sustainability of 431; Trust Fund 114; voucher system 457

Medicare Advantage 429, 432, 439

Medicare Improvements for Patients and Providers Act 2008 275, 500

Medicare Part A is the hospital insurance component of Medicare, 428, 431

Medicare Part B is optional insurance that covers physician's fees and outpatient services, 428–9

Medicare Part C/Medicare Advantage 429

Medicare Part D 105, 429–31

Medicare Payroll Tax 431, 438

Medicare Prescription Drug, Improvement, and Modernization Act 2003 is federal legislation that provides prescription drug coverage to Medicare beneficiaries. The Medicare prescription drug benefit is referred to as Part D, 430, 480

Medicare's Hospital Insurance (HI) Trust Fund 145, 428, 431

medication, overuse/foster care 446

Medigap policies 429

mental disabilities, under G. H. W. Bush 100

mental disorders, classification/definitions of 457

mental health *see also* mental illness: and Affordable Care Act 454; finance 414; initiatives 81–2; of Native Americans 47; parity 445–6, 457, 478; policies/programs 440–1; reform of 48–9; of veterans 67, 75, 446

Mental Health Act 1946 76, 81

Mental Health Bill of Rights Act 272

mental health care: funding 441; and National Association of Social Workers (NASW) 457–8

mental health centers 273, 444, 447, 511

mental health courts 399, 444

mental health initiatives, health model 461

mental health institutions, state 49

mental health needs, older adults 499

Mental Health Parity Act 1996 417, 445, 465

mental health policies/programs 447–8; evaluating 448–50; history/background 442–5; promoting effectiveness 455–6; strengths perspective 458

mental health professionals, preparing 445–6

mental health reform movement 49

mental health services: access to 441, 446, 459; children 446; managed care 444–5; older adults 478, 500; under Reagan 98; and stigma 461

Mental Health Systems Act 1980 443–4

mental health treatment, denial to African Americans 45

mental hygiene movement 442

mental illness *see also* mental health: and almshouses 42; and children 446; and civil rights 273, 444; in colonial America 48; community care 442–5; deinstitutionalization 82, 98, 124, 273, 442–5, 447; homelessness 273, 443, 447; institutional/community-based care 124; and Medicare/Medicaid 275, 441, 443, 447; and nursing homes 98, 441, 478; older adults 275; placements in prisons/nursing facilities 98, 273; and prisons 49, 98, 443, 444, 445; reinstitutionalization 443, 465; and rights 444, 458; right to refuse treatment 273; serious mental illness (SMI) 441, 443, 444, 458, 465; and slaves 45; stigma 441, 461, 511; youth 399

Mental Retardation and Community Mental Health Centers Construction Act 1963 and 1965 were federal legislation designed to reduce the number of patients in state mental hospitals and to develop a system of community mental health centers that would provide services to the deinstitutionalized people. Federal funds were provided to the states through block grants, 443, 447–8, 465

Mental Retardation Facilities and Community Mental Health Centers Construction Act 1963 81

mental retardation, initiatives 81

merchant seamen, Public Health Service 44

Mexican Americans: and education 266; treatment of/Independence to civil war 47

Mexican border, controlling immigration 266

micro-enterprise 357, 537

microfinance, business start-up 350

Middle Ages, welfare infrastructure 37

middle class: and policy initiatives 536; unemployment 307

Midgley, James 126
migration: African Americans to northern cities 77; Middle Ages 37–8
militancy, Native Americans 91 *see also* activism
military servicemen/women: combat roles/women 279; sexual identities of 271
military service, rate of black/white 299
millennial generation 483, 529, 536
Millennium Project 533–4
mini-blogging 238
minority groups: children under 18 484; civil rights of 255; mental health provision (19c.) 49; older adults 483–4; older adults/demographics 481; substance abuse/incarceration 454; and voting 112; youth/and juvenile justice system 398
minority workers: affirmative action 93; in education 94
miracle question 240
missions 41
mistrust, black community/of social services 45
monetarism/monetary policy posits that stable economic growth is best promoted by control of the rate of increase of the money supply (the total amount of money that is circulating in the economy) to match the capacity for productive growth, 134
monitoring: outcomes 231, 299; social service agency policies/practice 300
moral consequences, government provision of social welfare 128
morality: and claims 182, 183; women/TANF 101; and work 43
Moral Majority 89
moral obligation, intergenerational 496
moral reform, anti-poverty policy as 54
morals test, mothers' pensions 60
mortality, and social class 460
mortgage interest deductions 349
mothers' pensions 59–60
mothers, programs to support 59
motivations, of forecasts 518–19
Motor Voter Act 111, 284
Mott, Lucretia 68
Moynihan, Daniel Patrick 87
Multidimensional Poverty Index (MPI) 352, 357
Multi-Ethnic Placement Act (MEPA) 1994 379–81, 386
multigenerational families 496
multipurpose senior centers 487
Muslims, discrimination 293
mutual aid 35

NASW Code of Ethics (2008) *see* Code of Ethics (2008)
National Academy of Sciences (NAS) 311
National Adult Protective Services Association (NAPSA) 490
National Alliance on Mental Illness 273
National Alliance to End Homelessness 178
National American Woman Suffrage Association (NAWSA) 68
National Association for the Advancement of Colored People (NAACP) 59, 77
National Association of Black Social Workers (NABSW) 380
National Association of Colored Women's Clubs (NACWC) 58
National Association of Social Workers (NASW): definition of social work 3; establishment of 56, 77; and mental health care 457–8; model licensure bill 94; National Task Force on Gay Rights 269; PACE 235, 546; and policy practice 235; Policy Statement on Juvenile Justice and Delinquency Prevention 398
National Breakfast and School Lunch Programs 245
National Commission on Working Women 98–9
National Committee on Lesbian, Gay, Bisexual and Transgender Issues (NCLGBTI) 269
National Conference of Charities and Correction 56
National Congress of American Indians (NCAI) 91
national debt 145, 147
National Defense Authorization Act 269
National Family Caregiver Support Program 487, 508
National Farm Workers Association 80
National Institute of Health 500
National Institute of Mental Health (NIMH) part of the National Institute of Health in the Department of Health and Human Services (HHS), is the federal agency that is primarily responsible for research on mental and behavioral disorders, 76, 442
National Institute on Aging 477
National Institutes of Health (NIH) 442
National Juvenile Justice and Delinquency Prevention Coalition 374–5
National Labor Relations Act 1935 74
National Organization for Women (NOW) 89
National Task Force on Gay Rights 269
National Urban League 59, 262, 299
Native Americans *see also* Indian tribes: access to communication/information technology 265; activism 90, 91, 263; and adoption 92; appropriation of land 45, 46, 47, 51–2; assimilation of 91; child welfare 91–2, 403; civil rights 90–3, 263–5; culture 90, 91, 264, 376; cutting off of aid

90; example of strength based initiative 20–1; Independence to civil war 45; and land ownership 90; life expectancies of 345; and nursing home policies 297; oppression 90–1; physical/mental health of 47; poverty 93, 264; providing welfare to European immigrants 41; religions/and social welfare 31–2; religious freedom 264; relocation 90–1; rights of 52; social problems 91; sovereignty 91, 263, 264, 265; substance abuse 47; termination policies 91, 263; treatment of/Independence to civil war 46–7; unemployment 47, 265
naturalization process 50
natural resources, global competition for 530
Nazi racism 77
need(s): alternate understandings of 169–70; defining 2, 168, 170–2, 175–9, 204; determination 167, 173–5, 206–7; documenting 175–9; and external factors 11; groups involved in determination of 206–7; individual/and policy issues 7; placing client's at center 7, 196; and policy development 205–9; presenting effectively 21; problem-centered approaches to 10; recasting human 10–12; role of government in addressing 70; term 1–2
negative income tax 87
neglect is the failure of caregivers to provide for basic needs such as nutrition, shelter, emotional care, and supervision: *see also* abuse; child abuse; child protection; maltreatment: defined 367–8; and drug abuse 392; and poverty 404; rates of 391; reporting systems 372
neoconservatives are people who believe the government should have a more restricted role in promoting social welfare, and advocate a greater transfer of welfare responsibility from the government to the private sector, 136
neoliberals are people who support a more active government role in achieving economic growth and social justice, 136
networking, and policy practice skills 19
networks, social 502
neutral policies, reconsidering 297, 305
new conservatives 135–6
New Deal 67, 68, 70, 90, 95, 96, 134
New Democrats 100
New Federalism 97–100, 116, 444
New Frontier 82–3
new liberals 136–7
Nixon, Richard 87, 88, 89, 91
non-cash benefits, and poverty 311
non-cash programs, low-income families 327–30

non-citizens: battered 289; civil rights 305; Hispanics/ Latinos 266
non-Hispanic white population 320, 527
non-profit organizations, tax-exempt status 241
non-profit voluntary organizations 543
normalization is a policy whereby schools endeavor to create an environment for children with disabilities similar to that experienced by children without special needs: children with special needs 387; and placements 393
normative affective strategies 240
North American Free Trade Agreement (NAFTA) 159
not-for-profit sector 147
"Nothing about us without us" 287
nurseries, crisis/respite 396
nursing facilities, and the mentally ill 98
nursing facility placement, older adults 501
nursing facility placement, politicization of 97
Nursing Home Reform Act 480
nursing homes: culture change movement 498; and long-term care 479–80; Medicaid funding 297, 419, 449; and the mentally ill 98, 443, 478; profit-making 147
nursing staff, minimum standards for 498

Obama, Barack 107–11; advance directives 501; AIDS/ HIV 455; budget priorities/national debt 145; CHIPRA 433; and CLASS 490; and disabled people/ legislation 272; and federal government responsibility 117; Hispanic support 81; and Keynesian economics 134; LGBTQ legislation 269, 270, 271; Lilly Ledbetter Fair Pay Act 107, 279; and Medicare/civil rights 413; political capital of 137–8; responsible fatherhood 325; social media/election of 132, 536, 547; teen pregnancy 394; and unemployment 151
obesity: and food insecurity 194; and poverty 329, 503
objectives: locating 187; policy/analysis of 186–9
occupational segregation refers to the disproportionately high representation of women and people of color in the secondary labor market which also negatively influences the welfare of these groups because these jobs generally do not provide benefits such as health insurance (NASW, 2003b), 291
O'Connor, Sandra Day 106
Office of Adolescent Health 394–5
Office of Child Support Enforcement 384
Office of Economic Opportunity (OEO) 84

Office of Juvenile Justice and Delinquency Prevention (OJJDP) 374, 399
Office of Management and Budget (OMB) 139
Office on Disability 487
Oglala Lakota (Sioux) people, activism by 91
Old Age and Survivors' Insurance (OASI) 73
Old Age Insurance (OAI) 73
old-age retirement pensions 314–16
Old Age, Survivors, and Disability Insurance (OASDI) OASDI is a federal program that provides pensions to workers and their families when income is lost due to retirement, old age, or disability. It was expanded to include health insurance when Medicare was enacted in 1965, 40, 73, 116, 123 see also social security; and disabled people 315, 346; evaluation of 343–7; and people of color 324–5, 345; and poverty 73, 347, 477; reform proposals 346; regressive or progressive? 345–6; as social insurance program 356; solvency of 346–7, 494–5, 513; summary 353; and women 344–5; and young people 313–16
old age, when does it begin? 469–70
older adults see also elders: 85+ 481; abuse 275, 490, 491; advance directives 414; ageism 478; anti-discrimination policies 299; benefits/and work 131; as burden 453; civil rights 274–6, 304; claims-making 183–4; community inclusion 487; depression 478, 499; diversity in needs 481; and economic downturn 494; economic security 493–7, 512, 513; effect of losses 472, 478; employment 473, 487, 493, 494, 496, 504, 513; evaluation of policies/programs 491–503; families unable to support 72; and Great Depression 474; health care 497–501, 512; history/background of policies 473–86; home-and community-based services 504; and housing 486; income sources 493; information needs 503–4; long-term care 479–80, 498, 512; major policies/programs 486–91; Medicaid funding 190, 475; medical expenses 485; and Medicare 184, 428, 475, 497; mental health services 478, 500; mental illness 275; minority/and Social Security 494; minority groups 483–4; nursing facility placement 501; oldest old 484; outreach 488, 496; and policy change 505; political power 489; poverty 73, 310; and recessions 274; remaining in own homes 498; self-determination 299, 502; sexism 502; social engagement 501–3, 508, 512; social insurance for 113; SSI 477, 495, 496; stereotypes 469, 478; suicide 478; third age 504; and transportation 473, 486, 502, 508–9;
unemployment 478–9, 494; untreated pain 275; voting patterns 486, 488; women see women
Older Americans Act (OAA) 1965 is a federal law designed to improve the coordination of planning and programs for older adults and to support their efforts to remain in the community even when they needed long-term care, 85, 475, 478, 486–8, 512; amendments 2000 487
Older Women's League (OWL) 343, 506
Older Workers Benefit Protection Act (OWBPA) 274
oldest old 484
Olmstead vs. *L.C.* 272, 444
Omnibus Budget Reconciliation Act 1990 480
Omnibus Budget Reconciliation Act 1993 378, 480
Omnibus Budget Reconciliation Act (OBRA) 1981 97
ONE 238
One Million Moms for Gun Control 238
online resources 219 see also Internet
open markets, and liberalism 136
opposition, interacting with 238–9
oppressed groups: civil rights of 254; collaborating with 296; discrimination against 255; and George H. W. Bush 96; giving voice to 20; and inequalities 256; and strengths perspective 295; strengths/resources of 258
oppression: and elites 30; immigrants 110; Independence to civil war 45; Native Americans 91; people of color 63; and social policies 5
organizational skills, of social workers 220
Organization for Economic Co-operation and Development (OECD) 156
Orphan Trains 52, 53
Orshansky, Mollie 310
Other are groups with which one does not identify: policy making for the 255; service users as 13
Other America, The 82
Other Mandatory Spending 142–3
outcome benchmarks 163
outcome indicators, and oppressed groups 256
outcomes: across life span 513; analysis of 193–4; children/ethnic groups 256; children/negative 337; child welfare 390; client/evaluating 204; client/evaluation of policy effectiveness 17; client/policy evaluation 231–3; for clients 173; of clients 389; educational 305; evaluating policy 215–16; funding linked to 193; health outcomes 411, 464; information on differential 179; Medicaid 419; monitoring 232, 299; of policy alternatives 211; and social class 460; and social environment 460; that

need to change 257–8; unintended 211; voices of clients in evaluating 551
outdoor relief is aid provided to people in their homes or other non-institutional settings, 39
out-of-home placement, foster care/adoption 377
out-of-pocket payments 193, 427, 436, 451
outreach: and Affordable Care Act 450, 548–9; lack of 478; older adults 488, 496; rural communities 488
over-population, and environmental degredation 540
overservice/underservice, health care 414, 415
oversight, health care 415
ownership society 95

pain, untreated/older adults 275
pandemics are epidemics that occur across large geographic regions, 454–5
Panetta, Leon 111
parental involvement, policies to encourage 341
parental rights, termination of 382, 391
parity: of mental health 445–6, 457, 478; of substance abuse 457
Parks, Rosa 78, 79
participatory action research 225
partnerships with clients, policy development process 204
part-time work, lack of benefits 537
Patient-Centered Outcomes Research Institute (PCORI) 440
Patient Protection and Affordable Care Act 2010 109, 406, 409, 435–38, 464
patient protection, insurance programs 459
patient rights 415
Patient Safety and Abuse Prevention Act 490–1
Patient's Self-Determination Act 1990 275
Patriot Act 294
Patten, Simon N. 56
Paul Wellstone and Pete Domenici Mental Health Parity and Addiction Equity Act 2008 417, 445, 454, 465
Pay Check Fairness Act 276
pay, gender discrimination 82
payment bundling, health care 416
payroll taxes: FICA 315, 316; insurance premiums as 141; and Medicare 428, 431; OASDI premiums as 72, 116; and retirement benefits 495; suspension of 145
payroll tax holiday 316
Pearl Harbor 74
peer lending strategy 350, 352
Pell Grants 455

penalties, for not working 131
Pension Benefit Guaranty Corporation (PBGC) 489
Pension Protection Act 2006 489
pensions: and Civil War 474; defined benefit plans 474, 477; defined contribution plans 476, 477; disability 319–20; employee pensions 474, 476–7; Job-Specific Pension Programs 476; non-portability of 537; old-age retirement 314–15; recognizing younger carers 508; at risk 476–7; Social Security pension program 149; and stock markets 494; veterans 474
people of color: discrimination 291; and employment/ benefits 324–5; and OASDI 324–5, 345; oppression 63; poverty 103–4, 256, 320, 345; and recessions 292; unemployment 98; voting rights infringements 295; wages of 98, 291
people, strengths of 9
people with mental illness *see* mental illness
Perkins, Frances 70, 74
permanency for children 392
permanency planning, foster care/adoption 377, 381–2, 392
personal experience, and social policy 8
personally constructed views 170
Personal Responsibility and Work Opportunity Reconciliation Act (PRWORA) 1996 101, 117, 321, 325, 326, 423–4
person/environmental fit 540
person-in-environment 547
person, value of 131
Pew Research Center 471
pharmaceutical companies, lobbying by 105
phased retirement is a retirement approach whereby an individual can reduce the number of hours he or she works during the years leading up to retirement, 496, 537
Philadelphia Plan 1969 93
philanthropy: private 44; private/and social policy 56, 63
physical abuse 363, 368
physical disabilities, under G. H. W. Bush 100
physical environment, and health 540
physicians, Medicaid/Medicare 480
physician's role, managed care 415
Pierce, Franklin 49
Piven, Frances 86
placements: children with special needs 387; and normalization 393
planning, end-of-life care 500–1
Plessy vs. *Ferguson* 51, 77

plugging in the elderly 453

pluralism: creating policy 133; and diversity 551; and future social policy 542; and public-private partnerships 544

pluralistic process of creating policy means that no one particular group holds all the power, 133

policies/programs, effectiveness 191–2, 215, 231–2, 356

policy advocacy 229

policy agenda, and media/public opinion 207–8

policy alternatives: assessing feasibility of 211–13; developing 204, 209; strengths-based 238

policy analysis 168–72; benefits/services provided 189–90; cost-effectiveness/outcomes 193–4, 197; eligibility rules 190–1; of financing 192–3; framework 185–94, 229–30; goals/objectives 186–9; overview 203; service delivery systems 191–2; strengths perspective 196, 197

policy development 200, 242; assessing policy alternatives 211–13; client involvement 15; clients' perspectives 14; determining need/claims-making 205–9; enacting/implementing 213–15; frameworks for 15–17, 173–5; influences upon 208; initial steps 208–9; overview 203; process 202, 204; and stakeholders 210; steps in 202–16; strengths perspective 12, 210–11, 287; tasks in 242; unanticipated consequences 216

policy effectiveness 17, 191

policy goal is a statement of the desired human condition or social environment that is expected to result from implementation of the policy: achieving consensus 209–10; analysis of 186–7; crafting 209–11; influences on 210; legislative support for 228; negotiating 227–8; public support for 204; and reimbursement systems 193

policy(ies) *see also* programs; social policy; social welfare policy: child welfare 361, 364, 390, 403; civil rights 260–1, 291–5; creating equity/inequity 125; cultural contexts 531; disadvantaging women 277; effective responses to 548; evaluating 17, 188, 197, 215–16, 232, 387–400, 491–503; factors shaping future 525–34; family income support 401; framework/influence of historical approaches 34–6; future directions 534–47; implementation stage/failure of 548; income-support 312; intergenerational 492, 506–7, 513, 524; major 281–90; mental health 440–1, 442–5, 447–8, 458; and middle class support 536; neutral/reconsidering 297, 298–9, 305; older people/history and background 473–86; regulatory 122–3; selective 320–1; social welfare in U.S. *see* social welfare policy (U.S.); sustainability of 541; worsening/improving social conditions 535–7

policy impact analysis attempts to determine the consequences of policy interventions – before, during, and after their implementation – on the well-being of different social groups, 232–3, 242

policy innovations 213

policy makers: contacting/mini-blogging 238; getting on their agendas 223–6; interacting with 239–40; providing information to 226; raising awareness in 201; and strengths in target populations 20; types of 214; understanding of truth 17

policy making 120, 139

policy options, involving clients 227

policy practice: professional efforts to influence the development, enactment, implementation, or assessment of social policies, primarily to ensure social justice and equal access to basic social goods 5, 242; action planning 237–8; and advocacy 7–8; analyzing costs 230–1; basic skills/tasks 220–33; becoming involved in 233–41; building skills 18; and conflict resolution/consensus building 13; connecting values to 22–3; ecological perspective 217–19; evaluating policy/client outcomes 231–3; examining own perspective 223; focussed on funding 228; focussing efforts 238; getting on the agenda 223–6; getting policy enacted 228–31; identifying/defining target client population 221–3; identifying/developing abilities 17–23; including client perspectives 227; negotiating policy goals 227–8; seeking support in 234–6; and social workers 6–8, 201, 202, 217–18, 242; and strengths perspective 10–14; taking action 236–41; tasks 220–1, 242

Policy Statement on Juvenile Justice and Delinquency Prevention 398

Political Action for Candidate Election (PACE) 235, 546

political activism is defined as actions taken for the purpose of influencing the outcome of elections or government decision making 235–6 *see also* activism; facing limits on 240–1; social workers 546

political capital, of Obama/G.W. Bush 137–8

political context of social policy focuses on the pursuit and exercise of power in government or public affairs, 120

political effectiveness, of social workers 235

political involvement, and social engagement 132
political momentum, and social media 536
political philosophies 135–8
political power, older adults 486
political schools of thought 134–5
political skills: of clients 239; of social workers 220
political tools, insurance programs as 494
politicization: of black youth 78; of private providers 97
politics, conservative 95
pollution, and health 461, 532, 540
poor: able-bodied/deserving 38; stigmatization of 33; victim blaming 54; worthy/unworthy 33, 34, 39, 40, 41, 89, 180
poorhouses 473
Poor Laws, English 36–40, 63, 87
population *see also* demographics: Asian Americans 268; below poverty line 310; composition 526; diversity 551; growth of 37–8, 45, 484, 526, 527, 550–1; Hispanic Americans 81; non-Hispanic whites 527; by race/Hispanic origin 528; trends 482–3 *see also* demographics
population projection refers to the number of people who are expected to be in a given group in a specific year, 520
post-traumatic stress disorders (PTSD) 446
poverty: 16th C. (Eng) 38; absolute/relative 309, 355; African Americans 51, 292, 320, 368; and aging in the community 485–6; Alaskan Natives 93; alternative measures of 311; and the American family 103–5; anti-poverty programs 75, 82–3, 84, 86; Asian Americans 267; asset 308–9, 348; asset-based approaches 102, 352; basic needs perspective 308; beliefs regarding people in 36; capabilities perspective 308, 355; child/by race and ethnicity 367; and child maltreatment 366–7, 367, 400, 404; child poverty rate 158, 320, 337; children 73, 96, 113, 122, 279, 337, 360–1; children/African American 367; children of color 257; child/TANF 12; and class 307; deep 338; definitions of 308–11, 355; as denial of human rights 296; and devolution 356; and disabilities 257, 272; and education/children of color 122; and EITC 333; elderly women of color 257; explanations of 170; federal poverty thresholds 485–6; feminization of 279; global context 350, 352; growing/and child welfare 366–7; guidelines 311, 327; under G. W. Bush 107; Hispanic/Latino population 81, 320; increasing 164; and lack of education/health care 44; life span 505; maintaining people in 348; measuring 310; Mexican

Americans 266; middle class 307; Native Americans/Alaskan Natives 93, 264; as natural selection 33; non-Hispanic whites 320; and OASDI 73, 343, 477; and obesity 329, 503; older adults 73, 310; older women 279, 344, 345, 496; people of color 76, 103–4, 256, 320, 345; policies 505; and public policy 233; rates of 98, 103, 309; reduced/1960s 85; reducing childhood 537; religious/faith-based approaches to 34; and religious traditions 30–2; and single-parent households 104, 384; strengths-based approach to 84; structural 82, 106, 170; and TANF 12, 323, 324, 336–8; urban/rural 310; and wages 114; war on 82–7, 116; women 279, 320–1 *see also* older women
poverty index 309
poverty level 310
poverty line (also described as the poverty index threshold, or level, depending on the context) is a yearly cash income threshold determined by the federal government and used to classify individuals or families as poor, 309–10, 355, 495
poverty threshold 309–10, 355
power: and claim-making 182; of corporations 159, 182; of experts 172; of health care industry 456; of medical care v. social care 180; political/older adults 486; threats to 549
preconceptions 170
pre-existing conditions, and insurance 435, 436, 438
preferred reality means helping your clients to articulate what they want changed, 222, 223
pregnant women, and Medicaid 419
prejudice: and the Holocaust 75; against immigrants 47–8
preschool, universal 536
prescription drugs: costs 430, 451; Medicare 429–31, 450–1, 480; rebates 435
preventative initiatives: health care 416; Medicare 436
prevention: abuse 148, 373, 490; and life expectancy 503; teen pregnancy 394, 395, 404
primary care, incentives to doctors 480, 481
primary care providers, training for 437
prisons *see also* incarceration: juveniles in adult 370, 373; and the mentally ill 49, 98, 443, 444, 445; minority groups/substance abuse 454
privacy: and technology 529, 541–2; v. security 111, 294
private assistance, American Revolution 44
private contractors, managed care 543

private non-profit organizations, tax-exempt status 241

private nursing home industry, politicization of 97

private organizations, funding of 148

private providers, politicization of 97

private sector: initiatives 147; role of 147–8, 164; workers' pensions 476

private social policies 4

privatization is the practice of transferring ownership or control from government to private enterprise, 96; child welfare services 368, 395; future policy directions 542–4, 551; under G. W. Bush 105; since 1980s 147

privilege, heterosexual 269

problem-centered approaches: framework for policy development 15, 16; to need 10

problem-focussed interventions 8–9

problems: analysing/expanded viewpoint 175–85; defined as national 176; defining 170–2, 175–9, 179, 180, 196; documenting 175–9, 196; homelessness as national 176; and interventions and outcomes 181; personal 168

problems/deficits, of clients 11, 14

productive aging 496

programs *see also* names of individual programs; policy(ies); social programs: analysis/strength-based 197; core federal 150; eligibility requirements 131; major 281–90; retaining safety net 202; selective 126, 320–1; to support mothers/children 59; universal 125, 312, 313–20

Progressive Era 56, 58–62

progressive taxes require people with higher incomes to pay higher rates or proportions of their income, 141

Prohibition 61, 64, 67

projects, high-rise public housing 174

Promoting Safe and Stable Families (PSSF) program 379

promotion of health/wellness 465

prospective payment is a reimbursement strategy whereby the insurer determines ahead of time the average cost for a procedure such as an appendectomy or uncomplicated childbirth in a previous year and then prospectively (before treatment) sets an amount they will reimburse the provider, 414

protected classes 299

protection, for older adults 275

Protestant work ethic 33

protest march, Selma to Montgomery 283

provision of services, public funding 148

psychiatric social work 82

psychoactive drugs 443; children 446

psychotropic medications, children in foster care 465

public accommodations: equal access to 79; segregation 80

public aid, cutting off Native Americans 90

public assistance programs 72, 73

public charges, Hispanics/Latinos as 266

public funding: provision of services 148; of religious organizations 34

public health departments 412

public health expenditure 151

Public Health Service, establishment of 44

public hearings, and policy development 210

public housing 329

public income support programs, and CDAs/IDAs 352

public insurance deductions 141

public medical centers 450

public opinion: and policy agenda 208; and social policy 210

public policy(ies): creating equity/inequity 125; and poverty 233

public-private partnerships 44, 116, 401, 456, 544

public/private welfare system 130

public relief, in English colonies 41

public social policies 4

public support, for policy goals 204

Public Welfare Amendments 1962: Social Security Act 1935 82

public welfare, provided by religious organizations 34–5

public welfare recipients, dependency of 82

purchase-of-service (POS) contracting means that the government contracts with a private entities to provide services rather than providing services directly (Petr, 2004), 395

purchasing power parity (PPP) 156

Pure Food and Drug Act (1906) 59

quality of life 544

quality, of Medicaid care 425

quotas, racial 94, 112

race disparities, child poverty 366

racial justice, European ideas of 77

racial practices, questioning of/post WWII 77

racial profiling 294

racial quotas 94, 112

racial reforms, overturning of 51

racial tension, under G. H. W. Bush 99

racism is stereotyping and generalizing, usually negatively, about a group of people related by common descent or heredity often based on any or a combination of various physical features such as skin color, or eye shape, 255–6; and African Americans 56; and immigrants 62; Independence to civil war 45–9; Japanese Americans 75; Nazi 77; and oppression 79, 255, 460; and Settlement House Movement 55; women of color 292

rape victims 257; juveniles in adult prisons 369

rapid rehousing 181, 193

rationing: of health care 408; and social policies 169

Reagan, Ronald 95, 96–7, 120, 136, 145–6, 282, 444

reality: developing a preferred 222–3; different views of 172; social construction of 170

reasonable efforts, foster care/adoption 377–8, 393

Reauthorization of Violence Against Women Act 2005 and 2013 288–9

recessions: and child abuse 391; managing 70, 96; and older people 274; and people of color 292; and poverty 307; and safety net programs 164, 342; and service demand 1; and SNAP caseloads 338; and TANF 338–40

recidivism rates: and juvenile justice system 399; and zero tolerance policies 398

reciprocacy: as core value 544; intergenerational 509

reciprocal obligation 546

recognition, of social problems 169

recommodifying labor 131

Reconstruction, the 50–2

record keeping, and information technology 541

Recovery Act 151

recruitment/retention, of social workers 399

redistribution of income 154

redistributive process means that resources are redistributed from one group of people to another group, 143

reform: OASDI 346; proposals for 350

reform movements, women in 59, 63–4

refugees 293

Regents of the University of California vs. *Bakke* 94, 279–80

regressive taxes require people with lower incomes to pay higher rates or proportions of their income, 141

Regulating the Poor 86

regulations, discriminatory 298

regulatory policy 122–3

rehabilitation: and juvenile justice system 369, 398; vocational 101

Rehnquist, William 106

reimbursement rates 161; and Medicaid/Medicare 425, 451

reimbursement strategies, private providers/children in state custody 393

reimbursement systems, and policy goals 193

reinstitutionalization, people with mental illness 443, 465

re-languaging discussions 522

relationship building: with legislators 207, 228; media 226; and policy practice skills 19

relationships: reciprocacy in 492; social workers/ clients 296

relationship skills 220

relative poverty refers to a measure of who is poor influenced heavily by societal standards, whereby a threshold of income is determined that will allow people to afford what is generally considered to be an adequate standard of living by the citizenry at a given time in a society, 309, 355

religion, lack of affiliation with/welfare provision 105

religious conflicts 530

religious freedom, and Native Americans 264–5

religious groups: contemporary U.S. society 35; people not belonging to 35

religious institutions, providing social welfare 34–5, 97, 105, 543 *see also* faith-based initiatives

religious leaders, and civil rights 304

religious sites, Native American 264–5

religious traditions, and social welfare 30–2

relocation, Native Americans 90 *see also* land

reluctant welfare state, U.S. as 157

reporting systems, child abuse prevention 373, 391

repression, and climate of fear 294

reproductive rights 69

reproductive technologies: and ethical dilemmas 539; and exploitation 528

Republican Party 46, 108, 110, 134, 136

research: evaluating 196, 207; focussing on clients strengths/capacities 225; and interacting with policy makers 239; involving target population 181; participatory action 225; policy outcomes 215–16; and policy practice 241; policy/skills in 220; skills/ social workers 220; social 54

researchers, Settlement House workers as 55

research needs, effectiveness of strengths perspective 22

reservations, forced removal to 46

residential facilities, and family reunification 392

residual approach posits that the government should intervene only when the family, religious institutions, the marketplace, and other private entities are unable to adequately meet the needs of certain populations: income-support programs 129; public relief 41–2

resource allocation, involving clients 162

resources: for clients/web based 219; depletion of 531; of oppressed groups 258; rationing of 169

respect, for diversity 6

respect for the individual, values 20

Respecting the Rights of Hospital Patients to Receive Visitors and to Designate Surrogate Decision Makers for Medical Emergencies 413, 501

respite nurseries 396

responsibility(ies): of citizens 130; collective/solving social problems 21; governments/people in need 42; individual/personal 95; local 39, 102; for policy practice 39

restraint, used in schools 387

retirees, worthy 73

retirement *see also* pensions: credits/for caring 538; early 495; early/due to unemployment 346; and economic downturn 504; future policy directions 537–8; and global workers 538; mandatory 274, 478–9; old-age retirement pensions 314–16; phased 496, 537; private/public programs 474–5; as a process 537; raising age of 345; rates of 494; Social Security retirement benefits 95, 193; solvency of pension plans 490; taxes on benefits 495; transferability of benefits 537

retrenchment, and policy practice 242

retrospective payment system is a reimbursement strategy whereby the private provider submits a bill after services have been rendered and the insurer then reimburses the provider, 414

reunification, children with their families 381, 382, 388, 392–3, 403

reverse discrimination is defined as discrimination against the dominant group due to policies designed to redress discrimination against minority groups, 93, 279

Richmond, Mary 56, 67

right(s) *see also* human rights: of African Americans 45, 51; civil rights *see* civil rights; and claims-making 182, 184; to due process of law/equal protection of laws 50, 459; family 390–1; of fetus 106; human rights 293–5, 296; of immigrants 293; of Native Americans 52; older adults/self-determination 502; patient 415; people with mental illness 444, 458; poverty/deprivation as denial of 296; to refuse treatment 273; reproductive 69; right of appeal 459; of same-sex couples 413, 464; social/and citizenship 128; social welfare as 129; to treatment/to refuse treatment 458; voting 284; of women 43, 68, 89, 292, 305

right to refuse treatment, mental illness 273

risk: and advocacy 541; for clients in policy practice 239; and policy alternatives 211; of poverty 320

risk factors: child abuse 391; social isolation 501

risk shifting: federal government to states 95; to individuals 416, 438, 457; and older adults 457, 489–90, 499, 513; and pensions 477

Roberts, John 106

Roe vs. *Wade* 90, 106

roles, expanding clients 12–13

Roman society, social welfare 33

Romer vs. *Evans* 269

Roosevelt, Franklin D. 70, 71, 417

Roosevelt, Theodore 59

Roper vs. *Simmons* 370

rule-making process: policy implementation 214; and social workers 548

rules, discriminatory 298

rural communities: access to computers 529; aging in/poverty 485, 488; incentives to doctors 480; life expectancies/women 503; outreach 488

Ryan White Comprehensive AIDS Resources Emergency (CARE) Act 1990 454–5

safety, child 390–2

safety net programs: attacks on 536; and capacity building approach 537; economic downturn 350; holes in 307; positive impact of 342; retaining 202; and strengths perspective 342; TANF 337, 341; value of 311, 356; work-based/and diversity 535–7

sales taxes 141

same-sex civil unions 270

same-sex couples, rights of 413, 464

same-sex marriage 112, 136, 270

sanctions, TANF 325–7

sandwich generation 492, 538

San Francisco, homeless people initiative 191

Sanger, Margaret Higgins 68, 69

Saver's Credit 489

savings *see also* assets: disincentives to/EITC 334; dwindling 494; spend down requirement 425, 497

savings programs, universal/progressive 545

Scandinavia 130, 131

scapegoating, vulnerable populations 294

school-based policies/programs, supporting families 397

school meals 362

schools: corporal punishment 400; restraint/seclusion used in 387; zero tolerance policies 398, 404

school segregation: *Brown* vs. *Board of Education of Topeka* 77, 122, 261; challenge to 77; Hispanic Americans 80; Latinos 266

schools of social work 56

scientific charity 54, 55

seclusion, in schools 387

secondary labor market refers to the segment of the economy made up of the lowest paying jobs which are often temporary and disproportionately held by women and people of color, 291

security, v. civil liberties/privacy 111, 294

segregation: de facto segregation 291; Hispanic Americans 80; Jim Crow laws 51–2; occupational segregation 291; post war 77–8; racial/class in housing 77; school/challenge to 77, 261; school/ Latinos 266

selective policies/programs are defined as programs that provide benefits and services only to those segments of a population that meet specific eligibility requirements, 126, 320–1; income-support 312; means-testing 356; TANF 321–7

self-determination refers to people's ability to control their own destiny: core values 6, 14, 529; end-of-life 500; and interdependence 502; older adults/ children 299; right of older adults 502; and strengths perspective 173, 547

self-help organizations, African Americans 45, 58

self-interest, and social movements 180

separate but equal policy 122

September 11 104, 138, 184, 293, 522

serious mental illness (SMI) is a classification given to adults over age 18 who have been diagnosed with a major mental illness that results in functional impairment and substantially limits their ability to perform activities of daily living, 441, 443, 444, 445, 458, 465

service delivery systems: evaluation of 17; policy analysis 191–2; and resources 229

service development, student involvement in 17–18

service eligibility, and immigration status 265 *see also* eligibility requirements

service fragmentation means that many organizations will be providing services with little overall coordination or attention to overlapping

services or gaps in service, decentralization of service in, 543

Servicemen's Readjustment Act 1944 75

service provision: and Internet 541; policy analysis of 189–90

services: culturally competent 399; to families 368; loss of/failure to evaluate 232; provision of/public funding 148

service users *see also* client group: as other 13; solutions to problems 547; term 3

Settlement House Movement 54–5, 62, 63

settlement house workers: and child welfare 60; as early social workers 56; as researchers 55

sexism is discrimination based solely on gender, 255, 256, 292, 502

sexual abuse 368

sexual assault 257; juveniles in adult prisons 369

sexual harassment 292

sexually transmitted infections (STIs) 395

sexual orientation is defined as "the tendency to experience erotic or romantic responses to men, women, or both, and the resulting sense of oneself" (NASW, 2003d, p. 224), 268; and bullying 303; and discrimination 99, 290, 292, 304; and foster care 392; hate crimes 257, 269, 290, 304; and homophobia 256; oppressed groups 116; and social workers 255; and strengths perspective 173

sexual violence 277

shared responsibility payment 438

Shelby County vs. *Holder* 112, 284

Sherraden, Michael 348, 349, 351, 545

shootings, mass 110

should statements 179–80

Silver Haired Legislature 491

single mothers, income of 337

single-parent households 104, 365, 384

single-payer health care plan is a system under which the federal government would pay for basic health care for all citizens from public revenues (NASW 2003a), 109, 417, 439

skills: policy development 202; policy practice 220; value-clarifying 220

skin color, legal discrimination 77

Skocpol, Theda 60

slavery 42–3, 45, 50

SNAP *see* Supplemental Nutrition Assistance Program (SNAP)

social benefits, and labor unions 129

social capital *see also* assets: formation 545; older adults 502

social conditions, and social problems 168–9
social connections, building 133
social conscience hypotheses 128
social construction: of family violence 171–2; and forecasting 524; meaning 171; of reality 170; of teenage pregnancy 171
social constructionist approach posits that our explanations of all human interactions – including social problems – are based on views of reality that are socially and personally constructed (Gergen, 1999; Geertz, 1973), 170
social contentment, and social welfare 128
social contract 131, 509
social control 30, 35, 178, 188, 550
Social Darwinism was a social philosophy that applied Darwin's theory of evolution based on natural selection to human societies (Reid, 1995), 33, 54
social determinants of health: "the circumstances in which people are born, grow up, live, work, and age, as well as the systems put in place to deal with illness" (CDC, 2013), 407, 463; and Affordable Care Act 418–19, 425; and health disparities 407–8; importance of 460; and Medicaid 425
social development approach seeks to harmonize economic development with social welfare policy by redistributing wealth and resources in ways that also promote economic growth (Midgley, 1999), 159–60
Social Diagnosis 56
social engagement: older adults 475, 501–3, 508, 509, 512; and political involvement 132
social environment, and health outcomes 460
social exchange theory 502
social expenditure, categories of 156
social goods 129
Social Gospel 33, 71
social inclusion, and strengths perspective 160
social inclusion policies 162–3
social indicators, and oppressed groups 256
social insurance is a system whereby society recognizes the normal risks of living, and people and the government pool money to help out when misfortune, such as unemployment, injury, or sickness, strikes,: beginnings of 58; OASDI as 356; for older adults 113; as social welfare spending 150; workers' compensation 318–19
social interaction, older adults 508
socialism, democratic 134–5
social isolation: combatting 502; and Internet 504, 520; as risk factor 501

socialized medicine 109
social justice refers to the equitable distribution of societal resources to all people as well as equity and fairness in the social, economic and political spheres,: and child welfare system 389; and claims 182–3; and defining the problem 179; and economic efficiency 544; and eligibility rules 190; and empowerment theory/strengths perspective 296; and equal treatment claims 226; and government 113; and immigration policies 536; model 9; and social policy(ies) 23; and social welfare 135; and social work 296; and social workers 305; and strengths perspective 173; and tax expenditures 142; values 6, 14, 20
socially constructed views 170
social media: and activism 541, 548; and advocacy 238; creating community 536; election of Obama 536, 547; and interacting with policy makers 239; and political momentum 536
social mobilization, and forecasts 519
social movements 180
social networks 502
social niches 218–19
social policy(ies) *see also* policy(ies) are the laws, rules, and regulations that govern the benefits and services provided by governmental and private organizations to assist people in meeting their needs: advocacy 547; capacity building approach 129, 544; and capitalism 121; and child abuse 3–4; defined 1–2; economic/political context 120, 163; and elites/social control 113; as engine for growth 129; and environmental concerns 114; evaluation of 15, 173; factors shaping future 525–34; under G. H. W. Bush 96–7; goals/design 15, 173; and Great Depression 70; influence of Poor Laws 39–40; involvement of target group 173; and judiciary 77; negative outcomes of 22; and oppression 5, 51; perpetuating poverty 51; and personal experience 8; and pluralism 542; private 4; and private philanthropy 56; and public opinion 210; public/private 4; purposes of 168, 178; as rationing 169; regulatory policy 122–3; and service effectiveness 3; shaping 23; and social justice 23; and social work 3–8; and Supreme Court 139; transgenerational perspective 114, 116; and value choices 544; and well-being 544; and work requirements 551
social problems are concerns about the quality of life for large groups of people that are either held as a broad consensus among a population or voiced by social and economic elites (Chambers, 2000):

analysis 9, 175–85; causal theories 180–2; construction of 172; defining 204; Native Americans 92; privileged conceptions of 172; recasting 10–12; and social conditions 168–9; term 2

social programs are defined as the specified set of activities that are designed to solve social problems and/or meet basic human needs, 4 *see also* programs; adequacy of expenditure on 154–8; impetus for 123–5; private sector responsibility for 105; social development approach 160; and well-being 162

social reform: and federal government 52; movement/ Progressive Era 59; and Settlement House Movement 55

social research 54

social resources, loss of 502

social responsibility 162, 544

social rights: and citizenship 128; social welfare as 129

Social Security *see also* Old Age, Survivors, and Disability Insurance (OASDI): and control of women 127; and federal deficit 494; funding 343; and G. W. Bush 476–7; and minority elders 494; and national debt 145; support for 494; term 313; viability of 114

Social Security Act 1935 72–3; administrating 70; Child Welfare Services Program 363; and federal role/social welfare 184; and Medicare/Medicaid 419, 426; Public Welfare Amendments 1962 82; success of 113; and TANF 101, 324; and Townsend Movement 129

Social Security Administration (SSA) 313, 331, 413

Social Security and Medicare Board of Trustees 451

Social Security credits 344

Social Security Disability Insurance (SSDI) program 443

Social Security pension program 149

Social Security retirement benefits 95, 193

Social Security tax, as regressive 345–6

Social Security Trust Fund 145

Social Service Amendments 1974 83, 89

social service reforms, 1970s 88–9

social services: local government provision of 48; mistrust of/black community 45; and Native Americans 47, 92; pressures to reduce spending 98; privatized 543; skepticism of effectiveness of 83

social stratification 132

social unrest, and social welfare 129

social welfare refers to a nation's system of programs, benefits, and services that help people meet those social, economic, educational, and health needs

that are fundamental to the maintenance of society, 3 *see also* social welfare policy; welfare; 1970s initiatives 88–9; and children 4–5; and civil rights protection 44; conflicting views of 33; and control of women 129; devolution 97–8, 146, 338; early approaches 35; and economy 129; federal government responsibility for 59, 70, 101; GDP spent on 149; institutional/residual approaches 125–6, 129; and local government/communities 137; and new conservatives 135; privatization of 116; and religious institutions 35; and social contentment 128; and social justice 135; as social right 129; and social unrest 129; spending under Reagan 96, 97; and tax expenditures 151–4; U.S. expenditure/other countries 156–8

social welfare expenditures refers to all spending necessary to sustain the core federal and state social welfare programs, 149–60

social welfare policy *see also* policy(ies); social policy(ies): American Revolution 43–4; beginnings of 30–3; and capitalism 113; under Clinton 100; colonial era 41–3; economic/political schools of thought 133–5; expansion of/Progressive Era 58–62; and federal budgets 142; Independence to civil war 45–9; New Democrats 100; and work 42

social work can be defined as "the professional activity of helping individuals, groups or communities to enhance or restore their capacity for social functioning and creating societal conditions favorable to this goal" (National Association of Social Workers, 1973, p. 4), *see also* social workers: 1970s changes 94–5; core values 5–6, 173, 504; defined 3; ecological perspective 218; effective 201, 547; hospital 462; mission of 3; origins of 52–6; policy practice work *see* policy practice; psychiatric 82; and social justice 296; and social policy 3–8; and strengths perspective 8–17, 173

social work agencies, economy of 161–2

social workers *see also* social work: as activists 540; and advocacy 201; African American 56–7; and benefits for older people 495; and civil rights 298–301; educated in gerontology 480–1, 510, 514, 519–20; and electoral politics 546, 548, 551; and health care reform 458–60; and immigration enforcement 296; as instruments of social control/ assistance 550; and New Deal programs 70; and policy development process 217; and policy practice 6–8, 201, 202, 217–18, 242; political effectiveness of 235; political skills of 220; practicing globally 541;

as resource 225; role of 173, 215, 221, 399, 459, 465, 504; and rule-making process 548; and social justice 305

social work profession: building the 56; and Child-Saving Movement 63

social work settings, discrimination in 301

Social Work Speaks 235, 546

society, and inequalities 103

Society for the Prevention of Cruelty to Children 54, 363

sodomy laws 269

solution-focused approaches 20, 222, 240

solution-focused therapy 547

solutions, and identifying strengths 221

solvency, OASDI 346–7, 494–5, 513

Southern Christian Leadership Conference (SCLC) 78

sovereignty, Native Americans 91, 263, 264, 265

special educational needs, legislation for children with 385, 387

special needs: and adoption 382; children/ incarceration of 370; normalization 387

Special Supplemental Nutrition Program for Women, Infants, and Children (WIC) 4–5, 187, 328–9

Spencer, Herbert 33

spend down requirement 425, 497

spending: adequacy of/social problems 154–8; on children/older adults 506, 514; defense 100, 105, 184; on disabled people over 65 497; discretionary 140, 143, 145, 150, 164, 312; federal 142–5; government/as redistributive process 143; health care 151, 410–11, 412, 419, 464; mandatory 140, 142, 144, 145, 150, 151, 312, 361; Medicaid 419; Medicare 431; pressures to reduce social service 98; and social insurance 150; social welfare/under G.W. Bush 150–1; state spending policies 145–7; TANF 322; teen pregnancy 393

SSI benefits *see* Supplementary Security Income (SSI) program

stakeholders are those people who likely will experience either substantial gain or loss as a result of the policy change, 210

standards: CSWE 6; for foster care 382–3; social work education 76–7

Stanton, Elizabeth Cady 68

Starr, Helen Gates 55

state assistance, American Revolution 44

State Children's Health Insurance Program (SCHIP) is a program established under Title XXI of the Social Security Act to make health insurance for children more widely available, 102, 433, 435, 464

State Comprehensive Mental Health Services Plan Act 1986 444, 448, 465

State Health Insurance Assistance Programs (SHIP) 480

state jurisdiction, services to families 368

state level, executive branch 138

State of the Future Index (SOFI) 533–4

state(s): bicameral legislature 139; budgets 139–40; capacity building 107, 130–3, 164, 355; conservative movement view 108; enabling/capacity building 130–3; responsibility for social welfare 95; spending policies 145–7; and TANF 321, 338; voter identification laws 80, 281, 284, 295

status offenders 374

status quo, maintaining 239

step-down programs 231

stereotypes: Asian Americans 267; older people 453, 469, 478; of women 89

sterilization, involuntary 442, 539, 540

Stewart B. McKinney Homeless Assistance Act 1987 *see* McKinney-Vento Homeless Assistance Act

stigma, mental illness 441, 461, 511

stigmatization: and benefits 189; and means testing 190

stock market crash 1929 68

stock markets, and pensions 494

Stonewall Riot 269

stories, personal/and social policy 220, 401

story banks, and policy practice 225, 238

strangers: ambivalence towards 34; help for 33; and Judaism 30; limiting aid to 101

strengths: documenting 221; identifying 9, 221; of oppressed groups 258; recognizing clients' 202

strengths approach *see also* strengths perspective

strengths approach(es): claims-making 13; Code of Ethics (2008) 524; Economic Opportunity Act 1964 84; example of 20–1; forecasts 523–5; policy development 16, 205, 287; policy practice/values integral to 5–8; program analysis 197; reform of child welfare services 389; social engagement 502; social policy development 547; strategies for utilizing 225–6; and strengths perspective 10; term 2

strengths-based agenda, developing 505–8

strengths/goals, of client(s) 14, 20

strengths/needs-based (SNB) approach, child welfare practice 388

strengths perspective is a philosophical approach to social work that posits that the goals, strengths, and resources of people and their environment rather than their problems and pathologies should be the central focus of the helping process (Saleebey, 1992), *see also* strengths approach: analyzing benefits/services 189; and asset-based approached 102; benefits of 20–1; cautions regarding 21–2; child protection policy 390–7; delivery systems 191; and ecological approach 219; and eligibility rules 191; and empowerment theory 295; evaluating child welfare policies 387–400; and exclusion/discrimination 11; framework for policy development 15; and future social policy 550; and GI Bill of Rights 75; health model 461; integrating/benefits and cautions 19–22; juvenile justice system 397–9; legislation 129; mental health policies 458; and needs determination 173–5; in new era 547–9; OASDI 347; and older adults 472, 505, 512; and oppressed groups 295; policy analysis 186, 196; policy development 204, 210–11; and policy practice 10–15; policy/program goals 335; principles of 173, 174; promotion of health/wellness 465; reforming TANF 340–2; research 181; and role of social worker 221; and safety net programs 342; and self-determination 173, 547; and Settlement House Movement 55; and social inclusion 160; social welfare 44; and social work 8–17, 174; and social work values 14; and strengths approach 10; term 2

strengths/resources, of clients 11

stress, and child abuse 367, 391

stress models, coping 504

structural barriers 14, 15, 106, 173

structural causes, of unemployment/poverty 170

structural change, under G. H. W. Bush 96

structural discrimination refers to entrenched and long-lasting societal practices that favor one group over another based on group characteristics such as skin color, 258

student loans 350, 351, 455, 481

students: advocacy 236, 327, 389, 459, 549; and claims-making 206; helping immigrants become citizens 293; and marriage equality 271; from oppressed groups 20; and outreach 549; political activism 235–6; raising awareness/human trafficking 532

Students United for Marriage (SUM) 271

subsistence migration 38

substance abuse: access to services 446, 459; and child welfare system 390; and health care system 453–4; Native Americans 47; parity 457; SAMHSA 445, 448, 454; and serious mental illness (SMI) 445; treatment of 445, 453–5

Substance Abuse and Mental Health Services Administration (SAMHSA) 445, 448, 454

suffrage: all male citizens 50; barriers to 80; black/opposition to 50; women 50, 59, 67

suicide: assisted 276; children/in poverty 361; juveniles in adult prisons 369; LGBTQ youths 270; older adults 478; soldiers 446

Summer Food Service Program 245, 246–50

Sumner, William Graham 33

Supplemental Nutrition Assistance Program (SNAP) 86, 327–8, 356 *see also* Food Stamp Program; benefits 192, 245; caseloads/and recessions 338; eligibility requirements 265, 327, 328, 338; raising awareness of 496; summary 354; work requirements 326

Supplemental Poverty Measure 311

Supplemental Security Income (SSI) program is the federal program that provides assistance to people with limited or no income who are elderly, blind, or have disabilities, 88, 330–2; disabled people 443; limiting 101; older adults 346–7, 477, 495, 496; summary 354; transfer to states 97

supply-side economics is an economic school that advocates reduction in social programs so that tax dollars can instead be invested in the private sector to stimulate economic growth, 96, 134

Supporting Healthy Marriage (SHM) 325

support, long-term 397

Supreme Court: and affirmative action 99, 112, 280; gender gap 276; G. W. Bush administration 106; rulings 111; and same-sex marriage 112; and social policy 139

surrogate decision makers 414

survivors' insurance: divorcees 344; and OASDI 346

sustainability, of policies 541

Sweden 130, 131

systemic solutions 168

system replacement, and forecasts 519

Systems of Care (SOC) 388

TANF 12–13, 356; analysis of funding 193; block grants 322, 326, 338, 356; cash benefits 322; and child care 323, 324; and child well-being 337; and CSE 387; drug testing proposal 205; eligibility requirements 194, 321, 322, 349; eligibility rules 194; evaluation of 335, 336–8; family formation goals 325; and FAP 88; federal support 146; Funding Work Incentive Program 326; goals of 323, 324–5; history/development of 323; and Individual Development Accounts (IDAs) 349; marriage incentives 129; and Medicaid 424; and poverty 12, 323, 324, 336–8; and recessions 338–40; reforming/ strengths perspective 340–2; replacing AFDC 100, 101; sanctions 325–7; as selective program 321–7; and single women families 102; summary 353; work requirements 101, 129, 321, 322, 325–7, 337, 341; and worthy poor 40

taxation: and business interests 146; and Contract with America 101; and corporations 151, 182; and discretionary spending 140; and EITC 88, 333; excise taxes 439; federal income tax 59; FICA tax 316; funding reforms/social welfare 58; and global competitiveness 158; under G. W. Bush 103, 134; and inequalities 164; Medicare Payroll Tax 431; negative income tax 88; payroll taxes 72, 116, 141, 145, 315, 316, 331, 428, 495; progressive taxes 141; under Reagan 96, 134; regressive taxes 141; on retirement benefits 495; sales taxes 141; Saver's Credit 489; supply-side economics 134; tax breaks 142, 151, 182; tax credits 317; tax cuts/G. W. Bush 105, 111, 144; tax deductions 151; tax entitlements 152, 153–4; tax-exempt status 241; tax incentives 144, 151; tax revenues 156; tax strategies 141–7; on tobacco 142; and unemployment insurance 317; U.S./low rates of 157, 158

tax-exempt status, private non-profit organizations 241

tax expenditures are taxes that are not collected from particular groups in order to assist them in obtaining goods and services such as housing, health care, and education, 141–2, 151–4

Taylor, Jim 218, 219

Tea Party movement 108, 137

technology: and challenges 529; and privacy 529, 541, 542; and social work practice 552

teenage foster children 389

teenage pregnancy: causes/consequences 181; discharge planning 462; evaluation of policies 393–5; prevention 394, 395, 404; social construction of 171; strengths perspective 9; Teen Pregnancy Prevention Initiative (TTPI) 394

teenagers, homeless 1

Temperance Movement 61

Temporary Aid to Needy Families (TANF) *see* TANF

Temporary Emergency Relief Administration (TERA) 71

Tenant-Based Housing Assistance Program 330

Ten 'Old' Ideas for Using Technology in Macro Practice in New Ways 221

termination, Medicaid 423

termination policies, Native Americans 90, 91, 263

terrorism 111

Texas, annexation of 47

third age, older adults 504

threats, global 531

three-legged stool 493, 494, 513

three pillars of welfare 130

Thrifty Food Plan 310, 328

Tice, C. J. & Perkins, K. 44

Ticket to Work and Work Incentives Improvement Act 1999 101

time-limited benefits, unemployment 131

Title IV-E funds 377

Titmuss, Richard 128–9

Torah, the 30

torture 104

Towle, Charlotte 10–11, 70

Townsend Movement 72, 129, 184, 475

Toynbee Hall 55

traditional conservatives, laissez-faire economy 134

trafficking, victims of 289

Trail of Broken Treaties caravan 91

Trail of Tears 46

training *see also* education: for clients/in advocacy 239; foster carers 396; health/mental health and minority groups 457; Manpower Development Training Act (MDTA) 82; mental health providers 478; options/TANF families 340; for primary care providers 437; to schools of social work 56; and Settlement House Movement 55; and workforce 131

transaction costs refer to all costs incurred during government interventions including financial, economic, personal, and environmental costs, 123

transformative change 542

Transitional Medical Assistance program 340

transition plans, contraception advice 395

transition to adulthood, foster children 389, 403

translation services, CHIPRA 434

transnational grassroots organizations 532

transportation: and access to health care 511; and employment 336; and older adults 473, 486, 502, 508–9

transporting niches are environments where people can get the help they need to move out of entrapping niches, 219

trauma, identification of childhood 398

treaties, Native Americans/termination and violations of 46

Treaty of Guadalupe Hidalgo 47

tribal advocacy 264

tribal caring 297
tribal communities, health disparities 265
tribal sovereignty 263, 265, 305
Tribal Sovereignty Protection Initiative 264
Tribal Supreme Court Project 264
tribes: casino income 265; and ICWA 376–7
Truman, Harry S. 75, 417
trust busting 58
trust, lack of/in corporations 123
Tubman, Harriet 45
Twitter 132, 238, 239

ultra-conservatives 110
unanticipated consequences is defined as
  unexpected events that result from the
  implementation of a policy, 216
Underground Railroad 45
unemployment *see also* employment: African
  Americans 263, 292; and loss of benefits 149;
  middle class 307; Native Americans 47, 265 under
  Obama 151; older adults 478–9, 494; and payroll
  taxes 145; people of color 98; structural causes of
  170; time-limited benefits 131
unemployment insurance 316–18; groups not eligible
  317; and people of color 324–5
unforeseen events, and forecasts 523
uninsured people: adults 449; children 432, 449;
  immigrants 424, 438; numbers of 409, 417, 463;
  reducing numbers of 417, 428, 440
United Civil Rights Leadership 78
United Farm Workers (UFW) 80
United Kingdom, social safety net 536
United Nations: Multidimensional Poverty Index
  (MPI) 352, 357; policy and poverty 232–3; social
  development approach 160; United Nations
  Convention on the Rights of the Child 400
Uniting and Strengthening America by Providing
  Appropriate Tools Required to Intercept and
  Obstruct Terrorism Act of 2001 *see* Patriot Act
universal health care 109; benefits of 509; and
  Clinton 100; and Green Party 137; lack of/infant
  mortality 158; and Liberals 136; and NASW 455–6;
  and Obama 107, 109; in other countries 411, 438;
  and Patient Protection and Affordable care Act 2010
  464
universal income support 509
universal programs provide services and benefits to
  all citizens in a broad category, 125, 312, 313–20
university admission, racial quotas 112
unrest, and anti-poverty programs 86

upside-down welfare state 151
Urban Institute 361
urbanization: post civil war 52; and unwillingness to
  help others 128
Urban League 84
urban slums, and immigrants 47, 48
U.S. Census Bureau 310, 311, 520, 521
U.S. Children's Bureau 363–4
U.S. Citizenship and Immigration Services (USCIS)
  294
U.S. Department of Health and Human Services
  (USDHHS) 272, 311, 372, 382, 384, 391, 396, 414,
  448, 486
U.S. Department of Housing and Urban Development
  (HUD) 176, 193, 329
U.S. Social Security Board 11

vagrancy, 16th. C. (Eng) 38, 39
value-clarifying skills 220
values *see also* core values: and claims-making 183;
  connecting to policy practice 22–3; core social work
  5–6, 173, 504; and policy development 211–13;
  respect for the individual 20; self-determination 14;
  social justice 6, 14, 20; and strengths perspective 14
ventilation/intubation 453
vertical equity focuses on redistributing resources to
  people in need who possess fewer resources to
help equalise conditions, 124
vested interests 239
veterans: benefits 319–20; disabilities 319; mental
  health of 67, 75, 446; pensions 474; support for
  returning 75
victim blaming 9, 20, 21, 54
views: own/and policy practice 223; of reality/
  different 172; socially/personally constructed 170
violence: Arab Americans 293; domestic 182, 277,
  491; family/social construction of 171–2; gender-
  related 277; and globalization 530; gun 111; sexual
  277; against women 257, 277, 288–9
Violence Against Women Act (VAWA) 277, 288,
  289
vision, developing a shared 222
visioning: clients/of goals 174; clients/of solutions
  196; preferred future 240, 549–50
vocational rehabilitation 101
voice, giving/oppressed groups 20
Volstead Act 1919 61–2
volunteering: older adults 496; and policy practice
  skills 19
Volunteers in Service to America (VISTA) 84

voting: encouraging 234, 235, 546; Hispanic voters 81; Latino voters 266; literacy tests 283; and minorities 112; older adults 486, 488; proof of citizenship 284; voter I.D. laws 80, 281, 284, 295; voter registration 284, 295; voter turnout 235, 546; voting rights infringements 294
Voting Rights Act 1965 80, 111, 261, 283–4
voucher system, Medicare 457

wages: African American women 292; of agricultural workers 80; discrimination 289; future policy directions 537–8; living wage 337, 537; low 103; of people of color 98, 291; and poverty 114; of women 276, 279, 291
waivers, Medicaid 420, 450, 479
Wald, Lillian 60
War on Drugs 445
War on Poverty 82–7, 116
war on terror 293
war(s): Afghanistan/Iraq 104, 138; cost of 111, 144, 145; expanding welfare state in 67–76; and mental illness/veterans 446; U.S. and Mexico 47
Watergate scandal 89
wealth: and corporations 159; and human capital 134
wealth gap 347
wealth redistribution, capacity building approach 545
Weick, A. 461
welfare: public/provided by religious organizations 34–5; social welfare 3; three pillars of 130; U.S. concept of 130
welfare agencies, first federal 51
welfare capitalism 128
welfare indicators 157–8
welfare mother, term 183
welfare pluralists believe that society benefits when a variety of private groups as well as various levels of government participate in the provision of social welfare benefit and services, 157
welfare policy: controlling women 127; and the environment 540
welfare programs, other countries 130, 131
welfare recipients, dependency of 82
welfare rights movement 83
welfare rolls, cost of 83, 86
welfare state: to enabling state 113; evolution of modern 75–87; expanding in war/depression 67–76; as failed experiment 95
welfare system: 1970s 87–95; 1981–present 95–112; explanations for development of 126–30; lessons/

challenges 112–15; and libertarians 137; in new century 104–7; traditional and industrialization 127; U.S. 130
welfare-to-work (WTW) grants 326
well-being: child/and EITC 334; and globalization 159; and social policy 544
whistle blowers 294, 543
Whitehall Studies 460
white liberal groups, coalitions with black civil rights groups 77
white men, control by 43
white non-Hispanic: children/numbers of 367; population 551
Wilensky, H. L. and Lebeaux, C. N. 157
Wilson, Woodrow 68
Winslow, Edward 31
woman's rights groups 68
women *see also* women of color: abuse/older women 491; activists 59, 64; African Americans 292; births to unmarried 365; as caregivers 277, 508; centenarians 483; and civil rights 89, 276–9; and control/welfare policy 127, 129; and cultural conservatives 136; domestic violence 277, 491; economic development of 537; employment 99; income inequality 257; laws/working conditions 59; life expectancies 503; morality of/TANF 101; and OASDI 344–5; older adults 483; older/learning to control own lives 501; older/Medicare 451; older/poverty in 257, 277, 344, 495; organizations of 59; and poverty 320–1; under Reagan 98; in reform movements 59, 63–4; rights of 43, 68, 89, 292, 305; serving in combat 111; sexual violence 277; stereotypes of 89; suffrage 50, 59, 67; violence against 257, 277, 288–9; wages of 276, 279, 537; in workforce 336; workplace policies 535; and work requirements 535–6
Women, Infants, and Children (WIC): creation of 7; policy 187; Special Supplemental Nutrition Program 4–5, 187, 328–9; summary 354
women of color: negative outcomes 292; older 257, 320; poverty 257; racism 292; sexism 292
women's clubs 58
work *see also* employment; workers: and disabled people 272; and eligibility rules 317; female 291; harassment on the job 292; incentives/penalties for 131; jobs/future policy directions 537–8; moral importance of 43; and older adults 493; part-time/lack of benefits 537; Protestant work ethic 33; and social welfare policies 42; willingness to/precondition for assistance 72

work credits, and eligibility for benefits 314

workers *see also* employment; work; workforce: affirmative action 93; compensation 318–19; disabled 313; income of black 299; international 538; low income/life expectancies of 345; low-paid/women 127; Mexican in U.S. 47; policies supporting parenting role 397; protection for older 274; provisions for retired 73; and value of person 131

workforce *see also* workers: and education/training 131; and health care 408; older adults in 274, 504; and public education/health care 127; women in 336

Workforce Investment Act 326

workhouses were publicly funded establishments in which large numbers of laborers were brought together to perform some type of work and sometimes to receive job training, 39, 40, 42

working class activism 163

workplace exploitation, Chinese immigrants 267

workplace policies, supporting mothers 535

work relief programs 70

work requirements: and benefits 87, 89, 314, 551; and claims 183; Medicaid 326; Medicare 426; safety net programs 535–7; SNAP benefits 326; TANF 101, 129, 321, 323, 325–7, 337, 340

Works Progress Administration (WPA) 70

World Economic Forum 276

World Federation of United Nations Associations 533–4

World War I 67, 68

World War II: impact of 74–5; Japanese Americans/ internment of 75, 267

worthy/unworthy poor 33, 34, 39, 40, 41, 89, 180; children 52

Wounded Knee 91, 263

wrap-around services 231, 387, 397, 404

young people *see also* juvenile: disabled/receiving benefits 427; and health care reform 438; LGBTQ/ problems of 270; mental illness 399; and OASDI 313–16; support for older adults 505; support for Social Security 494

Young, Whitney Jn. 83

Young, Whitney M. 262

youth account ownership 351

zakat 31

zero tolerance policies, schools 398, 404

Taylor & Francis

eBooks

FOR LIBRARIES

ORDER YOUR **FREE 30 DAY** INSTITUTIONAL TRIAL TODAY!

Over 23,000 eBook titles in the Humanities, Social Sciences, STM and Law from some of the world's leading imprints.

Choose from a range of subject packages or create your own!

Benefits for **you**

▶ Free MARC records
▶ COUNTER-compliant usage statistics
▶ Flexible purchase and pricing options

Benefits for your **user**

▶ Off-site, anytime access via Athens or referring URL
▶ Print or copy pages or chapters
▶ Full content search
▶ Bookmark, highlight and annotate text
▶ Access to thousands of pages of quality research at the click of a button

For more information, pricing enquiries or to order a free trial, contact your local online sales team.

UK and Rest of World: **online.sales@tandf.co.uk**

US, Canada and Latin America:
e-reference@taylorandfrancis.com

www.ebooksubscriptions.com

ALPSP Award for BEST eBOOK PUBLISHER **2009 Finalist** sponsored by

 **Taylor & Francis** eBooks
Taylor & Francis Group

A flexible and dynamic resource for teaching, learning and research.

Custom Materials
DELIVER A MORE REWARDING EDUCATIONAL EXPERIENCE.

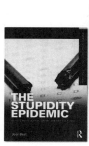

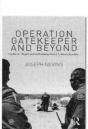

University Readers® Custom Publishing Evolved.

Routledge Taylor & Francis Group

The Social Issues Collection

This unique collection features 250 readings plus 45 recently added readings for undergraduate teaching in sociology and other social science courses. The social issues collection includes selections from Joe Nevins, Sheldon Elkand-Olson, Val Jenness, Sarah Fenstermaker, Nikki Jones, France Winddance Twine, Scott McNall, Ananya Roy, Joel Best, Michael Apple, and more.

1 Go to the website at
routledge.customgateway.com

2 Choose from almost 300 readings from Routledge & other publishers

3 Create your complete custom anthology

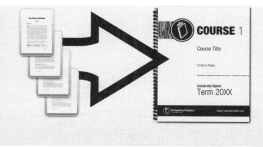

Learn more:
routledge.customgateway.com | 800.200.3908 x 501 | info@cognella.com

University Readers is an imprint of Cognella, Inc. ©1997-2013

NEW DIRECTIONS IN SOCIAL WORK

SERIES EDITOR: ALICE LIEBERMAN, UNIVERSITY OF KANSAS

New Directions in Social Work is an innovative, integrated series offering a uniquely distinctive teaching strategy for generalist courses in the social work curriculum, at both undergraduate and graduate levels. The series integrates five texts with custom websites housing interactive cases, companion readings, and a wealth of resources to enrich the teaching and learning experience.

Research for Effective Social Work Practice, Third Edition

Judy L. Krysik, Arizona State University and Jerry Finn, University of Washington, Tacoma

HB: 978-0-415-52100-0
PB: 978-0-415-51986-1
eBook: 978-0-203-07789-4

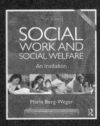

Social Work and Social Welfare, Third Edition

Anissa Taun Rogers, St. Louis University

HB: 978-0-415-52080-5
PB: 978-0-415-50160-6
eBook: 978-0-203-11931-0

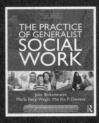

The Practice of Generalist Social Work, Third Edition

Julie Birkenmaier, Marla Berg-Weger, both at St. Louis University, and Martha P. Dewees, University of Vermont

HB: 978–0–415-51988–5
PB: 978–0–415-51989–2
eBook: 978–0–203–07098–7

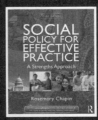

Social Policy for Effective Practice: A Strengths Approach, Third Edition

Rosemary Chapin, University of Kansas

HB: 978–0–415-51991–5
PB: 978–0–415-51992–2
eBook: 978–0–203–79476–0